# Microsoft® SQL Server® 2008 Internals

*Kalen Delaney*
*Paul S. Randal, Kimberly L. Tripp*
*Conor Cunningham, Adam Machanic*
*and Ben Nevarez*

PUBLISHED BY
Microsoft Press
A Division of Microsoft Corporation
One Microsoft Way
Redmond, Washington 98052-6399

Library of Congress Control Number: 2008940524

Printed and bound in the United States of America.

1 2 3 4 5 6 7 8 9   QWT   4 3 2 1 0 9

Distributed in Canada by H.B. Fenn and Company Ltd.

A CIP catalogue record for this book is available from the British Library.

Microsoft Press books are available through booksellers and distributors worldwide. For further information about international editions, contact your local Microsoft Corporation office or contact Microsoft Press International directly at fax (425) 936-7329. Visit our Web site at www.microsoft.com/mspress. Send comments to mspinput@microsoft.com.

**Acquisitions Editor:** Ken Jones
**Developmental Editor:** Sally Stickney
**Project Editor:** Lynn Finnel
**Editorial Production:** S4Carlisle Publishing Services
**Technical Reviewer:** Benjamin Nevarez; Technical Review services provided by Content Master, a member of CM Group, Ltd.
**Cover:** Tom Draper Design

Body Part No. X15-32079

*For Dan, forever . . . .*

*—Kalen*

# Contents at a Glance

# Table of Contents

**What do you think of this book? We want to hear from you!**

Microsoft is interested in hearing your feedback so we can continually improve our books and learning resources for you. To participate in a brief online survey, please visit:

**www.microsoft.com/learning/booksurvey/**

## 9  Plan Caching and Recompilation ......................... 525

**What do you think of this book? We want to hear from you!**

Microsoft is interested in hearing your feedback so we can continually improve our books and learning resources for you. To participate in a brief online survey, please visit:

**www.microsoft.com/learning/booksurvey/**

# Foreword

The developers who create products such as Microsoft SQL Server typically become experts in one area of the technology, such as access methods or query execution. They live and experience the product inside out and often know their component so deeply they acquire a "curse of knowledge": they possess so much detail about their particular domain, they find it difficult to describe their work in a way that helps customers get the most out of the product.

Technical writers who create product-focused books, on the other hand, experience a product outside in. Most of these authors acquire a broad, but somewhat shallow, surface knowledge of the products they write about and produce valuable books, usually filled with many screenshots, which help new and intermediate users quickly learn how to get things done with the product.

When the curse of knowledge meets surface knowledge, it leaves a gap where many of the great capabilities created by product developers don't get communicated in a way that allows customers, particularly intermediate to advanced users, to use a product to its full potential. This is where *Microsoft SQL Server 2008 Internals* comes in. This book, like those in the earlier "Inside SQL Server" series, is the definitive reference for how SQL Server really works. Kalen Delaney has been working with the SQL Server product team for over a decade, spending countless hours with developers breaking through the curse of knowledge and then capturing the result in an incredibly clear form that allows intermediate to advanced users to wring the most from the capabilities of SQL Server. In *Microsoft SQL Server 2008 Internals,* Kalen is joined by four SQL Server experts who also share the gift of breaking the curse. Conor Cunningham and Paul Randal have years of experience as SQL Server product developers, and each of them is both a deep technical expert and a gifted communicator. Kimberly Tripp and Adam Machanic both combine a passion to really understand how things work and to then effectively share it with others. Kimberly and Adam are both standing-room-only speakers at SQL Server events. This team has captured and incorporated the details of key architectural changes for SQL Server 2008, resulting in a new, comprehensive internals reference for SQL Server.

There is a litmus test you can use to determine if a technical product title deserves a "definitive reference" classification. It's a relatively easy test but a hard one for everybody to conduct. The test, quite simply, is to look at how many of the developers who created the product in question have a copy of the book on their shelves—and reference it. I can assure you that each version of *Inside Microsoft SQL Server* that Kalen has produced has met this test. *Microsoft SQL Server 2008 Internals* will, too.

*Dave Campbell*

*Technical Fellow*
*Microsoft SQL Server*

# Introduction

The book you are now holding is the evolutionary successor to the *Inside SQL Server* series, which included *Inside SQL Server 6.5, Inside SQL Server 7, Inside SQL Server 2000,* and *Inside SQL Server 2005* (in four volumes). The *Inside* series was becoming too unfocused, and the name "Inside" had been usurped by other authors and even other publishers. I needed a title that was much more indicative of what this book is really about.

*SQL Server 2008 Internals* tells you how SQL Server, Microsoft's flagship relational database product, works. Along with that, I explain how you can use the knowledge of how it works to help you get better performance from the product, but that is a side effect, not the goal. There are dozens of other books on the market that describe tuning and best practices for SQL Server. This one helps you understand why certain tuning practices work the way they do, and it helps you determine your own best practices as you continue to work with SQL Server as a developer, data architect, or DBA.

## Who This Book Is For

This book is intended to be read by anyone who wants a deeper understanding of what SQL Server does behind the scenes. The focus of this book is on the core SQL Server engine—in particular, the query processor and the storage engine. I expect that you have some experience with both the SQL Server engine and with the T-SQL language. You don't have to be an expert in either, but it helps if you aspire to become an expert and would like to find out all you can about what SQL Server is actually doing when you submit a query for execution.

This series doesn't discuss client programming interfaces, heterogeneous queries, business intelligence, or replication. In fact, most of the high-availability features are not covered, but a few, such as mirroring, are mentioned at a high level when we discuss database property settings. I don't drill into the details of some internal operations, such as security, because that's such a big topic it deserves a whole volume of its own.

My hope is that you'll look at the cup as half full instead of half empty and appreciate this book for what it does include. As for the topics that aren't included, I hope you'll find the information you need in other sources.

# What This Book Is About

*SQL Server Internals* provides detailed information on the way that SQL Server processes your queries and manages your data. It starts with an overview of the architecture of the SQL Server relational database system and then continues looking at aspects of query processing and data storage in 10 additional chapters, as follows:

- Chapter 1    SQL Server 2008 Architecture and Configuration
- Chapter 2    Change Tracking, Tracing, and Extended Events
- Chapter 3    Databases and Database Files
- Chapter 4    Logging and Recovery
- Chapter 5    Tables
- Chapter 6    Indexes: Internals and Management
- Chapter 7    Special Storage
- Chapter 8    The Query Optimizer
- Chapter 9    Plan Caching and Recompilation
- Chapter 10    Transactions and Concurrency
- Chapter 11    DBCC Internals

A twelfth chapter covering the details of reading query plans is available in the companion content (which is described in the next section). This chapter, called "Query Execution," was part of my previous book, *Inside SQL Server 2005: Query Tuning and Optimization*. Because 99 percent of the chapter is still valid for SQL Server 2008, we have included it "as is" for your additional reference.

## Companion Content

This book features a companion Web site that makes available to you all the code used in the book, organized by chapter. The companion content also includes an extra chapter from my previous book, as well as the "History of SQL Server" chapter from my book *SQL Server 2000*. The site also provides extra scripts and tools to enhance your experience and understanding of SQL Server internals. As errors are found and reported, they will also be posted online. You can access this content from the companion site at this address: *http://www.SQLServerInternals.com/companion*.

## System Requirements

To use the code samples, you'll need Internet access and a system capable of running SQL Server 2008 Enterprise or Developer edition. To get system requirements for SQL Server 2008 and to obtain a trial version, go to *http://www.microsoft.com/downloads*.

# Support for This Book

Every effort has been made to ensure the accuracy of this book and the contents of the companion Web site. As corrections or changes are collected, they will be added to a Microsoft Knowledge Base article.

Microsoft Press provides support for books at the following Web site:

*http://www.microsoft.com/learning/support/books/*

## Questions and Comments

If you have comments, questions, or ideas regarding the book, or questions that are not answered by visiting the sites above, please send them to Microsoft Press via e-mail to

*mspinput@microsoft.com*

Or via postal mail to

Microsoft Press
Attn: *Microsoft SQL Server 2008 Internals* Editor
One Microsoft Way
Redmond, WA 98052-6399

Please note that Microsoft software product support is not offered through the above addresses.

# Acknowledgments

As always, a work like this is not an individual effort, and for this current volume, it is truer than ever. I was honored to have four other SQL Server experts join me in writing *SQL Server 2008 Internals*, and I truly could not have written this book alone. I am grateful to Adam Machanic, Paul Randal, Conor Cunningham, and Kimberly Tripp for helping to make this book a reality. In addition to my brilliant co-authors, this book could never have seen the light of day with help and encouragement from many other people.

First on my list is you, the readers. Thank you to all of you for reading what I have written. Thank you to those who have taken the time to write to me about what you thought of the book and what else you want to learn about SQL Server. I wish I could answer every question in detail. I appreciate all your input, even when I'm unable to send you a complete reply. One particular reader of one of my previous books, *Inside SQL Server 2005: The Storage Engine*, deserves particular thanks. I came to know Ben Nevarez as a very astute reader who found some uncaught errors and subtle inconsistencies and politely and succinctly reported them to me through my Web site. After a few dozen e-mails, I started to look forward to Ben's e-mails and was delighted when I finally got the chance to meet him. Ben is now my most valued technical reviewer, and I am deeply indebted to him for his extremely careful reading of every one of the chapters.

As usual, the SQL Server team at Microsoft has been awesome. Although Lubor Kollar and Sunil Agarwal were not directly involved in much of the research for this book, I always knew they were there in spirit, and both of them always had an encouraging word whenever I saw them.

Boris Baryshnikov, Kevin Farlee, Marcel van der Holst, Peter Byrne, Sangeetha Shekar, Robin Dhamankar, Artem Oks, Srini Acharya, and Ryan Stonecipher met with me and responded to my (sometimes seemingly endless) e-mails. Jerome Halmans, Joanna Omel, Nikunj Koolar, Tres London, Mike Purtell, Lin Chan, and Dipti Sangani also offered valuable technical insights and information when responding to my e-mails. I hope they all know how much I appreciated every piece of information I received.

I am also indebted to Bob Ward, Bob Dorr, and Keith Elmore of the SQL Server Product Support team, not just for answering occasional questions but for making so much information about SQL Server available through white papers, conference presentations, and Knowledge Base articles. I am grateful to Alan Brewer and Gail Erickson for the great job they and their User Education team did putting together the SQL Server documentation in *SQL Server Books Online*.

And, of course, Buck Woody deserves my gratitude many times over. First from his job in the User Education group, then as a member of the SQL Server development team, he was always there when I had an unanswered question. His presentations and blog posts are always educational as well as entertaining, and his generosity and unflagging good spirits are a true inspiration.

I would also like to thank Leona Lowry and Cheryl Walter for finding me office space in the same building as most of the SQL Server team. The welcome they gave me was much appreciated.

I would like to extend my heartfelt thanks to all of the SQL Server MVPs, but most especially Erland Sommarskog. Erland wrote the section in Chapter 5 on collations just because he thought it was needed, and that someone who has to deal with only the 26 letters of the English alphabet could never do it justice. Also deserving of special mention are Tibor Karaszi and Roy Harvey, for all the personal support and encouragement they gave me. Other MVPs who inspired me during the writing of this volume are Tony Rogerson, John Paul Cook, Steve Kass, Paul Nielsen, Hugo Kornelis, Tom Moreau, and Linchi Shea. Being a part of the SQL Server MVP team continues to be one of the greatest honors and privileges of my professional life.

I am deeply indebted to my students in my "SQL Server Internals" classes, not only for their enthusiasm for the SQL Server product and for what I have to teach and share with them, but for all they have to share with me. Much of what I have learned has been inspired by questions from my curious students. Some of my students, such as Cindy Gross and Lara Rubbelke, have become friends (in addition to becoming Microsoft employees) and continue to provide ongoing inspiration.

Most important of all, my family continues to provide the rock-solid foundation I need to do the work that I do. My husband, Dan, continues to be the guiding light of my life after 24 years of marriage. My daughter, Melissa, and my three sons, Brendan, Rickey, and Connor, are now for the most part all grown, and are all generous, loving, and compassionate people. I feel truly blessed to have them in my life.

*Kalen Delaney*

# Paul Randal

I've been itching to write a complete description of what DBCC CHECKDB does for many years now—not least to get it all out of my head and make room for something else! When Kalen asked me to write the "Consistency Checking" chapter for this book, I jumped at the chance, and for that my sincere thanks go to Kalen. I'd like to give special thanks to two people from Microsoft, among the many great folks I worked with there (and in many cases still do). The first is Ryan Stonecipher, who I hired away from being an Escalation Engineer in SQL Product Support in late 2003 to work with me on DBCC, and who was suddenly thrust into complete ownership of 100,000+ lines of DBCC code when I become the team manager two months later. I couldn't have asked for more capable hands to take over my precious DBCC.... The second is Bob Ward, who heads up the SQL Product Support team and has been a great friend since my early days at Microsoft. We must have collaborated on hundreds of cases of corruption over the years, and I've yet to meet someone with more drive for solving customer problems and improving Microsoft SQL Server. Thanks must also go to Steve Lindell, the author of the original online consistency checking code for SQL Server 2000, who spent many hours patiently explaining how it worked in 1999. Finally, I'd like to thank my wife, Kimberly, who is, along with Katelyn and Kiera, the other passions in my life apart from SQL Server.

# Kimberly Tripp

First, I want to thank my good friend Kalen, for inviting me to participate in this title. After working together in various capacities—even having formed a company together back in 1996—it's great to finally have our ideas and content together in a book as deep and technical as this. In terms of performance tuning, indexes are critical; there's no better way to improve a system than by creating the *right* indexes. However, knowing what's right takes multiple components, some of which is only known after experience, after testing, and after seeing something in action. For this, I want to thank many of you—readers, students, conference attendees, customers—those of you who have asked the questions, shown me interesting scenarios, and stayed late to "play" and/or just figure it out. It's the deep desire to know why something is working the way that it is that keeps this product interesting to me and has always made me want to dive deeper and deeper into understanding what's really going on. For that, I thank the SQL team in general—the folks that I've met and worked with over the years have been inspiring, intelligent, and insightful. Specifically, I want to thank a few folks on the SQL team who have patiently, quickly, and thoroughly responded to questions about what's really going on and often, why: Conor Cunningham,

Cesar Galindo-Legaria, and from my early days with SQL Server, Dave Campbell, Nigel Ellis, and Rande Blackman. Gert E. R. Drapers requires special mention due to the many hours spent together over the years where we talked, argued, and figured it out. And, to Paul, my best friend and husband, who before that *was* also a good source of SQL information. We just don't talk about it anymore . . . at home. OK, maybe a little.

## Conor Cunningham

I'd like to thank Bob Beauchemin and Milind Joshi for their efforts to review my chapter, "The Query Optimizer," in this book for technical correctness. I'd also like to thank Kimberly Tripp and Paul Randal for their encouragement and support while I wrote this chapter. Finally, I'd like to thank all the members of the SQL Server Query Processor team who answered many technical questions for me.

## Adam Machanic

I would like to, first and foremost, extend my thanks to Kalen Delaney for leading the effort of this book from conception through reality. Kalen did a great job of keeping us focused and on task, as well as helping to find those hidden nuggets of information that make a book like this one great. A few Microsoft SQL Server team members dedicated their time to helping review my work: Jerome Halmans and Fabricio Voznika from the Extended Events team, and Mark Scurrell from the Change Tracking team. I would like to thank each of you for keeping me honest, answering my questions, and improving the quality of my chapter. Finally, I would like to thank Kate and Aura, my wife and daughter, who always understand when I disappear into the office for a day or two around deadline time.

# Chapter 1
# SQL Server 2008 Architecture and Configuration

*Kalen Delaney*

Microsoft SQL Server is Microsoft's premiere database management system, and SQL Server 2008 is the most powerful and feature-rich version yet. In addition to the core database engine, which allows you to store and retrieve large volumes of relational data, and the world-class Query Optimizer, which determines the fastest way to process your queries and access your data, dozens of other components increase the usability of your data and make your data and applications more available and more scalable. As you can imagine, no single book could cover all these features in depth. This book, *SQL Server 2008 Internals,* covers the main features of the core database engine.

Throughout this book, we'll delve into the details of specific features of the SQL Server Database Engine. In this first chapter, you'll get a high-level view of the components of that engine and how they work together. My goal is to help you understand how the topics covered in subsequent chapters fit into the overall operations of the engine.

In this chapter, however, we'll dig deeper into one big area of the SQL Server Database Engine that isn't covered later: the SQL operating system (SQLOS) and, in particular, the components related to memory management and scheduling. We'll also look at the metadata that SQL Server makes available to allow you to observe the engine behavior and data organization.

## SQL Server Editions

Each version of SQL Server comes in various editions, which you can think of as a subset of the product features, with its own specific pricing and licensing requirements. Although we won't be discussing pricing and licensing in this book, some of the information about editions is important, because of the features that are available with each edition. The editions available and the feature list that each supports is described in detail in *SQL Server Books Online,* but here we will list the main editions. You can verify what edition you are running with the following query:

```
SELECT SERVERPROPERTY('Edition');
```

There is also a server property called *EngineEdition* that you can inspect, as follows:

```
SELECT SERVERPROPERTY('EngineEdition');
```

The *EngineEdition* property returns a value of 2, 3, or 4 (1 is not a possible value), and this value determines what features are available. A value of 3 indicates that your SQL Server edition is either Enterprise, Enterprise Evaluation, or Developer. These three editions have exactly the same features and functionality. If your *EngineEdition* value is 2, your edition is either Standard or Workgroup, and fewer features are available. The features and behaviors discussed in this book will be the ones available in one of these two engine editions. The features in Enterprise edition (as well as in Developer edition and Enterprise Evaluation edition) that are not in Standard edition generally relate to scalability and high-availability features, but there are other Enterprise-only features as well. When we discuss such features that are considered Enterprise-only, we'll let you know. For full details on what is in each edition, see the *SQL Server Books Online* topic "Features Supported by the Editions of SQL Server 2008." (A value of 4 for *EngineEdition* indicates that your SQL Server edition is an Express edition, which includes SQL Server Express, SQL Server Express with Advanced Services, or Windows Embedded SQL. None of these versions will be discussed specifically.) There is also a *SERVERPROPERTY* property called *EditionID*, which allows you to differentiate between the specific editions within each of the different *EngineEdition* values (that is, it allows you to differentiate between Enterprise, Enterprise Evaluation, and Developer editions).

# SQL Server Metadata

SQL Server maintains a set of tables that store information about all the objects, data types, constraints, configuration options, and resources available to SQL Server. In SQL Server 2008, these tables are called the *system base tables*. Some of the system base tables exist only in the *master* database and contain system-wide information, and others exist in every database (including *master*) and contain information about the objects and resources belonging to that particular database. Beginning with SQL Server 2005, the system base tables are not always visible by default, in *master* or any other database. You won't see them when you expand the *tables* node in the Object Explorer in SQL Server Management Studio, and unless you are a system administrator, you won't see them when you execute the *sp_help* system procedure. If you log in as a system administrator and select from the catalog view (discussed shortly) called *sys.objects*, you can see the names of all the system tables. For example, the following query returns 58 rows of output on my SQL Server 2008 instance:

```
USE master;
SELECT name FROM sys.objects
WHERE type_desc = 'SYSTEM_TABLE';
```

But even as a system administrator, if you try to select data from one of the tables whose names are returned by the preceding query, you get a 208 error, indicating that the object name is invalid. The only way to see the data in the system base tables is to make a connection using the dedicated administrator connection (DAC), which we'll tell you about in the section entitled "The Scheduler," later in this chapter. Keep in mind that the system base tables are used for internal purposes only within the Database Engine and are not intended for general use. They are subject to change, and compatibility is not guaranteed. In SQL Server 2008, there are three types of system metadata objects. One type is Dynamic Management Objects, which we'll talk about later in this chapter when we discuss SQL Server scheduling and memory management. These Dynamic Management Objects don't really correspond to physical tables—they contain information gathered from internal structures to allow you to observe the current state of your SQL Server instance. The other two types of system objects are actually views built on top of the system base tables.

## Compatibility Views

Although you were allowed to see data in the system tables in versions of SQL Server before 2005, you weren't encouraged to do this. Nevertheless, many people used system tables for developing their own troubleshooting and reporting tools and techniques, providing result sets that aren't available using the supplied system procedures. You might assume that due to the inaccessibility of the system base tables, you would have to use the DAC to utilize your homegrown tools when using SQL Server 2005 or 2008. However, you still might be disappointed. Many of the names and much of the content of the SQL Server 2000 system tables have changed, so any code that used them is completely unusable even with the DAC. The DAC is intended only for emergency access, and no support is provided for any other use of it. To save you from this grief, SQL Server 2005 and 2008 offer a set of compatibility views that allow you to continue to access a subset of the SQL Server 2000 system tables. These views are accessible from any database, although they are created in the hidden resource database.

Some of the compatibility views have names that might be quite familiar to you, such as *sysobjects, sysindexes, sysusers,* and *sysdatabases.* Others, like *sysmembers* and *sysmessages,* might be less familiar. For compatibility reasons, the views in SQL Server 2008 have the same names as their SQL Server 2000 counterparts, as well as the same column names, which means that any code that uses the SQL Server 2000 system tables won't break. However, when you select from these views, you are not guaranteed to get exactly the same results that you get from the corresponding tables in SQL Server 2000. In addition, the compatibility views do not contain any metadata related to new SQL Server 2005 or 2008 features, such as partitioning or the Resource Governor. You should consider the compatibility views to be for backward compatibility only; going forward, you should consider using other metadata mechanisms, such as the catalog view discussed in the next section. All these compatibility views will be removed in a future version of SQL Server.

 **More Info**  You can find a complete list of names and the columns in these views in *SQL Server Books Online.*

SQL Server 2005 and 2008 also provide compatibility views for the SQL Server 2000 pseudotables, such as *sysprocesses* and *syscacheobjects*. Pseudotables are tables that are not based on data stored on disk but are built as needed from internal structures and can be queried exactly as if they are tables. SQL Server 2005 replaced these pseudotables with Dynamic Management Objects. Note that there is not always a one-to-one correspondence between the SQL Server 2000 pseudotables and the SQL Server 2005 and SQL Server 2008 Dynamic Management Objects. For example, for SQL Server 2008 to retrieve all the information available in *sysprocesses*, you must access three Dynamic Management Objects: *sys.dm_exec_connections*, *sys.dm_exec_sessions*, and *sys.dm_exec_requests*.

## Catalog Views

SQL Server 2005 introduced a set of catalog views as a general interface to the persisted system metadata. All the catalog views (as well as the Dynamic Management Objects and compatibility views) are in the *sys* schema, and you must reference the schema name when you access the objects. Some of the names are easy to remember because they are similar to the SQL Server 2000 system table names. For example, there is a catalog view called *objects* in the *sys* schema, so to reference the view, the following can be executed:

```
SELECT * FROM sys.objects;
```

Similarly, there are catalog views called *sys.indexes* and *sys.databases*, but the columns displayed for these catalog views are very different from the columns in the compatibility views. Because the output from these types of queries is too wide to reproduce, let me just suggest that you run these two queries yourself and observe the difference:

```
SELECT * FROM sys.databases;
SELECT * FROM sysdatabases;
```

The *sysdatabases* compatibility view is in the *sys* schema, so you can reference it as *sys.sysdatabases*. You can also reference it using *dbo.sysdatabases*. But again, for compatibility reasons, the schema name is not required, as it is for the catalog views. (That is, you cannot simply select from a view called *databases*; you must use the schema *sys* as a prefix.)

When you compare the output from the two preceding queries, you might notice that there are a lot more columns in the *sys.databases* catalog view. Instead of a bitmap *status* field that needs to be decoded, each possible database property has its own column in *sys.databases*. With SQL Server 2000, running the system procedure *sp_helpdb* decodes all these database options, but because *sp_helpdb* is a procedure, it is difficult to filter the results. As a view, *sys.databases* can be queried and filtered. For example, if you want to know which databases are in *simple* recovery mode, you can run the following:

```
SELECT name FROM sys.databases
WHERE recovery_model_desc = 'SIMPLE';
```

The catalog views are built on an inheritance model, so sets of attributes common to many objects don't have to be redefined internally. For example, *sys.objects* contains all the columns for attributes common to all types of objects, and the views *sys.tables* and *sys.views* contain all the same columns as *sys.objects*, as well as some additional columns that are relevant only to the particular type of objects. If you select from *sys.objects*, you get 12 columns, and if you then select from *sys.tables*, you get exactly the same 12 columns in the same order, plus 15 additional columns that aren't applicable to all types of objects but are meaningful for tables. In addition, although the base view *sys.objects* contains a subset of columns compared to the derived views such as *sys.tables*, it contains a superset of rows compared to a derived view. For example, the *sys.objects* view shows metadata for procedures and views in addition to that for tables, whereas the *sys.tables* view shows only rows for tables. So I can summarize the relationship between the base view and the derived views as follows: "The base views contain a subset of columns and a superset of rows, and the derived views contain a superset of columns and a subset of rows."

Just as in SQL Server 2000, some of the metadata appears only in the *master* database, and it keeps track of system-wide data, such as databases and logins. Other metadata is available in every database, such as objects and permissions. The *SQL Server Books Online* topic "Mapping System Tables to System Views" categorizes its objects into two lists—those appearing only in *master* and those appearing in all databases. Note that metadata appearing only in the *msdb* database is not available through catalog views but is still available in system tables, in the schema *dbo*. This includes metadata for backup and restore, replication, Database Maintenance Plans, Integration Services, log shipping, and SQL Server Agent.

As views, these metadata objects are based on an underlying Transact-SQL (T-SQL) definition. The most straightforward way to see the definition of these views is by using the *object_definition* function. (You can also see the definition of these system views by using *sp_helptext* or by selecting from the catalog view *sys.system_sql_modules*.) So to see the definition of *sys.tables*, you can execute the following:

```
SELECT object_definition (object_id('sys.tables'));
```

If you execute the preceding *SELECT* statement, you'll see that the definition of *sys.tables* references several completely undocumented system objects. On the other hand, some system object definitions refer only to objects that are documented. For example, the definition of the compatibility view *syscacheobjects* refers only to three Dynamic Management Objects (one view, *sys.dm_exec_cached_plans*, and two functions, *sys.dm_exec_sql_text* and *sys.dm_exec_plan_attributes*) that are fully documented.

The metadata with names starting with 'sys.dm_', such as the just-mentioned *sys.dm_exec_cached_plans*, are considered Dynamic Management Objects, and we'll be discussing them in the next section when we discuss the SQL Server Database Engine's behavior.

## Other Metadata

Although the catalog views are the recommended interface for accessing the SQL Server 2008 catalog, other tools are available as well.

### Information Schema Views

Information schema views, introduced in SQL Server 7.0, were the original system table–independent view of the SQL Server metadata. The information schema views included in SQL Server 2008 comply with the SQL-92 standard and all these views are in a schema called *INFORMATION_SCHEMA*. Some of the information available through the catalog views is available through the information schema views, and if you need to write a portable application that accesses the metadata, you should consider using these objects. However, the information schema views only show objects that are compatible with the SQL-92 standard. This means there is no information schema view for certain features, such as indexes, which are not defined in the standard. (Indexes are an implementation detail.) If your code does not need to be strictly portable, or if you need metadata about nonstandard features such as indexes, filegroups, the CLR, and SQL Server Service Broker, we suggest using the Microsoft-supplied catalog views. Most of the examples in the documentation, as well as in this and other reference books, are based on the catalog view interface.

### System Functions

Most SQL Server system functions are property functions, which were introduced in SQL Server 7.0 and greatly enhanced in SQL Server 2000. SQL Server 2005 and 2008 have enhanced these functions still further. Property functions give us individual values for many SQL Server objects and also for SQL Server databases and the SQL Server instance itself. The values returned by the property functions are scalar as opposed to tabular, so they can be used as values returned by *SELECT* statements and as values to populate columns in tables. Here is the list of property functions available in SQL Server 2008:

- *SERVERPROPERTY*
- *COLUMNPROPERTY*
- *DATABASEPROPERTY*
- *DATABASEPROPERTYEX*
- *INDEXPROPERTY*
- *INDEXKEY_PROPERTY*
- *OBJECTPROPERTY*
- *OBJECTPROPERTYEX*
- *SQL_VARIANT_PROPERTY*
- *FILEPROPERTY*

- *FILEGROUPPROPERTY*

- *TYPEPROPERTY*

- *CONNECTIONPROPERTY*

- *ASSEMBLYPROPERTY*

The only way to find out what the possible property values are for the various functions is to check *SQL Server Books Online*.

Some of the information returned by the property functions can also be seen using the catalog views. For example, the *DATABASEPROPERTYEX* function has a property called *Recovery* that returns the recovery model of a database. To view the recovery model of a single database, you can use the property function as follows:

```
SELECT DATABASEPROPERTYEX('msdb', 'Recovery');
```

To view the recovery models of all our databases, you can use the *sys.databases* view:

```
SELECT name, recovery_model, recovery_model_desc
FROM sys.databases;
```

> **Note** Columns with names ending in *_desc* are the so-called friendly name columns, and they are always paired with another column that is much more compact, but cryptic. In this case, the *recovery_model* column is a *tinyint* with a value of 1, 2, or 3. Both columns are available in the view because different consumers have different needs. For example, internally at Microsoft, the teams building the internal interfaces wanted to bind to more compact columns, whereas DBAs running adhoc queries might prefer the friendly names.

In addition to the property functions, the system functions include functions that are merely shortcuts for catalog view access. For example, to find out the database ID for the *AdventureWorks2008* database, you can either query the *sys.databases* catalog view or use the *DB_ID()* function. Both of the following *SELECT* statements should return the same result:

```
SELECT database_id
FROM sys.databases
WHERE name = 'AdventureWorks2008';
```

```
SELECT DB_ID('AdventureWorks2008');
```

## System Stored Procedures

System stored procedures are the original metadata access tool, in addition to the system tables themselves. Most of the system stored procedures introduced in the very first version of SQL Server are still available. However, catalog views are a big improvement over these procedures: you have control over how much of the metadata you see because you can query the views as if they were tables. With the system stored procedures, you basically have to accept the data that it returns. Some of the procedures allow parameters, but they are very limited. So for the *sp_helpdb* procedure, you can pass a parameter to see just one database's information or not pass a parameter and see information for all databases. However, if you want to see only databases that the login *sue* owns, or just see databases that are in a lower compatibility level, you cannot do it using the supplied stored procedure. Using the catalog views, these queries are straightforward:

```
SELECT name FROM sys.databases
WHERE suser_sname(owner_sid) ='sue';

SELECT name FROM sys.databases
WHERE compatibility_level < 90;
```

## Metadata Wrap-Up

Figure 1-1 shows the multiple layers of metadata available in SQL Server 2008, with the lowest layer being the system base tables (the actual catalog). Any interface that accesses the information contained in the system base tables is subject to the metadata security policies. For SQL Server 2008, that means that no users can see any metadata that they don't need to see or to which they haven't specifically been granted permissions. (There are a few exceptions, but they are very minor.) The "other metadata" refers to system information not contained in system tables, such as the internal information provided by the Dynamic Management Objects. Remember that the preferred interfaces to the system metadata are the catalog views and system functions. Although not all the compatibility views, *INFORMATION_SCHEMA* views, and system procedures are actually defined in terms of the catalog views, conceptually it is useful to think of them as another layer on top of the catalog view interface.

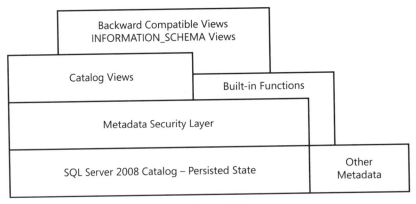

**FIGURE 1-1** Layers of metadata in SQL Server 2008

# Components of the SQL Server Engine

Figure 1-2 shows the general architecture of SQL Server, which has four major components. Three of those components, along with their subcomponents are shown in the figure: the relational engine (also called the *query processor*), the storage engine, and the SQLOS.

(The fourth component is the protocol layer, which is not shown.) Every batch submitted to SQL Server for execution, from any client application, must interact with these four components. (For simplicity, I've made some minor omissions and simplifications and ignored certain "helper" modules among the subcomponents.)

The protocol layer receives the request and translates it into a form that the relational engine can work with, and it also takes the final results of any queries, status messages, or error messages and translates them into a form the client can understand before sending them back to the client. The relational engine layer accepts T-SQL batches and determines what to do with them. For T-SQL queries and programming constructs, it parses, compiles, and optimizes the request and oversees the process of executing the batch. As the batch is executed, if data is needed, a request for that data is passed to the storage engine. The storage engine manages all data access, both through transaction-based commands and bulk operations such as backup, bulk insert, and certain DBCC commands. The SQLOS layer handles activities that are normally considered to be operating system responsibilities, such as thread management (scheduling), synchronization primitives, deadlock detection, and memory management, including the buffer pool.

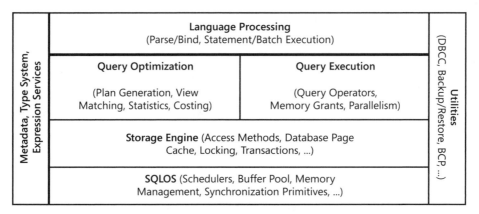

**FIGURE 1-2** The major components of the SQL Server Database Engine

## Observing Engine Behavior

SQL Server 2008 includes a suite of system objects that allow developers and database administrators to observe much of the internals of SQL Server. These metadata objects, introduced in SQL Server 2005, are called *Dynamic Management Objects*. These objects include both views and functions, but the vast majority are views. (Dynamic Management Objects are frequently referred to as Dynamic Management Views (DMVs) to reflect the fact that most of the objects are views.) You can access these metadata objects as if they reside in the *sys* schema, which exists in every SQL Server 2008 database, but they are not real tables that are stored on disk. They are similar to the pseudotables used in SQL Server 2000 for observing the active processes (*sysprocesses*) or the contents of the plan cache (*syscacheobjects*). However, the pseudotables in SQL Server 2000 do not provide any tracking of detailed resource usage and are not always directly usable to detect resource problems or state changes. Some of the DMVs allow tracking of detailed resource history, and there are more than 100 such objects that you can directly query and join with SQL *SELECT* statements, although not all of these objects are documented. The DMVs expose changing server state information that might span multiple sessions, multiple transactions, and multiple user requests. These objects can be used for diagnostics, memory and process tuning, and monitoring across all sessions in the server. They also provide much of the data available through the Management Data Warehouse's performance reports, which is a new feature in SQL Server 2008. (Note that *sysprocesses* and *syscacheobjects* are still available as compatibility views, which we mentioned in the section "SQL Server Metadata," earlier in this chapter.)

The DMVs aren't based on real tables stored in database files but are based on internal server structures, some of which we'll discuss in this chapter. We'll discuss further details about the DMVs in various places in this book, where the contents of one or more of the objects can illuminate the topics being discussed. The objects are separated into several categories based on the functional area of the information they expose. They are all in the *sys* schema and have a name that starts with *dm_*, followed by a code indicating the area of the server with which the object deals. The main categories we'll address are the following:

**dm_exec_***

Contains information directly or indirectly related to the execution of user code and associated connections. For example, *sys.dm_exec_sessions* returns one row per authenticated session on SQL Server. This object contains much of the same information that *sysprocesses* contains but has even more information about the operating environment of each session.

**dm_os_***

Contains low-level system information such as memory, locking, and scheduling. For example, *sys.dm_os_schedulers* is a DMV that returns one row per scheduler. It is primarily used to monitor the condition of a scheduler or to identify runaway tasks.

**dm_tran_***

Contains details about current transactions. For example, *sys.dm_tran_locks* returns information about currently active lock resources. Each row represents a currently active request to the lock management component for a lock that has been granted or is waiting to be granted.

**dm_io_***

Keeps track of I/O activity on networks and disks. For example, the function *sys.dm_io_virtual_file_stats* returns I/O statistics for data and log files.

**dm_db_***

Contains details about databases and database objects such as indexes. For example, *sys.dm_db_index_physical_stats* is a function that returns size and fragmentation information for the data and indexes of the specified table or view.

SQL Server 2008 also has Dynamic Management Objects for many of its functional components; these include objects for monitoring full-text search catalogs, change data capture (CDC) information, service broker, replication, and the CLR.

Now let's look at the major components of the SQL Server Database Engine.

# Protocols

When an application communicates with the Database Engine, the application programming interfaces (APIs) exposed by the protocol layer formats the communication using a Microsoft-defined format called a *tabular data stream (TDS) packet*. The SQL Server Network Interface (SNI) protocol layer on both the server and client computers encapsulates the TDS packet inside a standard communication protocol, such as TCP/IP or Named Pipes. On the server side of the communication, the network libraries are part of the Database Engine. On the client side, the network libraries are part of the SQL Native Client. The configuration of the client and the instance of SQL Server determine which protocol is used.

SQL Server can be configured to support multiple protocols simultaneously, coming from different clients. Each client connects to SQL Server with a single protocol. If the client program does not know which protocols SQL Server is listening on, you can configure the client to attempt multiple protocols sequentially. The following protocols are available:

**Shared Memory**   The simplest protocol to use, with no configurable settings. Clients using the Shared Memory protocol can connect only to a SQL Server instance running on the same computer, so this protocol is not useful for most database activity. Use this protocol for troubleshooting when you suspect that the other protocols are configured incorrectly. Clients using MDAC 2.8 or earlier cannot use the Shared Memory protocol. If such a connection is attempted, the client is switched to the Named Pipes protocol.

**Named Pipes**   A protocol developed for local area networks (LANs). A portion of memory is used by one process to pass information to another process, so that the output of one is the input of the other. The second process can be local (on the same computer as the first) or remote (on a networked computer).

**TCP/IP**   The most widely used protocol over the Internet. TCP/IP can communicate across interconnected networks of computers with diverse hardware architectures and operating systems. It includes standards for routing network traffic and offers advanced security features. Enabling SQL Server to use TCP/IP requires the most configuration effort, but most networked computers are already properly configured.

**Virtual Interface Adapter (VIA)**   A protocol that works with VIA hardware. This is a specialized protocol; configuration details are available from your hardware vendor.

### Tabular Data Stream Endpoints

SQL Server 2008 also allows you to create a TDS endpoint, so that SQL Server listens on an additional TCP port. During setup, SQL Server automatically creates an endpoint for each of the four protocols supported by SQL Server, and if the protocol is enabled, all users have access to it. For disabled protocols, the endpoint still exists but cannot be used. An additional endpoint is created for the DAC, which can be used only by members of the *sysadmin* fixed server role. (We'll discuss the DAC in more detail shortly.)

## The Relational Engine

As mentioned earlier, the relational engine is also called the query processor. It includes the components of SQL Server that determine exactly what your query needs to do and the best way to do it. In Figure 1-2, the relational engine is shown as two primary components: Query Optimization and Query Execution. By far the most complex component of the query processor, and maybe even of the entire SQL Server product, is the Query Optimizer, which determines the best execution plan for the queries in the batch. The Query Optimizer is discussed in great detail in Chapter 8, "The Query Optimizer"; in this section, we'll give you just a high-level overview of the Query Optimizer as well as of the other components of the query processor.

The relational engine also manages the execution of queries as it requests data from the storage engine and processes the results returned. Communication between the relational engine and the storage engine is generally in terms of OLE DB row sets. (*Row set* is the OLE DB term for a *result set*.) The storage engine comprises the components needed to actually access and modify data on disk.

### The Command Parser

The command parser handles T-SQL language events sent to SQL Server. It checks for proper syntax and translates T-SQL commands into an internal format that can be operated on. This internal format is known as a *query tree*. If the parser doesn't recognize the syntax, a syntax error is immediately raised that identifies where the error occurred. However, nonsyntax error messages cannot be explicit about the exact source line that caused the error. Because only the command parser can access the source of the statement, the statement is no longer available in source format when the command is actually executed.

### The Query Optimizer

The Query Optimizer takes the query tree from the command parser and prepares it for execution. Statements that can't be optimized, such as flow-of-control and Data Definition Language (DDL) commands, are compiled into an internal form. The statements that are optimizable are marked as such and then passed to the Query Optimizer. The Query Optimizer is mainly concerned with the Data Manipulation Language (DML) statements *SELECT, INSERT, UPDATE,* and *DELETE,* which can be processed in more than one way, and it is the Query Optimizer's job to determine which of the many possible ways is the best. It compiles an entire command batch, optimizes queries that are optimizable, and checks security. The query optimization and compilation result in an execution plan.

The first step in producing such a plan is to *normalize* each query, which potentially breaks down a single query into multiple, fine-grained queries. After the Query Optimizer normalizes a query, it *optimizes* it, which means that it determines a plan for executing that query. Query optimization is cost-based; the Query Optimizer chooses the plan that it determines would cost the least based on internal metrics that include estimated memory requirements, CPU utilization, and number of required I/Os. The Query Optimizer considers the type of statement requested, checks the amount of data in the various tables affected, looks at the indexes available for each table, and then looks at a sampling of the data values kept for each index or column referenced in the query. The sampling of the data values is called *distribution statistics*. (Statistics will be discussed in detail in Chapter 8.) Based on the available information, the Query Optimizer considers the various access methods and processing strategies that it could use to resolve a query and chooses the most cost-effective plan.

The Query Optimizer also uses pruning heuristics to ensure that optimizing a query doesn't take longer than it would take to simply choose a plan and execute it. The Query Optimizer doesn't necessarily perform exhaustive optimization. Some products consider every possible plan and then choose the most cost-effective one. The advantage of this exhaustive optimization is that the syntax chosen for a query theoretically never causes a performance difference, no matter what syntax the user employed. But with a complex query, it could take much longer to estimate the cost of every conceivable plan than it would to accept a good plan, even if it is not the best one, and execute it.

After normalization and optimization are completed, the normalized tree produced by those processes is compiled into the execution plan, which is actually a data structure. Each command included in it specifies exactly which table will be affected, which indexes will be used (if any), which security checks must be made, and which criteria (such as equality to a specified value) must evaluate to TRUE for selection. This execution plan might be considerably more complex than is immediately apparent. In addition to the actual commands, the execution plan includes all the steps necessary to ensure that constraints are checked. Steps for calling a trigger are slightly different from those for verifying constraints. If a trigger is included for the action being taken, a call to the procedure that comprises the trigger is appended. If the trigger is an *instead-of* trigger, the call to the trigger's plan replaces the actual data modification command. For *after* triggers, the trigger's plan is branched to right after the plan for the modification statement that fired the trigger, before that modification is committed. The specific steps for the trigger are not compiled into the execution plan, unlike those for constraint verification.

A simple request to insert one row into a table with multiple constraints can result in an execution plan that requires many other tables to be accessed or expressions to be evaluated as well. In addition, the existence of a trigger can cause many more steps to be executed. The step that carries out the actual *INSERT* statement might be just a small part of the total execution plan necessary to ensure that all actions and constraints associated with adding a row are carried out.

## The Query Executor

The query executor runs the execution plan that the Query Optimizer produced, acting as a dispatcher for all the commands in the execution plan. This module steps through each command of the execution plan until the batch is complete. Most of the commands require interaction with the storage engine to modify or retrieve data and to manage transactions and locking. More information on query execution, and execution plans, is available on the companion Web site, *http://www.SQLServerInternals.com/companion*.

# The Storage Engine

The SQL Server storage engine includes all the components involved with the accessing and managing of data in your database. In SQL Server 2008, the storage engine is composed of three main areas: access methods, locking and transaction services, and utility commands.

## Access Methods

When SQL Server needs to locate data, it calls the access methods code. The access methods code sets up and requests scans of data pages and index pages and prepares the OLE DB row sets to return to the relational engine. Similarly, when data is to be inserted, the access methods code can receive an OLE DB row set from the client. The access methods code contains components to open a table, retrieve qualified data, and update data. The access methods code doesn't actually retrieve the pages; it makes the request to the buffer manager, which ultimately serves up the page in its cache or reads it to cache from disk. When the scan starts, a look-ahead mechanism qualifies the rows or index entries on a page. The retrieving of rows that meet specified criteria is known as a *qualified retrieval*. The access methods code is employed not only for *SELECT* statements but also for qualified *UPDATE* and *DELETE* statements (for example, *UPDATE* with a WHERE clause) and for any data modification operations that need to modify index entries. Some types of access methods are listed below.

**Row and Index Operations**     You can consider row and index operations to be components of the access methods code because they carry out the actual method of access. Each component is responsible for manipulating and maintaining its respective on-disk data structures—namely, rows of data or B-tree indexes, respectively. They understand and manipulate information on data and index pages.

The row operations code retrieves, modifies, and performs operations on individual rows. It performs an operation within a row, such as "retrieve column 2" or "write this value to column 3." As a result of the work performed by the access methods code, as well as by the lock and transaction management components (discussed shortly), the row is found and appropriately locked as part of a transaction. After formatting or modifying a row in memory, the row operations code inserts or deletes a row. There are special operations that the row operations code needs to handle if the data is a Large Object (LOB) data type—*text, image,* or *ntext*—or if the row is too large to fit on a single page and needs to be stored as overflow data. We'll look at the different types of data storage structures in Chapters 5, "Tables," 6, "Indexes: Internals and Management," and 7, "Special Storage."

The index operations code maintains and supports searches on B-trees, which are used for SQL Server indexes. An index is structured as a tree, with a root page and intermediate-level and lower-level pages. (If the tree is very small, there might not be intermediate-level pages.) A B-tree groups records that have similar index keys, thereby allowing fast access to data by searching on a key value. The B-tree's core feature is its ability to balance the index tree. (*B* stands for *balanced.*) Branches of the index tree are spliced together or split apart as necessary so that the search for any given record always traverses the same number of levels and therefore requires the same number of page accesses.

**Page Allocation Operations**     The allocation operations code manages a collection of pages for each database and keeps track of which pages in a database have already been used, for what purpose they have been used, and how much space is available on each page. Each database is a collection of 8-KB disk pages that are spread across one or more physical files. (In Chapter 3, "Databases and Database Files," you'll find more details about the physical organization of databases.)

SQL Server uses 13 types of disk pages. The ones we'll be discussing in this book are data pages, two types of LOB pages, row-overflow pages, index pages, Page Free Space (PFS) pages, Global Allocation Map and Shared Global Allocation Map (GAM and SGAM) pages, Index Allocation Map (IAM) pages, Bulk Changed Map (BCM) pages, and Differential Changed Map (DCM) pages.

All user data is stored on data or LOB pages, and all index rows are stored on index pages. PFS pages keep track of which pages in a database are available to hold new data. Allocation pages (GAMs, SGAMs, and IAMs) keep track of the other pages. They contain no database rows and are used only internally. BCM and DCM pages are used to make backup and recovery more efficient. We'll explain these types of pages in Chapters 3 and 4, "Logging and Recovery."

**Versioning Operations**     Another type of data access, which was added to the product in SQL Server 2005, is access through the version store. Row versioning allows SQL Server to maintain older versions of changed rows. The row versioning technology in SQL Server supports Snapshot isolation as well as other features of SQL Server 2008, including online index builds and triggers, and it is the versioning operations code that maintains row versions for whatever purpose they are needed.

Chapters 3, 5, 6, and 7 deal extensively with the internal details of the structures that the access methods code works with: databases, tables, and indexes.

## Transaction Services

A core feature of SQL Server is its ability to ensure that transactions are *atomic*—that is, all or nothing. In addition, transactions must be durable, which means that if a transaction has been committed, it must be recoverable by SQL Server no matter what—even if a total system failure occurs one millisecond after the commit was acknowledged. There are actually four properties that transactions must adhere to: *atomicity, consistency, isolation,* and *durability,* called the *ACID properties.* we'll discuss all four of these properties in Chapter 10, "Transactions and Concurrency," when we discuss transaction management and concurrency issues.

In SQL Server, if work is in progress and a system failure occurs before the transaction is committed, all the work is rolled back to the state that existed before the transaction began. Write-ahead logging makes it possible to always roll back work in progress or roll forward committed work that has not yet been applied to the data pages. Write-ahead logging ensures that the record of each transaction's changes is captured on disk in the transaction log before a transaction is acknowledged as committed, and that the log records are always written to disk before the data pages where the changes were actually made are written. Writes to the transaction log are always synchronous—that is, SQL Server must wait for them to complete. Writes to the data pages can be asynchronous because all the effects can be reconstructed from the log if necessary. The transaction management component coordinates logging, recovery, and buffer management. These topics are discussed later in this book; at this point, we'll just look briefly at transactions themselves.

The transaction management component delineates the boundaries of statements that must be grouped together to form an operation. It handles transactions that cross databases within the same SQL Server instance, and it allows nested transaction sequences. (However, nested transactions simply execute in the context of the first-level transaction; no special action occurs when they are committed. And a rollback specified in a lower level of a nested transaction undoes the entire transaction.) For a distributed transaction to another SQL Server instance (or to any other resource manager), the transaction management component coordinates with the Microsoft Distributed Transaction Coordinator (MS DTC) service using operating system remote procedure calls. The transaction management component marks *save points*—points you designate within a transaction at which work can be partially rolled back or undone.

The transaction management component also coordinates with the locking code regarding when locks can be released, based on the isolation level in effect. It also coordinates with the versioning code to determine when old versions are no longer needed and can be removed from the version store. The isolation level in which your transaction runs determines how sensitive your application is to changes made by others and consequently how long your transaction must hold locks or maintain versioned data to protect against those changes.

SQL Server 2008 supports two concurrency models for guaranteeing the ACID properties of transactions: optimistic concurrency and pessimistic concurrency. Pessimistic concurrency guarantees correctness and consistency by locking data so that it cannot be changed; this is the concurrency model that every version of SQL Server prior to SQL Server 2005 used exclusively, and it is the default in both SQL Server 2005 and SQL Server 2008. SQL Server 2005 introduced optimistic concurrency, which provides consistent data by keeping older versions of rows with committed values in an area of *tempdb* called the *version store*. With optimistic concurrency, readers do not block writers and writers do not block readers, but writers still block writers. The cost of these nonblocking reads and writes must be considered. To support optimistic concurrency, SQL Server needs to spend more time managing the version store. In addition, administrators have to pay close attention to the *tempdb* database and plan for the extra maintenance it requires.

Five isolation-level semantics are available in SQL Server 2008. Three of them support only pessimistic concurrency: Read Uncommitted, Repeatable Read, and Serializable. Snapshot isolation level supports optimistic concurrency. The default isolation level, Read Committed, can support either optimistic or pessimistic concurrency, depending on a database setting.

The behavior of your transactions depends on the isolation level and the concurrency model you are working with. A complete understanding of isolation levels also requires an understanding of locking because the topics are so closely related. The next section gives an overview of locking; you'll find more detailed information on isolation, transactions, and concurrency management in Chapter 10.

**Locking Operations**    Locking is a crucial function of a multiuser database system such as SQL Server, even if you are operating primarily in the Snapshot isolation level with optimistic concurrency. SQL Server lets you manage multiple users simultaneously and ensures that the transactions observe the properties of the chosen isolation level. Even though readers do not block writers and writers do not block readers in Snapshot isolation, writers do acquire locks and can still block other writers, and if two writers try to change the same data concurrently, a conflict occurs that must be resolved. The locking code acquires and releases various types of locks, such as share locks for reading, exclusive locks for writing, intent locks taken at a higher granularity to signal a potential "plan" to perform some operation, and extent locks for space allocation. It manages compatibility between the lock types, resolves deadlocks, and escalates locks if needed. The locking code controls table, page, and row locks as well as system data locks.

**Note**  Concurrency, with locks or row versions, is an important aspect of SQL Server. Many developers are keenly interested in it because of its potential effect on application performance. Chapter 10 is devoted to the subject, so we won't go into it further here.

### Other Operations

Also included in the storage engine are components for controlling utilities such as bulk-load, DBCC commands, full-text index population and management, and backup and restore operations. DBCC is discussed in detail in Chapter 11, "DBCC Internals." The log manager makes sure that log records are written in a manner to guarantee transaction durability and recoverability; we'll go into detail about the transaction log and its role in backup and restore operations in Chapter 4.

# The SQLOS

The SQLOS is a separate application layer at the lowest level of the SQL Server Database Engine, that both SQL Server and SQL Reporting Services run atop. Earlier versions of SQL Server have a thin layer of interfaces between the storage engine and the actual operating system through which SQL Server makes calls to the operating system for memory allocation, scheduler resources, thread and worker management, and synchronization objects. However, the services in SQL Server that needed to access these interfaces can be in any part of the engine. SQL Server requirements for managing memory, schedulers, synchronization objects, and so forth have become more complex. Rather than each part of the engine growing to support the increased functionality, a single application layer has been designed to manage all operating system resources that are specific to SQL Server.

The two main functions of SQLOS are scheduling and memory management, both of which we'll talk about in detail later in this section. Other functions of SQLOS include the following:

**Synchronization**   Synchronization objects include spinlocks, mutexes, and special reader/ writer locks on system resources.

**Memory Brokers**   Memory brokers distribute memory allocation between various components within SQL Server, but do not perform any allocations, which are handled by the Memory Manager.

**SQL Server Exception Handling**   Exception handling involves dealing with user errors as well as system-generated errors.

**Deadlock Detection**   The deadlock detection mechanism doesn't just involve locks, but checks for any tasks holding onto resources, that are mutually blocking each other. We'll talk about deadlocks involving locks (by far the most common kind) in Chapter 10.

**Extended Events**   Tracking extended events is similar to the SQL Trace capability, but is much more efficient because the tracking runs at a much lower level than SQL Trace. In addition, because the extended event layer is so low and deep, there are many more types of events that can be tracked. The SQL Server 2008 Resource Governor manages resource usage using extended events. We'll talk about extended events in Chapter 2, "Change Tracking, Tracing, and Extended Events." (In a future version, all tracing will be handled at this level by extended events.)

**Asynchronous IO**   The difference between asynchronous and synchronous is what part of the system is actually waiting for an unavailable resource. When SQL Server requests a synchronous I/O, if the resource is not available the Windows kernel will put the thread on a wait queue until the resource becomes available. For asynchronous I/O, SQL Server requests that Windows initiate an I/O. Windows starts the I/O operation and doesn't stop the thread from running. SQL Server will then place the server session in an I/O wait queue until it gets the signal from Windows that the resource is available.

## NUMA Architecture

SQL Server 2008 is NUMA–aware, and both scheduling and memory management can take advantage of NUMA hardware by default. You can use some special configurations when you work with NUMA, so we'll provide some general background here before discussing scheduling and memory.

The main benefit of NUMA is scalability, which has definite limits when you use symmetric multiprocessing (SMP) architecture. With SMP, all memory access is posted to the same shared memory bus. This works fine for a relatively small number of CPUs, but problems appear when you have many CPUs competing for access to the shared memory bus. The trend in hardware has been to have more than one system bus, each serving a small set of processors. NUMA limits the number of CPUs on any one memory bus. Each group of processors has its own memory and possibly its own I/O channels. However, each CPU can access memory associated with other groups in a coherent way, and we'll discuss this a bit more later in the chapter. Each group is called a *NUMA node,* and the nodes are linked to each other by a high-speed interconnection. The number of CPUs within a NUMA node depends on the hardware vendor. It is faster to access local memory than the memory associated with other NUMA nodes. This is the reason for the name *Non-Uniform Memory Access.* Figure 1-3 shows a NUMA node with four CPUs.

SQL Server 2008 allows you to subdivide one or more physical NUMA nodes into smaller NUMA nodes, referred to as *software NUMA* or *soft-NUMA.* You typically use *soft-NUMA* when you have many CPUs and do not have hardware NUMA because soft-NUMA allows only for the subdividing of CPUs but not memory. You can also use soft-NUMA to subdivide hardware NUMA nodes into groups of fewer CPUs than is provided by the hardware NUMA. Your soft-NUMA nodes can also be configured to listen on their own ports.

Only the SQL Server scheduler and SNI are soft-NUMA–aware. Memory nodes are created based on hardware NUMA and are therefore not affected by soft-NUMA.

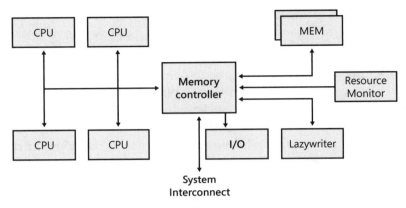

**FIGURE 1-3** A NUMA node with four CPUs

TCP/IP, VIA, Named Pipes, and shared memory can take advantage of NUMA round-robin scheduling, but only TCP and VIA can affinitize to a specific set of NUMA nodes. See *SQL Server Books Online* for how to use the SQL Server Configuration Manager to set a TCP/IP address and port to single or multiple nodes.

# The Scheduler

Prior to SQL Server 7.0, scheduling depended entirely on the underlying Microsoft Windows operating system. Although this meant that SQL Server could take advantage of the hard work done by Windows engineers to enhance scalability and efficient processor use, there were definite limits. The Windows scheduler knew nothing about the needs of a relational database system, so it treated SQL Server worker threads the same as any other process running on the operating system. However, a high-performance system such as SQL Server functions best when the scheduler can meet its special needs. SQL Server 7.0 and all subsequent versions are designed to handle their own scheduling to gain a number of advantages, including the following:

- A private scheduler can support SQL Server tasks using fibers as easily as it supports using threads.

- Context switching and switching into kernel mode can be avoided as much as possible.

> **Note** The scheduler in SQL Server 7.0 and SQL Server 2000 was called the *User Mode Scheduler* (UMS) to reflect the fact that it ran primarily in user mode, as opposed to kernel mode. SQL Server 2005 and 2008 call the scheduler the SOS Scheduler and improve on UMS even more.

One major difference between the SOS scheduler and the Windows scheduler is that the SQL Server scheduler runs as a cooperative rather than a preemptive scheduler. This means that it relies on the workers, threads, or fibers to yield voluntarily often enough so one process or thread doesn't have exclusive control of the system. The SQL Server product team has to make sure that its code runs efficiently and voluntarily yields the scheduler in appropriate places; the reward for this is much greater control and scalability than is possible with the Windows scheduler.

Even though the scheduler is not preemptive, the SQL Server scheduler still adheres to a concept of a quantum. Instead of SQL Server tasks being forced to give up the CPU by the operating system, SQL Server tasks can request to be put on a wait queue periodically, and if they have exceeded the internally defined quantum, and they are not in the middle of an operation that cannot be stopped, they will voluntarily relinquish the CPU.

# SQL Server Workers

You can think of the SQL Server scheduler as a logical CPU used by SQL Server workers. A worker can be either a thread or a fiber that is bound to a logical scheduler. If the Affinity Mask Configuration option is set, each scheduler is affinitized to a particular CPU. (We'll talk about configuration later in this chapter.) Thus, each worker is also associated with a single CPU. Each scheduler is assigned a worker limit based on the configured Max Worker Threads and the number of schedulers, and each scheduler is responsible for creating or destroying workers as needed. A worker cannot move from one scheduler to another, but as workers are destroyed and created, it can appear as if workers are moving between schedulers.

Workers are created when the scheduler receives a request (a task to execute) and there are no idle workers. A worker can be destroyed if it has been idle for at least 15 minutes, or if SQL Server is under memory pressure. Each worker can use at least half a megabyte of memory on a 32-bit system and at least 2 MB on a 64-bit system, so destroying multiple workers and freeing their memory can yield an immediate performance improvement on memory-starved systems. SQL Server actually handles the worker pool very efficiently, and you might be surprised to know that even on very large systems with hundreds or even thousands of users, the actual number of SQL Server workers might be much lower than the configured value for Max Worker Threads. Later in this section, we'll tell you about some of the Dynamic Management Objects that let you see how many workers you actually have, as well as scheduler and task information (discussed in the next section).

## SQL Server Schedulers

In SQL Server 2008, each actual CPU (whether hyperthreaded or physical) has a scheduler created for it when SQL Server starts. This is true even if the affinity mask option has been configured so that SQL Server is set to not use all the available physical CPUs. In SQL Server 2008, each scheduler is set to either ONLINE or OFFLINE based on the affinity mask settings, and the default is that all schedulers are ONLINE. Changing the affinity mask value can change the status of one or more schedulers to OFFLINE, and you can do this without having to restart your SQL Server. Note that when a scheduler is switched from ONLINE to OFFLINE due to a configuration change, any work already assigned to the scheduler is first completed and no new work is assigned.

## SQL Server Tasks

The unit of work for a SQL Server worker is a *request*, or a *task*, which you can think of as being equivalent to a single batch sent from the client to the server. Once a request is received by SQL Server, it is bound to a worker, and that worker processes the entire request before handling any other request. This holds true even if the request is blocked for some reason, such as while it waits for a lock or for I/O to complete. The particular worker does not handle any new requests but waits until the blocking condition is resolved and the request can be completed. Keep in mind that a session ID (SPID) is not the same as a task. A SPID is a connection or channel over which requests can be sent, but there is not always an active request on any particular SPID.

In SQL Server 2008, a SPID is not bound to a particular scheduler. Each SPID has a preferred scheduler, which is the scheduler that most recently processed a request from the SPID. The SPID is initially assigned to the scheduler with the lowest load. (You can get some insight into the load on each scheduler by looking at the *load_factor* column in the DMV *sys.dm_os_schedulers*.) However, when subsequent requests are sent from the same SPID, if another scheduler has a load factor that is less than a certain percentage of the average of the scheduler's entire load factor, the new task is given to the scheduler with the smallest load factor. There is a restriction that all tasks for one SPID must be processed by schedulers on the same NUMA node. The exception to this restriction is when a query is being executed as a parallel query across multiple CPUs. The optimizer can decide to use more CPUs that are available on the NUMA node processing the query, so other CPUs (and other schedulers) can be used.

## Threads vs. Fibers

As mentioned earlier, the UMS was designed to work with workers running on either threads or fibers. Windows fibers have less overhead associated with them than threads do, and multiple fibers can run on a single thread. You can configure SQL Server to run in fiber mode by setting the Lightweight Pooling option to 1. Although using less overhead and a "lightweight" mechanism sounds like a good idea, you should evaluate the use of fibers carefully.

Certain components of SQL Server don't work, or don't work well, when SQL Server runs in fiber mode. These components include SQLMail and SQLXML. Other components, such as heterogeneous and CLR queries, are not supported at all in fiber mode because they need certain thread-specific facilities provided by Windows. Although it is possible for SQL Server to switch to thread mode to process requests that need it, the overhead might be greater than the overhead of using threads exclusively. Fiber mode was actually intended just for special niche situations in which SQL Server reaches a limit in scalability due to spending too much time switching between thread contexts or switching between user mode and kernel mode. In most environments, the performance benefit gained by fibers is quite small compared to the benefits you can get by tuning in other areas. If you're certain you have a situation that could benefit from fibers, be sure to test thoroughly before you set the option on a production server. In addition, you might even want to contact Microsoft Customer Support Services (*http://support.microsoft.com/ph/2855*) just to be certain.

## NUMA and Schedulers

With a NUMA configuration, every node has some subset of the machine's processors and the same number of schedulers. If the machine is configured for hardware NUMA, the number of processors on each node will be preset, but for soft-NUMA that you configure yourself, you can decide how many processors are assigned to each node. There is still the same number of schedulers as processors, however. When SPIDs are first created, they are assigned to nodes on a round-robin basis. The Scheduler Monitor then assigns the SPID to the least loaded scheduler on that node. As mentioned earlier, if the SPID is moved to another scheduler, it stays on the same node. A single processor or SMP machine will be treated as a machine with a single NUMA node. Just like on an SMP machine, there is no hard mapping between schedulers and a CPU with NUMA, so any scheduler on an individual node can run on any CPU on that node. However, if you have set the Affinity Mask Configuration option, each scheduler on each node will be fixed to run on a particular CPU.

Every NUMA node has its own lazywriter (which we'll talk about in the section entitled "Memory," later in this chapter) as well as its own I/O Completion Port (IOCP), which is the network listener. Every node also has its own Resource Monitor, which is managed by a hidden scheduler. You can see the hidden schedulers in *sys.dm_os_schedulers*. Each Resource Monitor has its own SPID, which you can see by querying the *sys.dm_exec_requests* and *sys.dm_os_workers* DMVs, as shown here:

```
SELECT session_id,
    CONVERT (varchar(10), t1.status) AS status,
    CONVERT (varchar(20), t1.command) AS command,
    CONVERT (varchar(15), t2.state) AS worker_state
FROM sys.dm_exec_requests AS t1 JOIN sys.dm_os_workers AS t2
ON  t2.task_address = t1.task_address
WHERE command = 'RESOURCE MONITOR';
```

Every node has its own Scheduler Monitor, which can run on any SPID and runs in a preemptive mode. The Scheduler Monitor is a thread that wakes up periodically and checks each scheduler to see if it has yielded since the last time the Scheduler Monitor woke up (unless the scheduler is idle). The Scheduler Monitor raises an error (17883) if a nonidle thread has not yielded. The 17883 error can occur when an application other than SQL Server is monopolizing the CPU. The Scheduler Monitor knows only that the CPU is not yielding; it can't ascertain what kind of task is using it. The Scheduler Monitor is also responsible for sending messages to the schedulers to help them balance their workload.

## Dynamic Affinity

In SQL Server 2008 (in all editions except SQL Server Express), processor affinity can be controlled dynamically. When SQL Server starts up, all scheduler tasks are started on server startup, so there is one scheduler per CPU. If the affinity mask has been set, some of the schedulers are then marked as offline and no tasks are assigned to them.

When the affinity mask is changed to include additional CPUs, the new CPU is brought online. The Scheduler Monitor then notices an imbalance in the workload and starts picking workers to move to the new CPU. When a CPU is brought offline by changing the affinity mask, the scheduler for that CPU continues to run active workers, but the scheduler itself is moved to one of the other CPUs that are still online. No new workers are given to this scheduler, which is now offline, and when all active workers have finished their tasks, the scheduler stops.

## Binding Schedulers to CPUs

Remember that normally, schedulers are not bound to CPUs in a strict one-to-one relationship, even though there is the same number of schedulers as CPUs. A scheduler is bound to a CPU only when the affinity mask is set. This is true even if you specify that the affinity mask use all the CPUs, which is the default setting. For example, the default Affinity Mask Configuration value is 0, which means to use all CPUs, with no hard binding of scheduler to CPU. In fact, in some cases when there is a heavy load on the machine, Windows can run two schedulers on one CPU.

For an eight-processor machine, an affinity mask value of 3 (bit string 00000011) means that only CPUs 0 and 1 are used and two schedulers are bound to the two CPUs. If you set the affinity mask to 255 (bit string 11111111), all the CPUs are used, just as with the default. However, with the affinity mask set, the eight CPUs will be bound to the eight schedulers.

In some situations, you might want to limit the number of CPUs available but not bind a particular scheduler to a single CPU—for example, if you are using a multiple-CPU machine for server consolidation. Suppose that you have a 64-processor machine on which you are running eight SQL Server instances and you want each instance to use eight of the processors. Each instance has a different affinity mask that specifies a different subset of the 64 processors, so you might have affinity mask values 255 (0xFF), 65280 (0xFF00), 16711680 (0xFF0000), and 4278190080 (0xFF000000). Because the affinity mask is set, each instance has hard binding of scheduler to CPU. If you want to limit the number of CPUs but still not constrain a particular scheduler to running on a specific CPU, you can start SQL Server with trace flag 8002. This lets you have CPUs mapped to an instance, but within the instance, schedulers are not bound to CPUs.

### Observing Scheduler Internals

SQL Server 2008 has several Dynamic Management Objects that provide information about schedulers, workers, and tasks. These are primarily intended for use by Microsoft Customer Support Services, but you can use them to gain a greater appreciation for the information that SQL Server monitors.

> **Note**  All these objects (as well as most of the other Dynamic Management Objects) require a permission called *View Server State*. By default, only a SQL Server administrator has that permission, but it can be granted to others. For each of the objects, we will list some of the more useful or interesting columns and provide the description of each column taken from *SQL Server 2008 Books Online*. For the full list of columns, most of which are useful only to support personnel, you can refer to *SQL Server Books Online,* but even then, you'll find that some of the columns are listed as "for internal use only."

These Dynamic Management Objects are as follows:

**sys.dm_os_schedulers**   This view returns one row per scheduler in SQL Server. Each scheduler is mapped to an individual processor in SQL Server. You can use this view to monitor the condition of a scheduler or to identify runaway tasks. Interesting columns include the following:

 **parent_node_id**   The ID of the node that the scheduler belongs to, also known as the *parent node*. This represents a NUMA node.

 **scheduler_id**   The ID of the scheduler. All schedulers that are used to run regular queries have IDs of less than 255. Those with IDs greater than or equal to 255, such as the dedicated administrator connection scheduler, are used internally by SQL Server.

 **cpu_id**   The ID of the CPU with which this scheduler is associated. If SQL Server is configured to run with affinity, the value is the ID of the CPU on which the scheduler is supposed to run. If the affinity mask has not been specified, the *cpu_id* will be 255.

 **is_online**   If SQL Server is configured to use only some of the available processors on the server, this can mean that some schedulers are mapped to processors that are not in the affinity mask. If that is the case, this column returns 0. This means the scheduler is not being used to process queries or batches.

 **current_tasks_count**   The number of current tasks associated with this scheduler, including the following. (When a task is completed, this count is decremented.)

  ❏  Tasks that are waiting on a resource to be acquired before proceeding

  ❏  Tasks that are currently running or that are runnable and waiting to be executed

 **runnable_tasks_count**   The number of tasks waiting to run on the scheduler.

 **current_workers_count**   The number of workers associated with this scheduler, including workers that are not assigned any task.

 **active_workers_count**   The number of workers that have been assigned a task.

 **work_queue_count**   The number of tasks waiting for a worker. If *current_workers_count* is greater than *active_workers_count*, this work queue count should be 0 and the work queue should not grow.

*pending_disk_io_count*    The number of pending I/Os. Each scheduler has a list of pending I/Os that are checked every time there is a context switch to determine whether they have been completed. The count is incremented when the request is inserted. It is decremented when the request is completed. This number does not indicate the state of the I/Os.

*load_factor*    The internal value that indicates the perceived load on this scheduler. This value is used to determine whether a new task should be put on this scheduler or another scheduler. It is useful for debugging purposes when schedulers appear not to be evenly loaded. In SQL Server 2000, a task is routed to a particular scheduler. In SQL Server 2008, the routing decision is based on the load on the scheduler. SQL Server 2008 also uses a load factor of nodes and schedulers to help determine the best location to acquire resources. When a task is added to the queue, the load factor increases. When a task is completed, the load factor decreases. Using load factors helps the SQLOS balance the work load better.

*sys.dm_os_workers*    This view returns a row for every worker in the system. Interesting columns include the following:

*is_preemptive*    A value of 1 means that the worker is running with preemptive scheduling. Any worker running external code is run under preemptive scheduling.

*is_fiber*    A value of 1 means that the worker is running with lightweight pooling.

*sys.dm_os_threads*    This view returns a list of all SQLOS threads that are running under the SQL Server process. Interesting columns include the following:

*started_by_sqlserver*    Indicates the thread initiator. A 1 means that SQL Server started the thread and 0 means that another component, such as an extended procedure from within SQL Server, started the thread.

*creation_time*    The time when this thread was created.

*stack_bytes_used*    The number of bytes that are actively being used on the thread.

*affinity*    The CPU mask on which this thread is supposed to be running. This depends on the value in the *sp_configure* "affinity mask."

*locale*    The cached locale LCID for the thread.

*sys.dm_os_tasks*    This view returns one row for each task that is active in the instance of SQL Server. Interesting columns include the following:

*task_state*    The state of the task. The value can be one of the following:

- ❑ PENDING: Waiting for a worker thread
- ❑ RUNNABLE: Runnable but waiting to receive a quantum
- ❑ RUNNING: Currently running on the scheduler

❑   SUSPENDED: Has a worker but is waiting for an event

❑   DONE: Completed

❑   SPINLOOP: Processing a spinlock, as when waiting for a signal

*context_switches_count*   The number of scheduler context switches that this task has completed.

*pending_io_count*   The number of physical I/Os performed by this task.

*pending_io_byte_count*   The total byte count of I/Os performed by this task.

*pending_io_byte_average*   The average byte count of I/Os performed by this task.

*scheduler_id*   The ID of the parent scheduler. This is a handle to the scheduler information for this task.

*session_id*   The ID of the session associated with the task.

**sys.dm_os_waiting_tasks**   This view returns information about the queue of tasks that are waiting on some resource. Interesting columns include the following:

*session_id*   The ID of the session associated with the task.

*exec_context_id*   The ID of the execution context associated with the task.

*wait_duration_ms*   The total wait time for this wait type, in milliseconds. This time is inclusive of *signal_wait_time*.

*wait_type*   The name of the wait type.

*resource_address*   The address of the resource for which the task is waiting.

*blocking_task_address*   The task that is currently holding this resource.

*blocking_session_id*   The ID of the session of the blocking task.

*blocking_exec_context_id*   The ID of the execution context of the blocking task.

*resource_description*   The description of the resource that is being consumed.

## The Dedicated Administrator Connection (DAC)

Under extreme conditions such as a complete lack of available resources, it is possible for SQL Server to enter an abnormal state in which no further connections can be made to the SQL Server instance. Prior to SQL Server 2005, this situation meant that an administrator could not get in to kill any troublesome connections or even begin to diagnose the possible cause of the problem. SQL Server 2005 introduced a special connection called the *DAC* that was designed to be accessible even when no other access can be made.

Access via the DAC must be specially requested. You can connect to the DAC using the command-line tool SQLCMD, and specifying the *-A* (or */A*) flag. This method of connection is recommended because it uses fewer resources than the graphical user interface (GUI).

Through Management Studio, you can specify that you want to connect using DAC by preceding the name of your SQL Server with *ADMIN:* in the Connection dialog box.

For example, to connect to the default SQL Server instance on my machine, TENAR, we would enter **ADMIN:TENAR**. To connect to a named instance called SQL2008 on the same machine, we would enter **ADMIN:TENAR\SQL2008**.

The DAC is a special-purpose connection designed for diagnosing problems in SQL Server and possibly resolving them. It is not meant to be used as a regular user connection. Any attempt to connect using the DAC when there is already an active DAC connection results in an error. The message returned to the client says only that the connection was rejected; it does not state explicitly that it was because there already was an active DAC. However, a message is written to the error log indicating the attempt (and failure) to get a second DAC connection. You can check whether a DAC is in use by running the following query. If there is an active DAC, the query will return the SPID for the DAC; otherwise, it will return no rows.

```
SELECT s.session_id
FROM sys.tcp_endpoints as e JOIN sys.dm_exec_sessions as s
   ON e.endpoint_id = s.endpoint_id
WHERE e.name='Dedicated Admin Connection';
```

You should keep the following points in mind about using the DAC:

- By default, the DAC is available only locally. However, an administrator can configure SQL Server to allow remote connection by using the configuration option called *Remote Admin Connections*.

- The user logon to connect via the DAC must be a member of the *sysadmin* server role.

- There are only a few restrictions on the SQL statements that can be executed on the DAC. (For example, you cannot run *BACKUP* or *RESTORE* using the DAC.) However, it is recommended that you do not run any resource-intensive queries that might exacerbate the problem that led you to use the DAC. The DAC connection is created primarily for troubleshooting and diagnostic purposes. In general, you'll use the DAC for running queries against the Dynamic Management Objects, some of which you've seen already and many more of which we'll discuss later in this book.

- A special thread is assigned to the DAC that allows it to execute the diagnostic functions or queries on a separate scheduler. This thread cannot be terminated. You can kill only the DAC session, if needed. The DAC scheduler always uses the *scheduler_id* value of 255, and this thread has the highest priority. There is no lazywriter thread for the DAC, but the DAC does have its own IOCP, a worker thread, and an idle thread.

You might not always be able to accomplish your intended tasks using the DAC. Suppose you have an idle connection that is holding on to a lock. If the connection has no active task, there is no thread associated with it, only a connection ID. Suppose further that many other processes are trying to get access to the locked resource, and that they are blocked. Those connections still have an incomplete task, so they do not release their worker. If 255 such processes (the default number of worker threads) try to get the same lock, all available workers might get used up and no more connections can be made to SQL Server. Because the DAC has its own scheduler, you can start it, and the expected solution would be to kill the connection that is holding the lock but not do any further processing to release the lock. But if you try to use the DAC to kill the process holding the lock, the attempt fails. SQL Server would need to give a worker to the task to kill it, and no workers are available. The only solution is to kill several of the (blameless) blocked processes that still have workers associated with them.

 **Note**  To conserve resources, SQL Server 2008 Express edition does not support a DAC connection unless started with a trace flag 7806.

The DAC is not guaranteed to always be usable, but because it reserves memory and a private scheduler and is implemented as a separate node, a connection probably is possible when you cannot connect in any other way.

# Memory

Memory management is a huge topic, and to cover every detail of it would require a whole book in itself. My goal in this section is twofold: first, to provide enough information about how SQL Server uses its memory resources so you can determine whether memory is being managed well on your system; and second, to describe the aspects of memory management that you have control over so you can understand when to exert that control.

By default, SQL Server 2008 manages its memory resources almost completely dynamically. When allocating memory, SQL Server must communicate constantly with the operating system, which is one of the reasons the SQLOS layer of the engine is so important.

## The Buffer Pool and the Data Cache

The main memory component in SQL Server is the buffer pool. All memory not used by another memory component remains in the buffer pool to be used as a data cache for pages read in from the database files on disk. The buffer manager manages disk I/O functions for bringing data and index pages into the data cache so data can be shared among users. When other components require memory, they can request a buffer from the buffer pool. A buffer is a page in memory that's the same size as a data or index page. You can think of it as a page frame that can hold one page from a database. Most of the buffers taken from the buffer pool for other memory components go to other kinds of memory caches, the largest of which is typically the cache for procedure and query plans, which is usually called the *plan cache*.

Occasionally, SQL Server must request contiguous memory in larger blocks than the 8-KB pages that the buffer pool can provide, so memory must be allocated from outside the buffer pool. Use of large memory blocks is typically kept to a minimum, so direct calls to the operating system account for a small fraction of SQL Server memory usage.

## Access to In-Memory Data Pages

Access to pages in the data cache must be fast. Even with real memory, it would be ridiculously inefficient to scan the whole data cache for a page when you have gigabytes of data. Pages in the data cache are therefore hashed for fast access. *Hashing* is a technique that uniformly maps a key via a hash function across a set of hash buckets. A *hash table* is a structure in memory that contains an array of pointers (implemented as a linked list) to the buffer pages. If all the pointers to buffer pages do not fit on a single hash page, a *linked list* chains to additional hash pages.

Given a *dbid-fileno-pageno* identifier (a combination of the database ID, file number, and page number), the hash function converts that key to the hash bucket that should be checked; in essence, the hash bucket serves as an index to the specific page needed. By using hashing, even when large amounts of memory are present, SQL Server can find a specific data page in cache with only a few memory reads. Similarly, it takes only a few memory reads for SQL Server to determine that a desired page is not in cache and that it must be read in from disk.

> **Note** Finding a data page might require that multiple buffers be accessed via the hash buckets chain (linked list). The hash function attempts to uniformly distribute the *dbid-fileno-pageno* values throughout the available hash buckets. The number of hash buckets is set internally by SQL Server and depends on the total size of the buffer pool.

## Managing Pages in the Data Cache

You can use a data page or an index page only if it exists in memory. Therefore, a buffer in the data cache must be available for the page to be read into. Keeping a supply of buffers available for immediate use is an important performance optimization. If a buffer isn't readily available, many memory pages might have to be searched simply to locate a buffer to free up for use as a workspace.

In SQL Server 2008, a single mechanism is responsible both for writing changed pages to disk and for marking as free those pages that have not been referenced for some time. SQL Server maintains a linked list of the addresses of free pages, and any worker needing a buffer page uses the first page of this list.

Every buffer in the data cache has a header that contains information about the last two times the page was referenced and some status information, including whether the page is dirty (that is, it has been changed since it was read into disk). The reference information is used to implement the page replacement policy for the data cache pages, which uses an algorithm called *LRU-K*, which was introduced by Elizabeth O'Neil, Patrick O'Neil, and Gerhard Weikum (in the Proceedings of the ACM SIGMOD Conference, May 1993). This algorithm is a great improvement over a strict Least Recently Used (LRU) replacement policy, which has no knowledge of how recently a page was used. It is also an improvement over a Least Frequently Used (LFU) policy involving reference counters because it requires far fewer adjustments by the engine and much less bookkeeping overhead. An LRU-K algorithm keeps track of the last $K$ times a page was referenced and can differentiate between types of pages, such as index and data pages, with different levels of frequency. It can actually simulate the effect of assigning pages to different buffer pools of specifically tuned sizes. SQL Server 2008 uses a $K$ value of 2, so it keeps track of the two most recent accesses of each buffer page.

The data cache is periodically scanned from the start to the end. Because the buffer cache is all in memory, these scans are quick and require no I/O. During the scan, a value is associated with each buffer based on its usage history. When the value gets low enough, the dirty page indicator is checked. If the page is dirty, a write is scheduled to write the modifications to disk. Instances of SQL Server use a write-ahead log so the write of the dirty data page is blocked while the log page recording the modification is first written to disk. (We'll discuss logging in much more detail in Chapter 4.) After the modified page has been flushed to disk, or if the page was not dirty to start with, the page is freed. The association between the buffer page and the data page that it contains is removed by deleting information about the buffer from the hash table, and the buffer is put on the free list.

Using this algorithm, buffers holding pages that are considered more valuable remain in the active buffer pool whereas buffers holding pages not referenced often enough eventually return to the free buffer list. The instance of SQL Server determines internally the size of the free buffer list, based on the size of the buffer cache. The size cannot be configured.

## The Free Buffer List and the Lazywriter

The work of scanning the buffer pool, writing dirty pages, and populating the free buffer list is primarily performed by the individual workers after they have scheduled an asynchronous read and before the read is completed. The worker gets the address of a section of the buffer pool containing 64 buffers from a central data structure in the SQL Server Database Engine. Once the read has been initiated, the worker checks to see whether the free list is too small. (Note that this process has consumed one or more pages of the list for its own read.) If so, the worker searches for buffers to free up, examining all 64 buffers, regardless of how many it actually finds to free up in that group of 64. If a write must be performed for a dirty buffer in the scanned section, the write is also scheduled.

Each instance of SQL Server also has a thread called *lazywriter* for each NUMA node (and every instance has at least one) that scans through the buffer cache associated with that node. The lazywriter thread sleeps for a specific interval of time, and when it wakes up, it examines the size of the free buffer list. If the list is below a certain threshold, which depends on the total size of the buffer pool, the lazywriter thread scans the buffer pool to repopulate the free list. As buffers are added to the free list, they are also written to disk if they are dirty.

When SQL Server uses memory dynamically, it must constantly be aware of the amount of free memory. The lazywriter for each node queries the system periodically to determine the amount of free physical memory available. The lazywriter expands or shrinks the data cache to keep the operating system's free physical memory at 5 MB (plus or minus 200 KB) to prevent paging. If the operating system has less than 5 MB free, the lazywriter releases memory to the operating system instead of adding it to the free list. If more than 5 MB of physical memory is free, the lazywriter recommits memory to the buffer pool by adding it to the free list. The lazywriter recommits memory to the buffer pool only when it repopulates the free list; a server at rest does not grow its buffer pool.

SQL Server also releases memory to the operating system if it detects that too much paging is taking place. You can tell when SQL Server increases or decreases its total memory use by using one of SQL Server's tracing mechanisms to monitor Server Memory Change events (in the Server Event category). An event is generated whenever memory in SQL Server increases or decreases by 1 MB or 5 percent of the maximum server memory, whichever is greater. You can look at the value of the data element, called *Event Sub Class,* to see whether the change was an increase or a decrease. An *Event Sub Class* value of 1 means a memory increase; a value of 2 means a memory decrease. Tracing will be covered in detail in Chapter 2.

# Checkpoints

The checkpoint process also scans the buffer cache periodically and writes any dirty data pages for a particular database to disk. The difference between the checkpoint process and the lazywriter (or the worker threads' management of pages) is that the checkpoint process never puts buffers on the free list. The only purpose of the checkpoint process is to ensure that pages written before a certain time are written to disk, so that the number of dirty pages in memory is always kept to a minimum, which in turn ensures that the length of time SQL Server requires for recovery of a database after a failure is kept to a minimum. In some cases, checkpoints may find few dirty pages to write to disk if most of the dirty pages have been written to disk by the workers or the lazywriters in the period between two checkpoints.

When a checkpoint occurs, SQL Server writes a checkpoint record to the transaction log, which lists all the transactions that are active. This allows the recovery process to build a table containing a list of all the potentially dirty pages. Checkpoints occur automatically at regular intervals but can also be requested manually.

Checkpoints are triggered when any of the following occurs:

- A database owner (or backup operator) explicitly issues a *CHECKPOINT* command to perform a checkpoint in that database. In SQL Server 2008, you can run multiple checkpoints (in different databases) concurrently by using the *CHECKPOINT* command.

- The log is getting full (more than 70 percent of capacity) and the database is in autotruncate mode. (We'll tell you about autotruncate mode in Chapter 4.) A checkpoint is triggered to truncate the transaction log and free up space. However, if no space can be freed up, perhaps because of a long-running transaction, no checkpoint occurs.

- A long recovery time is estimated. When recovery time is predicted to be longer than the Recovery Interval configuration option, a checkpoint is triggered. SQL Server 2008 uses a simple metric to predict recovery time because it can recover, or redo, in less time than it took the original operations to run. Thus, if checkpoints are taken about as often as the recovery interval frequency, recovery completes within the interval. A recovery interval setting of 1 means that checkpoints occur about every minute so long as transactions are being processed in the database. A minimum amount of work must be done for the automatic checkpoint to fire; this is currently 10 MB of logs per minute. In this way, SQL Server doesn't waste time taking checkpoints on idle databases. A default recovery interval of 0 means that SQL Server chooses an appropriate value; for the current version, this is one minute.

- An orderly shutdown of SQL Server is requested, without the NOWAIT option. A checkpoint operation is then run in each database on the instance. An orderly shutdown occurs when you explicitly shut down SQL Server, unless you do so by using the *SHUTDOWN WITH NOWAIT* command. An orderly shutdown also occurs when the SQL Server service is stopped through Service Control Manager or the net stop command from an operating system prompt.

You can also use the *sp_configure* Recovery Interval option to influence checkpointing frequency, balancing the time to recover vs. any impact on run-time performance. If you're interested in tracing when checkpoints actually occur, you can use the SQL Server extended events *sqlserver.checkpoint_begin* and *sqlserver.checkpoint_end* to monitor checkpoint activity. (Details on extended events can be found in Chapter 2.)

The checkpoint process goes through the buffer pool, scanning the pages in a nonsequential order, and when it finds a dirty page, it looks to see whether any physically contiguous (on the disk) pages are also dirty so that it can do a large block write. But this means that it might, for example, write buffers 14, 200, 260, and 1,000 when it sees that buffer 14 is dirty. (Those pages might have contiguous disk locations even though they're far apart in the buffer pool. In this case, the noncontiguous pages in the buffer pool can be written as a single operation called a *gather-write*.) The process continues to scan the buffer pool until it gets to page 1,000. In some cases, an already written page could potentially be dirty again, and it might need to be written out to disk a second time.

The larger the buffer pool, the greater the chance that a buffer that has already been written will be dirty again before the checkpoint is done. To avoid this, SQL Server uses a bit associated with each buffer called a *generation number*. At the beginning of a checkpoint, all the bits are toggled to the same value, either all 0's or all 1's. As a checkpoint checks a page, it toggles the generation bit to the opposite value. When the checkpoint comes across a page whose bit has already been toggled, it doesn't write that page. Also, any new pages brought into cache during the checkpoint process get the new generation number so they won't be written during that checkpoint cycle. Any pages already written because they're in proximity to other pages (and are written together in a gather write) aren't written a second time.

In some cases checkpoints may issue a substantial amount of I/O, causing the I/O subsystem to get inundated with write requests which can severely impact read performance. On the other hand, there may be periods of relatively low I/O activity that could be utilized. SQL Server 2008 includes a command-line option that allows throttling of checkpoint I/Os. You can use the SQL Server Configuration Manager, and add the *–k* parameter, followed by a decimal number, to the list of startup parameters for the SQL Server service. The value specified indicates the number of megabytes per second that the checkpoint process can write. By using this *–k* option, the I/O overhead of checkpoints can be spread out and have a more measured impact. Remember that by default, the checkpoint process makes sure that SQL Server can recover databases within the recovery interval that you specify. If you enable this option, the default behavior changes, resulting in a long recovery time if you specify a very low value for the parameter. Backups may take a slightly longer time to finish because a checkpoint process that a backup initiates is also delayed. Before enabling this option on a production system, you should make sure that you have enough hardware to sustain the I/O requests that are posted by SQL Server and that you have thoroughly tested your applications on the system.

## Managing Memory in Other Caches

Buffer pool memory that isn't used for the data cache is used for other types of caches, primarily the plan cache. The page replacement policy, as well as the mechanism by which freeable pages are searched for, are quite a bit different than for the data cache.

SQL Server 2008 uses a common caching framework that is used by all caches except the data cache. The framework consists of a set of stores and the Resource Monitor. There are three types of stores: cache stores, user stores (which don't actually have anything to do with users), and object stores. The plan cache is the main example of a cache store, and the metadata cache is the prime example of a user store. Both cache stores and user stores use the same LRU mechanism and the same costing algorithm to determine which pages can stay and which can be freed. Object stores, on the other hand, are just pools of memory blocks and don't require LRU or costing. One example of the use of an object store is the SNI, which uses the object store for pooling network buffers. For the rest of this section, my discussion of stores refers only to cache stores and user stores.

The LRU mechanism used by the stores is a straightforward variation of the clock algorithm. Imagine a clock hand sweeping through the store, looking at every entry; as it touches each entry, it decreases the cost. Once the cost of an entry reaches 0, the entry can be removed from the cache. The cost is reset whenever an entry is reused.

Memory management in the stores takes into account both global and local memory management policies. Global policies consider the total memory on the system and enable the running of the clock algorithm across all the caches. Local policies involve looking at one store or cache in isolation and making sure it is not using a disproportionate amount of memory.

To satisfy global and local policies, the SQL Server stores implement two hands: external and internal. Each store has two clock hands, and you can observe these by examining the DMV *sys.dm_os_memory_cache_clock_hands*. This view contains one internal and one external clock hand for each cache store or user store. The external clock hands implement the global policy, and the internal clock hands implement the local policy. The Resource Monitor is in charge of moving the external hands whenever it notices memory pressure. There are many types of memory pressure, and it is beyond the scope of this book to go into all the details of detecting and troubleshooting memory problems. However, if you take a look at the DMV *sys.dm_os_memory_cache_clock_hands*, specifically at the *removed_last_round_count* column, you can look for a value that is very large compared to other values. If you notice that value increasing dramatically, that is a strong indication of memory pressure. The companion Web site for this book contains a comprehensive white paper called "Troubleshooting Performance Problems in SQL Server 2008," which includes many details on tracking down and dealing with memory problems.

The internal clock moves whenever an individual cache needs to be trimmed. SQL Server attempts to keep each cache reasonably sized compared to other caches. The internal clock hands move only in response to activity. If a worker running a task that accesses a cache notices a high number of entries in the cache or notices that the size of the cache is greater than a certain percentage of memory, the internal clock hand for that cache starts to free up memory for that cache.

### The Memory Broker

Because memory is needed by so many components in SQL Server, and to make sure each component uses memory efficiently, SQL Server uses a Memory Broker, whose job is to analyze the behavior of SQL Server with respect to memory consumption and to improve dynamic memory distribution. The Memory Broker is a centralized mechanism that dynamically distributes memory between the buffer pool, the query executor, the Query Optimizer, and all the various caches, and it attempts to adapt its distribution algorithm for different types of workloads. You can think of the Memory Broker as a control mechanism with a feedback loop. It monitors memory demand and consumption by component, and it uses the information that it gathers to calculate the optimal memory distribution across all components. It can broadcast this information to the component, which then uses the information to adapt its memory usage. You can monitor Memory Broker behavior by querying the Memory Broker ring buffer as follows:

```
SELECT * FROM sys.dm_os_ring_buffers
WHERE ring_buffer_type =
'RING_BUFFER_MEMORY_BROKER';
```

The ring buffer for the Memory Broker is updated only when the Memory Broker wants the behavior of a given component to change—that is, to grow, shrink, or remain stable (if it has previously been growing or shrinking).

## Sizing Memory

When we talk about SQL Server memory, we are actually talking about more than just the buffer pool. SQL Server memory is actually organized into three sections, and the buffer pool is usually the largest and most frequently used. The buffer pool is used as a set of 8-KB buffers, so any memory that is needed in chunks larger than 8 KB is managed separately.

The DMV called *sys.dm_os_memory_clerks* has a column called *multi_pages_kb* that shows how much space is used by a memory component outside the buffer pool:

```
SELECT type, sum(multi_pages_kb)
FROM sys.dm_os_memory_clerks
WHERE multi_pages_kb != 0
GROUP BY type;
```

If your SQL Server instance is configured to use Address Windowing Extensions (AWE) memory, that can be considered a third memory area. AWE is an API that allows a 32-bit application to access physical memory beyond the 32-bit address limit. Although AWE memory is measured as part of the buffer pool, it must be kept track of separately because only data cache pages can use AWE memory. None of the other memory components, such as the plan cache, can use AWE memory.

**Note** If AWE is enabled, the only way to get information about the actual memory consumption of SQL Server is by using SQL Server–specific counters or DMVs inside the server; you won't get this information from operating system–level performance counters.

## Sizing the Buffer Pool

When SQL Server starts, it computes the size of the virtual address space (VAS) of the SQL Server process. Each process running on Windows has its own VAS. The set of all virtual addresses available for process use constitutes the size of the VAS. The size of the VAS depends on the architecture (32- or 64-bit) and the operating system. VAS is just the set of all possible addresses; it might be much greater than the physical memory on the machine.

A 32-bit machine can directly address only 4 GB of memory and, by default, Windows itself reserves the top 2 GB of address space for its own use, which leaves only 2 GB as the maximum size of the VAS for any application, such as SQL Server. You can increase this by enabling a */3GB* flag in the system's Boot.ini file, which allows applications to have a VAS of up to 3 GB. If your system has more than 3 GB of RAM, the only way a 32-bit machine can get to it is by enabling AWE. One benefit of using AWE in SQL Server 2008 is that memory pages allocated through the AWE mechanism are considered locked pages and can never be swapped out.

On a 64-bit platform, the AWE Enabled configuration option is present, but its setting is ignored. However, the Windows policy option Lock Pages in Memory is available, although it is disabled by default. This policy determines which accounts can make use of a Windows feature to keep data in physical memory, preventing the system from paging the data to virtual memory on disk. It is recommended that you enable this policy on a 64-bit system.

On 32-bit operating systems, you have to enable the Lock Pages in Memory option when using AWE. It is recommended that you don't enable the Lock Pages in Memory option if you are not using AWE. Although SQL Server ignores this option when AWE is not enabled, other processes on the system may be affected.

> **Note** Memory management is much more straightforward on a 64-bit machine, both for SQL Server, which has so much more VAS to work with, and for an administrator, who doesn't have to worry about special operating system flags or even whether to enable AWE. Unless you are working only with very small databases and do not expect to need more than a couple of gigabytes of RAM, you should definitely consider running a 64-bit edition of SQL Server 2008.

Table 1-1 shows the possible memory configurations for various editions of SQL Server 2008.

**TABLE 1-1 SQL Server 2008 Memory Configurations**

| Configuration | VAS | Maximum Physical Memory | AWE/Locked Pages Support |
|---|---|---|---|
| Native 32-bit on 32-bit operating system with /3GB boot parameter | 2 GB | 64 GB | AWE |
| | 3 GB | 16 GB | AWE |
| 32-bit on x64 operating system (Windows on Windows) | 4 GB | 64 GB | AWE |
| Native 64-bit on x64 operating system | 8 terabyte | 1 terabyte | Locked Pages |
| Native 64-bit on IA64 operating system | 7 terabyte | 1 terabyte | Locked Pages |

In addition to the VAS size, SQL Server also calculates a value called *Target Memory,* which is the number of 8-KB pages that it expects to be able to allocate. If the configuration option Max Server Memory has been set, Target Memory is the lesser of these two values. Target Memory is recomputed periodically, particularly when it gets a memory notification from Windows. A decrease in the number of target pages on a normally loaded server might indicate a response to external physical memory pressure. You can see the number of target pages by using the Performance Monitor—examine the Target Server Pages counter in the *SQL Server: Memory Manager* object. There is also a DMV called *sys.dm_os_sys_info* that contains one row of general-purpose SQL Server configuration information, including the following columns:

*physical_memory_in_bytes*   The amount of physical memory available.

*virtual_memory_in_bytes*   The amount of virtual memory available to the process in user mode. You can use this value to determine whether SQL Server was started by using a 3-GB switch.

*bpool_commited*   The total number of buffers with pages that have associated memory. This does not include virtual memory.

*bpool_commit_target*   The optimum number of buffers in the buffer pool.

*bpool_visible*   The number of 8-KB buffers in the buffer pool that are directly accessible in the process virtual address space. When not using AWE, when the buffer pool has obtained its memory target (*bpool_committed = bpool_commit_target*), the value of *bpool_visible* equals the value of *bpool_committed*. When using AWE on a 32-bit version of SQL Server, *bpool_visible* represents the size of the AWE mapping window used to access physical memory allocated by the buffer pool. The size of this mapping window is bound by the process address space and, therefore, the visible amount will be smaller than the committed amount and can be reduced further by internal components consuming memory for purposes other than database pages. If the value of *bpool_visible* is too low, you might receive out-of-memory errors.

Although the VAS is reserved, the physical memory up to the target amount is committed only when that memory is required for the current workload that the SQL Server instance is handling. The instance continues to acquire physical memory as needed to support the workload, based on the users connecting and the requests being processed. The SQL Server instance can continue to commit physical memory until it reaches its target or the operating system indicates that there is no more free memory. If SQL Server is notified by the operating system that there is a shortage of free memory, it frees up memory if it has more memory than the configured value for Min Server Memory. Note that SQL Server does not commit memory equal to Min Server Memory initially. It commits only what it needs and what the operating system can afford. The value for Min Server Memory comes into play only after the buffer pool size goes above that amount, and then SQL Server does not let memory go below that setting.

As other applications are started on a computer running an instance of SQL Server, they consume memory, and SQL Server might need to adjust its target memory. Normally, this should be the only situation in which target memory is less than commit memory, and it should stay that way only until memory can be released. The instance of SQL Server adjusts its memory consumption, if possible. If another application is stopped and more memory becomes available, the instance of SQL Server increases the value of its target memory, allowing the memory allocation to grow when needed. SQL Server adjusts its target and releases physical memory only when there is pressure to do so. Thus, a server that is busy for a while can commit large amounts of memory that will not necessarily be released if the system becomes quiescent.

> **Note**  There is no special handling of multiple SQL Server instances on the same machine; there is no attempt to balance memory across all instances. They all compete for the same physical memory, so to make sure none of the instances becomes starved for physical memory, you should use the Min and Max Server Memory option on all SQL Server instances on a multiple-instance machine.

## Observing Memory Internals

SQL Server 2008 includes several Dynamic Management Objects that provide information about memory and the various caches. Like the Dynamic Management Objects containing information about the schedulers, these objects are intended primarily for use by Customer

Support Services to see what SQL Server is doing, but you can use them for the same purpose. To select from these objects, you must have the View Server State permission. Once again, we will list some of the more useful or interesting columns for each object; most of these descriptions are taken from *SQL Server Books Online:*

**sys.dm_os_memory_clerks**    This view returns one row per memory clerk that is currently active in the instance of SQL Server. You can think of a clerk as an accounting unit. Each store described earlier is a clerk, but some clerks are not stores, such as those for the CLR and for full-text search. The following query returns a list of all the types of clerks:

```
SELECT DISTINCT type FROM sys.dm_os_memory_clerks;
```

Interesting columns include the following:

**single_pages_kb**    The amount of single-page memory allocated, in kilobytes. This is the amount of memory allocated by using the single-page allocator of a memory node. This single-page allocator steals pages directly from the buffer pool.

**multi_pages_kb**    The amount of multiple-page memory allocated, in kilobytes. This is the amount of memory allocated by using the multiple-page allocator of the memory nodes. This memory is allocated outside the buffer pool and takes advantage of the virtual allocator of the memory nodes.

**virtual_memory_reserved_kb**    The amount of virtual memory reserved by a memory clerk. This is the amount of memory reserved directly by the component that uses this clerk. In most situations, only the buffer pool reserves VAS directly by using its memory clerk.

**virtual_memory_committed_kb**    The amount of memory committed by the clerk. The amount of committed memory should always be less than the amount of Reserved Memory.

**awe_allocated_kb**    The amount of memory allocated by the memory clerk by using AWE. In SQL Server, only buffer pool clerks (MEMORYCLERK_SQLBUFFERPOOL) use this mechanism, and only when AWE is enabled.

**sys.dm_os_memory_cache_counters**    This view returns a snapshot of the health of each cache of type userstore and cachestore. It provides run-time information about the cache entries allocated, their use, and the source of memory for the cache entries. Interesting columns include the following:

**single_pages_kb**    The amount of single-page memory allocated, in kilobytes. This is the amount of memory allocated by using the single-page allocator. This refers to the 8-KB pages that are taken directly from the buffer pool for this cache.

**multi_pages_kb**    The amount of multiple-page memory allocated, in kilobytes. This is the amount of memory allocated by using the multiple-page allocator of the memory node. This memory is allocated outside the buffer pool and takes advantage of the virtual allocator of the memory nodes.

> *multi_pages_in_use_kb* The amount of multiple-page memory being used, in kilobytes.
>
> *single_pages_in_use_kb* The amount of single-page memory being used, in kilobytes.
>
> *entries_count* The number of entries in the cache.
>
> *entries_in_use_count* The number of entries in use in the cache.

*sys.dm_os_memory_cache_hash_tables* This view returns a row for each active cache in the instance of SQL Server. This view can be joined to *sys.dm_os_memory_cache_counters* on the *cache_address* column. Interesting columns include the following:

> *buckets_count* The number of buckets in the hash table.
>
> *buckets_in_use_count* The number of buckets currently being used.
>
> *buckets_min_length* The minimum number of cache entries in a bucket.
>
> *buckets_max_length* The maximum number of cache entries in a bucket.
>
> *buckets_avg_length* The average number of cache entries in each bucket. If this number gets very large, it might indicate that the hashing algorithm is not ideal.
>
> *buckets_avg_scan_hit_length* The average number of examined entries in a bucket before the searched-for item was found. As above, a big number might indicate a less-than-optimal cache. You might consider running *DBCC FREESYSTEMCACHE* to remove all unused entries in the cache stores. You can get more details on this command in *SQL Server Books Online*.

*sys.dm_os_memory_cache_clock_hands* This DMV, discussed earlier, can be joined to the other cache DMVs using the *cache_address* column. Interesting columns include the following:

> *clock_hand* The type of clock hand, either external or internal. Remember that there are two clock hands for every store.
>
> *clock_status* The status of the clock hand: suspended or running. A clock hand runs when a corresponding policy kicks in.
>
> *rounds_count* The number of rounds the clock hand has made. All the external clock hands should have the same (or close to the same) value in this column.
>
> *removed_all_rounds_count* The number of entries removed by the clock hand in all rounds.

## NUMA and Memory

As mentioned earlier, one major reason for implementing NUMA is to handle large amounts of memory efficiently. As clock speed and the number of processors increase, it becomes increasingly difficult to reduce the memory latency required to use this additional processing power. Large L3 caches can help alleviate part of the problem, but this is only a limited solution. NUMA is the scalable solution of choice. SQL Server 2008 has been designed to take advantage of NUMA-based computers without requiring any application changes. Keep in mind that the NUMA memory nodes depend completely on the hardware NUMA configuration. If you define your own soft-NUMA, as discussed earlier, you will not affect the number of NUMA memory nodes. So, for example, if you have an SMP computer with eight CPUs and you create four soft-NUMA nodes with two CPUs each, you have only one MEMORY node serving all four NUMA nodes. Soft-NUMA does not provide memory to CPU affinity. However, there is a network I/O thread and a lazywriter thread for each NUMA node, either hard or soft.

The principal reason for using soft-NUMA is to reduce I/O and lazywriter bottlenecks on computers with many CPUs and no hardware NUMA. For instance, on a computer with eight CPUs and no hardware NUMA, you have one I/O thread and one lazywriter thread that could be a bottleneck. Configuring four soft-NUMA nodes provides four I/O threads and four lazywriter threads, which could definitely help performance.

If you have multiple NUMA memory nodes, SQL Server divides the total target memory evenly among all the nodes. So if you have 10 GB of physical memory and four NUMA nodes and SQL Server determines a 10-GB target memory value, all nodes eventually allocate and use 2.5 GB of memory as if it were their own. In fact, if one of the nodes has less memory than another, it must use memory from another one to reach its 2.5-GB allocation. This memory is called *foreign memory*. Foreign memory is considered local, so if SQL Server has readjusted its target memory and each node needs to release some, no attempt will be made to free up foreign pages first. In addition, if SQL Server has been configured to run on a subset of the available NUMA nodes, the target memory will *not* be limited automatically to the memory on those nodes. You must set the Max Server Memory value to limit the amount of memory.

In general, the NUMA nodes function largely independently of each other, but that is not always the case. For example, if a worker running on a node *N1* needs to access a database page that is already in node *N2*'s memory, it does so by accessing *N2*'s memory, which is called *nonlocal memory*. Note that nonlocal is not the same as foreign memory.

## Read-Ahead

SQL Server supports a mechanism called *read-ahead*, whereby the need for data and index pages can be anticipated and pages can be brought into the buffer pool before they're actually needed. This performance optimization allows large amounts of data to be processed effectively. Read-ahead is managed completely internally, and no configuration adjustments are necessary.

There are two kinds of read-ahead: one for table scans on heaps and one for index ranges. For table scans, the table's allocation structures are consulted to read the table in disk order. Up to 32 extents (32 * 8 pages/extent * 8,192 bytes/page = 2 MB) of read-ahead may be outstanding at a time. Four extents (32 pages) at a time are read with a single 256-KB scatter read. If the table is spread across multiple files in a file group, SQL Server attempts to distribute the read-ahead activity across the files evenly.

For index ranges, the scan uses level 1 of the index structure (the level immediately above the leaf) to determine which pages to read ahead. When the index scan starts, read-ahead is invoked on the initial descent of the index to minimize the number of reads performed. For instance, for a scan of *WHERE state* = 'WA', read-ahead searches the index for *key* = 'WA', and it can tell from the level-1 nodes how many pages must be examined to satisfy the scan. If the anticipated number of pages is small, all the pages are requested by the initial read-ahead; if the pages are noncontiguous, they're fetched in scatter reads. If the range contains a large number of pages, the initial read-ahead is performed and thereafter, every time another 16 pages are consumed by the scan, the index is consulted to read in another 16 pages. This has several interesting effects:

- Small ranges can be processed in a single read at the data page level whenever the index is contiguous.

- The scan range (for example, *state* = 'WA') can be used to prevent reading ahead of pages that won't be used because this information is available in the index.

- Read-ahead is not slowed by having to follow page linkages at the data page level. (Read-ahead can be done on both clustered indexes and nonclustered indexes.)

As you can see, memory management in SQL Server is a huge topic, and I've provided you with only a basic understanding of how SQL Server uses memory. This information should give you a start in interpreting the wealth of information available through the DMVs and troubleshooting. The companion Web site includes a white paper that offers many more troubleshooting ideas and scenarios.

# SQL Server Resource Governor

Having sufficient memory and scheduler resources available is of paramount importance in having a system that runs well. Although SQL Server and the SQLOS have many built-in algorithms to distribute these resources equitably, you often understand your resource needs better than the SQL Server Database Engine does.

## Resource Governor Overview

SQL Server 2008 Enterprise Edition provides you with an interface for assigning scheduler and memory resources to groups of processes based on your determination of their needs. This interface is called the *Resource Governor*, which has the following goals:

- Allow monitoring of resource consumption per workload, where a workload can be defined as a group of requests.

- Enable workloads to be prioritized.

- Provide a means to specify resource boundaries between workloads to allow predictable execution of those workloads where there might otherwise be resource contention

- Prevent or reduce the probability of runaway queries.

The Resource Governor's functionality is based on the concepts of workloads and resource pools, which are set up by the DBA. Using just a few basic DDL commands, you can define a set of workload groups, create a classifier function to determine which user sessions are members of which groups, and set up pools of resources to allow each workload group to have minimum and maximum settings for the amount of memory and the percentage of CPU resources that they can use.

Figure 1-4 illustrates a sample relationship between the classifier function applied to each session, workload groups, and resource pools. More details about groups and pools are provided throughout this section, but you can see in the figure that each new session is placed in a workload group based on the result of the classifier function. Also notice that there is a many-to-one relationship between groups and pools. Many workload groups can be assigned to the same pool, but each workload group only belongs on one pool.

## Enabling the Resource Governor

The Resource Governor is enabled using the DDL statement *ALTER RESOURCE GOVERNOR*. Using this statement, you can specify a classifier function to be used to assign sessions to a workload, enable or disable the Resource Governor, or reset the statistics being kept on the Resource Governor.

## Classifier Function

Once a classifier function has been defined and the Resource Governor enabled, the function is applied to each new session to determine the name of the workload group to which the session will be assigned. The session stays in the same group until its termination, unless it is assigned explicitly to a different group. There can only be a maximum of one classifier function active at any given time, and if no classifier function has been defined, all new sessions are assigned to a default group. The classifier function is typically based on properties of a connection, and determines the workload group based on system functions such as *SUSER_NAME(), SUSER_SNAME(), IS_SRVROLEMEMBER()*, and *IS_MEMBER()*, and on property functions like *LOGINPROPERTY* and *CONNECTIONPROPERTY*.

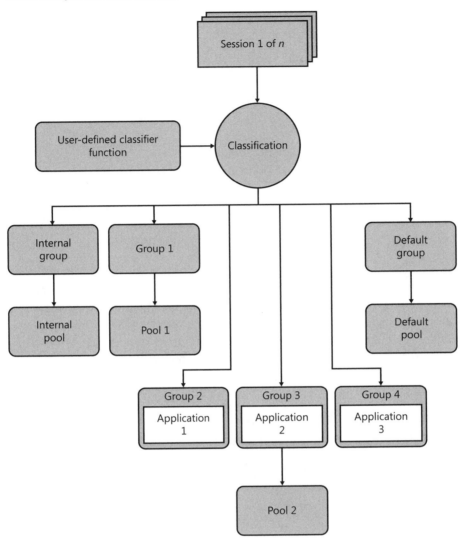

**FIGURE 1-4** Resource Governor components

## Workload Groups

A *workload group* is just a name defined by a DBA to allow multiple connections to share the same resources. There are two predefined workload groups in every SQL Server instance:

- **Internal group**   This group is used for the internal activities of SQL Server. Users are not able to add sessions to the internal group or affect its resource usage. However, the internal group can be monitored.

- **Default group**   All sessions are classified into this group when no other classifier rules could be applied. This includes situations where the classifier function resulted in a nonexistent group or when there was a failure of the classifier function.

Many sessions can be assigned to the same workload group, and each session can start multiple sequential tasks (or batches). Each batch can be composed of multiple statements, and some of those statements, such as stored procedure calls, can be broken down further. Figure 1-5 illustrates this relationship between workload groups, sessions, batches, and statements.

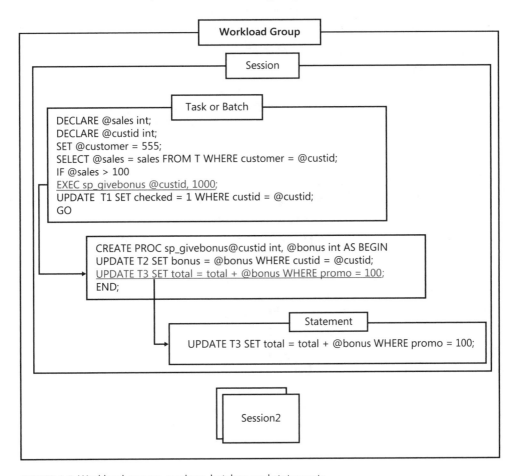

**FIGURE 1-5** Workload groups, sessions, batches, and statements

When you create a workload group, you give it a name and then supply values for up to six specific properties of the group. For any properties that aren't specified, there is a default value. In addition to the properties of the group, the group is assigned to a resource pool; and if no pool is specified, the default group is assumed. The six properties that can be specified are the following:

1. **IMPORTANCE**   Each workload group can have an importance of *low, medium,* or *high* within their resource pool. Medium is the default. This value determines the relative ratio of CPU bandwidth available to the group in a preset proportion (which is subject to change in future versions or services packs). Currently the weighting is low = 1, medium =3, and high = 9. This means that a scheduler tries to execute runnable sessions from high-priority

workload groups three times more often than sessions from groups with medium importance, and nine times more often than sessions from groups with low importance. It's up to the DBA to make sure not to have too many sessions in the groups with high importance, or not to assign a high importance to too many groups. If you have nine times as many sessions from groups with high importance than from groups with low importance, the end result will be that all the sessions will get equal time on the scheduler.

2. **REQUEST_MAX_MEMORY_GRANT_PERCENT**   This value specifies the maximum amount of memory that a single task from this group can take from the resource pool. This is the percent relative to the pool size specified by the pool's MAX_MEMORY_PERCENT value, not the actual amount of memory being used. This amount refers only to memory granted for query execution, and not for data buffers or cached plans, which can be shared by many requests. The default value is 25 percent, which means a single request can consume one-fourth of the pool's memory.

3. **REQUEST_MAX_CPU_TIME_SEC**   This value is the maximum amount of CPU time in seconds that can be consumed by any one request in the workload group. The default setting is 0, which means there is no limit on the CPU time.

4. **REQUEST_MEMORY_GRANT_TIMEOUT_SEC**   This value is the maximum time in seconds that a query waits for a resource to become available. If the resource does not become available, it may fail with a timeout error. (In some cases, the query may not fail, but it may run with substantially reduced resources.) The default value is 0, which means the server will calculate the timeout based on the query cost.

5. **MAX_DOP**   This value specifies the maximum degree of parallelism (DOP) for a parallel query, and the value takes precedence over the max degree of parallelism configuration option and any query hints. The actual run-time DOP is also bound by number of schedulers and availability of parallel threads. This MAX_DOP setting is a maximum limit only, meaning that the server is allowed to run the query using fewer processors than specified. The default setting is 0, meaning that the server handles the value globally. You should be aware of the following details about working with the MAX_DOP value:

   ❑ MAXDOP as query hint is honored so long as it does not exceed the workload group MAX_DOP value.

   ❑ MAXDOP as query hint always overrides the Max Degree of Parallelism configuration option.

   ❑ If the query is marked as serial at compile time, it cannot be changed back to parallel at run time regardless of workload group or configuration setting.

   ❑ Once the degree of parallelism is decided, it can be lowered only when memory pressure occurs. Workload group reconfiguration will not be seen for tasks waiting in the grant memory queue.

6. **GROUP_MAX_REQUESTS**   This value is the maximum number of requests allowed to be simultaneously executing in the workload group. The default is 0, which means unlimited requests.

Any of the properties of a workload group can be changed by using *ALTER WORKLOAD GROUP.*

## Resource Pools

A resource pool is a subset of the physical resources of the server. Each pool has two parts. One part does not overlap with other pools, which enables you to set a minimum value for the resource. The other part of the pool is shared with other pools, and this allows you to define the maximum possible resource consumption. The pool resources are set by specifying one of the following for each resource:

- MIN or MAX for CPU

- MIN or MAX for memory percentage

MIN represents the minimum guaranteed resource availability for CPU or memory and MAX represents the maximum size of the pool for CPU or memory.

The shared part of the pool is used to indicate where available resources can go if resources are available. However, when resources are consumed, they go to the specified pool and are not shared. This may improve resource utilization in cases where there are no requests in a given pool and the resources configured to the pool can be freed up for other pools.

Here are more details about the four values that can be specified for each resource pool:

1. **MIN_CPU_PERCENT**   This is a guaranteed average CPU bandwidth for all requests in the pool when there is CPU contention. SQL Server attempts to distribute CPU bandwidth between individual requests as fairly as possible and takes the *IMPORTANCE* property for each workload group into account. The default value is 0, which means there is no minimum value.

2. **MAX_CPU_PERCENT**   This is the maximum CPU bandwidth that all requests in the pool receive when there is CPU contention. The default value is 100, which means there is no maximum value. If there is no contention for CPU resources, a pool can consume up to 100 percent of CPU bandwidth.

3. **MIN_MEMORY_PERCENT**   This value specifies the amount of memory reserved for this pool that cannot be shared with other pools. If there are no requests in the pool but the pool has a minimum memory value set, this memory cannot be used for requests in other pools and is wasted. Within a pool, distribution of memory between requests is on a first-come-first-served basis. Memory for a request can also be affected by properties of the workload group, such as REQUEST_MAX_MEMORY_GRANT_PERCENT. The default value of 0 means that there is no minimum memory reserved.

4. **MAX_MEMORY_PERCENT** This value specifies the percent of total server memory that can be used by all requests in the specified pool. This amount can go up to 100 percent, but the actual amount is reduced by memory already reserved by the MIN_MEMORY_PERCENT value specified by other pools. MAX_MEMORY_PERCENT is always greater than or equal to MIN_MEMORY_PERCENT. The amount of memory for an individual request will be affected by workload group policy, for example, REQUEST_MAX_MEMORY_GRANT_PERCENT. The default setting of 100 means that all the server memory can be used for one pool. This setting cannot be exceeded, even if it means that the server will be underutilized.

Some extreme cases of pool configuration are the following:

- All pools define minimums that add up to 100 percent of the server resources. This is equivalent to dividing the server resources into nonoverlapping pieces regardless of the resources consumed inside any given pool.

- All pools have no minimums. All the pools compete for available resources, and their final sizes are based on resource consumption in each pool.

Resource Governor has two predefined resource pools for each SQL Server instance:

**Internal pool** This pool represents the resources consumed by the SQL Server itself. This pool always contains only the internal workload group and is not alterable in any way. There are no restrictions on the resources used by the internal pool. You are not able to affect the resource usage of the internal pool or add workload groups to it. However, you are able to monitor the resources used by the internal group.

**Default pool** Initially, the default pool contains only the default workload group. This pool cannot be dropped, but it can be altered and other workload groups can be added to it. Note that the default group cannot be moved out of the default pool.

## Pool Sizing

Table 1-2, taken from *SQL Server 2008 Books Online*, illustrates the relationships between the MIN and MAX values in several pools and how the effective MAX values are computed. The table shows the settings for the internal pool, the default pool, and two user-defined pools. The following formulas are used for calculating the effective MAX % and the shared %:

- Min(X,Y) means the smaller value of *X* and *Y*.

- Sum(X) means the sum of value *X* across all pools.

- Total shared % = 100 − sum(MIN %).

- Effective MAX % = min(X,Y).

- Shared % = Effective MAX % − MIN %.

**TABLE 1-2  MIN and MAX Values for Workload Groups**

| Pool Name | MIN % Setting | MAX % Setting | Calculated Effective MAX % | Calculated Shared % | Comment |
|---|---|---|---|---|---|
| internal | 0 | 100 | 100 | 0 | Effective MAX % and shared % are not applicable to the internal pool. |
| default | 0 | 100 | 30 | 30 | The effective MAX value is calculated as min(100,100−(20+50)) = 30. The calculated shared % is effective MAX − MIN = 30. |
| Pool 1 | 20 | 100 | 50 | 30 | The effective MAX value is calculated as min(100,100−50) = 50. The calculated shared % is effective MAX − MIN = 30. |
| Pool 2 | 50 | 70 | 70 | 20 | The effective MAX value is calculated as min(70,100−20) = 70. The calculated shared % is effective MAX − MIN = 20. |

Table 1-3, also taken from *SQL Server Books Online*, shows how the values above can change when a new pool is created. This new pool is Pool 3 and has a MIN % setting of 5.

**TABLE 1-3  MIN and MAX Values for Resource Pools**

| Pool Name | MIN % Setting | MAX % Setting | Calculated Effective MAX % | Calculated Shared % | Comment |
|---|---|---|---|---|---|
| internal | 0 | 100 | 100 | 0 | Effective MAX % and shared % are not applicable to the internal pool. |
| default | 0 | 100 | 25 | 30 | The effective MAX value is calculated as min(100,100−(20+50+5)) = 25. The calculated shared % is effective MAX − MIN = 25. |
| Pool 1 | 20 | 100 | 45 | 25 | The effective MAX value is calculated as min(100,100−55) = 45. The calculated shared % is effective MAX − MIN = 30. |
| Pool 2 | 50 | 70 | 70 | 20 | The effective MAX value is calculated as min(70,100−25) = 70. The calculated shared % is effective MAX − MIN = 20. |
| Pool 3 | 5 | 100 | 30 | 25 | The effective MAX value is calculated as min(100,100−70) = 30. The calculated shared % is effective MAX − MIN = 25. |

## Example

This section includes a few syntax examples of the Resource Governor DDL commands, to give a further idea of how all these concepts work together. This is not a complete discussion of all the possible DDL command options; for that, you need to refer to *SQL Server Books Online*.

```
--- Create a resource pool for production processing
--- and set limits.
USE master;
GO
CREATE RESOURCE POOL pProductionProcessing
WITH
(
    MAX_CPU_PERCENT = 100,
    MIN_CPU_PERCENT = 50
);
GO
--- Create a workload group for production processing
--- and configure the relative importance.
CREATE WORKLOAD GROUP gProductionProcessing
WITH
(
    IMPORTANCE = MEDIUM
)
--- Assign the workload group to the production processing
--- resource pool.
USING pProductionProcessing;
GO
--- Create a resource pool for off-hours processing
--- and set limits.
CREATE RESOURCE POOL pOffHoursProcessing
WITH
(
    MAX_CPU_PERCENT = 50,
    MIN_CPU_PERCENT = 0
);
GO
--- Create a workload group for off-hours processing
--- and configure the relative importance.
CREATE WORKLOAD GROUP gOffHoursProcessing
WITH
(
    IMPORTANCE = LOW
)
--- Assign the workload group to the off-hours processing
--- resource pool.
USING pOffHoursProcessing;
GO
--- Any changes to workload groups or resource pools require that the
--- resource governor be reconfigured.
ALTER RESOURCE GOVERNOR RECONFIGURE;
GO
USE master;
```

```
GO
CREATE TABLE tblClassifierTimeTable (
    strGroupName      sysname          not null,
    tStartTime        time             not null,
    tEndTime          time             not null
);
GO
--- Add time values that the classifier will use to
--- determine the workload group for a session.
INSERT into tblClassifierTimeTable
    VALUES('gProductionProcessing', '6:35 AM', '6:15 PM');
GO
--- Create the classifier function
CREATE FUNCTION fnTimeClassifier()
RETURNS sysname
WITH SCHEMABINDING
AS
BEGIN
    DECLARE @strGroup sysname
    DECLARE @loginTime time
    SET @loginTime = CONVERT(time,GETDATE())
    SELECT TOP 1 @strGroup = strGroupName
    FROM dbo.tblClassifierTimeTable
    WHERE tStartTime <= @loginTime and tEndTime >= @loginTime
    IF(@strGroup is not null)
    BEGIN
        RETURN @strGroup
    END
--- Use the default workload group if there is no match
--- on the lookup.
    RETURN N'gOffHoursProcessing'
END;
GO
--- Reconfigure the Resource Governor to use the new function
ALTER RESOURCE GOVERNOR with (CLASSIFIER_FUNCTION = dbo.fnTimeClassifier);
ALTER RESOURCE GOVERNOR RECONFIGURE;
GO
```

## Resource Governor Controls

The actual limitations of resources are controlled by your pool settings. In SQL Server 2008, you can control memory and CPU resources, but not I/O. It's possible that in a future version, more resource controls will become available. There is an important difference between the way that memory and CPU resources limits are applied.

You can think of the memory specifications for a pool as hard limits, and no pool will ever use more than its maximum memory setting. In addition, SQL Server always reserves the minimum memory for each pool, so that if no sessions in workload groups are assigned to a pool, its minimum memory reservation is unusable by other sessions.

However, CPU limits are soft limits, and unused scheduler bandwidth can be used by other sessions. The maximum values are also not always fixed upper limits. For example, if there are two pools, one with a maximum of 25 percent and the other with a maximum of 50 percent, as soon as the first pool has used its 25 percent of the scheduler, sessions from groups in the other pool can use all the remaining CPU resources. As soft limits, they can make CPU usage not quite as predictable as memory usage. Each session is assigned to a scheduler, as described in the previous section, with no regard to the workload group that the session is in. Assume a minimal situation with only two sessions running on a dual CPU instance. Each will most likely be assigned to a different scheduler, and the two sessions may be in two different workload groups in two different resource pools.

Assume that the session on CPU1 is from a workload group in the first pool that has a maximum CPU setting of 80 percent, and that the second session, on CPU2, is from a group in the second pool with a maximum CPU setting of 20 percent. Because these are only two sessions, they each use 100 percent of their scheduler or 50 percent of the total CPU resources on the instance. If CPU1 is then assigned another task from a workload group from the 20 percent pool, the situation changes. Tasks using the 20 percent pool have 20 percent of CPU1 but still have 100 percent of CPU2, and tasks using the 80 percent pool still have only 80 percent of CPU1. This means tasks running from the 20 percent pool have 60 percent of the total CPU resources, and the one task from the 80 percent pool has only 40 percent of the total CPU resources. Of course, as more and more tasks are assigned to the schedulers, this anomaly may work itself out, but because of the way that scheduler resources are managed across multiple CPUs, there is much less explicit control.

For testing and troubleshooting purposes, there may be times you want to be able to turn off all Resource Governor functionality easily. You can disable the Resource Governor with the command *ALTER RESOURCE GOVERNOR DISABLE*. You can then re-enable the Resource Governor with the command *ALTER RESOURCE GOVERNOR RECONFIGURE*. If you want to make sure the Resource Governor stays disabled, you can start your SQL Server instance with trace flag 8040 in this situation. When this trace flag is used, Resource Governor stays in the OFF state at all times and all attempts to reconfigure it fails. The same behavior results if you start your SQL Server instance in single-user mode using the *–m* and *–f* flags. If the Resource Governor is disabled, you should notice the following behaviors:

- Only the *internal* workload group and resource pool exist.
- Resource Governor configuration metadata are not loaded into memory.
- Your classifier function is never executed automatically.
- The Resource Governor metadata is visible and can be manipulated.

## Resource Governor Metadata

There are three specific catalog views that you'll want to take a look at when working with the Resource Governor.

- *sys.resource_governor_configuration*   This view returns the stored Resource Governor state.
- *sys.resource_governor_resource_pools*   This view returns the stored resource pool configuration. Each row of the view determines the configuration of an individual pool.

- *sys.resource_governor_workload_groups*   This view returns the stored workload group configuration.

There are also three DMVs devoted to the Resource Governor:

- *sys.dm_resource_governor_workload_groups*   This view returns workload group statistics and the current in-memory configuration of the workload group.

- *sys.dm_resource_governor_resource_pools*   This view returns information about the current resource pool state, the current configuration of resource pools, and resource pool statistics.

- *sys.dm_resource_governor_configuration*   This view returns a row that contains the current in-memory configuration state for the Resource Governor.

Finally, six other DMVs contain information related to the Resource Governor:

- *sys.dm_exec_query_memory_grants*   This view returns information about the queries that have acquired a memory grant or that still require a memory grant to execute. Queries that do not have to wait for a memory grant do not appear in this view. The following columns are added for the Resource Governor: *group_id, pool_id, is_small, ideal_memory_kb.*

- *sys.dm_exec_query_resource_semaphores*   This view returns the information about the current query-resource semaphore status. It provides general query-execution memory status information and allows you to determine whether the system can access enough memory. The *pool_id* column has been added for the Resource Governor.

- *sys.dm_exec_sessions*   This view returns one row per authenticated session on SQL Server. The *group_id* column has been added for the Resource Governor.

- *sys.dm_exec_requests*   This view returns information about each request that is executing within SQL Server. The *group_id* column is added for the Resource Governor.

- *sys.dm_exec_cached_plans*   This view returns a row for each query plan that is cached by SQL Server for faster query execution. The *pool_id* column is added for the Resource Governor.

- *sys.dm_os_memory_brokers*   This view returns information about allocations that are internal to SQL Server, which use the SQL Server memory manager. The following columns are added for the Resource Governor: *pool_id, allocations_db_per_sec, predicated_allocations_kb, overall_limit_kb.*

Although at first glance it may seem like the setup of the Resource Governor is unnecessarily complex, hopefully you'll find that being able to specify properties for both workload groups and resource pools provides you with the maximum control and flexibility. You can think of the workload groups as tools that give control to your developers, and the resource pools as administrator tools for limiting what the developers can do.

# SQL Server 2008 Configuration

In the second part of this chapter, we'll look at the options for controlling how SQL Server 2008 behaves. One main method of controlling the behavior of the Database Engine is to adjust configuration option settings, but you can configure behavior in a few other ways as well. We'll first look at using SQL Server Configuration Manager to control network protocols and SQL Server–related services. We'll then look at other machine settings that can affect the behavior of SQL Server. Finally, we'll examine some specific configuration options for controlling server-wide settings in SQL Server.

## Using SQL Server Configuration Manager

Configuration Manager is a tool for managing the services associated with SQL Server, configuring the network protocols used by SQL Server, and managing the network connectivity configuration from client computers connecting to SQL Server. It is installed as part of SQL Server. Configuration Manager is available by right-clicking the registered server in Management Studio, or you can add it to any other Microsoft Management Console (MMC) display.

## Configuring Network Protocols

A specific protocol must be enabled on both the client and the server for the client to connect and communicate with the server. SQL Server can listen for requests on all enabled protocols at once. The underlying operating system network protocols (such as TCP/IP) should already be installed on the client and the server. Network protocols are typically installed during Windows setup; they are not part of SQL Server setup. A SQL Server network library does not work unless its corresponding network protocol is installed on both the client and the server.

On the client computer, the SQL Native Client must be installed and configured to use a network protocol enabled on the server; this is usually done during Client Tools Connectivity setup. The SQL Native Client is a standalone data access API used for both OLE DB and ODBC. If the SQL Native Client is available, any network protocol can be configured for use with a particular client connecting to SQL Server. You can use SQL Server Configuration Manager to enable a single protocol or to enable multiple protocols and specify an order in which they should be attempted. If the Shared Memory protocol setting is enabled, that protocol is always tried first, but, as mentioned earlier in this chapter, it is available for communication only when the client and the server are on the same machine.

The following query returns the protocol used for the current connection, using the DMV *sys.dm_exec_connections*:

```
SELECT net_transport
FROM sys.dm_exec_connections
WHERE session_id = @@SPID;
```

# Default Network Configuration

The network protocols that can be used to communicate with SQL Server 2008 from another computer are not all enabled for SQL Server during installation. To connect from a particular client computer, you might need to enable the desired protocol. The Shared Memory protocol is enabled by default on all installations, but because it can be used to connect to the Database Engine only from a client application on the same computer, its usefulness is limited.

TCP/IP connectivity to SQL Server 2008 is disabled for new installations of the Developer, Evaluation, and SQL Express editions. OLE DB applications connecting with MDAC 2.8 cannot connect to the default instance on a local server using ".", "(local)", or (<blank>) as the server name. To resolve this, supply the server name or enable TCP/IP on the server. Connections to local named instances are not affected, nor are connections using the SQL Native Client. Installations in which a previous installation of SQL Server is present might not be affected.

Table 1-4 describes the default network configuration settings.

**TABLE 1-4  SQL Server 2008 Default Network Configuration Settings**

| SQL Server Edition | Type of Installation | Shared Memory | TCP/IP | Named Pipes | VIA |
|---|---|---|---|---|---|
| Enterprise | New | Enabled | Enabled | Disabled (available only locally) | Disabled |
| Enterprise (clustered) | New | Enabled | Enabled | Enabled | Disabled |
| Developer | New | Enabled | Disabled | Disabled (available only locally) | Disabled |
| Standard | New | Enabled | Enabled | Disabled (available only locally) | Disabled |
| Workgroup | New | Enabled | Enabled | Disabled (available only locally) | Disabled |
| Evaluation | New | Enabled | Disabled | Disabled (available only locally) | Disabled |
| Web | New | Enabled | Enabled | Disabled (available only locally) | Disabled |
| SQL Server Express | New | Enabled | Disabled | Disabled (available only locally) | Disabled |
| All editions | Upgrade or side-by-side installation | Enabled | Settings preserved from the previous installation | Settings preserved from the previous installation | Disabled |

# Managing Services

You can use Configuration Manager to start, pause, resume, or stop SQL Server–related services. The services available depend on the specific components of SQL Server you have installed, but you should always have the SQL Server service itself and the SQL Server Agent service. Other services might include the SQL Server Full-Text Search service and SQL Server Integration Services (SSIS). You can also use Configuration Manager to view the current properties of the services, such as whether the service is set to start automatically. Configuration Manager is the preferred tool for changing service properties rather than using Windows service management tools. When you use a SQL Server tool such as Configuration Manager to change the account used by either the SQL Server or SQL Server Agent service, the SQL Server tool automatically makes additional configurations, such as setting permissions in the Windows Registry so that the new account can read the SQL Server settings. Password changes using Configuration Manager take effect immediately without requiring you to restart the service.

## SQL Server Browser

One other related service that deserves special attention is the SQL Server Browser service. This service is particularly important if you have named instances of SQL Server running on a machine. SQL Server Browser listens for requests to access SQL Server resources and provides information about the various SQL Server instances installed on the computer where the Browser service is running.

Prior to SQL Server 2000, only one installation of SQL Server could be on a machine at one time, and there really was no concept of an "instance." SQL Server always listened for incoming requests on port 1433, but any port can be used by only one connection at a time. When SQL Server 2000 introduced support for multiple instances of SQL Server, a new protocol called *SQL Server Resolution Protocol (SSRP)* was developed to listen on UDP port 1434. This listener could reply to clients with the names of installed SQL Server instances, along with the port numbers or named pipes used by the instance. SQL Server 2005 replaced SSRP with the SQL Server Browser service, which is still used in SQL Server 2008.

If the SQL Server Browser service is not running on a computer, you cannot connect to SQL Server on that machine unless you provide the correct port number. However, if the SQL Server Browser service is not running, the following connections will not work:

- Connecting to a named instance without providing the port number or pipe
- Using the DAC to connect to a named instance or the default instance if it us not using TCP/IP port 1433
- Enumerating servers in Management Studio, Enterprise Manager, or Query Analyzer

It is recommended that the Browser Service be set to start automatically on any machine on which SQL Server will be accessed using a network connection.

# SQL Server System Configuration

You can configure the machine that SQL Server runs on, as well as the Database Engine itself, in several ways and through a variety of interfaces. We'll first look at some operating system–level settings that can affect the behavior of SQL Server. Next, we'll see some SQL Server options that can affect behavior that aren't especially considered to be configuration options. Finally, we'll examine the configuration options for controlling the behavior of SQL Server 2008, which are set primarily using a stored procedure interface called *sp_configure*.

## Operating System Configuration

For your SQL Server to run well, it must be running on a tuned operating system, on a machine that has been properly configured to run SQL Server. Although it is beyond the scope of this book to discuss operating system and hardware configuration and tuning, there are a few issues that are very straightforward but can have a major impact on the performance of SQL Server, and we will describe them here.

### Task Management

As you saw in the first part of this chapter, the operating system schedules all threads in the system for execution. Each thread of every process has a priority, and Windows executes the next available thread with the highest priority. By default, the operating system gives active applications a higher priority, but this priority setting may not be appropriate for a server application running in the background, such as SQL Server 2008. To remedy this situation, the SQL Server installation program modifies the priority setting to eliminate the favoring of foreground applications.

It's not a bad idea to double-check this priority setting periodically in case someone has set it back. You'll need to open the Advanced tab of the Performance Options dialog box.

If you're using Windows XP or Windows Server 2003, click the Start menu, right-click My Computer, and choose Properties. The System Properties dialog box opens. On the Advanced tab, click the Settings button in the Performance area. Again, select the Advanced tab.

If you're using Windows Server 2008, click the Start menu, right-click Computer, and choose Properties. The System information screen opens. Select Advanced System Settings from the list on the left to open the System Properties dialog box. Just as for Windows XP and Windows Server 2003, on the Advanced tab, click the Settings button in the Performance area. Again, select the Advanced tab. You should see the Performance Options dialog box, shown in Figure 1-6.

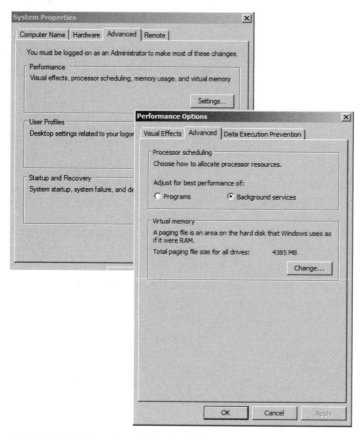

**FIGURE 1-6** Configuration of priority for background services

The first set of options is for specifying how to allocate processor resources, and you can adjust for the best performance of either programs or background services. Select Background Services so that all programs (both background and foreground) receive equal processor resources. If you plan to connect to SQL Server 2008 from a local client (that is, a client running on the same computer as the server), you can improve processing time by using this setting.

## System Paging File Location

If possible, you should place the operating system paging file on a different drive than the files used by SQL Server. This is vital if your system will be paging. However, a better approach is to add memory or change the SQL Server memory configuration to effectively eliminate paging. In general, SQL Server is designed to minimize paging, so if your memory configuration values are appropriate for the amount of physical memory on the system, such a small amount of page-file activity will occur that the file's location is irrelevant.

## Nonessential Services

You should disable any services that you don't need. In Windows Server 2003, you can right-click My Computer and choose Manage. Expand the Services And Applications node in the Computer Management tool, and click Services. In the right-hand pane, you see a list of all the services available on the operating system. You can change a service's startup property by right-clicking its name and choosing Properties. Unnecessary services add overhead to the system and use resources that could otherwise go to SQL Server. No unnecessary services should be marked for automatic startup. Avoid using a server that's running SQL Server as a domain controller, the group's file or print server, the Web server, or the Dynamic Host Configuration Protocol (DHCP) server. You should also consider disabling the Alerter, ClipBook, Computer Browser, Messenger, Network Dynamic Data Exchange (DDE), and Task Scheduler services, which are enabled by default but are not needed by SQL Server.

## Connectivity

You should run only the network protocols that you actually need for connectivity. You can use the SQL Server Configuration Manager to disable unneeded protocols, as described earlier in this chapter.

## Firewall Setting

Improper firewall settings are another system configuration issue that can inhibit SQL Server connectivity across your network. Firewall systems help prevent unauthorized access to computer resources and are usually desirable, but to access an instance of SQL Server through a firewall, you'll need to configure the firewall on the computer running SQL Server to allow access. Many firewall systems are available, and you'll need to check the documentation for your system for the exact details of how to configure it. In general, you'll need to carry out the following steps:

1.  Configure the SQL Server instance to use a specific TCP/IP port. Your default SQL Server uses port 1433 by default, but that can be changed. Named instances use dynamic ports by default, but that can also be changed using the SQL Server Configuration Manager.

2.  Configure your firewall to allow access to the specific port for authorized users or computers.

3.  As an alternative to configuring SQL Server to listen on a specific port and then opening that port, you can list the SQL Server executable (Sqlservr.exe) and the SQL Browser executable (Sqlbrowser.exe) when requiring a connection to named instances, as exceptions to the blocked programs. You can use this method when you want to continue to use dynamic ports.

## Trace Flags

*SQL Server Books Online* lists only about a dozen trace flags that are fully supported. You can think of trace flags as special switches that you can turn on or off to change the behavior of SQL Server. There are actually many dozens, if not hundreds, of trace flags. However, most were created for the SQL Server development team's internal testing of the product and were never intended for use by anybody outside Microsoft.

You can set trace flags on or off by using the *DBCC TRACEON* or *DBCC TRACEOFF* command or by specifying them on the command line when you start SQL Server using Sqlservr.exe. You can also use the SQL Server Configuration Manager to enable one or more trace flags every time the SQL Server service is started. (You can read about how to do that in *SQL Server Books Online*.) Trace flags enabled with *DBCC TRACEON* are valid only for a single connection unless you specified an additional parameter of –1, in which case they are active for all connections, even ones opened before you ran *DBCC TRACEON*. Trace flags enabled as part of starting the SQL Server service are enabled for all sessions.

A few of the trace flags are particularly relevant to topics covered in this book, and we will discuss particular ones when we describe topics that they are related to. For example, we already mentioned trace flag 8040 in conjunction with the Resource Governor.

> **Caution**  Because trace flags change the way SQL Server behaves, they can actually cause trouble if used inappropriately. Trace flags are not harmless features that you can experiment with just to see what happens, especially not on a production system. Using them effectively requires a thorough understanding of SQL Server default behavior (so that you know exactly what you'll be changing) and extensive testing to determine that your system really will benefit from the use of the trace flag.

# SQL Server Configuration Settings

If you choose to have SQL Server automatically configure your system, it dynamically adjusts the most important configuration options for you. It's best to accept the default configuration values unless you have a good reason to change them. A poorly configured system can destroy performance. For example, a system with an incorrectly configured memory setting can break an application.

In certain cases, tweaking the settings rather than letting SQL Server dynamically adjust them might lead to a tiny performance improvement, but your time is probably better spent on application and database designing, indexing, query tuning, and other such activities, which we'll talk about later in this book. You might see only a 5 percent improvement in performance by moving from a reasonable configuration to an ideal configuration, but a badly configured system can kill your application's performance.

SQL Server 2008 has 68 server configuration options that you can query using the catalog view *sys.configurations*.

You should change configuration options only when you have a clear reason for doing so, and you should closely monitor the effects of each change to determine whether the change improved or degraded performance. Always make and monitor changes one at a time. The server-wide options discussed here can be changed in several ways. All of them can be set via the *sp_configure* system stored procedure. However, of the 68 options, all but 16 are considered advanced options and are not manageable by default using *sp_configure*. You'll first need to change the Show Advanced Options option to be 1, as shown here:

```
EXEC sp_configure 'show advanced options', 1;
GO
RECONFIGURE;
GO
```

To see which options are advanced, you can again query the *sys.configurations* view and examine a column called *is_advanced,* which lets you see which options are considered advanced:

```
SELECT * FROM sys.configurations
WHERE is_advanced = 1;
GO
```

Many of the configuration options can also be set from the Server Properties dialog box in the Object Explorer window of Management Studio, but there is no single dialog box from which all configuration settings can be seen or changed. Most of the options that you can change from the Server Properties dialog box are controlled from one of the property pages that you reach by right-clicking the name of your SQL Server instance from Management Studio. You can see the list of property pages in Figure 1-7.

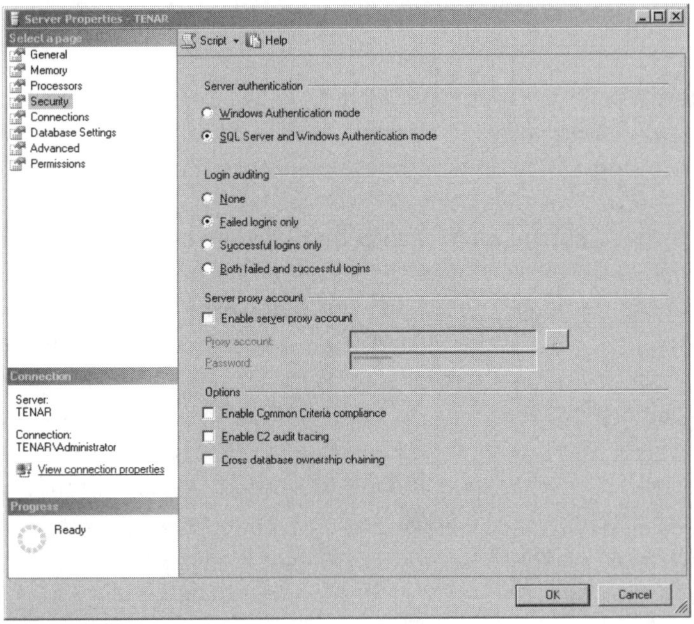

**FIGURE 1-7** List of server property pages in Management Studio

If you use the *sp_configure* stored procedure, no changes take effect until the *RECONFIGURE* command runs. In some cases, you might have to specify *RECONFIGURE WITH OVERRIDE* if you are changing an option to a value outside the recommended range. Dynamic changes take effect immediately upon reconfiguration, but others do not take effect until the server is restarted. If after running *RECONFIGURE,* an option's *run_value* and *config_value* as displayed by *sp_configure* are different, or if the value and value_in_use in *sys.configurations* are different, you must restart the SQL Server service for the new value to take effect. You can use the *sys.configurations* view to determine which options are dynamic:

```
SELECT * FROM sys.configurations
WHERE is_dynamic = 1;
GO
```

We won't look at every configuration option here—only the most interesting ones or ones that are related to SQL Server performance. In most cases, I'll discuss options that you should *not* change. Some of these are resource settings that relate to performance only in that they consume memory (for example, Locks). But if they are configured too high, they can rob a system of memory and degrade performance. We'll group the configuration settings by functionality. Keep in mind that SQL Server sets almost all these options automatically, and your applications work well without you ever looking at them.

## Memory Options

In the preceding section, you saw how SQL Server uses memory, including how it allocates memory for different uses and when it reads data from or writes data to disk. However, we did not discuss how to control how much memory SQL Server actually uses for these purposes.

**Min Server Memory and Max Server Memory**   By default, SQL Server adjusts the total amount of the memory resources it will use. However, you can use the Min Server Memory and Max Server Memory configuration options to take manual control. The default setting for Min Server Memory is 0 MB, and the default setting for Max Server Memory is 2147483647. If you use the *sp_configure* stored procedure to change both of these options to the same value, you basically take full control and tell SQL Server to use a fixed memory size. The absolute maximum of 2147483647 MB is actually the largest value that can be stored in the integer field of the underlying system table. It is not related to the actual resources of your system. The Min Server Memory option does not force SQL Server to acquire a minimum amount of memory at startup. Memory is allocated on demand based on the database workload. However, once the Min Server Memory threshold is reached, SQL Server does not release memory if it would be left with less than that amount. To ensure that each instance has allocated memory at least equal to the Min Server Memory value, therefore, we recommend that you execute a database server load shortly after startup. During normal server activity, the memory available per instance varies, but there is never less than the Min Server Memory value available for each instance.

**Set Working Set Size**   The configuration option Set Working Set Size is a setting from earlier versions, and it has been deprecated. This setting is ignored in SQL Server 2008, even though you do not receive an error message when you try to use this value.

**AWE Enabled**   This option enables the use of the AWE API to support large memory sizes on 32-bit systems. With AWE enabled, SQL Server 2008 can use as much memory as the Enterprise, Developer, or Standard editions allow. When running on Windows Server 2003 or Windows Server 2008, SQL Server reserves only a small portion of AWE-mapped memory when it starts. As additional AWE-mapped memory is required, the operating system dynamically allocates it to SQL Server. Similarly, if fewer resources are required, SQL Server can return AWE-mapped memory to the operating system for use by other processes or applications.

Use of AWE, in either Windows Server 2003 or Windows Server 2008, locks the pages in memory so that they cannot be written to the paging file. Windows has to swap out other applications if additional physical memory is needed, so the performance of those applications might suffer. You should therefore set a value for Max Server Memory when you have also enabled AWE.

If you are running multiple instances of SQL Server on the same computer, and each instance uses AWE-mapped memory, you should ensure that the instances perform as expected. Each instance should have a Min Server Memory setting. Because AWE-mapped memory cannot be swapped out to the page file, the sum of the Min Server Memory values for all instances should be less than the total physical memory on the computer.

If your SQL Server is set up for failover clustering and is configured to use AWE memory, you must ensure that the sum of the Max Server Memory settings for all the instances is less than the least physical memory available on any of the servers in the cluster. If the failover node has less physical memory than the original node, the instances of SQL Server may fail to start.

**User Connections**   SQL Server 2008 dynamically adjusts the number of simultaneous connections to the server if the User Connections configuration setting is left at its default of 0. Even if you set this value to a different number, SQL Server does not actually allocate the full amount of memory needed for each user connection until a user actually connects. When SQL Server starts, it allocates an array of pointers with as many entries as the configured value for User Connections. If you must use this option, do not set the value too high because each connection takes approximately 28 KB of overhead regardless of whether the connection is being used. However, you also don't want to set it too low because if you exceed the maximum number of user connections, you receive an error message and cannot connect until another connection becomes available. (The exception is the DAC connection, which can be used.) Keep in mind that the User Connections value is not the same as the number of users; one user, through one application, can open multiple connections to SQL Server. Ideally, you should let SQL Server dynamically adjust the value of the User Connections option.

> **Important**  The Locks configuration option is a setting from earlier versions, and it has been deprecated. This setting is ignored in SQL Server 2008, even though you do not receive an error message when you try to use this value.

## Scheduling Options

As described previously, SQL Server 2008 has a special algorithm for scheduling user processes using the SQLOS, which manages one scheduler per logical processor and makes sure that only one process can run on a scheduler at any given time. The SQLOS manages the assignment of user connections to workers to keep the number of users per CPU as balanced as possible. Five configuration options affect the behavior of the scheduler: Lightweight Pooling, Affinity Mask, Affinity64 Mask, Priority Boost, and Max Worker Threads.

**Affinity Mask and Affinity64 Mask**    From an operating system point of view, the ability of Windows to move process threads among different processors is efficient, but this activity can reduce SQL Server performance because each processor cache is reloaded with data repeatedly. By setting the Affinity Mask option, you can allow SQL Server to assign processors to specific threads and thus improve performance under heavy load conditions by eliminating processor reloads and reducing thread migration and context switching across processors. Setting an affinity mask to a *non-0* value not only controls the binding of schedulers to processors, but it also allows you to limit which processors are used for executing SQL Server requests.

The value of an affinity mask is a 4-byte integer, and each bit controls one processor. If you set a bit representing a processor to 1, that processor is mapped to a specific scheduler. The 4-byte affinity mask can support up to 32 processors. For example, to configure SQL Server to use processors 0 through 5 on an eight-way box, you would set the affinity mask to 63, which is equivalent to a bit string of 00111111. To enable processors 8 through 11 on a 16-way box, you would set the affinity mask to 3840, or 0000111100000000. You might want to do this on a machine supporting multiple instances, for example. You would set the affinity mask of each instance to use a different set of processors on the computer.

To cover more than 32 CPUs, you configure a 4-byte affinity mask for the first 32 CPUs and up to a 4-byte Affinity64 mask for the remaining CPUs. Note that affinity support for servers with 33 to 64 processors is available only on 64-bit operating systems.

You can configure the affinity mask to use all the available CPUs. For an eight-way machine, an Affinity Mask setting of 255 means that all CPUs will be enabled. This is not exactly the same as a setting of 0 because with the *nonzero* value, the schedulers are bound to a specific CPU, and with the *0* value, they are not.

**Lightweight Pooling**    By default, SQL Server operates in thread mode, which means that the workers processing SQL Server requests are threads. As we described earlier, SQL

Server also lets user connections run in fiber mode. Fibers are less expensive to manage than threads. The Lightweight Pooling option can have a value of 0 or 1; 1 means that SQL Server should run in fiber mode. Using fibers may yield a minor performance advantage, particularly when you have eight or more CPUs and all of the available CPUs are operating at or near 100 percent. However, the trade-off is that certain operations, such as running queries on linked servers or executing extended stored procedures, must run in thread mode and therefore need to switch from fiber to thread. The cost of switching from fiber to thread mode for those connections can be noticeable and in some cases offsets any benefit of operating in fiber mode.

If you're running in an environment using a high percentage of total CPU resources, and if System Monitor shows a lot of context switching, setting Lightweight Pooling to 1 might yield some performance benefit.

**Priority Boost**   If the Priority Boost setting is enabled, SQL Server runs at a higher scheduling priority. The result is that the priority of *every* thread in the server process is set to a priority of 13 in Windows 2000 and Windows Server 2003. Most processes run at the normal priority, which is 7. The net effect is that if the server is running a very resource-intensive workload and is getting close to maxing out the CPU, these normal priority processes are effectively starved.

The default Priority Boost setting is 0, which means that SQL Server runs at normal priority whether or not you're running it on a single-processor machine. There are probably very few sites or applications for which setting this option makes much difference, but if your machine is totally dedicated to running SQL Server, you might want to enable this option (setting it to 1) to see for yourself. It can potentially offer a performance advantage on a heavily loaded, dedicated system. As with most of the configuration options, you should use it with care. Raising the priority too high might affect the core operating system and network operations, resulting in problems shutting down SQL Server or running other operating system tasks on the server.

**Max Worker Threads**   SQL Server uses the operating system's thread services by keeping a pool of workers (threads or fibers) that take requests from the queue. It attempts to divide the worker threads evenly among the SQLOS schedulers so that the number of threads available to each scheduler is the Max Worker Threads setting divided by the number of CPUs. With 100 or fewer users, there are usually as many worker threads as active users (not just connected users who are idle). With more users, it often makes sense to have fewer worker threads than active users. Although some user requests have to wait for a worker thread to become available, total throughput increases because less context switching occurs.

The Max Worker Threads default value of 0 means that the number of workers is configured by SQL Server, based on the number of processors and machine architecture. For example, for a four-way 32-bit machine running SQL Server, the default is 256 workers. This does not mean that 256 workers are created on startup. It means that if a connection is waiting to be serviced and no worker is available, a new worker is created if the total is currently below 256. If this setting is configured to 256 and the highest number of simultaneously executing commands is, say, 125, the actual number of workers will not exceed 125. It might be even smaller than that because SQL Server destroys and trims away workers that are no longer being used. You should probably leave this setting alone if your system is handling 100 or fewer simultaneous connections. In that case, the worker thread pool will not be greater than 100.

Table 1-5 lists the default number of workers given your machine architecture and number of processors. (Note that Microsoft recommends 1024 as the maximum for 32-bit operating systems.)

**TABLE 1-5  Default Settings for Max Worker Threads**

| CPU | 32-Bit Computer | 64-Bit Computer |
| --- | --- | --- |
| Up to 4 processors | 256 | 512 |
| 8 processors | 288 | 576 |
| 16 processors | 352 | 704 |
| 32 processors | 480 | 960 |

Even systems that handle 4,000 or more connected users run fine with the default setting. When thousands of users are simultaneously connected, the actual worker pool is usually well below the Max Worker Threads value set by SQL Server because from the perspective of the database, most connections are idle even if the user is doing plenty of work on the client.

## Disk I/O Options

No options are available for controlling the disk read behavior of SQL Server. All the tuning options to control read-ahead in previous versions of SQL Server are now handled completely internally. One option is available to control disk write behavior. This option controls how frequently the checkpoint process writes to disk.

**Recovery Interval**   The Recovery Interval option can be configured automatically. SQL Server setup sets it to 0, which means autoconfiguration. In SQL Server 2008, this means that the recovery time should be less than one minute. This option lets the database administrator control the checkpoint frequency by specifying the maximum number of minutes that recovery should take, per database. SQL Server estimates how many data modifications it can roll forward in that recovery time interval. SQL Server then inspects the log of each database (every minute, if the recovery interval is set to the default of 0) and issues a checkpoint for each database that has made at least that many data modification operations since the last checkpoint. For databases with relatively small transaction logs, SQL Server issues a checkpoint when the log becomes 70 percent full, if that is less than the estimated number.

The Recovery Interval option does not affect the time it takes to undo long-running transactions. For example, if a long-running transaction takes two hours to perform updates before the server becomes disabled, the actual recovery takes considerably longer than the Recovery Interval value.

The frequency of checkpoints in each database depends on the amount of data modifications made, not on a time-based measure. So a database that is used primarily for read operations will not have many checkpoints issued. To avoid excessive checkpoints, SQL Server tries to make sure that the value set for the recovery interval is the minimum amount of time between successive checkpoints.

As discussed previously, most writing to disk doesn't actually happen during checkpoint operations. Checkpoints are just a way to guarantee that all dirty pages not written by other mechanisms are still written to the disk in a timely manner. For this reason, you should keep the Recovery Interval value set at 0 (self-configuring).

**Affinity I/O Mask and Affinity64 I/O Mask**    These two options control the affinity of a processor for I/O operations and work in much the same way as the two options for controlling processing affinity for workers. Setting a bit for a processor in either of these bit masks means that the corresponding processor is used *only* for I/O operations. You probably never need to set this option. However, if you do decide to use it, perhaps just for testing purposes, you should use it in conjunction with the Affinity Mask or Affinity64 Mask option and make sure the bits set do not overlap. You should thus have one of the following combinations of settings: 0 for both Affinity I/O Mask and Affinity Mask for a CPU, 1 for the Affinity I/O Mask option and 0 for Affinity Mask, or 0 for Affinity I/O Mask and 1 for Affinity Mask.

**Backup Compression Default**    Backup Compression is a new feature in SQL Server 2008, and for backward compatibility, the default value for backup compression is 0, meaning that backups are not compressed. Although only Enterprise edition instances can create a compressed backup, any edition of SQL Server 2008 can restore a compressed backup. When Backup Compression is enabled, the compression is performed on the server prior to writing, so it can greatly reduce the size of the backups and the I/O required to write the backups to the external device. The amount of space reduction depends on many factors, including the following:

- **The type of data in the backup**    For example, character data compresses more than other types of data.

- **Whether the data is encrypted**    Encrypted data compresses significantly less than equivalent unencrypted data. If transparent data encryption is used to encrypt an entire database, compressing backups might not reduce their size by much, if at all.

After the backup has been performed, you can inspect the *backupset* table in the *msdb* database to determine the compression ratio, using a statement like the following:

```
SELECT backup_size/compressed_backup_size FROM msdb..backupset;
```

Although compressed backups can use significantly fewer I/O resources, it can significantly increase CPU usage when performing the compression. This additional load can affect other operations occurring concurrently. To minimize this impact, you can consider using the Resource Governor to create a workload group for sessions performing backups and assign the group to a resource pool with a limit on its maximum CPU utilization.

The configured value is the instance-wide default for Backup Compression, but it can be overridden for a particular backup operation, by specifying WITH COMPRESSION or WITH NO_COMPRESSION. Compression can be used for any type of backup: full, log, differential or partial (file or filegroup).

> **Note**  The algorithm used for compressing backups is very different than the database compression algorithms. Backup Compression uses an algorithm very similar to zip, where it is just looking for patterns in the data. Data compression will be discussed in Chapter 7.

**Filestream Access Level**    Filestream integrates the Database Engine with your NTFS file system by storing BLOB data as files on the file system and allowing you to access this data either using T-SQL or Win32 file system interfaces to provide streaming access to the data. Filestream uses the Windows system cache for caching file data to help reduce any effect that filestream data might have on SQL Server performance. The SQL Server buffer pool is not used so that filestream does not reduce the memory available for query processing.

Prior to setting this configuration option to indicate the access level for filestream data, you must enable *FILESTREAM* externally using the SQL Server Configuration Manager (if you haven't enabled *FILESTREAM* during SQL Server setup). Using the SQL Server Configuration Manager, you can right-click the name of the SQL Server service and choose properties. The dialog box has a separate tab for *FILESTREAM* options. You must check the top box to enable *FILESTREAM* for T-SQL access, and then you can choose to enable *FILESTREAM* for file I/O streaming if you want.

After enabling *FILESTREAM* for your SQL Server instance, you then set the configuration value. The following values are allowed:

- *0 Disables FILESTREAM*   support for this instance
- *1 Enables FILESTREAM*   for T-SQL access
- *2 Enables FILESTREAM*   for T-SQL and Win32 streaming access

Databases that store filestream data must have a special filestream filegroup. We'll discuss filegroups in Chapter 3. More details about filestream storage will be covered in Chapter 7.

## Query Processing Options

SQL Server has several options for controlling the resources available for processing queries. As with all the other tuning options, your best bet is to leave the default values unless thorough testing indicates that a change might help.

**Min Memory Per Query**   When a query requires additional memory resources, the number of pages that it gets is determined partly by the Min Memory Per Query option. This option is relevant for sort operations that you specifically request using an ORDER BY clause, and it also applies to internal memory needed by merge-join operations and by hash-join and hash-grouping operations. This configuration option allows you to specify a minimum amount of memory (in kilobytes) that any of these operations should be granted before they are executed. Sort, merge, and hash operations receive memory in a very dynamic fashion, so you rarely need to adjust this value. In fact, on larger machines, your sort and hash queries typically get much more than the Min Memory Per Query setting, so you shouldn't restrict yourself unnecessarily. If you need to do a lot of hashing or sorting, however, and you have few users or a lot of available memory, you might improve performance by adjusting this value. On smaller machines, setting this value too high can cause virtual memory to page, which hurts server performance.

**Query Wait**   The Query Wait option controls how long a query that needs additional memory waits if that memory is not available. A setting of –1 means that the query waits 25 times the estimated execution time of the query, but it always waits at least 25 seconds with this setting. A value of 0 or more specifies the number of seconds that a query waits. If the wait time is exceeded, SQL Server generates error 8645:

```
Server: Msg 8645, Level 17, State 1, Line 1
A time out occurred while waiting for memory resources to execute the query. Re-run the
query.
```

Even though memory is allocated dynamically, SQL Server can still run out of memory if the memory resources on the machine are exhausted. If your queries time out with error 8645, you can try increasing the paging file size or even adding more physical memory. You can also try tuning the query by creating more useful indexes so that hash or merge operations aren't needed. Keep in mind that this option affects only queries that have to wait for memory needed by hash and merge operations. Queries that have to wait for other reasons are not affected.

**Blocked Process Threshold**   This option allows an administrator to request a notification when a user task has been blocked for more than the configured number of seconds. When Blocked Process Threshold is set to 0, no notification is given. You can set any value up to 86,400 seconds. When the deadlock monitor detects a task that has been waiting longer than the configured value, an internal event is generated. You can choose to be notified of this event in one of two ways. You can use SQL Trace to create a trace and capture event of type Blocked process report, which you can find in the Errors and Warnings category on the Events Select screen in SQL Server Profiler. So long as a resource stays blocked on a deadlock-detectable resource, the event is raised every time the deadlock monitor checks for a deadlock. An Extensible Markup Language (XML) string is captured in the Text Data column of the trace that describes the blocked resource and the resource being waited on. More information about deadlock detection is in Chapter 10.

Alternatively, you can use event notifications to send information about events to a service broker service. Event notifications can provide a programming alternative to defining a trace, and they can be used to respond to many of the same events that SQL Trace can capture. Event notifications, which execute asynchronously, can be used to perform an action inside an instance of SQL Server 2008 in response to events with very little consumption of memory resources. Because event notifications execute asynchronously, these actions do not consume any resources defined by the immediate transaction.

**Index Create Memory**   The Min Memory Per Query option applies only to sorting and hashing used during query execution; it does not apply to the sorting that takes place during index creation. Another option, Index Create Memory, lets you allocate a specific amount of memory for index creation. Its value is specified in kilobytes.

**Query Governor Cost Limit**   You can use the Query Governor Cost Limit option to specify the maximum number of seconds that a query can run. If you specify a nonzero, non-negative value, SQL Server disallows execution of any query that has an estimated cost exceeding that value. Specifying 0 (the default) for this option turns off the query governor, and all queries are allowed to run without any time limit.

**Max Degree Of Parallelism and Cost Threshold For Parallelism**   SQL Server 2008 lets you run certain kinds of complex queries simultaneously on two or more processors. The queries must lend themselves to being executed in sections. Here's an example:

```
SELECT AVG(charge_amt), category
FROM charge
GROUP BY category
```

If the charge table has 1,000,000 rows and there are 10 different values for *category*, SQL Server can split the rows into groups and have only a subset of the groups processed on each processor. For example, with a four-CPU machine, categories 1 through 3 can be averaged on the first processor, categories 4 through 6 can be averaged on the second processor, categories 7 and 8 can be averaged on the third, and categories 9 and 10 can be averaged on the fourth. Each processor can come up with averages for only its groups, and the separate averages are brought together for the final result.

During optimization, the Query Optimizer always finds the cheapest possible serial plan before considering parallelism. If this serial plan costs less than the configured value for the Cost Threshold For Parallelism option, no parallel plan is generated. Cost Threshold For Parallelism refers to the cost of the query in seconds; the default value is 5. If the cheapest serial plan costs more than this configured threshold, a parallel plan is produced based on assumptions about how many processors and how much memory will actually be available at runtime. This parallel plan cost is compared with the serial plan cost, and the cheaper one is chosen. The other plan is discarded.

A parallel query execution plan can use more than one thread; a serial execution plan, which is used by a nonparallel query, uses only a single thread. The actual number of threads used by a parallel query is determined at query plan execution initialization and is the DOP. The decision is based on many factors, including the Affinity Mask setting, the Max Degree Of Parallelism setting, and the available threads when the query starts executing.

You can observe when SQL Server is executing a query in parallel by querying the DMV *sys.dm_os_tasks*. A query that is running on multiple CPUs has one row for each thread, as follows:

```
SELECT
    task_address,
    task_state,
    context_switches_count,
    pending_io_count,
    pending_io_byte_count,
    pending_io_byte_average,
    scheduler_id,
    session_id,
    exec_context_id,
    request_id,
    worker_address,
    host_address
FROM sys.dm_os_tasks
ORDER BY session_id, request_id;
```

Be careful when you use the Max Degree Of Parallelism and Cost Threshold For Parallelism options—they have server-wide impact.

There are other configuration options that we will not mention, most of which deal with aspects of SQL Server that are beyond the scope of this book. These include options for configuring remote queries, replication, SQL Agent, C2 auditing, and full-text search. There is a Boolean option to disallow use of the CLR in programming SQL Server objects; it is off (0) by default. The Allow Updates option still exists but has no effect in SQL Server 2008. A few of the configuration options deal with programming issues, and you can get more details in *Inside SQL Server 2008: TSQL Programming*. These options include ones for dealing with recursive and nested triggers, cursors, and accessing objects across databases.

## The Default Trace

One final option that doesn't seem to fit into any of the other categories is called *Default Trace Enabled*. We mention it because the default value is 1, which means that as soon as SQL

Server starts, it runs a server-side trace, capturing a predetermined set of information into a predetermined location. None of the properties of this default trace can be changed; the only thing you can do is turn it off.

You can compare the default trace to the blackbox trace which has been available since SQL Server 7 (and is still available in SQL Server 2008), but the blackbox trace takes a few steps to create, and it takes even more steps to have it start automatically when your SQL Server starts. This default trace is so lightweight that you might find little reason to disable it. If you're not familiar with SQL Server tracing, you'll probably need to spend some time reading about tracing in Chapter 2.

The default trace output file is stored in the same directory in which you installed SQL Server, in the \Log subdirectory. So if you've installed SQL Server in the default location, the captured trace information for a default instance will be in the file C:\Program Files\Microsoft SQL Server\MSSQL10.MSSQLSSERVER\MSSQL\LOG\Log.trc. Every time you stop and restart SQL Server, or reach the maximum file size of 20 MB, a new trace file is created with a sequential numerical suffix, so the second trace file would be Log_01.trc, followed by Log_02.trc, and so on. If all the trace log files are removed or renamed, the next trace file starts at log.trc again. SQL Server will keep no more than five trace files per instance, so when the sixth file is created, the earliest one is deleted.

You can open the trace files created through the default trace mechanism by using the SQL Server Profiler, just as you can any other trace file, or you can copy to a table by using the system function *fn_trace_gettable* and view the current contents of the trace while the trace is still running. As with any server-side trace that writes to a file, the writing is done in 128-KB blocks. Thus, on a very low-use SQL Server instance, it might look like nothing is being written to the file for quite some time. You need 128 KB of data for any writes to the physical file to occur. In addition, when the SQL Server service is stopped, whatever events have accumulated for this trace will be written out to the file.

Unlike the blackbox trace, which captures every single batch completely and can get huge quickly, the default trace in SQL Server 2008 captures only a small set of events that were deemed likely to cause stability problems or performance degradation of SQL Server. The events include database file size change operations, error and warning conditions, full-text crawl operations, object *CREATE, ALTER,* and *DROP* operations, changes to permissions or object ownership, and memory change events.

Not only can you not change anything about the files saved or their locations, you can't add or remove events, the data captured along with the events, or the filters that might be applied to the events. If you want something slightly different than the default trace, you can disable the predefined trace and create your own with whatever events, data, and filters you choose. Of course, you must then make sure the trace starts automatically. This is not impossible to do, but we suggest that you leave the default trace on, in addition to whatever other traces you need, so that you know that at least some information about the activities taking place on your SQL Server is being captured.

# Final Words

In this chapter, I've looked at the general workings of the SQL Server engine, including the key components and functional areas that make up the engine. I've also looked at the interaction between SQL Server and the operating system. By necessity, I've made some simplifications throughout the chapter, but the information should provide some insight into the roles and responsibilities of the major components in SQL Server and the interrelationships among components.

This chapter also covered the primary tools for changing the behavior of SQL Server. The primary means of changing the behavior is by using configuration options, so we looked at the options that can have the biggest impact on SQL Server behavior, especially its performance. To really know when changing the behavior is a good idea, it's important that you understand how and why SQL Server works the way it does. My hope is that this chapter has laid the groundwork for you to make informed decisions about configuration changes.

# Chapter 2

# Change Tracking, Tracing, and Extended Events

*Adam Machanic*

As the Microsoft SQL Server engine processes user requests, a variety of actions can occur: data structures are interrogated; files are read from or written to; memory is allocated, deallocated, or accessed; data is read or modified; an error may be raised; and so on. Classified as a group, these actions can be referred to as the collection of *run-time events* that can occur within SQL Server.

From the point of view of a user—a DBA or database developer working with SQL Server—the fact that certain events are occurring may be interesting in the context of supporting debugging, auditing, and general server maintenance tasks. For example, it may be useful to track when a specific error is raised, every time a certain column is updated, or how much CPU time various stored procedures are consuming.

To support these kinds of user scenarios, the SQL Server engine is instrumented with a variety of infrastructures designed to support event consumption. These range from relatively simple systems such as triggers—which call user code in response to data modifications or other events—to the complex and extremely flexible Extended Events Engine, which is new in SQL Server 2008.

This chapter covers the key areas of each of the common event systems that you might encounter as a SQL Server DBA or database developer: triggers, event notifications, Change Tracking, SQL Trace, and extended events. Each of these has a similar basic goal—to react or report when something happens—but each works somewhat differently.

## The Basics: Triggers and Event Notifications

Although the majority of this chapter is concerned with larger and more complex eventing infrastructures, the basics of how SQL Server internally deals with events can be learned more easily through an investigation of triggers and event notifications; therefore, they are a good place to begin.

Triggers come in a couple of basic varieties. Data Manipulation Language (DML) triggers can be defined to fire on operations like inserts and updates, and Data Definition Language (DDL) triggers can be defined to fire on either server-level or database-level actions such as creating a login or dropping a table. DML triggers can fire instead of the triggering event, or after the event has completed but before the transaction is committed. DDL triggers can be configured to fire only after the event has completed, but again, before the transaction has committed. Event notifications are really nothing more than special-case DDL triggers that send a message to a SQL Service Broker queue rather than invoking user code. The most important difference is that they do not require a transaction and as a result support many non-transactional events—for example, a user disconnecting from the SQL Server instance—that standard DDL triggers do not.

## Run-Time Trigger Behavior

DML triggers and DDL triggers have slightly different run-time behaviors owing to their different modes of operation and the nature of the required data within the trigger. Because DDL triggers are associated with metadata operations, they require much less data than their DML counterparts.

DML triggers are resolved during DML compilation. After the query has been parsed, each table involved is checked via an internal function for the presence of a trigger. If triggers are found, they are compiled and checked for tables that have triggers, and the process recursively continues. During the actual DML operation, the triggers are fired and the rows in the inserted and deleted virtual tables are populated in *tempdb*, using the version store infrastructure.

DDL triggers and event notifications follow similar paths, which are slightly different from that of DML triggers. In both cases, the triggers themselves are resolved via a check only after the DDL change to which they are bound has been applied. DDL triggers and event notifications are fired after the DDL operation has occurred, as a post-operation step rather than during the operation as with DML triggers. The only major difference between DDL triggers and event notifications is that DDL triggers run user-defined code, whereas event notifications send a message to a Service Broker queue.

# Change Tracking

Change Tracking is a feature designed to help eliminate the need for many of the custom synchronization schemes that developers must often create from scratch during an application's lifetime. An example of this kind of system is when an application pulls data from the database into a local cache and occasionally asks the database whether any of the data has been updated, so that the data in the local store can be brought up to date. Most of these systems are implemented using triggers or timestamps, and they are often riddled with performance issues or subtle logic flaws. For example, schemes using timestamps often break down if the timestamp column is populated at insert time rather than at commit time. This can cause a problem if a large insert happens simultaneously with many smaller inserts, and the large insert commits later than smaller inserts that started afterward, thereby ruining the ascending nature of the timestamp. Triggers can remedy this particular problem, but they cause their own problems—namely, they can introduce blocking issues because they increase the amount of time needed for transactions to commit.

Unlike custom systems, Change Tracking is deeply integrated into the SQL Server relational engine and designed from the ground up with performance and scalability in mind. The system is designed to track data changes in one or more tables in a database and is designed to let the user easily determine the order in which changes occurred, as a means by which to support multitable synchronization. Changes are tracked synchronously as part of the transaction in which the change is made, meaning that the list of changed rows is always up to date and consistent with the actual data in the table.

Change Tracking is based on the idea of working forward from a baseline. The data consumer first requests the current state of all the rows in the tracked tables and is given a version number with each row. The baseline version number—effectively, the maximum version number that the system currently knows about—is also queried at that time and is recorded until the next synchronization request. When the request is made, the baseline version number is sent back to the Change Tracking system, and the system determines which rows have been modified since the first request. This way, the consumer needs to concern itself only with deltas; there is generally no reason to reacquire rows that have not changed. In addition to sending a list of rows that have changed, the system identifies the nature of the change since the baseline—a new row, an update to an existing row, or a deleted row. The maximum row version returned when requesting an update becomes the new baseline.

SQL Server 2008 includes two similar technologies that can be used to support synchronization: Change Tracking and Change Data Capture (the details of which are outside the scope of this book because it is not an engine feature per se—it uses an external log reader to do its work). It is worth spending a moment to discuss where and when Change Tracking should be used. Change Tracking is designed to support offline applications, occasionally connected applications, and other applications that don't need real-time notification as data is updated. The Change Tracking system sends back only the current versions of any rows requested after the baseline—incremental row states are not preserved—so the ideal Change Tracking application does not require the full history of a given row. As compared with Change Data Capture, which records the entire modification history of each row, Change Tracking is lighter weight and less applicable to auditing and data warehouse extract, transform, and load (ETL) scenarios.

## Change Tracking Configuration

Although Change Tracking is designed to track changes on a table-by-table basis, it is actually configured at two levels: the database in which the tables reside and the tables themselves. A table cannot be enabled for Change Tracking until the feature has been enabled in the containing database.

### Database-Level Configuration

SQL Server 2008 extends the *ALTER DATABASE* command to support enabling and disabling Change Tracking, as well as configuring options that define whether and how often the history of changes that have been made to participating tables is purged. To enable Change Tracking for a database with the default options, the following *ALTER DATABASE* syntax is used:

```
ALTER DATABASE AdventureWorks2008
SET CHANGE_TRACKING = ON;
```

Running this statement enables a configuration change to metadata that allows two related changes to occur once table-level configuration is enabled: First, a hidden system table will begin getting populated in the target database, should qualifying transactions occur (see the next section). Second, a cleanup task will begin eliminating old rows found in the internal table and related tables.

## Commit Table

The hidden table, known as the Commit Table, maintains one row for every transaction in the database that modifies at least one row in a table that participates in Change Tracking. At transaction commit time, each qualifying transaction is assigned a unique, ascending identifier called a Commit Sequence Number (CSN). The CSN is then inserted—along with the transaction identifier, log sequence information, begin time, and other data—into the Commit Table. This table is central to the Change Tracking process and is used to help determine which changes need to be synchronized when a consumer requests an update, by maintaining a sequence of committed transactions.

Although the Commit Table is an internal table and users can't access it directly, except administrators, via the dedicated administrator connection (DAC), it is still possible to view its columns and indexes by starting with the *sys.all_columns* catalog view. The physical name for the table is *sys.syscommitab*, and the following query returns six rows, as described in Table 2-1:

```
SELECT *
FROM sys.all_columns
WHERE object_id = OBJECT_ID('sys.syscommittab');
```

**TABLE 2-1** Columns in the *sys.syscommittab* System Table

| Column Name | Type | Description |
| --- | --- | --- |
| commit_ts | BIGINT | The ascending CSN for the transaction |
| xdes_id | BIGINT | The internal identifier for the transaction |
| commit_lbn | BIGINT | The log block number for the transaction |
| commit_csn | BIGINT | The instance-wide sequence number for the transaction |
| commit_time | DATETIME | The time the transaction was committed |
| dbfragid | INT | Reserved for future use |

The *sys.syscommitab* table has two indexes (which are visible via the *sys.indexes* catalog view): a unique clustered index on the *commit_ts* and *xdes_id* columns and a unique nonclustered index on the *xdes_id* column that includes the *dbfragid* column. None of the columns are nullable, so the per-row data size is 44 bytes for the clustered index and 20 bytes for the nonclustered index.

Note that this table records information about transactions, but none about which rows were actually modified. That related data is stored in separate system tables, created when Change Tracking is enabled on a user table. Because one transaction can span many different tables and many rows within each table, storing the transaction-specific data in a single central table saves a considerable number of bytes that need to be written during a large transaction.

All the columns in the *sys.syscommitab* table except *dbfragid* are visible via the new *sys.dm_tran_commit_table* DMV. This view is described by *SQL Server Books Online* as being included for "supportability purposes," but it can be interesting to look at for the purpose of learning how Change Tracking behaves internally, as well as to watch the cleanup task, discussed in the next section, in action.

## Internal Cleanup Task

Once Change Tracking is enabled and the Commit Table and related hidden tables fill with rows, they can begin taking up a considerable amount of space in the database. Consumers—that is, synchronizing databases and applications—may not need a change record beyond a certain point of time, and so keeping it around may be a waste. To eliminate this overhead, Change Tracking includes functionality to enable an internal task that removes change history on a regular basis.

When enabling Change Tracking using the syntax listed previously, the default setting, Remove History Older Than Two Days, is used. This setting can be specified when enabling Change Tracking using optional parameters to the *ALTER DATABASE* syntax:

```
ALTER DATABASE AdventureWorks2008
SET CHANGE_TRACKING = ON
(AUTO_CLEANUP=ON, CHANGE_RETENTION=1 hours);
```

The AUTO_CLEANUP option can be used to disable the internal cleanup task completely, and the CHANGE_RETENTION option can be used to specify the interval after which history should be removed, in an interval that can be defined by a number of minutes, hours, or days.

If enabled, the internal task runs once every 30 minutes and evaluates which transactions need to be removed by subtracting the retention interval from the current time and then using an interface into the Commit Table to find a list of transaction IDs older than that period. These transactions are then purged from both the Commit Table and other hidden Change Tracking tables.

The current cleanup and retention settings for each database can be queried from the *sys.change_tracking_databases* catalog view.

> **Note** When setting the cleanup retention interval, it is important to err on the side of being too long, to ensure that data consumers do not end up with a broken change sequence. If this does become a concern, applications can use the *CHANGE_TRACKING_MIN_VALID_VERSION* function to find the current minimum version number stored in the database. If the minimum version number is higher than the application's current baseline, the application has to resynchronize all data and take a new baseline.

## Table-Level Configuration

Once Change Tracking is enabled at the database level, specific tables must be configured to participate. By default, no tables are enlisted in Change Tracking as a result of the feature being enabled at the database level.

The *ALTER TABLE* command has been modified to facilitate enabling of Change Tracking at the table level. To turn on the feature, use the new ENABLE CHANGE_TRACKING option, as shown in the following example:

```
ALTER TABLE HumanResources.Employee
ENABLE CHANGE_TRACKING;
```

If Change Tracking has been enabled at the database level, running this statement causes two changes to occur. First, a new internal table is created in the database to track changes made to rows in the target table. Second, a hidden column is added to the target table to enable tracking of changes to specific rows by transaction ID. An optional feature called Column Tracking can also be enabled; this is covered in the section entitled "Column Tracking," later in this chapter.

## Internal Change Table

The internal table created by enabling Change Tracking at the table level is named *sys.change_tracking_[object id]*, where *[object id]* is the database object ID for the target table. The table can be seen by querying the *sys.all_objects* catalog view and filtering on the *parent_object_id* column based on the object ID of the table you're interested in, or by looking at the *sys.internal_tables* view for tables with an *internal_type* of 209.

The internal table has five static columns, plus at least one additional column depending on how many columns participate in the target table's primary key, as shown in Table 2-2.

**TABLE 2-2 Columns in the Internal Change Tracking Table**

| Column Name | Type | Description |
|---|---|---|
| *sys_change_xdes_id* | *BIGINT NOT NULL* | Transaction ID of the transaction that modified the row. |
| *sys_change_xdes_id_seq* | *BIGINT NOT NULL (IDENTITY)* | Sequence identifier for the operation within the transaction. |

**TABLE 2-2 Columns in the Internal Change Tracking Table**

| Column Name | Type | Description |
| --- | --- | --- |
| sys_change_operation | NCHAR(1) NULL | Type of operation that affected the row: insert, update, or delete. |
| sys_change_columns | VARBINARY(4100) NULL | List of which columns were modified (used for updates, only if column tracking is enabled). |
| sys_change_context | VARBINARY(128) NULL | Application-specific context information provided during the DML operation using the WITH CHANGE_ TRACKING_CONTEXT option. |
| k_[name]_[ord] | [type] NOT NULL | Primary key column(s) from the target table. [name] is the name of the primary key column, [ord] is the ordinal position in the key, and [type] is the data type of the column. |

Calculating the per-row overhead of the internal table is a bit trickier than for the Commit Table, as several factors can influence overall row size. The fixed cost includes 18 bytes for the transaction ID, CSN, and operation type, plus the size of the primary key from the target table. If the operation is an update and column tracking is enabled (as described in the section entitled "Column Tracking," later in this chapter), up to 4,100 additional bytes per row may be consumed by the *sys_change_columns* column. In addition, context information—such as the name of the application or user doing the modification—can be provided using the new WITH CHANGE_TRACKING_CONTEXT DML option (see the section entitled "Query Processing and DML Operations," later in this chapter), and this adds a maximum of another 128 bytes to each row.

The internal table has a unique clustered index on the transaction ID and transaction sequence identifier and no nonclustered indexes.

## Change Tracking Hidden Columns

In addition to the internal table created when Change Tracking is enabled for a table, a hidden 8-byte column is added to the table to record the transaction ID of the transaction that last modified each row. This column is not visible in any relational engine metadata (that is, catalog views and the like), but can be seen referenced in query plans as *$sys_change_xdes_id*. In addition, you may notice the data size of tables increasing accordingly after Change Tracking is updated. This column is removed, along with the internal table, if Change Tracking is disabled for a table.

**Note** The hidden column's value can be seen by connecting via the DAC and explicitly referencing the column name. It never shows up in the results of a *SELECT *** query.

# Change Tracking Run-Time Behavior

The various hidden and internal objects covered to this point each have a specific purpose when Change Tracking interfaces with the query processor at run time. Enabling Change Tracking for a table modifies the behavior of every subsequent DML operation against the table, in addition to enabling use of the *CHANGETABLE* function that allows a data consumer to find out which rows have changed and need to be synchronized.

## Query Processing and DML Operations

Once Change Tracking has been enabled for a given table, all existing query plans for the table that involve row modification are marked for recompilation. New plans that involve modifications to the rows in the table include an insert into the internal change table, as shown in Figure 2-1. Because the internal table represents all operations—inserts, updates, and deletes—by inserting new rows, the subtree added to each of the new query plans is virtually identical.

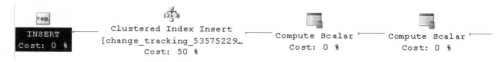

**FIGURE 2-1** Query plan subtree involving an insert into the internal change table

In addition to the insert into the internal table, the query processor begins processing a new DML option thanks to Change Tracking: the *WITH CHANGE_TRACKING_CONTEXT* function. This function allows the storage of up to 128 bytes of binary data, alongside other information about the change, in the internal table's *sys_change_context* column. This column can be used by developers to persist information about which application or user made a given change, using the Change Tracking system as a metadata repository with regard to row changes.

The syntax for this option is similar to a Common Table Expression and is applied at the beginning of the DML query, as in the following example:

```
DECLARE @context VARBINARY(128) =
    CONVERT(VARBINARY(128), SUSER_SNAME());

WITH CHANGE_TRACKING_CONTEXT(@context)
UPDATE AdventureWorks2008.HumanResources.Employee
SET
    JobTitle = 'Production Engineer'
WHERE
    JobTitle = 'Design Engineer';
```

**Note** This syntax is perfectly valid for tables that do not have Change Tracking enabled. However, in those cases, the query processor simply ignores the call to the *CHANGE_TRACKING_CONTEXT* function.

In addition to the insert into the internal table that occurs synchronously at the end of the transaction, an insert into the Commit Table also occurs at commit time. The inserted row contains the same transaction ID that is used both in the internal table and in the hidden column on the target table. A CSN is also assigned for the transaction at this time; this number can, therefore, be thought of as the version number that applies to all rows modified by the transaction.

## Column Tracking

When working with tables that have a large number of columns or tables with one or more extremely wide columns, the synchronization process can be optimized by not reacquiring the data from those columns that were not updated. To support this kind of optimization, Change Tracking includes a feature called Column Tracking, which works by recording, in the internal table and only in the case of an update operation, which columns were updated.

The column list is persisted within the internal table in the *sys_change_columns* column. Each column is stored as an integer, and a column list including as many as 1,024 columns can be stored. If more than 1,024 columns are modified in a transaction, the column list is not stored and the application must reacquire the entire row.

To enable Column Tracking, a switch called TRACK_COLUMNS_UPDATED is applied to the *ALTER TABLE* statement, as in the following example:

```
ALTER TABLE HumanResources.Employee
ENABLE CHANGE_TRACKING
WITH (TRACK_COLUMNS_UPDATED = ON);
```

Once enabled, the changed columns list is returned with the output of the *CHANGETABLE(CHANGES)* function, which is described in the next section. The bitmap can be evaluated for the presence of a particular column by using the *CHANGE_TRACKING_IS_COLUMN_IN_MASK* function.

> **Caution**  Be careful when enabling Column Tracking for active tables. Although this feature may help to optimize the synchronization process by resulting in fewer bytes being sent out at synchronization time, it also increases the number of bytes that must be written with each update against the target table. This may result in a net decrease in overall performance if the columns are not sufficiently large enough to balance the additional byte requirements of the bitmap.

## *CHANGETABLE* Function

The primary API that users can use to leverage the Change Tracking system is the *CHANGETABLE* function. This function has the dual purpose of returning the baseline version for all rows in the target table and returning a set containing only updated versions and related change information. The function accomplishes each of these tasks with the help of the various internal and hidden structures created and populated when Change Tracking is enabled for a given table or set of tables in a database.

*CHANGETABLE* is a system table-valued function, but unlike other table-valued functions, its result shape changes at run time based on input parameters. In VERSION mode, used for acquiring the baseline values of each row in the table, the function returns only a primary key, version number, and context information for each row. In CHANGES mode, used for getting a list of updated rows, the function also returns the operation that affected the change and the column list.

Because the VERSION mode for *CHANGETABLE* is designed to help callers get a baseline, calling the function in this mode requires a join to the target table, as in the following example:

```
SELECT
    c.SYS_CHANGE_VERSION,
    c.SYS_CHANGE_CONTEXT,
    e.*
FROM AdventureWorks2008.HumanResources.Employee e
CROSS APPLY CHANGETABLE
(
    VERSION AdventureWorks2008.HumanResources.Employee,
    (BusinessEntityId),
    (e.BusinessEntityId)
) c;
```

A quick walk-through of this example is called for here. In VERSION mode, the first parameter to the function is the target table. The second parameter is a comma-delimited list of the primary key columns on the target table. The third parameter is a comma-delimited list, in the same order, of the associated primary key columns from the target table as used in the query. The columns are internally correlated in this order to support the joins necessary to get the baseline versions of each row.

When this query is executed, the query processor scans the target table, visiting each row and getting the values for every column, along with the value of the hidden column (the last transaction ID that modified the row). This transaction ID is used as a key to join to the Commit Table to pick up the associated CSN and to populate the *sys_change_version* column. The transaction ID and primary key are also used to join to the internal tracking table in order to populate the *sys_change_context* column.

Once a baseline has been acquired, it is up to the data consumer to call the *CHANGE_TRACKING_CURRENT_VERSION* function, which returns the maximum Change Tracking version number currently stored in the database. This number becomes the baseline version number that the application can use for future synchronization requests. This number is passed into the *CHANGETABLE* function in CHANGES mode to get subsequent versions of the rows in the table, as in the following example:

```
DECLARE @last_version BIGINT = 8;

SELECT
    c.*
```

```
FROM CHANGETABLE
(
    CHANGES AdventureWorks2008.HumanResources.Employee,
    @last_version
) c;
```

This query returns a list of all changed rows since version 8, along with what operation
caused each row to be modified. Note that the output reflects only the most recent version
of the row as of the time that the query is run. For example, if a row existed as of version 8
and was subsequently updated three times and then deleted, this query shows only one
change for the row: a delete. This query includes in its output the primary keys that changed,
so it is possible to join to the target table to get the most recent version of each row that
changed. Care must be taken to use an OUTER JOIN in that case, as shown in the following
example, as a row may no longer exist if it was deleted:

```
DECLARE @last_version BIGINT = 8;

SELECT
    c.SYS_CHANGE_VERSION,
    c.SYS_CHANGE_OPERATION,
    c.SYS_CHANGE_CONTEXT,
    e.*
FROM CHANGETABLE
(
    CHANGES AdventureWorks2008.HumanResources.Employee,
    @last_version
) c
LEFT OUTER JOIN AdventureWorks2008.HumanResources.Employee e ON
    e.BusinessEntityID = c.BusinessEntityID;
```

When *CHANGETABLE* is run in CHANGES mode, the various internal structures are used
slightly differently than in the VERSION example. The first step of the process is to query the
Commit Table for all transaction IDs associated with CSNs greater than the one passed in to
the function. This list of transaction IDs is next used to query the internal tracking table for
the primary keys associated with changes rendered by the transactions. The rows that result
from this phase must be aggregated based on the primary key and transaction sequence
identifier from the internal table to find the most recent row for each primary key. No join
to the target table is necessary in this case unless the consumer would like to retrieve all
associated row values.

Because rows may be changing all the time—including while the application is requesting
a list of changes—it is important to keep consistency in mind when working with Change
Tracking. The best way to ensure consistent results is to either make use of SNAPSHOT
isolation if the application retrieves a list of changed keys and then subsequently requests
the row value, or READ COMMITTED SNAPSHOT isolation if the values are retrieved using
a JOIN. SNAPSHOT isolation and READ COMMITTED SNAPSHOT isolation are discussed in
Chapter 10.

# Tracing and Profiling

Query tuning, optimization, and general troubleshooting are all made possible through visibility into what's going on within SQL Server; it would be impossible to fix problems without being able to identify what caused them. SQL Trace is one of the more powerful tools provided by SQL Server to give you a real-time or near-real-time look at exactly what the database engine is doing, at a very granular level.

Included in the tracing toolset are 180 events that you can monitor, filter, and manipulate to get a look at anything from a broad overview of user logins down to such fine-grained information as the lock activity done by a specific session id (SPID). This data is all made available via SQL Server Profiler, as well as a series of server-side stored procedures and .NET classes, giving you the flexibility to roll a custom solution when a problem calls for one.

## SQL Trace Architecture and Terminology

SQL Trace is a SQL Server database engine technology, and it is important to understand that the client-side Profiler tool is really nothing more than a wrapper over the server-side functionality. When tracing, we monitor for specific events that are generated when various actions occur in the database engine. For example, a user logging onto the server or executing a query are each actions that cause events to fire. These events are fired by instrumentation of the database engine code; in other words, special code has been added to these and other execution paths that cause the events to fire when hit.

Each event has an associated collection of "columns," which are attributes that contain data collected when the event fires. For instance, in the case of a query, we can collect data about when the query started, how long it took, and how much CPU time it used. Finally, each trace can specify filters, which limit the results returned based on a set of criteria. One could, for example, specify that only events that took longer than 50 milliseconds should be returned.

With 180 events and 66 columns to choose from, the number of data points that can be collected is quite large. Not every column can be used with every event, but the complete set of allowed combinations is over 4,000. Thinking about memory utilization to hold all this data and the processor time needed to create it, you might be interested in how SQL Server manages to run efficiently while generating so much information. The answer is that SQL Server doesn't actually collect any data until someone asks for it—instead, the model is to selectively enable collection only as necessary.

### Internal Trace Components

The central component of the SQL Trace architecture is the *trace controller*, which is a shared resource that manages all traces created by any consumer. Throughout the database engine are various *event producers*; for example, they are found in the query processor, lock manager, and cache manager. Each of these producers is responsible for generating events that pertain to certain categories of server activity, but each of the producers is disabled by default and therefore generates no data. When a user requests that a trace be started for a certain event, a global bitmap in the trace controller is updated, letting the event producer know that at least one trace is listening, and causing the event to begin firing. Managed along with this bitmap is a secondary list of which traces are monitoring which events.

Once an event fires, its data is routed into a global event sink, which queues the event data for distribution to each trace that is actively listening. The trace controller routes the data to each listening trace based on its internal list of traces and watched events. In addition to the trace controller's own lists, each individual trace keeps track of which events it is monitoring, along with which columns are actually being used, as well as what filters are in place. The event data returned by the trace controller to each trace is filtered, and the data columns are trimmed down as necessary, before the data is routed to an *I/O provider.*

## Trace I/O Providers

The trace I/O providers are what actually send the data along to its final destination. The available output formats for trace data are either a file on the database server (or a network share) or a rowset to a client. Both providers use internal buffers to ensure that if the data is not consumed quickly enough (that is, written to disk or read from the rowset) that it will be queued. However, there is a big difference in how the providers handle a situation in which the queue grows beyond a manageable size.

The *file provider* is designed with a guarantee that no event data will be lost. To make this work even if an I/O slowdown or stall occurs, the internal buffers begin to fill if disk writes are not occurring quickly enough. Once the buffers fill up, threads sending event data to the trace begin waiting for buffer space to free up. To avoid threads waiting on trace buffers, it is imperative to ensure that tracing is performed using a sufficiently fast disk system. To monitor for these waits, watch the SQLTRACE_LOCK and IO_COMPLETION wait types.

The *rowset provider,* on the other hand, is not designed to make any data loss guarantees. If data is not being consumed quickly enough and its internal buffers fill, it waits up to 20 seconds before it begins jettisoning events to free buffers and get things moving. The SQL Server Profiler client tool sends a special error message if events are getting dropped, but you can also find out if you're headed in that direction by monitoring the TRACEWRITE wait type in SQL Server, which is incremented as threads are waiting for buffers to free up.

A background trace management thread is also started whenever at least one trace is active on the server. This background thread is responsible for flushing file provider buffers (which is done every four seconds), in addition to closing rowset-based traces that are considered to be expired (this occurs if a trace has been dropping events for more than 10 minutes). By flushing the file provider buffers only occasionally rather than writing the data to disk every time an event is collected, SQL Server can take advantage of large block writes, dramatically reducing the overhead of tracing, especially on extremely active servers.

A common question asked by DBAs new to SQL Server is why no provider exists that can write trace data directly to a table. The reason for this limitation is the amount of overhead that would be required for such activity. Because a table does not support large block writes, SQL Server would have to write the event data row by row. The performance degradation caused by event consumption would require either dropping a lot of events or, if a lossless guarantee were enforced, causing a lot of blocking to occur. Neither scenario is especially palatable, so SQL Server simply does not provide this ability. However, as we will see later in the chapter, it is easy enough to load the data into a table either during or after tracing, so this is not much of a limitation.

# Security and Permissions

Tracing can expose a lot of information about not only the state of the server, but also the data sent to and returned from the database engine by users. The ability to monitor individual queries down to the batch or even query plan level is at once both powerful and worrisome; even exposure of stored procedure input arguments can give an attacker a lot of information about the data in your database.

To protect SQL Trace from users that should not be able to view the data it exposes, versions of SQL Server prior to SQL Server 2005 allowed only administrative users (members of the *sysadmin* fixed server role) access to start traces. That restriction proved a bit too inflexible for many development teams, and as a result, it has been loosened.

## ALTER TRACE Permission

Starting with SQL Server 2005, a new permission exists, called ALTER TRACE. This is a server-level permission (granted to a login principal), and allows access to start, stop, or modify a trace, in addition to providing the ability to generate user-defined events.

**Tip** Keep in mind that the ALTER TRACE permission is granted at the server level, and access is at the server level; if a user can start a trace, he or she can retrieve event data no matter what database the event was generated in. The inclusion of this permission in SQL Server is a great step in the right direction for handling situations in which developers might need to run traces on production systems to debug application issues, but it's important not to grant this permission too lightly. It's still a potential security threat, even if it's not nearly as severe as giving someone full *sysadmin* access.

To grant ALTER TRACE permission to a login, use the *GRANT* statement as follows (in this example, the permission is granted to a server principal called "Jane"):

```
GRANT ALTER TRACE TO Jane;
```

## Protecting Sensitive Event Data

In addition to being locked down so that only certain users can use SQL Trace, the tracing engine itself has a couple of built-in security features to keep unwanted eyes—including those with access to trace—from viewing private information. SQL Trace automatically omits data if an event contains a call to a password-related stored procedure or statement. For example, a call to *CREATE LOGIN* that includes the WITH PASSWORD option is blanked out by SQL Trace.

 **Note** In versions of SQL Server before SQL Server 2005, SQL Trace automatically blanked out a query event if the string *sp_password* was found anywhere in the text of the query. This feature has been removed in SQL Server 2005 and SQL Server 2008, and you should not depend on it to protect your intellectual capital.

Another security feature of SQL Trace is knowledge of encrypted modules. SQL Trace does not return statement text or query plans generated within an encrypted stored procedure, user-defined function, or view. Again, this helps to safeguard especially sensitive data even from users who should have access to see traces.

# Getting Started: Profiler

SQL Server 2008 ships with Profiler, a powerful user interface tool that can be used to create, manipulate, and manage traces. This tool is the primary starting point for most tracing activity, and thanks to the ease with which it can help you get traces up and running, it is perhaps the most important SQL Server component available for quickly troubleshooting database issues. Profiler also adds a few features to the toolset that are not made possible by SQL Trace itself. This section discusses those features in addition to the base tracing capabilities.

## Profiler Basics

The Profiler tool can be found in the Performance Tools subfolder of the SQL Server 2008 Start Menu folder (which you get to by clicking Start and selecting All Programs, SQL Server 2008, Performance Tools, SQL Server Profiler). Once the tool is started, you see a blank screen. Click File, New Trace... and connect to a SQL Server instance. You are shown a Trace Properties dialog box with two tabs, General and Events Selection.

The General tab, shown in Figure 2-2, allows you to control how the trace is processed by the consumer. The default setting is to use the rowset provider, displaying the events in real time in the SQL Server Profiler window. Also available are options to save the events to a file (on either the server or the client), or to a table. However, we generally recommend that you avoid these options on a busy server.

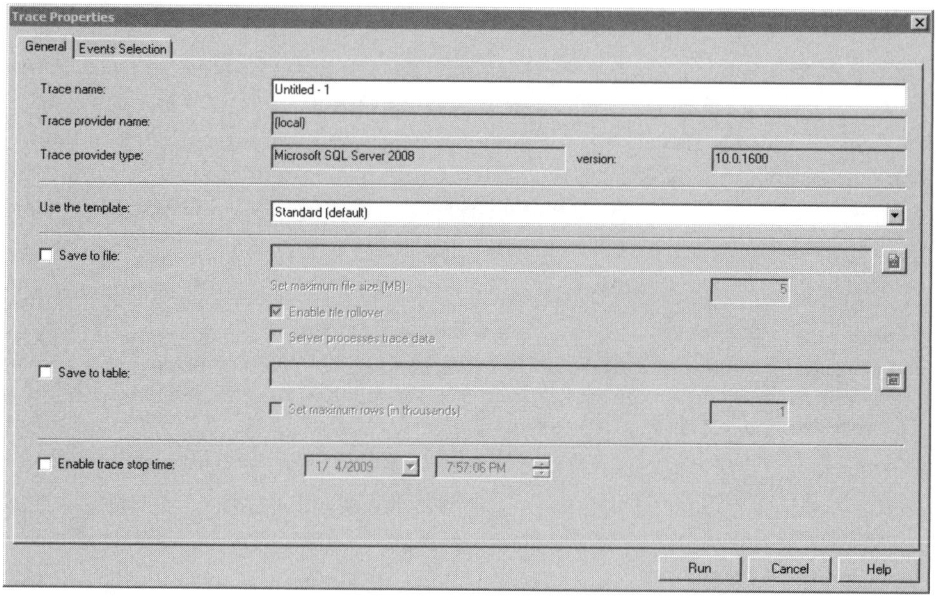

**FIGURE 2-2** Choosing the I/O provider for the trace

When you ask Profiler to save the events to a server-side file (by selecting the Server Processes Trace Data option), it actually starts two equivalent traces, one using the rowset provider and the other using the file provider. Having two traces means twice as much overhead, and that is generally not a good idea. See the section entitled "Server-Side Tracing and Collection," later in this chapter for information, on how to set up a trace using the file provider, which allows you to save to a server-side file efficiently. Saving to a client-side file does not use the file provider at all. Rather, the data is routed to the Profiler tool via the rowset provider and then saved from there to a file. This is more efficient than using Profiler to write to a server-side file, but you do incur network bandwidth because of using the rowset provider, and you also do not get the benefit of the lossless guarantee that the file provider offers.

> **Note** Seeing the Save To Table option, you might wonder why we stated earlier in this chapter that tracing directly to a table is not possible in SQL Trace. The fact is that SQL Trace exposes no table output provider. Instead, when you use this option, the Profiler tool uses the rowset provider and routes the data back into a table. If the table you save to is on the same server you're tracing, you can create quite a large amount of server overhead and bandwidth utilization, so if you must use this option we recommend saving the data to a table on a different server. Profiler also provides an option to save the data to a table *after* you're done tracing, and this is a much more scalable choice in most scenarios.

The Events Selection tab, shown in Figure 2-3, is where you'll spend most of your time configuring traces in Profiler. This tab allows you to select events that you'd like to trace, along with associated data columns. The default options, shown in Figure 2-3, collect data about any connections that exist when the trace starts (the *ExistingConnection* event) when a login or logout occurs (the *Audit Login* and *Audit Logout* events), when remote procedure calls complete (the *RPC:Completed* event), and when T-SQL batches start or complete (the *SQL:BatchCompleted* and *SQL:BatchStarting* events). By default, the complete list of both events and available data columns is hidden. Selecting the Show All Events and Show All Columns check boxes brings the available selections into the UI.

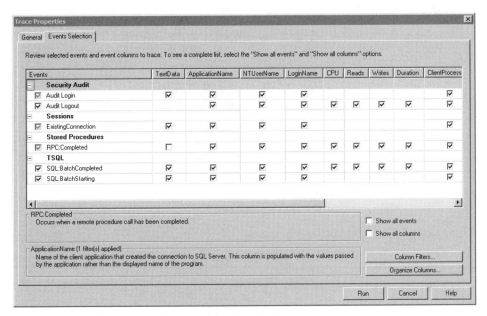

**FIGURE 2-3** Choosing event/column combinations for the trace

These default selections are a great starting point and can be used as the basis for a lot of commonly required traces. The simplest questions that DBAs generally answer using SQL Trace are based around query cost and/or duration. What are the longest queries, or the queries that are using the most resources? The default selections can help you answer those types of questions, but on an active server, a huge amount of data would have to be collected, which not only means more work for you to be able to answer your question, but also more work for the server to collect and distribute that much data.

To narrow your scope and help ensure that tracing does not cause performance issues, SQL Trace offers the ability to filter the events based on various criteria. Filtration is exposed in SQL Profiler via the Column Filters... button in the Events Selection tab. Click this button to bring up an Edit Filter dialog box similar to the one shown in Figure 2-4. In this example, we want to see only events with a duration greater than or equal to 200 milliseconds. This is just an arbitrary number; an optimal choice should be discovered iteratively as you build up your knowledge of the tracing requirements for your particular application. Keep raising this number until you mostly receive only the desired events (in this case, those with long durations) from your trace. By working this way, you can isolate the slowest queries in your system easily and quickly.

> **Tip**  The list of data columns made available by SQL Profiler for you to use as a filter is the same list of columns available in the outer Events Selection user interface. Make sure to select the Show All Columns check box to ensure that you see a complete list.

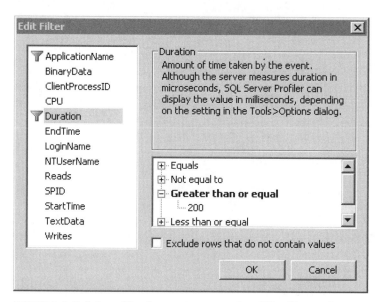

**FIGURE 2-4** Defining a filter for events greater than 200 milliseconds

Once events are selected and filters are defined, the trace can be started. In the Trace Properties dialog box, click Run. Because Profiler uses the rowset provider, data begins streaming back immediately. If you find that data is coming in too quickly for you to be able to read it, consider disabling auto scrolling using the Auto Scroll Window button on the SQL Profiler toolbar.

An important note on filters is that, by default, events that do not produce data for a specific column are not filtered if a trace defines a filter for that column. For example, the *SQL:BatchStarting* event does not produce duration data—the batch is considered to start more or less instantly the moment it is submitted to the server. Figure 2-5 shows a trace that we ran with a filter on the *Duration* column for values greater than 200 milliseconds. Notice that both the *ExistingConnection* and *SQL:BatchStarting* events are still returned even though they lack the *Duration* output column. To modify this behavior, select the Exclude Rows That Do Not Contain Values check box in the Edit Filter dialog box for the column for which you want to change the setting.

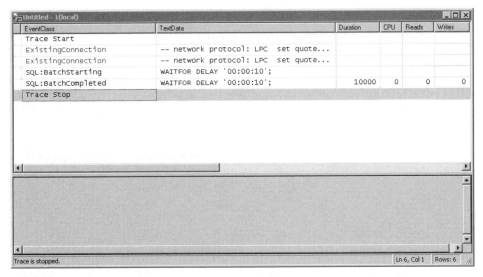

| EventClass | TextData | Duration | CPU | Reads | Writes |
|---|---|---|---|---|---|
| Trace Start | | | | | |
| ExistingConnection | -- network protocol: LPC  set quote... | | | | |
| ExistingConnection | -- network protocol: LPC  set quote... | | | | |
| SQL:BatchStarting | WAITFOR DELAY '00:00:10'; | | | | |
| SQL:BatchCompleted | WAITFOR DELAY '00:00:10'; | 10000 | 0 | 0 | 0 |
| Trace Stop | | | | | |

Trace is stopped.   Ln 6, Col 1   Rows: 6

**FIGURE 2-5** By default, trace filters treat empty values as valid for the sake of the filter.

## Saving and Replaying Traces

The functionality covered up through this point in the chapter has all been made possible by Profiler merely acting as a wrapper over what SQL Trace provides. In the section entitled "Server-Side Tracing and Collection," later in this chapter, we show you the mechanisms by which Profiler does its work. But first we'll get into the features offered by Profiler that make it more than a simple UI wrapper over the SQL Trace features.

When we discussed the General tab of the Trace Properties window earlier, we glossed over how the default events are actually set: They are included in the standard events template that ships with the product. A *template* is a collection of event and column selections, filters, and other settings that you can save to create reusable trace definitions. This feature can be extremely useful if you do a lot of tracing; reconfiguring the options each time you need them is generally not a good use of your time.

In addition to the ability to save your own templates, Profiler ships with nine predefined templates. Aside from the standard template that we already explored, one of the most important of these is the TSQL_Replay template, which is selected in Figure 2-6. This template selects a variety of columns for 15 different events, each of which are required for Profiler to be able to play back (or replay) a collected trace at a later time. By starting a trace using this template and then saving the trace data once collection is complete, you can do things such as use a trace as a test harness for reproducing a specific problem that might occur when certain stored procedures are called in the correct order.

To illustrate this functionality, we started a new trace using the TSQL_Replay template and sent two batches from each of two connections, as shown in Figure 2-7. The first SPID (53, in this case) selected 1, and then the second SPID (54) selected 2. Back to SPID 53, which

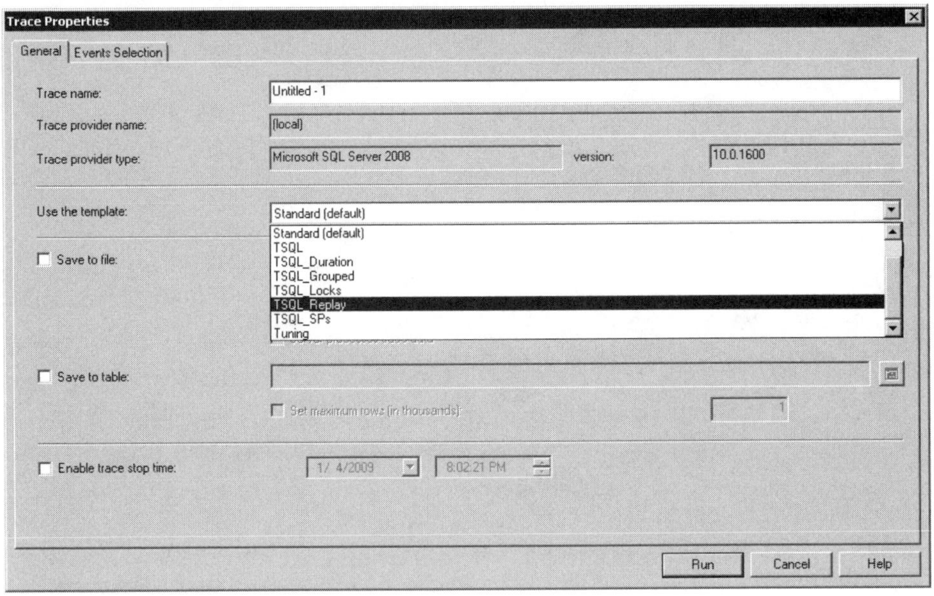

**FIGURE 2-6** Selecting the TSQL_Replay template

selected 3, and then finally back to SPID 54, which selected 4. The most interesting thing to note in the figure is the second column, *EventSequence*. This column can be thought of almost like the *IDENTITY* property for a table. Its value is incremented globally, as events are recorded by the trace controller, to create a single representation of the order in which events occurred in the server. This avoids problems that might occur when ordering by StartTime/EndTime (also in the trace, but not shown in Figure 2-7), as there will be no ties—the *EventSequence* is unique for every trace. The number is a 64-bit integer, and it is reset whenever the server is restarted, so it is unlikely that you can ever trace enough to run it beyond its range.

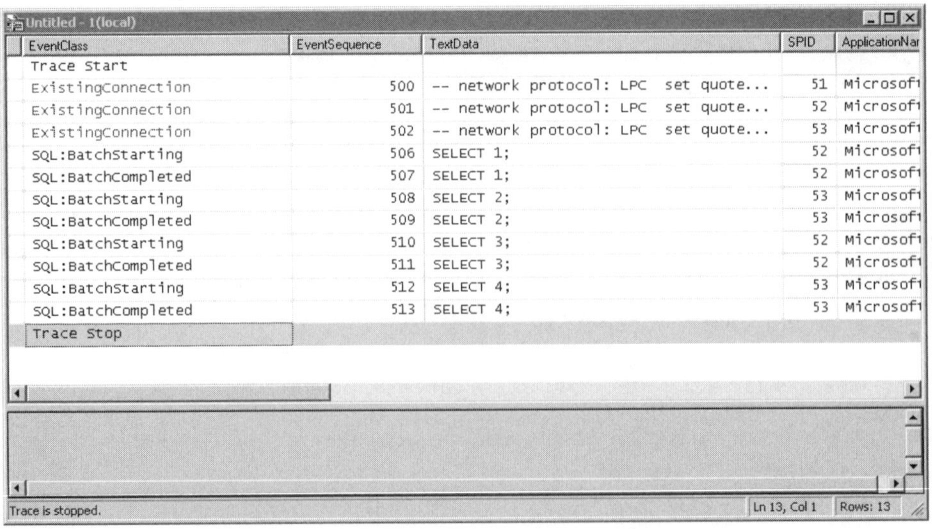

**FIGURE 2-7** Two SPIDs sending interleaved batches

Once the trace data has been collected, it must be saved and then reopened before a replay can begin. Profiler offers the following options for saving trace data, which are available from the File menu:

- The Trace File option is used to save the data to a file formatted using a proprietary binary format. This is generally the fastest way to save the data, and it is also the smallest in terms of bytes on disk.

- The Trace Table option is used to save the data to a new or previously created table in a database of your choosing. This option is useful if you need to manipulate or report on the data using T-SQL.

- The Trace XML File option saves the data to a text file formatted as XML.

- The Trace XML File For Replay option also saves the data to an XML text file, but only those events and columns needed for replay functionality are saved.

Any of these formats can be used as a basis from which to replay a trace, so long as you've collected all the required events and columns needed to do a replay (guaranteed when you use the TSQL_Replay template). We generally recommend using the binary file format as a starting point and saving to a table if manipulation using T-SQL is necessary. For instance, you might want to create a complex query that finds the top queries that use certain tables; something like that would be beyond the abilities of Profiler. With regard to the XML file formats, so far I have not found much use for them. But as more third-party tools hit the market that can use trace data, we may see more use cases.

Once the data has been saved to a file or table, the original trace window can be closed and the file or table reopened via the File menu in the Profiler tool. Once a trace is reopened in this way, a Replay menu appears on the Profiler toolbar, allowing you to start replaying the trace, stop the replay, or set a breakpoint—which is useful when you want to test only a small portion of a larger trace.

After clicking Start in Profiler, you are asked to connect to a server—either the server from which you did the collection, or another server if you want to replay the same trace somewhere else. After connecting, the Replay Configuration dialog box shown in Figure 2-8 is presented. The Basic Replay Options tab allows you to save results of the trace in addition to modifying how the trace is played back.

During the course of the replay, the same events used to produce the trace being replayed are traced from the server on which you replay. The Save To File and Save To Table options are used for a client-side save. No server-side option exists for saving playback results.

The Replay Options pane of the Replay Configurations dialog box is a bit confusing as worded. No matter which option you select, the trace is replayed on multiple threads, corresponding to at most the number you selected in the Number Of Replay Threads drop-down list. However, selecting the Replay Events In The Order They Were Traced option ensures that all events are played back in exactly the order in which they occurred, as based upon the *EventSequence* column. Multiple threads are still used to simulate multiple SPIDs. Selecting the Replay Events

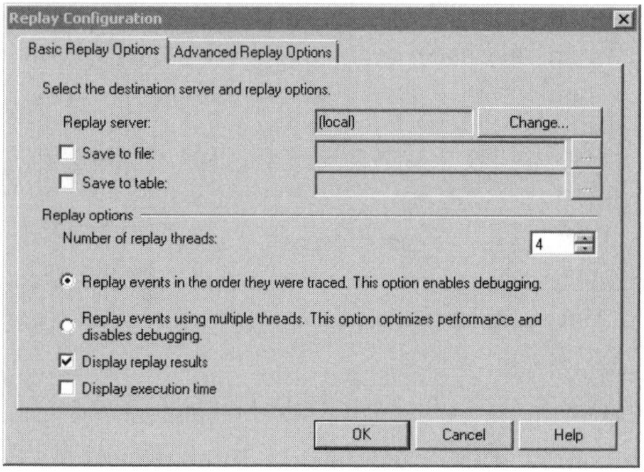

**FIGURE 2-8** The Replay Configuration dialog box

Using Multiple Threads option, on the other hand, allows Profiler to rearrange the order in which each SPID starts to execute events, in order to enhance playback performance. Within a given SPID, however, the order of events remains consistent with the *EventSequence*.

To illustrate this difference, we replayed the trace shown in Figure 2-7 twice, each using a different replay option. Figure 2-9 shows the result of the Replay In Order option, whereas Figure 2-10 shows the result of the Multiple Threads option. In Figure 2-9, the results show that the batches were started and completed in exactly the same order in which they were originally traced, whereas in Figure 2-10 the two participating SPIDs have had all their events grouped together rather than interleaved.

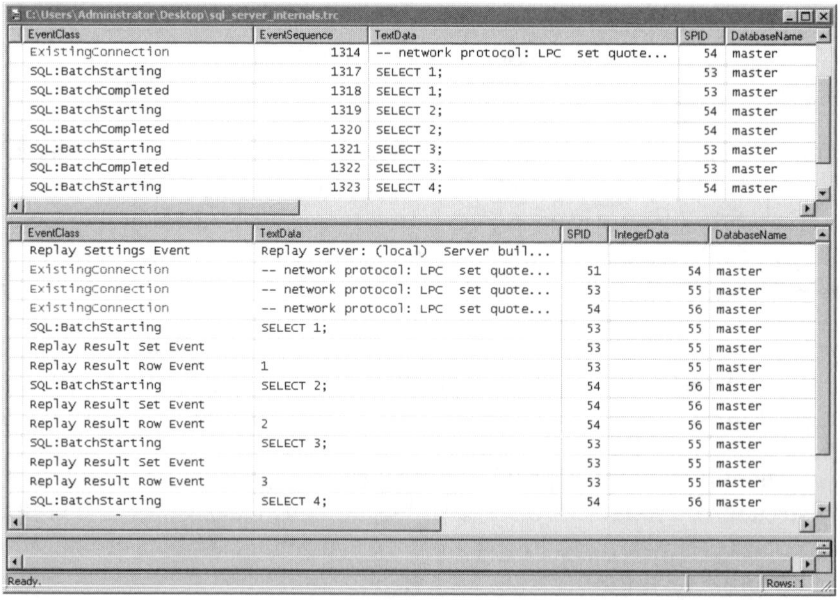

**FIGURE 2-9** Replay using the Replay In Order option

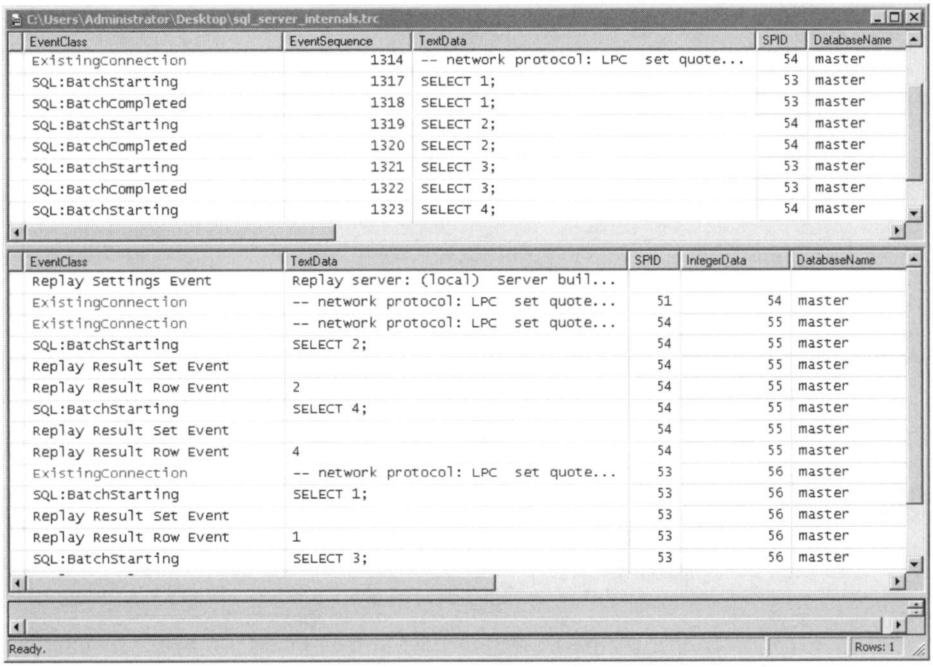

| EventClass | EventSequence | TextData | SPID | DatabaseName |
|---|---|---|---|---|
| ExistingConnection | 1314 | -- network protocol: LPC  set quote... | 54 | master |
| SQL:BatchStarting | 1317 | SELECT 1; | 53 | master |
| SQL:BatchCompleted | 1318 | SELECT 1; | 53 | master |
| SQL:BatchStarting | 1319 | SELECT 2; | 54 | master |
| SQL:BatchCompleted | 1320 | SELECT 2; | 54 | master |
| SQL:BatchStarting | 1321 | SELECT 3; | 53 | master |
| SQL:BatchCompleted | 1322 | SELECT 3; | 53 | master |
| SQL:BatchStarting | 1323 | SELECT 4; | 54 | master |

| EventClass | TextData | SPID | IntegerData | DatabaseName |
|---|---|---|---|---|
| Replay Settings Event | Replay server: (local)  Server buil... | | | |
| ExistingConnection | -- network protocol: LPC  set quote... | 51 | 54 | master |
| ExistingConnection | -- network protocol: LPC  set quote... | 54 | 55 | master |
| SQL:BatchStarting | SELECT 2; | 54 | 55 | master |
| Replay Result Set Event | | 54 | 55 | master |
| Replay Result Row Event | 2 | 54 | 55 | master |
| SQL:BatchStarting | SELECT 4; | 54 | 55 | master |
| Replay Result Set Event | | 54 | 55 | master |
| Replay Result Row Event | 4 | 54 | 55 | master |
| ExistingConnection | -- network protocol: LPC  set quote... | 53 | 56 | master |
| SQL:BatchStarting | SELECT 1; | 53 | 56 | master |
| Replay Result Set Event | | 53 | 56 | master |
| Replay Result Row Event | 1 | 53 | 56 | master |
| SQL:BatchStarting | SELECT 3; | 53 | 56 | master |

Ready.    Rows: 1

**FIGURE 2-10** Replay using the Multiple Threads option

The Multiple Threads option can be useful if you need to replay a lot of trace data where each SPID has no dependency upon other SPIDs. For example, this might be done to simulate, on a test server, a workload captured from a production system. On the other hand, the Replay In Order option is useful if you need to ensure that you can duplicate the specific conditions that occurred during the trace. For example, this might apply when debugging a deadlock or blocking condition that results from specific interactions of multiple threads accessing the same data.

Profiler is a full-featured tool that provides extensive support for both tracing and doing simple work with trace data, but if you need to do advanced queries against your collected data or run traces against extremely active production systems, Profiler falls short of the requirements. Again, Profiler is essentially nothing more than a wrapper over functionality provided within the database engine, and instead of using it for all stages of the trace lifestyle, we can exploit the tool directly to increase flexibility in some cases. In the following section, you learn how Profiler works with the database engine to start, stop, and manage traces, and how you can harness the same tools for your needs.

## Server-Side Tracing and Collection

Behind its nice user interface, Profiler is nothing more than a fairly lightweight wrapper over a handful of system stored procedures that expose the true functionality of SQL Trace. In this section, we explore which stored procedures are used and how to harness SQL Server Profiler as a scripting tool rather than a tracing interface.

The following system stored procedures are used to define and manage traces:

- *sp_trace_create* is used to define a trace and specify an output file location as well as other options that I'll cover in the coming pages. This stored procedure returns a handle to the created trace, in the form of an integer trace ID.

- *sp_trace_setevent* is used to add event/column combinations to traces based on the trace ID, as well as to remove them, if necessary, from traces in which they have already been defined.

- *sp_trace_setfilter* is used to define event filters based on trace columns.

- *sp_trace_setstatus* is called to turn on a trace, to stop a trace, and to delete a trace definition once you're done with it. Traces can be started and stopped multiple times over their lifespan.

## Scripting Server-Side Traces

Rather than delve directly into the syntax specifications for each of the stored procedures—all which are documented in detail in *SQL Server Books Online*—it is a bit more interesting to observe them in action. To begin, open up SQL Server Profiler, start a new trace with the default template, and clear all the events except for *SQL:BatchCompleted*, as shown in Figure 2-11.

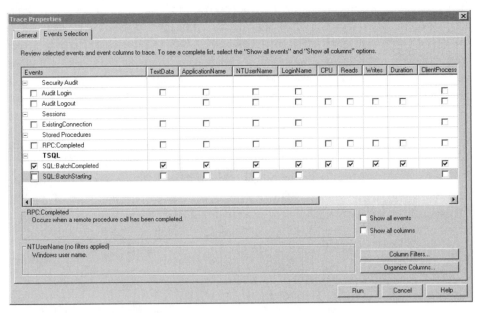

**FIGURE 2-11** Trace events with only *SQL:BatchCompleted* selected

Next, remove the default filter on the *ApplicationName* column (set to not pick up SQL Server Profiler events), and add a filter on *Duration* for greater than or equal to 10 milliseconds, as shown in Figure 2-12.

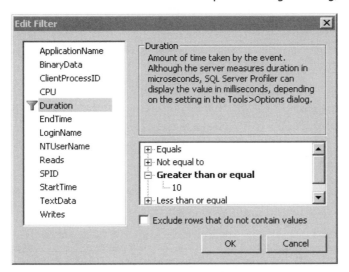

**FIGURE 2-12** Filter on *Duration* set to greater than or equal to 10 milliseconds

Once you're finished, click Run to start the trace, then immediately click Stop. Because of the workflow required by the SQL Profiler user interface, you must actually start a trace before you can script it. On the File menu, select Export, Script Trace Definition, and For SQL Server 2005 - 2008. This will produce a script similar to the following (edited for brevity and readability):

```
declare @rc int
declare @TraceID int
declare @maxfilesize bigint
set @maxfilesize = 5

exec @rc = sp_trace_create
    @TraceID output,
    0,
    N'InsertFileNameHere',
    @maxfilesize,
    NULL
if (@rc != 0) goto finish

-- Set the events
declare @on bit
set @on = 1
exec sp_trace_setevent @TraceID, 12, 15, @on
exec sp_trace_setevent @TraceID, 12, 16, @on
exec sp_trace_setevent @TraceID, 12, 1, @on
exec sp_trace_setevent @TraceID, 12, 9, @on
exec sp_trace_setevent @TraceID, 12, 17, @on
exec sp_trace_setevent @TraceID, 12, 6, @on
exec sp_trace_setevent @TraceID, 12, 10, @on
exec sp_trace_setevent @TraceID, 12, 14, @on
exec sp_trace_setevent @TraceID, 12, 18, @on
exec sp_trace_setevent @TraceID, 12, 11, @on
exec sp_trace_setevent @TraceID, 12, 12, @on
exec sp_trace_setevent @TraceID, 12, 13, @on
```

```
-- Set the Filters
declare @bigintfilter bigint

set @bigintfilter = 10000
exec sp_trace_setfilter @TraceID, 13, 0, 4, @bigintfilter

-- Set the trace status to start
exec sp_trace_setstatus @TraceID, 1

-- display trace id for future references
select TraceID=@TraceID

finish:
go
```

> **Note** An option also exists to script the trace definition for SQL Server 2000. The SQL Trace stored procedures did not change much between SQL Server 2000 and SQL Server 2005—and it did not change at all between SQL Server 2005 and SQL Server 2008—but several new events and columns were added to the product. Scripting for SQL Server 2000 simply drops from the script any events that are not backward-compatible.

This script is an extremely simple yet complete definition of a trace that uses the file provider. A couple of placeholder values need to be modified, but for the most part, it is totally functional. Given the complexity of working directly with the SQL Trace stored procedures, we generally define a trace using SQL Profiler's user interface, and then script it and work from there. This way, you get the best of both worlds: ease of use combined with the efficiency of server-side traces using the file provider.

This script does a few different things, so we will walk through each stage:

1. The script defines a few variables to be used in the process. The *@rc* variable is used to get a return code from *sp_trace_create*. The *@TraceID* variable holds the handle to the newly created trace. Finally, the *@maxfilesize* variable defines the maximum size (in megabytes) per trace file. When running server-side traces, the file provider can be configured to create *rollover files* automatically as the primary trace file fills up. This can be useful if you're working on a drive with limited space, as you can move previously filled files to another device. In addition, smaller files can make it easier to manipulate subsets of the collected data. Finally, rollover files also have their utility in high-load scenarios. However, most of the time these are not necessary, and a value of 5 is a bit small for the majority of scenarios.

2. The script calls the *sp_trace_create* stored procedure, which initializes—but does not start—the trace. The parameters specified here are the output parameter for the trace ID of the newly created trace; 0 for the options parameter—meaning that rollover files should not be used; a placeholder for a server-side file path, which should be changed before using this script; the maximum file size as defined by the *@maxfilesize* variable; and NULL for the stop date—this trace only stops when it is told to. Note that there is also

a final parameter in *sp_trace_create*, which allows the user to set the maximum number of rollover files. This parameter, called *@filecount* in the *sp_trace_create* documentation, was added in SQL Server 2005 and is not added automatically to the trace definition scripts created with the Script Trace Definition option. The *@filecount* parameter doesn't apply here because the options parameter was set to 0 and no rollover files are created, but it can be useful in many other cases. Note that because rollover files are disabled, if the maximum file size is reached, the trace automatically stops and closes.

> **Note** The file extension .trc is appended to the file path specified for the output trace file automatically. If you use the .trc extension in your file name (for example, C:\mytrace.trc), the file on disk is C:\mytrace.trc.trc.

3. *sp_trace_setevent* is used to define the event/column combinations used for the trace. In this case, to keep things simple, only event 12—*SQL:BatchCompleted*—is used. One call to *sp_trace_setevent* is required for each event/column combination used in the trace. As an aside, note that the *@on* parameter must be a *bit*. Because numeric literals in SQL Server 2005 and earlier are cast as integers implicitly by default, the local *@on* variable is needed to force the value to be treated appropriately by the stored procedure in those versions.

4. Once events are set, filters are defined. In this case, column 13 (*Duration*) is filtered using the *and* logical operator (the third parameter, with a value of 0) and the *greater than or equal to* comparison operator (the fourth parameter, with a value of 4). The actual value is passed in as the final parameter. Note that it is shown in the script in microseconds; SQL Trace uses microseconds for its durations, although the default standard of time in SQL Profiler is milliseconds. To change the SQL Profiler default, click Tools, Options, and then select the Show Values In Duration Column In Microseconds check box (note that microsecond durations are available in SQL Server 2005 and SQL Server 2008 only).

> **Note** SQL Trace offers both *and* and *or* logical operators that can be combined if multiple filters are used. However, there is no way to indicate parentheses or other grouping constructs, meaning that the order of operations is limited to left-to-right evaluation. This means that an expression such as *A and B or C and D* is logically evaluated by SQL Trace as (((A and B) or C) and D). However, SQL Trace internally breaks the filters into groups based on columns being filtered. So the expression *Column1=10 or Column1=20 and Column3=15 or Column3=25* is actually evaluated as (Column1=10 or Column1=20) and (Column3=15 or Column3=25). Not only is this somewhat confusing, but it can make certain conditions difficult or impossible to express. Keep in mind that in some cases, you may have to break up your filter criteria and create multiple traces to capture everything the way you intend to.

5. The trace has now been created, event and column combinations set, and filters defined. The final thing to do is actually start tracing. This is done via the call to *sp_trace_setstatus*, with a value of 1 for the second parameter.

## Querying Server-Side Trace Metadata

After modifying the file name placeholder appropriately and running the test script on my server, I received a value of 2 for the trace ID. Using a trace ID, you can retrieve a variety of metadata about the trace from the *sys.traces* catalog view, such as is done by the following query:

```
SELECT
    status,
    path,
    max_size,
    buffer_count,
    buffer_size,
    event_count,
    dropped_event_count
FROM sys.traces
WHERE id = 2;
```

This query returns the trace status, which is 1 (started) or 0 (stopped); the server-side path to the trace file (or NULL if the trace is using the rowset provider); the maximum file size (or again, NULL in the case of the rowset provider); information about how many buffers of what size are in use for processing the I/O; the number of events captured; and the number of dropped events (in this case, NULL if your trace is using the file provider).

> **Note** For readers migrating from SQL Server 2000, note that the *sys.traces* view replaces the older *fn_trace_getinfo* function. This older function returns only a small subset of the data returned by the *sys.traces* view, so it's definitely better to use the view going forward.

In addition to the *sys.traces* catalog view, SQL Server ships with a few other views and functions to help derive information about traces running on the server. They are described in the upcoming sections.

*fn_trace_geteventinfo*    This function returns the numeric combinations of events and columns selected for the trace, in a tabular format. The following T-SQL code returns this data for trace ID 2:

```
SELECT *
FROM fn_trace_geteventinfo(2);
```

The output from running this query on the trace created in the preceding script follows:

| eventid | columnid |
|---------|----------|
| 12      | 1        |
| 12      | 6        |
| 12      | 9        |
| 12      | 10       |
| 12      | 11       |

| eventid | columnid |
|---------|----------|
| 12      | 12       |
| 12      | 13       |
| 12      | 14       |
| 12      | 15       |
| 12      | 16       |
| 12      | 17       |
| 12      | 18       |

**sys.trace_events and sys.trace_columns**   The numeric representations of trace events and columns are not especially interesting on their own. To be able to query this data properly, a textual representation is necessary. The *sys.trace_events* and *sys.trace_columns* contain not only text describing the events and columns, respectively, but also other information such as data types for the columns and whether they are filterable. Combining these views with the previous query against the *fn_trace_geteventinfo* function, we can get a version of the same output that is much easier to read:

```
SELECT
    e.name AS Event_Name,
    c.name AS Column_Name
FROM fn_trace_geteventinfo(2) ei
JOIN sys.trace_events e ON ei.eventid = e.trace_event_id
JOIN sys.trace_columns c ON ei.columnid = c.trace_column_id;
```

The output from this query follows:

| Event_Name         | Column_Name     |
|--------------------|-----------------|
| SQL:BatchCompleted | TextData        |
| SQL:BatchCompleted | NTUserName      |
| SQL:BatchCompleted | ClientProcessID |
| SQL:BatchCompleted | ApplicationName |
| SQL:BatchCompleted | LoginName       |
| SQL:BatchCompleted | SPID            |
| SQL:BatchCompleted | Duration        |
| SQL:BatchCompleted | StartTime       |
| SQL:BatchCompleted | EndTime         |
| SQL:BatchCompleted | Reads           |
| SQL:BatchCompleted | Writes          |
| SQL:BatchCompleted | CPU             |

**fn_trace_getfilterinfo**   To get information about which filter values were set for a trace, the *fn_trace_getfilterinfo* function can be used. This function returns the column ID being filtered (which can be joined to the *sys.trace_columns* view for more information), the logical operator, comparison operator, and the value of the filter. The following code shows an example of its use:

```
SELECT
    columnid,
    logical_operator,
    comparison_operator,
    value
FROM fn_trace_getfilterinfo(2);
```

## Retrieving Data from Server-Side Traces

Once a trace is started, the obvious next move is to actually read the collected data. This is done using the *fn_trace_gettable* function. This function takes two parameters: The name of the first file from which to read the data, and the maximum number of rollover files to read from (should any exist). The following T-SQL reads the trace file located at C:\sql_server_internals.trc:

```
SELECT *
FROM fn_trace_gettable('c:\sql_server_internals.trc', 1);
```

A trace file can be read at any time, even while a trace is actively writing data to it. Note that this is probably not a great idea in most scenarios because it increases disk contention, thereby decreasing the speed with which events can be written to the table and increasing the possibility of blocking. However, in situations in which you're collecting data infrequently—such as when you've filtered for a very specific stored procedure pattern that isn't called often—this is an easy way to find out what you've collected so far.

Because *fn_trace_gettable* is a table-valued function, its uses within T-SQL are virtually limitless. It can be used to formulate queries, or it can be inserted into a table so that indexes can be created. In the latter case, it's probably a good idea to use *SELECT INTO* to take advantage of minimal logging:

```
SELECT *
INTO sql_server_internals
FROM fn_trace_gettable('c:\sql_server_internals.trc', 1);
```

Once the data has been loaded into a table, it can be manipulated any number of ways to troubleshoot or answer questions.

## Stopping and Closing Traces

When a trace is first created, it has the status of 0, stopped (or not yet started, in that case). A trace can be brought back to that state at any time using *sp_trace_setstatus*. To set trace ID 2 to a status of stopped, the following T-SQL code is used:

```
EXEC sp_trace_setstatus 2, 0;
```

Aside from the obvious benefit that the trace no longer collects data, there is another perk to doing this: Once the trace is in a stopped state, you can modify the event/column selections and filters using the appropriate stored procedures without re-creating the trace. This can be extremely useful if you need to make only a minor adjustment.

If you are actually finished tracing and do not wish to continue at a later time, you can remove the trace definition from the system altogether by setting its status to 2:

```
EXEC sp_trace_setstatus 2, 2;
```

> **Tip** Trace definitions are removed automatically in the case of a SQL Server service restart, so if you need to run the same trace again later, either save it as a Profiler template or save the script used to start it.

## Investigating the Rowset Provider

Most of this section has dealt with how to work with the file provider using server-side traces, but some readers are undoubtedly asking themselves how SQL Server Profiler interfaces with the rowset provider. The rowset provider and its interfaces are completely undocumented. However, because Profiler is doing nothing more than calling stored procedures under the covers, it is not too difficult to find out what's going on. As a matter of fact, you can use a somewhat recursive process: use Profiler to trace activity generated by itself.

A given trace session cannot capture all its own events (the trace won't be running yet when some of them occur), so to see how Profiler works, we need to set up two traces: an initial trace configured to watch for Profiler activity, and a second trace to produce the activity for the first trace to capture. To begin with, open SQL Profiler and create a new trace using the default template. In the Edit Filter dialog box, remove the default Not Like filter on *ApplicationName* and replace it with a Like filter on *ApplicationName* for the string *SQL Server Profiler%*. This filter captures all activity that is produced by any SQL Server Profiler session.

Start that trace, then load up another trace using the default template and start it. The first trace window now fills with calls to the various *sp_trace* stored procedures, fired via *RPC:Completed* events. The first hint that something different happens when using the rowset provider is the call made to *sp_trace_create*:

```
declare @p1 int;
exec sp_trace_create @p1 output,1,NULL,NULL,NULL;
select @p1;
```

The second parameter, used for options, is set to 1, a value not documented in *SQL Server Books Online*. This is the value that turns on the rowset provider. And the remainder of the parameters, which deal with file output, are populated with NULLs.

> **Tip** The *sp_trace_create options* parameter is actually a bit mask—multiple options can be set
> simultaneously. To do that, simply add up the values for each of the options you want. With only
> three documented values and one undocumented value, there aren't a whole lot of possible
> combinations, but it's still something to keep in mind.

Much of the rest of the captured activity looks familiar at this point; you see normal-looking
calls to *sp_trace_setevent*, *sp_trace_setfilter*, and *sp_trace_setstatus*. However, to see the
complete picture, you must stop the second trace (the one actually generating the trace
activity being captured). As soon as the second trace stops, the first trace captures the
following *RPC:Completed* event:

```
exec sp_executesql N'exec sp_trace_getdata @P1, 0',N'@P1 int',3;
```

In this case, 3 is the trace ID for the second trace on our system. Given this set of input
parameters, the *sp_trace_getdata* stored procedure streams event data back to the caller in a
tabular format and does not return until the trace is stopped.

Unfortunately, the tabular format produced by *sp_trace_getdata* is far from recognizable and
is not in the standard trace table format. By modifying the previous file-based trace, we can
produce a rowset-based trace using the following T-SQL code:

```
declare @rc int
declare @TraceID int

exec @rc = sp_trace_create
    @TraceID output,
    1,
    NULL,
    NULL,
    NULL
if (@rc != 0) goto finish

-- Set the events
declare @on bit
set @on = 1
exec sp_trace_setevent @TraceID, 12, 15, @on
exec sp_trace_setevent @TraceID, 12, 16, @on
exec sp_trace_setevent @TraceID, 12, 1, @on
exec sp_trace_setevent @TraceID, 12, 9, @on
exec sp_trace_setevent @TraceID, 12, 17, @on
exec sp_trace_setevent @TraceID, 12, 6, @on
exec sp_trace_setevent @TraceID, 12, 10, @on
exec sp_trace_setevent @TraceID, 12, 14, @on
exec sp_trace_setevent @TraceID, 12, 18, @on
exec sp_trace_setevent @TraceID, 12, 11, @on
exec sp_trace_setevent @TraceID, 12, 12, @on
exec sp_trace_setevent @TraceID, 12, 13, @on

-- Set the Filters
declare @bigintfilter bigint
```

```
set @bigintfilter = 10000
exec sp_trace_setfilter @TraceID, 13, 0, 4, @bigintfilter

-- Set the trace status to start
exec sp_trace_setstatus @TraceID, 1

-- display trace id for future references
select TraceID=@TraceID

exec sp_executesql
    N'exec sp_trace_getdata @P1, 0',
    N'@P1 int',
    @TraceID

finish:
go
```

Running this code, then issuing a *WAITFOR DELAY '00:00:10'* in another window, produces the following output (truncated and edited for brevity):

| ColumnId | Length | Data |
| --- | --- | --- |
| 65526 | 6 | 0xFEFF63000000 |
| 14 | 16 | 0xD707050002001D001 … |
| 65533 | 31 | 0x01010000000300000 … |
| 65532 | 26 | 0x0C000100060009000 … |
| 65531 | 14 | 0x0D000004080010270 … |
| 65526 | 6 | 0xFAFF00000000 |
| 65526 | 6 | 0x0C000E010000 |
| 1 | 48 | 0x57004100490054004 … |
| 6 | 8 | 0x4100640061006D00 |
| 9 | 4 | 0xC8130000 |
| 10 | 92 | 0x4D006900630072006 … |

Each of the values in the *columnid* column corresponds to a trace data column ID. The *length* and *data* columns are relatively self-explanatory—*data* is a binary-encoded value that corresponds to the collected column, and *length* is the number of bytes used by the *data* column. Each row of the output coincides with one column of one event. SQL Server Profiler pulls these events from the rowset provider via a call to *sp_trace_getdata* and performs a pivot to produce the human-readable output that we're used to seeing. This is yet another reason that the rowset provider can be less efficient than the file provider—sending so many rows can produce a huge amount of network traffic.

If you do require rowset provider–like behavior for your monitoring needs, luckily you do not need to figure out how to manipulate this data. SQL Server 2008 ships with a series of managed classes in the *Microsoft.SqlServer.Management.Trace* namespace, designed to help with setting up and consuming rowset traces. The use of these classes is beyond the scope of this chapter, but they are well documented in the SQL Server TechCenter and readers should have no trouble figuring out how to exploit what they offer.

# Extended Events

As useful as SQL Trace can be for DBAs and developers who need to debug complex scenarios within SQL Server, the fact is that it has some key limitations. First, its column-based architecture makes it difficult to add new events that don't fit nicely into the existing set of output columns. Second, large traces can have a greater impact on system performance than many DBAs prefer. Finally, SQL Trace is a tracing infrastructure only; it cannot be extended into other areas that a general-purpose eventing system can be used for.

The solution to all these problems is Extended Events (XE, XEvents, or X/Events for short, depending on which article or book you happen to be reading—we'll use the XE shorthand for the remainder of this chapter). Unlike SQL Trace, XE is designed as a general eventing system that can be used to fulfill tracing requirements but that also can be used for a variety of other purposes—both internal to the engine and external. Events in XE are not bound to a general set of output columns as are SQL Trace events. Instead, each XE event publishes its data using its own unique schema, making the system as flexible as possible. XE also answers some of the performance problems associated with SQL Trace. The system was engineered from the ground up with performance in mind, and so in most cases, events have minimal impact on overall system performance.

Due to its general nature, XE is much bigger and more complex than SQL Trace, and learning the system requires that DBAs understand a number of new concepts. In addition, because the system is new for SQL Server 2008, there is not yet UI support in the form of a Profiler or similar tool. Given the steep learning curve, many DBAs may be less than excited about diving in. However, as you will see in the remainder of this chapter, XE is a powerful tool and certainly worth learning today. The next several versions of SQL Server will see XE extended and utilized in a variety of ways, so understanding its foundations today is a good investment for the future.

## Components of the XE Infrastructure

The majority of the XE system lives in an overarching layer of SQL Server that is architecturally similar to the role of the SQL operating system (SQLOS). As a general-purpose eventing and tracing system, it must be able to interact with all levels of the SQL Server host process, from the query processing APIs all the way down into the storage engine. To accomplish its goals, XE exposes several types of components that work together to form the complete system.

## Packages

Packages are the basic unit within which all other XE objects ship. Each package is a collection of types, predicates, targets, actions, maps, and events—the actual user-configurable components of XE that you work with as you interact with the system. SQL Server 2008 ships with four packages, which can be queried from the *sys.dm_xe_packages* DMV, as in the following example:

```
SELECT *
FROM sys.dm_xe_packages;
```

Packages can interact with one another to avoid having to ship the same code in multiple contexts. For example, if one package exposes a certain action that can be bound to an event, any number of other events in other packages can use it. As a means by which to use this flexibility, Microsoft ships a package called *package0* with SQL Server 2008. This package can be considered the base; it contains objects designed to be used by all the other packages currently shipping with SQL Server, as well as those that might ship in the future.

In addition to *package0*, SQL Server ships with three other packages. The *sqlos* package contains objects designed to help the user interact with the SQLOS system. The *sqlserver* package, on the other hand, contains objects specific to the rest of the SQL Server system. The *SecAudit* package is a bit different; it contains objects designed for the use of SQL Audit, which is an auditing technology built on top of Extended Events. Querying the *sys.dm_xe_packages* DMV, you can see that this package is marked as *private* in the *capabilities_desc* column. This means that non-system consumers can't directly use the objects that it contains.

To see a list of all the objects exposed by the system, query the *sys.dm_xe_objects* DMV:

```
SELECT *
FROM sys.dm_xe_objects;
```

This DMV exposes a couple of key columns important for someone interested in exploring the objects. The *package_guid* column is populated with the same GUIDs that can be found in the *guid* column of the *sys.dm_xe_packages* DMV. The *object_type* column can be used to filter on specific types of objects. And just like *sys.dm_xe_packages*, *sys.dm_xe_objects* exposes a *capabilities_desc* column that is sometimes set to *private* for certain objects that are not available for use by external consumers. There is also a column called *description*, which purports to contain human-readable text describing each object, but this is a work in progress as of SQL Server 2008 RTM, and many of the descriptions are incomplete.

In the following sections, we explore, in detail, each of the object types found in *sys.dm_xe_objects*.

## Events

Much like SQL Trace, XE exposes a number of events that fire at various expected times as SQL Server goes about its duties. Also, just like with SQL Trace, various code paths throughout the product have been instrumented with calls that cause the events to fire when appropriate. New users of XE will find almost all the same events that SQL Trace exposes, plus many more. SQL Trace ships with 180 events in SQL Server 2008; XE ships with 254. This number increases for XE because many of the XE events are at a much deeper level than the SQL Trace events. For example, XE includes an event that fires each time a page split occurs. This allows a user to track splits at the query level, something that was impossible to do in previous versions of SQL Server.

The most important differentiator of XE events, compared with those exposed by SQL Trace, is that each event exposes its own output schema. These schemas are exposed in the *sys.dm_xe_object_columns* DMV, which can be queried for a list of output columns as in the following example:

```
SELECT *
FROM sys.dm_xe_object_columns
WHERE
    object_name = 'page_split';
```

In addition to a list of column names and column ordinal positions, this query also returns a list of data types associated with each column. These data types, just like every other object defined within the XE system, are contained within packages and each has its own entry in the *sys.dm_xe_objects* DMV. Columns can be marked *readonly* (per the *column_type* column), in which case they have a value defined in the *column_value* column, or they can be marked as *data*, which means that their values will be populated at run time. The *readonly* columns are metadata, used to store various information including a unique identifier for the type of event that fired and a version number so that different versions of the schema for each event can be independently tracked and used.

One of the handful of *readonly* attributes that is associated with each event is the CHANNEL for the event. This is a reflection of one of the XE design goals, to align with the Event Tracing for Windows (ETW) system. Events in SQL Server 2008 are categorized as Admin, Analytic, Debug, or Operational. The following is a description of each of these event channels:

- *Admin events* are those that are expected to be of most use to systems administrators, and this channel includes events such as error reports and deprecation announcements.

- *Analytic events* are those that fire on a regular basis—potentially thousands of times per second on a busy system—and are designed to be aggregated to support analysis about system performance and health. These include events around topics such as lock acquisition and SQL statements starting and completing.

- *Debug events* are those expected to be used by DBAs and support engineers to help diagnose and solve engine-related problems. This channel includes events that fire when threads and processes start and stop, various times throughout a scheduler's lifecycle, and for other similar themes.

- *Operational events* are those expected to be of most use to operational DBAs for managing the SQL Server service and databases. This channel's events relate to databases being attached, detached, started, and stopped, as well as issues such as the detection of database page corruption.

Providing such a flexible event payload system ensures that any consumer can use any exposed event, so long as the consumer knows how to read the schema. Events are designed such that the output of each instance of the event always includes the same attributes, exposed in the exact order defined by the schema, to minimize the amount of work required for consumers to processes bound events. Event consumers can also use this ordering guarantee to more easily ignore data that they are not interested in. For example, if a consumer knows that the first 16 bytes of a given event contains an identifier that is not pertinent to the consumer's requirements, these bytes can simply be disregarded rather than needlessly processed.

Although the schema of each event is predetermined before run time, the actual size of each instance of the event is not. Event payloads can include both fixed and variable-length data elements, in addition to non-schematized elements populated by actions (see the section entitled "Actions" later in this chapter, for more information). To reduce the probability of events overusing memory and other resources, the system sets a hard 32-MB upper limit on the data size of variable-length elements.

One thing you might notice about the list of columns returned for each event is that it is small compared with the number of columns available for each event in SQL Trace. For example, the XE *sql_statement_completed* event exposes only seven columns: *source_database_id, object_id, object_type, cpu, duration, reads,* and *writes.* SQL Trace users might be wondering where all the other common attributes are—session ID, login name, perhaps the actual SQL text that caused the event to fire. These are all available by binding to "actions" (described in the section entitled "Actions," later in this chapter) and are not populated by default by the event's schema. This design further adds to the flexibility of the XE architecture and keeps events themselves as small as possible, thereby improving overall system performance.

As with SQL Trace events, XE events are disabled by default and have virtually no overhead until they are enabled in an event session (the XE equivalent of a trace, covered later in this chapter). Also like SQL Trace events, XE events can be filtered and can be routed to various post-event providers for collection. The terminology here is also a bit different; filters in XE are called *predicates,* and the post-event providers are referred to as *targets,* covered in the sections entitled "Predicates" and "Targets," respectively, later in this chapter.

## Types and Maps

In the previous section, we saw that each event exposes its own schema, including column names and type information. Also mentioned was that each of the types included in these schemas is also defined within an XE package.

Two kinds of data types can be defined: scalar types and maps. A scalar type is a single value; something like an integer, a single Unicode character, or a binary large object. A map, on the other hand, is very similar to an enumeration in most object-oriented systems. The idea for a map is that many events have greater value if they can convey to the consumer some human-readable text about what occurred, rather than just a set of machine-readable values. Much of this text can be predefined—for example, the list of wait types supported by

SQL Server—and can be stored in a table indexed by an integer. At the time an event fires, rather than collecting the actual text, the event can simply store the integer, thereby saving large amounts of memory and processing resources.

Types and maps, like events, are visible in the *sys.dm_xe_objects* DMV. To see a list of both types and maps supported by the system, use the following query:

```
SELECT *
FROM sys.dm_xe_objects
WHERE
    object_type IN ('TYPE', 'MAP');
```

Although types are more or less self-describing, maps must expose their associated values so that consumers can display the human-readable text when appropriate. This information is available in a DMV called *sys.dm_xe_map_values*. The following query returns all the wait types exposed by the SQL Server engine, along with the map keys (the integer representation of the type) used within XE events that describe waits:

```
SELECT *
FROM sys.dm_xe_map_values
WHERE
    name = 'wait_types';
```

As of SQL Server 2008 RTM, virtually all the types are exposed via the *package0* package, whereas each of the four packages contain many of their own map values. This makes sense, given that a scalar type such as an integer does not need to be redefined again and again, whereas maps are more aligned to specific purposes.

It is also worth noting, from an architectural point of view, that some thought has been put into optimizing the type system by including pass-by-value and pass-by-reference semantics depending on the size of the object. Any object of 8 bytes or smaller is passed by value as the data flows through the system, whereas larger objects are passed by reference using a special XE-specific 8-byte pointer type.

## Predicates

As with SQL Trace events, XE events can be filtered so that only interesting events are recorded. You may wish to record, for example, only events that occur in a specific database, or which fired for a specific session ID. In keeping with the design goal of providing the most flexible experience possible, XE predicates are assigned on a per-event basis, rather than to the entire session. This is quite a departure from SQL Trace, where filters are defined at the granularity of the entire trace, and so every event used within the trace must abide by the overarching filter set. In XE, if it makes sense to only filter some events and to leave other events totally unfiltered—or filtered using a different set of criteria—that is a perfectly acceptable option.

From a metadata standpoint, predicates are represented in *sys.dm_xe_objects* as two different object types: *pred_compare* and *pred_source*. The *pred_compare* objects are comparison functions, each designed to compare instances of a specific data type, whereas the *pred_source* objects are extended attributes that can be used within predicates.

First, we'll take a look at the *pred_compare* objects. The following query against the *sys.dm_xe_objects* DMV returns all >= comparison functions that are available, by filtering on the *pred_compare* object type:

```
SELECT *
FROM sys.dm_xe_objects
WHERE
    object_type = 'pred_compare'
    AND name LIKE 'greater_than_equal%';
```

Running this query, you can see comparison functions defined for a number of base data types—integers, floating-point numbers, and various string types. Each of these functions can be used explicitly by an XE user, but the DDL for creating event sessions has been overloaded with common operators, so that this is unnecessary in the vast majority of cases. For example, if you use the >= operator to define a predicate based on two integers, the XE engine automatically maps the call to the *greater_than_equal_int64* predicate that you can see in the DMV. There is currently only one predicate that is not overloaded with an operator, a modulus operator that tests whether one input equally divides by the other. See the section entitled "Extended Events DDL and Querying," later in this chapter, for more information on how to use the comparison functions.

The other predicate object type—*pred_source*—requires a bit of background explanation. In the XE system, event predicates can filter on one of two types of attribute: a column exposed by the event itself—such as *source_database_id* for the *sql_statement_completed* event—or any of the external attributes (predicate sources) defined as *pred_source* in the *sys.dm_xe_objects* DMV. The available sources are returned by the following query:

```
SELECT *
FROM sys.dm_xe_objects
WHERE
    object_type = 'pred_source';
```

Each of these attributes—29 as of SQL Server 2008 RTM—can be bound to any event in the XE system and can be used anytime you need to filter on an attribute that is not carried by the event's own schematized payload. This lets you ask for events that fired for a specific session ID, for a certain user name, or—if you want to debug at a deeper level—on a specific thread or worker address. The important thing to remember is that these predicate sources are not carried by any of the events by default, and using them forces the XE engine to acquire the data in an extra step during event processing. For most of the predicates, the acquisition cost is quite small, but if you are using several of them, this cost can add up.

We explore when and how predicates fire in the section entitled "Lifecycle of an Event," later in this chapter.

## Actions

One quality of an eventing system is that as events fire, it may be prudent to exercise some external code. For example, consider DML triggers, which are events that fire in response to a DML action and exercise code in the form of the body of the trigger. Aside from doing some sort of work, external code can also retrieve additional information that might be important to the event; for example, a trigger can select data from another table in the system.

In XE, a type of object called an *action* takes on these dual purposes. Actions, if bound to an event, are synchronously invoked after the predicate evaluates to true and can both exercise code and write data back into the event's payload, thereby adding additional attributes. As mentioned in the section entitled "Events," earlier in this chapter, XE events are designed to be as lean as possible, including only a few attributes each by default. When dealing with predicates, the lack of a complete set of attributes can be solved using predicate sources, but these are only enabled for filtration. Using a predicate source does not cause its value to be stored along with the rest of the event data. The most common use of actions is to collect additional attributes not present by default on a given event.

It should by this point come as no surprise that to see a list of the available actions, a user should query *sys.dm_xe_objects*, as in the following example:

```
SELECT *
FROM sys.dm_xe_objects
WHERE
    object_type = 'action';
```

As of SQL Server 2008 RTM, XE ships with 37 actions, which include attributes that map to virtually every predicate source, should you wish to filter on a given source as well as include the actual value in your event's output. The list also includes a variety of other attributes, as well as a handful of actions that exercise only code and do not return any data to the event's payload.

Actions fire synchronously on an event immediately after the predicates are evaluated, but before control is returned to the code that caused the event to fire (for more information, see the section entitled "Lifecycle of an Event," later in this chapter). This is done to ensure that actions will be able to collect information as it happens and before the server state changes, which might be a potential problem were they fired asynchronously.

As a result of their synchronous design, actions bear some performance cost. The majority of them—such as those that mirror the available predicates—are relatively inexpensive to retrieve, but others can be costly. For example, an especially interesting action useful for debugging purposes is the *tsql_stack* action, which returns the entire nested stack of stored procedure and/or function calls that resulted in the event firing. Although very useful, this information is not available in the engine without briefly stopping execution of the current thread and walking the stack, so this action bears a heavier performance cost than, for example, retrieving the current session ID.

To see a list of those actions that do not return any data but rather only execute external code, filter on the *type_name* column of *sys.dm_xe_objects* for a "null" return value, as in the following query:

```
SELECT *
FROM sys.dm_xe_objects
WHERE
    object_type = 'action'
    and type_name = 'null';
```

Note that "null" in this example is actually a string and is not the same as a SQL NULL; *null* is the name of a type defined in *package0* and shows up in the list of objects of type *type*. There are three actions that do not return additional data: two of them perform mini-dumps and the other causes a debugger breakpoint to fire. All these are best used only when instructed to by product support—especially the debug break event, which stops the active thread upon which the breakpoint is hit, potentially blocking the entire SQL Server process depending on where the breakpoint is hit.

Much like predicates, actions are bound on an event-by-event basis rather than at the event session level, so a consumer can choose to invoke actions only when specific events fire within a larger session. Certain actions may not apply to every event in the system, and these will fail to bind with an error at session creation time, if a user attempts to bind them with an incompatible event.

From a performance point of view, aside from the synchronous nature of these actions, it is important to remember that actions that write data back to the event increase the size of each instance of the event. This means that not only do events take longer to fire and return control to the caller—because actions are synchronously executed—but once fired, the event also consumes more memory and requires more processing time to write to the target. The key, as is often the case with performance-related issues, is to maintain a balance between the data needs of the consumer and the performance needs of the server as a whole. Keeping in mind that actions are not free helps you to create XE sessions that have less of an impact on the host server.

## Targets

So far, we have seen events that fire when an instrumented code path is encountered, predicates that filter events so that only interesting data is collected, and actions that can add additional data to an event's payload. Once all this has taken place, the final package of event data needs to go somewhere to be collected. This destination for event data is one or more targets, which are the means by which XE events are consumed.

Targets are the final object type that has metadata exposed within *sys.dm_xe_objects*, and the list of available targets can be seen by running the following query:

```
SELECT *
FROM sys.dm_xe_objects
WHERE
    object_type = 'target';
```

SQL Server 2008 RTM ships with 13 targets—7 public and 6 private, for use only by SQL Audit. Of the 7 public targets, 3 are marked *synchronous* in the *capabilities_desc* column. These targets collect event data synchronously—much like actions—before control is returned to the code that caused the event to fire. The other five events, in comparison, are asynchronous, meaning that the data is buffered before being collected by the target at some point after the event fires. Buffering results in better performance for the code that caused the event to fire, but it also introduces latency into the process because the target may not collect the event for some time.

XE targets come in a variety of types that are both similar to and somewhat different from the I/O providers exposed by SQL Trace. Similar to the SQL Trace file provider is the XE *asynchronous_file_target*, which buffers data before writing it out to a proprietary binary file format. Another file-based option is the *etw_classic_sync_target*, which synchronously writes data to a file format suitable for consumption by any number of ETW-enabled readers. There is no XE equivalent for the SQL Trace streaming rowset provider.

The remaining five targets are quite different than what is offered by SQL Trace, and all store consumed data in memory rather than persisting it to a file. The most straightforward of these is the *ring_buffer* target, which stores data in a ring buffer with a user-configurable size. A ring buffer loops back to the start of the buffer when it fills and begins overwriting data collected earlier. This means that the buffer can consume an endless quantity of data without using all available system memory, but only the newest data is available at any given time.

Another target type is the *synchronous_event_counter* target, which synchronously counts the number of times events have fired. Along these same lines are two bucketizer targets—one synchronous and the other asynchronous—which create buckets based on a user-defined column, and count the number of times that events occur within each bucket. For example, a user could "bucketize" based on session ID, and the targets would count the number of events that fired for each SPID.

The final target type is called the *pair_matching* target, and it is designed to help find instances where a pair of events is expected to occur, but one or the other is not firing due to a bug or some other problem. The *pair_matching* target works by asynchronously collecting events defined by the user as begin events, and matching them to events defined by the user as end events. When a pair of successfully matched events is found, both events are dropped, leaving only those events that did not have a match. For an example of where this would be useful, consider lock acquisition in the storage engine. Each lock is acquired and—we hope—released within a relatively short period to avoid blocking. If blocking problems are occurring, it is possible that they are due to locks being acquired and held for longer than necessary. By using the *pair_matching* target in conjunction with the lock acquired and lock released events, it is easy to identify those locks that have been taken but not yet released.

Targets can often be used in conjunction with one another, and it is therefore possible to bind multiple targets to a single session, rather than having to create many sessions to collect the same data. For example, a user can create multiple bucketizing targets to simultaneously keep metadata counts based on different bucket criteria, while recording all the unaggregated data to a file for later evaluation.

As with the SQL Trace providers, some action must occur when more data enters the system than can be processed in a reasonable amount of time. When working with the synchronous targets, things are simple; the calling code waits until the target returns control, and the target waits until its event data has been fully consumed. With asynchronous targets, on the other hand, there are a number of configuration options that dictate how to handle the situation.

When event data buffers begin to fill up, the engine can take one of three possible actions depending on how the session was configured by the user. These actions are the following:

- **Block, waiting for buffer space to become available (no event loss)**   This is the same behavior characterized by the SQL Trace file provider, and can cause performance degradation.

- **Drop the waiting event (allow single event loss)**   In this case, the system drops only a single event at a time while waiting for more buffer space to free up. This is the default mode.

- **Drop a full buffer (allow multiple event loss)**   Each buffer can contain many events, and the number of events lost depends upon the size of the events in addition to the size of the buffers (which we will describe shortly).

The various options are listed here in decreasing order of their impact on overall system performance should buffers begin filling up, and in increasing order of the number of events that may be lost while waiting for buffers to become free. It is important to choose an option that reflects the amount of acceptable data loss while keeping in mind that blocking will occur should too restrictive an option be used. Liberal use of predicates, careful attention to the number of actions bound to each event, and attention to other configuration options all help users avoid having to worry about buffers filling up and whether the choice of these options is a major issue.

Along with the ability to specify what should happen when buffers fill up, a user can specify how much memory is allocated, how the memory is allocated across CPU or NUMA node boundaries, and how often buffers are cleared.

By default, one central set of buffers, consuming a maximum of 4 MB of memory, is created for each XE session (as described in the next section). The central set of buffers always contains three buffers, each consuming one-third of the maximum amount of memory specified. A user can override these defaults, creating one set of buffers per CPU or one set per NUMA node, and increasing or decreasing the amount of memory that each set of buffers consumes. In addition, a user can specify that events larger than the maximum allocated buffer memory should be allowed to fire. In that case, those events are stored in special large memory buffers.

Another default option is that buffers are cleared every 30 seconds or when they fill up. This option can be overridden by a user and a maximum latency set. This causes the buffers to be checked and cleared both at a specific time interval (specified as a number of seconds), in addition to when they fill up.

It is important to note that each of these settings applies not on a per-target basis, but rather to any number of targets that are bound to a session. We explore how this works in the next section.

## Event Sessions

We have now gone through each of the elements that make up the core XE infrastructure. Bringing each of these together into a cohesive unit at run time are sessions. These are the XE equivalent of a trace in SQL Trace parlance. A session describes the events that the user is interested in collecting, predicates against which the events should be filtered, actions that should fire in conjunction with the events, and finally targets that should be used for data collection at the end of the cycle.

Any number of sessions can be created by users with adequate server-level permission, and sessions are for the most part independent of one another, just as with SQL Trace. The main thread that links any number of sessions is a central bitmap that indicates whether a given event is enabled or disabled. An event can be enabled simultaneously in any number of sessions, but the global bitmap is used to avoid having to check each of those sessions at run time. Beyond this level, sessions are completely separate from one another, and each uses its own memory and has its own set of defined objects.

### Session-Scoped Catalog Metadata

Along with defining a set of events, predicates, actions, and targets, various XE configuration options are scoped at the session level. As with the objects that define the basis for XE, a number of views have been added to the metadata repository of SQL Server to support metadata queries about sessions.

The *sys.server_event_sessions* catalog view is the central metadata store for information about XE sessions. The view exposes one row per session defined on the SQL Server instance. Like traces in SQL Trace, XE sessions can be started and stopped at will. But unlike traces, XE sessions are persistent with regard to service restarts, and so querying the view before and after a restart show the same results unless a session has been explicitly dropped. A session can be configured to start itself automatically when the SQL Server instance starts; this setting can be seen via the *startup_state* column of the view.

Along with the central *sys.server_event_sessions* views are a number of other views describing details of how the session was configured. The *sys.server_event_session_events* view exposes one row per event bound to each session, and includes a predicate column that contains the definition of the predicate used to filter the event, if one has been set. There are similar views for actions and targets, namely: *sys.server_event_session_actions* and *sys.server_event_session_targets.* A final view, *sys.server_event_session_fields,* contains information about settings that can be customized for a given event or target. For example, the ring buffer target's memory consumption can be set to a specific amount by a user; if the target is used, the memory setting appears in this view.

## Session-Scoped Configuration Options

As mentioned in the section entitled "Targets," earlier in this chapter, a number of settings are set globally for a session and, in turn, influence the run-time behavior of the objects that make up the session.

The first set of session-scoped options includes those that we have already discussed: options that determine how asynchronous target buffers are configured, both from a memory and latency standpoint. These settings influence a process called the *dispatcher,* which is responsible for periodically collecting data from the buffers and sending it to each of the asynchronous targets bound to the session. The frequency with which the dispatcher is activated depends on how the memory and latency settings are configured. If a latency value of *infinite* is specified, the dispatcher does not collect data except when the buffers are full. Otherwise, the dispatcher collects data at the interval determined by the setting—as often as once a second.

The *sys.dm_xe_sessions* DMV can be used to monitor whether there are any problems dispatching asynchronous buffers. This DMV exposes one row per XE session that has been started and exposes a number of columns that can give a user insight into how buffers are being handled. The most important columns are the following:

- *regular_buffer_size* and *total_regular_buffers.* These columns expose the number of buffers created—based on the maximum memory and memory partitioning settings—as well as the size of each buffer. Knowing these numbers and estimating the approximate size for each event tells you how many events you might lose in case of a full buffer situation, should you make use of the allow multiple event loss option.

- *dropped_event_count* and *dropped_buffer_count.* These columns expose the number of events and/or buffers that have been dropped due to there not being enough free buffer space to accommodate incoming event data.

- *blocked_event_fire_time.* This column exposes the amount of time that blocking occurred, if the no event loss option was used.

Another session-scoped option that can be enabled is called *causality tracking.* This option enables users to use a SQL Server engine feature to help correlate events either when there are parent-child relationships between tasks on the same thread or when one thread causes activity to occur on another thread. In the engine code, these relationships are tracked by each task defining a GUID, known as an *activity ID.* When a child task is called, the ID is passed along and continues down the stack as subsequent tasks are called. If activity needs to pass to another thread, the ID is passed in a structure called a *transfer block,* and the same logic continues.

These identifiers are exposed via two XE actions: *package0.attach_activity_id* and *package0. attach_activity_id_xfer*. However, these actions cannot be attached to an event by a user creating a session. Instead, a user must enable the causality tracking option at the session level, which automatically binds the actions to every event defined for the session. Once the actions are enabled, both the activity ID and activity transfer ID are added to each event's payload.

## Lifecycle of an Event

The firing of an event means, at its core, that a potentially "interesting" point in the SQL Server code has been encountered. This point in the code calls a central function that handles the event logic, and several things happen, as described in this section and as illustrated in Figure 2-13.

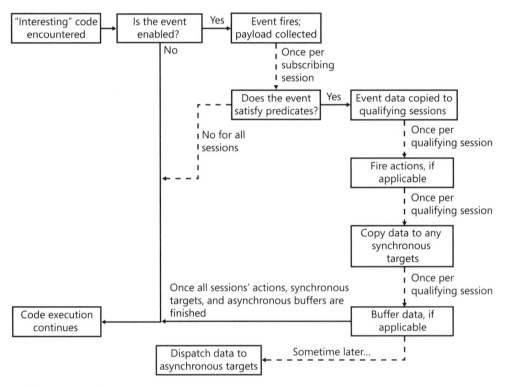

**FIGURE 2-13** The lifecycle of an extended event

Once an event has been defined within at least one session, a global bitmap is set to indicate that the event should fire when code that references it is encountered. Whether or not an event is enabled, the code must always perform this check; for events that are not enabled, the check involves a single code branch and adds virtually no overhead to the SQL Server process. If the event is not enabled, this is the end of the process and the code continues its normal execution path. Only if an event is enabled in one or more sessions must the event-specific code continue processing.

At this point, if enabled, the event fires and all the data elements associated with its schema are collected and packaged. The XE engine next finds each session that has the event enabled and synchronously (one session at a time) takes the following steps:

1. Check whether the event satisfies predicates defined for the event within the session. If not, the engine moves on to the next session without taking any further action.

2. If the predicates are satisfied, the engine copies the event data into the session's context. Any actions defined for the event within the session are then fired, followed by copying the event data to any synchronous targets.

3. Finally, the event data is buffered, if necessary, for any asynchronous targets used by the session.

Once each of these steps has been performed for each session, code execution resumes. It is important to stress that this all happens synchronously, while code execution blocks. Although each of these steps, and the entire system, has been designed for performance, users can still create problems by defining too many sessions, with too many actions or synchronous targets, for extremely active events such as those in the analytic channel. Care should be taken to avoid overusing the synchronous features, lest run-time blocking becomes an issue.

At some point after being buffered—depending on the event latency and memory settings for the session(s)—the event data is passed once more, to any asynchronous targets. At this point, the event data is removed from the buffer to make room for new incoming data.

To help track down problems with targets taking too long to consume the data and therefore causing waiting issues, the *sys.dm_xe_session_targets* DMV can be used. This DMV exposes one row per target defined by each active XE session, and includes a column called *execution_duration_ms*. This column indicates the amount of time that the target took to process the most recent event or buffer (depending on the target). If you see this number begin to climb, waiting issues are almost certainly occurring in SQL Server code paths.

## Extended Events DDL and Querying

To complete the overview of XE, we will take a quick tour of the session creation DDL and see how all the objects apply to what you can control when creating actual sessions. We will also look at an example of how to query some of the data collected by an XE session.

### Creating an Event Session

The primary DDL hook for XE is the *CREATE EVENT SESSION* statement. This statement allows users to create sessions and map all the various XE objects. An *ALTER EVENT SESSION* statement also exists, allowing a user to modify a session that has already been created. To modify an existing session, it must not be active.

The following T-SQL statement creates a session and shows how to configure all the XE features and options we have reviewed in the chapter:

```
CREATE EVENT SESSION [statement_completed]
ON SERVER
ADD EVENT
    sqlserver.sp_statement_completed,
ADD EVENT
    sqlserver.sql_statement_completed
    (
        ACTION
        (
            sqlserver.sql_text
        )
        WHERE
        (
            sqlserver.session_id = 53
        )
    )
ADD TARGET
    package0.ring_buffer
    (
        SET
            max_memory=4096
    )
WITH
(
    MAX_MEMORY = 4096KB,
    EVENT_RETENTION_MODE = ALLOW_SINGLE_EVENT_LOSS,
    MAX_DISPATCH_LATENCY = 1 SECONDS,
    MEMORY_PARTITION_MODE = NONE,
    TRACK_CAUSALITY = OFF,
    STARTUP_STATE = OFF
);
```

The session is called *statement_completed,* and two events are bound: *sp_statement_completed* and *sql_statement_completed,* both exposed by the *sqlserver* package. The *sp_statement_ completed* event has no actions or predicates defined, so it publishes to the session's target with its default set of attributes every time the event fires instance-wide. The *sql_statement_completed* event, on the other hand, has a predicate configured (the WHERE option) so that it publishes only for session ID 53. Note that the predicate uses the equality operator (=) rather than calling the *pred_compare* function for comparing two integers. The standard comparison operators are all defined; currently the only reason to call a function directly is for using the *divides_by_uint64* function, which determines whether one integer exactly divides by another (useful when working with the counter predicate source). Note also that the WHERE clause supports AND, OR, and parentheses—you can create complex predicates that combine many different conditions if needed.

When the *sql_statement_completed* event fires for session ID 53, the event session invokes the *sql_text* action. This action collects the text of the SQL statement that caused the event to fire and adds it to the event's data. After the event data has been collected, it is pushed to the *ring_buffer* target, which is configured to use a maximum of 4,096 KB of memory.

We have also configured some session-level options. The session's asynchronous buffers cannot consume more than 4,096 KB of memory, and should they fill up, we allow events to be dropped. That is probably not likely to happen, though, because we have configured the dispatcher to clear the buffers every second. Memory is not partitioned across CPUs—so we end up with three buffers—and we are not using causality tracking. Finally, after the session is created, it exists only as metadata; it does not start until we issue the following statement:

```
ALTER EVENT SESSION [statement_completed]
ON SERVER
STATE=START;
```

## Querying Event Data

Once the session is started, the ring buffer target is updated with new events (assuming there are any) every second. Each of the in-memory targets—the ring buffer, bucketizers, and event count targets—exposes its data in XML format in the *target_data* column of the *sys.dm_xe_session_targets* DMV. Given the fact that the data is in XML format, many DBAs who have not yet delved into XQuery may want to try it; we highly recommend learning how to query the data, given the richness of the information that can be retrieved using XE.

Consuming the XML in a tabular format requires knowledge of which nodes are present. In the case of the ring buffer target, a root node called *RingBufferTarget* includes one event node for each event that fires. The event node contains one data node for each attribute contained within the event data, and one "action" node for actions bound to the event. These data and action nodes contain three nodes each: one node called *type,* which indicates the data type; one called *value,* which includes the value in most cases; and one called *text* which is there for longer text values.

Explaining how to query every possible event and target is beyond the scope of this book, but a quick sample query based on the *statement_completed* session follows; you can use this query as a base from which to work up queries against other events and actions when working with the ring buffer target:

```
SELECT
    theNodes.event_data.value('(data/value)[1]', 'bigint') AS source_database_id,
    theNodes.event_data.value('(data/value)[2]', 'bigint') AS object_id,
    theNodes.event_data.value('(data/value)[3]', 'bigint') AS object_type,
    theNodes.event_data.value('(data/value)[4]', 'bigint') AS cpu,
    theNodes.event_data.value('(data/value)[5]', 'bigint') AS duration,
    theNodes.event_data.value('(data/value)[6]', 'bigint') AS reads,
    theNodes.event_data.value('(data/value)[7]', 'bigint') AS writes,
    theNodes.event_data.value('(action/value)[1]', 'nvarchar(max)') AS sql_text
FROM
(
    SELECT
        CONVERT(XML, st.target_data) AS ring_buffer
    FROM sys.dm_xe_sessions s
    JOIN sys.dm_xe_session_targets st ON
        s.address = st.event_session_address
    WHERE
        s.name = 'statement_completed'
) AS theData
CROSS APPLY theData.ring_buffer.nodes('//RingBufferTarget/event') theNodes (event_data);
```

This query converts the ring buffer data to an XML instance and then uses the *nodes* XML function to create one row per event node found. It then uses the ordinal positions of the various data elements within the event nodes to map the data to output columns. Of course, more advanced sessions require more advanced XQuery to determine the type of each event and do some case logic if the events involved in the session have different schemas—which, thankfully, the two in this example do not. Once you've gotten to this point, the data is just that—standard tabular data, which can be aggregated, joined, inserted into a table, or whatever else you want to do with it.

You can also read from the asynchronous file target via T-SQL, using the *sys.fn_xe_file_target_read_file* table-valued function. This function returns one row per event, but you still have to get comfortable with XML; the event's data, exposed in a column called *event_data,* is in an XML format similar to data in the ring buffer target. Eventually we can expect a user interface to bear some of the XML burden for us, but just as with SQL Trace, even the most powerful user interfaces aren't enough when complex analysis is required. Therefore, XML is here to stay for those DBAs who wish to be XE power users.

### Stopping and Removing the Event Session

Once you have finished reading data from the event session, it can be stopped using the following code:

```
ALTER EVENT SESSION [statement_completed]
ON SERVER
STATE=STOP;
```

Stopping the event session does not remove the metadata; to eliminate the session from the server completely, you must drop it using the following statement:

```
ALTER EVENT SESSION [statement_completed]
ON SERVER;
```

# Summary

SQL Server has many eventing systems that range from the simple—like triggers and event notifications—to the intricate—like XE. Each of these systems is designed to help both users and SQL Server itself work better by enabling arbitrary code execution or data collection when specific actions occur in the database engine. In this chapter, we explored the various hidden and internal objects used by Change Tracking to help support synchronization applications, the inner workings of the ubiquitous SQL Trace infrastructure, and the complex architecture of XE, the future of eventing within SQL Server. Events within SQL Server are extremely powerful, and we hope that this chapter has provided you with enough internal knowledge of these systems to understand how to better use the many eventing features in your day-to-day activities.

# Chapter 3
# Databases and Database Files

*Kalen Delaney*

Simply put, a Microsoft SQL Server database is a collection of objects that hold and manipulate data. A typical SQL Server instance has only a handful of databases, but it's not unusual for a single instance to contain several dozen databases. The technical limit for one SQL Server instance is 32,767 databases. But practically speaking, this limit would never be reached.

To elaborate a bit, you can think of a SQL Server database as having the following properties and features:

- It is a collection of many objects, such as tables, views, stored procedures, and constraints. The technical limit is $2^{31}-1$ (more than 2 billion) objects. The number of objects typically ranges from hundreds to tens of thousands.

- It is owned by a single SQL Server login account.

- It maintains its own set of user accounts, roles, schemas, and security.

- It has its own set of system tables to hold the database catalog.

- It is the primary unit of recovery and maintains logical consistency among objects within it. (For example, primary and foreign key relationships always refer to other tables within the same database, not in other databases.)

- It has its own transaction log and manages its own transactions.

- It can span multiple disk drives and operating system files.

- It can range in size from 2 MB to a technical limit of 524,272 terabytes.

- It can grow and shrink, either automatically or manually.

- It can have objects joined in queries with objects from other databases in the same SQL Server instance or on linked servers.

- It can have specific properties enabled or disabled. (For example, you can set a database to be read-only or to be a source of published data in replication.)

And here is what a SQL Server database is *not*:

- It is not synonymous with an entire SQL Server instance.

- It is not a single SQL Server table.

- It is not a specific operating system file.

Although a database isn't the same thing as an operating system file, it always exists in two or more such files. These files are known as SQL Server *database files* and are specified either at the time the database is created, using the *CREATE DATABASE* command, or afterward, using the *ALTER DATABASE* command.

# System Databases

A new SQL Server 2008 installation always includes four databases: *master*, *model*, *tempdb*, and *msdb*. It also contains a fifth, "hidden" database that you never see using any of the normal SQL commands that list all your databases. This database is referred to as the *resource database*, but its actual name is *mssqlsystemresource*.

## master

The *master* database is composed of system tables that keep track of the server installation as a whole and all other databases that are subsequently created. Although every database has a set of system catalogs that maintain information about objects that the database contains, the *master* database has system catalogs that keep information about disk space, file allocations and usage, system-wide configuration settings, endpoints, login accounts, databases on the current instance, and the existence of other servers running SQL Server (for distributed operations).

The *master* database is critical to your system, so always keep a current backup copy of it. Operations such as creating another database, changing configuration values, and modifying login accounts all make modifications to *master*, so you should always back up *master* after performing such actions.

## model

The *model* database is simply a template database. Every time you create a new database, SQL Server makes a copy of *model* to form the basis of the new database. If you'd like every new database to start out with certain objects or permissions, you can put them in *model*, and all new databases inherit them. You can also change most properties of the *model* database by using the *ALTER DATABASE* command, and those property values then are used by any new database you create.

## tempdb

The *tempdb* database is used as a workspace. It is unique among SQL Server databases because it's re-created—not recovered—every time SQL Server is restarted. It's used for temporary tables explicitly created by users, for worktables that hold intermediate results created internally by SQL Server during query processing and sorting, for maintaining row versions used in snapshot isolation and certain other operations, and for materializing static cursors and the keys of keyset cursors. Because the *tempdb* database is re-created, any objects or permissions that you create in the database are lost the next time you start your SQL Server instance. An alternative is to create the object in the *model* database, from which *tempdb* is copied. (Keep in mind that any objects that you create in the *model* database also are added to any new databases you create subsequently. If you want objects to exist only in *tempdb,* you can create a startup stored procedure that creates the objects every time your SQL Server instance starts.)

The *tempdb* database sizing and configuration is critical for optimal functioning and performance of SQL Server, so I'll discuss *tempdb* in more detail in its own section later in this chapter.

## The Resource Database

As mentioned, the *mssqlsystemresource* database is a hidden database and is usually referred to as the *resource database.* Executable system objects, such as system stored procedures and functions, are stored here. Microsoft created this database to allow very fast and safe upgrades. If no one can get to this database, no one can change it, and you can upgrade to a new service pack that introduces new system objects by simply replacing the resource database with a new one. Keep in mind that you can't see this database using any of the normal means for viewing databases, such as selecting from *sys.databases* or executing *sp_helpdb*. It also won't show up in the system databases tree in the Object Explorer pane of SQL Server Management Studio, and it does not appear in the drop-down list of databases accessible from your query windows. However, this database still needs disk space.

You can see the files in your default *binn* directory by using Microsoft Windows Explorer. My data directory is at C:\Program Files\Microsoft SQL Server\MSSQL10.MSSQLSERVER\ MSSQL\Binn; I can see a file called mssqlsystemresource.mdf, which is 60.2 MB in size, and mssqlsystemresource.ldf, which is 0.5 MB. The created and modified date for both of these files is the date that the code for the current build was frozen. It should be the same date that you see when you run *SELECT @@version*. For SQL Server 2008, the RTM build, this is 10.0.1600.22.

If you have a burning need to "see" the contents of *mssqlsystemresource,* a couple of methods are available. The easiest, if you just want to see what's there, is to stop SQL Server, make copies of the two files for the resource database, restart SQL Server, and then attach the copied files to create a database with a new name. You can do this by using Object Explorer in Management Studio or by using the *CREATE DATABASE FOR ATTACH* syntax to create a clone database, as shown here:

```
CREATE DATABASE resource_COPY
ON (NAME = data, FILENAME = 'C:\Program Files\Microsoft SQL Server\MSSQL.1\MSSQL\binn
        \mssqlsystemresource_COPY.mdf'),
   (NAME = log, FILENAME =
    'C:\Program Files\Microsoft SQL Server\MSSQL.1\MSSQL\binn\mssqlsystemresource_COPY.ldf')
    FOR ATTACH;
```

SQL Server treats this new *resource_COPY* database like any other user database, and it does not treat the objects in it as special in any way. If you want to change anything in the resource database, such as the text of a supplied system stored procedure, changing it in *resource_COPY* obviously does not affect anything else on your instance. However, if you start your SQL Server instance in single-user mode, you can make a single connection to your SQL Server, and that connection can use the *mssqlsystemresource* database. Starting an instance in single-user mode is not the same thing as setting a database to single-user mode. For details on how to start SQL Server in single-user mode, see the *SQL Server Books Online* entry for the sqlservr.exe application. In Chapter 6, "Indexes: Internals and Management," when I discuss database objects, I'll discuss some of the objects in the resource database.

## msdb

The *msdb* database is used by the SQL Server Agent service and other companion services, which perform scheduled activities such as backups and replication tasks, and the Service Broker, which provides queuing and reliable messaging for SQL Server. In addition to backups, objects in *msdb* support jobs, alerts, log shipping, policies, database mail, and recovery of damaged pages. When you are not actively performing these activities on this database, you can generally ignore *msdb*. (But you might take a peek at the backup history and other information kept there.) All the information in *msdb* is accessible from Object Explorer in Management Studio, so you usually don't need to access the tables in this database directly. You can think of the *msdb* tables as another form of system table: Just as you can never directly modify system tables, you shouldn't directly add data to or delete data from tables in *msdb* unless you really know what you're doing or are instructed to do so by a SQL Server technical support engineer. Prior to SQL Server 2005, it was actually possible to drop the *msdb* database; your SQL Server instance was still usable, but you couldn't maintain any backup history, and you weren't able to define tasks, alerts, or jobs or set up replication. There is an undocumented traceflag that allows you to drop the *msdb* database, but because the default *msdb* database is so small, I recommend leaving it alone even if you think you might never need it.

# Sample Databases

Prior to SQL Server 2005, the installation program automatically installed sample databases so you would have some actual data for exploring SQL Server functionality. As part of Microsoft's efforts to tighten security, SQL Server 2008 does not automatically install any sample databases. However, several sample databases are widely available.

## AdventureWorks

*AdventureWorks* actually comprises a family of sample databases that was created by the Microsoft User Education group as an example of what a "real" database might look like. The family includes: *AdventureWorks2008, AdventureWorksDW2008,* and *AdventureWorksLT2008,* as well as their counterparts created for SQL Server 2005: *AdventureWorks, AdventureWorksDW,* and *AdventureWorksLT.* You can download these databases from the Microsoft codeplex site at *http://www.codeplex.com/SqlServerSamples.* The database was designed to showcase SQL Server features, including the organization of objects into different schemas. These databases are based on data needed by the fictitious Adventure Works Cycles company. The *AdventureWorks* and *AdventureWorks2008* databases are designed to support OLTP applications and *AdventureWorksDW* and *AdventureWorksDW2008* are designed to support the business intelligence features of SQL Server and are based on a completely different database architecture. Both designs are highly normalized. Although normalized data and many separate schemas might map closely to a real production database's design, they can make it quite difficult to write and test simple queries and to learn basic SQL.

Database design is not a major focus of this book, so most of my examples use simple tables that I create; if more than a few rows of data are needed, I'll sometimes copy data from one or more *AdventureWorks2008* tables into tables of my own. It's a good idea to become familiar with the design of the *AdventureWorks* family of databases because many of the examples in *SQL Server Books Online* and in white papers published on the Microsoft Web site (*http://www.microsoft.com/ sqlserver/2008/en/us/white-papers.aspx*) use data from these databases.

Note that it is also possible to install an *AdventureWorksLT2008* (or *AdventureWorksLT*) database, which is a highly simplified and somewhat denormalized version of the *AdventureWorks* OLTP database and focuses on a simple sales scenario with a single schema.

## pubs

The *pubs* database is a sample database that was used extensively in earlier versions of SQL Server. Many older publications with SQL Server examples assume that you have this database because it was installed automatically on versions of SQL Server prior to SQL Server 2005. You can download a script for building this database from Microsoft's Web site, and I have also included the script with this book's companion content at *http://www.SQLServerInternals.com/companion.*

The *pubs* database is admittedly simple, but that's a feature, not a drawback. It provides good examples without a lot of peripheral issues to obscure the central points. You shouldn't worry about making modifications in the *pubs* database as you experiment with SQL Server features. You can rebuild the *pubs* database from scratch by running the supplied script. In a query window, open the file named Instpubs.sql and execute it. Make sure there are no current connections to *pubs* because the current *pubs* database is dropped before the new one is created.

## Northwind

The *Northwind* database is a sample database that was originally developed for use with Microsoft Office Access. Much of the pre–SQL Server 2005 documentation dealing with application programming uses *Northwind*. *Northwind* is a bit more complex than *pubs*, and, at almost 4 MB, it is slightly larger. As with *pubs*, you can download a script from the

Microsoft Web site to build it, or you can use the script provided with the companion content. The file is called Instnwnd.sql. In addition, some of the sample scripts for this book use a modified copy of *Northwind* called *Northwind2*.

# Database Files

A database file is nothing more than an operating system file. (In addition to database files, SQL Server also has *backup devices*, which are logical devices that map to operating system files or to physical devices such as tape drives. In this chapter, I won't be discussing files that are used to store backups.) A database spans at least two, and possibly several, database files, and these files are specified when a database is created or altered. Every database must span at least two files, one for the data (as well as indexes and allocation pages) and one for the transaction log.

SQL Server 2008 allows the following three types of database files:

- **Primary data files**   Every database has one primary data file that keeps track of all the rest of the files in the database, in addition to storing data. By convention, a primary data file has the extension .mdf.

- **Secondary data files**   A database can have zero or more secondary data files. By convention, a secondary data file has the extension .ndf.

- **Log files**   Every database has at least one log file that contains the information necessary to recover all transactions in a database. By convention, a log file has the extension .ldf.

In addition, SQL Server 2008 databases can have filestream data files and full-text data files. Filestream data files will be discussed in the section "Filestream Filegroups," later in this chapter, and in Chapter 7, "Special Storage." Full-text data files are created and managed completely, separately from your other database files and are beyond the scope of this book.

Each database file has five properties that can be specified when you create the file: a logical filename, a physical filename, an initial size, a maximum size, and a growth increment. (Filestream data files have only the logical and physical name properties.) The value of these properties, along with other information about each file, can be seen through the metadata view *sys.database_files*, which contains one row for each file used by a database. Most of the columns shown in *sys.database_files* are listed in Table 3-1. The columns not mentioned here contain information dealing with transaction log backups relevant to the particular file, and I'll discuss the transaction log in Chapter 4, "Logging and Recovery."

**TABLE 3-1**  The *sys.database_files* Catalog View

| Column | Description |
| --- | --- |
| *fileid* | The file identification number (unique for each database). |
| *file_guid* | GUID for the file. NULL = Database was upgraded from an earlier version of SQL Server. |

**TABLE 3-1** The *sys.database_files* Catalog View

| Column | Description |
|---|---|
| *type* | File type: |
| | 0 = Rows (includes full-text catalogs upgraded to or created in SQL Server 2008) |
| | 1 = Log |
| | 2 = FILESTREAM |
| | 3 = Reserved for future use |
| | 4 = Full-text (includes full-text catalogs from versions earlier than SQL Server 2008) |
| *type_desc* | Description of the file type: |
| | ROWS |
| | LOG |
| | FILESTREAM |
| | FULLTEXT |
| *data_space_id* | ID of the data space to which this file belongs. Data space is a filegroup. |
| | 0 = Log file. |
| *name* | The logical name of the file. |
| *physical_name* | Operating-system file name. |
| *state* | File state: |
| | 0 = ONLINE |
| | 1 = RESTORING |
| | 2 = RECOVERING |
| | 3 = RECOVERY_PENDING |
| | 4 = SUSPECT |
| | 5 = Reserved for future use |
| | 6 = OFFLINE |
| | 7 = DEFUNCT |
| *state_desc* | Description of the file state: |
| | ONLINE |
| | RESTORING |
| | RECOVERING |
| | RECOVERY_PENDING |
| | SUSPECT |
| | OFFLINE |
| | DEFUNCT |
| *size* | Current size of the file, in 8-KB pages. |
| | 0 = Not applicable |
| | For a database snapshot, size reflects the maximum space that the snapshot can ever use for the file. |

**TABLE 3-1** The *sys.database_files* Catalog View

| Column | Description |
|--------|-------------|
| *max_size* | Maximum file size, in 8-KB pages: |
| | 0 = No growth is allowed. |
| | –1 = File will grow until the disk is full. |
| | 268435456 = Log file will grow to a maximum size of 2 terabytes. |
| *growth* | 0 = File is a fixed size and will not grow. |
| | >0 = File will grow automatically. |
| | If *is_percent_growth* = 0, growth increment is in units of 8-KB pages, rounded to the nearest 64 KB. |
| | If *is_percent_growth* = 1, growth increment is expressed as a whole number percentage. |
| *is_media_read_only* | 1 = File is on read-only media. |
| | 0 = File is on read/write media. |
| *is_read_only* | 1 = File is marked read-only. |
| | 0 = File is marked read/write. |
| *is_sparse* | 1 = File is a sparse file. |
| | 0 = File is not a sparse file. |
| | (Sparse files are used with database snapshots, discussed later in this chapter.) |
| *is_percent_growth* | See description for *growth* column, above. |
| *is_name_reserved* | 1 = Dropped file name (name or physical_name) is reusable only after the next log backup. When files are dropped from a database, the logical names stay in a reserved state until the next log backup. This column is relevant only under the full recovery model and the bulk-logged recovery model. |

# Creating a Database

The easiest way to create a database is to use Object Explorer in Management Studio, which provides a graphical front end to the T-SQL commands that actually create the database and set its properties. Figure 3-1 shows the New Database dialog box, which represents the T-SQL *CREATE DATABASE* command for creating a new user database. Only someone with the appropriate permissions can create a database, either through Object Explorer or by using the *CREATE DATABASE* command. This includes anyone in the *sysadmin* role, anyone who has been granted CONTROL or ALTER permission on the server, and any user who has been granted CREATE DATABASE permission by someone with the *sysadmin* or *dbcreator* role.

When you create a new database, SQL Server copies the *model* database. If you have an object that you want created in every subsequent user database, you should create that object in *model* first. You can also use *model* to set default database options in all subsequently created databases. The *model* database includes 53 objects—45 system tables, 6 objects used for SQL Server Query Notifications and Service Broker, 1 table used for helping to manage filestream data, and 1 table for helping to manage change tracking. You can see these objects by selecting from the system table called *sys.objects*. However, if you run the procedure *sp_help* in the *model* database, it will list 1,978 objects. It turns out that most of these objects are not really stored in the *model* database but are accessible through it. In Chapter 5, "Tables," I'll tell you what the other kinds of objects are and how you can tell whether an object is really stored in a particular database. Most of the objects you see in *model* will show up when you run *sp_help* in any database, but your user databases will probably have more objects added to this list. The contents of *model* are just the starting point.

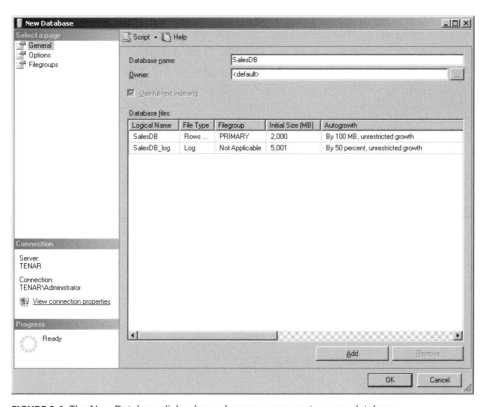

**FIGURE 3-1** The New Database dialog box, where you can create a new database

A new user database must be 3 MB or larger (including the transaction log), and the primary data file size must be at least as large as the primary data file of the *model* database. (The *model* database only has one file and cannot be altered to add more. So the size of the primary data file and the size of the database are basically the same for *model*.) Almost all the possible arguments to the *CREATE DATABASE* command have default values, so it's possible to create a database using a simple form of *CREATE DATABASE*, such as this:

```
CREATE DATABASE newdb;
```

This command creates the *newdb* database, with a default size, on two files whose logical names—*newdb* and *newdb_log*—are derived from the name of the database. The corresponding physical files, newdb.mdf and newdb_log.ldf, are created in the default data directory, which is usually determined at the time SQL Server is installed.

The SQL Server login account that created the database is known as the *database owner*, and that information is stored with the information about the database properties in the *master* database. A database can have only one actual owner, who always corresponds to a login name. Any login that uses any database has a user name in that database, which might be the same name as the login name but doesn't have to be. The login that is the owner of a database always has the special user name *dbo* when using the database it owns. I'll discuss database users later in this chapter when I tell you about the basics of database security. The default size of the data file is the size of the primary data file of the *model* database (which is 2 MB by default), and the default size of the log file is 0.5 MB. Whether the database name, *newdb*, is case-sensitive depends on the sort order that you chose during setup. If you accepted the default, the name is case-insensitive. (Note that the actual command *CREATE DATABASE* is case-insensitive, regardless of the case sensitivity chosen for data.)

Other default property values apply to the new database and its files. For example, if the LOG ON clause is not specified but data files are specified, SQL Server creates a log file with a size that is 25 percent of the sum of the sizes of all data files.

If the MAXSIZE clause isn't specified for the files, the file grows until the disk is full. (In other words, the file size is considered unlimited.) You can specify the values for *SIZE*, *MAXSIZE*, and *FILEGROWTH* in units of terabytes, GB, and MB (the default), or KB. You can also specify the *FILEGROWTH* property as a percentage. A value of 0 for *FILEGROWTH* indicates no growth. If no *FILEGROWTH* value is specified, the default growth increment for data files is 1 MB. The log file *FILEGROWTH* default is specified as 10 percent.

## A *CREATE DATABASE* Example

The following is a complete example of the *CREATE DATABASE* command, specifying three files and all the properties of each file:

```
CREATE DATABASE Archive
ON
PRIMARY
( NAME = Arch1,
FILENAME =
    'c:\program files\microsoft sql server\mssql.1\mssql\data\archdat1.mdf',
SIZE = 100MB,
MAXSIZE = 200MB,
FILEGROWTH = 20MB),
( NAME = Arch2,
FILENAME =
    'c:\program files\microsoft sql server\mssql.1\mssql\data\archdat2.ndf',
```

```
SIZE = 10GB,
MAXSIZE = 50GB,
FILEGROWTH = 250MB)
LOG ON
( NAME = Archlog1,
FILENAME =
    'c:\program files\microsoft sql server\mssql.1\mssql\data\archlog1.ldf',
SIZE = 2GB,
MAXSIZE = 10GB,
FILEGROWTH = 100MB);
```

# Expanding or Shrinking a Database

Databases can be expanded and shrunk automatically or manually. The mechanism for automatic expansion is completely different from the mechanism for automatic shrinkage. Manual expansion is also handled differently from manual shrinkage. Log files have their own rules for growing and shrinking; I'll discuss changes in log file size in Chapter 4.

> **Warning**  Shrinking a database or any data file is an extremely resource-intensive operation, and the only reason to do it is if you absolutely must reclaim disk space. Shrinking a data file can also lead to excessive logical fragmentation within your database. We'll discuss fragmentation in Chapter 6 and shrinking in Chapter 11, "DBCC Internals."

## Automatic File Expansion

Expansion can happen automatically to any one of the database's files when that particular file becomes full. The file property *FILEGROWTH* determines how that automatic expansion happens. The *FILEGROWTH* property that is specified when the file is first defined can be qualified using the suffix *TB, GB, MB, KB,* or *%*, and it is always rounded up to the nearest 64 KB. If the value is specified as a percentage, the growth increment is the specified percentage of the size of the file when the expansion occurs. The file property *MAXSIZE* sets an upper limit on the size.

Allowing SQL Server to grow your data files automatically is no substitute for good capacity planning before you build or populate any tables. Enabling autogrow might prevent some failures due to unexpected increases in data volume, but it can also cause problems. If a data file is full and your autogrow percentage is set to grow by 10 percent, if an application attempts to insert a single row and there is no space, the database might start to grow by a large amount (10 percent of 10,000 MB is 1,000 MB). This in itself can take a lot of time if fast file initialization (discussed in the next section) is not being used. The growth might take so long that the client application's timeout value is exceeded, which means the insert query fails. The query would have failed anyway if autogrow weren't set, but with autogrow enabled, SQL Server spends a lot of time trying to grow the file, and you won't be informed of the problem immediately. In addition, file growth can result in physical fragmentation on the disk.

With autogrow enabled, your database files still cannot grow the database size beyond the limits of the available disk space on the drives on which files are defined, or beyond the size specified in the *MAXSIZE* file property. So if you rely on the autogrow functionality to size your databases, you must still independently check your available hard disk space or the total file size. (The undocumented extended procedure *xp_fixeddrives* returns a list of the amount of free disk space on each of your local volumes.) To reduce the possibility of running out of space, you can watch the Performance Monitor counter SQL Server: Databases Object: Data File Size and set up a performance alert to fire when the database file reaches a certain size.

## Manual File Expansion

You can expand a database file manually by using the *ALTER DATABASE* command with the MODIFY FILE option to change the *SIZE* property of one or more of the files. When you alter a database, the new size of a file must be larger than the current size. To decrease the size of a file, you use the *DBCC SHRINKFILE* command, which I'll tell you about shortly.

## Fast File Initialization

SQL Server 2008 data files (but not log files) can be initialized instantaneously. This allows for fast execution of the file creation and growth. Instant file initialization adds space to the data file without filling the newly added space with zeros. Instead, the actual disk content is overwritten only as new data is written to the files. Until the data is overwritten, there is always the chance that a hacker using an external file reader tool can see the data that was previously on the disk. Although the SQL Server 2008 documentation describes the instant file initialization feature as an "option," it is not really an option within SQL Server. It is actually controlled through a Windows security setting called SE_MANAGE_VOLUME_NAME, which is granted to Windows administrators by default. (This right can be granted to other Windows users by adding them to the Perform Volume Maintenance Tasks security policy.) If your SQL Server service account is in the Windows Administrator role and your SQL Server is running on a Windows XP, Windows Server 2003, or Windows Server 2008 filesystem, instant file initialization is used. If you want to make sure your database files are zeroed out as they are created and expanded, you can use traceflag 1806 or deny SE_MANAGE_VOLUME_NAME rights to the account under which your SQL Server service is running.

## Automatic Shrinkage

The database property *autoshrink* allows a database to shrink automatically. The effect is the same as doing a *DBCC SHRINKDATABASE (dbname, 25)*. This option leaves 25 percent free space in a database after the shrink, and any free space beyond that is returned to the operating system. The thread that performs autoshrink shrinks databases at very frequent intervals, in some cases as often as every 30 minutes. Shrinking data files is so resource-intensive that it should be done only when there is no other way to reclaim needed disk space.

**Important** Automatic shrinking is never recommended. In fact, Microsoft has announced that the autoshrink option will be removed in a future version of SQL Server and you should avoid using it.

## Manual Shrinkage

You can shrink a database manually using one of the following DBCC commands:

```
DBCC SHRINKFILE ( {file_name | file_id }
[, target_size][, {EMPTYFILE | NOTRUNCATE | TRUNCATEONLY} ]  )

DBCC SHRINKDATABASE (database_name [, target_percent]
[, {NOTRUNCATE | TRUNCATEONLY} ]  )
```

### DBCC SHRINKFILE

*DBCC SHRINKFILE* allows you to shrink files in the current database. When you specify *target_size*, *DBCC SHRINKFILE* attempts to shrink the specified file to the specified size in megabytes. Used pages in the part of the file to be freed are relocated to available free space in the part of the file that is retained. For example, for a 15-MB data file, a *DBCC SHRINKFILE* with a *target_size* of 12 causes all used pages in the last 3 MB of the file to be reallocated into any free slots in the first 12 MB of the file. *DBCC SHRINKFILE* doesn't shrink a file past the size needed to store the data. For example, if 70 percent of the pages in a 10-MB data file are used, a *DBCC SHRINKFILE* command with a *target_size* of 5 shrinks the file to only 7 MB, not 5 MB.

### DBCC SHRINKDATABASE

*DBCC SHRINKDATABASE* shrinks all files in a database but does not allow any file to be shrunk smaller than its minimum size. The minimum size of a database file is the initial size of the file (specified when the database was created) or the size to which the file has been explicitly extended or reduced, using either the *ALTER DATABASE* or *DBCC SHRINKFILE* command. If you need to shrink a database smaller than its minimum size, you should use the *DBCC SHRINKFILE* command to shrink individual database files to a specific size. The size to which a file is shrunk becomes the new minimum size.

The numeric *target_percent* argument passed to the *DBCC SHRINKDATABASE* command is a percentage of free space to leave in each file of the database. For example, if you've used 60 MB of a 100-MB database file, you can specify a shrink percentage of 25 percent. SQL Server then shrinks the file to a size of 80 MB, and you have 20 MB of free space in addition to the original 60 MB of data. In other words, the 80-MB file has 25 percent of its space free. If, on the other hand, you've used 80 MB or more of a 100-MB database file, there is no way that SQL Server can shrink this file to leave 25 percent free space. In that case, the file size remains unchanged.

Because *DBCC SHRINKDATABASE* shrinks the database on a file-by-file basis, the mechanism used to perform the actual shrinking of data files is the same as that used with *DBCC SHRINKFILE* (when a data file is specified). SQL Server first moves pages to the front of files to free up space at the end, and then it releases the appropriate number of freed pages to the operating system. The actual internal details of how data files are shrunk will be discussed in Chapter 11.

> **Note**  Shrinking a log file is very different from shrinking a data file, and understanding how much you can shrink a log file and what exactly happens when you shrink it requires an understanding of how the log is used. For this reason, I will postpone the discussion of shrinking log files until Chapter 4.

As the warning at the beginning of this section indicated, shrinking a database or any data files is a resource-intensive operation. If you absolutely need to recover disk space from the database, you should plan the shrink operation carefully and perform it when it has the least impact on the rest of the system. You should never enable the AUTOSHRINK option, which will shrink *all* the data files at regular intervals and wreak havoc with system performance. Because shrinking data files can move data all around a file, it can also introduce fragmentation, which you then might want to remove. Defragmenting your data files can then have its own impact on productivity because it uses system resources. Fragmentation and defragmentation will be discussed in Chapter 6.

It is possible for shrink operations to be blocked by a transaction that has been enabled for either of the snapshot-based isolation levels. When this happens, *DBCC SHRINKFILE* and *DBCC SHRINKDATABASE* print out an informational message to the error log every five minutes in the first hour and then every hour after that. SQL Server also provides progress reporting for the *SHRINK* commands, available through the *sys.dm_exec_requests* view. Progress reporting will be discussed in Chapter 11.

# Using Database Filegroups

You can group data files for a database into filegroups for allocation and administration purposes. In some cases, you can improve performance by controlling the placement of data and indexes into specific filegroups on specific drives or volumes. The filegroup containing the primary data file is called the *primary filegroup*. There is only one primary filegroup, and if you don't ask specifically to place files in other filegroups when you create your database, *all* of your data files are in the primary filegroup.

In addition to the primary filegroup, a database can have one or more user-defined filegroups. You can create user-defined filegroups by using the *FILEGROUP* keyword in the *CREATE DATABASE* or *ALTER DATABASE* command.

Don't confuse the primary filegroup and the primary file. Here are the differences:

■ The primary file is always the first file listed when you create a database, and it typically has the file extension .mdf. The one special feature of the primary file is that it has pointers into a table in the *master* database (which you can access through the catalog view *sys.database_files*) that contains information about all the files belonging to the database.

■ The primary filegroup is always the filegroup that contains the primary file. This filegroup contains the primary data file and any files not put into another specific filegroup. All pages from system tables are always allocated from files in the primary filegroup.

## The Default Filegroup

One filegroup always has the property of *DEFAULT*. Note that *DEFAULT* is a property of a filegroup, not a name. Only one filegroup in each database can be the default filegroup. By default, the primary filegroup is also the default filegroup. A database owner can change which filegroup is the default by using the *ALTER DATABASE* command. When creating a table or index, it is created in the default filegroup if no specific filegroup is specified.

Most SQL Server databases have a single data file in one (default) filegroup. In fact, most users probably never know enough about how SQL Server works to know what a filegroup is. As a user acquires greater database sophistication, she might decide to use multiple devices to spread out the I/O for a database. The easiest way to do this is to create a database file on a RAID device. Still, there would be no need to use filegroups. At the next level of sophistication and complexity, the user might decide that she really wants multiple files—perhaps to create a database that uses more space than is available on a single drive. In this case, she still doesn't need filegroups—she can accomplish her goals using *CREATE DATABASE* with a list of files on separate drives.

More sophisticated database administrators might decide to have different tables assigned to different drives or to use the table and index partitioning feature in SQL Server 2008. Only then will they need to use filegroups. They can then use Object Explorer in Management Studio to create the database on multiple filegroups. Then they can right-click the database name in Object Explorer and create a script of the *CREATE DATABASE* command that includes all the files in their appropriate filegroups. They can save and reuse this script when they need to re-create the database or build a similar database.

### Why Use Multiple Files?

You might wonder why you would want to create a database on multiple files located on one physical drive. There's usually no performance benefit in doing so, but it gives you added flexibility in two important ways.

First, if you need to restore a database from a backup because of a disk crash, the new database must contain the same number of files as the original. For example, if your original database consisted of one large 120-GB file, you would need to restore it to a database with one file of that size. If you don't have another 120-GB drive immediately available, you cannot restore the database. If, however, you originally created the database on several smaller files, you have added flexibility during a restoration. You might be more likely to have several 40-GB drives available than one large 120-GB drive.

Second, spreading the database onto multiple files, even on the same drive, gives you the flexibility of easily moving the database onto separate drives if you modify your hardware configuration in the future. (Please refer to the section "Moving or Copying a Database," later in this chapter, for details.)

Objects that have space allocated to them, namely tables and indexes, are created on a particular filegroup. (They can also be created on a partition scheme, which is a collection of filegroups. I'll discuss partitioning and partition schemes in Chapter 7.) If the filegroup (or partition scheme) is not specified, objects are created on the default filegroup. When you add space to objects stored in a particular filegroup, the data is stored in a *proportional fill* manner, which means that if you have one file in a filegroup with twice as much free space as another, the first file has two extents (or units of space) allocated from it for each extent allocated from the second file. (I'll discuss extents in more detail in the section entitled "Space Allocation," later in this chapter.) It's recommended that you create all of your files to be the same size to avoid the issues of proportional fill.

You can also use filegroups to allow backups of parts of the database. Because a table is created on a single filegroup, you can choose to back up just a certain set of critical tables by backing up the filegroups in which you placed those tables. You can also restore individual files or filegroups in two ways. First, you can do a partial restore of a database and restore only a subset of filegroups, which must always include the primary filegroup. The database will be online as soon as the primary filegroup has been restored, but only objects created on the restored filegroups will be available. Partial restore of just a subset of filegroups can be a solution to allow very large databases to be available within a mandated time window. Alternatively, if you have a failure of a subset of the disks on which you created your database, you can restore backups of the filegroups on those disks on top of the existing database. This method of restoring also requires that you have log backups, so I'll discuss this topic in more detail in Chapter 4.

## A *FILEGROUP CREATION* Example

This example creates a database named *sales* with three filegroups:

- The primary filegroup, with the files *salesPrimary1* and *salesPrimary2*. The *FILEGROWTH* increment for both of these files is specified as 100 MB.
- A filegroup named *SalesGroup1*, with the files *salesGrp1File1* and *salesGrp1File2*.
- A filegroup named *SalesGroup2*, with the files *salesGrp2File1* and *salesGrp2File2*.

```
CREATE DATABASE Sales
ON PRIMARY
( NAME = salesPrimary1,
FILENAME =
    'c:\program files\microsoft sql server\mssql.1\mssql\data\salesPrimary1.mdf',
SIZE = 100,
MAXSIZE = 500,
FILEGROWTH = 100 ),
( NAME = salesPrimary2,
FILENAME =
    'c:\program files\microsoft sql server\mssql.1\mssql\data\salesPrimary2.ndf',
SIZE = 100,
MAXSIZE = 500,
FILEGROWTH = 100 ),
FILEGROUP SalesGroup1
( NAME = salesGrp1File1,
FILENAME =
    'c:\program files\microsoft sql server\mssql.1\mssql\data\salesGrp1File1.ndf',
SIZE = 500,
MAXSIZE = 3000,
FILEGROWTH = 500 ),
( NAME = salesGrp1File2,
FILENAME =
    'c:\program files\microsoft sql server\mssql.1\mssql\data\salesGrp1File2.ndf',
SIZE = 500,
MAXSIZE = 3000,
FILEGROWTH = 500 ),
FILEGROUP SalesGroup2
( NAME = salesGrp2File1,
FILENAME =
    'c:\program files\microsoft sql server\mssql.1\mssql\data\salesGrp2File1.ndf',
SIZE = 100,
MAXSIZE = 5000,
FILEGROWTH = 500 ),
( NAME = salesGrp2File2,
FILENAME =
    'c:\program files\microsoft sql server\mssql.1\mssql\data\salesGrp2File2.ndf',
SIZE = 100,
MAXSIZE = 5000,
FILEGROWTH = 500 )
LOG ON
( NAME = 'Sales_log',
FILENAME =
    'c:\program files\microsoft sql server\mssql.1\mssql\data\saleslog.ldf',
SIZE = 5MB,
MAXSIZE = 25MB,
FILEGROWTH = 5MB );
```

## Filestream Filegroups

I briefly mentioned filestream storage in Chapter 1, "SQL Server 2008 Architecture and Configuration," when I talked about configuration options. Filestream filegroups can be created when you create a database, just like regular filegroups can be, but you must specify that the filegroup is for filestream data by using the phrase CONTAINS FILESTREAM. Unlike regular filegroups, each filestream filegroup can contain only one file reference, and that file is specified as an operating system folder, not a specific file. The path up to the last folder must exist, and the last folder must not exist. So in my example, the path C:\Data must exist, but the *Reviews_FS* subfolder cannot exist when you execute the *CREATE DATABASE* command. Also unlike regular filegroups, there is no space preallocated to the filegroup and you do not specify size or growth information for the file within the filegroup. The file and filegroup will grow as data is added to tables that have been created with filestream columns:

```
CREATE DATABASE MyMovieReviews
ON
PRIMARY
  ( NAME = Reviews_data,
    FILENAME = 'c:\data\Reviews_data.mdf'),
FILEGROUP MovieReviewsFSGroup1 CONTAINS FILESTREAM
  ( NAME = Reviews_FS,
    FILENAME = 'c:\data\Reviews_FS')
LOG ON  ( NAME = Reviews_log,
    FILENAME = 'c:\data\Reviews_log.ldf');
GO
```

If you run the previous code, you should see a Filestream.hdr file and an $FSLOG folder in the C:\Data\Reviews_FS folder. The Filestream.hdr file is a FILESTREAM container header file. This file should not be modified or removed. For existing databases, you can add a filestream filegroup using *ALTER DATABASE,* which I'll cover in the next section. All data in all columns placed in the *MovieReviewsFSGroup1* is maintained and managed with individual files created in the *Reviews_FS* folder. I'll tell you more about the file organization within this folder in Chapter 7, when I talk about special storage formats.

# Altering a Database

You can use the *ALTER DATABASE* command to change a database's definition in one of the following ways:

- Change the name of the database.
- Add one or more new data files to the database. If you want, you can put these files in a user-defined filegroup. All files added in a single *ALTER DATABASE* command must go in the same filegroup.
- Add one or more new log files to the database.
- Remove a file or a filegroup from the database. You can do this only if the file or filegroup is completely empty. Removing a filegroup removes all the files in it.

- Add a new filegroup to a database. (Adding files to those filegroups must be done in a separate *ALTER DATABASE* command.) Modify an existing file in one of the following ways:

  - ❏ Increase the value of the *SIZE* property.

  - ❏ Change the *MAXSIZE* or *FILEGROWTH* property.

  - ❏ Change the logical name of a file by specifying a *NEWNAME* property. The value of *NEWNAME* is then used as the *NAME* property for all future references to this file.

  - ❏ Change the *FILENAME* property for files, which can effectively move the files to a new location. The new name or location doesn't take effect until you restart SQL Server. For *tempdb*, SQL Server automatically creates the files with the new name in the new location; for other databases, you must move the file manually after stopping your SQL Server instance. SQL Server then finds the new file when it restarts.

- Mark the file as OFFLINE. You should set a file to OFFLINE when the physical file has become corrupted and the file backup is available to use for restoring. (There is also an option to mark the whole database as OFFLINE, which I'll discuss shortly when I talk about database properties.) Marking a file as OFFLINE allows you to indicate that you don't want SQL Server to recover that particular file when it is restarted. Modify an existing filegroup in one of the following ways:

  - ❏ Mark the filegroup as READONLY so that updates to objects in the filegroup aren't allowed. The primary filegroup cannot be made READONLY.

  - ❏ Mark the filegroup as READWRITE, which reverses the READONLY property.

  - ❏ Mark the filegroup as the default filegroup for the database.

  - ❏ Change the name of the filegroup.

- Change one or more database options. (I'll discuss database options later in the chapter.)

The *ALTER DATABASE* command can make only one of the changes described each time it is executed. Note that you cannot move a file from one filegroup to another.

## *ALTER DATABASE* Examples

The following examples demonstrate some of the changes that you can make using the *ALTER DATABASE* command.

This example increases the size of a database file:

```
USE master
GO
ALTER DATABASE Test1
MODIFY FILE
( NAME = 'test1dat3',
SIZE = 2000MB);
```

The following example creates a new filegroup in a database, adds two 500-MB files to the filegroup, and makes the new filegroup the default filegroup. You need three *ALTER DATABASE* statements:

```
ALTER DATABASE Test1
ADD FILEGROUP Test1FG1;
GO
ALTER DATABASE Test1
ADD FILE
( NAME = 'test1dat4',
FILENAME =
    'c:\program files\microsoft sql server\mssql.1\mssql\data\t1dat4.ndf',
SIZE = 500MB,
MAXSIZE = 1000MB,
FILEGROWTH = 50MB),
( NAME = 'test1dat5',
FILENAME =
    'c:\program files\microsoft sql server\mssql.1\mssql\data\t1dat5.ndf',
SIZE = 500MB,
MAXSIZE = 1000MB,
FILEGROWTH = 50MB)
TO FILEGROUP Test1FG1;
GO
ALTER DATABASE Test1
MODIFY FILEGROUP Test1FG1 DEFAULT;
GO
```

# Databases Under the Hood

A database consists of user-defined space for the permanent storage of user objects such as tables and indexes. This space is allocated in one or more operating system files.

Databases are divided into logical pages (of 8 KB each), and within each file the pages are numbered contiguously from 0 to *x*, with the value *x* being defined by the size of the file. You can refer to any page by specifying a database ID, a file ID, and a page number. When you use the *ALTER DATABASE* command to enlarge a file, the new space is added to the end of the file. That is, the first page of the newly allocated space is page *x* + 1 on the file you're enlarging. When you shrink a database by using the *DBCC SHRINKDATABASE* or *DBCC SHRINKFILE* command, pages are removed starting at the highest-numbered page in the database (at the end) and moving toward lower-numbered pages. This ensures that page numbers within a file are always contiguous.

When you create a new database using the *CREATE DATABASE* command, it is given a unique database ID, and you can see a row for the new database in the *sys.databases* view. The rows returned in *sys.databases* include basic information about each database, such as its name, *database_id,* and creation date, as well as the value for each database option that can be set with the *ALTER DATABASE* command. I'll discuss database options in more detail later in the chapter.

# Space Allocation

The space in a database is used for storing tables and indexes. The space is managed in units called *extents*. An extent is made up of eight logically contiguous pages (or 64 KB of space). To make space allocation more efficient, SQL Server 2008 doesn't allocate entire extents to tables with small amounts of data. SQL Server 2008 has two types of extents:

- **Uniform extents**   These are owned by a single object; all eight pages in the extent can be used only by the owning object.

- **Mixed extents**   These are shared by up to eight objects.

SQL Server allocates pages for a new table or index from mixed extents. When the table or index grows to eight pages, all future allocations use uniform extents.

When a table or index needs more space, SQL Server needs to find space that's available to be allocated. If the table or index is still less than eight pages total, SQL Server must find a mixed extent with space available. If the table or index is eight pages or larger, SQL Server must find a free uniform extent.

SQL Server uses two special types of pages to record which extents have been allocated and which type of use (mixed or uniform) the extent is available for:

- **Global Allocation Map (GAM) pages**   These pages record which extents have been allocated for any type of use. A GAM has a bit for each extent in the interval it covers. If the bit is 0, the corresponding extent is in use; if the bit is 1, the extent is free. After the header and other overhead are accounted for, there are 8,000 bytes, or 64,000 bits, available on the page, so each GAM can cover about 64,000 extents, or almost 4 GB of data. This means that one GAM page exists in a file for every 4 GB of file size.

- **Shared Global Allocation Map (SGAM) pages**   These pages record which extents are currently used as mixed extents and have at least one unused page. Just like a GAM, each SGAM covers about 64,000 extents, or almost 4 GB of data. The SGAM has a bit for each extent in the interval it covers. If the bit is 1, the extent being used is a mixed extent and has free pages; if the bit is 0, the extent isn't being used as a mixed extent, or it's a mixed extent whose pages are all in use.

Table 3-2 shows the bit patterns that each extent has set in the GAM and SGAM pages, based on its current use.

**TABLE 3-2  Bit Settings in GAM and SGAM Pages**

| Current Use of Extent | GAM Bit Setting | SGAM Bit Setting |
| --- | --- | --- |
| Free, not in use | 1 | 0 |
| Uniform extent or full mixed extent | 0 | 0 |
| Mixed extent with free pages | 0 | 1 |

There are several tools available for actually examining the bits in the GAMs and SGAMs. Chapter 5 discusses the *DBCC PAGE* command which allows you to view the contents of a SQL Server database page using a query window. Because the page numbers of the GAMs and SGAMs are known, we can just look at pages 2 or 3. If we use format 3, which gives the most details, we can see that output displays which extents are allocated and which are not. Figure 3-2 shows the last section of the output using *DBCC PAGE* with format 3 for the first GAM page of my *AdventureWorks2008* database.

| (1:0) | - (1:24256) | = | ALLOCATED |
|---|---|---|---|
| (1:24264) | - | = | NOT ALLOCATED |
| (1:24272) | - (1:29752) | = | ALLOCATED |
| (1:29760) | - (1:30168) | = | NOT ALLOCATED |
| (1:30176) | - (1:30240) | = | ALLOCATED |
| (1:30248) | - (1:30256) | = | NOT ALLOCATED |
| (1:30264) | - (1:32080) | = | ALLOCATED |
| (1:32088) | - (1:32304) | = | NOT ALLOCATED |

**FIGURE 3-2** GAM page contents indicating allocation status of extents in a file

This output indicates that all the extents up through the one that starts on page 24,256 are allocated. This corresponds to the first 189 MB of the file. The extent starting at 24,264 is not allocated, but the next 5,480 pages are allocated.

We can also use a graphical tool called *SQL Internals Viewer* to look at which extents have been allocated. SQL Internals Viewer is a free tool available from *http://www.SQLInternalsViewer.com*, and is also available on this book's companion Web site. Figure 3-3 shows the main allocation page for my *master* database. GAMs and SGAMs have been combined in one display and indicate the status of every page, not just every extent. The green squares indicate that the SGAM is being used but the extent is not used, so there are pages available for single-page allocations. The blue blocks indicate that both the GAM bit and the SGAM bit are set, so the corresponding extent is completely unavailable. The gray blocks indicate that the extent is free.

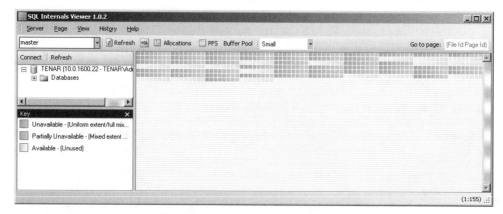

**FIGURE 3-3** SQL Internals Viewer indicating the allocation status of each page

If SQL Server needs to find a new, completely unused extent, it can use any extent with a corresponding bit value of 1 in the GAM page. If it needs to find a mixed extent with available space (one or more free pages), it finds an extent with a value in the SGAM of 1 (which always has a value in the GAM of 0). If there are no mixed extents with available space, it uses the GAM page to find a whole new extent to allocate as a mixed extent, and uses one page from that. If there are no free extents at all, the file is full.

SQL Server can locate the GAMs in a file quickly because a GAM is always the third page in any database file (that is, page 2). An SGAM is the fourth page (that is, page 3). Another GAM appears every 511,230 pages after the first GAM on page 2, and another SGAM appears every 511,230 pages after the first SGAM on page 3. Page 0 in any file is the File Header page, and only one exists per file. Page 1 is a Page Free Space (PFS) page. In Chapter 5, I'll say more about how individual pages within a table look and tell you about the details of PFS pages. For now, because I'm talking about space allocation, I'll examine how to keep track of which pages belong to which tables.

IAM pages keep track of the extents in a 4-GB section of a database file used by an allocation unit. An allocation unit is a set of pages belonging to a single partition in a table or index and comprises pages of one of three storage types: pages holding regular in-row data, pages holding Large Object (LOB) data, or pages holding row-overflow data. I'll discuss these regular in-row storage in Chapter 5, and LOB, row-overflow storage, and partitions in Chapter 7.

For example, a table on four partitions that has all three types of data (in-row, LOB, and row-overflow) has at least 12 IAM pages. Again, a single IAM page covers only a 4-GB section of a single file, so if the partition spans files, there will be multiple IAM pages, and if the file is more than 4 GB in size and the partition uses pages in more than one 4-GB section, there will be additional IAM pages.

An IAM page contains a 96-byte page header, like all other pages followed by an IAM page header, which contains eight page-pointer slots. Finally, an IAM page contains a set of bits that map a range of extents onto a file, which doesn't necessarily have to be the same file that the IAM page is in. The header has the address of the first extent in the range mapped by the IAM. The eight page-pointer slots might contain pointers to pages belonging to the relevant object contained in mixed extents; only the first IAM for an object has values in these pointers. Once an object takes up more than eight pages, all of its additional extents are uniform extents—which means that an object never needs more than eight pointers to pages in mixed extents. If rows have been deleted from a table, the table can actually use fewer than eight of these pointers. Each bit of the bitmap represents an extent in the range, regardless of whether the extent is allocated to the object owning the IAM. If a bit is on, the relative extent in the range is allocated to the object owning the IAM; if a bit is off, the relative extent isn't allocated to the object owning the IAM.

For example, if the bit pattern in the first byte of the IAM is 1100 0000, the first and second extents in the range covered by the IAM are allocated to the object owning the IAM and extents 3 through 8 aren't allocated to the object owning the IAM.

IAM pages are allocated as needed for each object and are located randomly in the database file. Each IAM covers a possible range of about 512,000 pages.

The internal system view called *sys.system_internals_allocation_units* has a column called *first_iam_page* that points to the first IAM page for an allocation unit. All the IAM pages for that allocation unit are linked in a chain, with each IAM page containing a pointer to the next in the chain. You can find out more about IAMs and allocation units in Chapters 5, 6, and 7 when I discuss object and index storage.

In addition to GAMs, SGAMs, and IAMs, a database file has three other types of special allocation pages. PFS pages keep track of how each particular page in a file is used. The second page (page 1) of a file is a PFS page, as is every 8,088th page thereafter. I'll talk about them more in Chapter 5. The seventh page (page 6) is called a Differential Changed Map (DCM) page. It keeps track of which extents in a file have been modified since the last full database backup. The eighth page (page 7) is called a Bulk Changed Map (BCM) page and is used when an extent in the file is used in a minimally or bulk-logged operation. I'll tell you more about these two kinds of pages when I talk about the internals of backup and restore operations in Chapter 4. Like GAM and SGAM pages, DCM and BCM pages have 1 bit for each extent in the section of the file they represent. They occur at regular intervals—every 511,230 pages.

You can see the details of IAMs and PFS pages, as well as DCM and BCM pages, using either *DBCC PAGE* or the SQL Internals Viewer. I'll show you more examples of the output of *DBCC PAGE* in later chapters as we cover more details of the different types of allocation pages.

# Setting Database Options

You can set several dozen options, or properties, for a database to control certain behavior within that database. Some options must be set to ON or OFF, some must be set to one of a list of possible values, and others are enabled by just specifying their name. By default, all the options that require ON or OFF have an initial value of OFF unless the option was set to ON in the *model* database. All databases created after an option is changed in *model* have the same values as *model*. You can easily change the value of some of these options by using Management Studio. You can set all of them directly by using the *ALTER DATABASE* command. (You can also use the *sp_dboption* system stored procedure to set some of the options, but that procedure is provided for backward compatibility only and is scheduled to be removed in the next version of SQL Server.)

Examining the *sys.databases* catalog view can show you the current values of all the options. The view also contains other useful information, such as database ID, creation date, and the Security ID (SID) of the database owner. The following query retrieves some of the most important columns from *sys.databases* for the four databases that exist on a new default installation of SQL Server:

```
SELECT name, database_id, suser_sname(owner_sid) as owner,
    create_date, user_access_desc, state_desc
FROM sys.databases
WHERE database_id <= 4;
```

The query produces this output, although the created dates may vary:

```
name    database_id owner create_date               user_access_desc state_desc
------  ----------- ----- ------------------------- ---------------- ----------
master  1           sa    2003-04-08 09:13:36.390   MULTI_USER       ONLINE
tempdb  2           sa    2008-04-19 12:02:35.327   MULTI_USER       ONLINE
model   3           sa    2003-04-08 09:13:36.390   MULTI_USER       ONLINE
msdb    4           sa    2008-03-21 01:54:05.240   MULTI_USER       ONLINE
```

The *sys.databases* view actually contains both a number and a name for the *user_access* and *state* information. Selecting all the columns from *sys.databases* would show you that the *user_access_desc* value of MULTI_USER has a corresponding *user_access* value of 0, and the *state_desc* value of ONLINE has a *state* value of 0. *SQL Server Books Online* shows the complete list of number and name relationships for the columns in *sys.databases*. These are just two of the database options displayed in the *sys.databases* view. The complete list of database options is divided into seven main categories: state options, cursor options, auto options, parameterization options, SQL options, database recovery options, and external access options. There are also options for specific technologies that SQL Server can use, including database mirroring, Service Broker activities, change tracking, database encryption, and snapshot isolation. Some of the options, particularly the SQL options, have corresponding SET options that you can turn on or off for a particular connection. Be aware that the ODBC or OLE DB drivers turn on a number of these SET options by default, so applications act as if the corresponding database option has already been set.

Here is a list of the options, by category. Options listed on a single line and values separated by vertical bars (|) are mutually exclusive.

## State options

1. SINGLE_USER | RESTRICTED_USER | MULTI_USER

2. OFFLINE | ONLINE | EMERGENCY

3. READ_ONLY | READ_WRITE

## Cursor options

1. CURSOR_CLOSE_ON_COMMIT { ON | OFF }

2. CURSOR_DEFAULT { LOCAL | GLOBAL }

## Auto options

1. AUTO_CLOSE { ON | OFF }

2. AUTO_CREATE_STATISTICS { ON | OFF }

3. AUTO_SHRINK { ON | OFF }

4. AUTO_UPDATE_STATISTICS { ON | OFF }

5. AUTO_UPDATE_STATISTICS_ASYNC { ON | OFF }

## Parameterization options

1. DATE_CORRELATION_OPTIMIZATION { ON | OFF }

2. PARAMETERIZATION { SIMPLE | FORCED }

## SQL options

1. ANSI_NULL_DEFAULT { ON | OFF }

2. ANSI_NULLS { ON | OFF }

3. ANSI_PADDING { ON | OFF }

4. ANSI_WARNINGS { ON | OFF }

5. ARITHABORT { ON | OFF }

6. CONCAT_NULL_YIELDS_NULL { ON | OFF }

7. NUMERIC_ROUNDABORT { ON | OFF }

8. QUOTED_IDENTIFIER { ON | OFF }

9. RECURSIVE_TRIGGERS { ON | OFF }

## Database recovery options

1. RECOVERY { FULL | BULK_LOGGED | SIMPLE }

2. TORN_PAGE_DETECTION { ON | OFF }

3. PAGE_VERIFY { CHECKSUM | TORN_PAGE_DETECTION | NONE }

## External access options

1. DB_CHAINING { ON | OFF }

2. TRUSTWORTHY { ON | OFF }

## Database mirroring options

1. PARTNER { = 'partner_server' }

2. | FAILOVER

3. | FORCE_SERVICE_ALLOW_DATA_LOSS

4. | OFF

5. | RESUME

6. | SAFETY { FULL | OFF }

7. | SUSPEND

8. | TIMEOUT *integer*

9. }

10. WITNESS { = 'witness_server' }| OFF }

### Service Broker options

1. ENABLE_BROKER | DISABLE_BROKER

2. NEW_BROKER

3. ERROR_BROKER_CONVERSATIONS

### Change Tracking options

1. CHANGE_TRACKING {= ON [ <change_tracking_settings> | = OFF}

### Database Encryption options

1. ENCRYPTION {ON | OFF}

### Snapshot Isolation options

1. ALLOW_SNAPSHOT_ISOLATION {ON | OFF }

2. READ_COMMITTED_SNAPSHOT {ON | OFF } [ WITH <termination> ]

## State Options

The state options control who can use the database and for what operations. There are three aspects to usability: The user access state determines which users can use the database; the status state determines whether the database is available to anybody for use; and the updateability state determines what operations can be performed on the database. You control each of these aspects by using the *ALTER DATABASE* command to enable an option for the database. None of the state options uses the keywords *ON* and *OFF* to control the state value.

### SINGLE_USER | RESTRICTED_USER | MULTI_USER

The three options SINGLE_USER, RESTRICTED_USER, and MULTI_USER describe the user access property of a database. They are mutually exclusive; setting any one of them unsets the others. To set one of these options for your database, you just use the option name. For example, to set the *AdventureWorks2008* database to single-user mode, use the following code:

```
ALTER DATABASE AdventureWorks2008 SET SINGLE_USER;
```

A database in SINGLE_USER mode can have only one connection at a time. A database in RESTRICTED_USER mode can have connections only from users who are considered "qualified"—those who are members of the *dbcreator* or *sysadmin* server role or the *db_owner* role for that database. The default for a database is MULTI_USER mode, which means anyone with a valid user name in the database can connect to it. If you attempt to change a database's state to a mode that is incompatible with the current conditions—for example, if you try to change the database to SINGLE_USER mode when other connections exist—the behavior of SQL Server is determined by the TERMINATION option you specify. I'll discuss termination options shortly.

To determine which user access value is set for a database, you can examine the *sys.databases* catalog view, as shown here:

```
SELECT USER_ACCESS_DESC FROM sys.databases
WHERE name = '<name of database>';
```

This query will return one of MULTI_USER, SINGLE_USER, or RESTRICTED_USER.

## OFFLINE | ONLINE | EMERGENCY

You use the OFFLINE, ONLINE, and EMERGENCY options to describe the status of a database. They are mutually exclusive. The default for a database is ONLINE. As with the user access options, when you use *ALTER DATABASE* to put the database in one of these modes, you don't specify a value of ON or OFF—you just use the name of the option. When a database is set to OFFLINE, it is closed and shut down cleanly and marked as offline. The database cannot be modified while the database is offline. A database cannot be put into OFFLINE mode if there are any connections in the database. Whether SQL Server waits for the other connections to terminate or generates an error message is determined by the TERMINATION option specified.

The following code examples show how to set a database's status value to OFFLINE and how to determine the status of a database:

```
ALTER DATABASE AdventureWorks2008 SET OFFLINE;
SELECT state_desc from sys.databases
WHERE name = 'AdventureWorks2008';
```

A database can be explicitly set to EMERGENCY mode, and that option will be discussed in Chapter 11, in conjunction with DBCC commands.

As shown in the preceding query, you can determine the current status of a database by examining the *state_desc* column of the *sys.databases* view. This column can return status values other than OFFLINE, ONLINE, and EMERGENCY, but those values are not directly settable using *ALTER DATABASE*. A database can have the status value RESTORING while it is in the process of being restored from a backup. It can have the status value RECOVERING during a restart of SQL Server. The recovery process is performed on one database at a time, and until SQL Server has finished recovering a database, the database has a status of RECOVERING. If the recovery process cannot be completed for some reason (most likely because one or more of the log files for the database is unavailable or unreadable), SQL Server gives the database the status of RECOVERY_PENDING. Your databases can also be put into RECOVERY_PENDING mode if SQL Server runs out of either log or data space during rollback recovery, or if SQL Server runs out of locks or memory during any part of the startup process. I'll go into more detail about the difference between rollback recovery and startup recovery in Chapter 4.

If all the needed resources, including the log files, are available, but corruption is detected during recovery, the database may be put in the SUSPECT state. You can determine the state value by looking at the *state_desc* column in the *sys.databases* view. A database is completely unavailable if it's in the SUSPECT state, and you will not even see the database listed if you run *sp_helpdb*. However, you can still see the status of a suspect database in the *sys.databases* view. In many cases, you can make a suspect database available for read-only operations by setting its status to EMERGENCY mode. If you really have lost one or more of the log files for a database, EMERGENCY mode allows you to access the data while you copy it to a new location. When you move from RECOVERY_ PENDING to EMERGENCY, SQL Server shuts down the database and then restarts it with a special flag that allows it to skip the recovery process. Skipping recovery can mean you have logically or physically inconsistent data—missing index rows, broken page links, or incorrect metadata pointers. By specifically putting your database in EMERGENCY mode, you are acknowledging that the data might be inconsistent but that you want access to it anyway.

## READ_ONLY | READ_WRITE

These options describe the updatability of a database. They are mutually exclusive. The default for a database is READ_WRITE. As with the user access options, when you use *ALTER DATABASE* to put the database in one of these modes, you don't specify a value of ON or OFF, you just use the name of the option. When the database is in READ_WRITE mode, any user with the appropriate permissions can carry out data modification operations. In READ_ONLY mode, no INSERT, UPDATE, or DELETE operations can be executed. In addition, because no modifications are done when a database is in READ_ONLY mode, automatic recovery is not run on this database when SQL Server is restarted, and no locks need to be acquired during any *SELECT* operations. Shrinking a database in READ_ONLY mode is not possible.

A database cannot be put into READ_ONLY mode if there are any connections to the database. Whether SQL Server waits for the other connections to terminate or generates an error message is determined by the TERMINATION option specified.

The following code shows how to set a database's updatability value to READ_ONLY and how to determine the updatability of a database:

```
ALTER DATABASE AdventureWorks2008 SET READ_ONLY;
SELECT name, is_read_only FROM sys.databases
WHERE name = 'AdventureWorks2008';
```

When READ_ONLY is enabled for database, the *is_read_only* column returns 1; otherwise, for a READ_WRITE database, it returns 0.

## Termination Options

As I just mentioned, several of the state options cannot be set when a database is in use or when it is in use by an unqualified user. You can specify how SQL Server should handle this situation by indicating a termination option in the *ALTER DATABASE* command. You can have SQL Server wait for the situation to change, generate an error message, or terminate the connections of unqualified users. The termination option determines the behavior of SQL Server in the following situations:

- When you attempt to change a database to SINGLE_USER and it has more than one current connection

- When you attempt to change a database to RESTRICTED_USER and unqualified users are currently connected to it

- When you attempt to change a database to OFFLINE and there are current connections to it

- When you attempt to change a database to READ_ONLY and there are current connections to it

The default behavior of SQL Server in any of these situations is to wait indefinitely. The following TERMINATION options change this behavior:

- **ROLLBACK AFTER integer [SECONDS]**   This option causes SQL Server to wait for the specified number of seconds and then break unqualified connections. Incomplete transactions are rolled back. When the transition is to SINGLE_USER mode, all connections are unqualified except the one issuing the *ALTER DATABASE* command. When the transition is to RESTRICTED_USER mode, unqualified connections are those of users who are not members of the *db_owner* fixed database role or the *dbcreator* and *sysadmin* fixed server roles.

- **ROLLBACK IMMEDIATE**   This option breaks unqualified connections immediately. All incomplete transactions are rolled back. Keep in mind that although the connection may be broken immediately, the rollback might take some time to complete. All work done by the transaction must be undone, so for certain operations, such as a batch update of millions of rows or a large index rebuild, you could be in for a long wait. Unqualified connections are the same as those described previously.

- **NO_WAIT**   This option causes SQL Server to check for connections before attempting to change the database state and causes the *ALTER DATABASE* command to fail if certain connections exist. If the database is being set to SINGLE_USER mode, the *ALTER DATABASE* command fails if any other connections exist. If the transition is to RESTRICTED_USER mode, the *ALTER DATABASE* command fails if any unqualified connections exist.

The following command changes the user access option of the *AdventureWorks2008* database to SINGLE_USER and generates an error if any other connections to the *AdventureWorks2008* database exist:

```
ALTER DATABASE AdventureWorks2008 SET SINGLE_USER WITH NO_WAIT;
```

## Cursor Options

The cursor options control the behavior of server-side cursors that were defined using one of the following T-SQL commands for defining and manipulating cursors: *DECLARE, OPEN, FETCH, CLOSE,* and *DEALLOCATE.*

- **CURSOR_CLOSE_ON_COMMIT {ON | OFF}**   When this option is set to ON, any open cursors are closed (in compliance with SQL-92) when a transaction is committed or rolled back. If OFF (the default) is specified, cursors remain open after a transaction is committed. Rolling back a transaction closes any cursors except those defined as *INSENSITIVE* or *STATIC*.

- **CURSOR_DEFAULT {LOCAL | GLOBAL}**   When this option is set to LOCAL and cursors aren't specified as GLOBAL when they are created, the scope of any cursor is local to the batch, stored procedure, or trigger in which it was created. The cursor name is valid only within this scope. The cursor can be referenced by local cursor variables in the batch, stored procedure, or trigger, or by a stored procedure output parameter. When this option is set to GLOBAL and cursors aren't specified as LOCAL when they are created, the scope of the cursor is global to the connection. The cursor name can be referenced in any stored procedure or batch executed by the connection.

## Auto Options

The auto options affect actions that SQL Server might take automatically. All these options are Boolean options, with a value of ON or OFF.

- **AUTO_CLOSE**   When this option is set to ON, the database is closed and shut down cleanly when the last user of the database exits, thereby freeing any resources. All file handles are closed, and all in-memory structures are removed so that the database is not using any memory. When a user tries to use the database again, it reopens. If the database was shut down cleanly, the database isn't initialized (reopened) until a user tries to use the database the next time SQL Server is restarted. The AUTO_CLOSE option is handy for personal SQL Server databases because it allows you to manage database files as normal files. You can move them, copy them to make backups, or even e-mail them to other users. However, you shouldn't use this option for databases accessed by an application that repeatedly makes and breaks connections to SQL Server. The overhead of closing and reopening the database between each connection will hurt performance.

- **AUTO_SHRINK**  When this option is set to ON, all of a database's files are candidates for periodic shrinking. Both data files and log files can be automatically shrunk by SQL Server. The only way to free space in the log files so that they can be shrunk is to back up the transaction log or set the recovery model to SIMPLE. The log files shrink at the point that the log is backed up or truncated. This option is never recommended.

- **AUTO_CREATE_STATISTICS**  When this option is set to ON (the default), the SQL Server Query Optimizer creates statistics on columns referenced in a query's WHERE or ON clause. Adding statistics improves query performance because the SQL Server Query Optimizer can better determine how to evaluate a query.

- **AUTO_UPDATE_STATISTICS**  When this option is set to ON (the default), existing statistics are updated if the data in the tables has changed. SQL Server keeps a counter of the modifications made to a table and uses it to determine when statistics are outdated. When this option is set to OFF, existing statistics are not automatically updated. (They can be updated manually.) Statistics will be discussed in more detail in Chapter 6 and Chapter 8, "The Query Optimizer."

## SQL Options

The SQL options control how various SQL statements are interpreted. They are all Boolean options. The default for all these options is OFF for SQL Server, but many tools, such as the Management Studio, and many programming interfaces, such as ODBC, enable certain session-level options that override the database options and make it appear as if the ON behavior is the default.

- **ANSI_NULL_DEFAULT**  When this option is set to ON, columns comply with the ANSI SQL-92 rules for column nullability. That is, if you don't specifically indicate whether a column in a table allows NULL values, NULLs are allowed. When this option is set to OFF, newly created columns do not allow NULLs if no nullability constraint is specified.

- **ANSI_NULLS**  When this option is set to ON, any comparisons with a NULL value result in UNKNOWN, as specified by the ANSI-92 standard. If this option is set to OFF, comparisons of non-Unicode values to NULL result in a value of TRUE if both values being compared are NULL.

- **ANSI_PADDING**   When this option is set to ON, strings being compared with each other are set to the same length before the comparison takes place. When this option is OFF, no padding takes place.

- **ANSI_WARNINGS**   When this option is set to ON, errors or warnings are issued when conditions such as division by zero or arithmetic overflow occur.

- **ARITHABORT**   When this option is set to ON, a query is terminated when an arithmetic overflow or division-by-zero error is encountered during the execution of a query. When this option is OFF, the query returns NULL as the result of the operation.

- **CONCAT_NULL_YIELDS_NULL**   When this option is set to ON, concatenating two strings results in a NULL string if either of the strings is NULL. When this option is set to OFF, a NULL string is treated as an empty (zero-length) string for the purposes of concatenation.

- **NUMERIC_ROUNDABORT**   When this option is set to ON, an error is generated if an expression will result in loss of precision. When this option is OFF, the result is simply rounded. The setting of ARITHABORT determines the severity of the error. If ARITHABORT is OFF, only a warning is issued and the expression returns a NULL. If ARITHABORT is ON, an error is generated and no result is returned.

- **QUOTED_IDENTIFIER**   When this option is set to ON, identifiers such as table and column names can be delimited by double quotation marks, and literals must then be delimited by single quotation marks. All strings delimited by double quotation marks are interpreted as object identifiers. Quoted identifiers don't have to follow the T-SQL rules for identifiers when QUOTED_IDENTIFIER is ON. They can be keywords and can include characters not normally allowed in T-SQL identifiers, such as spaces and dashes. You can't use double quotation marks to delimit literal string expressions; you must use single quotation marks. If a single quotation mark is part of the literal string, it can be represented by two single quotation marks (''). This option must be set to ON if reserved keywords are used for object names in the database. When it is OFF, identifiers can't be in quotation marks and must follow all T-SQL rules for identifiers.

- **RECURSIVE_TRIGGERS**   When this option is set to ON, triggers can fire recursively, either directly or indirectly. Indirect recursion occurs when a trigger fires and performs an action that causes a trigger on another table to fire, thereby causing an update to occur on the original table, which causes the original trigger to fire again. For example, an application updates table *T1*, which causes trigger *Trig1* to fire. *Trig1* updates table *T2*, which causes trigger *Trig2* to fire. *Trig2* in turn updates table *T1*, which causes *Trig1* to fire again. Direct recursion occurs when a trigger fires and performs an action that causes the same trigger to fire again. For example, an application updates table *T3*, which causes trigger *Trig3* to fire. *Trig3* updates table *T3* again, which causes trigger *Trig3* to fire again. When this option is OFF (the default), triggers can't be fired recursively.

## Database Recovery Options

The database option RECOVERY (FULL, BULK_LOGGED or SIMPLE) determines how much recovery can be done on a SQL Server database. It also controls how much information is logged and how much of the log is available for backups. I'll cover this option in more detail in Chapter 4.

Two other options also apply to work done when a database is recovered. Setting the TORN_PAGE_DETECTION option to ON or OFF is possible in SQL Server 2008, but that particular option will go away in a future version. The recommended alternative is to set the PAGE_VERIFY option to a value of TORN_PAGE_DETECTION or CHECKSUM. (So TORN_PAGE_DETECTION should now be considered a value, rather the name of an option.)

The PAGE_VERIFY options discover damaged database pages caused by disk I/O path errors, which can cause database corruption problems. The I/O errors themselves are generally caused by power failures or disk failures that occur when a page is being written to disk.

- **CHECKSUM**   When the PAGE_VERIFY option is set to CHECKSUM, SQL Server calculates a checksum over the contents of each page and stores the value in the page header when a page is written to disk. When the page is read from disk, a checksum is recomputed and compared with the value stored in the page header. If the values do not match, error message 824 (indicating a checksum failure) is reported.

- **TORN_PAGE_DETECTION**   When the PAGE_VERIFY option is set to TORN_PAGE_DETECTION, it causes a bit to be flipped for each 512-byte sector in a database page (8 KB) whenever the page is written to disk. It allows SQL Server to detect incomplete I/O operations caused by power failures or other system outages. If a bit is in the wrong state when the page is later read by SQL Server, it means that the page was written incorrectly. (A torn page has been detected.) Although SQL Server database pages are 8 KB, disks perform I/O operations using 512-byte sectors. Therefore, 16 sectors are written per database page. A torn page can occur if the system crashes (for example, because of power failure) between the time the operating system writes the first 512-byte sector to disk and the completion of the 8-KB I/O operation. When the page is read from disk, the torn bits stored in the page header are compared with the actual page sector information. Unmatched values indicate that only part of the page was written to disk. In this situation, error message 824 (indicating a torn page error) is reported. Torn pages are typically detected by database recovery if it is truly an incomplete write of a page. However, other I/O path failures can cause a torn page at any time.

- **NONE (No Page Verify Option)**   You can specify that that neither the CHECKSUM nor the TORN_PAGE_DETCTION value will be generated when a page is written, and these values will not be verified when a page is read.

Both checksum and torn page errors generate error message 824, which is written to both the SQL Server error log and the Windows event log. For any page that generates an

824 error when read, SQL Server inserts a row into the system table *suspect_pages* in the *msdb* database. (*SQL Server Books Online* has more information on "Understanding and Managing the suspect _pages Table.")

SQL Server retries any read that fails with a checksum, torn page, or other I/O error four times. If the read is successful in any one of those attempts, a message is written to the error log and the command that triggered the read continues. If the attempts fail, the command fails with error message 824.

You can "fix" the error by restoring the data or potentially rebuilding the index if the failure is limited to index pages. If you encounter a checksum failure, you can run *DBCC CHECKDB* to determine the type of database page or pages affected. You should also determine the root cause of the error and correct the problem as soon as possible to prevent additional or ongoing errors. Finding the root cause requires investigating the hardware, firmware drivers, BIOS, filter drivers (such as virus software), and other I/O path components.

In SQL Server 2008 and SQL Server 2005, the default is CHECKSUM. In SQL Server 2000, TORN_PAGE_ DETECTION was the default, and CHECKSUM was not available. If you upgrade a database from SQL Server 2000, the PAGE_VERIFY value will be NONE or TORN_PAGE_ DETECTION. You should always consider using CHECKSUM. Although TORN_PAGE_DETECTION uses fewer resources, it provides less protection than CHECKSUM. Keep in mind that if you enable CHECKSUM on a database upgraded from SQL Server 2000, that a checksum value is computed only on pages that are modified.

> **Note**  Prior to SQL Server 2008, neither CHECKSUM nor TORN_PAGE_DETECTION was available in the *tempdb* database.

## Other Database Options

Of the other categories of database options, two more will be covered in later chapters. The snapshot isolation options will be discussed in Chapter 10, "Transactions and Concurrency." and the change tracking options were covered in Chapter 2. The others are beyond the scope of this book.

# Database Snapshots

An interesting feature added to the product in SQL Server 2005 Enterprise Edition is database snapshots, which allow you to create a point-in-time, read-only copy of any database. In fact, you can create multiple snapshots of the same source database at different points in time. The actual space needed for each snapshot is typically much less than the space required for the original database because the snapshot stores only pages that have changed, as will be discussed shortly.

Database snapshots allow you to do the following:

- Turn a database mirror into a reporting server. (You cannot read from a database mirror, but you can create a snapshot of the mirror and read from that.)

- Generate reports without blocking or being blocked by production operations.

- Protect against administrative or user errors.

You'll probably think of more ways to use snapshots as you gain experience working with them.

## Creating a Database Snapshot

The mechanics of snapshot creation are straightforward—you simply specify an option for the *CREATE DATABASE* command. There is no graphical interface for creating a database snapshot through Object Explorer, so you must use the T-SQL syntax. When you create a snapshot, you must include each data file from the source database in the *CREATE DATABASE* command, with the original logical name and a new physical name and path. No other properties of the files can be specified, and no log file is used.

Here is the syntax to create a snapshot of the *AdventureWorks2008* database, putting the snapshot files in the SQL Server 2008 default data directory:

```
CREATE DATABASE AdventureWorks_snapshot ON
( NAME = N'AdventureWorks_Data',
  FILENAME =
 N'C:\Program Files\Microsoft SQL Server\MSSQL10.MSSQLSERVER\MSSQL\
   Data\AW_data_snapshot.mdf')
AS SNAPSHOT OF AdventureWorks2008;
```

Each file in the snapshot is created as a sparse file, which is a feature of the NTFS file system. (Don't confuse sparse files with sparse columns available in SQL Server 2008.) Initially, a sparse file contains no user data, and disk space for user data has not been allocated to it. As data is written to the sparse file, NTFS allocates disk space gradually. A sparse file can potentially grow very large. Sparse files grow in 64-KB increments; thus, the size of a sparse file on disk is always a multiple of 64 KB.

The snapshot files contain only the data that has changed from the source. For every file, SQL Server creates a bitmap that is kept in cache, with a bit for each page of the file, indicating whether that page has been copied to the snapshot. Every time a page in the source is updated, SQL Server checks the bitmap for the file to see if the page has already been copied, and if it hasn't, it is copied at that time. This operation is called a *copy-on-write operation*. Figure 3-4 shows a database with a snapshot that contains 10 percent of the data (one page) from the source.

When a process reads from the snapshot, it first accesses the bitmap to see whether the page it wants is in the snapshot file or is still the source. Figure 3-5 shows read operations from the same database as in Figure 3-4. Nine of the pages are accessed from the source database, and one is accessed from the snapshot because it has been updated on the source. When a process reads from a snapshot database, no locks are taken no matter what isolation level

Percent copied 10%

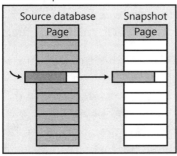

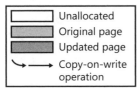

**FIGURE 3-4** A database snapshot that contains one page of data from the source database

Percent copied 10%

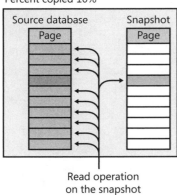

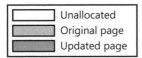

**FIGURE 3-5** Read operations from a database snapshot, reading changed pages from the snapshot and unchanged pages from the source database

you are in. This is true whether the page is read from the sparse file or from the source database. This is one of the big advantages of using database snapshots.

As mentioned earlier, the bitmap is stored in cache, not with the file itself, so it is always readily available. When SQL Server shuts down or the database is closed, the bitmaps are lost and need to be reconstructed at database startup. SQL Server determines whether each page is in the sparse file as it is accessed, and then it records that information in the bitmap for future use.

The snapshot reflects the point in time when the *CREATE DATABASE* command is issued—that is, when the creation operation commences. SQL Server checkpoints the source database and records a synchronization Log Sequence Number (LSN) in the source database's transaction log. As you'll see in Chapter 4, when I talk about the transaction log, the LSN is a way to determine a specific point in time in a database. SQL Server then runs recovery on the source database so that any uncommitted transactions are rolled back in the snapshot. So although the sparse file for the snapshot starts out empty, it might not stay that way for long. If transactions are in progress at the time the snapshot is created, the recovery process has to undo uncommitted transactions before the snapshot database can be usable, so the snapshot contains the original versions of any page in the source that contains modified data.

Snapshots can be created only on NTFS volumes because they are the only volumes that support the sparse file technology. If you try to create a snapshot on a FAT or FAT32 volume, you'll get an error like one of the following:

```
Msg 1823, Level 16, State 2, Line 1
A database snapshot cannot be created because it failed to start.
```

```
Msg 5119, Level 16, State 1, Line 1
Cannot make the file "E:\AW_snapshot.MDF" a sparse file. Make sure the file system supports
sparse files.
```

The first error is basically the generic failure message, and the second message provides more details about why the operation failed.

## Space Used by Database Snapshots

You can find out the number of bytes that each sparse file of the snapshot is currently using on disk by looking at the Dynamic Management Function *sys.dm_io_virtual_file_stats*, which returns the current number of bytes in a file in the *size_on_disk_bytes* column. This function takes *database_id* and *file_id* as parameters. The database ID of the snapshot database and the file IDs of each of its sparse files are displayed in the *sys.master_files* catalog view. You can also view the size in Windows Explorer by right-clicking the file name and looking at the properties, as shown in Figure 3-6. The Size value is the maximum size, and the size on disk should be the same value that you see using *sys.dm_io_virtual_file_stats*. The maximum size should be about the same size the source database was when the snapshot was created.

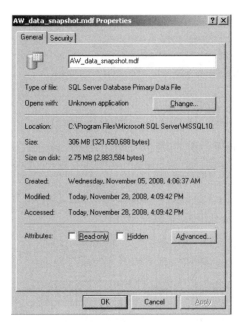

**FIGURE 3-6** The snapshot file's Properties dialog box in Windows Explorer showing the current size of the sparse file as the size on disk

Because it is possible to have multiple snapshots for the same database, you need to make sure you have enough disk space available. The snapshots start out relatively small, but as the source database is updated, each snapshot grows. Allocations to sparse files are made in fragments called *regions,* in units of 64 KB. When a region is allocated, all the pages are zeroed out except the one page that has changed. There is then space for seven more changed pages in the same region, and a new region is not allocated until those seven pages are used.

It is possible to overcommit your storage. This means that under normal circumstances, you can have many times more snapshots than you have physical storage for, but if the snapshots grow, the physical volume might run out of space. (Note that this can happen when running online *DBCC CHECKDB,* and related commands, which use a hidden snapshot during processing. You have no control of the placement of the hidden snapshot that the commands use—they're placed on the same volume that the files of the parent database reside on. If this happens, the DBCC uses the source database and acquires table locks. You can read lots more details of the internals of the DBCC commands in Chapter 11.) Once the physical volume runs out of space, the write operations to the source cannot copy the Before image of the page to the sparse file. The snapshots that cannot write their pages out are marked as suspect and are unusable, but the source database continues operating normally. There is no way to "fix" a suspect snapshot; you must drop the snapshot database.

## Managing Your Snapshots

If any snapshots exist on a source database, the source database cannot be dropped, detached, or restored. In addition, you can basically replace the source database with one of its snapshots by reverting the source database to the way it was when a snapshot was made. You do this by using the *RESTORE* command:

```
RESTORE DATABASE AdventureWorks2008
FROM DATABASE_SNAPSHOT = 'AdventureWorks_snapshot';
```

During the revert operation, both the snapshot and the source database are unavailable and are marked as "In restore." If an error occurs during the revert operation, the operation tries to finish reverting when the database starts again. You cannot revert to a snapshot if multiple snapshots exist, so you should first drop all snapshots except the one you want to revert to. Dropping a snapshot is like using any other *DROP DATABASE* operation. When the snapshot is deleted, all the NTFS sparse files are also deleted.

Keep in mind these additional considerations regarding database snapshots:

■ Snapshots cannot be created for the *model, master,* or *tempdb* database. (Internally, snapshots can be created to run the online DBCC checks on the *master* database, but they cannot be created explicitly.)

■ A snapshot inherits the security constraints of its source database, and because it is read-only, you cannot change the permissions.

■ If you drop a user from the source database, the user is still in the snapshot.

■ Snapshots cannot be backed up or restored, but backing up the source database works normally; it is unaffected by database snapshots.

■ Snapshots cannot be attached or detached.

■ Full-text indexing is not supported on database snapshots, and full-text catalogs are not propagated from the source database.

# The *tempdb* Database

In some ways, the *tempdb* database is just like any other database, but it has some unique behaviors. Not all of them are relevant to the topic of this chapter, so I will provide some references to other chapters where you can find additional information.

As mentioned previously, the biggest difference between *tempdb* and all the other databases in your SQL Server instance is that *tempdb* is re-created—not recovered—every time SQL Server is restarted. You can think of *tempdb* as a workspace for temporary user objects and internal objects explicitly created by SQL Server itself.

Every time *tempdb* is re-created, it inherits most database options from the model database. However, the recovery model is not copied because *tempdb* always uses simple recovery, which will be discussed in detail in Chapter 4. Certain database options cannot be set for *tempdb*, such as OFFLINE and READONLY. You also cannot drop the *tempdb* database.

In the SIMPLE recovery model, the *tempdb* database's log is constantly being truncated, and it can never be backed up. No recovery information is needed because every time SQL Server is started, *tempdb* is completely re-created; any previous user-created temporary objects (that is, all your tables and data) disappear.

Logging for *tempdb* is also different than for other databases. (Normal logging will be discussed in Chapter 4.) Many people assume that there is no logging in *tempdb*, but this is not true. Operations within *tempdb* are logged so that transactions on temporary objects can be rolled back, but the records in the log contain only enough information to roll back a transaction, not to recover (or redo) it.

As I mentioned previously, recovery is run on a database as one of the first steps in creating a snapshot. We can't recover *tempdb*, so we cannot create a snapshot of it, and this means we can't run *DBCC CHECKDB* using a snapshot (or, in fact, most of the DBCC validation commands). Another difference with running DBCC in *tempdb* is that SQL Server skips all allocation and catalog checks. Running *DBCC CHECKDB* (or *CHECKTABLE*) in *tempdb* acquires a Shared Table lock on each table as it is checked. (Locking will be discussed in Chapter 10.)

## Objects in *tempdb*

Three types of objects are stored in *tempdb*: user objects, internal objects, and the version store, used primarily for snapshot isolation.

### User Objects

All users have the privileges to create and use local and global temporary tables that reside in *tempdb*. (Local and global table names have the # or ## prefix, respectively. However, by default, users don't have the privileges to use *tempdb* and then create a table there, unless the table name is prefaced with # or ##.) But you can easily grant the privileges in an autostart procedure that runs each time SQL Server is restarted.

Other user objects that need space in *tempdb* include table variables and table-valued functions. The user objects that are created in *tempdb* are in many ways treated just like user objects in any other database. Space must be allocated for them when they are populated, and the metadata needs to be managed. You can see user objects by examining the system catalog views, such as *sys.objects*, and information in the *sys.partitions* and *sys.allocation_units* views will allow you to see how much space is taken up by user objects. I'll discuss these views in Chapters 5 and 7.

### Internal Objects

Internal objects in *tempdb* are not visible using the normal tools, but they still take up space from the database. They are not listed in the catalog views because their metadata is stored only in memory. The three basic types of internal objects are work tables, work files, and sort units.

Work tables are created by SQL Server during the following operations:

- Spooling, to hold intermediate results during a large query

- Running *DBCC CHECKDB* or *DBCC CHECKTABLE*

- Working with XML or *varchar(MAX)* variables

- Processing SQL Service Broker objects

- Working with static or keyset cursors

Work files are used when SQL Server is processing a query that uses a hash operator, either for joining or aggregating data.

Sort units are created when a sort operation takes place, and this occurs in many situations in addition to a query containing an ORDER BY clause. SQL Server uses sorting to build an index, and it might use sorting to process queries involving grouping. Certain types of joins might require that SQL Server sort the data before performing the join. Sort units are created in *tempdb* to hold the data as it is being sorted. SQL Server can also create sort units in user databases in addition to *tempdb*, in particular when creating indexes. As you'll see in Chapter 6, when you create an index, you have the option to do the sort in the current user database or in *tempdb*.

## Version Store

The version store supports technology for row-level versioning of data. Older versions of updated rows are kept in *tempdb* in the following situations:

- When an AFTER trigger is fired

- When a Data Modification Language (DML) command is executed in a database that allows snapshot transactions

- When multiple active result sets (MARS) are invoked from a client application

- During online index builds or rebuilds when there is concurrent DML on the index

Versioning and snapshot transactions are discussed in detail in Chapter 10.

## Optimizations in *tempdb*

Because *tempdb* is used for many internal operations in SQL Server 2008 than in previous versions, you have to take care in monitoring and managing it. The next section presents some best practices and monitoring suggestions. In this section, I tell you about some of the internal optimizations in SQL Server that allow *tempdb* to manage objects much more efficiently.

## Logging Optimizations

As you know, every operation that affects your user database in any way is logged. In *tempdb*, however, this is not entirely true. For example, with logging update operations, only the original data (the "before" image) is logged, not the new values (the after image). In addition, the commit operations and committed log records are not flushed to disk synchronously in *tempdb*, as they are in other databases.

## Allocation and Caching Optimizations

Many of the allocation optimizations are used in all databases, not just *tempdb*. However, *tempdb* is most likely the database in which the greatest number of new objects are created and dropped during production operations, so the impact on *tempdb* is greater than on user databases. In SQL Server 2008, allocation pages are accessed very efficiently to determine where free extents are available; you should see far less contention on the allocation pages than in previous versions. SQL Server 2008 also has a very efficient search algorithm for finding an available single page from mixed extents. When a database has multiple files, SQL Server 2008 has a very efficient proportional fill algorithm that allocates space to multiple data files, proportional to the amount of free space available in each file.

Another optimization specific to *tempdb* prevents you from having to allocate any new space for some objects. If a work table is dropped, one IAM page and one extent are saved (for a total of nine pages), so there is no need to deallocate and then reallocate the space if the same work table needs to be created again. This dropped work table cache is not very big and has room for only 64 objects. If a work table is truncated internally and the query plan that uses that worktable is still in the plan cache, again the first IAM page and the first extent are saved. For these truncated tables, there is no specific limitation on the number of objects that can be cached; it depends only on the available memory space.

User objects in *tempdb* can also have some of their space cached if they are dropped. For a small table of less than 8 MB, dropping a user object in *tempdb* causes one IAM page and one extent to be saved. However, if the table has had any additional DDL performed, such as creating indexes or constraints, or if the table was created using dynamic SQL, no caching is done.

For a large table, the entire drop is performed as a deferred operation. Deferred drop operations are in fact used in every database as a way to improve overall throughput because a thread does not need to wait for the drop to complete before proceeding with its next task. Like the other allocation optimizations that are available in all databases, the deferred drop probably provides the most benefit in *tempdb*, which is where tables are most likely to be dropped during production operations. A background thread eventually cleans up the space allocated for dropped tables, but until then, the allocated space remains. You can detect this space by looking at the *sys.allocation_units* system view for rows with a *type* value of 0, which indicates a dropped object; you will also see that the column called *container_id* is 0, which indicates that the allocated space does not really belong to any object. I'll look at *sys.allocation_units* and the other system views that keep track of space usage in Chapter 5.

## Best Practices

By default, your *tempdb* database is created on only one data file. You will probably find that multiple files give you better I/O performance and less contention on the global allocation structures (the GAM, SGAM, and PFS pages). An initial recommendation is that you have one file per CPU, but your own testing based on your data and usage patterns might indicate more or less than that. For the greatest efficiency with the proportional fill algorithm, the files should be the same size. The downside of multiple files is that every object will have multiple IAM pages and there will be more switching costs as objects are accessed. It will also take more effort just to manage the files. No matter how many files you have, they should be on the fastest disks you can afford. One log file should be sufficient, and that should also be on a fast disk.

To determine the optimum size of your *tempdb*, you must test your own applications with your data volumes, but knowing when and how *tempdb* is used can help you make preliminary estimates. Keep in mind that there is only one *tempdb* for each SQL Server instance, so one badly behaving application can affect all other users in all other applications. In Chapter 10, I'll explain how to determine the size of the version store. All these factors affect the space needed for your *tempdb*. Finally, in Chapter 11, I'll look at how the DBCC consistency checking commands use *tempdb* and how to determine the *tempdb* space requirements.

Database options for *tempdb* should rarely be changed, and some options are not applicable to *tempdb*. In particular, the autoshrink option is ignored in *tempdb*. In any case, shrinking *tempdb* is not recommended unless your workload patterns have changed significantly. If you do need to shrink your *tempdb*, you're probably better off shrinking each file individually. Keep in mind that the files might not be able to shrink if any internal objects or version store pages need to be moved. The best way to shrink *tempdb* is to ALTER the database, change the files' sizes, and then stop and restart SQL Server so *tempdb* is rebuilt to the desired size. You should allow your *tempdb* files to autogrow only as a last resort and only to prevent errors due to running out of room. You should not rely on autogrow to manage the size of your *tempdb* files. Autogrow causes a delay in processing when you can probably least afford it, although the impact is somewhat less if you use instant file initialization. You should determine the size of *tempdb* through testing and planning so that *tempdb* can start with as much space as it needs and won't have to grow while your applications are running.

Here are some tips for making optimum use of your *tempdb*. Later chapters will elaborate on why these suggestions are considered best practices:

- Take advantage of *tempdb* object caching.
- Keep your transactions short, especially those that use snapshot isolation, MARS, or triggers.

- If you expect a lot of allocation page contention, force a query plan that uses *tempdb* less.

- Avoid page allocation and deallocation by keeping columns that are to be updated at a fixed size rather than a variable size (which can implement the *UPDATE* as a *DELETE* followed by an *INSERT*).

- Do not mix long and short transactions from different databases (in the same instance) if versioning is being used.

## *tempdb* Space Monitoring

Quite a few tools, stored procedures, and system views report on object space usage, as discussed in Chapters 5 and 7. However, one set of system views reports information only for *tempdb*. The simplest view is *sys.dm_db_file_space_usage*, which returns one row for each data file in *tempdb*. It returns the following columns:

- *database_id* (even though the *DBID* 2 is the only one used)

- *file_id*

- *unallocated_extent_page_count*

- *version_store_reserved_page_count*

- *user_object_reserved_page_count*

- *internal_object_reserved_page_count*

- *mixed_extent_page_count*

These columns can show you how the space in *tempdb* is being used for the three types of storage: user objects, internals objects, and version store.

Two other system views are similar to each other:

- **sys.dm_db_task_space_usage**   This view returns one row for each active task and shows the space allocated and deallocated by the task for user objects and internal objects. If no tasks are being run by a session, this view still gives you one row for the session, with all the space values showing 0. No version store information is reported because that space is not associated with any particular task or session. Every running task starts with zeros for all the space allocation and deallocation values.

- **sys.dm_db_session_space_usage**   This view returns one row for each session, with the cumulative values for space allocated and deallocated by the session for user objects and internal objects, for all tasks that have been completed. In general, the space allocated values should be the same as the space deallocated values, but if there are deferred drop operations, allocated values will be greater than the deallocated values. Keep in mind that this information is not available to all users; a special permission called *VIEW SERVER STATE* is needed to select from this view.

# Database Security

Security is a huge topic that affects almost every action of every SQL Server user, including administrators and developers, and it deserves an entire book of its own. However, some areas of the SQL Server security framework are crucial to understanding how to work with a database or with any objects in a SQL Server database, so I can't leave the topic completely untouched in this book.

SQL Server manages a hierarchical collection of entities. The most prominent of these entities are the server and databases in the server. Underneath the database level are objects. Each of these entities below the server level is owned by individuals or groups of individuals. The SQL Server security framework controls access to the entities within a SQL Server instance. Like any resource manager, the SQL Server security model has two parts: authentication and authorization.

*Authentication* is the process by which the SQL Server validates and establishes the identity of an individual who wants to access a resource. *Authorization* is the process by which SQL Server decides whether a given identity is allowed to access a resource.

In this section, I'll discuss the basic issues of database access and then describe the metadata where information on database access is stored. I'll also tell you about the concept of schemas and describe how they are used to access objects.

The following two terms now form the foundation for describing security control in SQL Server 2008:

- **Securable**   A *securable* is an entity on which permissions can be granted. Securables include databases, schemas, and objects.

- **Principal**   A *principal* is an entity that can access securables. A *primary principal* represents a single user (such as a SQL Server login or a Windows login); a *secondary principal* represents multiple users (such as a role or a Windows group).

## Database Access

Authentication is performed at two different levels in SQL Server. First, anyone who wants to access any SQL Server resource must be authenticated at the server level. SQL Server 2008 security provides two basic methods for authenticating logins: Windows Authentication and SQL Server Authentication. In Windows Authentication, SQL Server login security is integrated directly with Windows security, allowing the operating system to authenticate SQL Server users. In SQL Server Authentication, an administrator creates SQL Server login accounts within SQL Server, and any user connecting to SQL Server must supply a valid SQL Server login name and password.

Windows Authentication uses *trusted connections,* which rely on the impersonation feature of Windows. Through impersonation, SQL Server can take on the security context of the Windows user account initiating the connection and test whether the SID has a valid privilege level. Windows impersonation and trusted connections are supported by any of the available network libraries when connecting to SQL Server.

Under Windows Server 2003 and Windows Server 2008, SQL Server can use Kerberos to support mutual authentication between the client and the server, as well as to pass a client's security credentials between computers so that work on a remote server can proceed using the credentials of the impersonated client. With Windows Server 2003 and Windows Server 2008, SQL Server uses Kerberos and delegation to support Windows authentication as well as SQL Server authentication.

The authentication method (or methods) used by SQL Server is determined by its security mode. SQL Server can run in one of two security modes: Windows Authentication mode (which uses only Windows authentication) and Mixed mode (which can use either Windows authentication or SQL Server authentication, as chosen by the client). When you connect to an instance of SQL Server configured for Windows Authentication mode, you cannot supply a SQL Server login name, and your Windows user name determines your level of access to SQL Server.

One advantage of Windows authentication has always been that it allows SQL Server to take advantage of the security features of the operating system, such as password encryption, password aging, and minimum and maximum length restrictions on passwords. When running on Windows Server 2003 or Windows Server 2008, SQL Server authentication can also take advantage of Windows password policies. Take a look at the *ALTER LOGIN* command in *SQL Server Books Online* for the full details. Also note that if you choose Windows Authentication during setup, the default SQL Server *sa* login is disabled. If you switch to Mixed mode after setup, you can enable the *sa* login using the *ALTER LOGIN* command. You can change the authentication mode in Management Studio by right-clicking on the server name, choosing Properties, and then selecting the Security page. Under Server authentication, select the new server authentication mode, as shown in Figure 3-7.

Under Mixed mode, Windows-based clients can connect using Windows authentication, and connections that don't come from Windows clients or that come across the Internet can connect using SQL Server authentication. In addition, when a user connects to an instance of SQL Server that has been installed in Mixed mode, the connection can always supply a SQL Server login name explicitly. This allows a connection to be made using a login name distinct from the user name in Windows.

All login names, whether from Windows or SQL Server authentication, can be seen in the *sys.server_principals* catalog view, which also contains a SID for each server principal. If the principal is a Windows login, the SID is the same one that Windows uses to validate the user's access to Windows resources. The view contains rows for server roles, Windows groups, and logins mapped to certificates and asymmetric keys, but I will not discuss those principals here.

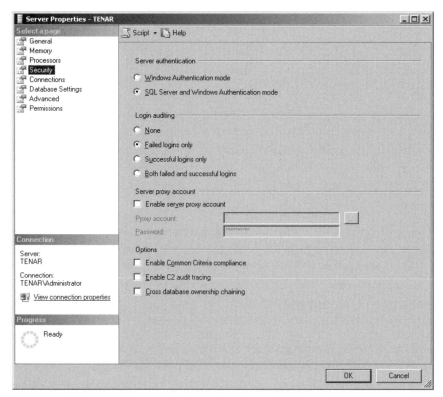

**FIGURE 3-7** Choosing an authentication mode for your SQL Server instance in the Server Properties dialog box

## Managing Database Security

Login names can be the owners of databases, as seen in the *sys.databases* view, which has a column for the SID of the login that owns the database. Databases are the only resource owned by login names. As you'll see, all objects within a database are owned by database principals.

The SID used by a principal determines which databases that principal has access to. Each database has a *sys.database_principals* catalog view, which you can think of as a mapping table that maps login names to users in that particular database. Although a login name and a user name can have the same value, they are separate things. The following query shows the mapping of users in the *AdventureWorks2008* database to login names, and it also shows the default schema (which I will discuss shortly) for each database user:

```
SELECT s.name as [Login Name], d.name as [User Name],
    default_schema_name as [Default Schema]
  FROM sys.server_principals s
    JOIN sys.database_principals d
  ON d.sid = s.sid;
```

In my *AdventureWorks2008* database, these are the results I receive:

```
Login Name User Name  Default Schema
---------- ----------  --------------
sa         dbo         dbo
sue        sue         sue
```

Note that the login *sue* has the same value for the user name in this database. There is no guarantee that other databases that *sue* has access to will use the same user name. The login name *sa* has the user name *dbo*. This name is a special login that is used by the *sa* login, by all logins in the *sysadmin* role, and by whatever login is listed in *sys.databases* as the owner of the database. Within a database, it is users, not logins, who own objects, and users, not logins, to whom permissions are granted.

The preceding results also indicate the default schema for each user in my *AdventureWorks2008* database. In this case, the default schema is the same as the user name, but that doesn't have to be the case, as you'll see in the next section.

## Databases vs. Schemas

In the ANSI SQL-92 standard, a *schema* is defined as a collection of database objects that are owned by a single user and form a single namespace. A *namespace* is a set of objects that cannot have duplicate names. For example, two tables can have the same name only if they are in separate schemas, so no two tables in the same schema can have the same name. You can think of a schema as a container of objects. (In the context of database tools, a schema also refers to the catalog information that describes the objects in a schema or database. In SQL Server Analysis Services, a schema is a description of multidimensional objects such as cubes and dimensions.)

## Principals and Schemas

Prior to SQL Server 2005, there was a *CREATE SCHEMA* command, but it effectively did nothing because there was an implicit relationship between users and schemas that could be changed or removed. In fact, the relationship was so close that many users of these earlier versions of SQL Server were unaware that users and schemas are different things. Every user was the owner of a schema that has the same name as the user. If you created a user *sue*, for example, SQL Server 2000 created a schema called *sue*, which was *sue*'s default schema.

In SQL Server 2005 and SQL Server 2008, users and schemas are two separate things. To understand the difference between users and schemas, think of the following: Permissions are granted to users, but objects are placed in schemas.

The command *GRANT CREATE TABLE TO sue* refers to the user *sue*. Let's say *sue* then creates a table, as follows:

```
CREATE TABLE mytable (col1 varchar(20));
```

This table is placed in *sue*'s default schema, which may be the schema *sue*. If another user wants to retrieve data from this table, he can issue this statement:

```
SELECT col1 FROM sue.mytable;
```

In this statement, *sue* refers to the schema that contains the table.

Schemas can be owned by either primary or secondary principals. Although every object in a SQL Server 2008 database is owned by a user, you never reference an object by its owner; you reference it by the schema in which it is contained. In most cases, the owner of the schema is the same as the owner of all objects within the schema. The metadata view *sys.objects* contains a column called *principal_id*, which contains the *user_id* of an object's owner if it is not the same as the owner of the object's schema. In addition, a user is never added to a schema; schemas contain objects, not users. For backward compatibility, if you execute the *sp_adduser* or *sp_grantdbaccess* procedure to add a user to a database, SQL Server 2008 creates both a user and a schema of the same name, and it makes the schema the default schema for the new user. However, you should get used to using the new *DDL CREATE USER* and *CREATE SCHEMA* commands because *sp_adduser* and *sp_grantdbaccess* have been deprecated. When you create a user, you can specify a default schema if you want, but the default for the default schema is the *dbo* schema.

## Default Schemas

When you create a new database in SQL Server 2008, several schemas are included in it. These include *dbo*, *INFORMATION_SCHEMA*, and *guest*. In addition, every database has a schema called *sys*, which provides a way to access all the system tables and views. Finally, every fixed database role except *public* has a schema of the same name in SQL Server 2008.

Users can be assigned a default schema that might or might not exist when the user is created. A user can have at most one default schema at any time. As mentioned earlier, if no default schema is specified for a user, the default schema for the user is *dbo*. A user's default schema is used for name resolution during object creation or object reference. This can be both good news and bad news for backward compatibility. The good news is that if you've upgraded a database from SQL Server 2000, which has many objects in the *dbo* schema, your code can continue to reference those objects without having to specify the schema explicitly. The bad news is that for object creation, SQL Server tries to create the object in the *dbo* schema rather than in a schema owned by the user creating the table. The user might not have permission to create objects in the *dbo* schema, even if that is the user's default schema. To avoid confusion, in SQL Server 2008 you should always specify the schema name for all object access as well as object management.

> **Note** When a login in the *sysadmin* role creates an object with a single part name, the schema is always *dbo*. However, a *sysadmin* can explicitly specify an alternate schema in which to create an object.

To create an object in a schema, you must satisfy the following conditions:

- The schema must exist.

- The user creating the object must have permission to create the object (through *CREATE TABLE, CREATE VIEW, CREATE PROCEDURE,* and so on), either directly or through role membership.

- The user creating the object must be the owner of the schema or a member of the role that owns the schema, or the user must have ALTER rights on the schema or have the ALTER ANY SCHEMA permission in the database.

# Moving or Copying a Database

You might need to move a database before performing maintenance on your system, after a hardware failure, or when you replace your hardware with a newer, faster system. Copying a database is a common way to create a secondary development or testing environment. You can move or copy a database by using a technique called *detach and attach* or by backing up the database and restoring it in the new location.

## Detaching and Reattaching a Database

You can detach a database from a server by using a simple stored procedure. Detaching a database requires that no one is using the database. If you find existing connections that you can't terminate, you can use the *ALTER DATABASE* command and set the database to SINGLE_USER mode using one of the termination options that breaks existing connections. Detaching a database ensures that no incomplete transactions are in the database and that there are no dirty pages for this database in memory. If these conditions cannot be met, the detach operation fails. Once the database is detached, the entry for it is removed from the *sys.databases* catalog view and from the underlying system tables.

Here is the command to detach a database:

```
EXEC sp_detach_db <name of database>;
```

Once the database has been detached, from the perspective of SQL Server, it's as if you had dropped the database. No metadata for the database remains within the SQL Server instance, and the only time there might be a trace of it is when your *msdb* database contains backup and restore history for the database that has not yet been deleted. But the history of when backups and restores were done would provide no information about the structure or content of the database. If you are planning to reattach the database later, it's a good idea to record the properties of all the files that were part of the database.

**Note** The *DROP DATABASE* command also removes all traces of the database from your instance, but dropping a database is more severe than detaching. SQL Server makes sure that no one is connected to the database before dropping it, but it doesn't check for dirty pages or open transactions. Dropping a database also removes the physical files from the operating system, so unless you have a backup, the database is really gone.

To attach a database, you can use the *CREATE DATABASE* command with the FOR ATTACH option. (There is a stored procedure, *sp_attach_db*, but it is deprecated and not recommended in SQL Server 2008.) The *CREATE DATABASE* command gives you control over all the files and their placement and is not limited to only 16 files like *sp_attach_db* is. *CREATE DATABASE* has no such limit—in fact, you can specify up to 32,767 files and 32,767 file groups for each database. The syntax summary for the *CREATE DATABASE* command showing the attach options is shown here:

```
CREATE DATABASE database_name
    ON <filespec> [ ,...n ]
    FOR { ATTACH
        | ATTACH_REBUILD_LOG }
```

Note that only the primary file is required to have a <filespec> entry because the primary file contains information about the location of all the other files. If you'll be attaching existing files with a different path than when the database was first created or last attached, you must have additional <filespec> entries. In any event, all the data files for the database must be available, whether or not they are specified in the *CREATE DATABASE* command. If there are multiple log files, they must all be available.

However, if a read/write database has a single log file that is currently unavailable and if the database was shut down with no users or open transactions before the attach operation, FOR ATTACH rebuilds the log file and updates information about the log in the primary file. If the database is read-only, the primary file cannot be updated, so the log cannot be rebuilt. Therefore, when you attach a read-only database, you must specify the log file or files in the FOR ATTACH clause.

Alternatively, you can use the FOR ATTACH_REBUILD_LOG option, which specifies that the database will be created by attaching an existing set of operating system files. This option is limited to read/write databases. If one or more transaction log files are missing, the log is rebuilt. There must be a <filespec> entry specifying the primary file. In addition, if the log files are available, SQL Server uses those files instead of rebuilding the log files, so the FOR ATTACH_REBUILD_LOG will function as if you used FOR ATTACH.

If your transaction log is rebuilt by attaching the database, using the FOR ATTACH_REBUILD_LOG breaks the log backup chain. You should consider making a full backup after performing this operation.

You typically use FOR ATTACH_REBUILD_LOG when you copy a read/write database with a large log to another server where the copy will be used mostly or exclusively for read operations and therefore require less log space than the original database.

Although the documentation says that you should use *CREATE DATABASE FOR ATTACH* only on databases that were previously detached using *sp_detach_db,* sometimes following this recommendation isn't necessary. If you shut down the SQL Server instance, the files are closed, just as if you had detached the database. However, you are not guaranteed that all dirty pages from the database were written to disk before the shutdown. This should not cause a problem when you attach such a database if the log file is available. The log file has a record of all completed transactions, and a full recovery is performed when the database is attached to make sure the database is consistent. One benefit of using the *sp_detach_db* procedure is that SQL Server records the fact that the database was shut down cleanly, and the log file does not have to be available to attach the database. SQL Server builds a new log file for you. This can be a quick way to shrink a log file that has become much larger than you would like, because the new log file that *sp_attach_db* creates for you would be the minimum size—less than 1 MB.

## Backing Up and Restoring a Database

You can also use backup and restore to move a database to a new location, as an alternative to detach and attach. One benefit of this method is that the database does not need to come offline at all because backup is a completely online operation. Because this book is not a how-to book for database administrators, you should refer to the bibliography in the companion content for several excellent book recommendations about the mechanics of backing up and restoring a database and to learn best practices for setting up a backup-and-restore plan for your organization. Nevertheless, some issues relating to backup-and-restore processes can help you understand why one backup plan might be better suited to your needs than another, so I will discuss backup and restore briefly in Chapter 4. Most of these issues involve the role of the transaction log in backup-and-restore operations.

## Moving System Databases

You might need to move system databases as part of a planned relocation or scheduled maintenance operation. If you move a system database and later rebuild the *master* database, you must move the system database again because the rebuild operation installs all system databases to their default location. The steps for moving *tempdb, model,* and *msdb* are slightly different than for moving the *master* database.

> **Note**  In SQL Server 2008, the *mssqlsystemresource* database cannot be moved. If you move the files for this database, you will not be able to restart your SQL Server service. This is incorrectly documented in the RTM edition of *SQL Server 2008 Books Online,* which indicates that the *mssqlsystemresource* database can be moved, but this misinformation may be corrected in a later refresh.

Here are the steps for moving an undamaged system database (that is, not the *master* database):

1. For each file in the database to be moved, use the *ALTER DATABASE* command with the MODIFY FILE option to specify the new physical location.

2. Stop the SQL Server instance.

3. Physically move the files.

4. Restart the SQL Server instance.

5. Verify the change by running the following query:

```
SELECT name, physical_name AS CurrentLocation, state_desc
FROM sys.master_files
WHERE database_id = DB_ID(N'<database_name>');
```

If the system database needs to be moved because of a hardware failure, the solution is a bit more problematical because you might not have access to the server to run the *ALTER DATABASE* command. Here are the steps to move a damaged system database (other than the *master* database or the resource database):

1. Stop the instance of SQL Server if it has been started.

2. Start the instance of SQL Server in *master-only* recovery mode (by specifying traceflag 3608) by entering one of the following commands at the command prompt:

```
-- If the instance is the default instance:
NET START MSSQLSERVER /f /T3608

-- For a named instance:
NET START MSSQL$instancename /f /T3608
```

3. For each file in the database to be moved, use the *ALTER DATABASE* command with the MODIFY FILE option to specify the new physical location. You can use either Management Studio or the SQLCMD utility.

4. Exit Management Studio or the SQLCMD utility.

5. Stop the instance of SQL Server.

6. Physically move the file or files to the new location.

7. Restart the instance of SQL Server without traceflag 3608. For example, run *NET START MSSQLSERVER*.

8. Verify the change by running the following query:

```
SELECT name, physical_name AS CurrentLocation, state_desc
FROM sys.master_files
WHERE database_id = DB_ID(N'<database_name>');
```

## Moving the *master* Database

Full details on moving the *master* database can be found in *SQL Server Books Online,* but I will summarize the steps here. The biggest difference between moving this database and moving other system databases is that you must go through the SQL Server Configuration Manager.

To move the *master* database, follow these steps.

1. Open the SQL Server Configuration Manager. Right-click the desired instance of SQL Server, choose Properties, and then click the Advanced tab.

2. Edit the Startup Parameters values to point to the new directory location for the *master* database data and log files. If you want, you can also move the SQL Server error log files. The parameter value for the data file must follow the *–d* parameter, the value for the log file must follow the *–l* parameter, and the value for the error log must follow the *–e* parameter, as shown here:

```
-dE:\SQLData\master.mdf;
-lE:\SQLData\mastlog.ldf;
-eE:\ SQLData\LOG\ERRORLOG
```

3. Stop the instance of SQL Server and physically move the files for to the new location.

4. Restart the instance of SQL Server.

5. Verify the file change for the *master* database by running the following query:

```
SELECT name, physical_name AS CurrentLocation, state_desc
FROM sys.master_files
WHERE database_id = DB_ID('master');
```

# Compatibility Levels

Each new version of SQL Server includes a large number of new features, many of which require new keywords and also change certain behaviors that existed in earlier versions. To provide maximum backward compatibility, Microsoft allows you to set the compatibility level of a database running on a SQL Server 2008 instance to one of the following modes: 100, 90, or 80. All newly created databases in SQL Server 2008 have a compatibility level of 100 unless you change the level for the *model* database. A database that has been upgraded or attached from an older version has its compatibility level set to the version from which the database was upgraded.

All the examples and explanations in this book assume that you're using a database in 100 compatibility mode, unless otherwise noted. If you find that your SQL statements behave differently than the ones in the book, you should first verify that your database is in 100 compatibility mode by executing this command:

```
SELECT compatibility_level FROM sys.databases
WHERE name =  '<database name>';
```

To change to a different compatibility level, use the *ALTER DATABASE* command:

```
ALTER DATABASE <database name>
SET COMPATIBILITY_LEVEL =  <compatibility-level>;
```

> **Note**  The compatibility-level options are intended to provide a transition period while you're upgrading a database or an application to SQL Server 2008. I strongly suggest that you try to change your applications so that compatibility options are not needed. Microsoft doesn't guarantee that these options will continue to work in future versions of SQL Server.

Not all changes in behavior from older versions of SQL Server can be duplicated by changing the compatibility level. For the most part, the differences have to do with whether new reserved keywords and new syntax are recognized, and they do not affect how your queries are processed internally. For example, if you change to compatibility level 80, you don't make the system tables viewable or do away with schemas. But because the word *MERGE* is a new reserved keyword in SQL Server 2008 (compatibility level 100), by setting your compatibility level to 80 or 90, you can create a table called *MERGE* without using any special delimiters—or a table that you already have in a SQL Server 2005 database continues to be accessible if the database stays in the 90 compatibility level.

For a complete list of the behavioral differences between the compatibility levels and the new reserved keywords, see the documentation for *ALTER DATABASE Compatibility Level* in *SQL Server Books Online.*

## Summary

A database is a collection of objects such as tables, views, and stored procedures. Although a typical SQL Server installation has many databases, it always includes the following three: *master*, *model*, and *tempdb*. An installation usually also includes *msdb*, but that database can be removed. (To remove *msdb* requires a special traceflag and is rarely recommended.) A SQL Server instance also includes the *mssqlsystemresource* database that cannot be seen using the normal tools. Every database has its own transaction log; integrity constraints among objects keep a database logically consistent.

Databases are stored in operating system files in a one-to-many relationship. Each database has at least one file for data and one file for the transaction log. You can increase and decrease the size of databases and their files easily, either manually or automatically.

# Chapter 4
# Logging and Recovery

*Kalen Delaney*

In Chapter 3, "Databases and Database Files," I told you about the data files that are created to hold information in a Microsoft SQL Server database. Every database also has at least one file that stores its transaction log. I referred to SQL Server transaction logs and log files in Chapter 3, but I did not really go into detail about how a log file is different from a data file and exactly how SQL Server uses its log files. In this chapter, I tell you about the structure of SQL Server log files and how they're managed when transaction information is logged. I explain how SQL Server log files grow and when and how a log file can be reduced in size. Finally, I look at how log files are used during SQL Server backup and restore operations and how they are affected by your database's recovery model.

## Transaction Log Basics

The transaction log records changes made to the database and stores enough information to allow SQL Server to recover the database. The recovery process takes place every time a SQL Server instance is started, and it can take place every time SQL Server restores a database or a log from backup. *Recovery* is the process of reconciling the data files and the log. Any changes to the data that the log indicates have been committed must appear in the data files, and any changes that are not marked as committed must not appear in the data files. The log also stores information needed to roll back an operation if SQL Server receives a request to roll back a transaction from the client (using the *ROLLBACK TRAN* command) or if an error, such as a deadlock, generates an internal *ROLLBACK*.

Physically, the transaction log is one or more files associated with a database at the time the database is created or altered. Operations that perform database modifications write records in the transaction log that describe the changes made (including the page numbers of the data pages modified by the operation), the data values that were added or removed, information about the transaction that the modification was part of, and the date and time of the beginning and end of the transaction. SQL Server also writes log records when certain internal events happen, such as checkpoints. Each log record is labeled with a Log Sequence Number (LSN) that is guaranteed to be unique. All log entries that are part of the same transaction are linked so that all parts of a transaction can be located easily for both undo activities (as with a rollback) and redo activities (during system recovery).

The Buffer Manager guarantees that the transaction log will be written before the changes to the database are written. (This is called *write-ahead logging*.) This guarantee is possible because SQL Server keeps track of its current position in the log by means of the LSN. Every time a page is changed, the LSN corresponding to the log entry for that change is written into the header of the data page. Dirty pages can be written to the disk only when the LSN on the page is less than or equal to the LSN for the last record written to the log. The Buffer Manager also guarantees that log pages are written in a specific order, making it clear which log blocks must be processed after a system failure, regardless of when the failure occurred.

The log records for a transaction are written to disk before the commit acknowledgement is sent to the client process, but the actual changed data might not have been physically written out to the data pages. Although the writes to the log are asynchronous, at commit time the thread must wait for the writes to complete to the point of writing the commit record in the log for the transaction. (SQL Server must wait for the commit record to be written so that it knows the relevant log records are safely on the disk.) Writes to data pages are completely asynchronous. That is, writes to data pages need only be posted to the operating system, and SQL Server can check later to see that they were completed. They don't have to be completed immediately because the log contains all the information needed to redo the work, even in the event of a power failure or system crash before the write completes. The system would be much slower if it had to wait for every I/O request to complete before proceeding.

Logging involves demarcating the beginning and end of each transaction (and savepoints, if a transaction uses them). Between the beginning and ending demarcations is information about the changes made to the data. This information can take the form of the actual "before and after" data, or it can refer to the operation that was performed so that those values can be derived. The end of a typical transaction is marked with a Commit record, which indicates that the transaction must be reflected in the database's data files or redone if necessary. A transaction aborted during normal runtime (not system restart) due to an explicit rollback or something like a resource error (for example, an out-of-memory error) actually undoes the operation by applying changes that undo the original data modifications. The records of these changes are written to the log and marked as "compensation log records."

As mentioned previously, there are two types of recovery, both of which have the goal of making sure the log and the data agree. A *restart recovery* runs every time SQL Server is started. The process runs on each database because each database has its own transaction log. Your SQL Server error log reports the progress of restart recovery, and for each database, the error log tells you how many transactions were rolled forward and how many were rolled back. This type of recovery is sometimes referred to as *crash recovery* because a crash, or unexpected stopping of the SQL Server service, requires the recovery process to be run when the service is restarted. If the service was shut down cleanly with no open transactions in any database, only minimal recovery is necessary upon system restart. In SQL Server 2008, restart recovery can be run on multiple databases in parallel, each handled by a different thread.

The other type of recovery, *restore recovery* (or *media recovery*), is run by request when a restore operation is executed. This process makes sure that all the committed transactions in the backup of the transaction log are reflected in the data and that any transactions that did not complete do not show up in the data. I'll talk more about restore recovery later in the chapter.

Both types of recovery must deal with two situations: when transactions are recorded as committed in the log but not yet written to the data files, and when changes to the data files don't correspond to committed transactions. These two situations can occur because committed log records are written to the log files on disk every time a transaction commits. Changed data pages are written to the data files on disk completely asynchronously, every time a checkpoint occurs in a database. As I mentioned in Chapter 1, "SQL Server 2008 Architecture and Configuration," data pages can also be written to disk at other times, but the regularly occurring checkpoint operations give SQL Server a point at which *all* changed (or dirty) pages are known to have been written to disk. Checkpoint operations also write log records from transactions in progress to disk because the cached log records are also considered to be dirty.

If the SQL Server service stops after a transaction commits but before the data is written out to the data pages, when SQL Server starts and runs recovery, the transaction must be rolled forward. SQL Server essentially redoes the transaction by reapplying the changes indicated in the transaction log. All the transactions that need to be redone are processed first (even though some of them might need to be undone later during the next phase). This is called the *redo* phase of recovery.

If a checkpoint occurs before a transaction is committed, it writes the uncommitted changes out to disk. If the SQL Server service then stops before the commit occurs, the recovery process finds the changes for the uncommitted transactions in the data files, and it has to roll back the transaction by undoing the changes reflected in the transaction log. Rolling back all the incomplete transactions is called the *undo* phase of recovery.

> **Note**  I'll continue to refer to recovery as a system startup function, which is its most common role by far. However, remember that recovery is also run during the final step of restoring a database from backup or attaching a database, and can also be forced manually. In addition, recovery is run when creating a database snapshot, during database mirroring, or when failing over to a database mirror.

Later in this chapter, I'll cover some special issues related to recovery during a database restore. These include the three recovery models that you can set using the *ALTER DATABASE* statement and the ability to place a named marker in the log to indicate a specific point to recover to. The discussion that follows deals with recovery in general, whether it's performed when the SQL Server service restarts or when a database is being restored from a backup.

# Phases of Recovery

During recovery, only changes that occurred or were in progress since the last checkpoint are evaluated to determine if they need to be redone or undone. Any transactions that completed prior to the last checkpoint, either by being committed or rolled back, are accurately reflected in the data pages, and no additional work needs to be done for them during recovery.

The recovery algorithm has three phases, which center around the last checkpoint record in the transaction log. The three phases are illustrated in Figure 4-1.

**Phase 1: Analysis**    The first phase is a forward pass starting at the last checkpoint record in the transaction log. This pass determines and constructs a dirty page table (DPT) consisting of pages that might have been dirty at the time SQL Server stopped. An active transaction table is also built that consists of uncommitted transactions at the time SQL Server stops.

**Phase 2: Redo**    This phase returns the database to the state it was in at the time the SQL Server service stopped. The starting point for this forward pass is the start of the oldest uncommitted transaction. The minimum LSN in the DPT is the first time SQL Server expects to have to redo an operation on a page, but it needs to redo the logged operations starting all the way back at the start of the oldest open transaction so that the necessary locks can be acquired. (Prior to SQL Server 2005, it was just allocation locks that needed to be reacquired. In SQL 2005 and later, all locks for those open transactions need to be reacquired.)

**Phase 3: Undo**    This phase uses the list of active transactions (uncommitted at the time SQL Server came down) which were found in Phase 1 (Analysis). It rolls each of these active transactions back individually. SQL Server follows the links between entries in the transaction log for each transaction. Any transaction that was not committed at the time SQL Server stopped is undone so that none of the changes are actually reflected in the database.

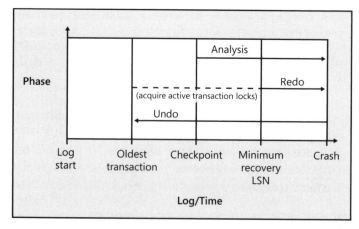

**FIGURE 4-1** The three phases of the SQL Server recovery process

SQL Server uses the log to keep track of the data modifications that were made, as well as any locks that were applied to the objects being modified. This allows SQL Server to support a feature called *fast recovery* when SQL Server is restarted (in the Enterprise and Developer editions only). With fast recovery, the database is available as soon as the redo phase is finished. The same locks that were acquired during the original modification can be reacquired to keep other processes from accessing the data that needs to have its changes undone; all other data in the database remains available. Fast recovery cannot be done during media recovery, but it is used by database mirroring recovery, which uses a hybrid of media recovery and restart recovery.

In addition, SQL Server uses multiple threads to process the recovery operations on the different databases simultaneously, so databases with higher ID numbers don't have to wait for all databases with lower ID numbers to be completely recovered before their own recovery process starts.

## Page LSNs and Recovery

Every database page has an LSN in the page header that reflects the location in the transaction log of the last log entry that modified a row on this page. Each log record for changes to a data page has two LSNs associated with it. In addition to the LSN for the actual log record, it also keeps track of the LSN, which was on the data page before the change recorded by this log record. During a redo operation of transactions, the LSNs on each log record are compared to the page LSN of the data page that the log entry modified. If the page LSN is equal to the previous page LSN in the log record, the operation indicated in the log entry is redone. If the LSN on the page is equal to or higher than the actual LSN for this log record, SQL Server skips the *REDO* operation. These two possibilities are illustrated in Figure 4-2. The LSN on the page cannot be between the previous and current values for the log record.

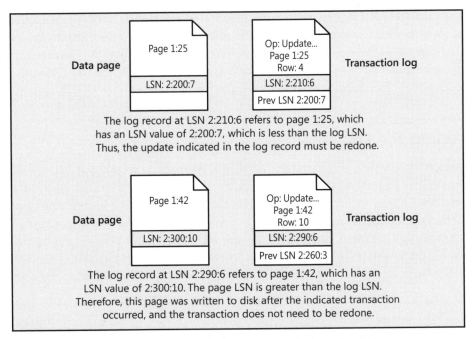

**FIGURE 4-2** Comparing LSNs to decide whether to process the log entry during recovery

Because recovery finds the last checkpoint record in the log (plus transactions that were still active at the time of the checkpoint) and proceeds from there, recovery time is short, and all changes committed before the checkpoint can be purged from the log or archived. Otherwise, recovery could take a long time and transaction logs could become unreasonably large. A transaction log cannot be truncated prior to the point of the earliest transaction that is still open, no matter how many checkpoints have occurred since the transaction started and no matter how many other transactions have started or completed. If a transaction remains open, the log must be preserved because it's still not clear whether the transaction is done or ever will be done. The transaction might ultimately need to be rolled back or rolled forward.

> **Note**  Truncating of the transaction log is a logical operation and merely marks parts of the log as no longer needed, so the space can be reused. Truncation is not a physical operation and does not reduce the size of the transaction log files on disk. To reduce the physical size, a shrink operation must be performed.

Some SQL Server administrators have noted that the transaction log seems unable to be truncated, even after the log has been backed up. This problem often results from a user opening a transaction and then forgetting about it. For this reason, from an application development standpoint, you should ensure that transactions are kept short. Another possible reason for an inability to truncate the log relates to a table being replicated using transactional replication when the replication log reader hasn't processed all the relevant log records yet. This situation is less common, however, because typically a latency of only a few seconds occurs while the log reader does its work. You can use *DBCC OPENTRAN* to look for the earliest open transaction or the oldest replicated transaction not yet processed and then take corrective measures (such as killing the offending process or running the *sp_repldone* stored procedure to allow the replicated transactions to be purged). I'll discuss problems with transaction management and some possible solutions in Chapter 10, "Transactions and Concurrency." I'll discuss shrinking of the log in the next section.

## Reading the Log

Although the log contains a record of every change made to a database, it is not intended to be used as an auditing tool. The transaction log is used to enable SQL Server to guarantee recoverability in case of statement or system failure and to allow a system administrator to take backups of the changes to a SQL Server database. If you want to keep a readable record of changes to a database, you have to do your own auditing. You can do this by creating a trace of SQL Server activities, using SQL Server Profiler or one of the tracing mechanisms in SQL Server, as discussed in Chapter 2, "Change Tracking, Tracing, and Extended Events."

> **Note**  You might be aware that some third-party tools can read the transaction log and show you all the operations that have taken place in a database and can allow you to roll back any of those operations. The developers of these tools spent tens of thousands of hours looking at byte-level dumps of the transaction log files and correlating that information with the output of an undocumented *DBCC LOG* command. Once they had a product on the market, Microsoft started working with them, which made their lives a bit easier in subsequent releases. However, no such tools are available for SQL Server 2008.

Although you might assume that reading the transaction log directly would be interesting or even useful, it's usually just too much information. If you know in advance that you want to keep track of what your server running SQL Server is doing, you're much better off defining a trace with the appropriate filter to capture just the information that is useful to you.

# Changes in Log Size

No matter how many physical files have been defined for the transaction log, SQL Server always treats the log as one contiguous stream. For example, when the *DBCC SHRINKDATABASE* command (discussed in Chapter 3) determines how much the log can be shrunk, it does not consider the log files separately but instead determines the shrinkable size based on the entire log.

## Virtual Log Files

The transaction log for any database is managed as a set of virtual log files (VLFs) whose size is determined internally by SQL Server based on the total size of all the log files and the growth increment used when enlarging the log. When a log file is first created, it always has between 2 and 16 VLFs. If the file size is 1 MB or less, SQL Server divides the size of the log file by the minimum VLF size [31 * 8 KB] to determine the number of VLFs. If the log file size is between 1 and 64 MB, SQL Server splits the log into 4 VLFs. If the log file is greater than 64 MB but less than or equal to 1 GB, 8 VLFs are created. If the size is more than 1 GB, there will be 16 VLFs. When the log grows, the same formula is used to determine how many new VLFs to add. A log always grows in units of entire VLFs and can be shrunk only to a VLF boundary. (Figure 4-3 illustrates a physical log file, along with several VLFs.)

A VLF can be in one of four states:

**Active**   The active portion of the log begins at the minimum LSN representing an active (uncommitted) transaction. The active portion of the log ends at the last LSN written. Any VLFs that contain any part of the active log are considered active VLFs. (Unused space in the physical log is not part of any VLF.) Figure 4-3 contains two active VLFs.

**Recoverable**   The portion of the log preceding the oldest active transaction is needed only to maintain a sequence of log backups for restoring the database to a former state.

**Reusable**   If transaction log backups are not being maintained or if you have already backed up the log, VLFs before the oldest active transaction are not needed and can be reused. Truncating or backing up the transaction log changes recoverable VLFs into reusable VLFs. For the purpose of determining which VLFs are reusable, active transactions include more than just open transactions. The earliest active transaction may be a transaction marked for replication that has not yet been processed, the beginning of a log backup operation, or the beginning of an internal diagnostic scan that SQL Server performs periodically.

**Unused**   One or more VLFs at the physical end of the log files might not have been used yet if not enough logged activity has taken place or if earlier VLFs have been marked as reusable and then reused.

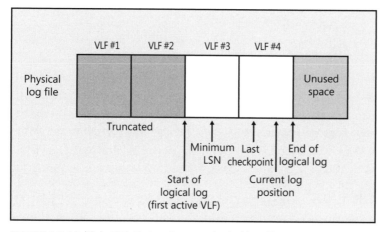

**FIGURE 4-3** Multiple VLFs that make up a physical log file

## Observing Virtual Log Files

You can observe the same key properties of virtual log files by executing the undocumented command *DBCC LOGINFO*. This command takes no parameters, so it must be run in the database for which you want information. It returns one row for each VLF. When I run this command in my *AdventureWorks2008* database, I get the following eight rows returned (not all columns are shown):

| FileId | FileSize | StartOffset | FSeqNo | Status | CreateLSN |
|--------|----------|-------------|--------|--------|-----------|
| 2 | 458752 | 8192 | 42 | 2 | 0 |
| 2 | 458752 | 466944 | 41 | 0 | 0 |
| 2 | 458752 | 925696 | 43 | 2 | 0 |
| 2 | 712704 | 1384448 | 44 | 2 | 0 |
| 2 | 4194304 | 2097152 | 47 | 2 | 44000000085601161 |
| 2 | 4194304 | 6291456 | 46 | 2 | 44000000085601161 |
| 2 | 4194304 | 10485760 | 40 | 2 | 44000000085601161 |
| 2 | 4194304 | 14680064 | 0 | 0 | 44000000085601161 |

The number of rows tells me how many VLFs are in my database. The *FileID* column indicates which of the log's physical files contains the VLF; for my *AdventureWorks2008* database, there is only one physical log file. *FileSize* and *StartOffset* are indicated in bytes, so you can see that the first VLF starts after 8192 bytes, which is the number of bytes in a page. The first physical page of a log file contains header information, not log records, so the VLF is considered to start on the second page. The *FileSize* column is actually redundant for most rows because the size value can be computed by subtracting the *StartOffset* values for two successive VLFs. The rows are listed in physical order, but that is not always the order in which the VLFs have been used. The use order (logical order) is reflected in the column called *FSeqNo* (which stands for File Sequence Number).

In the output shown previously, you can see that the rows are listed in physical order according to the *StartOffset*, but the logical order does not match. The *FSeqNo* values indicate that the seventh VLF is actually the first one in use (logical) order; the last one in use order is the fifth VLF in physical order. The *Status* column indicates whether the VLF is reusable. A status of 2 means that it is either active or recoverable; a status of 0 indicates that it is reusable or completely unused. (A completely unused VLF has a *FSeqNo* value of 0, as in the eighth row of my output.) As I mentioned previously, truncating or backing up the transaction log changes recoverable VLFs into reusable VLFs, so a status of 2 changes to a status of 0 for all VLFs that don't include active log records. In fact, that's one way to tell which VLFs are active: the VLFs that still have a status of 2 after a log backup or truncation must contain records from active transactions. VLFs with a status of 0 can be reused for new log records, and the log does not need to grow to keep track of the activity in the database. On the other hand, if all the VLFs in the log have a status of 2, SQL Server needs to add new VLFs to the log to record new transaction activity. One last column shown in the *DBCC LOG* output shown previously is called *CreateLSN*. That column contains an LSN value; in fact, it is the current LSN at the time the VLF was added to the transaction log. If the *CreateLSN* value is 0, it means the VLF was part of the original log file created when the database was created. You can also tell how many VLFs were added in any one operation by noticing which VLFs have the same value for *CreateLSN*. In my output, the *CreateLSN* values indicate that my log file only grew once, and four new VLFs were added at the same time.

## Multiple Log Files

I mentioned previously that SQL Server treats multiple physical log files as if they were one sequential stream. This means that all the VLFs in one physical file are used before any VLFs in the second file are used. If you have a well-managed log that is regularly backed up or truncated, you might never use any log files other than the first one. If none of the VLFs in multiple physical log files is available for reuse when a new VLF is needed, SQL Server adds new VLFs to each physical log file in a round-robin fashion.

You can actually see the order of usage of different physical files by examining the output of *DBCC LOGINFO*. The first column is the *file_id* of the physical file. If we can capture the output of *DBCC LOGINFO* into a table, we can then sort it in a way that is useful to us. The following code creates a table called *sp_loginfo* that can hold the output of *DBCC LOGINFO*. Because the table is created in the master database and starts with the three characters 'sp_', it can be accessed and modified in any database:

```
USE master
GO
IF EXISTS  (SELECT 1 FROM sys.tables
                          WHERE name = 'sp_LOGINFO')
       DROP TABLE sp_loginfo;
GO
CREATE TABLE sp_LOGINFO
(FileId tinyint,
 FileSize bigint,
 StartOffset bigint,
 FSeqNo int,
 Status tinyint,
 Parity tinyint,
 CreateLSN numeric(25,0) );
GO
```

The following code creates a new database called *TWO_LOGS* and then copies a large table from the *AdventureWorks2008* sample database into *TWO_LOGS*, causing the log to grow:

```
USE Master
GO
IF EXISTS (SELECT * FROM sys.databases
                         WHERE name = 'TWO_LOGS')
    DROP DATABASE TWO_LOGS;
GO
CREATE DATABASE TWO_LOGS
  ON PRIMARY
  (NAME = Data ,
    FILENAME =
    'C:\Program Files\Microsoft SQL Server\MSSQL10.MSSQLSERVER\MSSQL\DATA\TWO_LOGS.mdf'
        , SIZE = 100 MB)
  LOG ON
  (NAME = TWO_LOGS1,
    FILENAME =
    'C:\Program Files\Microsoft SQL Server\MSSQL10.MSSQLSERVER\MSSQL\DATA\TWO_LOGS1.ldf'
        , SIZE = 5 MB
        , MAXSIZE = 2 GB),
  (NAME = TWO_LOGS2,
    FILENAME =
    'C:\Program Files\Microsoft SQL Server\MSSQL10.MSSQLSERVER\MSSQL\DATA\TWO_LOGS2.ldf'
        , SIZE = 5 MB);
GO
```

If you run *DBCC LOGINFO*, you'll notice that it returns VLFs sorted by *FileID*, and initially, the file sequential number values (*FSeqNo*) are also in order:

```
USE TWO_LOGS
GO
DBCC LOGINFO;
GO
```

Now we can insert some rows into the database, by copying from another table:

```
SELECT * INTO Orders
    FROM AdventureWorks2008.Sales.SalesOrderDetail;
GO
```

If you run *DBCC LOGINFO* again, you see that after the *SELECT INTO* operation, even though there are many more rows for each *FileID*, the output is still sorted by *FileID*, and *FSeqNo* values are not related at all. Instead, we can save the output of *DBCC LOGINFO* in the *sp_loginfo* table, and sort by *FSeqNo:*

```
TRUNCATE TABLE sp_LOGINFO;
INSERT INTO sp_LOGINFO
    EXEC ('DBCC LOGINFO');
GO
-- Unused VLFs have a Status of 0, so the CASE forces those to the end
SELECT * FROM sp_LOGINFO
ORDER BY CASE FSeqNo WHEN 0 THEN 9999999 ELSE FSeqNo END;
GO
```

The output of the *SELECT* is shown here:

| FileId | StartOffset | FSeqNo | Status | CreateLSN |
|--------|-------------|--------|--------|-----------|
| 2 | 8192 | 43 | 0 | 0 |
| 2 | 1253376 | 44 | 0 | 0 |
| 2 | 2498560 | 45 | 0 | 0 |
| 2 | 3743744 | 46 | 0 | 0 |
| 3 | 8192 | 47 | 0 | 0 |
| 3 | 1253376 | 48 | 0 | 0 |
| 3 | 2498560 | 49 | 0 | 0 |
| 3 | 3743744 | 50 | 0 | 0 |
| 2 | 5242880 | 51 | 0 | 50000000247200092 |
| 2 | 5496832 | 52 | 0 | 50000000247200092 |
| 3 | 5242880 | 53 | 0 | 51000000035600288 |
| 3 | 5496832 | 54 | 0 | 51000000035600288 |
| 2 | 5767168 | 55 | 0 | 53000000037600316 |
| 2 | 6021120 | 56 | 0 | 53000000037600316 |
| 3 | 5767168 | 57 | 0 | 56000000010400488 |
| 3 | 6021120 | 58 | 0 | 56000000010400488 |
| 2 | 6356992 | 59 | 0 | 58000000007200407 |
| 2 | 6610944 | 60 | 0 | 58000000007200407 |
| 3 | 6356992 | 61 | 0 | 60000000025600218 |
| 3 | 6610944 | 62 | 0 | 60000000025600218 |
| 2 | 7012352 | 63 | 0 | 62000000023900246 |
| 2 | 7266304 | 64 | 0 | 62000000023900246 |
| 3 | 7012352 | 65 | 0 | 64000000037100225 |
| 3 | 7266304 | 66 | 0 | 64000000037100225 |
| 2 | 7733248 | 67 | 0 | 66000000037600259 |
| 2 | 7987200 | 68 | 0 | 66000000037600259 |
| 2 | 8241152 | 69 | 0 | 66000000037600259 |
| 3 | 7733248 | 70 | 0 | 68000000035500288 |
| 3 | 7987200 | 71 | 0 | 68000000035500288 |

| 3 | 8241152 | 72 | 0 | 68000000035500288 |
|---|---------|----|---|-------------------|
| 2 | 8519680 | 73 | 0 | 71000000037300145 |
| 2 | 8773632 | 74 | 0 | 71000000037300145 |
| 2 | 9027584 | 75 | 0 | 71000000037300145 |
| 3 | 8519680 | 76 | 0 | 75000000018700013 |
| 3 | 8773632 | 77 | 2 | 75000000018700013 |
| 3 | 9027584 | 0  | 0 | 75000000018700013 |

Now you can notice that after the first eight initial VLFs are used (the ones with a *CreateLSN* value of 0), the VLFs alternate between the physical files. Because of the amount of log growth each time, several new VLFs are created, first from *FileID* 2 and then from *FileID* 3. The last VLF added to *FileID* 3 has not been used yet.

So there is really no reason to use multiple physical log files if you have done thorough testing and have determined the optimal size of your database's transaction log. However, if you find that the log needs to grow more than expected and if the volume containing the log does not have sufficient free space to allow the log to grow enough, you might need to create a second log file on another volume.

## Automatic Truncation of Virtual Log Files

SQL Server assumes you're not maintaining a sequence of log backups if any of the following is true:

- You have configured the database to truncate the log on a regular basis by setting the recovery model to SIMPLE.

- You have never taken a full database backup.

Under any of these circumstances, SQL Server truncates the database's transaction log every time it gets "full enough." (I'll explain this in a moment.) The database is considered to be in autotruncate mode.

Remember that truncation means that all log records prior to the oldest active transaction are invalidated and all VLFs not containing any part of the active log are marked as reusable. It does not imply shrinking of the physical log file. In addition, if your database is a publisher in a replication scenario, the oldest open transaction could be a transaction marked for replication that has not yet been replicated.

"Full enough" means that there are more log records than can be redone during system startup in a reasonable amount of time—the *recovery interval*. You can change the recovery interval manually by using the *sp_configure* stored procedure or by using SQL Server Management Studio, as discussed in Chapter 1. However, it is best to let SQL Server autotune this value. In most cases, this recovery interval value is set to one minute. By default, *sp_configure* shows zero minutes, meaning SQL Server autotunes the value. SQL Server bases its recovery interval on the estimate that 10 MB worth of transactions can be recovered in one minute.

The actual log truncation is invoked by the checkpoint process, which is usually sleeping and is awakened only on demand. Each time a user thread calls the log manager, the log manager checks the size of the log. If the size exceeds the amount of work that can be recovered during the recovery interval, the checkpoint thread is woken up. The checkpoint thread checkpoints the database and then truncates the inactive portion of the log.

In addition, if the log ever gets to 70 percent full while the database is in autotruncate mode, the log manager wakes the checkpoint thread to force a checkpoint. Growing the log is much more expensive than truncating it, so SQL Server truncates the log whenever it can.

> **Note**  If the log manager is never needed, the checkpoint process won't be invoked and the truncation never happens. If you have a database in autotruncate mode, for which the transaction log has VLFs with a status of 2, you do not see the status change to 0 until some logging activity is required in the database.

If the log is regularly truncated, SQL Server can reuse space in the physical file by cycling back to an earlier VLF when it reaches the end of the physical log file. In effect, SQL Server recycles the space in the log file that is no longer needed for recovery or backup purposes. My *AdventureWorks2008* database is in this state because I have never made a full database backup.

## Maintaining a Recoverable Log

If a log backup sequence *is* being maintained, the part of the log before the minimum LSN cannot be overwritten until those log records have actually been backed up. The VLF status stays at 2 until the log backup occurs. After the log backup, the status changes to 0 and SQL Server can cycle back to the beginning of the file. Figure 4-4 depicts this cycle in a simplified fashion. As you can see from the *FSeqNo* values in the earlier output from the *AdventureWorks2008* database, SQL Server does not always reuse the log files in their physical sequence.

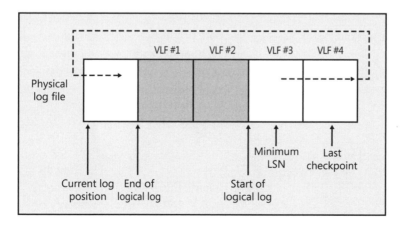

**FIGURE 4-4**  The active portion of the log cycling back to the beginning of the physical log file

> **Note** If a database is not in autotruncate mode and you are not performing regular log backups, your transaction log is never truncated. If you are doing only full database backups, you must truncate the log manually to keep it at a manageable size.

The easiest way to tell whether a database is in autotruncate mode is by using the catalog view called *sys.database_recovery_status* and looking in the column called *last_log_backup_lsn*. If that column value is null, the database is in autotruncate mode.

You can actually observe the difference between a database that is in autotruncate mode and a database that isn't by running a simple script in the *pubs* database, which is shown at the end of this paragraph. This script works so long as you have never made a full backup of the *pubs* database. If you have never made any modifications to *pubs*, and you installed it using the *Instpubs.sql* script, the size of its transaction log file is just about 0.75 MB, which is the size at creation. The following script creates a new table in the *pubs* database, inserts three records, and then updates those records 1,000 times. Each update is an individual transaction, and each one is written to the transaction log. However, you should note that the log does not grow at all, and the number of VLFs does not increase even after 3,000 update records are written. (If you've already taken a backup of *pubs*, you might want to re-create the database before trying this example. You can do that by running the script *Instpubs.sql* again, which you can download from the companion Web site, *http://www.SQLServerInternals.com/companion*.) However, even though the number of VLFs does not change, you see that the *FSeqNo* values change. Log records are being generated, and as each VLF is reused, it gets a new *FSeqNo* value:

```
USE pubs;
-- First look at the VLFs for the pubs database
DBCC LOGINFO;
-- Now verify that pubs is in auto truncate mode
SELECT last_log_backup_lsn
FROM master.sys.database_recovery_status
WHERE database_id = db_id('pubs');
GO
CREATE TABLE newtable (a int);
GO
INSERT INTO newtable VALUES (10);
INSERT INTO newtable VALUES (20);
INSERT INTO newtable VALUES (30);
GO
SET NOCOUNT ON
DECLARE @counter int;
SET @counter = 1 ;
WHILE @counter < 1000 BEGIN
    UPDATE newtable SET a = a + 1;
    SET @counter = @counter + 1;
END;
```

Now make a backup of the *pubs* database after making sure that the database is not in the SIMPLE recovery model. I'll discuss recovery models later in this chapter, but for now, you can just make sure that *pubs* is in the appropriate recovery model by executing the following command:

```
ALTER DATABASE pubs SET RECOVERY FULL;
```

You can use the following statement to make the backup, substituting the path shown with the path to your SQL Server installation, or the path to any backup location:

```
BACKUP DATABASE pubs to disk =
    'c:\Program Files\Microsoft SQL Server\MSSQL.1\MSSQL\backup\pubs.bak';
```

As soon as you make the full backup, you can verify that the database is not in autotruncate mode, again by looking at the *database_recovery_status* view:

```
SELECT last_log_backup_lsn
FROM master.sys.database_recovery_status
WHERE database_id = db_id('pubs');
```

This time, you should get a non-null value for *last_log_backup_lsn* to indicate that log backups are expected. Next, run the update script again, starting with the *DECLARE* statement. You should see that the physical log file has grown to accommodate the log records added and that there are more VLFs. The initial space in the log could not be reused because SQL Server assumed that you were saving that information for transaction log backups.

Now you can try to shrink the log back down again. The first thing that you need to do is truncate the log, which you can do by setting the recovery model to SIMPLE as follows:

```
ALTER DATABASE pubs SET RECOVERY SIMPLE;
```

If you then issue the following command, or if you issue the *DBCC SHRINKDATABASE* command for the *pubs* database, SQL Server shrinks the log file:

```
DBCC SHRINKFILE (2);
```

At this point, you should notice that the physical size of the log file has been reduced. If a log is truncated without any shrink command issued, SQL Server marks the space used by the truncated records as available for reuse but does not change the size of the physical file.

In SQL Server 7.0, where this log architecture was first introduced, running the preceding commands exactly as specified did not always shrink the physical log file. When the log file did not shrink, it was because the active part of the log was located at the end of the physical file. Physical shrinking can take place only from the end of the log, and the active portion is never shrinkable. To remedy this situation, you had to enter some dummy transactions after truncating the log to force the active part of the log to move around to the beginning of the file. In versions later than SQL Server 7.0, this process is unnecessary. If a shrink command has already been issued, truncating the log internally generates a series of NO-OP (or dummy) log records that force the active log to move from the physical end of the file. Shrinking happens as soon as the log is no longer needed.

## Automatic Shrinking of the Log

Remember that truncating is not shrinking. A database should be truncated so that it is most shrinkable, and if the log is in autotruncate mode and the autoshrink option is set, the log is physically shrunk at regular intervals.

If a database has the autoshrink option on, an autoshrink process kicks in every 30 minutes (as discussed in Chapter 3) and determines the size to which the log should be shrunk. The log manager accumulates statistics on the maximum amount of log space used in the 30-minute interval between autoshrink processes. The autoshrink process marks the shrinkpoint of the log as 125 percent of the maximum log space actually used or the minimum size of the log, whichever is larger. (Minimum size is the creation size of the log or the size to which it has been manually increased or decreased.) The log then shrinks to that size whenever it gets the chance, which is when it gets truncated or backed up. It's possible to have autoshrink without having the database in autotruncate mode, although you cannot guarantee that the log actually shrinks. For example, if the log is never backed up, none of the VLFs are marked as reusable, so no shrinking can take place.

As a final note, you need to be aware that just because a database is in autotruncate mode, you cannot guarantee that the log won't grow. (It is the converse that you can be sure of— that if a database is not in autotruncate mode, the log *will* grow.) *Autotruncate* means only that VLFs that are considered recoverable are marked as reusable at regular intervals. But VLFs in an active state are not affected. If you have a long-running transaction (which might be a transaction that someone forgot to commit), all the VLFs that contain any log records since that long-running transaction started are considered active and can never be reused. One uncommitted transaction can mean the difference between a very manageable transaction log size and a log that uses more disk space than the database itself and continues to grow.

## Log File Size

You can see the current size of the log file for all databases, as well as the percentage of the log file space that has been used, by running the command *DBCC SQLPERF('logspace')*. However, because it is a DBCC command, it's hard to filter the rows to get just the rows for a single database. Instead, you can use the dynamic management view *sys.dm_os_performance_counters* and retrieve the percentage full for each database's log:

```
SELECT instance_name as [Database],
       cntr_value as "LogFullPct"
FROM sys.dm_os_performance_counters
WHERE counter_name LIKE 'Percent Log Used%'
    AND instance_name not in ('_Total', 'mssqlsystemresource')
    AND cntr_value > 0;
```

The final condition is needed to filter out databases that have no log file size reported. This includes any database that is unavailable because it has not been recovered or is in a suspect state, as well as any database snapshots, which have no transaction log.

# Backing Up and Restoring a Database

As you probably know by now, this book is not intended to be a how-to book for database administrators. The bibliography in the companion content lists several excellent books that can teach you the mechanics of making database backups and restoring and can offer best practices for setting up a backup-and-restore plan for your organization. Nevertheless, some important issues relating to backup and restore processes can help you understand why one backup plan might be better suited to your needs than another. Most of these issues involve the role the transaction log plays in backup and restore operations, so I'll discuss the main ones in this section.

## Types of Backups

No matter how much fault tolerance you have implemented on your database system, it is no replacement for regular backups. Backups can provide a solution to accidental or malicious data modifications, programming errors, and natural disasters (if you store backups in a remote location). If you opt for the fastest possible speed for data file access at the cost of fault tolerance, backups provide insurance in case your data files are damaged. In addition, backups are also the preferred way to manage copying of databases to other machines or other instances.

If you're using a backup to restore lost data, the amount of data that is potentially recoverable depends on the type of backup. SQL Server 2008 has four main types of backups (and a couple of variations on those types):

**Full backup**   A full database backup basically copies all the pages from a database onto a backup device, which can be a local or network disk file, or a local tape drive.

**Differential backup**   A differential backup copies only the extents that were changed since the last full backup was made. The extents are copied onto a specified backup device. SQL Server can tell quickly which extents need to be backed up by examining the bits on the Differential Changed Map (DCM) pages for each data file in the database. DCM pages are big bitmaps, with one bit representing an extent in a file, just like the Global Allocation Map (GAM) and Shared Global Allocation Map (SGAM) pages that I discussed in Chapter 3. Each time a full backup is made, all the bits in the DCM are cleared to 0. When any page in an extent is changed, its corresponding bit in the DCM page is changed to 1.

**Log backup**   In most cases, a log backup copies all the log records that have been written to the transaction log since the last full or log backup was made. However, the exact behavior of the *BACKUP LOG* command depends on your database's recovery mode setting. I'll discuss recovery modes shortly.

**File and filegroup backup**   File and filegroup backups are intended to increase flexibility in scheduling and media handling compared to full backups, in particular for very large databases. File and filegroup backups are also useful for large databases that contain data with varying update characteristics, meaning some filegroups allow both read and write operations and some are read-only.

> **More Info**  For full details on the mechanics of defining backup devices, making backups, and scheduling backups to occur at regular intervals, consult *SQL Server Books Online* or one of the SQL Server administration books listed in the bibliography in the online companion content.

A full backup can be made while your database is in use. This is considered a "fuzzy" backup—that is, it is not an exact image of the state of the database at any particular point in time. The backup threads just copy extents, and if other processes need to make changes to those extents while the backup is in progress, they can do so.

To maintain consistency for either full, differential, or file backups, SQL Server records the current log sequence number (LSN) at the time the backup starts and again at the time the backup ends. This allows the backup to capture the relevant parts of the log as well. The relevant part starts with the oldest active transaction at the time of the first recorded LSN and ends with the second recorded LSN.

As I mentioned previously, what gets recorded with a log backup depends on the recovery model that you are using. So before I talk about log backup in detail, I'll tell you about recovery models.

## Recovery Models

As I said in Chapter 3 when I discussed database options, the RECOVERY option has three possible values: FULL, BULK_LOGGED, or SIMPLE. The value that you choose determines the size of your transaction log, the speed and size of your transaction log backups (or whether you can make log backups at all), as well as the degree to which you are at risk of losing committed transactions in case of media failure.

### FULL Recovery Model

The FULL recovery model provides the least risk of losing work in the case of a damaged data file. If a database is in this mode, all operations are fully logged. This means that in addition to logging every row added with the *INSERT* operation, removed with the *DELETE* operation, or changed with the *UPDATE* operation, SQL Server also writes to the transaction log in its entirety every row inserted using a *bcp* or *BULK INSERT* operation. If you experience a media failure for a database file and need to recover a database that was in FULL recovery mode and you've been making regular transaction log backups preceded by a full database backup, you can restore to any specified point in time up to the time of the last log backup. In addition, if your log file is available after the failure of a data file, you can restore up to the last transaction committed before the failure. SQL Server 2008 also supports a feature called *log marks*, which allows you to place reference points in the transaction log. If your database is in FULL recovery mode, you can choose to recover to one of these log marks.

In FULL recovery mode, SQL Server also fully logs *CREATE INDEX* operations. When you restore from a transaction log backup that includes index creations, the recovery operation is much faster because the index does not have to be rebuilt—all the index pages have been captured as part of the database backup. Prior to SQL Server 2000, SQL Server logged only the fact that an index had been built, so when you restored from a log backup, the entire index would have to be built all over again.

So FULL recovery mode sounds great, right? As always, there are trade-offs. The biggest trade-off is that the size of your transaction log files can be enormous, so it can take much longer to make log backups than with releases prior to SQL Server 2000.

## BULK_LOGGED Recovery Model

The BULK_LOGGED recovery model allows you to restore a database completely in case of media failure and also gives you the best performance and least log space usage for certain bulk operations. In FULL recovery mode, these operations are fully logged, but in BULK_LOGGED recovery mode, they are logged only minimally. This can be much more efficient than normal logging because in general, when you write data to a user database, you must write it to disk twice: once to the log and once to the database itself. This is because the database system uses an undo/redo log so it can roll back or redo transactions when needed. Minimal logging consists of logging only the information that is required to roll back the transaction without supporting point-in-time recovery. These bulk operations include:

- *SELECT INTO*

  ❑ This command always creates a new table in the default filegroup.

- Bulk import operations, including the following:

  ❑ The *BULK INSERT* command

  ❑ The *bcp* executable

- The *INSERT INTO . . . SELECT* command, when data is selected using the *OPENROWSET(BULK. . .)* function.

- The *INSERT INTO . . . SELECT* command, when more than an extent's worth of data is being inserted into a table without nonclustered indexes and the TABLOCK hint is used. If the destination table is empty, it can have a clustered index. If the destination table is already populated, it cannot. (This option can be useful to create a new table in a nondefault filegroup with minimal logging. The *SELECT INTO* command does not allow specifying a filegroup.)

- Partial updates to columns having a large value data type (which will be discussed in Chapter 7, "Special Storage").

- Using the .WRITE clause in the *UPDATE* statement when inserting or appending new data.

- *WRITETEXT* and *UPDATETEXT* statements when inserting or appending new data into LOB data columns (text, ntext, or image).

  - Minimal logging is not used in these cases when existing data is updated.

- Index operations

  - *CREATE INDEX*, including indexes on views

  - *ALTER INDEX REBUILD* or *DBCC DBREINDEX*

  - *DROP INDEX*. The creation of the new heap is minimally logged, but the page deallocation is always fully logged.

When you execute one of these bulk operations, SQL Server logs only the fact that the operation occurred and information about space allocations. Every data file in a SQL Server 2008 database has at least one special page called a Bulk Changed Map (BCM) page, or also called a Minimally Logged Map (ML Map) page, which is managed much like the GAM and SGAM pages that I discussed in Chapter 3 and the DCM pages that I mentioned previously. Each bit on a BCM page represents an extent, and if the bit is 1, it means that this extent has been changed by a minimally logged bulk operation since the last transaction log backup. A BCM page is located on the eighth page of every data file and every 511,230 pages thereafter. All the bits on a BCM page are reset to 0 every time a log backup occurs.

Because of the ability to minimally log bulk operations, the operations themselves can potentially be carried out much faster than in FULL recovery mode. However, the speed improvement is not guaranteed. The only guarantee with minimally logged operations is that the log itself is smaller. Minimal logging might actually be slower than fully logged operations in certain cases. Although there are not as many log records to write, with minimal logging SQL Server forces the data pages to be flushed to disk before the transaction commits. This forced flushing of the data pages can be very expensive, especially when the I/O for these pages is random. You can contrast this to full logging, which is always sequential I/O. If you don't have a fast I/O subsystem, it can become very noticeable that minimal logging is slower than full logging.

In general, minimal logging does not mean no logging, and it doesn't minimize logging for all operations. It is a feature that minimizes the amount of logging for the operations described previously, and if you have a high-performance I/O subsystem, performance likely improves as well. But on lower-end machines, minimally logged operations are slower than fully logged operations.

If your database is in BULK_LOGGED mode and you have not actually performed any bulk operations, you can restore your database to any point in time or to a named log mark because the log contains a full sequential record of all changes to your database.

The trade-off to having a smaller log comes during the backing up of the log. In addition to copying the contents of the transaction log to the backup media, SQL Server scans the BCM pages and backs up all the modified extents along with the transaction log itself. The log file itself stays small, but the backup of the log can be many times larger. So the log backup takes more time and might take up a lot more space than in FULL recovery mode. The time it takes to restore a log backup made in BULK_LOGGED recovery mode is similar to the time it takes to restore a log backup made in FULL recovery mode. The operations don't have to be redone; all the information necessary to recover all data and index structures is available in the log backup.

## SIMPLE Recovery Model

The SIMPLE recovery model offers the simplest backup-and-restore strategy. Your transaction log is truncated whenever a checkpoint occurs, which happens at regular, frequent intervals. Therefore, the only types of backups that can be made are those that don't require log backups. These types of backups are full database backups, differential backups, partial full and differential backups, and filegroup backups for read-only filegroups. You get an error if you try to back up the log while in SIMPLE recovery mode. Because the log is not needed for backup purposes, sections of it can be reused as soon as all the transactions that it contains are committed or rolled back, and the transactions are no longer needed for recovery from server or transaction failure. In fact, as soon as you change your database to SIMPLE recovery model, the log is truncated.

Keep in mind that SIMPLE logging does not mean no logging. What's "simple" is your backup strategy, because you never need to worry about log backups. However, all operations are logged in SIMPLE mode, even though some operations may have fewer log records in that mode than in FULL mode. A log for a database in SIMPLE mode might not grow as much as a database in FULL mode because the bulk operations discussed earlier in this chapter also are minimally logged in SIMPLE mode. This does not mean you don't have to worry about the size of the log in SIMPLE mode. As in any recovery mode, log records for active transactions cannot be truncated, and neither can log records for any transaction that started after the oldest open transaction. So if you have large or long-running transactions, you still might need lots of log space.

## Compatibility with Database Options

Microsoft introduced these recovery models in SQL Server 2000 and intended them to replace the *select into/bulkcopy* and *trunc. log on chkpt.* database options. SQL Server 7.0 and earlier versions required that the *select into/bulkcopy* option be set for you to perform a *SELECT INTO* or bulk copy operation. The *trunc. log on chkpt.* option forced your transaction log to be truncated every time a checkpoint occurred in the database. This option was recommended only for test or development systems, not for production servers. You can still set these options by using the *sp_dboption* procedure, but not by using the *ALTER DATABASE* command. However, with versions later than SQL Server 7.0, changing either of these options using *sp_dboption* also changes your recovery model, and changing your recovery model changes the value of one or both of these options, as you'll see here. The recommended method for changing your database recovery mode is to use the *ALTER DATABASE* command:

```
ALTER DATABASE <database_name>
    SET RECOVERY [FULL | BULK_LOGGED | SIMPLE]
```

To see what mode your database is in, you can inspect the *sys.databases* view. For example, this query returns the recovery mode and the state of the *AdventureWorks2008* database:

```
SELECT name, database_id, suser_sname(owner_sid) as owner ,
        state_desc, recovery_model_desc
FROM sys.databases
WHERE name = 'AdventureWorks2008'
```

As I just mentioned, you can change the recovery mode by changing the database options. For example, if your database is in FULL recovery mode and you change the *select into/bulkcopy* option to *true*, your database recovery mode changes to BULK_LOGGED. Conversely, if you force the database back into FULL mode by using *ALTER DATABASE,* the value of the *select into/ bulkcopy* option changes. If you're using SQL Server 2008 Standard or Enterprise edition, the *model* database starts in FULL recovery mode, so all your new databases will also be in FULL mode. You can change the mode of the *model* database or any other user database by using the *ALTER DATABASE* command.

To make best use of your transaction log, you can switch between FULL and BULK_LOGGED mode without worrying about your backup scripts failing. Prior to SQL Server 2000, once you performed a *SELECT INTO* command or a bulk copy, you could no longer back up your transaction log. So if you had automatic log backup scripts scheduled to run at regular intervals, they would break and generate an error. This can no longer happen. You can run *SELECT INTO* or bulk copy in any recovery mode, and you can back up the log in either FULL or BULK_LOGGED mode. You might want to switch between FULL and BULK_LOGGED modes if you usually operate in FULL mode but occasionally need to perform a bulk operation quickly. You can change to BULK_LOGGED and pay the price later when you back up the log; the backup simply takes longer and is larger.

You can't easily switch to and from SIMPLE mode if you're trying to maintain a sequence of log backups. Switching into SIMPLE mode is no problem, but when you switch back to FULL or BULK_LOGGED, you need to plan your backup strategy and be aware that there are no log backups up to that point. So when you use the *ALTER DATABASE* command to change from SIMPLE to FULL or BULK_LOGGED, you should first make a complete database backup in order for the change in behavior to be complete. Remember that in SIMPLE recovery mode, your transaction log is truncated at regular intervals. This recovery mode isn't recommended for production databases, where you need maximum transaction recoverability. The only time that SIMPLE mode is really useful is in test and development situations or for small databases that are primarily read-only. I suggest that you use FULL or BULK_LOGGED for your production databases and switch between those modes whenever you need to.

## Choosing a Backup Type

If you're responsible for creating the backup plan for your data, you need to choose not only a recovery model but also the kind of backup to make. I mentioned the three main types: full, differential, and log. In fact, you can use all three types together. To accomplish any type of full restore of a database, you must make a full database backup occasionally, to use as a starting point for other types of backups. In addition, you may choose among a differential backup, a log backup, or a combination of both. Here are the characteristics of these last two types, which can help you decide between them.

A differential backup

- Is faster if your environment includes a lot of changes to the same data. It backs up only the most recent change, whereas a log backup captures every individual update.

- Captures the entire B-tree structures for new indexes, whereas a log backup captures each individual step in building the index.

- Is cumulative. When you recover from a media failure, only the most recent differential backup needs to be restored because it contains all the changes since the last full database backup.

A log backup

- Allows you to restore to any point in time because it is a sequential record of all changes.

- Can be made after the database media fails, so long as the log is available. This allows you to recover right up to the point of the failure. The last log backup (called the tail of the log) must specify the WITH NO_TRUNCATE option in the *BACKUP LOG* command if the database itself is unavailable.

- Is sequential and discrete. Each log backup contains completely different log records. When you use a log backup to restore a database after a media failure, all log backups must be applied in the order that they were made.

Remember that backups can be created as compressed backups, as briefly discussed in Chapter 1. This can greatly reduce the amount of time and space required to actually create the backup (full, differential, or log) on the backup device. The algorithm for compressing backups is very different than the algorithms used for row or page data compression. I elaborate on the differences in Chapter 7.

## Restoring a Database

How often you make each type of backup determines two things: how fast you can restore a database and how much control you have over which transactions are restored. Consider the schedule in Figure 4-5, which shows a database fully backed up on Sundays. The log is backed up daily, and a differential backup is made on Tuesdays and Thursdays. A drive failure occurs on a Friday. If the failure does not include the log files, or if you have mirrored them using RAID 1, you should back up the tail of the log with the NO_TRUNCATE option.

 **Warning** If you are operating in BULK_LOGGED recovery mode, backing up the log also backs up any data that was changed with a *BULK_LOGGED* operation, so you might need to have more than just the log file available to back up the tail of the log. You also need to have available any filegroups containing data inserted by a minimally logged operation.

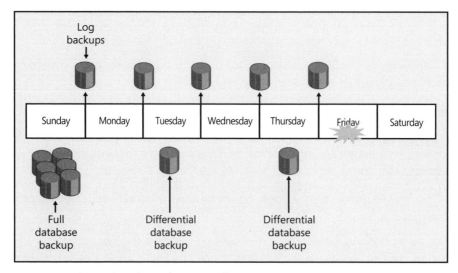

**FIGURE 4-5** The combined use of log and differential backups, which reduces total restore time

To restore this database after a failure, you must start by restoring the full backup made on Sunday. This does two things: it copies all the data and index extents, as well as all the log blocks, from the backup media to the database files, and it applies all the transactions in the log. You must determine whether incomplete transactions are rolled back. You can opt to recover the database by using the WITH RECOVERY option of the *RESTORE* command. This rolls back any incomplete transactions and opens the database for use. No further restoring can be done. If you choose not to roll back incomplete transactions by specifying the WITH NORECOVERY option, the database is left in an inconsistent state and is not usable.

If you choose WITH NORECOVERY, you can then apply the next backup. In the scenario depicted in Figure 4-5, you would restore the differential backup made on Thursday, which would copy all the changed extents back into the data files. The differential backup also contains the log records spanning the time the differential backup was being made, so you have to decide whether to recover the database. Complete transactions are always rolled forward, but you determine whether incomplete transactions are rolled back.

After the differential backup is restored, you must restore, in sequence, all the log backups made after the differential backup was made. This includes the tail of the log backed up after the failure if you were able to make this last backup.

> **Note** Restore recovery (media recovery) is similar to restart recovery, which I described previously in this chapter, but it is a *REDO-only* operation. It includes an analysis pass to determine how much work might need to be done, and then a roll-forward pass to redo completed transactions and return the database to the state it was in when the backup was complete. Unlike restart restore recovery, you have control over when the rollback pass is done. It should not be done until all the rolling forward from all the backups has been applied. Once a *RESTORE WITH RECOVERY* is specified, after the redo pass, the database is restarted and SQL Server runs a restart recovery to undo incomplete transactions. In addition, SQL Server might need to make some adjustments to metadata after the recovery is complete, so no access to the database is allowed until all phases of recovery are finished. In other words, you don't have the option to use "fast" recovery as part of a *RESTORE*.

## Backing Up and Restoring Files and Filegroups

SQL Server 2008 allows you to back up individual files or filegroups. This can be useful in environments with extremely large databases. You can choose to back up just one file or filegroup each day, so the entire database does not have to be backed up as often. This also can be useful when you have an isolated media failure on a single drive and you think that restoring the entire database would take too long.

Here are some details to keep in mind about backing up and restoring files and filegroups:

- Individual files and filegroups with the *read-write* property can be backed up only when your database is in FULL or BULK_LOGGED recovery mode because you must apply log backups after you restore a file or filegroup, and you can't make log backups in SIMPLE mode. Read-only filegroups and the files in them can be backed up in SIMPLE mode.

- You can restore individual file or filegroup backups from a full database backup.

- Immediately before restoring an individual file or filegroup, you must back up the transaction log. You must have an unbroken chain of log backups from the time the file or filegroup backup was made.

- After restoring a file or filegroup backup, you must restore all the transaction logs made between the time you backed up the file or filegroup and the time you restored it. This guarantees that the restored files are in sync with the rest of the database.

For example, suppose that you back up filegroup *FG1* at 10 A.M. on Monday. The database is still in use, and changes happen to data in *FG1* and transactions are processed that change data in both *FG1* and other filegroups. You back up the log at 4 P.M. More transactions are processed that change data in both *FG1* and other filegroups. At 6 P.M., a media failure occurs and you lose one or more of the files that make up *FG1*.

To restore, you must first back up the tail of the log containing all changes that occurred between 4 P.M. and 6 P.M. The tail of the log is backed up using the special WITH NO_TRUNCATE option, but you can also use the NORECOVERY option. When backing up the tail of the log WITH NORECOVERY, the database is put into the RESTORING state and can prevent an accidental background change from interfering with the restore sequence.

You can then restore *FG1* using the *RESTORE DATABASE* command, specifying just filegroup *FG1*. Your database is not in a consistent state because the restored *FG1* has changes only through 10 A.M., and the rest of the database has changes through 6 P.M. However, SQL Server knows when the last change was made to the database because each page in a database stores the LSN of the last log record that changed that page. When restoring a filegroup, SQL Server makes a note of the maximum LSN in the database. You must restore log backups until the log reaches at least the maximum LSN in the database, and you do not reach that point until you apply the 6 P.M. log backup.

## Partial Backups

A partial backup can be based either on a full or a differential backup, but a partial backup does not contain all the filegroups. Partial backups contain all the data in the primary filegroup and all the read-write filegroups. In addition, you can specify that any read-only files also be backed up. If the entire database is marked as read-only, a partial backup contains only the primary filegroup. Partial backups are particularly useful for very large databases (VLDBs) using the SIMPLE recovery model because they allow you to back up only specific filegroups, even without having log backups.

## Page Restore

SQL Server 2008 also allows you to restore individual pages. When SQL Server detects a damaged page, it marks it as suspect and stores information about the page in the *suspect_pages* table in the *msdb* database.

Damaged pages can be detected when activities such as the following take place:

- A query needs to read a page.
- *DBCC CHECKDB* or *DBCC CHECKTABLE* is being run.
- *BACKUP* or *RESTORE* is being run.
- You are trying to repair a database with *DBCC DBREPAIR*.

Several types of errors can require a page to be marked as suspect and entered into the *suspect_pages* table. These can include checksum and torn page errors, as well as internal consistency problems, such as a bad page ID in the page header. The column *event_type* in the *suspect_pages* table indicates the reason for the status of the page, which usually reflects the reason the page has been entered into the *suspect_pages* table. *SQL Server Books Online* lists the following possible values for the *event_type* column:

| *event_type* value | Description |
|---|---|
| 1 | 823 error caused by an operating system CDC error or 824 errors other than a bad checksum or a torn page (for example, a bad page ID). |
| 2 | Bad checksum. |
| 3 | Torn page. |
| 4 | Restored. (The page was restored after it was marked as bad.) |
| 5 | Repaired. (DBCC repaired the page.) |
| 7 | Deallocated by DBCC. |

Some of the errors recorded in the *suspect_pages* table might be transient errors, such as an I/O error that occurs because a cable has been disconnected. Rows can be deleted from the *suspect_pages* table by someone with the appropriate permissions, such as someone in the *sysadmin* server role. In addition, not all errors that cause a page to be inserted in the *suspect_pages* table require that the page be restored. A problem that occurs in cached data, such as in a nonclustered index, might be resolved by rebuilding the index. If a *sysadmin* drops a nonclustered index and rebuilds it, the corrupt data, although fixed, is not indicated as fixed in the *suspect_pages* table.

Page restore is specifically intended to replace pages that have been marked as suspect because of an invalid checksum or a torn write. Although multiple database pages can be restored at once, you aren't expected to be replacing a large number of individual pages. If you do have many damaged pages, you should probably consider a full file or database restore. In addition, you should probably try to determine the cause of the errors; if you discover a pending device failure, you should do your full file or database restore to a new location. Log restores must be done after the page restores to bring the new pages up to date with the rest of the database. Just as with file restore, the log backups are applied to the database files containing a page that is being recovered.

In an online page restore, the database is online for the duration of the restore, and only the data being restored is offline. Note that not all damaged pages can be restored with the database online.

> **Note**  Online page restore is allowed only in SQL Server 2008 Enterprise Edition.

*SQL Server Books Online* lists the following basic steps for a page restore:

1. Obtain the page IDs of the damaged pages to be restored. A checksum or torn write error returns the page ID, which is the information needed for specifying the pages. You can also get page IDs from the *suspect_pages* table.

2. Start a page restore with a full, file, or filegroup backup that contains the page or pages to be restored. In the *RESTORE DATABASE* statement, use the PAGE clause to list the page IDs of all the pages to be restored. The maximum number of pages that can be restored in a single file is 1,000.

3. Apply any available differentials required for the pages being restored.

4. Apply the subsequent log backups.

5. Create a new log backup of the database that includes the final LSN of the restored pages—that is, the point at which the last restored page was taken offline. The final LSN, which is set as part of the first restore in the sequence, is the redo target LSN. Online roll-forward of the file containing the page can stop at the redo target LSN. To learn the current redo target LSN of a file, see the *redo_target_lsn* column of *sys.master_files*.

6. Restore the new log backup. Once this new log backup is applied, the page restore is complete and the pages are usable. All the pages that were bad are affected by the log restore. All other pages have a more recent LSN in their page header, and there is nothing to redo. In addition, no UNDO phase is needed for page-level restore.

## Partial Restore

SQL Server 2008 lets you do a partial restore of a database in emergency situations. Although the description and the syntax look similar to file and filegroup backup and restore, there is a big difference. With file and filegroup restore, you start with a complete database and replace one or more files or filegroups with previously backed up versions. With a partial database restore, you don't start with a full database. You restore individual filegroups, which must include the primary filegroup containing all the system tables, to a new location. Any filegroups that you don't restore are treated as offline when you attempt to refer to data stored on them. You can then restore log backups or differential backups to bring the data in those filegroups to a later point in time. This allows you the option of recovering the data from a subset of tables after an accidental deletion or modification of table data. You can use the partially restored database to extract the data from the lost tables and copy it back into your original database.

## Restoring with Standby

In normal recovery operations, you have the choice of either running recovery to roll back incomplete transactions or not running recovery at all. If you run recovery, no further log backups can be restored and the database is fully usable. If you don't run recovery, the database is inconsistent and SQL Server won't let you use it at all. You have to choose one or the other because of the way log backups are made.

For example, in SQL Server 2008, log backups do not overlap—each log backup starts where the previous one ended. Consider a transaction that makes hundreds of updates to a single table. If you back up the log during the update and then after it, the first log backup has the beginning of the transaction and some of the updates, and the second log backup has the remainder of the updates and the commit. Suppose that you then need to restore these log backups after restoring the full database. If you run recovery after restoring the first log backup, the first part of the transaction is rolled back. If you then try to restore the second log backup, it starts in the middle of a transaction, and SQL Server won't have information about what the beginning of the transaction was. You certainly can't recover transactions from this point because their operations might depend on this update that you've partially lost. SQL Server, therefore, does not allow any more restoring to be done. The alternative is not to run recovery to roll back the first part of the transaction and instead to leave the transaction incomplete. SQL Server takes into account that the database is inconsistent and does not allow any users into the database until you finally run recovery on it.

What if you want to combine the two approaches? It would be nice to be able to restore one log backup and look at the data before restoring more log backups, particularly if you're trying to do a point-in-time recovery, but you won't know what the right point is. SQL Server provides an option called STANDBY that allows you to recover the database and still restore more log backups. If you restore a log backup and specify WITH STANDBY = '<some filename>', SQL Server rolls back incomplete transactions but keeps track of the rolled-back work in the specified file, which is known as a *standby file*. The next restore operation reads the contents of the standby file and redoes the operations that were rolled back, and then it restores the next log. If that restore also specifies WITH STANDBY, incomplete transactions again are rolled back, but a record of those rolled-back transactions is saved. Keep in mind that you can't modify any data if you've restored WITH STANDBY (SQL Server generates an error message if you try), but you can read the data and continue to restore more logs. The final log must be restored WITH RECOVERY (and no standby file is kept) to make the database fully usable.

# Summary

In addition to one or more data files, every database in a SQL Server instance has one or more log files that keep track of changes to that database. (Remember that database snapshots do not have log files because no changes are ever made directly to a snapshot.) SQL Server uses the transaction log to guarantee consistency of your data, at both a logical and a physical level. In addition, an administrator can make backups of the transaction log to make restoring a database more efficient. An administrator or database owner can also set a database's recovery mode to determine the level of detail stored in the transaction log.

# Chapter 5
# Tables

*Kalen Delaney*

In this chapter, we'll start with a basic introduction to tables and continue into some very detailed examinations of their internal structures. Simply put, a *table* is a collection of data about a specific *entity* (a person, place, or thing) that has a discrete number of named *attributes* (for example, quantity or type). Tables are at the heart of Microsoft SQL Server and the relational model in general. In SQL Server, a table is often referred to as a *base table* to emphasize where data is stored. Calling it a base table also distinguishes it from a *view*—a virtual table that's an internal query referencing one or more base tables or other views.

Attributes of a table's data (such as color, size, quantity, order date, and supplier's name) take the form of named *columns* in the table. Each instance of data in a table is represented as a single entry, or *row* (formally called a *tuple*). In a true relational database, each row in a table is unique and has a unique identifier called a *primary key*. (SQL Server, in accordance with the ANSI SQL standard, doesn't require you to make a row unique or declare a primary key. However, because both of these concepts are central to the relational model, I recommend that you always implement them.)

Most tables have some relationship to other tables. For example, in a typical order-entry system, the *orders* table has a *customer_number* column for keeping track of the customer number for an order, and *customer_number* also appears in the *customer* table. Assuming that *customer_ number* is a unique identifier, or primary key, of the *customer* table, a foreign key relationship is established by which *orders* and *customer* tables can subsequently be joined.

So much for the 30-second database design primer. You can find plenty of books that discuss logical database and table design, but this isn't one of them. I'll assume that you understand basic database theory and design and that you generally know what your tables will look like. The rest of this chapter discusses the internals of tables in SQL Server 2008.

## Creating Tables

To create a table, SQL Server uses the ANSI SQL standard *CREATE TABLE* syntax. SQL Server Management Studio provides a front-end, fill-in-the-blank table designer that can sometimes make your job easier. Ultimately, the SQL syntax is always sent to SQL Server to create a table, no matter what interface you use. In this chapter, I'll emphasize direct use of the Data Definition Language (DDL) rather than discuss the GUI tools. You should keep all DDL commands in a script so you can run them easily at a later time to re-create the table. (Even if you use one of the friendly front-end tools, it's critical that you are able to re-create the table later.) Management

Studio and other front-end tools can create and save operating system files using the SQL DDL commands necessary to create any object. This DDL is essentially source code, and you should treat it as such. Keep a backup copy. You should also consider keeping these files under version control using a source control product such as Microsoft Visual SourceSafe.

At the basic level, creating a table requires little more than knowing what you want to name it, what columns it contains, and what range of values (domain) each column can store. Here's the basic syntax for creating the *customer* table in the *dbo* schema, with three fixed-length character (*char*) columns. (Note that this table definition isn't necessarily the most efficient way to store data because it always requires 46 bytes per entry for data plus a few bytes of overhead, regardless of the actual length of the data.)

```
CREATE TABLE dbo.customer
(
name          char(30),
phone         char(12),
emp_id        char(4)
);
```

This example shows each column on a separate line for readability. As far as the SQL Server parser is concerned, white spaces created by tabs, carriage returns, and the spacebar are identical. From the system's standpoint, the following *CREATE TABLE* example is identical to the preceding one, but it's harder to read from a user's standpoint:

```
CREATE TABLE customer (name char(30), phone char(12), emp_id char(4));
```

## Naming Tables and Columns

A table is always created within one schema of one database. Tables also have owners, but unlike in versions of SQL Server prior to 2005, the table owner is not used to access the table. The schema is used for all object access. Normally, a table is created in the default schema of the user who is creating it, but the *CREATE TABLE* statement can specify the schema in which the object is to be created. A user can create a table only in a schema for which the user has *ALTER* permissions. Any user in the *sysadmin*, *db_ddladmin*, or *db_owner* roles can create a table in any schema. A database can contain multiple tables with the same name, so long as the tables are in different schemas. The full name of a table has three parts, in the following form:

database_name.schema_name.table_name

The first two parts of the three-part name specification have default values. The default for the name of the database is whatever database context in which you're currently working. The *schema_name* actually has two possible defaults when querying. If no schema name is specified when you reference an object, SQL Server first checks for an object in your default schema. If there is no such table in your default schema, SQL Server then checks to see if there is an object of the specified name in the *dbo* schema.

> **Note** To access a table or other object in a schema other than your default schema or the *dbo* schema, you must include the schema name along with the table name. In fact, you should get in the habit of always including the schema name when referring to any object in SQL Server 2008. Not only does this remove any possible confusion about which schema you are interested in, but it can lead to some performance benefits.
>
> The *sys* schema is a special case. For compatibility views, such as *sysobjects,* SQL Server accesses the object in the *sys* schema prior to any object you might have created with the same name. Obviously, it is not a good idea to create an object of your own called *sysobjects,* as you will never be able to access it. Compatibility views can also be accessed through the *dbo* schema, so the objects *sys.sysobjects* and *dbo.sysobjects* are the same. For catalog views and Dynamic Management Objects, you must specify the *sys* schema to access the object.

You should make column names descriptive, and because you'll use them repeatedly, you should avoid wordiness. The name of the column (or any object in SQL Server, such as a table or a view) can be whatever you choose, so long as it conforms to the SQL Server rule for regular identifiers: it must consist of a combination of 1 through 128 letters, digits, or the symbols #, $, @, or _.

> **More Info** Alternatively, you can use a delimited identifier that includes any characters you like. For more about identifier rules, see "Identifiers" in *SQL Server Books Online*. The discussion there applies to all SQL Server object names, not just column names.

In some cases, you can access a table using a four-part name, in which the first part is the name of the SQL Server instance. However, you can refer to a table using a four-part name only if the SQL Server instance has been defined as a linked server. You can read more about linked servers in *SQL Server Books Online;* I won't discuss them further here.

## Reserved Keywords

Certain reserved keywords, such as *TABLE, CREATE, SELECT,* and *UPDATE,* have special meaning to the SQL Server parser, and collectively they make up the SQL language implementation. You should avoid using reserved keywords for your object names. In addition to the SQL Server reserved keywords, the SQL-92 standard has its own list of reserved keywords. In some cases, this list is more restrictive than the SQL Server list; in other cases, it's less restrictive. *SQL Server Books Online* includes both lists.

Watch out for the SQL-92 reserved keywords. Some of the words aren't reserved keywords in SQL Server yet, but they might become reserved keywords in a future SQL Server version. If you use a SQL-92 reserved keyword, you might end up having to alter your application before upgrading it if the word becomes a SQL Server reserved keyword.

## Delimited Identifiers

You can't use keywords in your object names unless you use a delimited identifier. In fact, if you use a delimited identifier, not only can you use keywords as identifiers, but you can also use any other string as an object name—whether or not it follows the rules for identifiers. This includes spaces and other nonalphanumeric characters that are normally not allowed. Two types of delimited identifiers exist:

- Bracketed identifiers, which are delimited by square brackets ([*object name*])

- Quoted identifiers, which are delimited by double quotation marks (*"object name"*)

You can use bracketed identifiers in any environment, but to use quoted identifiers, you must enable a special option using SET QUOTED_IDENTIFIER ON. If you turn on QUOTED_IDENTIFIER, double quotes are interpreted as referencing an object. To delimit string or date constants, you must use single quotes.

Let's look at some examples. Because *column* is a reserved keyword, the first statement that follows is illegal in all circumstances. The second statement is illegal unless QUOTED_IDENTIFIER is on. The third statement is legal in any circumstance:

```
CREATE TABLE dbo.customer(name char(30), column char(12), emp_id char(4));

CREATE TABLE dbo.customer(name char(30), "column" char(12), emp_id char(4));

CREATE TABLE dbo.customer(name char(30), [column] char(12), emp_id char(4));
```

The SQL Native Client ODBC driver and SQL Native Client OLE DB Provider for SQL Server automatically set QUOTED_IDENTIFIER to ON when connecting. You can configure this in ODBC data sources, ODBC connection attributes, or OLE DB connection properties. You can determine whether this option is on or off for your session by executing the following query:

```
SELECT quoted_identifier
FROM sys.dm_exec_sessions
WHERE session_id = @@spid;
```

A result value of 1 indicates that QUOTED_IDENTIFIER is ON. If you're using Management Studio, you can check the setting by running the preceding command in a query window or by choosing Options from the Tools menu and then expanding the Query Execution/SQL Server node and examining the ANSI properties information, as shown in Figure 5-1.

**Tip** Technically, you can use delimited identifiers with all object and column names, so you never have to worry about reserved keywords. However, I don't recommend this. Many third-party tools for SQL Server don't handle quoted identifiers well, and they can make your code difficult to read. Using quoted identifiers might also make upgrading to future versions of SQL Server more difficult.

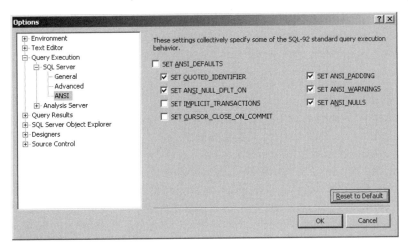

**FIGURE 5-1** Examining the ANSI properties for a connection in Management Studio

Rather than using delimited identifiers to protect against reserved keyword problems, you should simply adopt some simple naming conventions. For example, you can precede column names with the first few letters of the table name and an underscore. This naming style makes the column or object name more readable and also greatly reduces your chances of encountering a keyword or reserved word conflict.

## Naming Conventions

Many organizations and multiuser development projects adopt standard naming conventions. This is generally a good practice. For example, assigning a standard moniker of *cust_id* to represent a customer number in every table clearly shows that all the tables share common data. If an organization instead uses several monikers in the tables to represent a customer number, such as *cust_id*, *cust_num*, *customer_number*, and *customer_#*, it won't be as obvious that these monikers represent common data.

One naming convention is the Hungarian-style notation for column names. Hungarian-style notation is a widely used practice in C programming, whereby variable names include information about their data types. This notation uses names such as *sint_nn_custnum* to indicate that the *custnum* column is a small integer (*smallint* of 2 bytes) and is NOT NULL (doesn't allow nulls). Although this practice makes good sense in C programming, it defeats the data type independence that SQL Server provides; therefore, I recommend against using it.

## Data Types

SQL Server provides many data types, most of which are straightforward. Choosing the appropriate data type is simply a matter of mapping the domain of values you need to store to the corresponding data type. In choosing data types, you want to avoid wasting storage space while allowing enough space for a sufficient range of possible values over the life of your application. Discussing the details about all the possible considerations when programming with the various data types is beyond the scope of this book. For the most part, I'll just cover some of the basic issues related to dealing with the various data types.

## Choosing a Data Type

The decision about what data type to use for each column depends primarily on the nature of the data the column holds and the operations you want to perform on the data. The five basic data type categories in SQL Server 2008 are numeric, character, date and time, Large Object (LOB), and miscellaneous. SQL Server 2008 also supports a variant data type called *sql_variant*. Values stored in a *sql_variant* column can be of almost any data type. I'll discuss LOB columns in Chapter 7, "Special Storage," because their storage format is different than that of other data types discussed in this chapter. In this section, I'll examine some of the issues related to storing data of different data types.

## Numeric Data Types

You should use numeric data types for data on which you want to perform numeric comparisons or arithmetic operations. Your main decisions are the maximum range of possible values you want to be able to store and the accuracy you need. The tradeoff is that data types that can store a greater range of values take up more space.

Numeric data types can also be classified as either exact or approximate. Exact numeric values are guaranteed to store exact representations of your numbers. Approximate numeric values have a far greater range of values, but the values are not guaranteed to be stored precisely. The greatest range of values that exact numeric values can store data is $-10^{38} + 1$ to $10^{38} - 1$. Unless you need numbers with greater magnitude, I recommend that you not use the approximate numeric data types.

The exact numeric data types can be divided into two groups: integers and decimals. Integer types range in size from 1 to 8 bytes, with a corresponding increase in the range of possible values. The *money* and *smallmoney* data types are included frequently among the integer types because internally they are stored in the same way. For the *money* and *smallmoney* data types, it is understood that the rightmost four digits are after the decimal point. For the other integer types, no digits come after the decimal point. Table 5-1 lists the integer data types along with their storage size and range of values.

The decimal and numeric data types allow a high degree of accuracy and a large range of values. For those two synonymous data types, you can specify a *precision* (the total number of digits stored) and a *scale* (the maximum number of digits to the right of the decimal point). The maximum number of digits that can be stored to the left of the decimal point is precision – scale (that is, subtract the scale from precision to get the number of digits). Two different decimal values can have the same precision and very different ranges. For example, a column defined as decimal (8,4) can store values from –9,999.9999 to 9,999.9999, and a column defined as decimal (8,0) can store values from –99,999,999 to 99,999,999.

**TABLE 5-1  Range and Storage Requirements for Integer Data Types**

| Data Type | Range | Storage (Bytes) |
|---|---|---|
| *bigint* | $-2^{63}$ to $2^{63}-1$ | 8 |
| *int* | $-2^{31}$ to $2^{31}-1$ | 4 |
| *Smallint* | $-2^{15}$ to $2^{15}-1$ | 2 |
| *Tinyint* | 0 to 255 | 1 |
| *Money* | $-922,337,203,685,477.5808$ to $922,337,203,685,477.5807$, with accuracy of one ten-thousandth of a monetary unit | 8 |
| *Smallmoney* | $-214,748.3648$ to $214,748.3647$, with accuracy of one ten-thousandth of a monetary unit | 4 |

Table 5-2 shows the storage space required for decimal and numeric data based on the defined precision.

**TABLE 5-2  Storage Requirements for Decimal and Numeric Data Types**

| Precision | Storage (Bytes) |
|---|---|
| 1 to 9 | 5 |
| 10 to 19 | 9 |
| 20 to 28 | 13 |
| 29 to 38 | 17 |

> **Note**  SQL Server 2005 SP2 added a feature to allow decimal data to be stored in a variable amount of space. This can be useful when you have some values that need a high degree of precision, but most of the values in the column need only a few bytes, or are 0 or NULL. *Vardecimal,* unlike *varchar,* is not a data type, but rather a property of a table which is set by using the *sp_tableoption* procedure, and in SQL Server 2005, it must also be enabled for the database. In SQL Server 2008, all databases except the *master, model, tempdb,* and *msdb* databases always allow tables to have the *vardecimal storage format* property enabled.
>
> Although the vardecimal storage format can reduce the storage size of the data, it comes at the cost of adding additional CPU overhead. Once the *vardecimal* property is enabled for a table, all *decimal* data in the table is stored as variable-length data. This includes all indexes on *decimal* data and all log records that include *decimal* data.

Changing the value of the *vardecimal storage format* property of a table is an offline operation and SQL Server exclusively locks the table that is being modified until all the decimal data is converted to the new format. The vardecimal storage format has been deprecated, so I will not be describing the details of the internal storage for *vardecimal* data. For new development, it is recommended that you use SQL Server's compression capabilities to minimize your storage requirement for data that requires a variable number of bytes. I will discuss data compression in Chapter 7.

## Date and Time Data Types

SQL Server 2008 supports six data types for storing date and time information: *datetime* and *smalldatetime* have been available since the very first version and four new types were added in SQL Server 2008: *date, time, datetime2,* and *datetimeoffset.* The difference between these types is the range of possible dates, the number of bytes needed for storage, whether both date and time are stored (or just the date or just the time), and whether time zone information is incorporated into the stored value. Table 5-3, taken from *SQL Server 2008 Books Online,* shows the range and storage requirements for each of the date and time data types.

**TABLE 5-3  SQL Server Date and Time Data Types Range and Storage Requirements**

| Type | Format | Range | Accuracy | Storage Size (bytes) | User-Defined Fractional Second Precision |
|---|---|---|---|---|---|
| *time* | *hh:mm:ss [.nnnnnnn]* | 00:00:00.0000000 through 23:59:59.9999999 | 100 nanoseconds | 3 to 5 | Yes |
| *date* | *YYYY-MM-DD* | 0001-01-01 through 9999-12-31 | 1 day | 3 | No |
| *smalldatetime* | *YYYY-MM-DD hh:mm:ss* | 1900-01-01 through 2079-06-06 | 1 minute | 4 | No |
| *datetime* | *YYYY-MM-DD hh:mm:ss [.nnn]* | 1753-01-01 through 9999-12-31 | 0.00333 second | 8 | No |
| *datetime2* | *YYYY-MM-DD hh:mm:ss [.nnnnnnn]* | 0001-01-01 00:00:00.0000000 through 9999-12-31 23:59:59.9999999 | 100 nanoseconds | 6 to 8 | Yes |
| *datetimeoffset* | *YYYY-MM-DD hh:mm:ss [.nnnnnnn] [+\|-]hh:mm* | 0001-01-01 00:00:00.0000000 through 9999-12-31 23:59:59.9999999 (in UTC) | 100 nanoseconds | 8 to 10 (2 bytes for time zone data) | Yes |

If no date is supplied, the default of January 1, 1900, is assumed; if no time is supplied, the default of 00:00:00.000 (midnight) is assumed.

**Note** If you're new to SQL Server date and time data, you might be surprised that for the original *datetime* data type, the earliest possible date that can be stored is January 1, 1753. This was done for historical reasons, and started with the original Sybase specification for the *datetime* data type. In what we sometimes refer to as the Western world, there have been two calendars in modern time: the Julian and the Gregorian calendars. These calendars were a number of days apart (depending on which century you look at), so when a culture that used the Julian calendar moved to the Gregorian calendar, they dropped between 10 to 13 days from the calendar. Great Britain made this shift in 1752, and in that year, September 2 was followed by September 14. Sybase decided not to store dates earlier than 1753 because the date arithmetic functions would be ambiguous. However, other countries made the change at other times, and in Turkey, the calendar was not shifted until 1927.

Internally, values for all the date and time data types are stored completely differently from how you enter them or how they are displayed. Dates and times are always stored as two separate components: a date component and a time component.

For the original *datetime* data types, *datetime* and *smalldatetime*, the data is stored internally as two separate components. For *datetime* values, the data is stored as two 4-byte values, the first (for the date) being the number of days before or after the base date of January 1, 1900, and the second (for the time) being the number of clock ticks after midnight, with each tick representing 3.33 milliseconds, or 1/300 of a second. You can actually see these two parts if you convert a *datetime* value to a binary string of 8 hexadecimal bytes. For *smalldatetime* values, each component is stored in 2 bytes. The date is stored as the number of days after January 1, 1900, and the time is stored as the number of minutes after midnight.

The following example shows how to see the component parts of the current date and time, stored in a variable of type *datetime*, retrieved using the parameterless system function *CURRENT_TIMESTAMP*. The first *CONVERT* operation shows the full hexadecimal byte string that stores the *datetime* value. The second *CONVERT* displays the first four bytes converted to an integer and the third *CONVERT* displays the second four bytes converted to an integer. Because we're storing current date and time in a local variable, we can be sure we're using the same value for all the *CONVERT* operations:

```
DECLARE @today datetime
SELECT @today = CURRENT_TIMESTAMP
SELECT @today AS [CURRENT TIMESTAMP];
SELECT CONVERT (varbinary(8), @today) AS [INTERNAL FORMAT];
SELECT CONVERT (int, SUBSTRING (CONVERT (varbinary(8), @today), 1, 4))
        AS [DAYS AFTER 1/1/1900];
SELECT CONVERT (int, SUBSTRING (CONVERT (varbinary(8), @today), 5, 4))
        AS [TICKS AFTER MIDNIGHT];
```

These are the results when the code runs on July 10, 2008:

```
CURRENT TIMESTAMP
-----------------------
2008-07-10 17:29:11.967
```

```
INTERNAL FORMAT
------------------
0x00009AD501202BD6

DAYS AFTER 1/1/1900
-------------------
39637

TICKS AFTER MIDNIGHT
--------------------
18885590
```

Microsoft used the opportunity when adding new *date* and *time* data types in SQL Server 2008 to change the internal representation of dates and times completely. Dates are now stored as a three-byte positive number, representing the number of days after January 1, 0001. For the *datetimeoffset* type, an additional two bytes are used to store a time offset, in hours and minutes, from UTC. Note that although internally, the base date for the new date and data types is January 1, 0001, when SQL Server is interpreting a date value where the actual date is not specified, January 1, 1900, is the default. For example, if you try to insert the string '01:15:00' into a *datetime2* column, SQL Server interprets this as a time of 1:15 on January 1, 1900.

All the new types that contain time information (*time*, *datetime2*, and *datetimeoffset*) allow you to specify the precision of the time component by following the data type name with a number between 1 and 7 indicating the desired scale. The default, if no scale is specified, is to assume a scale of 7. Table 5-4 shows what each of the possible scale values means in terms of the precision and storage requirement of the stored data values.

**TABLE 5-4** Scale Values for Time Data with Storage Requirements and Precision

| Specified Scale | Result (precision, scale) | Column Length (bytes) | Fractional Seconds (precision) |
|---|---|---|---|
| none | (16,7) | 5 | 7 |
| (0) | (8,0) | 3 | 0–2 |
| (1) | (10,1) | 3 | 0–2 |
| (2) | (11,2) | 3 | 0–2 |
| (3) | (12,3) | 4 | 3–4 |
| (4) | (13,4) | 4 | 3–4 |
| (5) | (14,5) | 5 | 5–7 |
| (6) | (15,6) | 5 | 5–7 |
| (7) | (16,7) | 5 | 5–7 |

For a quick look at what the information in Table 5-4 means, you can run the following three conversions:

```
SELECT CAST(CURRENT_TIMESTAMP AS time);
SELECT CAST(CURRENT_TIMESTAMP AS time(2));
SELECT CAST(CURRENT_TIMESTAMP AS time(7));
```

I got the following results. Note that the scale value determines the number of decimal digits and that the value for *time* is identical to *time*(7):

```
17:39:43.0830000
17:39:43.08
17:39:43.0830000
```

Internally, the time is computed using the following formula, assuming *H* is hours, *M* is minutes, *S* is seconds, *F* is fractional sections, and *D* is scale (number of decimal digits):

$$(((H * 60) + M) * 60 + S) * 10^D + F$$

For example, the value 17:39:43.08, with *time(2)* format, would be stored internally as

$$(((17 * 60) + 39) * 60 + 43) * 10^2 + 083, \text{ or } 6358383$$

The same time, stored as *time*(7) would be

$$(((17 * 60) + 39) * 60 + 43) * 10^7 + 083, \text{ or } 635830000083$$

In the section entitled "Internal Storage," later in this chapter, we'll see what this data looks like when stored in a data row.

SQL Server 2008 provides dozens of functions for working with *date* and *time* data, as well as dozens of different formats that can be used for interpreting and displaying date and time values. It is beyond the scope of this book to cover date and time data in that level of detail. However, the most important thing to understand about these types is that what you see is not what is actually stored on disk. The on-disk format, whether you're using the old *datetime* and *smalldatetime* types or any of the new types, is completely unambiguous, but it is not very user-friendly. You need to make sure that you provide input data in a format that is also unambiguous. For example, the value '3/4/48' is *not* unambiguous. Does it represent March 4 or April 3, and is the year 1948, 2048, or perhaps 48 (almost 2,000 years ago)? The ISO 8601 format is an international standard with unambiguous specification. In addition this format is not affected by your session's *SET DATEFORMAT* or *SET LANGUAGE* settings. Using this format, March 4, 1948, could be represented as 19480304 or 1948-03-04.

## Character Data Types

Character data types come in four varieties. They can be fixed-length or variable-length strings of single-byte characters (*char* and *varchar*) or fixed-length or variable-length strings of Unicode characters (*nchar* and *nvarchar*). Unicode character strings need two bytes for each stored character; use them when you need to represent characters that can't be stored in the single-byte characters that are sufficient for storing most of the characters in the English and European alphabets. Single-byte character strings can store up to 8,000 characters, and Unicode character strings can store up to 4,000 characters. You should know the type of data that you are dealing with to decide between single-byte and double-byte character strings. Keep in mind that the catalog view *sys.types* reports the length in number of bytes, not in number of characters. In SQL Server 2005 and SQL Server 2008, you can also define a variable-length character string with a MAX length. Columns defined as *varchar(max)* are treated as normal variable-length columns when the actual length is less than or equal to 8,000 bytes, and they are treated as a large object value (mentioned later in this section and covered in detail in Chapter 7) when the actual length is greater than 8,000 bytes.

Deciding whether to use a variable-length or a fixed-length data type is a more difficult decision, and it isn't always straightforward or obvious. As a general rule, variable-length data types are most appropriate when you expect significant variation in the size of the data for a column and when the data in the column won't be changed frequently.

Using variable-length data types can yield important storage savings. It can sometimes result in a minor performance loss, and at other times it can result in improved performance. A row with variable-length columns requires special offset entries to be internally maintained. These entries keep track of the actual length of the column. Calculating and maintaining the offsets requires slightly more overhead than does a pure fixed-length row, which needs no such offsets. This task requires a few addition and subtraction operations to maintain the offset value. However, the extra overhead of maintaining these offsets is generally inconsequential, and this alone would not make a significant difference on most, if any, systems.

Another potential performance issue with variable-length fields is the cost of increasing the size of a row on a page that is almost full. If a row with variable-length columns uses only part of its maximum length and is later updated to a longer length, the enlarged row might no longer fit on the same page. If the table has a clustered index, the row must stay in the same position relative to the other rows, so the solution is to split the page and move some of the rows from the page with the enlarged row onto a newly linked page. This can be an expensive operation. Chapter 6, "Indexes: Internals and Management," describes the details of page splitting and moving rows. If the table has no clustered index, the row can move to a new location and leave a forwarding pointer in the original location. I'll talk about forwarding pointers later in this chapter.

On the other hand, using variable-length columns can sometimes improve performance because it can allow more rows to fit on a page. But the efficiency results from more than simply requiring less disk space. A data page for SQL Server is 8 KB (8,192 bytes), of which 8,096 bytes are available to store data. (The rest is for internal use to keep track of structural information about the page and the object to which it belongs.) One I/O operation brings back the entire page. If you can fit 80 rows on a page, a single I/O operation brings back 80 rows. But if you can fit 160 rows on a page, one I/O operation is essentially twice as efficient. In operations that scan for data and return lots of adjacent rows, this can amount to a significant performance improvement. The more rows you can fit per page, the better your I/O and cache-hit efficiency is.

For example, consider a simple customer table. Suppose that you could define it in two ways: fixed-length and variable-length, as shown in Figures 5-2 and 5-3.

Columns that contain addresses, names, or URLs all have data that varies significantly in length. Let's look at the differences between choosing fixed-length columns and choosing variable-length columns. In Figure 5-2, which uses all fixed-length columns, every row uses 384 bytes for data regardless of the number of characters actually inserted in the row. SQL Server also needs an additional 10 bytes of overhead for every row in this table, so each row needs a total of 394 bytes for storage. But let's say that even though the table must accommodate addresses and names up to the specified size, the average row is only half the maximum size.

```
USE testdb
GO

CREATE TABLE customer_fixed
(
cust_id                smallint       NULL,
cust_name              char(50)       NULL,
cust_addr1             char(50)       NULL,
cust_addr2             char(50)       NULL,
cust_city              char(50)       NULL,
cust_state             char(2)        NULL,
cust_postal_code       char(10)       NULL,
cust_phone             char(20)       NULL,
cust_fax               char(20)       NULL,
cust_email             char(30)       NULL,
cust_web_url           char(100)      NULL,
)
```

**FIGURE 5-2** A customer table with all fixed-length columns

```
USE testdb
GO

CREATE TABLE customer_var
(
cust_id                smallint       NULL,
cust_name              varchar(50)    NULL,
cust_addr1             varchar(50)    NULL,
cust_addr2             varchar(50)    NULL,
cust_city              varchar(50)    NULL,
cust_state             char(2)        NULL,
cust_postal_code       varchar(10)    NULL,
cust_phone             varchar(20)    NULL,
cust_fax               varchar(20)    NULL,
cust_email             varchar(30)    NULL,
cust_web_url           varchar(100)   NULL
)
```

**FIGURE 5-3** A customer table with variable-length columns

In Figure 5-3, assume that for all the variable-length (*varchar*) columns the average entry is actually only about half the maximum. Instead of a row length of 394 bytes, the average length is 224 bytes. This length is computed as follows: The *smallint* and *char(2)* columns total 4 bytes. The *varchar* columns' maximum total length is 380, half of which is 190 bytes. And a 2-byte overhead exists for each of nine *varchar* columns, for 18 bytes. Add 2 more bytes for any row that has one or more variable-length columns. In addition, these rows require the same 10 bytes of overhead that the fixed-length rows from Figure 5-2 require, regardless of the presence of variable-length fields. So the total is 4 + 190 + 18 + 2 + 10, or 224. (I'll discuss the actual meaning of each of these bytes of overhead later in this chapter.)

In the fixed-length example in Figure 5-2, you always fit 20 rows on a data page (8,096/394, discarding the remainder). In the variable-length example in Figure 5-3, you can fit an average of 36 rows per page (8,096/224). The table using variable-length columns will consume about half as many pages in storage, a single I/O operation retrieves almost twice as many rows, and a page cached in memory is twice as likely to contain the row you want.

> **More Info**  You need additional overhead bytes for each row if you are using snapshot isolation. I'll discuss this concurrency option, as well as the extra row overhead needed to support it, in Chapter 10, "Transactions and Concurrency."

When you choose lengths for columns, don't be wasteful—but don't be cheap, either. Allow for future needs, and realize that if the additional length doesn't change how many rows fit on a page, the additional size is free anyway. Consider again the examples in Figures 5-2 and 5-3. The *cust_id* is declared as a *smallint*, meaning that its maximum positive value is 32,767 (unfortunately, SQL Server doesn't provide any unsigned *int* or unsigned *smallint* data types), and it consumes 2 bytes of storage. Although 32,767 customers might seem like a lot to a new company, the company might be surprised by its own success and find in a couple of years that 32,767 is too limited.

The database designers might regret that they tried to save 2 bytes and didn't simply make the data type an *int*, using 4 bytes but with a maximum positive value of 2,147,483,647. They'll be especially disappointed if they realize they didn't really save any space. If you compute the rows-per-page calculations just discussed, increasing the row size by 2 bytes, you'll see that the same number of rows still fit on a page. The additional 2 bytes are free—they were simply wasted space before. They never cause fewer rows per page in the fixed-length example, and they'll rarely cause fewer rows per page even in the variable-length case.

So which strategy wins? Potentially better update performance? Or more rows per page? Like most questions of this nature, no one answer is right. It depends on your application. If you understand the tradeoffs, you can make the best choice. Now that you know the issues, this general rule merits repeating: Variable-length data types are most appropriate when you expect significant variation in the size of the data for that column and when the column won't be updated frequently.

## Character Data Collation

For many data types, the rules to compare and sort are straightforward. No matter whom you ask, 12 is always greater than 11, and even if people may write dates in different ways, August 20, 2008, is never the same as August 21, 2007. But for character data, this principle doesn't apply. Most people would sort *csak* before *cukor*, but in an Hungarian dictionary, they come in the opposite order. And is *STREET* equal to *Street* or not? Also, how are characters with diacritic marks, such as accents or umlauts, sorted?

Because different users have different preferences and needs, character data in SQL Server are always associated with a *collation*. A collation is a set of rules that defines how character data are sorted and compared, and how language-dependent functions such as *UPPER* and *LOWER* work. The collation also determines the character repertoire for the single-byte data types, *char, varchar,* and *text*. Metadata in SQL Server (that is, names of tables, variables, etc.) are also subject to collation rules.

**Determining Which Collation to Use**   You can define which collation to use at several levels in SQL Server. When you create a table, you can define the collation for each character column. If you don't supply a collation, the database collation is used.

The database collation also determines the collation for the metadata in the database. So in a database with a case-insensitive collation, you can use *MyTable* or *MYTABLE* to refer to a table which was created with the name *mytable*, but in a database with a case-sensitive collation, you must refer to it as *mytable*. The database collation also determines the collation for string literals and for data in character variables.

You can specify the database collation when you create a database. If you do not, the server collation is used. Under some fairly restricted circumstances, the *ALTER DATABASE* statement permits you to change the database collation. (Basically, if you have any CHECK constraints in the database, you cannot change the collation.) This will rebuild the system tables to reflect the new collation rules in the metadata. However, columns in user tables are left unchanged, and you need to change these yourself. For details on all restrictions, please see the *ALTER DATABASE* topic in *SQL Server Books Online*.

The server collation is used by the system databases *master, model, tempdb,* and *msdb*. (The resource database, on the other hand, always has the same collation, Latin1_General_CI_AI.) The server collation is also the collation for variable names, so on a server with a case-insensitive collation, @a and @A are the same variable, but they are two different ones if the server collation is case-sensitive. You select the server collation at setup.

Finally, you can use the COLLATE clause to force the collation in an expression. One situation where you need to do this is when the same expression includes two columns with different collations. This results in a *collation conflict*, and SQL Server requires you to resolve it with the COLLATE clause.

**Available Collations**   To see the available collations, you can run the query

```
SELECT * FROM fn_helpcollations();
```

When running this query on a SQL Server 2008 instance, the result contains 2,397 collations. There are another 112 collations that are deprecated and not listed by fn_helpcollations.

Collations fall into two main groups: Windows collations and SQL Server collations. SQL Server collations are mainly former collations retained for compatibility reasons. Nevertheless, the collation SQL_Latin1_General_CP1_CI_AS is one of the most commonly used ones because it is the default collation when you install SQL Server on a machine with English (United States) as the system locale.

**Windows Collations**     Windows collations take their definition from Microsoft Windows. SQL Server does not go out and query Windows for collation rules; rather, the SQL Server team has copied the collation definitions into SQL Server. The collations in Windows typically are modified with new releases of Windows to adapt to changes in the Unicode standard, and because collations determine in which order data appear in indexes, SQL Server cannot accept that the definition of a collation changes because you move a database to a different Windows version.

***The Anatomy of a Collation Name***     Windows collations come in families, with 18 collations in each family. All collations in the same family start with the same *collation designator*, which indicates which language or group of languages the collation family supports.

The collation designator is followed by tokens that indicate the nature of the collation. The collation can be a binary collation, in which case the token is BIN or BIN2. For the other 16 collations, the tokens are CI/CS to indicate case sensitivity/insensitivity, AI/AS to indicate accent sensitivity/insensitivity, KS to indicate kanatype sensitivity, and WS to indicate width sensitivity.

If CI is part of the collation name, the strings *smith* and *SMITH* are equal, but they are different if CS is in the name. Likewise, if the collation is AI, *cote, coté, côte,* and *côté* are all equal, but in an AS collation, they are different. Kanatype relates to Japanese text only, and in a kanatype-sensitive collation, katakana and hiragana counterparts are considered different. Width sensitivity refers to East Asian languages for which there exists both half-width and full-width forms of some characters. KI and WI tokens do not exist, but kanatype and width insensitivity are implied if KS and WS are absent.

The following are some examples of collation names:

- **Latin1_General_CI_AS**     A case-insensitive, accent-sensitive collation for Western European languages such as English, German, and Italian

- **Finnish_Swedish_CS_AS**     A case-sensitive and accent-sensitive collation for Finnish and Swedish

- **Japanese_CI_AI_KS_WS**     A collation that is insensitive to case and accent and sensitive to kanatype and width differences

- **Turkish_BIN2**     A binary collation for Turkish

***Different Versions of the Same Collation***     A collation designator may include a version number that indicates in which version of SQL Server the collation was added. The lack of a version number means that the collation was one of the original collations in SQL Server 2000; 90 indicates that the collation was added in SQL Server 2005; and 100 means that it was added in SQL Server 2008.

SQL Server 2008 added new collations for languages and language groups for which a collation already existed. So there is now both Latin1_General and Latin1_General_100, Finnish_Swedish and Finnish_Swedish_100, and other collation pairs.

These additions reflect the changes in Windows. The old collations are based on the collations in Windows 2000, and the new _100 collations are based on the collations in Windows 2008.

> **Caution**  If you plan to access your SQL Server 2008 instance as a linked server from SQL Server 2005, you should avoid using the new _100 collations because if you try to access such a column from SQL Server 2005, you get the error message, "An invalid tabular data stream (TDS) collation was encountered."

***The Single-Byte Character Types***   The single-byte character data types, *char, varchar,* and *text,* can represent only 255 possible characters, and the *code page* of the collation determines which 255 characters are available. In most code pages, the characters from 32 to 127 are always the same, taken from the ASCII standard, and remaining characters are selected to fit a certain language area. For instance, CP1252, also known as Latin-1, supports Western European languages such as English, French, Swedish, and others. CP1250 is for the Cyrillic script, CP1251 is for Eastern European languages, and so on.

When it comes to other operations—sorting, comparing, lower/upper, and so on—in a Windows collation, the rules are exactly the same for the single-byte data types and the double-byte Unicode data types. There is one exception to this: in a binary collation, sorting is done by character codes, and the order in the single-byte code page can be different from the order in Unicode. For instance, in a Polish collation, *char(209)* prints Ń (a capital N with an acute accent), whereas *unicode(N'Ń')* prints 323, which is the code point in Unicode for this character. (The code points in Unicode agree with the code points in Latin-1, but that applies only to the range 160-255.) Microsoft has added some extra characters to their version of Latin-1. One example of this is the Euro(€) character, which is *char(128)* in a collation based on CP1252, but in Unicode, code point 128 is a nonprinting character, and *unicode(N'€')* prints 8364.

There are some collations that do not map to a single-byte code page. You can use these collations only with Unicode data types. For instance, if you run the code

```
CREATE TABLE NepaleseTest
    (abc char(5) COLLATE Nepali_100_CI_AS NOT NULL);
```

you get the following error message:

```
Msg 459, Level 16, State 2, Line 1
Collation 'Nepali_100_CI_AS' is supported on Unicode data types only and cannot be applied
to char, varchar or text data types.
```

To view the code page for a collation, you can use the *collationproperty* function, as in this example:

```
SELECT collationproperty('Latin1_General_CS_AS', 'CodePage');
```

This returns 1252. For a collation that supports Unicode only, you get 0 in return. (If you get NULL back, you have misspelled the collation name or the word *CodePage*.)

You cannot use Unicode-only collations as the server collation.

***Sort Order*** The collation determines the sort order. When a Windows collation is insensitive (such as case or accents), this also applies to the sort order. For instance, in a case-insensitive collation, differences in case do not affect how the data is sorted. In a sensitive collation, case, accent, kanatype, and width affect the sorting, but only with a secondary weight. That is, these properties affect the sorting only when no other differences exist.

To illustrate this, consider this table:

```
CREATE TABLE #words (word    nvarchar(20) NOT NULL,
                     wordno tinyint PRIMARY KEY CLUSTERED);
INSERT #words
   VALUES(N'cloud',  1), (N'CSAK',    6), (N'cukor',   11),
         (N'Oblige', 2), (N'Opera',   7), (N'Öl',      12),
         (N'résumé', 3), (N'RESUME',  8), (N'RÉSUMÉ',  13),
         (N'resume', 4), (N'resumes', 9), (N'résumés', 14),
         (N'ŒIL',    5), (N'œil',    10);
```

To examine how a collation works, we use the query shown here. We start by looking at the commonly used collation Latin1_General_CI_AS:

```
WITH collatedwords (collatedword, wordno) AS (
   SELECT word COLLATE Latin1_General_CI_AS, wordno
   FROM    #words
)
SELECT collatedword, rank = dense_rank() OVER(ORDER BY collatedword),
       wordno
FROM    collatedwords
ORDER   BY collatedword;
```

When I ran the query, I got this result:

```
collatedword    rank    wordno
--------------  ------  ------
cloud           1       1
CSAK            2       6
cukor           3       11
Oblige          4       2
ŒIL             5       5
œil             5       10
Öl              6       12
Opera           7       7
RESUME          8       8
resume          8       4
résumé          9       3
RÉSUMÉ          9       13
resumes         10      9
résumés         11      14
```

The *rank* column gives the ranking in the sort order. We can see that for the words that differ only in case, the ranking is the same. We can also see from the output that sometimes the uppercase version comes first, and sometimes the lowercase version comes first. This is something that is entirely arbitrary, and it's perfectly possible that you will see a different order for these pairs if you run the query yourself.

If we change the collation to Latin1_General_CS_AS, we get this result:

```
collatedword    rank    wordno
--------------  ------  ------
cloud           1       1
CSAK            2       6
cukor           3       11
Oblige          4       2
œil             5       10
ŒIL             6       5
Öl              7       12
Opera           8       7
resume          9       4
RESUME          10      8
résumé          11      3
RÉSUMÉ          12      13
resumes         13      9
résumés         14      14
```

All entries now have a different ranking. The lowercase forms come before the uppercase forms when no other difference exists because in Windows collations, lowercase always has a lower secondary weight than uppercase.

Let's now see what happens with a different language. Here's a test for the collation Hungarian_CI_AI:

```
collatedword    rank    wordno
--------------  ------  ------
cloud           1       1
cukor           2       11
CSAK            3       6
Oblige          4       2
ŒIL             5       5
œil             5       10
Opera           6       7
Öl              7       12
RÉSUMÉ          8       13
RESUME          8       8
résumé          8       3
resume          8       4
resumes         9       9
résumés         9       14
```

The words *CSAK* and *öl* now sort after *cukor* and *Opera*. This is because in the Hungarian alphabet, CS and Ö are letters on their own. You can also see that in this CI_AI collation, all four forms of *résumé* have the same rank.

In these examples, the data type for the column was *nvarchar,* but if you change the table to use *varchar* and rerun the examples, you get the same results.

***Character Ranges and Collations*** The sort order applies not only to ORDER BY clauses, but also to operators such as > and ranges in LIKE expressions. For instance, note the following code:

```
SELECT * FROM #words
WHERE word COLLATE Latin1_General_CI_AS > 'opera';
SELECT * FROM #words
WHERE word COLLATE Latin1_General_CS_AS > 'opera';
```

The first *SELECT* lists six words, whereas the second lists seven (because in a case-sensitive collation, *Opera* is > *opera*).

If you are used to character ranges from regular expressions in other languages, you may fall into the following trap when trying to select the words that start with an uppercase letter:

```
SELECT * FROM #words WHERE word LIKE '[A-Z]%';
```

But even with a case-sensitive collation, this code usually lists all 14 words. (In some languages, *Ö* sorts as a separate letter after *Z*, so it does not fall into the specified range.) The range *A–Z* is also subject to the collation rules. This also has another consequence: change *cloud* to *aloud* in the list. Using a case-sensitive collation, *SELECT* now returns only 13 rows. Because *a* sorts before *A*, the range *A–Z* does not include *a*.

As you can see, this can be a bit confusing. My advice is that you be very careful when using ranges with character data. If you need to do it, make sure that you really test the edge cases to ensure that you don't exclude any data inadvertently.

***Binary Collations*** In a binary collation, no secondary weights exist, and characters sort by their code points in the character set. So with Latin1_General_BIN2 in the previous example, we get

| collatedword | rank | wordno |
| --- | --- | --- |
| CSAK | 1 | 6 |
| Oblige | 2 | 2 |
| Opera | 3 | 7 |
| RESUME | 4 | 8 |
| RÉSUMÉ | 5 | 13 |
| cloud | 6 | 1 |
| cukor | 7 | 11 |
| resume | 8 | 4 |
| resumes | 9 | 9 |
| résumé | 10 | 3 |
| résumés | 11 | 14 |
| Öl | 12 | 12 |
| ŒIL | 13 | 5 |
| œil | 14 | 10 |

Now the words with the uppercase first letters *C*, *O*, and *R* come before those with the lowercase *c*, *o*, and *r*, as they do in the ASCII standard. *Öl* and the two forms of *œil* have code points beyond the first 127 ASCII codes and therefore come at the end of the list.

Because binary collations are based on the code points and they may be different in the single-byte code page and in Unicode, the order can be different for single-byte and Unicode data types. For instance, if you change the data type in #words to *varchar* and run the example with Latin1_General_BIN2 again, you find that *Öl* now comes last.

As you recall from the previous discussion, two types of binary collations exist, BIN and BIN2. Of these, the BIN collations are earlier collations, and if you need to use a binary collation in new development, you should use a BIN2 collation. To understand the difference between the two, we need to look at a Unicode string in its binary representation. For instance, consider

```
SELECT convert(varbinary, N'ABC');
```

This code returns 0x410042004300. The ASCII code for *A* is 65, or 41 in hexadecimal. And in Unicode, *A* is U+0041. (Unicode characters are often written as U+XXXX, where XXXX is the code point in hexadecimal notation.) But converted to *varbinary*, it appears as 4100. This is because PC architecture is *little endian*, which means that the least significant byte is stored first. (The reason for this is beyond the scope of this book to explain.)

Therefore, to sort *nvarchar* data by their code points properly, SQL Server should not just look at the byte string but swap each word to get the correct code points. And this is exactly what the BIN2 collations do. The older BIN collations perform this swap only for the first character, and then perform a byte-per-byte comparison for remaining characters. To illustrate the difference between the two types of binary collations and also true byte-sort, here is an example where we use the characters *Z* (U+005A) and *Ń* (N with grave accent; U+0143):

```
SELECT n, str, convert(binary(6), str) AS bytestr,
       row_number() OVER(ORDER BY convert(varbinary, str))
         AS bytesort,
       row_number() OVER(ORDER BY str COLLATE Latin1_General_BIN)
         AS collate_BIN,
       row_number() OVER(ORDER BY str COLLATE Latin1_General_BIN2)
         AS collate_BIN2
FROM  (VALUES(1, N'ZZZ'), (2, N'ZŃŃ'), (3, N'ŃZZ'), (4, N'ŃŃŃ'))
      AS T(n, str)
ORDER BY n;
```

Here is the result:

| n | str | bytestr | bytesort | collate_BIN | collate_BIN2 |
|---|-----|---------|----------|-------------|--------------|
| 1 | ZZZ | 0x5A005A005A00 | 4 | 2 | 1 |
| 2 | ZŃŃ | 0x5A0043014301 | 3 | 1 | 2 |
| 3 | ŃZZ | 0x43015A005A00 | 2 | 4 | 3 |
| 4 | ŃŃŃ | 0x430143014301 | 1 | 3 | 4 |

You can see that in the *collate_BIN2* column, the rows are numbered according to their code points in Unicode. In the *bytesort* column, on the other hand, they are numbered in reverse order because the least significant byte in the character code takes precedence. Finally, in the *collate_BIN* column, the two entries that start with *Z* are sorted first, but in reverse order with regards to *collate_BIN2*.

**SQL Server Collations**    The SQL Server collations (known as *SQL collations* for short) is a much smaller group than the Windows collations. In total, there are 76 SQL collations, of which 1 is deprecated.

A SQL collation uses two different rule sets. One is for single-byte data types, and the other is for Unicode data types. The rules for single-byte data types are defined by SQL Server itself, and derive from the days when SQL Server did not support Unicode. When you work with Unicode data, a SQL collation uses the same rules as the matching Windows collation. To see which Windows collation a certain SQL collation matches, you can view the *description* column in the output from *fn_helpcollations()*.

The name of a SQL collation always starts with *SQL_* followed by a language indicator, similar to the name of a Windows collation. Likewise, names for SQL collations include *CI/CS* and *AI/AS* to indicate case and accent sensitivity. Some binary SQL collations also exist. In contrast to names for Windows collations, SQL collations always include the code page for single-byte characters in the name. For some reason, though, CP1252, Windows Latin-1, appears as CP1 in the names.

Many SQL collations relate to American National Standards Institute (ANSI) code pages, that is, code pages used by non-Unicode Windows applications. But there are also SQL collations for the OEM code pages CP437 and CP850; that is, code pages used in the command-line window. There are even a few SQL collations for EBCDIC.

*Sort Orders*    With a SQL collation, you can get different results depending on the data type. For instance, in the example with the 14 words, if we run it with *word* as *nvarchar* and with the commonly used SQL collation SQL_Latin1_General_CP1_CI_AS, the result is the same as when we used Latin1_General_CI_AS. But if you change *word* to be *varchar*, you get this result:

```
collatedword    rank    wordno
-------------   ------  ------
ŒIL             1       5
œil             2       10
cloud           3       1
CSAK            4       6
cukor           5       11
Oblige          6       2
Öl              7       12
Opera           8       7
RESUME          9       8
resume          9       4
résumé          10      3
RÉSUMÉ          10      13
resumes         11      9
résumés         12      14
```

Now the two forms of *œil* come first and they have different ranks, despite the collation being case insensitive. In this collation, a few accented letters sort as if they were punctuation characters. (The others are *Š*, *Ý*, and *Ž*.) Other differences in SQL_Latin1_General_CP1_CI_AS between the single-byte and Unicode data types include how punctuation characters are sorted. However, so long as your data mainly consist of the digits 0–9 and the English letters A–Z, these differences likely will not be significant to you.

***Tertiary Collations***   Just like Windows collations, SQL collations have primary and secondary weights, but it does not stop there. A total of 32 of the SQL collations also have *tertiary weights*. With one exception, the tertiary collations are all case insensitive. The purpose of the tertiary weight is to give preference to uppercase, so when everything else is equal in the entire ORDER BY clause, uppercase words sort first. In some tertiary collations, this is indicated by *Pref* appearing in the name, whereas in other tertiary collations, this is implicit. You find the full list of tertiary collations in *SQL Server Books Online* in the topic for the built-in function *TERTIARY_WEIGHTS*.

To study the tertiary collations, we use a different table with different words as follows:

```
CREATE TABLE #prefwords
           (word    char(3) COLLATE SQL_Latin1_General_Pref_CP1_CI_AS
                          NOT NULL,
            wordno int NOT NULL PRIMARY KEY NONCLUSTERED,
            tert   AS tertiary_weights(word));
CREATE CLUSTERED INDEX word_ix ON #prefwords (word);
--CREATE INDEX tert_ix on #prefwords(word, tert)
go
INSERT #prefwords (word, wordno)
   VALUES ('abc', 1), ('abC', 4), ('aBc', 7),
          ('aBC', 2), ('Abc', 5), ('ABc', 8),
          ('AbC', 3), ('ABC', 6);
go
SELECT word, wordno, rank = dense_rank() OVER(ORDER BY word),
       rowno = row_number() OVER (ORDER BY word)
FROM   #prefwords
ORDER  BY word--, wordno;
```

The output from this query is

```
word    wordno    rank    rowno
------  --------  ------  -----
ABC     6         1       8
ABc     8         1       6
AbC     3         1       7
Abc     5         1       5
aBC     2         1       4
aBc     7         1       3
abC     4         1       2
abc     1         1       1
```

You can see that all words have the same rank; nevertheless, uppercase letters consistently come before lowercase. And in the *rowno* column, rows are numbered in opposite order, which is likely to be by chance. That is, the tertiary weight affects only the ORDER BY at the end of the query, but not the ORDER BY for the *dense_rank* and *row_number* functions.

Now, if you look at the query plan for this query, you find a Sort operator, which is surprising, given there is a clustered index on *word*. If you go one step back in the plan, you find a Compute Scalar operator, and if you press F4, you can see that this operator defines [Expr1005] = Scalar Operator(tertiary_weights([tempdb].[dbo].[#prefwords].[word])), and if you look at the Sort operator, you see that it sorts by *word* and Expr1005. That is, the tertiary weight is not stored in the index, but computed at run time.

This is where the function *TERTIARY_WEIGHTS* comes in. This function accepts parameters of the types *char, varchar*, and *text* and returns a non-NULL value if the input value is not from a tertiary collation. *SQL Server Books Online* suggests that you can add a computed column with this function and then add an index on the character column and the computed column, like the *tert_ix* in the previous script. If you uncomment the creation of *tert_ix* in the previous script and also comment out the *rank* and *rowno* columns from the *SELECT* statement, you see a plan without any Sort operator. Thus the function *TERTIARY_WEIGHTS* can help to improve performance with tertiary collations.

Now see what happens if we uncomment *wordno* from the ORDER BY clause, so that the query now reads:

```
SELECT word, wordno
FROM   #prefwords
ORDER  BY word, wordno;
```

This is the output:

```
word    wordno
------  ------
abc     1
aBC     2
AbC     3
abC     4
Abc     5
ABC     6
aBc     7
ABc     8
```

That is, the tertiary weight only matters when there is no other difference in the entire ORDER BY clause. Needless to say, the query plan again includes the Sort operator.

**Collations Defined During SQL Server Setup**   When you install SQL Server, you need to select a server collation. This is an important choice, because if you make an incorrect selection, you cannot easily change this later. You will essentially have to reinstall SQL Server.

The SQL Server Setup provides a default collation, and this will always be a CI_AS collation— that is, a collation that is sensitive to accents but insensitive to case, kanatype, and width.

Setup selects the collation designator for the default collation from the *system locale*—that is, the locale that applies on the system level, which may be different from the regional settings for your own Windows user. The default is always a Windows collation, except in one very notable case: if your system locale is English (United States), the default is SQL_Latin1_General_CP1_CI_AS. The reason for this seemingly odd default is backward compatibility.

When different versions of the same language exist, the default depends on whether your system locale existed in previous versions of Windows or was added in Windows 2008. So, for instance, for English (United Kingdom) and German (Germany) the default is Latin1_General_CI_AS, whereas for English (Singapore) and Swahili (Kenya), the default is Latin1_General_100_CI_AS. Again, the reason for this variation is backward compatibility. For the full list of default collations, see the topic "Collation Settings in Setup" in *SQL Server Books Online.*

Although Setup suggests a default collation, it is far from certain that this default is the best for your server. You should make a conscious, deliberate decision. If you install a server to run a third-party product, you should consult the vendor's documentation to see if it has any recommendations or requirements for the application. If you plan to migrate databases from an earlier version of SQL Server, you should probably select the same collation for the new server as for your existing server. As I noted earlier, if you plan to access the server as a linked server from SQL Server 2005, you should avoid the new _100 collations.

Another thing to beware of is that your Windows administrator may have installed a U.S. English version of Windows, leaving the system locale as English (United States) even if the local language is something else. If this is the case on your server, and you do not pay attention when you install SQL Server, you may end up with a collation that does not fit well with the language in your country.

Some languages have multiple appropriate choices. For instance, for German, the default is Latin1_General_CI_AS, but you can also use any of the German_Phonebook collations (in which *ä, ö,* and *ü* sort as *ae, oe,* and *ue*).

***Running the Installation Wizard***   When you run the Installation Wizard for SQL Server 2008, you need to be observant because the collation selection is not on a page of its own but appears on a second tab on the Server Configuration page. You'll have to watch carefully because the collation tab is not displayed when you get to the *Server Configuration* screen. You'll see a screen asking for information about the service accounts to use. When you select the *collation* tab on that screen, you see something like Figure 5-4.

This screenshot was taken on a machine with the system locale set to Swedish, and thus the default collation is Finnish_Swedish_CI_AS. (As you can see, you can also set the collation for Analysis Services on this tab, but that is beyond the scope of this book.)

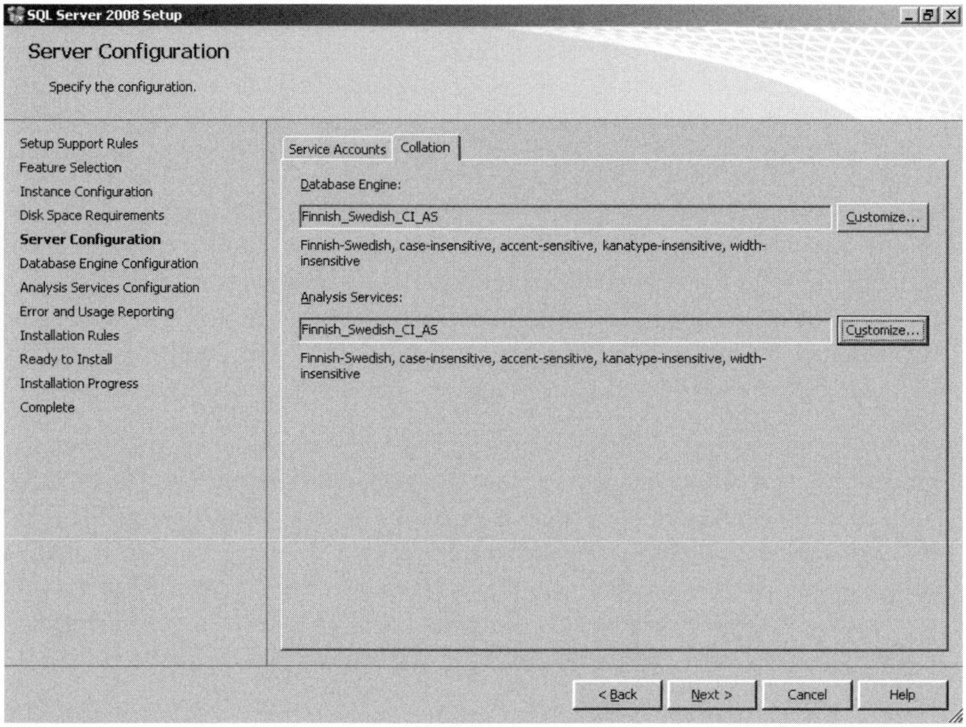

**FIGURE 5-4** Setting the server configuration

Figure 5-5 shows you what you see when you press Customize.

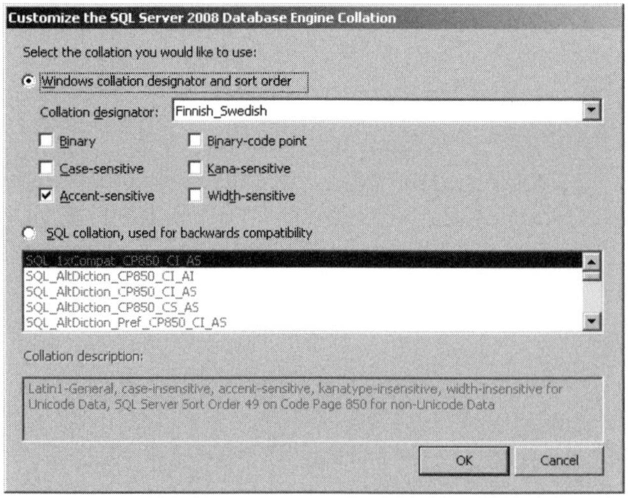

**FIGURE 5-5** Customize the collation properties

You can use an option button to select whether to use a Windows collation or a SQL collation. If you select a Windows collation, there is a drop-down list where you can select the Collation designator. Below that are check boxes to select case sensitivity and other features. The choice

*Binary* gives you a BIN collation, whereas *Binary-code point* gives you a BIN2 collation. If you select to use a SQL collation, there is a single list box that lists all SQL collations.

**Performance Considerations**    Does the choice of collation affect performance? Yes, but in many cases only marginally, and your most important criteria should be to choose the collation that best meet your users' needs. However, there are a few situations where the collation can have quite drastic effects.

Generally, binary collations give you the best performance, but in most applications, they do not give a very good user experience.

So long as you work with *varchar* data, the SQL collations perform almost equally well. The SQL collations include rules only for the 255 characters in the code page covered by the collation. A Windows collation always works with the full rules of Unicode internally, even for single-byte data. Thus, the internal routines for SQL collations are far less complex than those for Unicode.

The Windows collations have some differences between collation families where some are faster than others. A special case is the case-insensitive Latin1_General and Latin1_General_100 collations, which appear to perform better than any other collation family when you work with Unicode data. Contrary to what you may expect, case-sensitive collations do not give better performance; rather, their rate is a few percentage points slower in many operations. But, again, this is not something that you should pay too much attention to. If your users expect to see data sorted according to, say, the Danish alphabet, there is no reason to select Latin1_General_CI_AS just because it operates a little faster. What's the point of a faster operation that doesn't do what your users need? Also, keep in mind that a typical query includes so many other components that the effect of the collation is likely to be lost in the noise.

*A Trap with SQL Server Collations*    The collation really does matter in a few situations, though. Consider the following:

```
SELECT col FROM tbl WHERE indexedcol = @value;
```

For this query, the collation does not have much impact so long as the column and @value has the same data type. Neither is there an issue, if the column has a Unicode data type and @value is *char* or *varchar*. But if the column is single-byte and @value is Unicode, there is an issue because the data-type precedence rules in SQL Server. The *char* and *varchar* data types have lower precedence than *nchar* and *nvarchar*, so the column is converted to the type of the value, and this has ramifications for how the index can be used.

If the column has a Windows collation, SQL Server can still seek the index, albeit with a more complex filter, so compared to a query without conversion, you can expect the execution time to double or triple. But it is when the column has a SQL collation that this query becomes really problematic. The index does not serve any purpose after the conversion because in a SQL collation, the rules are entirely different for single-byte and Unicode data. SQL Server can at best scan the index. In a big table, performance can be drastically affected, with execution times that are 100 or 1,000 times more than for a properly written query. Thus, if you opt to use a SQL collation, you need to watch that you don't mix *varchar* and *nvarchar* casually.

Another case where the collation can make a huge difference is when SQL Server has to look at almost all characters in the strings. For instance, look at the following:

```
SELECT COUNT(*) FROM tbl WHERE longcol LIKE '%abc%';
```

This may execute 10 times faster or more with a binary collation than a nonbinary Windows collation. And with *varchar* data, this executes up to seven or eight times faster with a SQL collation than with a Windows collation. If you have a *varchar* column, you can speed this up by forcing the collation as follows:

```
SELECT COUNT(*) FROM tbl
WHERE longcol COLLATE SQL_Latin1_General_CP_CI_AS LIKE '%abc%';
```

If your column is *nvarchar*, you have to force a binary collation instead, but that would only be possible if users can accept a case-sensitive search.

The same considerations apply to the functions *CHARINDEX* and *PATINDEX*.

## Special Data Types

I'll end this section on data types by showing you a few additional data types that you might find useful.

**Binary Data Types**    These data types are *binary* and *varbinary*. They are used to store strings of bits, and the values are entered and displayed using their hexadecimal (hex) representation, which is indicated by a prefix of *0x*. So a hex value of 0x270F corresponds to a decimal value of 9,999 and a bit string of 0010011100001111. In hex, each two displayed characters represent a byte, so the value of 0x270F represents 2 bytes. You need to decide whether you want your data to be fixed or variable length, and you can use some of the same considerations discussed previously for deciding between *char* and *varchar* to make your decision. The maximum length of *binary* or *varbinary* data is 8,000 bytes.

***bit* Data Type**    The *bit* data type can store a 0 or a 1 and can consume only a single bit of storage space. However, if there is only one bit column in a table, it will take up a whole byte. Up to eight-bit columns are stored in a single byte.

**LOB Data Types**    SQL Server 2008 allows you to define columns with the *MAX* attribute: *varchar(MAX), nvarchar(MAX),* and *varbinary(MAX).* If the number of bytes actually inserted into these columns exceeds the maximum of 8,000, these columns are stored using a special storage format for LOB data. The special storage format is the same one as used for the data types *text, ntext,* and *image,* but because those types will be discontinued in a future version of SQL Server, it is recommend that you use the variable-length data types with the MAX specifier for all new development. The *varchar(MAX)* (or *text)* data type can store up to $2^{31} - 1$ non-Unicode characters, *nvarchar(MAX)* (or *ntext*) can store up to 2^30 – 1 (half as many) Unicode characters, and *varbinary(MAX)* (or *image*) can store up to 2^31 – 1 bytes of binary data. In addition, *varbinary(MAX)* data can be stored as filestream data. We'll cover filestream data in more detail in Chapter 7, as well as look at the storage structures for LOB data.

*cursor* **Data Type**   The *cursor* data type can hold a reference to a cursor. Although you can't declare a column in a table to be of type *cursor*, this data type can be used for output parameters and local variables. I've included the *cursor* data type in this list for completeness, but I won't be talking more about it.

*rowversion* **Data Type**   The *rowversion* data type is a synonym for what was formerly called a *timestamp*. When using the *timestamp* data type name, many people might assume that the data has something to do with dates or times, but it doesn't. A column of type *rowversion* holds an internal sequence number that SQL Server automatically updates every time the row is modified. The value of any *rowversion* column is actually unique within an entire database, and a table can have only one column of type *rowversion*. Any operation that modifies any *rowversion* column in the database generates the next sequential value. The actual value stored in a *rowversion* column is seldom important by itself. The column is used to detect whether a row has been modified since the last time it was accessed by determining whether the *rowversion* value has changed.

*sql_variant* **Data Type**   The *sql_variant* data type allows a column to hold values of any data type except *text*, *ntext*, *image*, *XML*, user-defined data types, variable-length data types with the MAX specifier, or *rowversi*on (*timestamp*). I'll describe the internal storage of *sql_variant* data later in this chapter.

**Spatial Data Type**   SQL Server 2008 provides two data types for storing spatial data. The *geometry* data type supports planar, or Euclidean (flat-earth), data. The *geometry* data type conforms to the Open Geospatial Consortium (OGC) Simple Features for SQL Specification version 1.1.0. The *geography* data type stores ellipsoidal (round-earth) data, such as Global Positioning Satellite (GPS) latitude and longitude coordinates. These data types have their own methods for accessing and manipulating the data, as well as their own special extended index structures, which are different than the normal SQL Server indexes. Any further discussion of the access methods and storage of spatial data is beyond the scope of this book.

*table* **Data Type**   The *table* data type can be used to store the result of a function and can be used as the data type of local variables. Columns in tables cannot be of type *table*.

*xml* **Data Type**   The *xml* data type lets you store XML documents and fragments in a SQL Server database. You can use the *xml* data type as a column type when you create a table, or as the data type for variables, parameters, and the return value of a function. XML data has its own methods for retrieval and manipulation. I will not be covering details of working with *xml* data in this book.

***uniqueidentifier* Data Type**    The *uniqueidentifier* data type is sometimes referred to as a globally unique identifier (GUID) or universal unique identifier (UUID). A GUID or UUID is a 128-bit (16-byte) value generated in a way that, for all practical purposes, guarantees uniqueness among every networked computer in the world. It is becoming an important way to identify data, objects, software applications, and applets in distributed systems. Because there are some very interesting aspects to the way the *uniqueidentifier* data type is generated and manipulated, I'll give you a bit more detail about it.

The T-SQL language supports the system functions *NEWID* and *NEWSEQUENTIALID*, which you can use to generate *uniqueidentifier* values. A column or variable of data type *uniqueidentifier* can be initialized to a value in one of the following two ways:

- Using the system-supplied function *NEWID* or *NEWSEQUENTIALID* as a default value.

- Using a string constant in the following form (32 hexadecimal digits separated by hyphens): *xxxxxxxx-xxxx-xxxx-xxxx-xxxxxxxxxxxx*. (Each *x* is a hexadecimal digit in the range 0 through 9 or *a* through *f*.)

This data type can be quite cumbersome to work with, and the only operations that are allowed against a *uniqueidentifier* value are comparisons (=, <>, <, >, <=, >=) and checking for NULL. However, using this data type internally can offer several advantages.

One reason to use the *uniqueidentifier* data type is that the values generated by *NEWID* or *NEWSEQUENTIALID* are guaranteed to be globally unique for any machine on a network because the last six bytes of a *uniqueidentifier* value make up the node number for the machine. When the SQL Server machine does not have an Ethernet/Token Ring (IEEE 802.*x*) address, there is no node number and the generated GUID is guaranteed to be unique among all GUIDs generated on that computer. However, the possibility exists that another computer without an Ethernet/Token Ring address will generate the identical GUID. The GUIDs generated on computers with network addresses are guaranteed to be globally unique.

The primary reason that SQL Server needed a way to generate a GUID was for use in merge replication, in which identifier values for the same table could be generated on any one of many different SQL Server machines. There needed to be a way to determine whether two rows really were the same row and there had to be no way that two rows not referring to the same entity would have the same identifier. Using GUID values provides that functionality. Two rows with the same GUID value must indicate that they really are the same row.

The difference between the *NEWSEQUENTIALID* and the *NEWID* functions is that *NEWSEQUENTIALID* creates a GUID that is greater than any GUID previously generated by this function on a specified computer and can be used to introduce a sequence to your GUID values. This turns out to increase greatly the scalability of systems using merge replication. If the *unqiueidentifer* values are being used as the clustered key for the replicated tables, the new rows are then inserted in random disk pages. (You'll see the details in Chapter 6, when clustered indexes are discussed in detail.) If the machines involved are performing a large amount of I/O operations, the nonsequential GUID generated by the *NEWID* function results in lots of random B-tree lookups and inefficient insert operations. The new function, *NEWSEQUENTIALID*, which is a wrapper around the Windows function *UuidCreateSequential*, does some byte scrambling and creates an ordering to the generated UUID values.

The list of *uniqueidentifier* values can't be exhausted. This is not the case with other data types frequently used as unique identifiers. In fact, SQL Server uses this data type internally for row-level merge replication. A *uniqueidentifier* column can have a special property called *ROWGUIDCOL*; at most, one *uniqueidentifier* column can have this property per table. The *ROWGUIDCOL* property can be specified as part of the column definition in *CREATE TABLE* and *ALTER TABLE ADD column*, or it can be added or dropped for an existing column using *ALTER TABLE ALTER COLUMN*.

You can reference a *uniqueidentifier* column with the *ROWGUIDCOL* property using the keyword *ROWGUIDCOL* in a query. This is similar to referencing an identity column using the *IDENTITYCOL* keyword. The *ROWGUIDCOL* property does not imply any automatic value generation, and if automatic value generation is needed, the *NEWID* function should be defined as the default value of the column. You can have multiple *uniqueidentifier* columns per table, but only one of them can have the *ROWGUIDCOL* property. You can use the *uniqueidentifier* data type for whatever reason you come up with, but if you're using one to identify the current row, an application must have a generic way to ask for it without needing to know the column name. That's what the *ROWGUIDCOL* property does.

## Much Ado About NULL

The issue of whether to allow NULL has become a heated debate for many in the industry, and the discussion here may outrage a few people. However, my intention isn't to engage in a philosophical debate. Pragmatically, dealing with NULL brings added complexity to the storage engine because SQL Server keeps a special bitmap in every row to indicate which nullable columns actually *are* NULL. If NULLs are allowed, SQL Server must decode this bitmap for every row accessed. Allowing NULL also adds complexity in application code, which can often lead to bugs. You must always add special logic to account for the case of NULL.

As the database designer, you might understand the nuances of NULL and three-valued logic in aggregate functions when you do joins and when you search by values. In addition, you must also consider whether your development staff really understands how to work with NULLs. I recommend, if possible, that you use all NOT NULL columns and define *default* values for missing or unknown entries (and possibly make such character columns *varchar* if the default value is significantly different in size from the typical entered value).

In any case, it's good practice to declare NOT NULL or NULL explicitly when you create a table. If no such declaration exists, SQL Server assumes NOT NULL. (In other words, no NULLs are allowed.) This might surprise many people who assume that the default for SQL Server is to allow NULLs. The reason for this misconception is that most of the tools and interfaces for working with SQL Server enable a session setting that makes it the default to allow NULLs. However, you can set the default to allow NULLs by using a session setting or a database option, which, as I just mentioned, is what most tools and interfaces already do. If you script your DDL and then run it against another server that has a different default setting, you get different results if you don't declare NULL or NOT NULL explicitly in the column definition.

Several database options and session settings can control the behavior of SQL Server regarding NULL values. You can set database options using the *ALTER DATABASE* command, as I showed you in Chapter 3, "Databases and Database Files." And you can enable session settings for one connection at a time using the *SET* command.

> **Note**  The database option *ANSI null default* corresponds to the two session settings ANSI_NULL_DFLT_ON and ANSI_NULL_DFLT_OFF. When the *ANSI null default* database option is false (the default setting for SQL Server), new columns created with the *ALTER TABLE* and *CREATE TABLE* commands are, by default, NOT NULL if the nullability status of the column isn't explicitly specified. SET ANSI_NULL_DFLT_OFF and SET ANSI_NULL_DFLT_ON are mutually exclusive options that indicate whether the database option should be overridden. When on, each option forces the opposite option off. Neither option, when off, turns the opposite option on—it only discontinues the current on setting.

You use the function *GETANSINULL* to determine the default nullability for your current session. This function returns 1 when new columns allow null values and the column or data type nullability wasn't defined explicitly when the table was created or altered. I strongly recommend declaring NULL or NOT NULL explicitly when you create a column. This removes all ambiguity and ensures that you're in control of how the table is built, regardless of the default nullability setting.

The database option *concat null yields null* corresponds to the session setting *SET CONCAT_NULL_YIELDS_NULL*. When *CONCAT_NULL_YIELDS_NULL* is on, concatenating a NULL value with a string yields a NULL result. For example, *SELECT* 'abc' + NULL yields NULL. When *SET CONCAT_NULL_YIELDS_NULL* is off, concatenating a NULL value with a string yields the string itself. In other words, the NULL value is treated as an empty string. For example, *SELECT* 'abc' + NULL yields *abc*. If the session-level setting isn't specified, the value of the database option *concat null yields null* applies.

The database option *ANSI nulls* corresponds to the session setting *SET ANSI_NULLS*. When this option is set to ON, all comparisons to a NULL value evaluate to UNKNOWN. When it is set to OFF, comparisons of values to a NULL value evaluate to TRUE if both values are NULL. In addition, when this option is set to ON, your code must use the condition IS NULL to determine whether a column has a NULL value. When this option is set to OFF, SQL Server allows = NULL as a synonym for IS NULL and <> NULL as a synonym for IS NOT NULL.

A fourth session setting is *ANSI_DEFAULTS*. Setting this to ON is a shortcut for enabling both *ANSI_NULLS* and *ANSI_NULL_DFLT_ON,* as well as other session settings not related to NULL handling. The SQL Server ODBC driver and the SQL Server OLE DB provider automatically set *ANSI_DEFAULTS* to ON. You can change the *ANSI_NULLS* setting when you define your data source name (DSN). You should be aware that the tool you are using to connect to SQL Server might set certain options ON or OFF.

The following query shows the values for all the SET options in your current session, and if you have VIEW SERVER STATE permission, you can change or remove the WHERE clause to return information about other sessions as follows:

```
SELECT * FROM sys.dm_exec_sessions
WHERE session_id = @@spid;
```

As you can see, you can configure and control the treatment and behavior of NULL values in several ways, and you might think it would be impossible to keep track of all the variations. If you try to control every aspect of NULL handling separately within each individual session, you can cause immeasurable confusion and even grief. However, most of the issues become moot if you follow a few basic recommendations:

- Never allow NULL values in your tables.
- Include a specific NOT NULL qualification in your table definitions.
- Don't rely on database properties to control the behavior of NULL values.

If you must use NULLs in some cases, you can minimize problems by always following the same rules, and the easiest rules to follow are the ones that ANSI already specifies.

In addition, certain database designs allow for NULL values in a large number of columns and in a large number of rows. SQL Server 2008 introduces the concept of sparse columns. Sparse columns reduce the space requirements for NULL values at the cost of more overhead to retrieve NOT NULL values. So the biggest benefit from sparse columns is found when a large percentage of your data is NULL. I'll discuss sparse column storage in Chapter 7.

There are a couple of other storage considerations to be aware of when allowing your columns to be NULL. For fixed-length columns (that are not defined to be sparse), the column always uses the full defined length, even when storing NULL. For example, a column defined as *char(200)* always uses 200 bytes whether it is NULL or not. Variable-length columns are different and do not take up any space for the actual data storage of NULLs. That doesn't mean there is no space requirement at all, as we'll see later in this chapter when I describe the internal storage mechanisms.

# User-Defined Data Types

A user-defined data type (UDT) provides a convenient way for you to guarantee consistent use of underlying native data types for columns known to have the same domain of possible values. For example, perhaps your database stores various phone numbers in many tables. Although no single, definitive way exists to store phone numbers, consistency is important in this database. You can create a *phone_number* UDT and use it consistently for any column in any table that keeps track of phone numbers to ensure that they all use the same data type. Here's how to create this UDT:

```
CREATE TYPE phone_number FROM varchar(20) NOT NULL;
```

And here's how to use the new UDT when you create a table:

```
CREATE TABLE customer
(
cust_id                smallint       NOT NULL,
cust_name              varchar(50)    NOT NULL,
cust_addr1             varchar(50)    NOT NULL,
cust_addr2             varchar(50)    NOT NULL,
cust_city              varchar(50)    NOT NULL,
cust_state             char(2)        NOT NULL,
cust_postal_code       varchar(10)    NOT NULL,
cust_phone             phone_number   NOT NULL,
cust_fax               varchar(20)    NOT NULL,
cust_email             varchar(30)    NOT NULL,
cust_web_url           varchar(100)   NOT NULL
);
```

When the table is created, internally the *cust_phone* data type is known to be *varchar(20)*. Notice that both *cust_phone* and *cust_fax* are *varchar(20)*, although *cust_phone* has that declaration through its definition as a UDT.

Information about the columns in your tables is available through the catalog view *sys.columns*, which we'll look at in more detail in the section entitled "Internal Storage," later in this chapter. For now, we'll just look at a basic query to show us two columns in *sys.columns*, one containing a number representing the underlying system data type and one containing a number representing the data type used when creating the table. The following query selects all the rows from *sys.columns* and displays the *column_id*, the column name, the data type values, and the maximum length, and then displays the results:

```
SELECT column_id, name, system_type_id, user_type_id,
        type_name(user_type_id) as user_type_name, max_length
FROM sys.columns
WHERE object_id=object_id('customer');
```

| column_id | type_name | system_type_id | user_type_id | user_type_name | max_length |
| --- | --- | --- | --- | --- | --- |
| 1 | cust_id | 52 | 52 | smallint | 2 |
| 2 | cust_name | 167 | 167 | varchar | 50 |
| 3 | cust_addr1 | 167 | 167 | varchar | 50 |

| 4 | cust_addr2 | 167 | 167 | varchar | 50 |
| 5 | cust_city | 167 | 167 | varchar | 50 |
| 6 | cust_state | 175 | 175 | char | 2 |
| 7 | cust_postal_code | 167 | 167 | varchar | 10 |
| 8 | cust_phone | 167 | 257 | phone_number | 20 |
| 9 | cust_fax | 167 | 167 | varchar | 20 |
| 10 | cust_email | 167 | 167 | varchar | 30 |
| 11 | cust_web_url | 167 | 167 | varchar | 100 |

You can see that both the *cust_phone* and *cust_fax* columns have the same *system_type_id* value, although the *cust_phone* column shows that the *user_type_id* is a UDT (*user_type_id* = 257). The type is resolved when the table is created, and the UDT can't be dropped or changed so long as a table is currently using it. Once declared, a UDT is static and immutable, so no inherent performance penalty occurs in using a UDT instead of the native data type.

The use of UDTs can make your database more consistent and clear. SQL Server implicitly converts between compatible columns of different types (either native types or UDTs of different types).

Currently, UDTs don't support the notion of subtyping or inheritance, nor do they allow a DEFAULT value or a CHECK constraint to be declared as part of the UDT itself. These powerful object-oriented concepts will likely make their way into future versions of SQL Server. These limitations notwithstanding, UDT functionality is a dynamic and often underused feature of SQL Server.

# *IDENTITY* Property

It is common to provide simple counter-type values for tables that don't have a natural or efficient primary key. Columns such as *cust_id* are usually simple counter fields. The *IDENTITY* property makes generating unique numeric values easy. *IDENTITY* isn't a data type; it's a column property that you can declare on a whole number data type such as *tinyint*, *smallint*, *int*, *bigint*, or numeric/decimal (with which only a scale of zero makes any sense). Each table can have only one column with the *IDENTITY* property. The table's creator can specify the starting number (seed) and the amount that this value increments or decrements. If not otherwise specified, the seed value starts at 1 and increments by 1, as shown in this example:

```
CREATE TABLE customer
(
cust_id     smallint      IDENTITY   NOT NULL,
cust_name   varchar(50)   NOT NULL
);
```

To find out which seed and increment values were defined for a table, you can use the *IDENT_SEED(tablename)* and *IDENT_INCR(tablename)* functions. Take a look at this statement:

```
SELECT IDENT_SEED('customer'), IDENT_INCR('customer')
```

It produces the following result for the *customer* table because values weren't declared explicitly and the default values were used.

```
1    1
```

This next example explicitly starts the numbering at 100 (seed) and increments the value by 20:

```
CREATE TABLE customer
(
cust_id      smallint      IDENTITY(100, 20)  NOT NULL,
cust_name    varchar(50)   NOT NULL
);
```

The value automatically produced with the *IDENTITY* property is normally unique, but that isn't guaranteed by the *IDENTITY* property itself, nor are the *IDENTITY* values guaranteed to be consecutive. (I will expand on the issues of nonunique and nonconsecutive *IDENTITY* values later in this section.) For efficiency, a value is considered used as soon as it is presented to a client doing an *INSERT* operation. If that client doesn't ultimately commit the *INSERT*, the value never appears, so a break occurs in the consecutive numbers. An unacceptable level of serialization would exist if the next number couldn't be parceled out until the previous one was actually committed or rolled back. (And even then, as soon as a row was deleted, the values would no longer be consecutive. Gaps are inevitable.)

> **Note** If you need exact sequential values without gaps, *IDENTITY* isn't the appropriate feature to use. Instead, you should implement a *next_number*-type table in which you can make the operation of bumping the number contained within it part of the larger transaction (and incur the serialization of queuing for this value).

To temporarily disable the automatic generation of values in an identity column, you use the SET IDENTITY_INSERT tablename ON option. In addition to filling in gaps in the identity sequence, this option is useful for tasks such as bulk-loading data in which the previous values already exist. For example, perhaps you're loading a new database with customer data from your previous system. You might want to preserve the previous customer numbers but have new ones automatically assigned using *IDENTITY*. The SET option was created exactly for cases like this.

Because the SET option allows you to determine your own values for an *IDENTITY* column, the *IDENTITY* property alone doesn't enforce uniqueness of a value within the table. Although *IDENTITY* generates a unique number if IDENTITY_INSERT has never been enabled, the uniqueness is not guaranteed once you have used the SET option. To enforce uniqueness (which you'll almost always want to do when using *IDENTITY*), you should also declare a UNIQUE or PRIMARY KEY constraint on the column. If you insert your own values for an identity column (using SET IDENTITY_INSERT), when automatic generation resumes, the next value is the next incremented value (or decremented value) of the highest value that exists in the table, whether it was generated previously or explicitly inserted.

**Tip** If you use the *bcp* utility for bulk-loading data, be aware of the *-E* (uppercase) parameter if your data already has assigned values that you want to keep for a column that has the *IDENTITY* property. You can also use the *T-SQL BULK INSERT* command with the KEEPIDENTITY option. For more information, see the SQL Server documentation for *bcp* and *BULK INSERT*.

The keyword *IDENTITYCOL* automatically refers to the specific column in a table that has the *IDENTITY* property, whatever its name. If that column is *cust_id*, you can refer to the column as *IDENTITYCOL* without knowing or using the column name, or you can refer to it explicitly as *cust_id*. For example, the following two statements work identically and return the same data:

```
SELECT IDENTITYCOL FROM customer;
SELECT cust_id FROM customer;
```

The column name returned to the caller is *cust_id*, not *IDENTITYCOL*, in both cases.

When inserting rows, you must omit an identity column from the column list and VALUES section. (The only exception is when the IDENTITY_INSERT option is on.) If you do supply a column list, you must omit the column for which the value will be supplied automatically. Here are two valid *INSERT* statements for the *customer* table shown previously:

```
INSERT customer VALUES ('ACME Widgets');
INSERT customer (cust_name) VALUES ('AAA Gadgets');
```

Selecting these two rows produces this output:

```
cust_id      cust_name
-------      ---------
1            ACME Widgets
2            AAA Gadgets
```

In applications, it's sometimes desirable to know immediately the value produced by *IDENTITY* for subsequent use. For example, a transaction might first add a new customer and then add an order for that customer. To add the order, you probably need to use the *cust_id*. Rather than selecting the value from the *customer* table, you can simply select the special system function *@@IDENTITY*, which contains the last identity value used by that connection. It doesn't necessarily provide the last value inserted in the table, however, because another user might have subsequently inserted data. If multiple *INSERT* statements are carried out in a batch on the same or different tables, the variable has the value for the last statement only. In addition, if an *INSERT* trigger fires after you insert the new row, and if that trigger inserts rows into a table with an identity column, *@@IDENTITY* does not have the value inserted by the original *INSERT* statement. To you, it might look like you're inserting and then immediately checking the value, as follows:

```
INSERT customer (cust_name) VALUES ('AAA Gadgets');
SELECT @@IDENTITY;
```

However, if a trigger were fired for the *INSERT*, the value of *@@IDENTITY* might have changed.

You might find two other functions useful when working with identity columns: *SCOPE_IDENTITY* and *IDENT_CURRENT*. *SCOPE_IDENTITY* returns the last identity value inserted into a table in the same scope, which could be a stored procedure, trigger, or batch. So if we replace *@@IDENTITY* with the *SCOPE_IDENTITY* function in the preceding code snippet, we can see the identity value inserted into the *customer* table. If an *INSERT* trigger also inserted a row that contained an identity column, it would be in a different scope, like this:

```
INSERT customer (cust_name) VALUES ('AAA Gadgets');
SELECT SCOPE_IDENTITY();
```

In other cases, you might want to know the last identity value inserted in a specific table from any application or user. You can get this value using the *IDENT_CURRENT* function, which takes a table name as an argument:

```
SELECT IDENT_CURRENT('customer');
```

This doesn't always guarantee that you can predict the next identity value to be inserted because another process could insert a row between the time you check the value of *IDENT_CURRENT* and the time you execute your *INSERT* statement.

You can't define the *IDENTITY* property as part of a UDT, but you can declare the *IDENTITY* property on a column that uses a UDT. A column that has the *IDENTITY* property must always be declared NOT NULL (either explicitly or implicitly); otherwise, error number 8147 results from the *CREATE TABLE* statement and *CREATE* won't succeed. Likewise, you can't declare the *IDENTITY* property and a *DEFAULT* on the same column. To check that the current identity value is valid based on the current maximum values in the table, and to reset it if an invalid value is found (which should never be the case), use the *DBCC CHECKIDENT*(tablename) statement.

Identity values are fully recoverable. If a system outage occurs while an insert activity is taking place with tables that have identity columns, the correct value is recovered when SQL Server restarts. SQL Server does this during the checkpoint processing by flushing the current identity value for all tables. For activity beyond the last checkpoint, subsequent values are reconstructed from the transaction log during the standard database recovery process. Any inserts into a table that have the *IDENTITY* property are known to have changed the value, and the current value is retrieved from the last *INSERT* statement (post-checkpoint) for each table in the transaction log. The net result is that when the database is recovered, the correct current identity value is also recovered.

In rare cases, the identity value can get out of sync. If this happens, you can use the *DBCC CHECKIDENT* command to reset the identity value to the appropriate number. In addition, the RESEED option to this command allows you to set a new starting value for the identity sequence. See the online documentation for complete details.

# Internal Storage

This section describes how SQL Server actually stores table data. In addition, it explores the basic system metadata that keeps track of data storage information. Although you can use SQL Server effectively without understanding the internals of data storage, a detailed knowledge of how SQL Server stores data helps you develop efficient applications.

When you create a table, one or more rows are inserted into a number of system tables to manage that table and SQL Server provides catalog views built on top of the system tables that allow you to explore their contents. At minimum, you can see metadata for your new table in the *sys.tables*, *sys.indexes*, and *sys.columns* catalog views. When you define the new table with one or more constraints, you also can see information in the *sys.check_constraints*, *sys.default_constraints*, *sys.key_constraints*, or *sys.foreign_keys* view. For every table created, a single row that contains the name, object ID, and ID of the schema containing the new table (among other items) is available through the *sys.tables* view. Remember that the *sys.tables* view inherits all the columns from *sys.objects* (which shows information relevant to all types of objects) and then includes additional columns pertaining only to tables. The *sys.columns* view shows you one row for each column in the new table, and each row contains information such as the column name, data type, and length. Each column receives a column ID, which initially corresponds to the order in which you specified the columns when you created the table—that is, the first column listed in the *CREATE TABLE* statement has a column ID of 1, the second column has a column ID of 2, and so on. Figure 5-6 shows the rows returned by the *sys.tables* and *sys.columns* views when you create a table. (Not all columns are shown for each view.)

```
CREATE TABLE dbo.employee (
               emp_lname   varchar(15)    NOT NULL,
               emp_fname   varchar(10)    NOT NULL,
               address     varchar(30)    NOT NULL,
               phone       char(12)       NOT NULL,
               job_level   smallint       NOT NULL
)


sys.tables      object_id   name                schema_id   type_desc
                ----------- ------------------- ----------- -------------------
                917578307   employee            1           USER_TABLE


sys.columns     object_id   column_id   name          system_type_id max_length
                ----------- ----------- ------------- -------------- ----------
                917578307   1           emp_lname     167            15
                917578307   2           emp_fname     167            10
                917578307   3           address       167            30
                917578307   4           phone         175            12
                917578307   5           job_level     52             2
```

**FIGURE 5-6** Basic catalog information stored after a table is created

**Note** There can be gaps in the column ID sequence if the table is altered to drop columns. However, the information schema view (*INFORMATION_SCHEMA.COLUMNS*) gives you a value called *ORDINAL_POSITION* because that is what the ANSI SQL standard demands. The ordinal position is the order the column will be listed when you *SELECT* * on the table. So the *column_id* is not necessarily the ordinal position of that column.

## The *sys.indexes* Catalog View

In addition to *sys.columns* and *sys.tables*, the *sys.indexes* view returns at least one row for each table. In versions of SQL Server prior to SQL Server 2005, the *sysindexes* table contains all the physical storage information for both tables and indexes, which are the only objects that actually use storage space. The *sysindexes* table has columns to keep track of the space used by all tables and indexes, the physical location of each index root page, and the first page of each table and index. (In Chapter 6, you'll see more about root pages and what the "first" page actually means.) In SQL Server 2008, the compatibility view sys.*sysindexes* contains much of the same information, but it is incomplete because of changes in the storage organization introduced in SQL Server 2005. The *sys.indexes* catalog view contains only basic property information about indexes, such as whether the index is clustered or nonclustered, unique or nonunique, and other properties, which are discussed in Chapter 6. To get all the storage information in SQL Server 2005 or SQL Server 2008 that previous versions provided in the *sysindexes* table, we have to look at two other catalog views in addition to *sys.indexes*: *sys.partitions* and *sys.allocation_units* (or alternatively, the undocumented *sys.system_internals_allocation_units*). I'll discuss the basic contents of these views shortly, but first let's focus on *sys.indexes*.

You might be aware that if a table has a clustered index, the table's data is actually considered part of the index, so the data rows are actually index rows. For a table with a clustered index, SQL Server has a row in *sys.indexes* with an *index_id* value of 1 and the *name* column in *sys.indexes* contains the name of the index. The name of the table that is associated with the index can be determined from the *object_id* column in *sys.indexes*. If a table has no clustered index, there is no organization to the data itself, and we call such a table a *heap*. A heap in *sys.indexes* table has an *index_id* value of 0, and the *name* column contains NULL. Every additional index has a row in *sys.indexes* with an *index_id* value between 2 and 250 or between 256 and 1,005. (The values 251 – 255 are reserved.) Because as many as 999 nonclustered indexes can be on a single table and there is one row for the heap or clustered index, every table has between 1 and 1,000 rows in the *sys.indexes* view for relational indexes. A table can have additional rows in *sys.indexes* for XML indexes. Metadata for XML indexes is available in the *sys.xml_indexes* catalog view, which inherits columns from the *sys.indexes* view. Two main features in SQL Server 2008 make it most efficient to use more than one catalog view to keep track of storage information. First, SQL Server has the ability to store a table or index on multiple partitions, so the space used by each partition, as well as the partition's location, must be kept track of separately. Second, table and index data can be stored in three different formats, which are regular row data, row-overflow data, and LOB data. Both row-overflow data and LOB data can be part of an index, so each index has to keep track of its special format data separately. So each table can have multiple indexes, and each table and index can be stored on multiple partitions, and each partition needs to keep track of data in up to three formats. I'll discuss indexes in Chapter 6, and I'll discuss the storage of row-overflow data and LOB data, as well as partitioned tables and indexes, in Chapter 7.

## Data Storage Metadata

Each heap and index has a row in *sys.indexes*, and each table and index in a SQL Server 2008 database can be stored on multiple partitions. The *sys.partitions* view contains one row for each partition of each heap or index. Every heap or index has at least one partition, even if you haven't specifically partitioned the structure, but one table or index can have up to 1,000 partitions. So there is a one-to-many relationship between *sys.indexes* and *sys.partitions*. The *sys.partitions* view contains a column called *partition_id* as well as the *object_id* and *index_id*, so we can join *sys.indexes* to *sys.partitions* on the *object_id* and *index_id* columns to retrieve all the partition ID values for a particular table or index. The term used in SQL Server 2008 to describe a subset of a table or index on a single partition is *hobt*, which stands for Heap Or B-Tree and is pronounced (you guessed it) "hobbit." (A B-tree is the storage structure used for indexes.) The *sys.partitions* view includes a column called *hobt_id*, and in SQL Server 2008, there is always a one-to-one relationship between *partition_id* and *hobt_id*. In fact, you can see that these two columns in the *sys.partitions* table always have the same value.

Each partition (whether for a heap or an index) can have three types of rows, each stored on its own set of pages. These types are called *in-row data pages* (for our "regular" data or index information), *row-overflow data pages*, and *LOB data pages*. A set of pages of one particular type for one particular partition is called an *allocation unit*, so the final catalog view I need to tell you about is *sys.allocation_units*. The *sys.allocation_units* view contains one, two, or three rows per partition because each heap or index on each partition can have as many as three allocation units. There is always an allocation unit for regular in-row pages, but there might also be an allocation unit for LOB data and one for row-overflow data. Figure 5-7 shows the relationship between *sys.indexes*, *sys.partitions*, and *sys.allocation_units*.

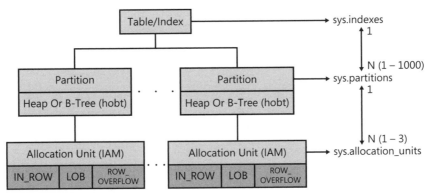

**FIGURE 5-7** The relationship between *sys.indexes*, *sys.partitions*, and *sys.allocation_units*

## Querying the Catalog Views

Let's look at a specific example now to see information in these three catalog views. Let's first create the table shown earlier in Figure 5-6. You can create it in any database, but I suggest either using *tempdb*, so the table is dropped automatically the next time you restart your SQL Server instance, or creating a new database just for testing. Many of my examples assume a database called *test*:

```
CREATE TABLE dbo.employee(
            emp_lname   varchar(15)   NOT NULL,
            emp_fname   varchar(10)   NOT NULL,
            address     varchar(30)   NOT NULL,
            phone       char(12)      NOT NULL,
            job_level   smallint      NOT NULL
);
```

This table has one row in *sys.indexes* and one in *sys.partitions*, as we can see when we run the following queries. I am including only a few of the columns from *sys.indexes,* but *sys.partitions* only has six columns, so I have retrieved them all:

```
SELECT  object_id, name, index_id, type_desc
FROM sys.indexes
WHERE object_id=object_id('dbo.employee');

SELECT *
FROM sys.partitions
WHERE object_id=object_id('dbo.employee');
```

Here are my results (yours might vary slightly because your ID values are probably different):

```
object_id   name    index_id    type_desc
----------- ------- ----------- ------------
5575058     NULL    0           HEAP

partition_id       object_id  index_id  partition_number  hobt_id            rows
----------------   ---------  --------  ----------------  -----------------  -----
72057594038779904  5575058    0         1                 72057594038779904  0
```

Each row in the *sys.allocation_units* view has a unique *allocation_unit_id* value. Each row also has a value in the column called *container_id* that can be joined with *partition_id* in *sys.partitions*, as shown in this query:

```
SELECT object_name(object_id) AS name,
    partition_id, partition_number AS pnum,  rows,
    allocation_unit_id AS au_id, type_desc as page_type_desc,
    total_pages AS pages
FROM sys.partitions p JOIN sys.allocation_units a
  ON p.partition_id = a.container_id
WHERE object_id=object_id('dbo.employee');
```

Again, for this simple table, I get only one row because there is only one partition, no nonclustered indexes, and only one type of data (IN_ROW_DATA). Here is the result:

```
name      partition_id      pnum   rows   au_id             page_type_desc pages
-----     ---------------   ------ ------ ----------------  -------------- -----
employee  72057594038779904  1      0      72057594043301888 IN_ROW_DATA    0
```

Now let's add some new columns to the table that need to be stored on other types of pages. *Varchar* data can be stored on row-overflow pages if the total row size exceeds the maximum of 8,060 bytes. By default, text data is stored on text pages. For *varchar* data that is stored on row-overflow pages, and for text data, there is additional overhead in the row itself to store a pointer to the off-row data. We'll look at the details of row-overflow and text data storage later in this section, and we'll look at *ALTER TABLE* at the end of this chapter, but now I just want to look at the additional rows in *sys.allocation_units:*

```
ALTER TABLE dbo.employee ADD resume_short varchar(8000);
ALTER TABLE dbo.employee ADD resume_long text;
```

If we run the preceding query that joins *sys.partitions* and *sys.allocation_units*, we get the following three rows:

```
name      partition_id            pnum   rows   au_id               page_type_desc      pages
--------  ----------------------  ------ ------ ------------------- ------------------- -----
employee  72057594038779904        1      0      72057594043301888   IN_ROW_DATA         0
employee  72057594038779904        1      0      72057594043367424   ROW_OVERFLOW_DATA   0
employee  72057594038779904        1      0      72057594043432960   LOB_DATA            0
```

You might also want to add an index or two and check the contents of these catalog views again. You should notice that just adding a clustered index does not change the number of rows in *sys.allocation_units*, but it does change the *partition_id* numbers because the entire table is rebuilt internally when you create a clustered index. Adding a nonclustered index adds at least one more row to *sys.allocation_units* to keep track of the pages for that index. The following query joins all three views—*sys.indexes, sys.partitions,* and *sys.allocation_units*—to show you the table name, index name and type, page type, and space usage information for the *dbo.employee* table:

```
SELECT  convert(char(8),object_name(i.object_id)) AS table_name,
    i.name AS index_name, i.index_id, i.type_desc as index_type,
    partition_id, partition_number AS pnum,  rows,
    allocation_unit_id AS au_id, a.type_desc as page_type_desc,
    total_pages AS pages
FROM sys.indexes i JOIN sys.partitions p
      ON i.object_id = p.object_id AND i.index_id = p.index_id
    JOIN sys.allocation_units a
      ON p.partition_id = a.container_id
WHERE i.object_id=object_id('dbo.employee');
```

Because I have not inserted any data into this table, you should notice that the values for rows and pages are all 0. When I discuss actual page structures, we'll insert data into our tables so we can look at the internal storage of the data at that time. The queries I've run so far do not provide us with any information about the location of pages in the various allocation units. In SQL Server 2000, the *sysindexes* table contains three columns that indicate where data is located; these columns are called *first*, *root*, and *firstIAM*. These columns are still available in SQL Server 2008 (with slightly different names: *first_page*, *root_page*, and *first_iam_page*), but they can be seen only in an undocumented view called *sys.system_internals_allocation_units*. This view is identical to *sys.allocation_units* except for the addition of these three additional columns, so you can replace *sys.allocation_units* with *sys.system_internals_allocation_units* in the preceding allocation query and add these three extra columns to the select list. Keep in mind that as an undocumented object, this view is for internal use only and is subject to change (as are other views starting with *system_internals*). Forward compatibility is not guaranteed.

# Data Pages

Data pages are the structures that contain user data that has been added to a database's tables. As we saw earlier, there are three varieties of data pages, each of which stores data in a different format. There are pages for in-row data, pages for row-overflow data, and pages for LOB data. As with all other types of pages in SQL Server, data pages have a fixed size of 8 KB, or 8,192 bytes. They consist of three major components: the page header, data rows, and the row offset array, as shown in Figure 5-8.

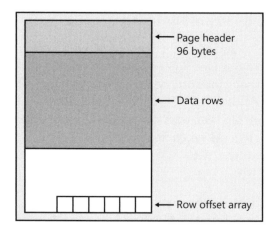

**FIGURE 5-8** The structure of a data page

## Page Header

As you can see in Figure 5-8, the page header occupies the first 96 bytes of each data page (leaving 8,096 bytes for data, row overhead, and row offsets). Table 5-5 shows some of the information shown when we examine the page header.

**TABLE 5-5 Information Available by Examining the Page Header**

| Field | Meaning |
|---|---|
| pageID | The file number and page number of this page in the database |
| nextPage | The file number and page number of the next page if this page is in a page chain |
| prevPage | The file number and page number of the previous page if this page is in a page chain |
| Metadata: ObjectId | The ID of the object to which this page belongs |
| Metadata: PartitionId | The ID of the partition that this page is part of |
| Metadata: AllocUnitId | The ID of the allocation unit that contains this page |
| LSN | The Log Sequence Number (LSN) corresponding to the last log entry that changed this page |
| slotCnt | The total number of slots (rows) used on this page |
| Level | The level of this page in an index (which always is 0 for leaf pages) |
| indexId | The index ID of this page (always 0 for data pages) |
| freeData | The byte offset of the first free space on this page |
| Pminlen | The number of bytes in fixed-length portion of rows |
| freeCnt | The number of free bytes on the page |
| reservedCnt | The number of bytes reserved by all transactions |
| xactreserved | The number of bytes reserved by the most recently started transaction |
| tornBits | A bit string containing 1 bit per sector for detecting torn page writes (or checksum information if *torn_page_detection* is not on) |
| flagBits | A 2-byte bitmap that contains additional information about the page |

## Data Rows for In-Row Data

Following the page header is the area in which the table's actual data rows are stored. The maximum size of a single data row is 8,060 bytes of in-row data. Rows can also have row-overflow and LOB data stored on separate pages. The number of rows stored on a given page varies depending on the structure of the table and on the data being stored. A table that has all fixed-length columns is always able to store the same number of rows per page; variable-length rows can store as many rows that fit based on the actual length of the data entered. Keeping the row length shorter allows more rows to fit on a page, thus reducing I/O and improving the cache-hit ratio.

## Row Offset Array

The row offset array is a block of 2-byte entries, each indicating the offset on the page at which the corresponding data row begins. Every row has a 2-byte entry in this array (as discussed earlier, when I mentioned the 10 overhead bytes needed by every row). Although these bytes aren't stored in the row with the data, they do affect the number of rows that fit on a page.

The row offset array indicates the logical order of rows on a page. For example, if a table has a clustered index, SQL Server stores the rows in the order of the clustered index key. This doesn't mean the rows are physically stored on the page in the order of the clustered index key. Rather, slot 0 in the offset array refers to the first row in the clustered index key order, slot 1 refers to the second row, and so forth. As we'll see shortly when we examine an actual page, the physical location of these rows can be anywhere on the page.

## Examining Data Pages

You can view the contents of a data page by using the *DBCC PAGE* command, which allows you to view the page header, data rows, and row offset table for any given page in a database. Only a system administrator can use *DBCC PAGE*. But because you typically won't need to view the contents of a data page, you won't find information about *DBCC PAGE* in the SQL Server documentation. Nevertheless, in case you want to use it, here's the syntax:

```
DBCC PAGE ({dbid | dbname}, filenum, pagenum[, printopt])
```

The *DBCC PAGE* command includes the parameters shown in Table 5-6. The code and results following Table 5-6 show sample output from *DBCC PAGE* with a *printopt* value of 1. Note that *DBCC TRACEON(3604)* instructs SQL Server to return the results to the client. Without this traceflag, no output is returned for the *DBCC PAGE* command.

**TABLE 5-6** Parameters of the *DBCC Page* Command

| Parameter | Description |
| --- | --- |
| Dbid | The ID of the database containing the page |
| Dbname | The name of the database containing the page |
| Filenum | The file number containing the page |
| Pagenum | The page number within the file |
| Printopt | An optional print option; takes one of these values: |
| | ■ 0 Default; prints the buffer header and page header |
| | ■ 1 Prints the buffer header, page header, each row separately, and the row offset table |
| | ■ 2 Prints the buffer and page headers, the page as a whole, and the offset table |
| | ■ 3 Prints the buffer header, page header, each row separately, and the row offset table; each row is followed by each of its column values listed separately |

```
DBCC TRACEON(3604);
GO
DBCC PAGE (pubs, 1, 157, 1);
GO
```

```
PAGE: (1:157)
BUFFER:
BUF @0x038E697C
bpage = 0x0C3AA000              bhash = 0x00000000              bpageno = (1:157)
bdbid = 11                      breferences = 0                 bUse1 = 60722
bstat = 0xc00009                blog = 0x3212159                bnext = 0x00000000


PAGE HEADER:
Page @0x0C3AA000
m_pageId = (1:157)             m_headerVersion = 1             m_type = 1
m_typeFlagBits = 0x4           m_level = 0                     m_flagBits = 0x200
m_objId (AllocUnitId.idObj) = 27    m_indexId (AllocUnitId.idInd) = 256
Metadata: AllocUnitId = 72057594039697408
Metadata: PartitionId = 72057594038779904            Metadata: IndexId = 1
Metadata: ObjectId = 2105058535    m_prevPage = (0:0)          m_nextPage = (0:0)
pminlen = 24                   m_slotCnt = 23                 m_freeCnt = 6010
m_freeData = 2136              m_reservedCnt = 0              m_lsn = (18:350:2)
m_xactReserved = 0            m_xdesId = (0:0)                m_ghostRecCnt = 0
m_tornBits = 1967525613


Allocation Status
GAM (1:2) = ALLOCATED           SGAM (1:3) = NOT ALLOCATED
PFS (1:1) = 0x60 MIXED_EXT ALLOCATED   0_PCT_FULL            DIFF (1:6) = CHANGED
ML (1:7) = NOT MIN_LOGGED


DATA:
Slot 0, Offset 0x631, Length 88, DumpStyle BYTE
Record Type = PRIMARY_RECORD          Record Attributes =  NULL_BITMAP VARIABLE_COLUMNS
Record Size = 88
Memory Dump @0x6292C631
00000000:    30001800 34303820 3439362d 37323233 †0...408 496-7223
00000010:    43413934 303235ff 09000000 05003300 †CA94025ÿ .....3.
00000020:    38003f00 4e005800 3137322d 33322d31 †8.?.N.X.172-32-1
00000030:    31373657 68697465 4a6f686e 736f6e31 †176WhiteJohnson1
00000040:    30393332 20426967 67652052 642e4d65 †0932 Bigge Rd.Me
00000050:    6e6c6f20 5061726b †††††††††††††††††††nlo Park


Slot 1, Offset 0xb8, Length 88, DumpStyle BYTE
Record Type = PRIMARY_RECORD          Record Attributes =  NULL_BITMAP VARIABLE_COLUMNS
Record Size = 88
Memory Dump @0x6292C0B8
00000000:    30001800 34313520 3938362d 37303230 †0...415 986-7020
```

```
00000010:   43413934 363138ff 09000000 05003300   †CA94618ÿ .....3.
00000020:   38004000 51005800 3231332d 34362d38   †8.@.Q.X.213-46-8
00000030:   39313547 7265656e 4d61726a 6f726965   †915GreenMarjorie
00000040:   33303920 36337264 2053742e 20233431   †309 63rd St. #41
00000050:   314f616b 6c616e64 †††††††††††††††††††10akland
```

Slot 2, Offset 0x110, Length 85, DumpStyle BYTE
Record Type = PRIMARY_RECORD        Record Attributes =  NULL_BITMAP VARIABLE_COLUMNS
Record Size = 85
Memory Dump @0x6292C110

```
00000000:   30001800 34313520 3534382d 37373233   †0...415 548-7723
00000010:   43413934 373035ff 09000000 05003300   †CA94705ÿ .....3.
00000020:   39003f00 4d005500 3233382d 39352d37   †9.?.M.U.238-95-7
00000030:   37363643 6172736f 6e436865 72796c35   †766CarsonCheryl5
00000040:   38392044 61727769 6e204c6e 2e426572   †89 Darwin Ln.Ber
00000050:   6b656c65 79††††††††††††††††††††††††††††keley
```

**/* Data for slots 3 through 20 not shown */**

Slot 21, Offset 0x1c0, Length 89, DumpStyle BYTE
Record Type = PRIMARY_RECORD        Record Attributes =  NULL_BITMAP VARIABLE_COLUMNS
Record Size = 89
Memory Dump @0x6292C1C0

```
00000000:   30001800 38303120 3832362d 30373532   †0...801 826-0752
00000010:   55543834 313532ff 09000000 05003300   †UT84152ÿ .....3.
00000020:   39003d00 4b005900 3839392d 34362d32   †9.=.K.Y.899-46-2
00000030:   30333552 696e6765 72416e6e 65363720   †035RingerAnne67
00000040:   53657665 6e746820 41762e53 616c7420   †Seventh Av.Salt
00000050:   4c616b65 20436974 79†††††††††††††††††††Lake City
```

Slot 22, Offset 0x165, Length 91, DumpStyle BYTE
Record Type = PRIMARY_RECORD        Record Attributes =  NULL_BITMAP VARIABLE_COLUMNS
Record Size = 91
Memory Dump @0x6292C165

```
00000000:   30001800 38303120 3832362d 30373532   †0...801 826-0752
00000010:   55543834 313532ff 09000000 05003300   †UT84152ÿ .....3.
00000020:   39003f00 4d005b00 3939382d 37322d33   †9.?.M.[.998-72-3
00000030:   35363752 696e6765 72416c62 65727436   †567RingerAlbert6
00000040:   37205365 76656e74 68204176 2e53616c   †7 Seventh Av.Sal
00000050:   74204c61 6b652043 697479†††††††††††††††t Lake City
```

```
OFFSET TABLE:
Row - Offset
22 (0x16) - 357 (0x165)
21 (0x15) - 448 (0x1c0)
20 (0x14) - 711 (0x2c7)
19 (0x13) - 1767 (0x6e7)
18 (0x12) - 619 (0x26b)
17 (0x11) - 970 (0x3ca)
16 (0x10) - 1055 (0x41f)
15 (0xf) - 796 (0x31c)
14 (0xe) - 537 (0x219)
13 (0xd) - 1673 (0x689)
12 (0xc) - 1226 (0x4ca)
11 (0xb) - 1949 (0x79d)
10 (0xa) - 1488 (0x5d0)
9 (0x9) - 1854 (0x73e)
8 (0x8) - 1407 (0x57f)
7 (0x7) - 1144 (0x478)
6 (0x6) - 96 (0x60)
5 (0x5) - 2047 (0x7ff)
4 (0x4) - 884 (0x374)
3 (0x3) - 1314 (0x522)
2 (0x2) - 272 (0x110)
1 (0x1) - 184 (0xb8)
0 (0x0) - 1585 (0x631)


DBCC execution completed. If DBCC printed error messages, contact your system administrator.
```

As you can see, the output from *DBCC PAGE* is divided into four main sections: BUFFER, PAGE HEADER, DATA, and OFFSET TABLE (really the offset array). The BUFFER section shows information about the buffer for the given page. A *buffer* in this context is the in-memory structure that manages a page, and the information in this section is relevant only when the page is in memory.

The PAGE HEADER section in the output from *DBCC PAGE* displays the data for all the header fields on the page. (Table 5-5 shows the meaning of most of these fields.) The DATA section contains information for each row. When *DBCC PAGE* is used with a *printopt* value of 1 or 3, *DBCC PAGE* indicates the slot position of each row, the offset of the row on the page, and the length of the row. The row data is divided into three parts. The left column indicates the byte position within the row where the displayed data occurs. The next section contains the actual data stored on the page, displayed in four columns of eight hexadecimal digits each. The right column contains an ASCII character representation of the data. Only character data is readable in this column, although some of the other data might be displayed.

The OFFSET TABLE section shows the contents of the row offset array at the end of the page. In the output from *DBCC PAGE*, you can see that this page contains 23 rows, with the first row (indicated by slot 0) beginning at offset 1585 (0x631). The first row physically stored on the page is actually row 6, with an offset in the row offset array of 96. *DBCC PAGE* with a *printopt* value of 1 displays the rows in slot number order, even though, as you can see by the offset of each of the slots, that it isn't the order in which the rows physically exist on the page. If you use *DBCC PAGE* with a *printopt* value of 2, you see a dump of all 8,096 bytes of the page (after the header) in the order they are stored on the page.

## The Structure of Data Rows

A table's data rows have the general structure shown in Figure 5-9 (so long as the data is stored in uncompressed form). We call this format the FixedVar format, because the data for all fixed-length columns is stored first, followed by the data for all variable-length columns. Table 5-7 shows the information stored in each FixedVar row. (In Chapter 7, we'll see the format of rows stored in a different format, used when the data on the page is compressed.)

Status Bits A contains a bitmap indicating properties of the row. The bits have the following meanings:

- **Bit 0**   Versioning information. In SQL Server 2008, this is always 0.

- **Bits 1 through 3**   Taken as a three-bit value, 0 indicates a primary record, 1 indicates a forwarded record, 2 indicates a forwarding stub, 3 indicates an index record, 4 indicates a blob fragment or row-overflow data, 5 indicates a ghost index record, 6 indicates a ghost data record, and 7 indicates a ghost version record. (I'll discuss forwarded records in the section entitled "Moving Rows," later in this chapter, and ghost records in Chapter 6.)

- **Bit 4**   Indicates that a NULL bitmap exists. In SQL Server 2008, a NULL bitmap is always present, even if no NULLs are allowed in any column.

- **Bit 5**   Indicates that variable-length columns exist in the row.

- **Bit 6**   Indicates that the row contains versioning information.

- **Bit 7**   Not used in SQL Server 2008.

Only one bit is used in the Status Bits B field, indicating that the record is a ghost forwarded record.

You can see in both Figure 5-9 and Table 5-7 that the third and fourth bytes indicate the length of the fixed-length portion of the row. As Figure 5-9 explains, it is the length excluding the 2 bytes for the number of columns, and the NULL bitmap, which is variable length depending on the total number of columns in the table. Another way to interpret the data in these bits is as the location in the row where the number of columns can be found. For example, if the third and fourth bytes (bytes 2-3) contain the value 0x0016, which is decimal 22, it means not only that there are 22 bytes in the row before the value for number of columns, but that the value for the number of columns can be found at byte 22. In some of the figures in this chapter and later ones, bytes 2-3 may be identified as the position to find the number of columns.

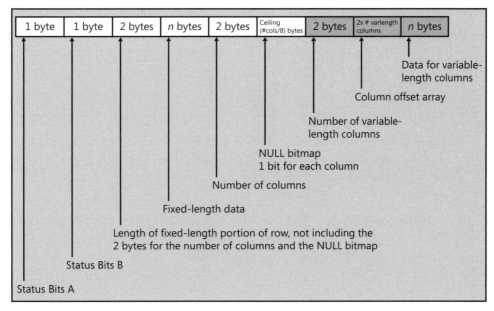

**FIGURE 5-9** The structure of data rows

**TABLE 5-7 Information Stored in a Table's Data Rows**

| Information | Mnemonic | Size |
|---|---|---|
| Status Bits A | TagA | 1 byte |
| Status Bits B | TagB | 1 byte |
| Fixed-length size | Fsize | 2 bytes |
| Fixed-length data | Fdata | Fsize − 4 |
| Number of columns | Ncol | 2 bytes |
| NULL bitmap (1 bit for each column in the table; a 1 indicates that the corresponding column is NULL or that the bit is unused.) | Nullbits | Ceiling (Ncol / 8) |
| Number of variable-length columns stored in row | VarCount | 2 bytes |
| Variable column offset array | VarOffset | 2 * VarCount |
| Variable-length data | VarData | VarOff[VarCount] - (Fsize + 4 + Ceiling (Ncol / 8) + 2 * VarCount) |

Within each block of fixed-length or variable-length data, the data is stored in the column order in which the table was created. For example, suppose a table is created with the following statement:

```
CREATE TABLE Test1
(
Col1 int          NOT NULL,
Col2 char(25)     NOT NULL,
```

```
Col3 varchar(60)     NULL,
Col4 money           NOT NULL,
Col5 varchar(20)     NOT NULL
);
```

The fixed-length data portion of this row contains the data for *Col1*, followed by the data for *Col2*, followed by the data for *Col4*. The variable-length data portion contains the data for *Col3*, followed by the data for *Col5*. For rows that contain only fixed-length data, the following is true:

- The first hexadecimal digit of the first byte of the data row is 1, indicating that no variable-length columns exist. (The first hexadecimal digit comprises bits 4 through 7; bits 6 and 7 are always 0, and if there are no variable-length columns, bit 5 is also 0. Bit 4 is always 1, so the value of the four bits is displayed as 1.)

- The data row ends after the NULL bitmap, which follows the fixed-length data (that is, the shaded portion shown in Figure 5-9 won't exist in rows with only fixed-length data).

- The total length of every data row is the same.

A data row that has any variable-length columns has a column offset array in the data row with a 2-byte entry for each non-NULL variable-length column, indicating the position within the row where the column ends. (The terms *offset* and *position* aren't exactly interchangeable. *Offset* is 0-based, and *position* is 1-based. A byte at an offset of 7 is in the eighth byte position in the row.) There are some special issues storing variable-length columns with a NULL value, and I'll discuss this issue in the section entitled "NULLs and Variable-Length Columns," later in this chapter.

## Finding a Physical Page

Before we examine specific data, we need to digress a bit. The examples that follow use the *DBCC PAGE* command to examine the physical database pages. To run this command, I need to know what page numbers are used to store rows for a table. I mentioned previously that a value for *first_page* was stored in an undocumented view called *sys.system_internals_allocation_units*, which is almost identical to the *sys.allocation_units* view. First, let me create a table (that will be used in the following section) and insert a single row into it:

```
USE tempdb;
CREATE TABLE Fixed
(
Col1 char(5)      NOT NULL,
Col2 int          NOT NULL,
Col3 char(3)      NULL,
Col4 char(6)      NOT NULL
);
INSERT Fixed VALUES ('ABCDE', 123, NULL, 'CCCC');
```

The following query gives me the value for *first_page* in the *Fixed* table:

```
SELECT object_name(object_id) AS name,
    rows, type_desc as page_type_desc,
    total_pages AS pages, first_page
```

```
FROM sys.partitions p  JOIN sys.system_internals_allocation_units a
   ON p.partition_id = a.container_id
WHERE object_id=object_id('dbo.Fixed');
```

RESULTS:

```
name    rows    page_type_desc    pages  first_page
-----   ----    --------------    -----  --------------
Fixed   1       IN_ROW_DATA       2      0xCF0400000100
```

I can then take the value of *first_page* from the preceding *sys.system_internals_allocation_units* output (0xCF0400000100) and convert it to a file and page address. (The value that you get for *first_page* most likely will be different than the one I got.) In hexadecimal notation, each set of two hexadecimal digits represents a byte. I first had to swap the bytes to get 00 01 00 00 04 CF. The first two groups represent the 2-byte file number; the last four groups represent the page number. So the file is 0x0001, which is 1, and the page number is 0x000004CF, which is 1231 in decimal.

Unless you particularly enjoy playing with hexadecimal conversions, you might want to use one of three other options for determining the actual page numbers associated with your SQL Server tables. First you can create the function shown here to convert a 6-byte hexadecimal page number value (such as 0xCF0400000100) to a *file_number:page_number* format:

```
CREATE FUNCTION convert_page_nums (@page_num binary(6))
   RETURNS varchar(11)
AS
  BEGIN
   RETURN(convert(varchar(2), (convert(int, substring(@page_num, 6, 1))
         * power(2, 8)) +
             (convert(int, substring(@page_num, 5, 1)))) + ':' +
               convert(varchar(11),
  (convert(int, substring(@page_num, 4, 1)) * power(2, 24)) +
  (convert(int, substring(@page_num, 3, 1)) * power(2, 16)) +
  (convert(int, substring(@page_num, 2, 1)) * power(2, 8)) +
  (convert(int, substring(@page_num, 1, 1)))) )
  END;
```

You can then execute this *SELECT* to call the function:

```
SELECT dbo.convert_page_nums(0xCF0400000100);
```

You should get back the result *1:1231*.

> **Warning** SQL Server does not guarantee that the *first_page* column in *sys.system_internals_allocation_units* always indicates the first page of a table. (The view is undocumented, after all.) I've found that *first_page* is reliable until you begin to perform deletes and updates on the data in the table.

The second option for determining the actual page numbers is to use another undocumented command called *DBCC IND*. Because most of the information returned is relevant only to indexes, I won't discuss this command in detail until Chapter 6. However, for a sneak preview, you can run the following command and note the values in the first two columns of output (labeled *PageFID* and *PagePID*) in the row where *PageType* = 1, which indicates that the page is a data page:

```
DBCC IND(tempdb, Fixed, -1);
```

If you weren't in *tempdb*, you would replace *tempdb* with the name of whatever database you were in when you created this table. The values for *PageFID* and *PagePID* should be the same value you used when you converted the hexadecimal string for the *first_page* value. In my case, I see that *PageFID* value is 1 and the *PagePID* value is 1231. So those are the values I use when calling *DBCC PAGE*.

The third method for obtaining file and page number information involves using an undocumented function, *sys.fn_PhysLocFormatter,* in conjunction with an undocumented value, *%%physloc%%,* to return the physical row location in your result rows along with data values from a table. This can be useful if you want to find which page in a table contains a particular value. *DBCC IND* can be used to find all the pages in a table but not specifically the pages containing a particular row. However, *sys.fn_PhysLocFormatter* can show you only data pages for the data that is returned in a *SELECT* statement. We can use this function to get the pages used by our data in the table *Fixed,* as follows:

```
SELECT sys.fn_PhysLocFormatter (%%physloc%%) AS RID, * FROM Fixed;
GO
```

Here are my results:

```
RID          Col1    Col2          Col3   Col4
------------ ------- ------------- ------ ------
(1:1231:1)   ABCDE   123           NULL   CCCC
```

Once you have the *FileID* and *PageID* values, you can use *DBCC PAGE*. For a larger table, we could use *sys.fn_PhysLocFormatter* to get the the pages only for the specific rows that were returned by the conditions in our WHERE clause.

> **Caution** The *%%physloc%%* value is not understood by the relational engine, which means that if you use *%%physloc%%* in a WHERE clause, SQL Server has to examine every row to see which ones are on the page indicated by *%%physloc%%*. It is not able to use *%%physloc%%* to find the row. Another way of looking at this is that *%%physloc%%* can be returned as output to report on a physical row location, but cannot be used as input to find a particular location in a table. The *%%physloc%%* value was introduced as a debugging feature by the SQL Server product development team and is not intended to be used (and is not supported) in production applications.

The two examples that follow illustrate how fixed-length and variable-length data rows are stored.

## Storage of Fixed-Length Rows

First, let's look at the simpler case of an all fixed-length row using the table I just built in the preceding section:

```
CREATE TABLE Fixed
(
Col1 char(5)      NOT NULL,
Col2 int          NOT NULL,
Col3 char(3)      NULL,
Col4 char(6)      NOT NULL
);
```

When this table is created, you should be able to execute the following queries against the *sys.indexes* and *sys.columns* views to receive the information similar to the results shown:

```
SELECT object_id,  type_desc,
    indexproperty(object_id, name, 'minlen') as min_row_len
    FROM sys.indexes where object_id=object_id('Fixed');

SELECT  column_id, name, system_type_id, max_length as max_col_len
FROM sys.columns
WHERE object_id=object_id('Fixed');
```

**RESULTS:**

| object_id | type_desc | minlen |
| --- | --- | --- |
| 53575229 | HEAP | 22 |

| column_id | name | system_type_id | max_length |
| --- | --- | --- | --- |
| 1 | Col1 | 175 | 5 |
| 2 | Col2 | 56 | 4 |
| 3 | Col3 | 175 | 3 |
| 4 | Col4 | 175 | 6 |

> **Note** The *sysindexes* compatibility view contains columns called *minlen* and *xmaxlen*, which store the minimum and maximum length of a row. In SQL Server 2008, these values are not available in any of the catalog views, but you can get them by using undocumented parameters to the *indexproperty* function. As with all undocumented features, keep in mind that they are not supported by Microsoft and future compatibility is not guaranteed.
>
> For tables containing only fixed-length columns, the value returned for *minlen* by the *indexproperty* function equals the sum of the column lengths (from *sys.columns.max_length*) plus 4 bytes. It doesn't include the 2 bytes for the number of columns, or the bytes for the NULL bitmap.

To look at a specific data row in this table, you must first insert a new row. If you didn't insert this row in the preceding section, insert it now:

```
INSERT Fixed VALUES ('ABCDE', 123, NULL, 'CCCC');
```

Figure 5-10 shows this row's actual contents on the data page.

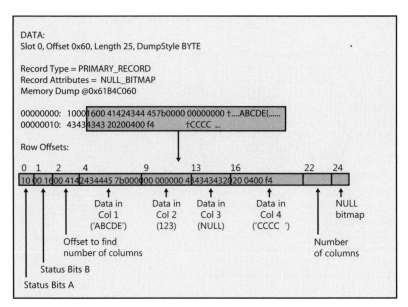

**FIGURE 5-10** A data row containing all fixed-length columns

I was able to get the page contents by running the *DBCC PAGE* command, using the file and page number obtained using one of the methods that I described previously:

```
DBCC PAGE(tempdb, 1, 1231, 1);
```

Reading the output of *DBCC PAGE* takes a bit of practice. First, note that the output shows the data rows in groups of 4 bytes at a time. The shaded area in Figure 5-10 has been expanded to show the bytes in an expanded form.

The first byte is Status Bits A, and its value (0x10) indicates that only bit 4 is on, and because bit 5 is not on, we know the row has no variable-length columns. The second byte in the row (Status Bits B) is unused. The third and fourth bytes (1600) indicate the length of the fixed-length fields, which is also the column offset in which the *Ncol* value can be found. (As a multibyte numeric value, this information is stored in a byte-swapped form, so the value is really 0x0016, which translates to 22.) To know where in the row between offsets 4 and 22 each column actually is located, we need to know the offset of each column. In SQL Server 2000, the *syscolumns* system table has a column indicating the offset within the row. Although you can still select from the compatibility view called *syscolumns* in SQL Server 2005, the results you get back are not reliable. The offsets can be found in an undocumented view called *sys.system_internals_partition_columns* that we can then join to *sys.partitions* to get the information about the referenced objects and join to *sys.columns* to get other information about each column.

Here is a query to return basic column information, including the offset within the row for each column. I will use the same query for other tables later in this chapter, and I will refer to it as the "column detail query."

```
SELECT  c.name AS column_name, column_id, max_inrow_length,
        pc.system_type_id, leaf_offset
 FROM sys.system_internals_partition_columns pc
    JOIN sys.partitions p
      ON p.partition_id = pc.partition_id
    JOIN sys.columns c
        ON column_id = partition_column_id
          AND c.object_id = p.object_id
WHERE p.object_id=object_id('Fixed');
```

RESULTS:

| column_name | column_id | max_inrow_length | system_type_id | leaf_offset |
| --- | --- | --- | --- | --- |
| Col1 | 1 | 5 | 175 | 4 |
| Col2 | 2 | 4 | 56 | 9 |
| Col3 | 3 | 3 | 175 | 13 |
| Col4 | 4 | 6 | 175 | 16 |

So now we can find the data in the row for each column simply by using the offset value in the preceding results: the data for column *Col1* begins at offset 4, the data for column *Col2* begins at offset 9, and so on. As an *int*, the data in *Col2* (7b000000) must be byte-swapped to give the value 0x0000007b, which is equivalent to 123 in decimal.

Note that the 3 bytes of data for *Col3* are all zeros, representing an actual NULL in the column. Because the row has no variable-length columns, the row ends 3 bytes after the data for column *Col4*. The 2 bytes starting right after the fixed-length data at offset 22 (0400, which is byte-swapped to yield 0x0004) indicate that four columns are in the row. The last byte is the NULL bitmap. The value of 0xf4 is 11110100 in binary, and bits are shown from high order to low order. The low-order four bits represent the four columns in the table, 0100, which indicates that only the third column actually IS NULL. The high-order four bits are 1111 because those bits are unused. The NULL bitmap must have a multiple of eight bits, and if the number of columns is not a multiple of 8, some bits are unused.

## Storage of Variable-Length Rows

Now let's look at the somewhat more complex case of a table with variable-length data. Each row has three *varchar* columns and two fixed-length columns:

```
CREATE TABLE Variable
(
Col1 char(3)       NOT NULL,
Col2 varchar(250)  NOT NULL,
Col3 varchar(5)    NULL,
Col4 varchar(20)   NOT NULL,
Col5 smallint      NULL
);
```

When this table is created, you should be able to execute the following queries against the *sys.indexes*, *sys.partitions*, *sys.system_internals_partition_columns*, and *sys.columns* views to receive the information similar to the results shown here:

```
SELECT object_id,  type_desc,
    indexproperty(object_id, name, 'minlen') as minlen
    FROM sys.indexes where object_id=object_id('Variable');

SELECT  name, column_id, max_inrow_length, pc.system_type_id, leaf_offset
  FROM sys.system_internals_partition_columns pc
    JOIN sys.partitions p
        ON p.partition_id = pc.partition_id
    JOIN sys.columns c
        ON column_id = partition_column_id AND c.object_id = p.object_id
WHERE p.object_id=object_id('Variable');
```

RESULTS:

| object_id | type_desc | minlen |
|-----------|-----------|--------|
| 69575286  | HEAP      | 9      |

| column_name | column_id | max_inrow_length | system_type_id | leaf_offset |
|-------------|-----------|------------------|----------------|-------------|
| Col1        | 1         | 3                | 175            | 4           |
| Col2        | 2         | 250              | 167            | -1          |
| Col3        | 3         | 5                | 167            | -2          |
| Col4        | 4         | 20               | 167            | -3          |
| Col5        | 5         | 2                | 52             | 7           |

Now you can insert a row into the table as follows:

```
INSERT Variable VALUES
    ('AAA', REPLICATE('X', 250), NULL, 'ABC', 123);
```

The *REPLICATE* function is used here to simplify populating a column; this function builds a string of 250 *X*s to be inserted into *Col2*.

You can see the details of this row as stored on the page in the *DBCC PAGE* output in Figure 5-11. The location of the fixed-length columns can be found by using the *leaf_offset* value in *sys.system_internals_partition_columns*, in the preceding query results. In this table, *Col1* begins at offset 4 and *Col5* begins at offset 7. Variable-length columns are not shown in the query output with a specific byte offset because the offset can be different in each row. Instead, the row itself holds the ending position of each variable-length column within that row in a part of the row called the *Column Offset Array*. The query output shows that *Col2* has an *leaf_offset* value of –1, which means that *Col2* is the first variable-length column; an offset for *Col3* of –2 means that *Col3* is the second variable-length column, and an offset of –3 for *Col4* means that *Col4* is the third variable-length column.

To find the variable-length columns in the data row itself, you first locate the column offset array in the row. Right after the 2-byte field indicating the total number of columns (0x0500) and the NULL bitmap with the value 0xe4, a 2-byte field exists with the value 0x0300 (or 3, decimal) indicating that three variable-length fields exist. Next comes the column offset array. Three 2-byte values indicate the ending position of each of the three variable-length columns: 0x0e01 is byte-swapped to 0x010e, so the first variable byte column ends at position 270. The next 2-byte offset is also 0x0e01, so that column has no length and has nothing stored in the variable data area. Unlike with fixed-length fields, if a variable-length field has a NULL value, it takes no room in the data row. SQL Server distinguishes between a *varchar* containing NULL and an empty string by determining whether the bit for the field is 0 or 1 in the NULL bitmap. The third 2-byte offset is 0x1101, which, when byte-swapped, gives us 0x0111. This means the row ends at position 273 (and is 273 bytes long).

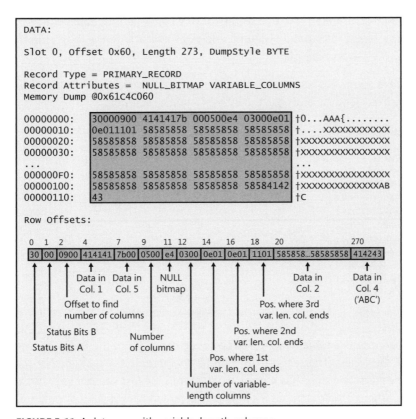

**FIGURE 5-11** A data row with variable-length columns

The total storage space needed for a row depends on a number of factors. Variable-length columns add more overhead to a row, and their actual size is probably unpredictable. Even for fixed-length columns, the number of bytes of overhead can change depending on the number of columns in the table. In the example illustrated earlier in this chapter in Figure 5-2, I mentioned that 10 bytes of overhead exist if a row contains all fixed-length columns. For that table 10 is the correct number. The size of the NULL bitmap needs to be long enough to store a bit for every column in the row. In the Figure 5-2 example, the table has 11 columns, so the NULL bitmap needs to be 2 bytes. In the examples illustrated by Figures 5-10 and 5-11, the tables have fewer than eight columns, so the NULL bitmaps need only a single byte. Don't forget that the total row overhead must also include the 2 bytes for each row in the row offset table at the bottom of the page.

## NULLS and Variable-Length Columns

As mentioned previously, fixed-length columns are always the same length, even if the column contains NULL. For variable-length columns, NULLs don't take any space in the variable-length data part of the row. However, as we saw in Figure 5-11, there is still a 2-byte column offset entry for each variable-length column, so we can't say that they take no space at all. However, if a zero-length value is stored at the end of the list of variable-length data columns, SQL Server does not store any information about it and does not include the 2 bytes in the column offset array. Let's look at an example.

The following table allows NULLs in each of its character columns, and they are all variable length. The only fixed-length column is the integer identity column:

```
CREATE TABLE dbo.null_varchar
    (
      id INT PRIMARY KEY IDENTITY(1,1),
      col1 VARCHAR(10) NULL,
      col2 VARCHAR(10) NULL,
      col3 VARCHAR(10) NULL,
      col4 VARCHAR(10) NULL,
      col5 VARCHAR(10) NULL,
      col6 VARCHAR(10) NULL,
      col7 VARCHAR(10) NULL,
      col8 VARCHAR(10) NULL,
      col9 VARCHAR(10) NULL,
      col10 VARCHAR(10) NULL
    );
GO
```

I'll insert four rows into this table. The first has a single character in the last *varchar* column, and NULLs in all the others. The second has a single character in the first *varchar* column, and NULLs in all the others. The third has a single character in the last *varchar* column, and empty strings in all the others. The fourth has a single character in the first *varchar* column, and empty strings in all the others:

```
SET NOCOUNT ON
INSERT INTO null_varchar(col10)
    SELECT 'a';
INSERT INTO null_varchar(col1)
    SELECT 'b';
INSERT INTO null_varchar
    SELECT '','','','','','','','','','c';
INSERT INTO null_varchar
    SELECT 'd','','','','','','','','','';
GO
```

Now I can use *DBCC IND* and *DBCC PAGE* (as shown previously) to look at the page containing these four rows.

Here is the first row (with the column offset array shaded):

```
Slot 0, Offset 0x60, Length 35, DumpStyle BYTE
Record Type = PRIMARY_RECORD          Record Attributes =  NULL_BITMAP VARIABLE_COLUMNS
Record Size = 35
Memory Dump @0x66B4C060
00000000:   30000800 01000000 0b00fe03 0a002200 †0.........þ...".
00000010:   22002200 22002200 22002200 22002200 †".".".".".".".".
00000020:   230061†††††††††††††††††††††††††††††††#.a
```

There are nine entries in the column offset array with the value (after byte-swapping) of hex 22, or decimal 18, and one entry with the decimal value 19. The value of 18 for the first nine positions indicates that data ends in the same position as the column offset array ends, and SQL Server determines that this means those nine columns are empty. But empty could mean either NULL or an empty string. By looking at the NULL bitmap, in positions 11 and 12, we see fe03, which is hex 03fe after byte-swapping. Looking at this in binary we see 0000001111111110. The column positions are shown from right to left. This table has only 11 columns, so the last five bits in the NULL bitmap are ignored. The rest of the string indicates the first and last columns are not NULL, but all the other columns are NULL.

The 10th value in the column offset array is hex 23, or decimal 19, which means that data ends at offset 19, which contains the ASCII code 61, representing *a*.

Here is the second row (with the column offset array shaded):

```
Slot 1, Offset 0x83, Length 17, DumpStyle BYTE
Record Type = PRIMARY_RECORD          Record Attributes =  NULL_BITMAP VARIABLE_COLUMNS
Record Size = 17
Memory Dump @0x66B4C083
00000000:   30000800 02000000 0b00fc07 01001100 †0.........ü.....
00000010:   62†††††††††††††††††††††††††††††††††††b
```

There are several important differences to note, between this row and the preceding one. First, the column offset array contains only a single value, which is the ending position for the first variable-length column. The 1100 bytes are byte-swapped to 0011, and converted to 17 decimal, which is the offset where the ASCII code for *b* (that is, 62) is located. Immediately preceding the column offset array is the 2-byte value indicating the number of variable-length columns. The first row had a hex value of 000a here, indicating 10 variable-length columns. The second row has 0001, which means only one of the variable-length columns is actually stored in the row. We just saw that zero-length columns prior to columns containing data do use the column offset array, but in this case, because all the zero-length columns are after the non-NULL, only the non-NULL column is represented here. If you look at the NULL bitmap, you'll see fc07, which is hex 07fc after byte-swapping. Looking at this in binary, we see 0000011111111100, indicating that the first two columns are not NULL, but all the rest are.

If you look at the rows containing empty strings instead of NULLs, the output should be exactly the same, except for the NULL bitmap. Here is the third row (slot 2) and the fourth row (slot 3), with the NULL bitmaps shaded:

```
Slot 2, Offset 0x94, Length 35, DumpStyle BYTE
Record Type = PRIMARY_RECORD          Record Attributes =  NULL_BITMAP VARIABLE_COLUMNS
Record Size = 35
Memory Dump @0x66B4C094
00000000:    30000800 03000000 0b000000 0a002200 †0.............".
00000010:    22002200 22002200 22002200 22002200 †".".".".".".".".
00000020:    230063†††††††††††††††††††††††††††††††#.c
```

```
Slot 3, Offset 0xb7, Length 17, DumpStyle BYTE
Record Type = PRIMARY_RECORD          Record Attributes =  NULL_BITMAP VARIABLE_COLUMNS
Record Size = 17
Memory Dump @0x66B4C0B7
00000000:    30000800 04000000 0b000000 01001100 †0...............
00000010:    63†††††††††††††††††††††††††††††††††††d
```

For both the third and fourth rows, the NULL bitmap is all zeros, indicating that none of the columns are NULL. The first and third rows differ only in the actual character value stored and in the NULL bitmap. The second and fourth rows differ in the same way.

If we insert a row with all NULLs in the *varchar* columns, the row storage changes a bit more. Here is what it would look like:

```
Slot 4, Offset 0xc8, Length 12, DumpStyle BYTE
Record Type = PRIMARY_RECORD          Record Attributes =  NULL_BITMAP
Record Size = 12
Memory Dump @0x66B4C0C8
00000000:    10000800 05000000 0b000000 †††††††††††.......
```

This row looks just like an all fixed-length row and ends right after the NULL bitmap. Bit 5 in the first byte (Status Bits A) has been set to 0 to indicate that there are no variable-length columns stored in this row.

## Storage of Date and Time Data

I described the storage of date and time data types earlier in this chapter, and now that we've had some practice looking at the actual on-disk storage, let's look at some date and time data. The following table stores all the different data and time data types in a single row, and all of the different possible scales for time data. (Remember that *datetime2* and *datetimeoffset* can also indicate a scale for the time component, but the time values look no different than the time values stored with the simple *time* data type.) The table also includes single-column character values, which I use just so I can find the other values easily in the single row of hex data that *DBCC PAGE* gives me:

```
CREATE TABLE times (
    a char(1),
    dt1 datetime,
```

```
     b char(1),
     sd smalldatetime,
     c char(1),
     dt2 datetime2,
     d char(1),
     dt date,
     e char(1),
     dto datetimeoffset,
     f char(1),
     t time,
     g char(1),
     t0 time(0),
     h char(1),
     t1 time(1),
     i char(1),
     t2 time(2),
     j char(1),
     t3 time(3),
     k char(1),
     t4 time(4),
     l char(1),
     t5 time(5),
     m char(1),
     t6 time(6),
     n char(1),
     t7 time(7));
GO
```

Now I'll insert one one-row data, with the same time value provided for each date or time column. The data types that need a date component assume a default date of January 1, 1900:

```
INSERT INTO times
SELECT
    'a', '01:02:03.123',
    'b', '01:02:03.123',
    'c', '01:02:03.123',
    'd', '01:02:03.123',
    'e', '01:02:03.123',
    'f', '01:02:03.123',
    'g', '01:02:03.123',
    'h', '01:02:03.123',
    'i', '01:02:03.123',
    'j', '01:02:03.123',
    'k', '01:02:03.123',
    'l', '01:02:03.123',
    'm', '01:02:03.123',
    'n', '01:02:03.123';
```

Here is the *DBCC PAGE* output for this row. I have shaded the single-character column data to use as dividers:

```
00000000:   10005800 61090b11 00000000 00623e00 †..X.a     ......b>.
00000010:   00006330 7c27ab08 5b950a64 5b950a65 †..c0|'".[?.d[?.e
```

```
00000020:    307c27ab 085b950a 00006630 7c27ab08 †0|'".[?...f0|'".
00000030:    678b0e00 686f9100 6958ae05 6a73cf38 †g?..ho?.iX®.jsÏ8
00000040:    006b7e1a 38026cec 08311600 6d3859ea †.k~.8.lì.1..m8Yê
00000050:    dd006e30 7c27ab08 1c000000 0000††††††Ý.n0|'".......
```

Table 5-8 shows the translation into decimal format for each of these values. Here are some points to notice:

- For the *datetime* and *smalldatetime* data types, the date value is stored as 0, meaning that the date is the base of 'January 1, 1900'. For the other types that store a date, the date value is stored as 693595, which represents the number of days after the new internal base date of January 1, 0001. To compute the corresponding date, you can use the *dateadd* function:

```
SELECT DATEADD(dd, 693595, CAST('0001/1/1' AS datetime2));
```

- This will return the value '1900-01-01' 00:00:00.00', which is the default when no date is specified.

- The fractional seconds component is the last *N* digits of the time component, where *N* is the scale of the time data, as listed in the table definition. So for the *time(7)* value, the fractional seconds are .1230000; for the *time(4)*, the fractional seconds are .1230; for the *time(1)* value, the fractional seconds are .1; and for the *time(0)* value, there are no fractional sections.

- Whatever remains in the time portion after the appropriate number of digits are removed for the fractional seconds is the hours, minutes, and seconds value. Because the same time value was used for all the columns in the table, the time values all start with the same four digits: 3723. Previously, I showed you the formula for converting a time value to an integer; here, I'll do the reverse, using the modulo operator (%) and integer division. SQL Server uses the following conversions to determine the hours, minutes, and seconds from 3723:

```
SELECT hours =  (3723 / 60) / 60;
SELECT minutes = (3723 / 60) % 60;
SELECT seconds = 3723 % 60;

RESULT:
hours
-----------
1

minutes
-----------
2

seconds
-----------
3
```

- The column storing *datetimeoffset* data has 2 extra bytes to store the *timezone* offset. Two bytes are needed because the offset is stored as the number of hours and minutes (1 byte for each) from Coordinated Universal Time (UTC).

**TABLE 5-8**  **Translation of Various Date and Time Values**

| Column Name | Data Type and Bytes Used | Value Stored in Row | Byte-Swapped Date | Time | Decimal Values Date | Time |
|---|---|---|---|---|---|---|
| dt1 | Datetime -8- | 090b110000 000000 | 00 00 00 00 | 00 11 0b 09 | 0 | 1116937 |
| sd | Small datetime -4- | 3e000000 | 00 00 | 00 3e | 0 | 62 |
| dt2 | datetime2 -8- | 307c27ab0 85b950a | 0a 95 5b | 08 ab 27 7c 30 | 693595 | 37231230000 |
| dt | date -3- | 5b950a | 0a 95 5b | (none) | 693595 | (none) |
| dto | datetime offset -10- | 307c27ab08 5b950a00 00 | 0a 95 5b | 08 ab 27 7c 30 | 693595 | 37231230000 |
| t | time -5- | 307c27ab08 | (none) | 08 ab 27 7c 30 | (none) | 37231230000 |
| t0 | time(0) -3- | 8b0e00 | (none) | 00 0e 8b | (none) | 3723 |
| t1 | time(1) -3- | 6f9100 | (none) | 00 91 6f | (none) | 37231 |
| t2 | time(2) -3- | 58ae05 | (none) | 05 ae 58 | (none) | 372312 |
| t3 | time(3) -4- | 73cf3800 | (none) | 00 38 cf 73 | (none) | 3723123 |
| t4 | time(4) -4- | 7e1a3802 | (none) | 02 38 1a 7e | (none) | 37231230 |
| t5 | time(5) -5- | ec08311600 | (none) | 00 16 31 08 ec | (none) | 372312300 |
| t6 | time(6) -5- | 3859eadd00 | (none) | 00 dd ea 59 38 | (none) | 3723123000 |
| t7 | time(7) -5- | 307c27ab08 | (none) | 08 ab 27 7c 30 | (none) | 37231230000 |

# Storage of *sql_variant* Data

The *sql_variant* data type provides support for columns that contain any or all of the SQL Server base data types except LOBs and variable-length columns with the MAX qualifier, *rowversion* (*timestamp*), XML, and the types that can't be defined for a column in a table, namely *cursor* and *table*. For instance, a column can contain a *smallint* value in some rows, a *float* value in others, and a *char* value in the remainder.

This feature was designed to support what appears to be semistructured data in products sitting above SQL Server. This semistructured data exists in conceptual tables that have a fixed number of columns of known data types and one or more optional columns whose type might not be known in advance. An example is e-mail messages in Microsoft Office Outlook and Microsoft Exchange. With the *sql_variant* data type, you can pivot a conceptual table into a real, more compact table with sets of property-value pairs. Here is a graphical example: the conceptual table shown in Table 5-9 has three rows of data. The fixed columns are the ones that exist in every row. Each row can also have values for one or more of the three different properties, which have different data types.

**TABLE 5-9  A Conceptual Table with an Arbitrary Number of Columns and Data Types**

| Row | Fixed Columns | Property 1 | Property 2 | Property 3 |
|-----|---------------|------------|------------|------------|
| row -1 | XXXXXX | value-11 | | value -13 |
| row -2 | YYYYYY | value-22 | | |
| row -3 | ZZZZZZ | value-31 | value-32 | |

This can be pivoted into Table 5-10, where the fixed columns are repeated for each different property that appears with those columns. The column called *value* can be represented by *sql_variant* data and be a different data type for each different property.

**TABLE 5-10  Semistructured Data Stored Using the *sql_variant* Data Type**

| Fixed Columns | Property | Value |
|---------------|----------|-------|
| XXXXXX | property-1 | value-11 |
| XXXXXX | property-3 | value-13 |
| YYYYYY | property-2 | value-22 |
| ZZZZZZ | property-1 | value-31 |
| ZZZZZZ | property-2 | value-32 |

Internally, columns of type *sql_variant* are always considered variable length. Their storage structure depends on the type of data, but the first byte of every *sql_variant* field always indicates the actual data type being used in that row.

I'll create a simple table with a *sql_variant* column and insert a few rows into it so we can observe the structure of the *sql_variant* storage.

```
USE testdb;
GO
CREATE TABLE variant (a int, b sql_variant);
GO
INSERT INTO variant VALUES (1, 3);
INSERT INTO variant VALUES (2, 3000000000);
INSERT INTO variant VALUES (3, 'abc');
INSERT INTO variant VALUES (4, current_timestamp);
```

SQL Server decides what data type to use in each row based on the data supplied. For example, the *3* in the first *INSERT* is assumed to be an integer. In the second *INSERT*, the *3000000000* is larger than the biggest possible integer, so SQL Server assumes a decimal with a precision of 10 and a scale of 0. (It could have used a *bigint*, but that would need more storage space.) We can now use *DBCC IND* to find the first page of the table and use *DBCC PAGE* to see its contents as follows:

```
DBCC IND (testdb, variant, -1);
-- (I got a value of file 1, page 2508 for the data page in this table)
GO
DBCC TRACEON (3604);
DBCC PAGE (testdb, 1, 2508, 1);
```

Figure 5-12 shows the contents of the four rows. I won't go into the details of every single byte because most are the same as what we've already examined.

The difference between the three rows starts at bytes 13 to 14, which indicate the position where the first variable-length column ends. Because there is only one variable-length column, this is also the length of the row. The *sql_variant* data begins at byte 15. Byte 15 is the code for the data type. You can find the codes in the *system_type_id* column of the *sys.types* catalog view. I've reproduced the relevant part of that view here:

```
system_type_id    name
---------------   ----------------------
34                image
35                text
36                uniqueidentifier
40                date
41                time
42                datetime2
43                datetimeoffset
48                tinyint
52                smallint
56                int
58                smalldatetime
59                real
60                money
61                datetime
62                float
98                sql_variant
99                ntext
104               bit
106               decimal
108               numeric
122               smallmoney
127               bigint
165               varbinary
167               varchar
173               binary
175               char
189               timestamp
231               nvarchar
231               sysname
239               nchar
240               hierarchyid
240               geometry
240               geography
241               xml
```

DATA:


Slot 0, Offset 0x60, Length 21, DumpStyle BYTE
Record Type = PRIMARY_RECORD        Record Attributes =  NULL_BITMAP VARIABLE_COLUMNS
Record Size = 21


Memory Dump @0x62B7C060
00000000: 30000800 01000000 02000001 00150038 †0.............8
00000010: 01030000 00††††††††††††††††††††††††.....

Slot 1, Offset 0x75, Length 24, DumpStyle BYTE
Record Type = PRIMARY_RECORD        Record Attributes =  NULL_BITMAP VARIABLE_COLUMNS
Record Size = 24
Memory Dump @0x62B7C075


00000000: 30000800 02000000 02000001 0018006c †0.............l
00000010: 010a0001 005ed0b2 †††††††††††††††††††.....^Ð²

Slot 2, Offset 0x8d, Length 26, DumpStyle BYTE
Record Type = PRIMARY_RECORD        Record Attributes =  NULL_BITMAP VARIABLE_COLUMNS
Record Size = 26
Memory Dump @0x62B7C08D


00000000: 30000800 03000000 02000001 001a00a7 †0.............§
00000010: 01401f08 d0003461 6263†††††††††††††††.@..Ð.4abc

Slot 3, Offset 0xa7, Length 25, DumpStyle BYTE

Record Type = PRIMARY_RECORD        Record Attributes =  NULL_BITMAP VARIABLE_COLUMNS
Record Size = 25
Memory Dump @0x62B7C0A7


00000000: 30000800 04000000 02000001 0019003d †0.............=
00000010: 0183de14 01299b00 00††††††††††††††††.Þ..)...

OFFSET TABLE:

Row - Offset
3 (0x3) - 167 (0xa7)
2 (0x2) - 141 (0x8d)
1 (0x1) - 117 (0x75)
0 (0x0) - 96 (0x60)

**FIGURE 5-12** Rows containing *sql_variant* data

In our table, we have the data types 38 hex (which is 56 decimal and *int*), 6C hex (which is 108 decimal, which is numeric), A7 hex (which is 167 decimal and *varchar*), and 3D hex (which is 61 decimal and *datetime*). Following the byte for data type is a byte representing the version of the *sql_variant* format, and that is always 1 in SQL Server 2008. Following the version, there can be one of the following four sets of bytes:

- For numeric and decimal: 1 byte for the precision and 1 byte for the scale

- For strings: 2 bytes for the maximum length and 4 bytes for the collation ID

- For *binary* and *varbinary*: 2 bytes for the maximum length

- For all other types: no extra bytes

These bytes are then followed by the actual data in the *sql_variant* column.

# Constraints

Constraints provide a powerful yet easy way to enforce the data integrity in your database. Data integrity comes in three forms:

**Entity integrity**   Ensures that a table has a primary key. In SQL Server 2008, you can guarantee entity integrity by defining PRIMARY KEY or UNIQUE constraints or by building unique indexes. Alternatively, you can write a trigger to enforce entity integrity, but this is usually far less efficient.

**Domain integrity**   Ensures that data values meet certain criteria. In SQL Server 2008, domain integrity can be guaranteed in several ways. Choosing appropriate data types can ensure that a data value meets certain conditions—for example, that the data represents a valid date. Other approaches include defining CHECK constraints or FOREIGN KEY constraints, or writing a trigger. You might also consider DEFAULT constraints as an aspect of enforcing domain integrity.

**Referential integrity**   Enforces relationships between two tables, a referenced table, and a referencing table. SQL Server allows you to define FOREIGN KEY constraints to enforce referential integrity, and you can also write triggers for enforcement. It's crucial to note that there are always two sides to referential integrity enforcement. If data is updated or deleted from the referenced table, referential integrity ensures that any data in the referencing table that refers to the changed or deleted data is handled in some way. On the other side, if data is updated or inserted into the referencing table, referential integrity ensures that the new data matches a value in the referenced table.

In this section, I'll briefly describe some of the internal aspects of managing constraints. Constraints are also called *declarative data integrity* because they are part of the actual table definition. This is in contrast to *programmatic data integrity*, which uses stored procedures or triggers.

Here are the five types of constraints:

- PRIMARY KEY

- UNIQUE

- FOREIGN KEY

- CHECK

- DEFAULT

You might also sometimes see the *IDENTITY* property and the nullability of a column described as constraints. I typically don't consider these attributes to be constraints; instead, I think of them as properties of a column, for two reasons. First, each constraint has its own row in the *sys.objects* catalog view, but *IDENTITY* and nullability information is not available in *sys.objects*, only in *sys.columns* and *sys.identity_columns*. This makes me think that these properties are more like data types, which are also viewable through *sys.columns*. Second, when you use the *SELECT INTO* command to make a copy of a table, all column names and data types are copied, as well as *IDENTITY* information and column nullability, but constraints are *not* copied to the new table. This makes me think that *IDENTITY* and nullability are more a part of the actual table structure than the constraints are.

## Constraint Names and Catalog View Information

The following simple *CREATE TABLE* statement, which includes a primary key on the table, creates a PRIMARY KEY constraint along with the table, and the constraint has a very cryptic-looking name:

```
CREATE TABLE customer
(
cust_id      int          IDENTITY  NOT NULL   PRIMARY KEY,
cust_name    varchar(30)  NOT NULL
);
```

If you don't supply a constraint name in the *CREATE TABLE* or *ALTER TABLE* statement that defines the constraint, SQL Server comes up with a name for you.

The constraint produced from the preceding simple statement has a name very similar to the nonintuitive name *PK__customer__3BD0198E35BCFE0A*. (The hexadecimal number at the end of the name most likely will be different for a *customer* table that you create.) All types of single-column constraints use this naming scheme, which I'll explain shortly. The advantage of explicitly naming your constraint rather than using the system-generated name is greater clarity. The constraint name is used in the error message for any constraint violation, so creating a name such as *CUSTOMER_PK* probably makes more sense to users than a name such as *PK__customer__0856260D*. You should choose your own constraint names if such error messages are visible to your users. The first two characters *(PK)* show the constraint type—*PK* for PRIMARY KEY, *UQ* for UNIQUE, *FK* for FOREIGN KEY, *CK* for CHECK, and *DF* for DEFAULT. Next are two underscore characters, which are used as a separator.

**Tip**  You might be tempted to use one underscore to conserve characters and to avoid having to truncate as much. However, it's common to use a single underscore in a table name or a column name, both of which appear in the constraint name. Using two underscore characters distinguishes the kind of a name it is and where the separation occurs.

> **Note**  Constraint names are schema-scoped, which means they all share the same namespace and hence must be unique within a schema. Within a schema, you cannot have two tables with the same name for any of their constraints.

Next comes the table name (*customer*), which is limited to 116 characters for a PRIMARY KEY constraint and slightly fewer characters for all other constraint names. For all constraints other than PRIMARY KEY and UNIQUE, there are two more underscore characters for separation, followed by the next sequence of characters, which is the column name. The column name is truncated to five characters if necessary. If the column name has fewer than five characters, the length of the table name portion can be slightly longer.

Finally, the hexadecimal representation of the object ID for the constraint comes after another separator. This value is used in the *object_id* column of the *sys.objects* catalog view. Object names are limited to 128 characters in SQL Server 2008, so the total length of all the portions of the constraint name must also be less than or equal to 128.

Several catalog views contain constraint information. They all inherit the columns from the *sys.objects* view and include additional columns specific to the type of constraint. These views are

- *sys.key_constraints*
- *sys.check_constraints*
- *sys.default_constraints*
- *sys.foreign_keys*

The *parent_object_id* column, which indicates which object contains the constraint, is actually part of the base *sys.objects* view, but for objects that have no "parent," this column is 0.

## Constraint Failures in Transactions and Multiple-Row Data Modifications

Many bugs occur in application code because developers don't understand how the failure of a constraint affects a multiple-statement transaction declared by the user. The biggest misconception is that any error, such as a constraint failure, automatically aborts and rolls back the entire transaction. On the contrary, after an error is raised, it's up to the transaction to proceed and ultimately commit or to roll back. This feature provides the developer with the flexibility to decide how to handle errors. (The semantics are also in accordance with the ANSI SQL-92 standard for COMMIT behavior.)

Because many developers have handled transaction errors incorrectly and because it can be tedious to add an error check after every command, SQL Server includes a SET option called XACT_ABORT that causes SQL Server to abort a transaction if it encounters any error during the transaction. The default setting is OFF, which is consistent with ANSI-standard behavior.

A final comment about constraint errors and transactions: a single data modification statement (such as an *UPDATE* statement) that affects multiple rows is automatically an atomic operation, even if it's not part of an explicit transaction. If such an *UPDATE* statement finds 100 rows that meet the criteria of the WHERE clause but one row fails because of a constraint violation, no rows will be updated. I discuss implicit and explicit transactions a bit more in Chapter 10.

### The Order of Integrity Checks

The modification of a given row fails if any constraint is violated or if a trigger rolls back the operation. As soon as a failure in a constraint occurs, the operation is aborted, subsequent checks for that row aren't performed, and no triggers fire for the row. Hence, the order of these checks can be important, as the following list shows:

1. Defaults are applied as appropriate.

2. NOT NULL violations are raised.

3. CHECK constraints are evaluated.

4. FOREIGN KEY checks of *referencing* tables are applied.

5. FOREIGN KEY checks of *referenced* tables are applied.

6. The UNIQUE and PRIMARY KEY constraints are checked for correctness.

7. Triggers fire.

# Altering a Table

SQL Server 2008 allows existing tables to be modified in several ways. Using the *ALTER TABLE* command, you can make the following types of changes to an existing table:

- Change the data type or the *NULL* property of a single column.

- Add one or more new columns, with or without defining constraints for those columns.

- Add one or more constraints.

- Drop one or more constraints.

- Drop one or more columns.

- Enable or disable one or more constraints (applies only to CHECK and FOREIGN KEY constraints).

- Enable or disable one or more triggers.

- Rebuild a table or a partition to change the compression settings or remove fragmentation. (Fragmentation is discussed in Chapter 6, and compression is discussed in Chapter 7.)

- Change the lock escalation behavior of a table. (Locks and lock escalation are discussed in Chapter 10.)

# Changing a Data Type

By using the ALTER COLUMN clause of *ALTER TABLE*, you can modify the data type or the *NULL* property of an existing column. But be aware of the following restrictions:

- The modified column can't be a *text*, *image*, *ntext*, or *rowversion (timestamp)* column.
- If the modified column is the *ROWGUIDCOL* for the table, only *DROP ROWGUIDCOL* is allowed; no data type changes are allowed.
- The modified column can't be a computed or replicated column.
- The modified column can't have a PRIMARY KEY or FOREIGN KEY constraint defined on it.
- The modified column can't be referenced in a computed column.
- The modified column can't have the type changed to *timestamp*.
- If the modified column participates in an index, the only type changes that are allowed are increasing the length of a variable-length type (for example, *varchar*(10) to *varchar*(20)), changing nullability of the column, or both.
- If the modified column has a UNIQUE or CHECK constraint defined on it, the only change allowed is altering the length of a variable-length column. For a UNIQUE constraint, the new length must be greater than the old length.
- If the modified column has a default defined on it, the only changes that are allowed are increasing or decreasing the length of a variable-length type, changing nullability, or changing the precision or scale.
- The old type of the column should have an allowed implicit conversion to the new type.
- The new type always has ANSI_PADDING semantics if applicable, regardless of the current setting.
- If conversion of an old type to a new type causes an overflow (arithmetic or size), the *ALTER TABLE* statement is aborted.

Here's the syntax and an example of using the ALTER COLUMN clause of the *ALTER TABLE* statement:

SYNTAX:

```
ALTER TABLE table-name ALTER COLUMN column-name
        { type_name [ ( prec [, scale] ) ] [COLLATE <collation name> ]
          [ NULL | NOT NULL ]
          | {ADD | DROP} {ROWGUIDCOL | PERSISTED}  }
```

EXAMPLE:

```
/* Change the length of the emp_lname column in the employee
   table from varchar(15) to varchar(30) */
ALTER TABLE employee
   ALTER COLUMN emp_name varchar(30);
```

## Adding a New Column

You can add a new column, with or without specifying column-level constraints. If the new column doesn't allow NULLs, isn't an identity column, and isn't a *rowversion* (or *timestamp* column), the new column must have a default constraint defined (unless no data is in the table yet). SQL Server populates the new column in every row with a NULL, the appropriate identity or *rowversion* value, or the specified default. If the newly added column is nullable and has a default constraint, the existing rows of the table are not filled with the default value, but rather with NULL values. You can override this restriction by using the WITH VALUES clause so that the existing rows of the table are filled with the specified default value.

## Adding, Dropping, Disabling, or Enabling a Constraint

You can use *ALTER TABLE* to add, drop, enable, or disable a constraint. The trickiest part of using *ALTER TABLE* to manipulate constraints is that the word *CHECK* can be used in three different ways:

- To specify a CHECK constraint.

- To defer the checking of a newly added constraint. In the following example, we're adding a constraint to validate that *cust_id* in *orders* matches a *cust_id* in *customer*, but we don't want the constraint applied to existing data:

```
ALTER TABLE orders
    WITH NOCHECK
    ADD FOREIGN KEY (cust_id) REFERENCES customer (cust_id);
```

 **Note** Instead of using WITH NOCHECK, I could use WITH CHECK to force the constraint to be applied to existing data, but that's unnecessary because it's the default behavior.

- To enable or disable a constraint. In this example, we enable all the constraints on the *employee* table:

```
ALTER TABLE employee
    CHECK CONSTRAINT ALL;
```

The only types of constraints that can be disabled are CHECK constraints and FOREIGN KEY constraints, and disabling tells SQL Server not to validate new data as it is added or updated. You should use caution when disabling and re-enabling constraints. If a constraint was part of the table when the table was created or was added to the table using the WITH CHECK option, SQL Server knows that the data conforms to the data integrity requirements of the constraint. The SQL Server Query Optimizer can then take advantage of this knowledge in some cases. For example, if you have a constraint that requires *col1* to be greater than 0, and then an application submits a query looking for all rows where *col1* < 0, if the constraint has always been in effect, the Optimizer knows that no rows can satisfy this query and the plan is a very simple plan. However, if the constraint has been disabled and re-enabled without using the WITH CHECK option, there is no guarantee that some of the data in the table won't meet the integrity requirements. You might not have any data less than or equal to 0, but the Optimizer cannot know that when it is devising the plan; all the Optimizer knows is that the constraint cannot be trusted. The catalog views *sys.check_constraints* and *sys.foreign_keys* each have a column called *is_not_trusted*. If you re-enable a constraint and don't use the WITH CHECK option to tell SQL Server to revalidate all existing data, the *is_not_trusted* column is set to 1.

Although you cannot use *ALTER TABLE* to disable or enable a PRIMARY KEY or UNIQUE constraint, you can use the *ALTER INDEX* command to disable the associated index. I'll discuss *ALTER INDEX* in Chapter 6. You can use *ALTER TABLE* to drop PRIMARY KEY and UNIQUE constraints, but you need to be aware that dropping one of these constraints automatically drops the associated index. In fact, the only way to drop those indexes is by altering the table to remove the constraint.

**Note** You can't use *ALTER TABLE* to modify a constraint definition. You must use *ALTER TABLE* to drop the constraint and then use *ALTER TABLE* to add a new constraint with the new definition.

## Dropping a Column

You can use *ALTER TABLE* to remove one or more columns from a table. However, you can't drop the following columns:

- A replicated column
- A column used in an index
- A column used in a CHECK, FOREIGN KEY, UNIQUE, or PRIMARY KEY constraint
- A column associated with a default defined using the *DEFAULT* keyword or bound to a default object
- A column to which a rule is bound

You can drop a column using the following syntax:

```
ALTER TABLE table-name
    DROP COLUMN column-name [, next-column-name]...
```

**Note** Notice the syntax difference between dropping a column and adding a new column: the word *COLUMN* is required when dropping a column but not when you add a new column to a table.

## Enabling or Disabling a Trigger

You can enable or disable one or more (or all) triggers on a table using the *ALTER TABLE* command.

## Internals of Altering Tables

Note that not all the *ALTER TABLE* variations require SQL Server to change every row when the *ALTER TABLE* is issued. SQL Server can carry out an *ALTER TABLE* command in three basic ways:

- It might need to change only metadata.

- It might need to examine all the existing data to make sure it is compatible with the change but only needs to make changes to metadata.

- It might need to change every row physically.

In many cases, SQL Server can just change the metadata (primarily the data seen through *sys.columns*) to reflect the new structure. In particular, the data isn't touched when a column is dropped, when a new column is added and NULL is assumed as the new value for all rows, when the length of a variable-length column is increased, or when a non-nullable column is changed to allow NULLs. The fact that data isn't touched when a column is dropped means that the disk space of the column is not reclaimed. You might have to reclaim the disk space of a dropped column when the row size of a table approaches or has exceeded its limit. You can reclaim space by creating a clustered index on the table or rebuilding an existing clustered index by using *ALTER INDEX*, as we'll see in Chapter 6.

Some changes to a table's structure require that the data be examined but not modified. For example, when you change the nullability property to disallow NULLs, SQL Server must first make sure there are no NULLs in the existing rows. A variable-length column can be shortened when all the existing data is within the new limit, so the existing data must be checked. If any rows have data longer than the new limit specified in the *ALTER TABLE*, the command fails. So you do need to be aware that for a huge table, this can take some time. Changing a fixed-length column to a shorter type, such as changing an *int* column to *smallint* or changing a *char(10)* to *char(8)*, also requires examining all the data to verify that all the existing values can be stored in the new type. However, even though the new data type takes up fewer bytes, the rows on the physical pages are not modified. If you have created a table with an *int* column, which needs 4 bytes in each row, all rows will use the full 4 bytes. After altering the table to change the *int* to *smallint*, we are restricted in the range of data values we can insert, but the rows continue to use 4 bytes for each value, instead of the 2 bytes that *smallint* requires. You can verify this by using the *DBCC PAGE* command. Changing a *char(10)* to *char(8)* displays similar behavior, and the rows continue to use 10 bytes for that column, but only 8 are allowed to have new data inserted. It is not until the table is rebuilt by creating or re-creating a clustered index that the *char(10)* columns are actually re-created to become *char(8)*.

Other changes to a table's structure require SQL Server to change every row physically, and as it makes the changes, it has to write the appropriate records to the transaction log, so these changes can be extremely resource intensive for a large table. One example of this type of change is adding a new column that doesn't allow NULL, in which case you must specify a default column value. SQL Server physically adds the column with the default to each row. Note that when adding a new column that allows NULLs, the change is a metadata-only operation.

Another negative side effect of altering tables happens when a column is altered to increase its length. In this case, the old column is not actually replaced. Rather, a new column is added to the table, and *DBCC PAGE* shows you that the old data is still there. I'll let you explore the page dumps for this situation on your own, but we can see some of this unexpected behavior by just looking at the column offsets using the column detail query that I showed you earlier in this chapter.

First, create a table with all fixed-length columns, including a *smallint* in the first position:

```
CREATE TABLE change
(col1 smallint, col2 char(10), col3 char(5));
```

Now look at the column offsets:

```
SELECT  c.name AS column_name, column_id, max_inrow_length, pc.system_type_id, leaf_offset
  FROM sys.system_internals_partition_columns pc
    JOIN sys.partitions p
      ON p.partition_id = pc.partition_id
    JOIN sys.columns c
        ON column_id = partition_column_id
          AND c.object_id = p.object_id
WHERE p.object_id=object_id('change');
```

RESULTS:

| column_name | column_id | max_inrow_length | system_type_id | leaf_offset |
| --- | --- | --- | --- | --- |
| col1 | 1 | 2 | 52 | 4 |
| col2 | 2 | 10 | 175 | 6 |
| col3 | 3 | 5 | 175 | 16 |

Now change *smallint* to *int*:

```
ALTER TABLE change
    ALTER COLUMN col1 int;
```

Finally, run the column detail query again to see that *col1* now starts much later in the row and that no column starts at offset 4 immediately after the row header information. This new column creation due to an *ALTER TABLE* takes place even before any data has been placed in the table:

| column_name | column_id | max_inrow_length | system_type_id | leaf_offset |
| --- | --- | --- | --- | --- |
| col1 | 1 | 4 | 56 | 21 |
| col2 | 2 | 10 | 175 | 6 |
| col3 | 3 | 5 | 175 | 16 |

Another drawback to the behavior of SQL Server in not actually dropping the old column is that we are now more severely limited in the size of the row. The row size now includes the old column, which is no longer usable or visible (unless you use *DBCC PAGE*). For example, if I create a table with a couple of large fixed-length character columns, as shown here, I can then ALTER the *char(2000)* column to be *char(3000)*:

```
CREATE TABLE bigchange
(col1 smallint, col2 char(2000), col3 char(1000));

ALTER TABLE bigchange
   ALTER COLUMN col2 char(3000);
```

At this point, the length of the rows should be just over 4,000 bytes because there is a 3,000-byte column, a 1,000-byte column, and a *smallint*. However, if I try to add another 3,000-byte column, it fails:

```
ALTER TABLE bigchange
   ADD col4 char(3000);

Msg 1701, Level 16, State 1, Line 1
Creating or altering table 'bigchange' failed because the minimum row size would be 9009,
including 7 bytes of internal overhead. This exceeds the maximum allowable table row size
of 8060 bytes.
```

However, if I just create a table with two 3,000-byte columns and a 1,000-byte column, there is no problem:

```
CREATE TABLE nochange
(col1 smallint, col2 char(3000), col3 char(1000), col4 char(3000));
```

Note that there is no way to *ALTER* a table to rearrange the logical column order or to add a new column in a particular position in the table. A newly added column always gets the next highest *column_id* value. When you execute *SELECT \** on a table or look at the metadata with *sp_help*, the columns are always returned in *column_id* order. If you need a different order, you have several options:

- Don't use *SELECT \**; always *SELECT* a list of columns in the order that you want to have them returned.

- Create a view on the table that *SELECT*s the columns in the order you want them, and then you can *SELECT \** from the view or run *sp_help* on the view.

- Create a new table, copy the data from the old table, drop the old table, and rename the new table to the old name. Don't forget to re-create all constraints, indexes, and triggers.

You might think that Management Studio can add a new column in a particular position or rearrange the column order, but this is not true. Behind the scenes, the tool is actually using the preceding third option and creating a completely new table with all new indexes, constraints, and triggers. If you wonder why simply adding a new column to an existing (large) table is taking a long time, this is probably the reason.

# Heap Modification Internals

We've seen how SQL Server stores data in a heap. Now we'll look at what SQL Server actually does internally when your heap data is modified. Modifying data in an index, which includes a table with a clustered index, is a completely separate topic and will be covered in detail in Chapter 6. As a rule of thumb, you should always have a clustered index on a table. There are some cases in which you might be better off with a heap, such as when the most important factor is the speed of *INSERT* operations, but until you do thorough testing to establish that you have one of these cases, it's better to have a clustered index than to have no organization to your data at all. In Chapter 6, you'll see the benefits and tradeoffs of clustered and nonclustered indexes and examine some guidelines for their use. For now, we'll look only at how SQL Server deals with the data modifications on tables without clustered indexes.

## Allocation Structures

As discussed in Chapter 3, SQL Server allocates one or more IAM pages for each object, to keep track of which extents in each file belong to that object. If the table is a heap, using the IAMs is the only way for SQL Server to find all the extents belonging to the table, because the individual data pages of a table are not connected in a doubly linked list, the way they are if the table has a clustered index. Pages at each level of an index are linked, and because the data is considered the leaf level of a clustered index, SQL Server does maintain the linkage. However, for a heap, no such linked list connects the pages to each other. The only way that SQL Server determines which pages belong to a table is by inspecting the IAMs for the table.

Another special allocation structure is particularly useful when SQL Server is performing data modification operations, and that is the Page Free Space (PFS) structure. PFS pages keep track of how much space is free on each page, so that *INSERT* operations in a heap know where space is available for the new data, and *UPDATE* operations know where a row can be moved. I briefly mentioned PFS pages in Chapter 3, and I told you that these pages contained 1 byte for each page in a 8,088-page range of a file. This is much less dense than Global Allocation Maps (GAMs), Shared Global Allocation Maps (SGAMs), and IAMs, which contain one bit per extent.) Figure 5-13 shows the structure of a byte on a PFS page. Only the last three bits are used to indicate the page fullness, and four of the other five bits each have a meaning.

Here is the way the bits are interpreted:

- **Bit 1**   This bit indicates whether the page is actually allocated or not. For example, a uniform extent can be allocated to an object, but all of the pages in the extent might not be allocated. To tell which pages within an allocated extent are actually used, SQL Server needs to look at this bit in the appropriate byte in the PFS page.

- **Bit 2**   Indicates whether or not the corresponding page is from a mixed extent.

- **Bit 3**   Indicates that this page is an IAM page. Remember that IAM pages are not located at known locations in a file.

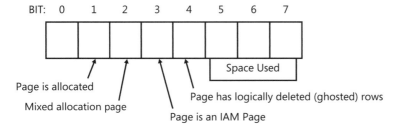

FIGURE 5-13 Meaning of the bits in a PFS byte

- **Bit 4**   Indicates that this page contains ghost records. As we'll see, SQL Server uses a background cleanup thread to remove ghost records, and these bits on the PFS pages help SQL Server find those pages that need to be cleaned up. (Ghost records only show up in indexes or when using row-level versioning, so they won't be discussed further in this chapter.)

- **Bits 5 through 7**   Taken as a three-bit value, the values 0 to 4 indicate the page fullness as follows:

  - ❑   0: The page is empty.

  - ❑   1: The page is 1–50 percent full.

  - ❑   2: The page is 51–80 percent full.

  - ❑   3: The page is 81–95 percent full.

  - ❑   4: The page is 96–100 percent full.

PFS pages are at known locations within each data file. The second page (page 1) of a file is a PFS page, as is every 8,088th page thereafter.

## Inserting Rows

When inserting a new row into a table, SQL Server must determine where to put it. When a table has no clustered index—that is, when the table is a heap—a new row is always inserted wherever room is available in the table. I've discussed how IAMs and the PFS pages keep track of which extents in a file already belong to a table and which of the pages in those extents have space available. Even without a clustered index, space management is quite efficient. If no pages with space are available, SQL Server tries to find unallocated pages from existing uniform extents that already belong to the object. If none exists, SQL Server must allocate a whole new extent to the table. Chapter 3 discussed how the GAMs and SGAMs were used to find extents available to be allocated to an object.

# Deleting Rows

When you delete rows from a table, you have to consider what happens both to the data pages and the index pages. Remember that the data is actually the leaf level of a clustered index, and deleting rows from a table with a clustered index happens the same way as deleting rows from the leaf level of a nonclustered index. Deleting rows from a heap is managed in a different way, as is deleting from node pages of an index.

## Deleting Rows from a Heap

SQL Server 2008 doesn't reorganize space on a page automatically when a row is deleted. As a performance optimization, the compaction doesn't occur until a page needs additional contiguous space for inserting a new row. You can see this in the following example, which deletes a row from the middle of a page and then inspects that page using *DBCC PAGE:*

```
USE testdb;
GO

CREATE TABLE smallrows
(
    a int identity,
    b char(10)
);
GO

INSERT INTO smallrows
    VALUES ('row 1');
INSERT INTO smallrows
    VALUES ('row 2');
INSERT INTO smallrows
    VALUES ('row 3');
INSERT INTO smallrows
    VALUES ('row 4');
INSERT INTO smallrows
    VALUES ('row 5');
GO

DBCC IND (testdb, smallrows, -1);
-- Note the FileID and PageID from the row where PageType = 1
--    and use those values with DBCC PAGE (I got FileID 1 and PageID 4536)

DBCC TRACEON(3604);
GO
DBCC PAGE(testdb, 1, 4536,1);
```

Here is the output from *DBCC PAGE*:

```
DATA:

Slot 0, Offset 0x60, Length 21, DumpStyle BYTE
Record Type = PRIMARY_RECORD        Record Attributes =  NULL_BITMAP
Memory Dump @0x61D9C060
00000000:   10001200 01000000 726f7720 31202020 †........row 1
00000010:   20200200 fc†††††††††††††††††††††††††††  ...

Slot 1, Offset 0x75, Length 21, DumpStyle BYTE
Record Type = PRIMARY_RECORD        Record Attributes =  NULL_BITMAP
Memory Dump @0x61D9C075
00000000:   10001200 02000000 726f7720 32202020 †........row 2
00000010:   20200200 fc†††††††††††††††††††††††††††  ...

Slot 2, Offset 0x8a, Length 21, DumpStyle BYTE
Record Type = PRIMARY_RECORD        Record Attributes =  NULL_BITMAP
Memory Dump @0x61D9C08A
00000000:   10001200 03000000 726f7720 33202020 †........row 3
00000010:   20200200 fc†††††††††††††††††††††††††††  ...

Slot 3, Offset 0x9f, Length 21, DumpStyle BYTE
Record Type = PRIMARY_RECORD        Record Attributes =  NULL_BITMAP
Memory Dump @0x61D9C09F
00000000:   10001200 04000000 726f7720 34202020 †........row 4
00000010:   20200200 fc†††††††††††††††††††††††††††  ...

Slot 4, Offset 0xb4, Length 21, DumpStyle BYTE
Record Type = PRIMARY_RECORD        Record Attributes =  NULL_BITMAP
Memory Dump @0x61D9C0B4
00000000:   10001200 05000000 726f7720 35202020 †........row 5
00000010:   20200200 fc†††††††††††††††††††††††††††  ...

OFFSET TABLE:
Row - Offset
4 (0x4) - 180 (0xb4)
3 (0x3) - 159 (0x9f)
2 (0x2) - 138 (0x8a)
1 (0x1) - 117 (0x75)
0 (0x0) - 96 (0x60)
```

Now we'll delete the middle row (WHERE a = 3) and look at the page again:

```
DELETE FROM smallrows
WHERE a = 3;
GO

DBCC PAGE(testdb, 1, 4536,1);
GO
```

Here is the output from the second execution of *DBCC PAGE:*

```
DATA:
Slot 0, Offset 0x60, Length 21, DumpStyle BYTE
Record Type = PRIMARY_RECORD        Record Attributes =  NULL_BITMAP
```

```
Memory Dump @0x61B6C060
00000000:    10001200 01000000 726f7720 31202020 †........row 1
00000010:    20200200 fc††††††††††††††††††††††††††  ...
```

```
Slot 1, Offset 0x75, Length 21, DumpStyle BYTE
Record Type = PRIMARY_RECORD         Record Attributes =  NULL_BITMAP
Memory Dump @0x61B6C075
00000000:    10001200 02000000 726f7720 32202020 †........row 2
00000010:    20200200 fc††††††††††††††††††††††††††  ...
```

```
Slot 3, Offset 0x9f, Length 21, DumpStyle BYTE
Record Type = PRIMARY_RECORD         Record Attributes =  NULL_BITMAP
Memory Dump @0x61B6C09F
00000000:    10001200 04000000 726f7720 34202020 †........row 4
00000010:    20200200 fc††††††††††††††††††††††††††  ...
```

```
Slot 4, Offset 0xb4, Length 21, DumpStyle BYTE
Record Type = PRIMARY_RECORD         Record Attributes =  NULL_BITMAP
Memory Dump @0x61B6C0B4
00000000:    10001200 05000000 726f7720 35202020 †........row 5
00000010:    20200200 fc††††††††††††††††††††††††††  ...
```

```
OFFSET TABLE:
Row - Offset
4 (0x4) - 180 (0xb4)
3 (0x3) - 159 (0x9f)
2 (0x2) - 0 (0x0)
1 (0x1) - 117 (0x75)
0 (0x0) - 96 (0x60)
```

Note that in the heap, the row offset array at the bottom of the page shows that the third row (at slot 2) is now at offset 0 (which means there really is no row using slot 2), and the row using slot 3 is at its same offset as before the delete. No data on the page is moved when the *DELETE* occurs. The row doesn't show up in the page when you use *printopt* 1 or 3 for *DBCC PAGE*. However, if you dump the page with *printopt* 2, you still see the bytes for 'row 3'. They are not physically removed from the page, but the 0 in the row offset array indicates that the space is not used now and can be used by a new row.

In addition to space on pages not being reclaimed, empty pages in heaps frequently cannot be reclaimed. Even if you delete all the rows from a heap, SQL Server does not mark the empty pages as unallocated, so the space is not available for other objects to use. The dynamic management view (DMV) *sys.dm_db_partition_stats* still shows the space as belonging to the heap table. One way to avoid this problem is to request a table lock when the delete is being performed, and we'll look at lock hints in Chapter 10. If this problem has already occurred, and you are showing more space belonging to a table than it really has, you can build a clustered index on the table to reorganize the space and then drop the index.

## Reclaiming Pages

When the last row is deleted from a data page, the entire page is deallocated. The exception is if the table is a heap, as I discussed previously. (If the page is the only one remaining in the table, it isn't deallocated. A table always contains at least one page, even if it's empty.) Deallocation of a data page results in the deletion of the row in the index page that pointed to the deallocated data page. Index pages are deallocated if an index row is deleted (which, again, might occur as part of a delete/insert update strategy), leaving only one entry in the index page. That entry is moved to its neighboring page, and then the empty page is deallocated.

The discussion so far has focused on the page manipulation necessary for deleting a single row. If multiple rows are deleted in a single *DELETE* operation, you must be aware of some other issues.

## Updating Rows

SQL Server can update rows in several different ways, automatically and invisibly choosing the fastest update strategy for the specific operation. In determining the strategy, SQL Server evaluates the number of rows affected, how the rows will be accessed (via a scan or an index retrieval, and via which index), and whether changes to the index keys will occur. Updates can happen either in place, by just changing one column's value to a new value in the original row, or as a delete followed by an insert. In addition, updates can be managed by the query processor or by the storage engine. In this section, we'll examine only whether the update happens in place or whether SQL Server treats it as two separate operations: delete the old row and insert a new row.

### Moving Rows

What happens if a row has to move to a new location in the table? In SQL Server 2008, this can happen for a couple of different reasons. In Chapter 6, we'll look at the structure of indexes and see that the value in a table's clustered index column (or columns) determines the location of the row. So, if the value of the clustered key is changed, the row most likely has to move within the table.

If it will still have the same row locator (in other words, the clustering key for the row stays the same), no nonclustered indexes have to be modified. If a table has no clustered index (in other words, if it's a heap), a row may move because it no longer fits on the original page. This can happen whenever a row with variable-length columns is updated to a new, larger size so that it no longer fits in the original location. As you'll see when we cover index structures in Chapter 6, every nonclustered index on a heap contains pointers to the data rows that are the actual physical location of the row, including the file number, page number, and row number. So that the nonclustered indexes do not all have to be updated just because a row moves to a different physical location, SQL Server leaves a forwarding pointer in the original location when a row has to move.

Let's look at an example to see these forwarding pointers. I'll create a table that's much like the one I created for doing *DELETE* operations, but this table has a third column of variable length. After I populate the table with five rows, which fills the page, I'll update one of the rows to make its third column much longer. The row no longer fits on the original page and has to move. I can use *DBCC IND* to get the page numbers used by the table as follows:

```
USE testdb;
GO
DROP TABLE bigrows;
GO
CREATE TABLE bigrows
(   a int IDENTITY ,
    b varchar(1600),
    c varchar(1600));
GO
INSERT INTO bigrows
    VALUES (REPLICATE('a', 1600), '');
INSERT INTO bigrows
    VALUES (REPLICATE('b', 1600), '');
INSERT INTO bigrows
    VALUES (REPLICATE('c', 1600), '');
INSERT INTO bigrows
    VALUES (REPLICATE('d', 1600), '');
INSERT INTO bigrows
    VALUES (REPLICATE('e', 1600), '');
GO
UPDATE bigrows
SET c = REPLICATE('x', 1600)
WHERE a = 3;
GO

DBCC IND (testdb, bigrows, -1);

DBCC IND (testdb, bigrows, -1);
-- Note the FileID and PageID from the rows where PageType = 1
--    and use those values with DBCC PAGE (I got FileID 1 and
--      PageID values of 2252 and 4586.

RESULTS:
PageFID PagePID
------- -----------
1       2252
1       4586

DBCC TRACEON(3604);
GO
DBCC PAGE(testdb, 1, 2252, 1);
GO
```

I won't show you the entire output from the *DBCC PAGE* command, but I'll show you what appears in the slot where the row with a = 3 formerly appeared:

```
Slot 2, Offset 0x1feb, Length 9, DumpStyle BYTE
Record Type = FORWARDING_STUB        Record Attributes =
Memory Dump @0x61ADDFEB
00000000:    04ea1100 00010000 00††††††††††††††††††.........
```

The value of 4 in the first byte means that this is just a forwarding stub. The 0011ea in the next 3 bytes is the page number to which the row has been moved. Because this is a hexadecimal value, we need to convert it to 4586 decimal. The next group of 4 bytes tells us that the page is at slot 0, file 1. If you then use *DBCC PAGE* to look at that page, page 4,586, you can see what the forwarded record looks like, and you can see that the Record Type indicates FORWARDED_RECORD.

## Managing Forward Pointers

Forward pointers allow you to modify data in a heap without worrying about having to make drastic changes to the nonclustered indexes. If a row that has been forwarded must move again, the original forwarding pointer is updated to point to the new location. You'll never end up with a forwarding pointer pointing to another forwarding pointer. In addition, if the forwarded row shrinks enough to fit in its original place, the record might move back to its original place (if there is still room on that page), and the forward pointer would be eliminated.

A future version of SQL Server might include some mechanism for performing a physical reorganization of the data in a heap, which would get rid of forward pointers. Note that forward pointers exist only in heaps, and that the *ALTER TABLE* option to reorganize a table won't do anything to heaps. You can defragment a nonclustered index on a heap but not the table itself. Currently, when a forward pointer is created, it stays there forever—with only a few exceptions. The first exception is the case I already mentioned, in which a row shrinks and returns to its original location. The second exception is when the entire database shrinks. The bookmarks are actually reassigned when a file is shrunk. The shrink process never generates forwarding pointers. For pages that were removed because of the shrink process, any forwarded rows or stubs they contain are effectively "unforwarded." Other cases in which the forwarding pointers are removed are the obvious ones: if the forwarded row is deleted, or if a clustered index is built on the table so that it is no longer a heap.

> **More Info**  To get a count of forward records in a table, you can look at the output from the *sys.dm_db_ index_physical_stats* function, which will be discussed in Chapter 6.

## Updating in Place

In SQL Server 2008, updating a row in place is the rule rather than the exception. This means that the row stays in exactly the same location on the same page and only the bytes affected are changed. In addition, the log contains a single record for each such updated row unless the table has an update trigger on it or is marked for replication. In these cases, the update still happens in place, but the log contains a delete record followed by an insert record.

In cases where a row can't be updated in place, the cost of a not-in-place update is minimal because of the way the nonclustered indexes are stored and because of the use of forwarding pointers, as described previously. In fact, you can have an update not-in-place for which the row stays on the original page. Updates happen in place if a heap is being updated (and no forwarding pointer is required), or if a table with a clustered index is updated without any change to the clustering keys. You can also get an update in place if the clustering key changes but the row does not need to move at all. For example, if you have a clustered index on a last-name column containing consecutive key values of *Able, Becker,* and *Charlie,* you might want to update *Becker* to *Baker.* Because the row stays in the same location even after the clustered index key changes, SQL Server performs this as an update in place. On the other hand, if you update *Able* to *Buchner,* the update cannot occur in place but the new row might stay on the same page.

### Updating Not in Place

If your update can't happen in place because you're updating clustering keys, the update occurs as a delete followed by an insert. In some cases, you'll get a hybrid update: some of the rows are updated in place and some aren't. If you're updating index keys, SQL Server builds a list of all the rows that need to change as both a *DELETE* and an *INSERT* operation. This list is stored in memory, if it's small enough, and is written to *tempdb* if necessary. This list is then sorted by key value and operator (*DELETE* or *INSERT*). If the index whose keys are changing isn't unique, the *DELETE* and *INSERT* steps are then applied to the table. If the index is unique, an additional step is carried out to collapse *DELETE* and *INSERT* operations on the same key into a single update operation.

> **More Info**  The Query Optimizer determines whether this special *UPDATE* method is appropriate, and this internal optimization, called *Split/Sort/Collapse,* is described in detail in Chapter 8, "The Query Optimizer."

# Summary

Tables are at the heart of relational databases in general and SQL Server in particular. In this chapter, we looked at the internal storage issues of various data types, in particular comparing fixed- and variable-length data types. We saw that SQL Server 2008 provides multiple options for storing variable-length data, including data that is too long to fit on a single data page, and you saw that it's simplistic to think that using variable-length data types is either always good or always bad. SQL Server provides user-defined data types for support of domains, and it provides the *IDENTITY* property to make a column produce auto-sequenced numeric values. You also saw how data is physically stored in data pages, and we queried some of the metadata views that provide information from the underlying (and inaccessible) system tables. SQL Server also provides constraints, which offer a powerful way to ensure your data's logical integrity.

# Chapter 6
# Indexes: Internals and Management

*Kalen Delaney, with Kimberly L. Tripp and Paul S. Randal*

Microsoft SQL Server doesn't have a configuration option or a knob that allows you to make it run faster; there's no magic bullet. However, indexes—when created and designed appropriately—are probably the closest thing to a magic bullet. The right index, created for the right query, can take query execution time from hours down to seconds. There's absolutely no other way to see these kinds of gains—adding hardware, or tweaking configuration options often only give marginal gains. What is it about indexes that can make a query request drop from millions of I/Os to only a few? And does just any index improve performance? Unfortunately, great performance doesn't just happen; all indexes are not equal, nor is just any index going to improve performance. In fact, over-indexing is often worse than under-indexing. You can't just "index every column" and expect SQL Server to improve.

So how do you know how to create the best indexes? Honestly, it takes multiple pieces—knowing your data, knowing your workload, and knowing how SQL Server works. In terms of how SQL Server works, there are multiple components: index internals, statistics, query optimization, and maintenance. In this chapter, we focus on index internals and maintenance—expanding these topics to give you creation best practices and optimal base indexing strategies. By knowing how SQL Server physically stores indexes as well as how the storage engine accesses and manipulates these physical structures, you are better equipped to create the *right* indexes for your workload. In addition, this information helps to prepare you for Chapter 8, "The Query Optimizer," as you can visualize the choices (in terms of physical structures) from which SQL Server can choose and why some structures are more effective than others for certain requests.

This chapter is split into multiple sections. The first section explains index usage and concepts and internals. In this section, you learn how indexes are stored and how they work for data retrieval. The second section dives into what happens when data is modified—both how it happens and how SQL Server guarantees consistency. In this section, you also learn the potential effects of data modifications on indexes, such as fragmentation. Finally, the third section discusses index management and maintenance.

## Overview

Think of the indexes you might see in your everyday life—those in books and other documents. Suppose that you're trying to create an index in SQL Server using the *CREATE INDEX* statement and you're using two SQL Server references to find out how to write the statement. One reference is the (hypothetical) *Microsoft SQL Server Transact-SQL Language Reference Manual,* which we'll refer to as the "T-SQL Reference." Assume that this book is just an alphabetical list of all the SQL Server keywords, commands, procedures, and functions. The other reference is this book: *Microsoft SQL Server 2008 Internals.* You can find information quickly in either book about indexes, even though the two books are organized differently.

In the T-SQL Reference, all the commands and keywords are organized alphabetically. You know that *CREATE INDEX* is near the front with all the other *CREATE* statements, so you can just ignore most of the rest of the book. Keywords and phrases are shown at the top of each page to tell you what commands are on that page. Thus, you can flip through just a few pages quickly and end up at a page that has *CREATE DATABASE* on it, and you know that *CREATE INDEX* appears shortly thereafter. Now, if you flipped forward and came to *CREATE VIEW* without passing *CREATE INDEX*, you'd know that *CREATE INDEX* was missing from the book, as the commands and keywords are organized alphabetically. (Of course, this is just an example—*CREATE INDEX* would certainly be in the T-SQL Reference.)

Next, you try to find *CREATE INDEX* in *Microsoft SQL Server 2008 Internals.* This book is *not* ordered alphabetically by commands and keywords, but there's an index at the back of the book, and all the index entries are organized alphabetically. So, again, you can use the fact that *CREATE INDEX* is near the front of the alphabet and find it quickly. However, unlike in the T-SQL Reference, once you find the words *CREATE INDEX*, you won't see nice, neat examples right in front of you. The index only gives you pointers—it tells you what pages to look at. In fact, it might list many pages in the book. And, if you look up *CREATE TABLE* in the book's index, you might find dozens of pages listed. Finally, if you look up the stored procedure, *sp_addumpdevice* (a completely deprecated command), you won't find it in the index at all because it's not described in this book.

The point is that these two searches are analogous to using a clustered index (in the case of the book's contents actually being ordered) and a nonclustered index (in the case of the lookup from the index into the book). If a table is clustered, the table data is logically stored in the clustering key order, just as the T-SQL Reference has all the main topics in order. Once you find the data you're looking for, your search is complete. In a nonclustered index, the index is a completely separate structure from the data itself. Once you find what you're looking for in the index, you have to follow some sort of reference pointer to get to the actual data. Although a nonclustered index in SQL Server is very much like the index in the back of a book, it is not exactly the same.

## SQL Server Index B-trees

In SQL Server, indexes are organized using a B-tree structure, as shown in Figure 6-1. *B-tree* stands for "balanced tree," and SQL Server uses a special kind called *B+ trees* (pronounced "b-plus trees") *that are not kept strictly balanced in all ways at all times.* Unlike a normal tree, B-trees are always inverted, with their root (a single page) at the top and their leaf level at the bottom. The existence of intermediate levels depends on multiple factors. *B-tree* is an overloaded term used in different ways by different people—either to mean the entire index structure or just the non-leaf levels. In this book, the term *B-tree* means the entire index structure.

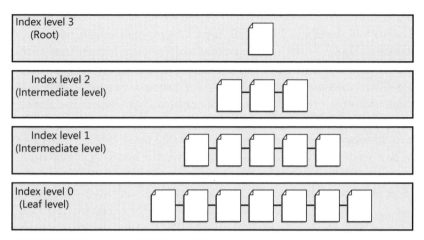

**FIGURE 6-1** A B-tree for a SQL Server index

What's interesting about these B-trees in SQL Server is how they are constructed and what is contained in each level. Structurally, indexes might change a small amount based on whether or not multiple CPUs are used to create or rebuild them (which is explained in more detail in the section "MAXDOP," later in this chapter), but for the most part, the size and width of the tree are based on the definition of the index and the number and size of rows in the table. To show this, we give a few examples starting with the general terms and definitions. First, indexes have two primary components: a leaf level and one or more non-leaf levels. The non-leaf levels are interesting to understand and discuss, but simply put, they're used for navigation (mostly for navigating to the leaf level). However, the first intermediate level is also used in fragmentation analysis and to drive read-ahead during large range scans of the index.

To understand these structures, we start with defining the leaf level in generic terms (meaning that these basic concepts apply to both clustered and nonclustered indexes). The leaf level of an index contains *something* (we discuss the specifics when we get into the topic of physical index structures later in the chapter) for every row of the table in indexed order. In this discussion, we are focusing on traditional indexes and those created without filters, which refers to a new SQL Server 2008 feature called *filtered indexes*.

Non-leaf levels exist to *help navigate to a row* at the leaf level but the architecture is rather straightforward. Each non-leaf level stores *something* for every page of the level below—and levels are added until the index builds up to a root of one page. Each higher non-leaf level in the index (that is, farther away from the leaf level) is smaller than the one below it because each row at a level contains only the minimum key value that can be on each page of the level below, plus a pointer to that page. Although it sounds like this could result in a lot of levels (that is, a tall tree), the limitation on the size of the key (which has a maximum of 900 bytes or 16 columns—whichever comes first) in SQL Server helps to keep index trees relatively small.

In fact, in the example that we show coming up—which has an index with fairly wide rows and a key definition that is at the maximum size—the tree size of this example index (at the time the index is created) is only eight levels deep.

To see this tree (and the computations used to determine its size), we use an example where the leaf level of the index contains 1,000,000 "rows." We put quotes around rows because these are not necessarily data rows—these are just leaf-level rows of *any* index. Later in the chapter—when we discuss the physical structures of each specific index—you will see exactly what leaf-level rows are and how they are structured. However, for this example, we're focused on an abstract "index" where we're concerned only about the leaf and non-leaf levels—as well as how they're structured within the confines of SQL Server pages (8-KB pages). In this example, our leaf-level rows are 4,000 bytes, which means we can store only two rows per page. For a table with 1,000,000 rows, the leaf level of our index would have 500,000 pages. Relatively speaking, this is a fairly wide row structure; however, we are not wasting a lot of space on the page. If our leaf-level page had two 3,000-byte rows we'd still only fit two rows per page, but then we'd have 2,000 bytes of wasted space. (This would be an example of internal fragmentation, which is discussed in the section entitled "Fragmentation," later in this chapter.)

Now, why are these just "rows" and not specifically data rows? The reason is that this leaf level *could* be the leaf level for a clustered index (therefore data rows) *or* these leaf-level rows could be rows in a nonclustered index that uses *INCLUDE* (which was added in SQL Server 2005) to add non-key columns to the leaf level of the index. When *INCLUDE* is used, leaf-level pages can contain wider rows (wider than the 900-byte or 16-column key maximum). Again, although this doesn't currently sound interesting, we explain later in this chapter why this can be beneficial. In this example, the leaf level of this index would be 4 GB in size (500,000 8-KB pages) at the time it's created. This structure, depending on its definition could become larger—and possibly very fragmented—if a lot of new data is added. However (and again depending on its definition), there are ways to control how fragmented this index becomes when data is volatile (we look at this topic further in multiple sections later in this chapter). In this case, the leaf level of the index is large because of "row" width. And, using the maximum of 900 bytes means that you can fit only eight (8,096 bytes per page/900 bytes per row) rows per non-leaf level page. However, using this maximum, the resulting tree (up to a root of one page) would be *relatively* small and result only in eight levels—as shown here. In fact, improving scalability is the primary reason for the limit to an index key of 900 bytes or 16 columns—whichever comes first:

- Root page of non-leaf level (Level 7) = 2 rows = 1 page (8 rows per page)

- Intermediate non-leaf level (Level 6) = 16 rows = 2 pages (8 rows per page)

- Intermediate non-leaf level (Level 5) = 123 rows = 16 pages (8 rows per page)

- Intermediate non-leaf level (Level 4) = 977 rows = 123 pages (8 rows per page)

- Intermediate non-leaf level (Level 3) = 7,813 rows = 977 pages (8 rows per page)

- Intermediate non-leaf level (Level 2) = 62,500 rows = 7,813 pages (8 rows per page)

- Intermediate non-leaf level (Level 1) = 500,000 rows = 62,500 pages (8 rows per page)

- Leaf level (Level 0) = 1,000,000 rows = 500,000 pages (2 rows per page)

An index with a smaller key size would scale even faster. Imagine the same leaf-level pages as shown previously (1,000,000 rows at 2 rows per page) but with a smaller index key and therefore a smaller row size in the non-leaf levels (including some space for overhead) of only 20 bytes, you can fit 404 rows per non-leaf-level page:

- Root page of non-leaf level (Level 3) = 4 rows = 1 page (404 rows per page)

- Intermediate non-leaf level (Level 2) = 1,238 rows = 4 pages (404 rows per page)

- Intermediate non-leaf level (Level 1) = 500,000 rows = 1,238 pages (404 rows per page)

- Leaf level (Level 0) = 1,000,000 rows = 500,000 pages (2 rows per page)

In this second example, not only is the initial index only four levels, but it can have an additional 130,878,528 rows added (the maximum possible number of rows is 404*404*404*2—or 131,878,528—minus the number of rows that already exist—1,000,000) before it would require another level. Think of it like this—the root page currently allows 404 entries; however, we're only storing 4 (and the existing non-leaf levels are not entirely 100 percent full). This is only a theoretical maximum, but without any other factors—such as fragmentation—a four-level tree would be able to seek into a table with over 131 million rows (again, with this small index key size). This means that a lookup into this index which uses the tree to navigate down to the corresponding row requires only four I/Os. And because the trees are balanced, finding any record requires the same amount of resources. Retrieval speed is consistent because the index has the same depth throughout. An index can become fragmented—and pages can become less dense—but these trees do not become unbalanced. This is something we look at later in this chapter when we cover index maintenance.

It's not critical to memorize all the math that was used to show these examples, but understanding the true scalability of indexes—especially with reasonably created keys—means you are likely to create more effective indexes (that is, more efficient, with narrower keys). In addition, there are tools inside SQL Server to help you see the actual structures (no math required). Most importantly, the size of an index (and the number of levels) depends on three things—the index definition, whether or not the base table has a clustered index, and the number of pages in the leaf level of the indexes. The number of leaf-level pages is directly tied to both row size and the number of rows in the table. This does not mean that the goal when defining indexes is to have only very narrow indexes—in fact, extremely narrow indexes usually have fewer uses than slightly wider indexes. It just means that you should understand the implications of different indexing choices and decisions. In addition, features such as *INCLUDE* and filtered indexes can profoundly affect the index in both size and usefulness. However, knowing how SQL Server works and the internal structures of indexes are a large part of finding the right balance between having too many and too few indexes, but most importantly, of having the right indexes.

# Tools for Analyzing Indexes

To expose and understand index structures fully, there are a few tools that we're going to use. To make the scenarios easier to understand, we need to get a feel for which tool is the most appropriate to use and when. In addition, this section focuses on an overview of the options for execution, as well as some tips and tricks. However, details on analyzing various aspects of the output can be found throughout this chapter.

## Using the *dm_db_index_physical_stats* DMV

The *sys.dm_db_index_physical_stats* function is one of the most useful functions to determine table structures. DMV can give you insight into whether or not your table has a clustered index, how many nonclustered indexes exist, and whether or not your table (and each index) has row-overflow or Large Object (LOB) data. Most importantly, it can expose to you the entire structure and its state of health. This particular DMV is a function that requires five parameters, all with defaults. If you set all the parameters to their defaults and do not filter the rows or the columns, the function returns 21 columns of data for (almost) every level of every index on every table on every partition in every database of the current SQL Server instance. You would request that information as follows:

```
SELECT * FROM sys.dm_db_index_physical_stats (NULL, NULL, NULL, NULL, NULL);
```

When executed on a very small SQL Server instance, with only the *AdventureWorks2008, pubs,* and *Northwind* databases in addition to the system databases, more than 390 rows are returned. Obviously, 21 columns and 390 rows is too much output to illustrate here, so this is a command that you should play with to get some experience. However, it's unlikely that you actually want to see every index on every table in every database (although that can have some benefits on smaller instances such as a development instance). To distill this to a more targeted execution, let's look at the parameters now:

- *database_id*   The first parameter must be specified as a number, but you can embed the *DB_ID* function as a parameter if you want to specify the database by name. If you specify NULL, which is the default, the function returns information about all databases. If the database ID is NULL, the next three parameters must also be NULL (which is their default value). In addition, this function must be executed in a database that has a compatibility mode of at least 90 (indicating SQL Server 2005). If, for some reason, your database is not running in at least compatibility mode 90, then executing this query from *master* and specifying a database name (DB_ID('databasename')) or the specific ID means that you can execute this without changing the target database's compatibility mode.

- *object_id*   The second parameter is the object ID, which must also be a number, not a name. Again, the NULL default means you want information about all objects, and in that case, the next two parameters, *index _id* and *partition_id,* must be NULL. Just as for the database ID, you can use an embedded function (*OBJECT_ID*) to get the object ID if you know the object name. As a word of caution, if you're executing this from a different database than your current database, you should use a three-part object name with the *OBJECT_ID* function, including the database name and the schema name.

- *index_id*   The third parameter allows you to specify the index ID from a particular table, and again, the default of NULL indicates that you want all the indexes. A handy fact to remember here is that the clustered index on a table always has an *index_id* of 1.

- *partition_number*   The fourth parameter indicates the partition number, and NULL means you want information for all the partitions. Remember that if you haven't explicitly created a table or index on a partition scheme, SQL Server internally considers it to be built on a single partition.

- *mode*   The fifth and last parameter is the only one for which the default NULL does not result in returning the most information. The last parameter indicates the level of information that you want returned (and therefore directly affects the speed of execution) when querying this function. When the function is called, SQL Server traverses the page chains for the allocated pages for the specified partitions of the table or index. Unlike *DBCC SHOWCONTIG* in SQL Server 2000, which usually requires a shared (S) table lock, *sys.dm_db_index_physical_stats* (and *DBCC SHOWCONTIG* in SQL Server 2005) requires only an Intent-Shared (IS) table lock, which is compatible with most other kinds of locks, as discussed in Chapter 10, "Transactions and Concurrency." Valid inputs are DEFAULT, NULL, LIMITED, SAMPLED, and DETAILED. The default is NULL, which corresponds to LIMITED. Here is what the latter three values mean:

  - ❑ **LIMITED**   The LIMITED mode is the fastest and scans the smallest number of pages. For an index, it scans only the first non-leaf (or intermediate) level of the index. For a heap, a scan is avoided by using the table's IAMs and then the associated Page Free Space (PFS) pages to define the allocation of the table. This allows SQL Server to obtain details about fragmentation in terms of page order (more on this later in the chapter) but not page density (or other details that can only be calculated from actually reading the leaf-level pages). In other words, it's fast but not quite as detailed. More specifically, this corresponds to the WITH FAST option of the now-deprecated *DBCC SHOWCONTIG* command.

  - ❑ **SAMPLED**   The SAMPLED mode returns physical characteristics based on a 1-percent sample of all the pages in the index or heap, plus the page order from reading the pages at the first intermediate level. However, if the index has less than 10,000 pages total, SQL Server converts SAMPLED to DETAILED.

  - ❑ **DETAILED**   The DETAILED mode scans all pages and returns all physical characteristics (both page order and page density) for all levels of the index. This is incredibly helpful when analyzing a small table but can take quite a bit of time for larger tables. It could also essentially "flush" your buffer pool if the index being processed is larger than the buffer pool.

You must be careful when using the built-in *DB_ID* or *OBJECT_ID* functions. If you specify an invalid name or simply misspell the name, you do not receive an error message and the value returned is NULL. However, because NULL is a valid parameter, SQL Server just assumes that this is what you meant to use. For example, to see all the previously described information, but only for the *AdventureWorks2008* database, you might mistype the name as follows:

```
SELECT * FROM sys.dm_db_index_physical_stats
        (DB_ID ('AdventureWorks208'), NULL, NULL, NULL, NULL);
```

There is no such database as *AdventureWorks208*, so the *DB_ID* function returns NULL, and it is as if you had called the function with all NULL parameters. No error or warning is given.

You might be able to guess from the number of rows returned that you made an error, but of course, if you have no idea how much output you are expecting, it might not be immediately obvious. *SQL Server Books Online* suggests that you can avoid this issue by capturing the IDs into variables and error-checking the values in the variables before calling the *sys.dm_db_index_physical_stats* function, as shown in this code:

```
DECLARE @db_id SMALLINT;
DECLARE @object_id INT;

SET @db_id = DB_ID (N'AdventureWorks2008');
SET @object_id = OBJECT_ID (N'AdventureWorks2008.Person.Address');


IF (@db_id IS NULL OR @object_id IS NULL)
BEGIN
    IF @db_id IS NULL
    BEGIN
        PRINT N'Invalid database';
    END;
    ELSE IF @object_id IS NULL
    BEGIN
        PRINT N'Invalid object';
    END
END
ELSE
SELECT *
FROM sys.dm_db_index_physical_stats
    (@db_id, @object_id, NULL, NULL, NULL);
```

Another more insidious problem is that the *OBJECT_ID* function is called based on your current database, before any call to the *sys.dm_db_index_physical_stats* function is made. So if you are in the *AdventureWorks2008* database but want information from a table in the *pubs* database, you could try running the following code:

```
SELECT *
FROM sys.dm_db_index_physical_stats
        (DB_ID (N'pubs'), OBJECT_ID (N'dbo.authors'), NULL, NULL, NULL);
```

However, because there is no *dbo.authors* table in the current database (*AdventureWorks2008*), *@object_id* is passed as NULL, and you get all the information from all the objects in *pubs*.

If an object with the same name exists in two databases, the problem may be even harder to detect. If there were a *dbo.authors* table in *AdventureWorks2008*, the ID for that table would be used to try to retrieve data from the *pubs* database—and it's unlikely that the *authors* table has the same ID even if it exists in both databases. SQL Server returns an error if the ID returned by *object_id()* does not match any object in the specified database, but if does match the object ID for another table, the details for *that* table are produced, potentially causing even more confusion. The following script shows the error:

```
USE AdventureWorks2008;
GO

CREATE TABLE dbo.authors
    (ID CHAR(11), name varchar(60));
GO

SELECT *
FROM sys.dm_db_index_physical_stats
        (DB_ID (N'pubs'), OBJECT_ID (N'dbo.authors'), NULL, NULL, NULL);
```

When you run the preceding *SELECT*, the *dbo.authors* ID is determined based on the current environment, which is still *AdventureWorks2008*. But when SQL Server tries to use that ID (which does not exist) in *pubs*, the following error is generated:

```
Msg 2573, Level 16, State 40, Line 1
Could not find table or object ID 295672101. Check system catalog.
```

The best solution is to fully qualify the table name, either in the call to the *sys.dm_db_index_ physical_stats* function itself or, as in the code sample shown earlier, to use variables to get the ID of the fully qualified table name. If you write wrapper procedures to call the *sys.dm_db_index_physical_stats* function, you can concatenate the database name onto the object name before retrieving the object ID, thereby avoiding the problem. Because the output of this function is a bit cryptic, you might find it beneficial to write your own procedure to access this function and return the information in a slightly friendlier fashion.

In summary, this DMV is incredibly useful for determining the size and health of your indexes; however, you need to know how to work with it to get only the specific information in which you're interested. But even for a subset of tables or indexes, and with careful use of the available parameters, you still might get more data back than you want. Because *sys.dm_db_index_physical_stats* is a table-valued function, you can add your own filters to the results being returned. For example, you can choose to look at the results for just the nonclustered indexes. Using the available parameters, your only choices are to see all the indexes or only one particular index. If we make the third parameter NULL to specify all indexes, we can then add a filter in a WHERE clause to indicate that we want only nonclustered index rows (WHERE *index_id* > 1). Note that while a WHERE clause may limit the number of rows returned it does not necessarily limit the tables and indexes analyzed.

## Using *DBCC IND*

The *DBCC IND* command (introduced in Chapter 5, "Tables") is undocumented but widely known and used. It is safe to use on production systems. The command has four parameters, but only the first three are required. The following code shows the command syntax:

```
DBCC IND ( { 'dbname' | dbid }, { 'objname' | objid },
    { nonclustered indid | 1 | 0 | -1 | -2 } [, partition_number]  )
```

The first parameter is the database name or the database ID. The second parameter is an object name or object ID within the database; the object can be either a table or an indexed view. The third parameter is a specific nonclustered index ID (2-250 or 256-1005) or the values 1, 0, –1, or –2. The values for this parameter have the following meanings:

- **0**   Displays information for in-row data pages and in-row IAM pages of the specified object.

- **1**   Displays information for all pages, including IAM pages, data pages, and any existing LOB pages or row-overflow pages of the requested object. If the requested object has a clustered index, the index pages are included.

- **–1**   Displays information for all IAMs, data pages, and index pages for all indexes on the specified object. This includes LOB and row-overflow data.

- **–2**   Displays information for all IAMs for the specified object.

- **Nonclustered index ID**   Displays information for all IAMs, data pages, and index pages for one index. This includes LOB and row-overflow data that might be part of the index's included columns.

The final parameter was new for SQL Server 2005 and is optional (to maintain backward compatibility with scripts that might use *DBCC IND* from SQL Server 2000). It specifies a particular partition number, and if no value is specified or a 0 is given, information for all partitions is displayed.

Unlike *DBCC PAGE* (discussed in Chapter 5), SQL Server does not require that you enable trace flag 3604 before running *DBCC IND*. However, because it's likely that you will want to investigate pages using *DBCC PAGE*, after determining the pages owned by an index, it's a good idea to turn the trace flag on at the beginning of your script.

The columns in the result set are described in Table 6-1. Note that all page references have the file and page component conveniently split between two columns, so you don't have to do any conversion.

**TABLE 6-1** **Column Descriptions for *DBCC IND* Output**

| Column | Meaning |
| --- | --- |
| *PageFID* | File ID containing the page |
| *PagePID* | Page number within that file |
| *IAMFID* | File ID containing the IAM managing this page |
| *IAMPID* | Page number within that file of the IAM managing this page |
| *ObjectID* | Object ID |
| *IndexID* | Index ID—valid values are 0–250 and 256–1005 (described later) |
| *PartitionNumber* | Partition number within the table or index for this page |
| *PartitionID* | ID for the partition containing this page (unique in the database) |
| *iam_chain_type* | Type of allocation unit this page belongs to: in-row data, row-overflow data, or LOB data |
| *PageType* | Page type: 1 = data page, 2 = index page, 3 = TEXT_MIXED_PAGE, 4 = TEXT_TREE_PAGE, 10 = IAM page |
| *IndexLevel* | Level of index; 0 is the leaf level and levels are counted up from the leaf to the root page (of an index structure with *IndexID* of 1–1005) |
| *NextPageFID* | File ID containing the next page at this level |
| *NextPagePID* | Page number within that file for next page at this level |
| *PrevPageFID* | File ID containing the previous page at this level |
| *PrevPagePID* | Page number within that file for previous page at this level |

Some of the return values were described in Chapter 5 because they are equally relevant to heaps. When dealing with indexes, we also can look at the *IndexID* column, which is 0 for a heap, 1 for pages of a clustered index, and a number between 2 and 1,005 for the pages of a nonclustered index pages. In SQL Server 2008, a table can have up to 1,000 total indexes (1 clustered and 999 nonclustered). Although 1,005 is higher than would be expected (2–1,000 would be sufficient for 999 nonclustered indexes), the range of nonclustered index IDs skips 251–255 because 255 had special meaning in earlier releases (it was used for the LOB values in a table) and 251–254 were unused. To simplify any backward-compatibility issues, this range (251–255) has been skipped in SQL Server 2008.

The *IndexLevel* value allows us to see at what level of the index tree a page is located, with a value of 0 meaning the leaf level. The highest value for any particular index is, therefore, the root page of that index, and you should be able to verify that the root page is the same value you get from the *sys.system_internals_allocation_units* view in the *root_page* column. The remaining four columns indicate the page linkage at each level of each index. For each page, there is a file ID and page ID for the next page and a file ID and page ID for the previous page. Of course, for the root pages, all these values are 0. You can also determine the first page by finding one with zeros for the previous page, and you can find the last page because it has zeros for the next page. Because the output of this DBCC command is too wide to display in a page of a book, and because it's likely that you want to reorder the result set, we are not going to reproduce it here. If you wish to view it, you can use a script that stores the output of this command into a table. Once we have this information in a table, we can query it and retrieve just the columns in which we are interested. Here is a script that creates a table called *sp_tablepages* with columns to hold all the returned information from *DBCC IND*. Note that any object created in the *master* database with a name that starts with *sp_* can be accessed from any database, without having to qualify it with the database name:

```
USE master;
GO
CREATE TABLE sp_tablepages
(PageFID  tinyint,
  PagePID int,
  IAMFID   tinyint,
  IAMPID  int,
  ObjectID  int,
  IndexID  tinyint,
  PartitionNumber tinyint,
  PartitionID bigint,
  iam_chain_type  varchar(30),
  PageType  tinyint,
  IndexLevel  tinyint,
  NextPageFID  tinyint,
  NextPagePID  int,
  PrevPageFID  tinyint,
  PrevPagePID int,
  Primary Key (PageFID, PagePID));
```

The following code truncates the *sp_tablepages* table and then fills it with *DBCC IND* results from the *Sales.SalesOrderDetail* table in the *AdventureWorks2008* database:

```
TRUNCATE TABLE sp_tablepages;
INSERT INTO sp_tablepages
    EXEC ('DBCC IND (AdventureWorks2008, [Sales.SalesOrderDetail], -1)');
```

Once you have the results of *DBCC IND* in a table, you can select any subset of rows or columns that you are interested in. We use *sp_tablepages* to report on *DBCC IND* information for many examples in this chapter. You can then use *DBCC PAGE* to examine index pages, just as you do for data pages. However, if you use *DBCC PAGE* with style 3 to print out the details of each column on each row on an index page, the output looks quite different. We see some examples as we analyze the physical structures of indexes next.

# Understanding Index Structures

As we discussed earlier in this chapter, index structures are divided into two basic components of the index: the leaf level and the non-leaf level(s). The details in this section help you to better understand what's specifically stored within these portions of your indexes and how they differ based on index type.

# The Dependency on the Clustering Key

The leaf level of a clustered index contains the data, not just the index keys. So the answer to the question "What else is in the leaf level of a clustered index besides the key value?" is "Everything else"—that is, all the columns of every row in the table are in the leaf level of a clustered index. Another way to say this is that when a clustered index is created, the data becomes the leaf level of the clustered index. At the time a clustered index is created, data in the table is copied and ordered by the clustering key. Once created, a clustered index is maintained logically rather than physically. This order is maintained through a doubly linked list called a *page chain*. (Note that pages in a heap are not linked in any way to each other.) The order of pages in the page chain, and the order of rows on the data pages, is based on the definition of the clustered index. Deciding on which column(s) to cluster is an important performance consideration.

Because the actual page chain for the data pages can be ordered in only one way, a table can have only one clustered index. And, in general, most tables perform better when the table is clustered. However, the clustering key needs to be chosen wisely. And, to appropriately choose a clustering key, you must understand how the clustered index works, as well as the internal dependencies on the clustering key (especially as far as the nonclustered indexes are concerned).

The dependencies of the nonclustered indexes on the clustering key have been in SQL Server since the storage engine was rearchitected in SQL Server 7.0. It all starts with how rows are identified (and looked up) when using a nonclustered index to reference a corresponding row within the table. If a table has a clustered index, then rows are identified (and looked up by) their clustering key. If the table does not have a clustered index, then rows are identified (and looked up by) their physical row identifier (RID), described in more detail later in this chapter. This process of looking up corresponding data rows in the base table is known as a *[bookmark] lookup*, which is named after the analogy that nonclustered indexes reference a place within a book, as a bookmark does.

Nonclustered indexes contain only the data as defined by the index. When looking up a row within a nonclustered index, you often need to go to the actual data row for additional data that's not part of the nonclustered index. To retrieve this additional data, you must look into the table for that data. For the purpose of this section, we focus only on how the bookmark lookup is performed when a table is clustered.

First, and foremost, all clustered indexes must be unique. The primary reason why a clustered index must be unique is so that nonclustered index entries can point to exactly one specific row. Consider the problem that would occur if a table were clustered by a nonunique value of last name. If a nonclustered index existed on a unique value, such as social security number, and a query looked into the index for a specific social security number of 123-45-6789 and found that its clustering key was 'Smith,' then if multiple rows with a last name of Smith existed, the question would be—which one? How would the specific row with a social security number of 123-45-6789 be located efficiently?

For a clustering key to be used effectively, all nonclustered index entries must refer to exactly one row. Because that pointer is the clustering key in SQL Server, then the clustering key must be unique. If you build a clustered index without specifying the *UNIQUE* keyword, SQL Server guarantees uniqueness internally by adding a hidden uniquifier column to the rows when necessary.

> **Note** In *SQL Server Books Online*, the word *uniquifier* is written as uniqueifier; however, the internal tools—such as *DBCC PAGE*—spell it as we've spelled it here.

This uniquifier is a 4-byte integer value added to the data row when the row's clustering key is not unique. Once added, it becomes part of the clustering key, meaning that it is duplicated in every nonclustered index. You can see whether or not a specific row has this extra value when you review the actual structure of index rows, as we will see later in this chapter.

Second, if a clustering key is used to look up the corresponding data rows from a nonclustered index into the clustered index (the data) then the clustering key is the most overly duplicated data in a table; all the columns that make up the clustering key are included in every nonclustered index in addition to being in the actual data row. As a result, the width of the clustering key is important. Consider a clustered index with a 64-byte clustering key on a table with 12 nonclustered indexes and 1 million rows. Without counting internal and structural overhead, the overhead required just to store the clustering key (to support the lookup) in every nonclustered index is 732 MB compared to only 92 MB if the clustering key were only 8 bytes and only 46 MB if the clustering key were only 4 bytes. Although this is just a rough estimate, it shows that you waste a lot of space (and potentially buffer pool memory) if you have an overly wide clustering key. However, it's not just about space alone; this also translates into performance and efficiency of your nonclustered indexes. And, in general, you don't want your nonclustered indexes to be unnecessarily wide.

Third, and because the clustering key is the most redundant data within your entire table, you should be sure to choose a clustering key that is *not* volatile. If a clustering key changes, then it can have multiple negative effects. First, it can cause record relocation within the clustered index (which can cause page splits and fragmentation, which we discuss in more detail later in this chapter). Second, it causes every nonclustered index to be modified (so that the value of the clustering key is correct for the relevant nonclustered index rows). This wastes time and space, causes fragmentation which then requires maintenance, and adds unnecessary overhead to every modification of the column(s) that make up the clustering key.

These three attributes—unique, narrow, and static—also (but not always) apply to a well-chosen primary key, and because you can have only one primary key (and only one clustering key), SQL Server uses a unique clustered index to enforce a primary key constraint (when no index type is defined in the primary key definition). However, this is not always known by the table's creator. And, if the primary key doesn't adhere to these criteria (for example, when the primary key has been chosen from the data's natural key, which, for example, is a wide, 100-byte combination of seven columns that is unique only when combined), then using a clustered index to enforce uniqueness and duplicating the entire 100-byte combination of columns in every nonclustered index can have very negative side effects. So, for some unsuspecting database developers, a very wide clustering key may have been created for them because of these defaults. The good news is that you can define the primary key to be nonclustered and easily create a clustered index on a different column (or set of columns); however, you have to know when—and how—to do this.

Finally, a table's clustering key should also be chosen so as to minimize fragmentation for inserts (fragmentation is discussed in more detail later in this chapter). Although only the logical order of a clustered index is maintained after it is created, the maintenance of this structure does have overhead. If rows consistently need to enter the table at random entry points (for example, inserts into a table ordered by last name), then that table's logical order is slightly more expensive to maintain than a table that's always adding rows to the end of the table (for example, inserts into a table ordered by order number, which is—or should be—an ever-increasing identity column).

More details will be available as we review the internals of indexes later in the chapter, but to summarize our discussion thus far, the clustering key should be chosen not only based on table usage (and, it's really hard to say "always" or "never" with regard to the clustering key) but also based on the internal dependencies that SQL Server has on the clustering key. For the latter, the clustering key should be unique, narrow, and static—and preferably, ever-increasing.

Examples of good clustering keys are the following:

- A single column key defined with an ever-increasing identity column (for example, a 4-byte *int* or an 8-byte *bigint*).

- A composite key defined with an ever-increasing date column (first), followed by a second column that uniquely identifies the rows—like an identity column. This can be very useful for date-based partitioned tables and tables where the data is inserted in increasing date-based order as it offers an additional benefit for range queries on date. Examples of this include a 12-byte composite key comprised of *SalesDate* (8 bytes) and *SalesNumber* (4-byte *int*) or, in SQL Server 2008, a date column that does not include time. However, date alone is not a good clustering key because it is not unique (and requires a uniquifier).

- A GUID column can be used successfully as a clustering key because it's clearly unique, relatively narrow (16 bytes wide), and likely to be static. However, as a clustering key, a GUID is appropriate only when it follows an ever-increasing pattern. Some GUIDs—depending on how there are generated—may cause a tremendous amount of fragmentation. If the GUID is generated outside SQL Server (like in a client application) or generated inside SQL Server using the *NEWID()* function, then fragmentation reduces the effectiveness of this column as a clustering key. If possible, consider using the *NEWSEQUENTIALID()* function instead (for ever-increasing GUIDs) or choosing a different clustering key. If you still want to use a GUID as a primary key and it's not ever-increasing, you can make it a nonclustered index instead of a clustered index.

In summary, there are no absolutes to choosing a clustering key; there are only general best practices which work well for most tables. However, if a table has only one index—and no nonclustered indexes—then the nonclustered index dependencies on the clustering key are no longer relevant and a clustered index can take any form. However, most tables are likely to have at least a few nonclustered indexes, and most tables perform better with a clustered index. Because this is the case, a clustered index with a well-chosen clustering key is always the first step to better performance. The second step is "finding the right balance" in your nonclustered indexes by choosing appropriate—and usually a relatively minimal number of—nonclustered indexes.

## Nonclustered Indexes

As shown earlier, there are two primary components of all indexes—the leaf level and the non-leaf level(s). For a clustered index, the leaf level *is* the data. For a nonclustered index, the leaf level is a separate and additional structure that has a copy of some of the data. Specifically, a nonclustered index depends on its definition to form the leaf level. The leaf level of a nonclustered index consists of the index key (as per the definition of the index), any included columns (using the *INCLUDE* feature added in SQL Server 2005), and the data row's bookmark value (either the clustering key if the table is clustered or the row's physical RID if the table is a heap). A nonclustered index has exactly the same number of rows as there are rows in the table, unless a filter predicate is used when the index is defined. Filtered indexes are new in SQL Server 2008 and are discussed in more detail later in this chapter.

In terms of *how* the nonclustered index is used, there are really two ways—either to help point to the data (similar to an index in the back of a book, using bookmark lookups, as discussed earlier) or to answer a query directly. When a nonclustered index has all the data as requested by the query, this is known as *query covering*, and the index is called a *covering index*. When a nonclustered index covers a query, the nonclustered index can be used to answer a query directly and a bookmark lookup (which can be expensive for a nonselective query) can be avoided. This can be one of the most effective ways to improve range query performance.

The bookmark lookup of a row occurs when a nonclustered index does not have all the data required by the query but the query is driven by a predicate that the index can help to find. If a table has a clustered index, the nonclustered index is used to drive the query to find the corresponding data row by using the clustering key. If the table is a heap (in other words, it has no clustered index), the lookup value is an 8-btye RID, which is an actual row locator in the form *FileID:PageID:SlotNumber*. This 8-byte row identifier breaks down into 2 bytes for the *FileID*, 4 bytes for the *PageID*, and 2 bytes for the *SlotNumber*. We will see exactly how these lookup values are used when we review data access later in this chapter.

The presence or absence of a nonclustered index doesn't affect how the data pages are organized, so you're not restricted to having only one nonclustered index per table, as is the case with clustered indexes. In SQL Server 2008, each table can include as many as 999 nonclustered indexes (up from 249 in SQL Server 2005), but you'll usually want to have far fewer than that (with a few exceptions, such as filtered indexes).

In summary, nonclustered indexes do not affect the base table; however, the base table's structure—either a heap or a table with a clustered index—affects the structure of your nonclustered indexes. This is something to consider and understand if you want to minimize wasted overhead and achieve the best performance.

## Constraints and Indexes

As mentioned earlier, an unsuspecting database developer might have a clustered index unintentionally due to having created a PRIMARY KEY constraint on their table. The idea for using constraints comes from relational theory, where a table has entity identifiers defined (to understand table relationships and help to join tables in a normalized schema). When constraints are defined on a table in SQL Server, both PRIMARY KEY and UNIQUE KEY constraints can enforce certain aspects of entity integrity within the database.

For a PRIMARY KEY constraint, SQL Server enforces two things: first, that all the columns involved in the PRIMARY KEY do not allow NULL values, and second, that the PRIMARY KEY value is unique within the table. If any of the columns allow NULL values, the PRIMARY KEY constraint cannot be created. To enforce uniqueness, SQL Server creates a UNIQUE index on the columns that make up the PRIMARY KEY constraint. The default index type, if not specified, is a unique clustered index.

For a UNIQUE constraint, SQL Server allows the columns that make up the UNIQUE constraint to allow NULLs, but it does not allow all columns to be NULL for more than one row. To enforce uniqueness for the UNIQUE constraint, SQL Server creates a unique index on the columns that make up the constraint. The default index type, if not specified, is a unique nonclustered index.

When you declare a PRIMARY KEY or UNIQUE constraint, the underlying index structure that is created is the same as if you had used the *CREATE INDEX* command directly. However, there are some differences in terms of usage and features. For example, a constraint-based index cannot have other features added (such as included columns or filters, features that are discussed later in this chapter), but a UNIQUE index can have these features while still enforcing uniqueness over the key definition of the index. And when referencing a UNIQUE index—which does not support a constraint—you cannot reference indexes with filters. However, an index that doesn't use filters or an index that uses included columns can be referenced. These can be powerful options to use to minimize the total number of indexes and yet still create a reference with a FOREIGN KEY constraint.

The names of the indexes that are built to support these constraints are the same as the constraint names. In terms of internal storage and how these indexes work, there is no difference between unique indexes created using the *CREATE INDEX* command and indexes created to support constraints. The Query Optimizer makes decisions based on the presence of the unique index rather than on whether the column was declared as a constraint or not. In other words, *how* the index was created is irrelevant to the Query Optimizer.

# Index Creation Options

In terms of creating indexes, the *CREATE INDEX* command is relatively straightforward:

```
CREATE [ UNIQUE ] [ CLUSTERED | NONCLUSTERED ] INDEX index_name
    ON <object> ( column [ ASC | DESC ] [ ,...n ] )
    [ INCLUDE ( column_name [ ,...n ] ) ]
    [ WHERE <filter_predicate> ]
```

The required parts of an index are the index name, the key definition, and the table on which this index is defined. An index can have non-key columns included in the leaf level of the index, using *INCLUDE*. An index can be defined over the entire rowset of the table—which is the default—or, new in SQL Server 2008, can be limited to only the rows as defined by a filter, using WHERE <filter_predicate>. We discuss both of these as we analyze the physical structures of nonclustered indexes.

However, *CREATE INDEX* has some additional options available for specialized purposes. You can add a WITH clause to the *CREATE INDEX* command:

```
[WITH
([FILLFACTOR = fillfactor]
[[,] [PAD_INDEX] = { ON | OFF }]
[[,] DROP_EXISTING  = { ON | OFF }]
[[,] IGNORE_DUP_KEY = { ON | OFF }]
[[,] SORT_IN_TEMPDB = { ON | OFF }]
[[,] STATISTICS_NORECOMPUTE  = { ON | OFF }]
[[,] ALLOW_ROW_LOCKS = { ON | OFF }]
[[,] ALLOW_PAGE_LOCKS = { ON | OFF }]
[[,] MAXDOP = max_degree_of_parallelism]
[[,] ONLINE = { ON | OFF }] )]
```

The FILLFACTOR, PAD_INDEX, DROP_EXISTING, SORT_IN_TEMPDB, and ONLINE index creation options are predominantly defined and used for index maintenance. To use them appropriately, you must better understand the physical structures of indexes as well as how data modifications work. We cover these options in detail in the section entitled "Managing Index Structures," later in this chapter. The remaining options are described here.

## IGNORE_DUP_KEY

You can ensure the uniqueness of an index key by defining it as UNIQUE or by defining a PRIMARY KEY or UNIQUE constraint. If an *UPDATE* or *INSERT* statement would affect multiple rows, or if even one row is found that would cause duplicates of keys defined as unique, the entire statement is aborted and no rows are affected. Alternatively, when you create a UNIQUE index, you can use the IGNORE_DUP_KEY option so that a duplicate key error on a multiple-row *INSERT* won't cause the entire statement to be rolled back. The nonunique row is discarded, and all other rows are inserted. IGNORE_DUP_KEY doesn't allow the uniqueness of the index to be violated; instead, it makes a violation in a multiple-row data modification nonfatal to all the nonviolating rows.

## STATISTICS_NORECOMPUTE

The STATISTICS_NORECOMPUTE option determines whether the statistics on the index should be updated automatically. Every index maintains a histogram representing the distribution of values for the leading column of the index. Among other things, the Query Optimizer uses these statistics to determine the usefulness of a particular index when choosing a query plan. As data is modified, the statistics get increasingly out of date, and this can lead to less-than-optimal query plans if the statistics are not updated. In Chapter 3, "Databases and Database Files," you learned about the database option AUTO_UPDATE_STATISTICS, which enables all statistics in a database to be updated automatically when needed. In general, the database option should be enabled. However, if desired, a specific statistic or index can be set to not update automatically, using the STATISTICS_NORECOMPUTE option. Adding this clause overrides an *ON* value for the AUTO_UPDATE_STATISTICS database option. If the database option is set to *OFF,* you cannot override that behavior for a particular index, and in that case, all statistics in the database must be updated manually using *UPDATE STATISTICS* or *sp_updatestats*. To see if the statistics for a given table are set to auto-update, as well as the last time they were updated, use *sp_autostats <table_name>*.

## MAXDOP

The option MAXDOP controls the maximum number of processors that can be used for index creation. It can override the server configuration option *max degree of parallelism* for index building. Allowing multiple processors to be used for index creation can greatly enhance the performance of index build operations. As with other parallel operations, the Query Optimizer determines at run time the actual number of processors to use, based on the current load on the system. The MAXDOP value just sets a maximum. Multiple processors can be used for index creation only when you run SQL Server Enterprise or SQL Server Developer editions. And, when used, each processor builds an equal-sized chunk of the index in parallel. When this occurs, the tree might not be perfectly balanced, and the math that's used to determine the theoretical minimum number of required pages differs from the actual number, as each parallel thread builds a separate tree. Once each of the threads have completed, the trees are essentially concatenated together. SQL Server can use any extra page space that's reserved during this parallel process for later modifications.

## Index Placement

A final clause in the *CREATE INDEX* command allows you to specify the placement of the index:

```
[ ON { partition_scheme_name ( column_name )
     | filegroup_name } ]
```

You can specify that an index should either be placed on a particular filegroup or partitioned according to a predefined partition scheme. By default, if no filegroup or partition scheme is specified, the index is placed on the same filegroup as the base table. We discussed filegroups in Chapter 3 and you will learn about table and index partitioning in Chapter 7, "Special Storage."

## Constraints and Indexes

The issue of whether a unique index should be defined using a UNIQUE or PRIMARY KEY constraint or through the *CREATE INDEX* command is a common concern and a frequent source of confusion. As mentioned earlier, there is no internal difference in structure, or in the Query Optimizer's choices, for a unique clustered index built using the *CREATE INDEX* command or one that was built to support a PRIMARY KEY constraint. The difference is really a design issue, so it is beyond the scope of this book, which deals with SQL Server internals. However, one simple distinction can be made; a constraint is a logical construct and an index is a physical one. When you build an index, you are asking SQL Server to create a physical structure that takes up storage space and must be maintained during data modifications. When you define a constraint, you are defining a property of your data and expecting SQL Server to enforce that property, but you are not telling SQL Server *how* to enforce it. In the current version, SQL Server enforces PRIMARY KEY and UNIQUE constraints by creating unique indexes, but there is no requirement that it do so. In a future release, SQL Server could enforce this through another mechanism, although it is unlikely to do so because of backward compatibility issues.

# Physical Index Structures

Index pages have almost the same structure as data pages except that they store index records instead of data records. As with all other types of pages in SQL Server, index pages use a fixed size of 8 KB, or 8,192 bytes. Index pages also have a 96-byte header, and there is an offset array at the end of the page with 2 bytes for each row to indicate the offset of that row on the page. A nonclustered index can have all three allocation units associated with it: IN_ROW_DATA, ROW_OVERFLOW_DATA, and LOB_DATA. Each index has a row in the *sys.indexes* catalog view, with an *index_id* value of either 1 (for a clustered index) or a number between 2 and 250 or between 256 and 1005 (indicating a nonclustered index). Remember that SQL Server has reserved values between 251 and 255.

## Index Row Formats

Index rows are structured just like data rows, with two main exceptions. First, an index row cannot have *SPARSE* columns. If a *SPARSE* column is used in an index definition (and there are some limitations as to where a *SPARSE* column can be used in indexes, such as that it cannot be used in a PRIMARY KEY), then the column is created in the index row as if it had not been defined as *SPARSE*. Second, if a clustered index is created and the index is not defined as unique, then the duplicate key values include a uniquifier.

There are a couple of other differences in structure between index and data rows. An index row does not use the *TagB* or *Fsize* row header values. In place of the *Fsize* field, which indicates where the fixed-length portion of a row ends, the page header *pminlen* value is used to decode an index row. The *pminlen* value indicates the offset at which the fixed-length data portion of the row ends. If the index row has no variable-length or nullable columns, that is the end of the row. Only if the index row has nullable columns are the field called *Ncol* and the null bitmap both present. The *Ncol* field contains a value indicating how many columns are in the index row; this value is needed to determine how many bits are in the null bitmap. Data rows have an *Ncol* field and null bitmap whether or not any columns allow NULL, but index rows have only a null bitmap and an *Ncol* field if NULLs are allowed in any of the columns of the index. Table 6-2 shows the general format of an index row.

**TABLE 6-2  Information Stored in an Index Row**

| Information | Mnemonic | Size |
| --- | --- | --- |
| Status Bits A | *TagA*<br>Some of the relevant bits are:<br>■  Bits 1 through 3:<br>Taken as a 3-bit value.<br>0 indicates a primary record.<br>3 indicates an index record.<br>5 indicates a ghost index record.<br>(Ghost records are discussed later in this chapter.)<br>■  Bit 4:<br>Indicates that a NULL bitmap exists.<br>■  Bit 5:<br>Indicates that variable-length columns exist in the row. | 1 byte |
| Fixed-length data | *Fdata* | *pminlen*—1 |
| Number of columns | *Ncol* | 2 bytes |
| NULL bitmap (1 bit for each column in the table; a 1 indicates that the corresponding column is NULL) | *Nullbits* | Ceiling (*Ncol* / 8) |
| Number of variable-length columns; only present if > 0 | *VarCount* | 2 bytes |
| Variable column offset array; only present if *VarCount* > 0 | *VarOffset* | 2 * *VarCount* |
| Variable-length data, if any | *VarData* | |

The specific column data stored in an index row depends on the type of index and the level in which that index row is located.

## Clustered Index Structures

The leaf level of a clustered index is the data itself. When a clustered index is created, the data is physically copied and ordered based on the clustering key (as discussed earlier in this chapter). There is no difference between the row structure of a clustered index and the row structure of a heap, except in one case: when the clustering key has not been defined with the UNIQUE attribute. In this case, SQL Server must guarantee uniqueness internally, and to do this, each duplicate row requires an additional uniquifier value.

### Clustered Index Rows with a Uniquifier

As mentioned earlier, if your clustered index was not created with the *UNIQUE* property, SQL Server adds a 4-byte integer to make each nonunique key value unique. Because the clustering key is used to identify the base rows being referenced by nonclustered indexes (the bookmark lookup), there needs to be a unique way to refer to each row in a clustered index.

SQL Server adds the uniquifier only when necessary—that is, when duplicate keys are added to the table. As an example, we create a small table with all fixed-length columns and then add a clustered, nonunique index to the table:

```
USE AdventureWorks2008;
GO

CREATE TABLE Clustered_Dupes
  (Col1 CHAR(5)    NOT NULL,
   Col2 INT        NOT NULL,
   Col3 CHAR(3)    NULL,
   Col4 CHAR(6)    NOT NULL);
GO

CREATE CLUSTERED INDEX Cl_dupes_col1 ON Clustered_Dupes(col1);
```

If you look at the row in the *sysindexes* compatibility view for this table, you notice something unexpected:

```
SELECT indid, keycnt, name FROM sysindexes
WHERE id = OBJECT_ID ('Clustered_Dupes');

RESULT:
indid  keycnt name
------ ------ --------------
1      2      Cl_dupes_col1
```

The column called *keycnt*, which indicates the number of keys an index has, has a value of 2. (Note that this column is available only in the compatibility view *sysindexes*, not in the catalog view *sys.indexes*.) If this index had the *UNIQUE* property, the *keycnt* value would be 1. Because creating a clustered index on a nonunique key is not recommended—it wastes time and space with the process of making rows unique—we'll skip a full analysis of this structure. However, there is a script named ExaminingtheClusteredIndexUniquifier. sql included with this chapter's resource materials in the companion content (which can be found at *http://www.SQLServerInternals.com/companion*). The script creates and analyzes the clustered index row structure when the clustering key is not defined as UNIQUE.

## The Non-Leaf Level(s) of a Clustered Index

To navigate to the leaf level of an index, a B-tree is created, which includes the data rows in the leaf level. Each row in the non-leaf levels has one entry for every page of the level below (later in this chapter, we look more into what this specifically looks like with each index type) and this entry includes an index key value and a 6-byte pointer to reference the page. In this case, the page pointer is in the format of 2 bytes for the *FileID* and 4 bytes for the *PageNumberInTheFile*. SQL Server does not need an 8-byte RID because the slot number does not need to be stored. The index key part of the entry always indicates the minimum value that could be on the pointed-to page. Note that they do not necessarily indicate the *actual* lowest value, just the lowest *possible* value for the page (as when the row with the lowest key value on a page is deleted, the index row in the level above is not updated).

## Analyzing a Clustered Index Structure

To better illustrate how the clustered index is stored as well as traversed, we review specific structures created in a sample database called *IndexInternals*. For this example, we review an *Employee* table created with a clustered index on the PRIMARY KEY.

> **Note**  The *IndexInternals* sample database is available for download. A few tables exist in this database already. Review the *EmployeeCaseStudy-TableDefinition.sql* script to see the table definitions, and then move to the *EmployeeCaseStudy-AnalyzeStructures.sql* script to analyze the structures. A backup of this database and a zip file containing the solution can be found in the companion content.

Here is the table definition for the *Employee* table, as it already exists within the *IndexInternals* database:

```
CREATE TABLE Employee
   (EmployeeID      INT          NOT NULL      IDENTITY,
   LastName         NCHAR(30)    NOT NULL,
   FirstName        NCHAR(29)    NOT NULL,
   MiddleInitial    NCHAR(1)     NULL,
   SSN              CHAR(11)     NOT NULL,
   OtherColumns     CHAR(258)    NOT NULL      DEFAULT 'Junk');
GO
```

The *Employee* table was created using a few deviations from normal best practices to make the structures somewhat predictable (for example, easier math and easier visualization). First, all columns have fixed widths even if when data values vary. Not all columns should be variable just because the data values vary, but when your column is over 20 characters and your data varies (and is not overly volatile), then it's best to consider variable-width character columns rather than fixed-width columns, to save space and for better *INSERT* performance. (*UPDATE* performance may be compromised, especially when updates make the variable-width column larger.) We discuss this in more detail in the section on fragmentation later in this chapter. In these specific tables, fixed-width columns are used to ensure a predictable row size and to help in better visualizing the data structures.

In this case, and including overhead, the data rows of the *Employee* table are exactly 400 bytes per row (using a filler column called *OtherColumns,* which adds 258 bytes of junk at the end of the data row). A row size of 400 bytes means that we can fit 20 rows per data page (8,096 bytes per page/400 bytes per row = 20.24, which translates into 20 rows per page because the IN_ROW portion of the data row cannot span pages). To calculate how large our tables are, we need to know how many rows these tables contain. And, in the *IndexInternals* database, this table has already been set up with exactly 80,000 rows. At 20 rows per page, this table requires 4,000 data pages to store its 80,000 rows.

In the current table definition, this table is a heap. For the *Employee* table, we define the clustered index by using a PRIMARY KEY constraint:

```
-- Add the CLUSTERED PRIMARY KEY for Employee
ALTER TABLE Employee
  ADD CONSTRAINT EmployeePK
    PRIMARY KEY CLUSTERED (EmployeeID);
GO
```

To investigate our *Employee* table further, we use *sys.dm_db_index_physical_stats* to determine the number of pages within the table, as well as the number of levels within our indexes. We can confirm the index structures using the DMV to see the number of levels as well as the number of pages within each level:

```
SELECT index_depth AS D
    , index_level AS L
    , record_count AS 'Count'
    , page_count AS PgCnt
    , avg_page_space_used_in_percent AS 'PgPercentFull'
    , min_record_size_in_bytes AS 'MinLen'
    , max_record_size_in_bytes AS 'MaxLen'
    , avg_record_size_in_bytes AS 'AvgLen'
FROM sys.dm_db_index_physical_stats
    (DB_ID ('IndexInternals')
    , OBJECT_ID ('IndexInternals.dbo.Employee')
    , 1, NULL, 'DETAILED');
GO
```

```
RESULT:
D   L   Count   PgCnt   PgPercentFull       MinLen  MaxLen  AvgLen
--- --- ------- ------- ------------------- ------- ------- ------
3   0   80000   4000    99.3081294786261    400     400     400
3   1   4000    7       91.7540400296516    11      11      11
3   2   7       1       1.09957993575488    11      11      11
```

The clustered index for this table has a leaf level of 4,000 pages, which is as expected, given that we have 80,000 rows at 20 rows per page. From the *MinLen* (*min_record_size_in_bytes*) column, we can see our row length in the leaf level is 400 bytes; however, the row length of the non-leaf levels is only 11 bytes. This structure is easily broken down as 4 bytes for the integer column (*EmployeeID*) on which the clustered index is defined, 6 bytes for our page pointer, and 1 byte for row overhead. Only 1 byte is needed for overhead because our index row contains only fixed-width columns and none of those columns allow NULLs (therefore, we do not need a NULL bitmap in the index pages). In addition, you can see that there are 4,000 rows in the first level above the leaf level because level 1 has a *Count* (*record_count*) of 4,000. In fact, in level 1 there are only seven pages [shown as *PgCnt* (*page_count*)], and in level 2, you can see that *Count* shows as 7. This refers back to earlier in this chapter, when we explained that each level up the tree contains a pointer for every page of the level below it. If a level has 4,000 pages, then the next level up has 4,000 rows. You can see a more detailed version of this structure in Figure 6-2.

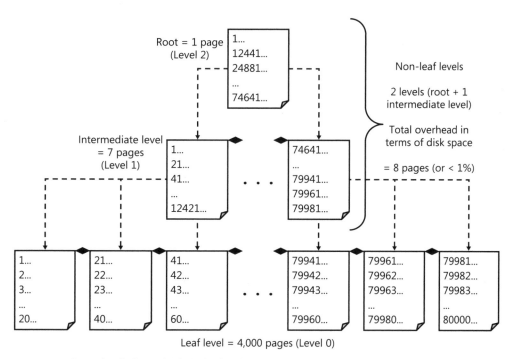

**FIGURE 6-2** Page details for multiple index levels

To understand both traversal as well as linkage further, you can use the *DBCC IND* command to see which pages have which data, as well as which pages precede and follow various pages in all levels of the index. In this case, we insert the results of *DBCC IND* into our *sp_tablepages* table in the *master* database so that we can access (and order) only specific columns of information:

```
TRUNCATE TABLE sp_tablepages;
INSERT sp_tablepages
        EXEC ('DBCC IND (IndexInternals, Employee, 1)');
GO

SELECT IndexLevel
    , PageFID
    , PagePID
    , PrevPageFID
    , PrevPagePID
    , NextPageFID
    , NextPagePID
FROM sp_tablepages
ORDER BY IndexLevel DESC, PrevPagePID;
GO
```

```
RESULT (abbreviated):
IndexLevel PageFID PagePID    PrevPageFID PrevPagePID NextPageFID NextPagePID
---------- ------- ---------- ----------- ----------- ----------- -----------
2          1       234        0           0           0           0

1          1       232        0           0           1           233
1          1       233        1           232         1           235
1          1       235        1           233         1           236
1          1       236        1           235         1           237
1          1       237        1           236         1           238
1          1       238        1           237         1           239
1          1       239        1           238         0           0

0          1       168        0           0           1           169
0          1       169        1           168         1           170
<snip>
0          1       4230       1           4229        1           4231
0          1       4231       1           4230        0           0

NULL       1       157        0           0           0           0
```

Because this table was created when the database was empty and because the clustered index was built after loading the data into a staging area (this is solely a separate location used for temporarily storing data—in this case, a different filegroup), this table's clustered index was able to use a completely contiguous range of pages within file 1. However, they are not completely contiguous from the root down because indexes are built from the leaf level up to the root as the rows are ordered for each of the levels. The most important thing to understand, however, is navigation. Imagine the following query:

```
SELECT e.*
FROM dbo.Employee AS e
WHERE e.EmployeeID = 27682;
```

To find all the data for a row with an *EmployeeID* of 27682 (remember, this is the clustering key value), SQL Server starts at the root page and navigates down to the leaf level. Based on the output shown previously, the root page is page 234 in *FileID* 1 (you can see this because the root page is the only page at the highest index level (*IndexLevel* = 2). To analyze the root page, we use *DBCC PAGE* with output style 3—and we make sure that the query window in SQL Server Management Studio is set to return grid results. The reason for this is that when using output style 3, the tabular set of a non-leaf page is returned to the grid results, separating the rows from the page header, which is returned to the messages window:

```
DBCC PAGE (IndexInternals, 1, 234, 3);
GO
```

```
RESULT:
FileId PageId Row     Level ChildFileId ChildPageId EmployeeID (key) KeyHashValue
------ ------ ------- ----- ----------- ----------- ---------------- ------------
1      234    0       2     1           232         NULL             NULL
1      234    1       2     1           233         12441            NULL
1      234    2       2     1           235         24881            NULL
1      234    3       2     1           236         37321            NULL
```

| 1 | 234 | 4 | 2 | 1 | 237 | 49761 | NULL |
| 1 | 234 | 5 | 2 | 1 | 238 | 62201 | NULL |
| 1 | 234 | 6 | 2 | 1 | 239 | 74641 | NULL |

Reviewing the output from *DBCC PAGE* for the root page, we can see the *EmployeeID* values at the start of each "child page" in the *EmployeeID* (key) column. And because these are based on ordered rows in the level below, we solely need to find the appropriate range. For the third page, you can see a low value of 24881, and for the fourth page, a low value of 37321. So if the value 27682 exists, it would have to be in the index area defined by this particular range. For navigational purposes, we must navigate down the tree using page (*ChildPageId*) 235 in *FileID* (*ChildFileId*) 1. To see this page's contents, we can again use *DBCC PAGE* with output style 3:

```
DBCC PAGE (IndexInternals, 1, 235, 3);
GO
```

```
RESULT (abbreviated):
FileId  PageId  Row    Level ChildFileId ChildPageId EmployeeID (key) KeyHashValue
------- ------  ------ ----- ----------- ----------- ---------------- ------------
1       235     0      1     1           1476        24881            NULL
...
1       235     139    1     1           1615        27661            NULL
1       235     140    1     1           1616        27681            NULL
1       235     141    1     1           1617        27701            NULL
...
1       235     621    1     1           2097        3730             NULL
```

Finally, if a row with an *EmployeeID* of 27682 exists, it must be on page 1,616 of *FileID* 1. Let's see if it is:

```
DBCC TRACEON(3604);
GO
DBCC PAGE (IndexInternals, 1, 1616, 3);
GO


...

Slot 1 Column 1 Offset 0x4 Length 4 Length (physical) 4
EmployeeID = 27682

Slot 1 Column 2 Offset 0x8 Length 60 Length (physical) 60
LastName = Arbariol

Slot 1 Column 3 Offset 0x44 Length 58 Length (physical) 58
FirstName = Burt

Slot 1 Column 4 Offset 0x7e Length 2 Length (physical) 2
MiddleInitial = R

Slot 1 Column 5 Offset 0x80 Length 11 Length (physical) 11
SSN = 373-00-8368

Slot 1 Column 6 Offset 0x8b Length 258 Length (physical) 258
OtherColumns = Junk
...
```

> **Note** *DBCC PAGE* returns all the details for the page; that is, the header and all data rows. In this condensed output, we see only the converted row values from output style 3 for our *EmployeeID* value of interest (27682). The header and all other rows have been removed.

By having traversed the structure for a row, we have reviewed two things—the index internals and the process by which a single data row can be found using a clustering key value. This method is used when performing a bookmark lookup from a nonclustered index to retrieve the data when the table is clustered. To understand fully how nonclustered indexes are used, we also need to know how a nonclustered index is stored and how it is traversed to get to the data.

# Nonclustered Index Structures

The contents of the leaf level of a nonclustered index depend on many factors: the definition of the nonclustered index key, the base table's structure (either a heap or a clustered index), the existence of any nonclustered index features such as included columns or filtered indexes, and finally, whether or not the nonclustered index is defined as unique.

To best understand nonclustered indexes, we continue using our *IndexInternals* database. This time, however, we review nonclustered indexes on two tables: the *Employee* table, which is clustered by the PRIMARY KEY constraint on the *EmployeeID* column, and the *EmployeeHeap* table, which does not have a clustered index. The *EmployeeHeap* table is an exact copy of the *Employee* table; however, it uses a nonclustered PRIMARY KEY constraint on the *EmployeeID* column instead of a clustered one. This is the first structure we review.

## Nonclustered Index Rows on a Heap

The *EmployeeHeap* table has exactly the same definition and data as the *Employee* table used in the prior example. Here is the *EmployeeHeap* table definition:

```
CREATE TABLE EmployeeHeap
    (EmployeeID      INT        NOT NULL      IDENTITY,
     LastName        NCHAR(30)  NOT NULL,
     FirstName       NCHAR(29)  NOT NULL,
     MiddleInitial   NCHAR(1)   NULL,
     SSN             CHAR(11)   NOT NULL,
     OtherColumns    CHAR(258)  NOT NULL      DEFAULT 'Junk');
GO
```

As with the *Employee* table, the data rows of the *EmployeeHeap* table are exactly 400 bytes per row and with 80,000 rows, this table also requires 4,000 data pages. To see the physical size of the data, you can use the *sys.dm_db_index_physical_stats* DMV discussed at the beginning of this chapter. We can confirm that this table is exactly the same (in terms of data) as the leaf level of the clustered index by using the DMV to see the number of pages, as well as the row length for the index with an *index_id* of 0 (the third parameter to the DMV):

```
SELECT index_depth AS D
    , index_level AS L
    , record_count AS 'Count'
    , page_count AS PgCnt
    , avg_page_space_used_in_percent AS 'PgPercentFull'
    , min_record_size_in_bytes AS 'MinLen'
    , max_record_size_in_bytes AS 'MaxLen'
    , avg_record_size_in_bytes AS 'AvgLen'
FROM sys.dm_db_index_physical_stats
    (DB_ID ('IndexInternals')
    , OBJECT_ID ('IndexInternals.dbo.EmployeeHeap')
    , 0, NULL, 'DETAILED');
GO


RESULT:
D   L   Count   PgCnt   PgPercentFull       MinLen  MaxLen  AvgLen
--- --- ------  ------- ------------------  ------- ------- ------
1   0   80000   4000    99.3081294786261    400     400     400
```

For the *EmployeeHeap* table, all the constraints are going to be created using nonclustered indexes. The following commands create the PRIMARY KEY as a nonclustered index on the *EmployeeID* column and a UNIQUE KEY as a nonclustered index on the *SSN* column:

```
-- Add a NONCLUSTERED PRIMARY KEY for EmployeeHeap
ALTER TABLE EmployeeHeap
  ADD CONSTRAINT EmployeeHeapPK
    PRIMARY KEY NONCLUSTERED (EmployeeID);
GO


-- Add the NONCLUSTERED UNIQUE KEY on SSN for EmployeeHeap
ALTER TABLE EmployeeHeap
  ADD CONSTRAINT SSNHeapUK
    UNIQUE NONCLUSTERED (SSN);
GO
```

To determine what's in the leaf level of a nonclustered index built on a heap, we first review the structure of the nonclustered index as shown by the DMV. For nonclustered indexes, we supply the specific index ID for parameter 3. To see the index ID assigned, we can use a query against *sys.indexes:*

```
SELECT index_depth AS D
    , index_level AS L
    , record_count AS 'Count'
    , page_count AS PgCnt
    , avg_page_space_used_in_percent AS 'PgPercentFull'
    , min_record_size_in_bytes AS 'MinLen'
    , max_record_size_in_bytes AS 'MaxLen'
    , avg_record_size_in_bytes AS 'AvgLen'
FROM sys.dm_db_index_physical_stats
    (DB_ID ('IndexInternals')
```

```
         , OBJECT_ID ('IndexInternals.dbo.EmployeeHeap')
         , 2, NULL, 'DETAILED');
GO
```

```
RESULT:
D   L   Count   PgCnt   PgPercentFull      MinLen   MaxLen   AvgLen
--- ---  ------  ------  ------------------ -------  -------  ------
2   0   80000   149     99.477291821102    13       13       13
2   1   149     1       23.9065974796145   11       11       11
```

In this case, the leaf level of the nonclustered index (level 0) shows a record count of 80,000 (based on the fact that there are 80,000 rows in the table) and a minimum, maximum, and average length of 13 (these are fixed-width index rows). This breaks down very clearly and easily—the nonclustered index is defined on the *EmployeeID* column (an integer of 4 bytes); the table is a heap so the data row's bookmark (the physical RID) is 8 bytes; and because this is a fixed-width row with no columns that allow NULL values, the row overhead is 1 byte (4 + 8 + 1 = 13 bytes). To see the data stored more specifically, we can use *DBCC IND* to review the leaf-level pages of this index:

```
TRUNCATE TABLE sp_tablepages;
INSERT sp_tablepages
        EXEC ('DBCC IND (IndexInternals, EmployeeHeap, 2)');
GO

SELECT IndexLevel
     , PageFID
     , PagePID
     , PrevPageFID
     , PrevPagePID
     , NextPageFID
     , NextPagePID
FROM sp_tablepages
ORDER BY IndexLevel DESC, PrevPagePID;
GO
```

```
RESULT (abbreviated):
IndexLevel PageFID PagePID    PrevPageFID PrevPagePID NextPageFID NextPagePID
---------- ------- ---------- ----------- ----------- ----------- -----------
1          1       8608       0           0           0           0

0          1       8544       0           0           1           8545
0          1       8545       1           8544        1           8546
...
0          1       8755       1           8754        1           8756
0          1       8756       1           8755        0           0

NULL       1       254        0           0           0           0
```

The root page is on page 8608 of *FileID* 1. Leaf-level pages are labeled with an *IndexLevel* of 0, so the first page of the leaf level is on page 8544 of *FileID* 1. To review the data on this page, we can use *DBCC PAGE* with output style 3. (The output for this leaf-level index page shows only the first 8 rows and the last 3 rows, out of a total of 539 rows.)

```
DBCC PAGE (IndexInternals, 1, 8544, 3);
GO
```

```
RESULT (abbreviated):
FileId PageId   Row    Level  EmployeeID (key)  HEAP RID              KeyHashValue
------ -------- ------ ------ ----------------  --------------------  ----------------
1      8544     0      0      1                 0xF500000001000000    (010086470766)
1      8544     1      0      2                 0xF500000001000100    (020068e8b274)
1      8544     2      0      3                 0xF500000001000200    (03000d8f0ecc)
1      8544     3      0      4                 0xF500000001000300    (0400b4b7d951)
1      8544     4      0      5                 0xF500000001000400    (0500d1d065e9)
1      8544     5      0      6                 0xF500000001000500    (06003f7fd0fb)
1      8544     6      0      7                 0xF500000001000600    (07005a186c43)
1      8544     7      0      8                 0xF500000001000700    (08000c080f1b)
...
1      8544     536    0      537               0xD211000001001000    (190098ec2ef0)
1      8544     537    0      538               0xD211000001001100    (1a0076439be2)
1      8544     538    0      539               0xD211000001001200    (1b001324275a)
```

From the output of *DBCC PAGE*, you can see that the leaf-level page of a nonclustered index on a heap has the index key column value (in this case, the *EmployeeID*), plus the actual data row's RID. The final value displayed is called *KeyHashValue*, which is not actually stored in the index row. It is a fixed-length string derived using a hash formula on all the key columns. This value is used to represent the row in certain other tools. One such tool that is discussed in Chapter 10 is the *sys.dm_tran_locks* DMV that shows the locks that are being held. When a lock is held on an index row, the list of locks displays *KeyHashValue* to indicate which key (or index row) is locked.

The RID can be converted to the *FileID:PageID:SlotNumber* format by using the following function:

```
CREATE FUNCTION convert_RIDs (@rid BINARY(8))
    RETURNS VARCHAR(30)
AS
    BEGIN
    RETURN (
        CONVERT (VARCHAR(5),
            CONVERT(INT, SUBSTRING(@rid, 6, 1)
            + SUBSTRING(@rid, 5, 1)) )
        + ':' +
        CONVERT(VARCHAR(10),
            CONVERT(INT, SUBSTRING(@rid, 4, 1)
            + SUBSTRING(@rid, 3, 1)
            + SUBSTRING(@rid, 2, 1)
            + SUBSTRING(@rid, 1, 1)) )
        + ':' +
        CONVERT(VARCHAR(5),
            CONVERT(INT, SUBSTRING(@rid, 8, 1)
            + SUBSTRING(@rid, 7, 1)) ) )
    END;
GO
```

With this function, you can find out the specific page number on which a row resides. For example, a row with an *EmployeeID* of 6 has a hexadecimal RID of 0xF500000001000500:

```
SELECT dbo.convert_RIDs (0xF500000001000500);
GO

RESULT:
1:245:5
```

Using the function, this converts to 1:245:5, which is comprised of *FileID* 1, *PageID* 245, and *SlotNumber* 5. To view this specific page, we can use *DBCC PAGE* and then review the data on slot 5 (to see if this is in fact the row with *EmployeeID* of 6):

```
DBCC PAGE (IndexInternals, 1, 245, 3);
GO

Slot 5 Column 1 Offset 0x4 Length 4 Length (physical) 4
EmployeeID = 6

Slot 5 Column 2 Offset 0x8 Length 60 Length (physical) 60
LastName = Anderson

Slot 5 Column 3 Offset 0x44 Length 58 Length (physical) 58
FirstName = Dreaxjktgvnhye

Slot 5 Column 4 Offset 0x7e Length 2 Length (physical) 2
MiddleInitial =

Slot 5 Column 5 Offset 0x80 Length 11 Length (physical) 11
SSN = 250-07-9751

Slot 5 Column 6 Offset 0x8b Length 258 Length (physical) 258
OtherColumns = Junk
...
```

In this case, you have seen the structure of a nonclustered index row in the leaf level of the nonclustered index, as well as how a bookmark lookup is performed using the heap's RID from the nonclustered index to the heap.

In terms of navigation, imagine the following query:

```
SELECT e.*
FROM dbo.EmployeeHeap AS e
WHERE e.EmployeeID = 27682;
```

Because this table is a heap, only nonclustered indexes can be used to navigate this data efficiently. And, in this case, we have a nonclustered index on *EmployeeID*. The first step is to go to the root page (as shown in the *DBCC IND* output earlier, the root page is page 8608 of *FileID* 1):

```
DBCC PAGE (IndexInternals, 1, 8608, 3);
GO
```

```
RESULT:
FileId  PageId  Row      Level  ChildFileId  ChildPageId  EmployeeID (key)  KeyHashValue
------- ------  -------  -----  -----------  -----------  ----------------  ------------
1       8608    0        1      1            8544         NULL              NULL
1       8608    1        1      1            8545         540               NULL
...
1       8608    49       1      1            8593         26412             NULL
1       8608    50       1      1            8594         26951             NULL
1       8608    51       1      1            8595         27490             NULL
1       8608    52       1      1            8596         28029             NULL
1       8608    53       1      1            8597         28568             NULL
1       8608    54       1      1            8598         29107             NULL
...
1       8608    147      1      1            8755         79234             NULL
1       8608    148      1      1            8756         79773             NULL
```

Using the *EmployeeID* column in this output, you can see a low value of 27490 for the child page 8595 in *FileID* 1, and then the next page has a low value of 28029. So if an *EmployeeID* of 27682 exists, it would have to be in the index area defined by this particular range. Then we must navigate down the tree using page (*ChildPageId*) 8595 in *FileID* (*ChildFileId*) 1. To see this page's contents, we can again use *DBCC PAGE* with output style 3:

```
DBCC PAGE (IndexInternals, 1, 8595, 3);
GO
```

```
RESULT:
FileId  PageId      Row     Level   EmployeeID (key)  HEAP RID            KeyHashValue
------  ----------- ------  ------  ----------------  ------------------  --------------
1       8595        0       0       27490             0x1617000001000900  (6200aa3b160b)
1       8595        1       0       27491             0x1617000001000A00  (6300cf5caab3)
...
1       8595        191     0       27681             0x2017000001000000  (2100fcdaf887)
1       8595        192     0       27682             0x2017000001000100  (220012754d95)
1       8595        193     0       27683             0x2017000001000200  (23007712f12d)

...
1       8595        538     0       28028             0x3117000001000700  (7c00b4675dbf)
```

> **Note**  The output returns 539 rows. In this condensed output, we see the first two rows, the last row, and then three rows surrounding the value of interest (27682).

From this point, you know how the navigation continues. SQL Server translates the data row's RID into the format of *FileID:PageID:SlotNumber* and proceeds to look up the corresponding data row in the heap.

## Nonclustered Index Rows on a Clustered Table

For nonclustered indexes on a table that has a clustered index, the leaf-level row structure is similar to that of a nonclustered index on a heap. The leaf level of the nonclustered index contains the index key and the bookmark lookup value (the clustering key). However, if the nonclustered index key has some columns in common with the clustering key, SQL Server stores the common columns only once in the nonclustered index row. For example, if the key of your clustered index is *EmployeeID,* and you have a nonclustered index on (*Lastname, EmployeeID, SSN*), then the index rows do not store the value of *EmployeeID* twice. In fact, the number of columns and the column order do not matter. For this example (as it's not generally a good practice to have a wide clustering key), imagine a clustering key that is defined on columns *b, e,* and *h*. The following nonclustered indexes would have these column(s) added to make up the nonclustered index leaf-level rows (the columns—if any—that are added to the leaf level of the nonclustered index, are italicized and bolded):

| Nonclustered Index Key | Nonclustered Leaf-Level Row |
| --- | --- |
| a | a, ***b, e, h*** |
| c, h, e | c, h, e, ***b*** |
| e | e, ***b, h*** |
| h | h, ***e, b*** |
| b, c, d | b, c, d, ***e, h*** |

To review the physical structures of a nonclustered index created on a table that is clustered, we review the UNIQUE constraint on the *SSN* column of the *Employee* table:

```
-- Add the NONCLUSTERED UNIQUE KEY on SSN for Employee
ALTER TABLE Employee
    ADD CONSTRAINT EmployeeSSNUK
        UNIQUE NONCLUSTERED (SSN);
GO
```

To gather information on the data size and number of levels, we use the DMV. However, before we can use the DMV, we need the specific index ID for parameter 3. To see the index ID assigned to this nonclustered index, we can use a query against *sys.indexes:*

```
SELECT name AS IndexName, index_id
FROM sys.indexes
WHERE [object_id] = OBJECT_ID ('Employee');
GO

RESULT:
IndexName          index_id
---------------- --------
EmployeePK         1
EmployeeSSNUK      2

SELECT index_depth AS D
     , index_level AS L
     , record_count AS 'Count'
     , page_count AS PgCnt
     , avg_page_space_used_in_percent AS 'PgPercentFull'
     , min_record_size_in_bytes AS 'MinLen'
```

```
    , max_record_size_in_bytes AS 'MaxLen'
    , avg_record_size_in_bytes AS 'AvgLen'
FROM sys.dm_db_index_physical_stats
    (DB_ID ('IndexInternals')
    , OBJECT_ID ('IndexInternals.dbo.Employee')
    , 2, NULL, 'DETAILED');
GO


RESULT:
D   L       Count   PgCnt   PgPercentFull     MinLen   MaxLen   AvgLen
--  ------- ------- ------- ----------------- -------- ------- ------
2   0       80000   179     99.3661106992834  16       16       16
2   1       179     1       44.2055843834939  18       18       18
```

In this case, the leaf level of the nonclustered index (level 0) shows a record count of 80,000 (there are 80,000 rows in the table) and a minimum, maximum, and average length of 16 (these are fixed-width index rows). This breaks down very clearly and easily—the nonclustered index is defined on the *SSN* column (a fixed-width character column of 11 bytes), the table has a clustering key of *EmployeeID* so the data row's bookmark (the clustering key) is 4 bytes, and because this row is a fixed-width row with no columns that allow NULL values, the row overhead is 1 byte (11 + 4 + 1 = 16 bytes). To see the data stored more specifically, we can use *DBCC IND* to review the leaf-level pages of this index:

```
TRUNCATE TABLE sp_tablepages;
INSERT sp_tablepages
        EXEC ('DBCC IND (IndexInternals, Employee, 2)');
GO


SELECT IndexLevel
    , PageFID
    , PagePID
    , PrevPageFID
    , PrevPagePID
    , NextPageFID
    , NextPagePID
FROM sp_tablepages
ORDER BY IndexLevel DESC, PrevPagePID;
GO


RESULT (abbreviated):
IndexLevel PageFID PagePID     PrevPageFID PrevPagePID NextPageFID NextPagePID
---------- ------- ----------- ----------- ----------- ----------- -----------
1          1       4328        0           0           0           0

0          1       4264        0           0           1           4265
0          1       4265        1           4264        1           4266
...
0          1       4505        1           4504        1           4506
0          1       4506        1           4505        0           0

NULL       1       158         0           0           0           0
```

The root page is on page 4328 of *FileID* 1. Leaf-level pages are labeled with an *IndexLevel* of 0, so the first page of the leaf level is on page 4264 of *FileID* 1. To review the data on this page, we can use *DBCC PAGE* with format 3:

```
DBCC PAGE (IndexInternals, 1, 4264, 3);
GO
```

```
RESULT (abbreviated):
FileId PageId     Row    Level  SSN (key)    EmployeeID  KeyHashValue
------ ---------- ------ ------ -----------  ----------- ----------------
1      4264       0      0      000-00-0184  31101       (fd00604642ee)
1      4264       1      0      000-00-0236  22669       (fb00de40fee1)
1      4264       2      0      000-00-0395  18705       (0101d993da83)
...
1      4264       446    0      013-00-5906  44969       (ff00355b1727)
1      4264       447    0      013-00-5982  7176        (03012415a3e8)
1      4264       448    0      013-00-6001  11932       (f100f75a17a4)
```

From the output of *DBCC PAGE*, you can see that the leaf-level page of a nonclustered index on a clustered table has actual column values for both the index key (in this case, the *SSN* column) and the data row's bookmark, which in this case is the *EmployeeID*. And this is an actual value, copied into the leaf level of the nonclustered index. Had the clustering key been wider, the leaf level of the nonclustered index would have been wider as well.

In terms of navigation, review the following query:

```
SELECT e.*
FROM dbo.Employee AS e
WHERE e.SSN = '123-45-6789';
```

To find all the data for a row with a *SSN* of 123-45-6789, SQL Server starts at the root page and navigates down to the leaf level. Based on the output shown previously, the root page is in page 4328 of *FileID* 1 (you can see this because the root page is the only page at the highest index level (*IndexLevel* = 1). We could perform the same analysis as before and follow the navigation through the B-tree, but this is left as an exercise for you, if you wish.

## Nonunique Nonclustered Index Rows

You now know that the leaf level of a nonclustered index must have a bookmark because from the leaf level, you want to be able to find the actual data row. The non-leaf levels of a nonclustered index need only help us traverse down to pages at the lower levels. In the case of a unique nonclustered index (such as in the previous examples of PRIMARY KEY and UNIQUE constraint indexes), the non-leaf level rows contain only the nonclustered index key values and the child-page pointer. However, if the index is *not* unique, the non-leaf level rows contain the nonclustered index key values, the child-page pointer, and the bookmark value. In other words, the bookmark value is added to the nonclustered index key in a nonunique, nonclustered index to guarantee uniqueness (as the bookmark, by definition, must be unique).

Keep in the mind that for the purposes of creating the index rows, SQL Server doesn't care whether the keys in the nonunique index actually contain duplicates. If the index is not defined to be unique, even if all the values are unique, the non-leaf index rows always contain the bookmark.

You can easily see this by creating the following three indexes to review both their leaf and non-leaf level row sizes:

```
CREATE NONCLUSTERED INDEX TestTreeStructure
ON Employee (SSN);
GO

CREATE UNIQUE NONCLUSTERED INDEX TestTreeStructureUnique1
ON Employee (SSN);
GO

CREATE UNIQUE NONCLUSTERED INDEX TestTreeStructureUnique2
ON Employee (SSN, EmployeeID);
GO

SELECT si.[name] AS iname
    , index_depth AS D
    , index_level AS L
    , record_count AS 'Count'
    , page_count AS PgCnt
    , avg_page_space_used_in_percent AS 'PgPercentFull'
    , min_record_size_in_bytes AS 'MinLen'
    , max_record_size_in_bytes AS 'MaxLen'
    , avg_record_size_in_bytes AS 'AvgLen'
FROM sys.dm_db_index_physical_stats
    (DB_ID ('IndexInternals')
    , OBJECT_ID ('IndexInternals.dbo.Employee')
    , NULL, NULL, 'DETAILED') ps
    INNER JOIN sys.indexes si
        ON ps.[object_id] = si.[object_id]
            AND ps.[index_id] = si.[index_id]
WHERE ps.[index_id] > 2;
GO
```

```
RESULT:
iname                        D L Count PgCnt PgPercentFull    MinLen MaxLen AvgLen
--------------------------   - - ----- ----- ---------------- ------ ------ ------
TestTreeStructure            2 0 80000 179   99.3661106992834 16     16     16
TestTreeStructure            2 1 179   1     53.0516431924883 22     22     22
TestTreeStructureUnique1     2 0 80000 179   99.3661106992834 16     16     16
TestTreeStructureUnique1     2 1 179   1     44.2055843834939 18     18     18
TestTreeStructureUnique2     2 0 80000 179   99.3661106992834 16     16     16
TestTreeStructureUnique2     2 1 179   1     53.0516431924883 22     22     22
```

Notice that the leaf level (level 0) of all three indexes is identical in all columns: *Count* (*record_count*), *PgCnt* (*page_count*), *PgPercentFull* (*avg_space_used_in_percent*), and all three length columns. For the non-leaf level of the indexes (which are very small), you can see that the lengths vary—for the first (*TestTreeStructure*) and the third (*TestTreeStructureUnique2*), the non-leaf levels are identical. The first index has the *EmployeeID* added because it's the clustering key (therefore the bookmark). The third index has *EmployeeID* already in the index—there's no need to add it again. However, in the first index, because it was not defined as unique, SQL Server had to add the clustering key all the way up the tree. For the second index—which was unique on *SSN* alone—SQL Server did not include *EmployeeID* all the way up the tree. If you're interested, you can continue to analyze these structures using *DBCC IND* and *DBCC PAGE* to view the physical row structures further.

## Nonclustered Index Rows with Included Columns (Using *INCLUDE*)

In all nonclustered indexes so far, we have focused on the physical aspects of indexes created by constraints or indexes created to test physical structures. Nowhere have we approached the limits of index key size, which are 900 bytes or 16 columns, whichever comes first. The reason that these limits exist is to help to ensure index tree scalability. However, this has also traditionally limited the maximum number of columns that can be indexed.

In some cases, adding columns in an index allows SQL Server to eliminate the bookmark lookup when accessing data for a range query, a concept called *covering indexes*. A covering index is a nonclustered index in which all the information needed to satisfy a query can be found in the leaf level, so SQL Server doesn't have to access the data pages at all. This can be a powerful tool for optimizing some of your more complex range-based queries.

Instead of adding columns to the nonclustered index key, and making the tree deeper, columns for a covering index can be added to the index rows without becoming part of the key using the *INCLUDE* syntax. It is a very simple addition to your *CREATE INDEX* command:

```
CREATE [UNIQUE] [CLUSTERED | NONCLUSTERED] INDEX index_name
   ON table_name (column_name [ASC | DESC][,...n])
      [ INCLUDE ( column_name [ ,...n ] ) ]
```

These columns listed after the keyword *INCLUDE* allow you to exceed the 900-byte or 16-key column limits in the leaf level of a nonclustered index. The included columns appear only in the leaf level and do not affect the sort order of the index rows in any way. In certain situations, SQL Server can silently add an included column to your indexes. This might happen when an index is created on a partitioned table and no ON filegroup or ON *partition_scheme_name* is specified.

## Nonclustered Index Rows with Filters (Filtered Indexes)

Without using filters, the leaf level of a nonclustered index contains one index row for every row of data in the table, in logical order based on the index definition. New in SQL Server 2008, you can add a filter predicate to your nonclustered index definition. This allows SQL Server to create nonclustered index rows only for data that matches your predicate, thus limiting the size of the nonclustered index. This can be extremely useful if you have one of the following situations:

- When a column contains mostly NULL values and where queries retrieve only the rows where the data is NOT NULL. This is especially useful when combined with *SPARSE* columns.

- When a column contains only a limited number of interesting values or you want to enforce uniqueness only for a set of values. For example, what if you wanted to allow NULL values for the *SSN* column of the *Employee* table? Using a constraint, SQL Server allows only a single row to be NULL. However, using a filtered index you can create a unique index over only the rows where the *SSN* is not NULL. The syntax would look like the following:

```
CREATE UNIQUE NONCLUSTERED INDEX SSN_NOT_NULLs
ON Employee (SSN)
WHERE SSN IS NOT NULL;
```

- When queries retrieve only a particular range of data and you want to add indexes to this data but not the entire table. For example, you have a table which is partitioned by month and covers three years worth of data (2008, 2007, and 2006) and a team wants to heavily analyze data in the fourth quarter of 2007. Instead of creating wider nonclustered indexes for all your data, you can create indexes (possibly using *INCLUDE* as well) that focus only on:

```
WHERE SalesDate > '20071001' AND SalesDate < '20080101';
```

The end result of an index created with a filter is that the leaf level of the nonclustered index contains a row only if the row matches the filter definition. And the column over which the filter is defined does not need to be in the key, or even in an included column; however, that can help to make the index more useful for certain queries. You can use *DBCC IND*, *DBCC PAGE*, and, the previously mentioned, DMVs to review the size and structure for indexes with filters.

# Special Index Structures

SQL Server 2008 allows you to create several special kinds of indexes: indexes on computed columns, indexes on views, spatial indexes, full-text indexes, and XML indexes. This section covers the requirements and the structural differences of creating these types of indexes.

## Indexes on Computed Columns and Indexed Views

Without indexes, some of these constructs—computed columns and views—are purely logical. There is no physical storage for the data involved. A computed column is not stored with the table data; it is recomputed every time a row is accessed (unless the computed column is marked as PERSISTED). A view does not save any data; it basically saves a *SELECT* statement that is executed again every time the data in the view is accessed. With these special indexes, SQL Server actually materializes what was only logical data into the physical leaf level of an index.

## Prerequisites

Before you can create indexes on either computed columns or views, certain prerequisites must be met. The biggest issue is that SQL Server must be able to guarantee that given the identical base table data, the same values are always returned for any computed columns or for the rows in a view (that is, the computed columns and views are *deterministic*). To guarantee that the same values are always generated, these special indexes have three categories of requirements. First, a number of session-level options must be set to a specific value. Second, there are some restrictions on the functions that can be used within the computed column or view definition. The third requirement, which applies only to indexed views, is that the tables that the view is based on must meet certain criteria.

## SET Options

The following seven SET options can affect the resulting value of an expression or predicate, so you must set them as shown to create indexed views or indexes on computed columns:

```
SET CONCAT_NULL_YIELDS_NULL ON
SET QUOTED_IDENTIFIER ON
SET ANSI_NULLS ON
SET ANSI_PADDING ON
SET ANSI_WARNINGS ON
SET NUMERIC_ROUNDABORT OFF
```

Note that all the options have to be ON except the NUMERIC_ROUNDABORT option, which has to be OFF. Technically, the option ARITHABORT must also be set to ON. And, when your database is set to 90 compatibility mode or higher, setting ANSI_WARNINGS to ON automatically sets ARITHABORT to ON, so you do not need to set it separately. If any of these options are not set as specified, you get an error message when you try to create a special index. In addition, if you've already created one of these indexes, after which you change the SET option settings, and then attempt to modify the computed column or view on which the index is based, you get an error. If you issue a *SELECT* that normally should use the index, and if the SET options do not have the values indicated, the index is ignored but no error is generated.

There are a couple of ways to determine whether the SET options are set appropriately before you create one of these special indexes. You can use the function *SESSIONPROPERTY* to test the settings for your current connection. A returned value of 1 means that the setting is ON, and a 0 means that it is OFF. The following example checks the current session setting for the option NUMERIC_ROUNDABORT:

```
SELECT SESSIONPROPERTY ('NUMERIC_ROUNDABORT');
```

Alternatively, you can use the *sys.dm_exec_sessions* DMV to check the SET options for any connection. The following query returns the values for five of the previously discussed six SET options for the current session:

```
SELECT quoted_identifier, arithabort, ansi_warnings,
       ansi_padding, ansi_nulls, concat_null_yields_null
FROM sys.dm_exec_sessions
WHERE session_id = @@spid;
```

Unfortunately, NUMERIC_ROUNDABORT is not included in the *sys.dm_exec_sessions* DMV results. There is no way to see the setting for that value for any other connections besides the current one.

## Permissible Functions

A function is either *deterministic* or *nondeterministic*. If the function returns the same result every time it is called with the same set of input values, it is deterministic. If it can return different results when called with the same set of input values, it is nondeterministic. For the purposes of indexes, a function is considered deterministic if it always returns the same values for the same input values when all the SET options have the required settings. Any function used in a computed column's definition or used in the *SELECT* list or WHERE clause of an indexable view must be deterministic.

**More Info**  *SQL Server Books Online* contains a complete list of which supplied functions are deterministic and which are nondeterministic. Some functions can be either deterministic or nondeterministic, depending on how they are used, and *SQL Server Books Online* also describes these functions.

It might seem that the list of nondeterministic functions is quite restrictive, but SQL Server must be able to guarantee that the values stored in the index are consistent. In some cases, the restrictions might be overly cautious, but the downside of being not cautious enough would be that your indexed views or indexes on computed columns are meaningless. The same restrictions apply to functions you use in your own user-defined functions (UDFs)—that is, your own functions cannot be based on any nondeterministic built-in function. You can verify the determinism property of any function by using the *OBJECTPROPERTY* function:

```
SELECT OBJECTPROPERTY (object_id('<function_name>'), 'IsDeterministic')
```

Even if a function is deterministic, if it contains *float* or *real* expressions, the result of the function might vary with different processors depending on the processor architecture or microcode version. Expressions or functions containing values of the data type *float* or *real* are therefore considered to be *imprecise*. To guarantee consistent values even when moving a database from one machine to another (by detaching and attaching, or by performing backup and restore), imprecise values can be used only in key columns of indexes if they are physically stored in the database and not recomputed. An imprecise value can be used if it is the value of a stored column in a table or if it is a computed column that is marked as persisted. We discuss persisted columns in more detail in the upcoming section entitled "Indexes on Computed Columns."

## Schema Binding

To create an indexed view, a requirement on the table itself is that the definition of any underlying object's schema cannot change. To prevent a change in schema definition, the *CREATE VIEW* statement allows the WITH SCHEMABINDING option. When you specify WITH SCHEMABINDING, the *SELECT* statement that defines the view must include the two-part names (*schema.object*) of all referenced tables. You can't drop the table or alter the columns that participate in a view created with the WITH SCHEMABINDING clause unless you've dropped that view or changed the view so that it's no longer schemabound. Otherwise, SQL Server raises an error. If any of the tables on which the view is based are owned by someone other than the user creating the view, the view creator doesn't automatically have the right to create the view with schema binding because that would restrict the table's owner from making changes to her own table. A user must be granted REFERENCES permission on a table to create a view with schema binding on that table. We will see an example of schema binding in a moment.

## Indexes on Computed Columns

SQL Server 2008 allows you to build indexes on deterministic, precise (and persisted imprecise) computed columns where the resulting data type is otherwise indexable. This means that the column's data type cannot be any of the LOB data types (such as *text, varchar(max)*, or *XML*). Such a computed column can be an index key, included column, or part of a PRIMARY KEY or UNIQUE constraint. You cannot define a FOREIGN KEY, CHECK, or DEFAULT constraint on a computed column, and computed columns are always considered nullable unless you enclose the expression in the *ISNULL* function. When you create an index on computed columns, the six previously mentioned SET options must first have the correct values set.

Here's an example:

```
CREATE TABLE t1 (a INT, b as 2*a);
GO
CREATE INDEX i1 ON t1 (b);
GO
```

If any of your SET options does not have the correct value when you create the table, you get this message when you try to create the index:

```
Server: Msg 1935, Level 16, State 1, Line 2
Cannot create index. Object '<tname>' was created with the following SET options off:
    '<option(s)>'.
```

If more than one option has an incorrect value, the error message reports them all.

Here's an example that creates a table with a nondeterministic computed column:

```
CREATE TABLE t2 (a INT, b DATETIME, c AS DATENAME(MM, b));
GO
CREATE INDEX i2 ON t2 (c);
GO
```

When you try to create the index on the computed column *c*, you get this error:

```
Msg 2729, Level 16, State 1, Line 1
Column 'c' in table 't2' cannot be used in an index or statistics or as a partition key
    because it is nondeterministic.
```

Column *c* is nondeterministic because the month value of *DATENAME()* can have different values depending on the language you're using.

**Using the *COLUMNPROPERTY* Function**    You can use the *IsDeterministic* column property to determine before you create an index on a computed column (or on a view) whether that column is deterministic. If you specify this property, the *COLUMNPROPERTY* function returns 1 if the column is deterministic and 0 otherwise. The result is undefined for columns that are neither computed columns nor columns in a view, so you should consider checking the *IsComputed* property before you check the *IsDeterministic* property. The following example detects that column *c* in table *t2* in the previous example is nondeterministic:

```
SELECT COLUMNPROPERTY (OBJECT_ID('t2'), 'c', 'IsDeterministic');
```

The value 0 is returned, which means that column *c* is nondeterministic. Note that the *COLUMNPROPERTY* function requires an object ID for the first argument and a column name for the second argument.

However, the *COLUMNPROPERTY* function also has a property of *IsIndexable*. That's probably the easiest to use for a quick check, but it won't give you the reason if the column is not indexable. For that, you should check these other properties.

## Implementation of a Computed Column

If you create a clustered index on a computed column, the computed column is no longer a virtual column in the table. The computed value physically exists in the rows of the table, which is the leaf level of the clustered index. Updates to the columns that the computed column is based on also update the computed column in the table itself. For example, in the *t1* table created previously, if we insert a row with the value 10 in column *a*, the row is created with both the values 10 and 20 in the actual data row. If we then update the 10 to 15, the second column is updated automatically to 30.

**Persisted Columns**    The ability to mark a computed column as PERSISTED (a feature introduced in SQL Server 2005) allows storage of computed values in a table, even before you build an index. In fact, this feature was added to the product to allow columns of computed values from underlying table columns of type *float* or *real* to have indexes built on them. The alternative, when you want an index on such a column, would be to drop and re-create the underlying column, which can involve an enormous amount of overhead on a large table.

Here's an example. In the *Northwind* database, the *Order Details* table has a column called *Discount* that is of type *real*. The following code adds a computed column called *Final* that shows the total price for an item after the discount is applied. The statement to build an index on *Final* fails because the resultant column involving the *real* value is imprecise and not persisted:

```
USE Northwind;
GO
ALTER TABLE [Order Details]
    ADD Final AS
    (Quantity * UnitPrice) - Discount * (Quantity * UnitPrice);
GO
```

```
CREATE INDEX OD_Final_Index on [Order Details](Final);
GO

Error Message:
Msg 2799, Level 16, State 1, Line 1
Cannot create index or statistics 'OD_Final_Index' on table 'Order Details'
    because the computed column 'Final' is imprecise and not persisted. Consider removing
    column from index or statistics key or marking computed column persisted.
```

Without persisted computed columns, the only way to create an index on a computed column containing the final price would be to drop the *Discount* column from the table and redefine it. Any existing indexes on *Discount* would have to be dropped as well, and then rebuilt. With persisted computed columns, all you need to do is drop the computed column (which is a metadata-only operation) and then redefine it as a persisted computed column. You can then build the index on the column:

```
ALTER TABLE [Order Details]
    DROP COLUMN Final;
GO
ALTER TABLE [Order Details]
    ADD Final AS
    (Quantity * UnitPrice) - Discount * (Quantity * UnitPrice) PERSISTED;
GO
CREATE INDEX OD_Final_Index on [Order Details](Final);
```

When determining whether you have to use the PERSISTED option, use the *COLUMNPROPERTY* function and the *IsPrecise* property to determine whether a deterministic column is precise:

```
SELECT COLUMNPROPERTY (OBJECT_ID ('Order Details'), 'Final', 'IsPrecise');
```

You can also use persisted computed columns when you define partitions. A computed column that is used as the partitioning column must be explicitly marked as PERSISTED, whether it is precise or imprecise. We look at partitioning in Chapter 7.

## Indexed Views

Indexed views in SQL Server are similar to what other products call *materialized views*. One of the most important benefits of indexed views is the ability to materialize summary aggregates of large tables. For example, consider a customer table containing rows for several million U.S.-based customers, from which you want information regarding customers in each state. You can create a view based on a *GROUP BY* query, grouping by state and containing the count of orders per state. Normal views are only named, saved queries and do not store the results. Every time the view is referenced, the aggregation to produce the grouped results must be recomputed. When you create an index on the view, the aggregated data is stored in the leaf level of the index. So instead of millions of customer rows, your indexed view has only 50 rows—one for each state. Your aggregate reporting queries can then be processed using the indexed views without having to scan the underlying, large tables.

The first index you must build on a view is a clustered index, and because the clustered index contains all the data at its leaf level, this index actually does the materialization of the view. The view's data is physically stored at the leaf level of the clustered index.

## Additional Requirements

In addition to the requirement that all functions used in the view must be deterministic, and that the required SET options must be set to the appropriate values, the view definition can't contain any of the following:

- *TOP*
- LOB columns
- *DISTINCT*
- *MIN, MAX, COUNT(*), COUNT(<expression>), STDEV, VARIANCE, AVG*
- *SUM* on a nullable expression
- A derived table
- The *ROWSET* function
- Another view (you can reference only base tables)
- *UNION*
- Subqueries, OUTER joins, or self-joins
- Full-text predicates (*CONTAINS, FREETEXT*)
- *COMPUTE, COMPUTE BY*
- *ORDER BY*

Also, if the view definition contains *GROUP BY*, the *SELECT* list must include the aggregate *COUNT_BIG (*)*. *COUNT_BIG* returns a *BIGINT*, which is an 8-byte integer. A view that contains *GROUP BY* can't contain *HAVING, CUBE, ROLLUP,* or *GROUP BY ALL*. Also, all *GROUP BY* columns must appear in the *SELECT* list. Note that if your view contains both *SUM* and *COUNT_BIG (*)*, you can compute the equivalent of the *AVG* aggregate function even though *AVG* is not allowed in indexed views. Although these restrictions might seem severe, remember that they apply to the view definitions, not to the queries that might use the indexed views.

To verify that you've met all the requirements, you can use the *OBJECTPROPERTY* function's *IsIndexable* property. The following query tells you whether you can build an index on a view called *Product Totals*:

```
SELECT OBJECTPROPERTY (OBJECT_ID ('Product_Totals'), 'IsIndexable');
```

A return value of 1 means you've met all requirements and can build an index on the view.

## Creating an Indexed View

The first step in building an index on a view is to create the view itself. Here's an example from the *AdventureWorks2008* database:

```
USE AdventureWorks2008;
GO
CREATE VIEW Vdiscount1
WITH SCHEMABINDING
AS SELECT SUM (UnitPrice*OrderQty) AS SumPrice
    , SUM (UnitPrice * OrderQty * (1.00 - UnitPriceDiscount))
        AS SumDiscountPrice
    , COUNT_BIG (*) AS Count
    , ProductID
FROM Sales.SalesOrderDetail
GROUP BY ProductID;
```

Notice the WITH SCHEMABINDING clause and the specification of the schema name (*Sales*) for the table. At this point, we have a normal view—a stored *SELECT* statement that uses no storage space. In fact, if we look at the data in *sys.dm_db_partition_stats* for this view, we see that no rows are returned:

```
SELECT si.name AS index_name,
     ps.used_page_count, ps.reserved_page_count, ps.row_count
FROM sys.dm_db_partition_stats AS ps
    JOIN sys.indexes AS si
        ON ps.[object_id] = si.[object_id]
WHERE ps.[object_id] = OBJECT_ID ('dbo.Vdiscount1');
```

To create an indexed view, you must first create a *unique clustered index*. The clustered index on a view contains all the data that makes up the view definition. This statement defines a unique clustered index for the view:

```
CREATE UNIQUE CLUSTERED INDEX VDiscount_Idx ON Vdiscount1 (ProductID);
```

Once the indexed view has been created, re-run the previous *SELECT* statement to see the pages materialized by the index on the view.

```
RESULT:
index_name      used_page_count      reserved_page_count  row_count
-------------   --------------------  -------------------- ---------
VDiscountIdx    4                     4                    266
```

Data that comprises the indexed view is persistent, with the indexed view storing the data in the clustered index's leaf level. You could construct something similar by using temporary tables to store the data you're interested in. But a temporary table is static and doesn't reflect changes to underlying data. In contrast, SQL Server automatically maintains indexed views, updating information stored in the clustered index whenever anyone changes data that affects the view.

After you create the unique clustered index, you can create multiple nonclustered indexes on the view. You can determine whether a view is indexed by using the *OBJECTPROPERTY* function's *IsIndexed* property. For the *Vdiscount1* indexed view, the following statement returns a 1, which means the view is indexed:

```
SELECT OBJECTPROPERTY (OBJECT_ID ('Vdiscount1'), 'IsIndexed');
```

Once a view is indexed, metadata about space usage and location is available through the catalog views, just as for any other index.

## Using an Indexed View

One of the most valuable benefits of indexed views is that your queries don't have to reference a view directly to use the index on the view. Consider the *Vdiscount1* indexed view. Suppose that you issue the following *SELECT* statement:

```
SELECT ProductID, total_sales = SUM (UnitPrice * OrderQty)
FROM  Sales.SalesOrderDetail
GROUP BY ProductID;
```

The Query Optimizer recognizes that the precomputed sums of all the *UnitPrice * OrderQty* values for each *ProductID* are already available in the index for the *Vdiscount1* view. The Query Optimizer evaluates the cost of using that indexed view in processing the query, and the indexed view very likely is used to access the information required to satisfy this query—the *Sales.SalesOrderDetail* table might never be touched at all.

> **Note** Although you can create indexed views in any edition of SQL Server 2008, for the Query Optimizer to consider using them even when they aren't referenced in the query, the engine edition of your SQL Server 2008 must be Enterprise, Developer, or Evaluation.

Just because you have an indexed view doesn't mean the Query Optimizer will always choose it for the query's execution plan. In fact, even if you reference the indexed view directly in the FROM clause, the Query Optimizer might access the base table directly instead. To make sure that an indexed view in your FROM clause is not expanded into its underlying *SELECT* statement, you can use the NOEXPAND hint in the FROM clause. Some of the internals of index selection, query optimization, and indexed view usage are discussed in more detail in Chapter 8.

## Full-Text Indexes

Full-text indexes are special-purpose indexes that support the full-text search feature—the ability to search efficiently through character and binary columns in a table. The specifics of creating and using full-text indexes are beyond the scope of this book, but *SQL Server Books Online* has a comprehensive section describing full-text indexing.

Full-text indexes are inverted, stacked, and compressed indexes that are stored in the database in internal tables for convenience. The full-text index data is stored in regular index rows in the internal tables, but the majority of the row is opaque to everything except the full-text engine itself (tools like *DBCC PAGE* cannot properly crack open all fields in the rows).

The storage for full-text indexes is the same as for regular indexes, but as they are stored as internal tables, regular methods of finding their structures do not work. For instance, the

*HumanResources.JobCandidate* table in the *AdventureWorks2008* database has a full-text index. To find the object IDs of the internal table(s) in which the full-text index is stored, the following T-SQL can be used to query the *sys.internal_tables* catalog view:

```
USE AdventureWorks2008;
GO
SELECT [name], [object_id] FROM sys.internal_tables
WHERE parent_object_id = OBJECT_ID ('HumanResources.JobCandidate');
GO

RESULT:
name                                            object_id
----------------------------------------------- -----------
fulltext_index_docidstatus_1333579789           2046630334
fulltext_docidfilter_1333579789                 2062630391
fulltext_indexeddocid_1333579789                2078630448
fulltext_avdl_1333579789                        2094630505
```

The regular methods for examining index structures can then be employed, using the object ID returned from *sys.internal_tables*. The same method works for spatial indexes and XML indexes, described next.

As you can see, internal tables have a different root in the system catalogs compared to regular tables and indexes, although their space usage is tracked in exactly the same way (using IAM pages) and their structures are the same as regular indexes. The *SQL Server Books Online* section "Internal Tables" contains a detailed explanation of them, including an entity-relationship diagram of the relevant system catalogs and various queries to view information about them.

## Spatial Indexes

A spatial index contains a decomposed view of all values in a spatial data type column in a table. The decomposed values are used for fuzzy-pruning of matching values during spatial comparison operations. As for full-text indexes, the specifics of creating and using spatial indexes are beyond the scope of this book, but *SQL Server Books Online* has an excellent section describing them. See the topic "Spatial Indexing Overview."

A spatial index is a clustered index that is stored as an internal table. Apart from storing the decomposed spatial values, it has exactly the same structure as a regular index.

## XML Indexes

An XML index provides an efficient mechanism for searching XML BLOB values by storing a shredded representation of the XML data that can be searched with regular B-tree methods, instead of having to walk through a (potentially large) XML BLOB. As with full-text and spatial indexes, the specifics of creating and using XML indexes are beyond the scope of this book, but *SQL Server Books Online* has an excellent section describing them. See the topic "Indexes on XML Data Types."

There are two types of XML indexes; primary XML indexes and secondary XML indexes. A primary XML index is a shredded representation of each value in the XML column being indexed, with one row for each node in the XML BLOB. A primary XML index is a clustered index and is stored as an internal table. A secondary XML index is a nonclustered index on the primary XML index and provides the same function as a regular nonclustered index; a different access path to the data using a different sort order. The internal structures of these indexes are the same as those for regular indexes.

# Data Modification Internals

We've seen how SQL Server stores data and index information. Now we look at what SQL Server actually does internally when your data is modified. We've seen how clustered indexes define logical order to your data and how a heap is nothing more than a collection of unordered pages. We've seen how nonclustered indexes are structures stored separately from the data and how that data is a copy of the actual table's data, defined by the index definition. And, as a rule of thumb, you should always have a clustered index on a table. The SQL Customer Advisory Team published a white paper in mid-2007 that compares various table structures and essentially supports this view; see *http://www.microsoft.com/ technet/prodtechnol/sql/bestpractice/clusivsh.mspx*. In this section, we review how SQL Server deals with the existence of indexes when processing data modification statements.

Note that for every *INSERT, UPDATE,* and *DELETE* operation on a table, the equivalent operation also happens to every nonclustered index on the table. The mechanisms described in this section apply equally to clustered and nonclustered indexes. Any modifications to the table are made to the heap or clustered index first, then to each nonclustered index in turn.

In SQL Server 2008, the exception to this rule is filtered indexes, where the filter predicate means the filtered nonclustered index may not have a matching row for the table row being modified. When changes are made to the table, the filtered index predicate is evaluated to determine whether it is necessary to apply the same operation to the filtered nonclustered index.

## Inserting Rows

When inserting a new row into a table, SQL Server must determine where to put the data, as well as insert a corresponding row into each nonclustered index. Each operation follows the same pattern: modify the appropriate data page (based on whether or not the table has a clustered index) and then insert the corresponding index rows into the leaf level of each nonclustered index.

When a table has no clustered index—that is, when the table is a heap—a new row is always inserted wherever room is available in the table. In Chapter 3, you learned how IAMs keep track of which extents in a file already belong to a table and in Chapter 5, you saw how the PFS pages indicate which of the pages in those extents have available space. If no pages with space are available, SQL Server tries to find unallocated pages from existing uniform extents that already belong to the object. If none exists, SQL Server must allocate a whole new extent to the table. Chapter 3 discussed how the Global Allocated Maps (GAMs) and Shared Global Allocation Maps (SGAMs) are used to find extents available to be allocated to an object. So, although locating space in which to do an *INSERT* is relatively efficient using the PFS and IAM, because the location of a row (on *INSERT*) is not defined, determining where to place a row within a heap is usually less efficient than if the table has a clustered index.

For an *INSERT* into a table with a clustered index and for index rows being inserted into nonclustered indexes, the row (regardless of whether it's a data row or an index row) always has a specific location within the index where it must be inserted, based on the value the new row has for the index key columns. An *INSERT* occurs either when the new row is the direct result of an *INSERT* or when it's the result of an *UPDATE* statement that either causes the row to move or for an index key column to change. When a row has to move to a new page, the *UPDATE* statement is internally executed using a *DELETE* followed by an *INSERT* (the *DELETE/ INSERT* strategy). New rows are inserted based on their index key position, and SQL Server splices in a new page via a page split if the current leaf level (a data page if this is the clustered index or an index page if this is a nonclustered index) has no room. Because the index dictates a particular ordering for the rows in the leaf level of the index, every new row has a specific location where it belongs. If there's no room for the new row on the page where it belongs, a new page must be allocated and linked into the B-tree. If possible, this new page is allocated from the same extent as the other pages to which it is linked. If the extent is already full (which is usually the case), a new extent (eight pages or 64 KB) is allocated to the object. As described in Chapter 3, SQL Server uses the GAM pages to find an available extent.

## Splitting Pages

After SQL Server finds the new page, the original page must be split; half the rows (the first half based on the slot array on the page) are left on the original page, and the other half are moved to the new page (or as close to a 50/50 split as possible). In some cases, SQL Server finds that even after the split, there's not enough room for the new row, which, because of variable-length fields, could potentially be much larger than any of the existing rows on the pages. As part of the split, SQL Server must add a corresponding entry for every new page into the parent page of the level above. One row is added if only a single split is needed. However, if the new row still won't fit after a single split, there can be potentially multiple new pages and multiple additions to the parent page. For example, consider a page with 32 rows on it. Suppose that SQL Server tries to insert a new row with 8,000 bytes. It splits the page once, and the new 8,000-byte row won't fit. Even after a second split, the new row won't fit. Eventually, SQL Server recognizes that the new row cannot fit on a page with any other rows, and it allocates a new page to hold only the new row. Quite a few splits occur, resulting in many new pages, and many new rows on the parent page.

An index tree is always searched from the root down, so during an *INSERT* operation, it is split on the way down. This means that while the index is being searched on an *INSERT*, the index is protected in anticipation of possibly being updated. The protection mechanism is a latch, which you can think of as something like a lock. (Locks are discussed in detail in Chapter 10.)

A latch is acquired while a page is being read from or written to disk and protects the physical integrity of the contents of the page. A parent node is latched (and protected) until the child node's needed split(s) are complete and no further updates to the parent node are required from the current operation. Then the parent latch can be released safely.

Before the latch on a parent node is released, SQL Server determines whether the page can accommodate another two rows; if not, it splits the page. This occurs only if the page is being searched with the objective of adding a row to the index. The goal is to ensure that the parent page always has room for the row or rows that result from a child page splitting. (Occasionally, this results in pages being split that don't need to be—at least not yet. In the long run, it's a performance optimization that helps to minimize deadlocks in an index and allows for free space to be added for future rows that may require it.) The type of split depends on the type of page being split: a root page of an index, an intermediate index page, or a leaf-level page. And, when a split occurs, it is committed independently of the transaction that caused the page to split (using special internal transactions called *system transactions*). Therefore, even if the *INSERT* transaction is rolled back, the split is not rolled back.

## Splitting the Root Page of an Index

If the root page of an index needs to be split for a new index row to be inserted, two new pages are allocated to the index. All the rows from the root are split between these two new pages, and the new index row is inserted into the appropriate place on one of these pages. The original root page is still the root, but now it has only two rows on it, pointing to each of the newly allocated pages. Keeping the original root page means that an update to the index metadata in the system catalogs (that contains a pointer to the index root page) is avoided. A root page split creates a new level in the index. Because indexes are usually only a few levels deep and typically very scalable, this type of split doesn't occur often.

## Splitting an Intermediate Index Page

An intermediate index page split is accomplished simply by locating the midpoint of the index keys on the page, allocating a new page, and then copying the lower half of the old index page into the new page. A new row is added to the index page in the level above the page that split, corresponding to the newly added page. Again, this doesn't occur often, although it's much more common than splitting the root page.

## Splitting a Leaf-Level Page

A leaf-level page split is the most interesting and potentially common case, and it's probably the only split that you, as a developer or DBA, should be concerned with. The mechanism is the same for splitting clustered index data pages or nonclustered index leaf-level index pages.

Data pages split only under *INSERT* activity and only when a clustered index exists on the table. Although splits are caused only by *INSERT* activity, that activity can be a result of an *UPDATE* statement, not just an *INSERT* statement. As you're about to learn, if the row can't be updated in place or at least on the same page, the update is performed as a *DELETE* of the original row followed by an *INSERT* of the new version of the row. The insertion of the new row can cause a page to split.

Splitting a leaf-level (data or index) page is a complicated operation. Much like an intermediate index page split, it's accomplished by locating the midpoint of the index keys on the page, allocating a new page, and then copying half of the old page into the new page. It requires that the index manager determine the page on which to locate the new row and then handle large rows that don't fit on either the old page or the new page. When a data page is split, the clustered index key values don't change, so the nonclustered indexes aren't affected.

Let's look at what happens to a page when it splits. The following script creates a table with large rows—so large, in fact, that only five rows fit on a page. Once the table is created and populated with five rows, we find its first (and only, in this case) page by inserting the output of *DBCC IND* in the *sp_tablepages* table, finding the information for the data page with no previous page, and then using *DBCC PAGE* to look at the contents of the page. Because we don't need to see all 8,020 bytes of data on the page, we look at only the slot array at the end of the page and then see what happens to those rows when we insert a sixth row:

```
USE AdventureWorks2008;
GO

DROP TABLE bigrows;
GO

CREATE TABLE bigrows
(
    a int  primary key,
    b varchar(1600)
);
GO

/* Insert five rows into the table */
INSERT INTO bigrows
    VALUES (5, REPLICATE('a', 1600));
INSERT INTO bigrows
    VALUES (10, replicate('b', 1600));
INSERT INTO bigrows
    VALUES (15, replicate('c', 1600));
INSERT INTO bigrows
    VALUES (20, replicate('d', 1600));
INSERT INTO bigrows
    VALUES (25, replicate('e', 1600));
GO

TRUNCATE TABLE sp_tablepages;
INSERT INTO sp_tablepages
    EXEC ('DBCC IND ( AdventureWorks2008, bigrows, -1)'  );
GO
```

```
SELECT PageFID, PagePID
FROM sp_tablepages
WHERE PageType = 1;
GO
```

```
RESULTS: (Yours may vary.)
PageFID PagePID
------- -----------
1       742
```

```
DBCC TRACEON(3604);
GO
DBCC PAGE(AdventureWorks2008, 1, 742, 1);
GO
```

Here is the slot array from the *DBCC PAGE* output:

```
Row - Offset
4 (0x4) - 6556 (0x199c)
3 (0x3) - 4941 (0x134d)
2 (0x2) - 3326 (0xcfe)
1 (0x1) - 1711 (0x6af)
0 (0x0) - 96 (0x60)
```

Now we insert one more row and look at the slot array again:

```
INSERT INTO bigrows
    VALUES (22, REPLICATE('x', 1600));
GO
DBCC PAGE (AdventureWorks2008, 1, 742, 1);
GO
```

The new page always contains the second half of the rows from the original page, but the new row value may be inserted on either page depending on the value of its index keys. In this example, the new row, with a clustered key value of 22, would have been inserted in the second half of the page. So when this page split occurs, the first three rows stay on page 742, the original page. You can inspect the page header to find the location of the next page, which contains the new row.

The page number is indicated by the *m_nextPage* field. This value is expressed as a *file number:page number* pair, in decimal, so you can easily use it with the *DBCC PAGE* command. In this case, *m_nextPage* returned a value of 1:21912 (nowhere near the current page). Using *DBCC PAGE* for the "next page" shows the rows there:

```
DBCC PAGE (AdventureWorks2008, 1, 21912, 1);
```

Here's the slot array after the *INSERT* for the second page:

```
Row - Offset
2 (0x2) - 1711 (0x6af)
1 (0x1) - 3326 (0xcfe)
0 (0x0) - 96 (0x60)
```

Note that after the page split, three rows are on the page: the last two original rows, with keys of 20 and 25, and the new row, with a key of 22. If you examine the actual data on the page, you notice that the new row is at slot position 1, even though the row itself is physically the last one on the page. Slot 1 (with value 22) starts at offset 3,326, and slot 2 (with value 25) starts at offset 1,711. The clustered key ordering of the rows is indicated by the slot number of the row, not by the physical position on the page. If a table has a clustered index, the row at slot 1 always has a key value less than the row at slot 2 and greater than the row at slot 0. Only the slot numbers are rearranged, not the data. This is an optimization so that only a small number of offsets are rearranged instead of the entire page's contents. It is a myth that rows in an index are always stored in the exact same physical order as their keys—in fact, SQL Server can store the rows anywhere on a page so long as the slot array provides the correct logical ordering.

Page splits are expensive operations, involving updates to multiple pages (the page being split, the new page, the page that used to be the *m_nextPage* of the page being split, and the parent page), all of which are fully logged. As such, you want to minimize the frequency of page splits in your production system, especially during peak usage times. You can avoid negatively affecting performance by minimizing splits. Splits can often be minimized by choosing a better clustering key (one where new rows are inserted at the end of the table, rather than randomly, as with a GUID clustering key) or, especially when splits are caused by update to variable-width columns, by reserving some free space on pages using the FILLFACTOR option when you're creating or rebuilding the indexes. You can use this setting to your advantage during your least busy operational hours by periodically rebuilding (or reorganizing) the indexes with the desired FILLFACTOR. That way, the extra space is available during peak usage times, and you save the overhead of splitting then. The pros and cons of various maintenance options are discussed later in this chapter.

## Deleting Rows

When you delete rows from a table, you have to consider what happens both to the data pages and the index pages. Remember that the data is actually the leaf level of a clustered index, and deleting rows from a table with a clustered index happens the same way as deleting rows from the leaf level of a nonclustered index. Deleting rows from a heap is managed in a different way, as is deleting from non-leaf pages of an index.

### Deleting Rows from a Heap

SQL Server 2008 doesn't automatically compact space on a page when a row is deleted. As a performance optimization, the compaction doesn't occur until a page needs additional contiguous space for inserting a new row. You can see this in the following example, which deletes a row from the middle of a page and then inspects that page using *DBCC PAGE:*

```
USE AdventureWorks2008;
GO
```

```
CREATE TABLE smallrows
(
    a int identity,
    b char(10)
);
GO

INSERT INTO smallrows
    VALUES ('row 1');
INSERT INTO smallrows
    VALUES ('row 2');
INSERT INTO smallrows
    VALUES ('row 3');
INSERT INTO smallrows
    VALUES ('row 4');
INSERT INTO smallrows
    VALUES ('row 5');
GO

TRUNCATE TABLE sp_tablepages;
INSERT INTO sp_tablepages
    EXEC ('DBCC IND (AdventureWorks2008, smallrows, -1)' );

SELECT PageFID, PagePID
FROM sp_tablepages
WHERE PageType = 1;

Results:
PageFID PagePID
------- -----------
1       4536

DBCC TRACEON(3604);
GO
DBCC PAGE(AdventureWorks2008, 1, 4536,1);
```

Here is the output from *DBCC PAGE*:

```
DATA:

Slot 0, Offset 0x60, Length 21, DumpStyle BYTE
Record Type = PRIMARY_RECORD        Record Attributes =  NULL_BITMAP
Memory Dump @0x61D9C060
00000000:    10001200 01000000 726f7720 31202020 †........row 1
00000010:    20200200 fc†††††††††††††††††††††††††††  ...

Slot 1, Offset 0x75, Length 21, DumpStyle BYTE
Record Type = PRIMARY_RECORD        Record Attributes =  NULL_BITMAP
Memory Dump @0x61D9C075
00000000:    10001200 02000000 726f7720 32202020 †........row 2
00000010:    20200200 fc†††††††††††††††††††††††††††  ...

Slot 2, Offset 0x8a, Length 21, DumpStyle BYTE
Record Type = PRIMARY_RECORD        Record Attributes =  NULL_BITMAP
Memory Dump @0x61D9C08A
```

```
00000000:   10001200 03000000 726f7720 33202020 †........row 3
00000010:   20200200 fc†††††††††††††††††††††††††  ...
```

```
Slot 3, Offset 0x9f, Length 21, DumpStyle BYTE
Record Type = PRIMARY_RECORD        Record Attributes =  NULL_BITMAP
Memory Dump @0x61D9C09F
00000000:   10001200 04000000 726f7720 34202020 †........row 4
00000010:   20200200 fc†††††††††††††††††††††††††  ...
```

```
Slot 4, Offset 0xb4, Length 21, DumpStyle BYTE
Record Type = PRIMARY_RECORD        Record Attributes =  NULL_BITMAP
Memory Dump @0x61D9C0B4
00000000:   10001200 05000000 726f7720 35202020 †........row 5
00000010:   20200200 fc†††††††††††††††††††††††††  ...
```

```
OFFSET TABLE:
Row - Offset
4 (0x4) - 180 (0xb4)
3 (0x3) - 159 (0x9f)
2 (0x2) - 138 (0x8a)
1 (0x1) - 117 (0x75)
0 (0x0) - 96 (0x60)
```

Now we delete the middle row (WHERE $a$ = 3) and look at the page again:

```
DELETE FROM smallrows
WHERE a = 3;
GO

DBCC PAGE(AdventureWorks2008, 1, 4536, 1);
GO
```

Here is the output from the second execution of *DBCC PAGE:*

```
DATA:
Slot 0, Offset 0x60, Length 21, DumpStyle BYTE
Record Type = PRIMARY_RECORD        Record Attributes =  NULL_BITMAP
Memory Dump @0x61B6C060
00000000:   10001200 01000000 726f7720 31202020 †........row 1
00000010:   20200200 fc†††††††††††††††††††††††††  ...
```

```
Slot 1, Offset 0x75, Length 21, DumpStyle BYTE
Record Type = PRIMARY_RECORD        Record Attributes =  NULL_BITMAP
Memory Dump @0x61B6C075
00000000:   10001200 02000000 726f7720 32202020 †........row 2
00000010:   20200200 fc†††††††††††††††††††††††††  ...
```

```
Slot 3, Offset 0x9f, Length 21, DumpStyle BYTE
Record Type = PRIMARY_RECORD        Record Attributes =  NULL_BITMAP
Memory Dump @0x61B6C09F
00000000:   10001200 04000000 726f7720 34202020 †........row 4
00000010:   20200200 fc†††††††††††††††††††††††††  ...
```

```
Slot 4, Offset 0xb4, Length 21, DumpStyle BYTE
Record Type = PRIMARY_RECORD        Record Attributes =  NULL_BITMAP
Memory Dump @0x61B6C0B4
```

```
00000000:    10001200 05000000 726f7720 35202020 †........row 5
00000010:    20200200 fc†††††††††††††††††††††††††† ...
```

```
OFFSET TABLE:
Row - Offset
4 (0x4) - 180 (0xb4)
3 (0x3) - 159 (0x9f)
2 (0x2) - 0 (0x0)
1 (0x1) - 117 (0x75)
0 (0x0) - 96 (0x60)
```

Using *DBCC PAGE* with style 1 on a heap, the row doesn't show up in the page itself—only in the slot array. The slot array at the bottom of the page shows that the third row (at slot 2) is now at offset 0 (which means there really is no row using slot 2), and the row using slot 3 is at its same offset as before the *DELETE*. The data on the page is *not* compacted.

In addition to space on pages not being reclaimed, empty pages in heaps frequently cannot be reclaimed. Even if you delete all the rows from a heap, SQL Server does not mark the empty pages as unallocated, so the space is not available for other objects to use. The catalog view *sys.dm_db_partition_stats* still shows the space as belonging to the heap.

## Deleting Rows from a B-tree

In the leaf level of an index, either clustered or nonclustered, rows are marked as *ghost records* when they are deleted. This means that the row stays on the page, but a bit is changed in the row header to indicate that the row is really deleted (a *ghost*). The page header also reflects the number of ghost records on a page. Ghost records are used for several purposes. They can be used to make rollbacks much more efficient—if the row hasn't been removed physically, all SQL Server has to do to roll back a *DELETE* is to change the bit indicating that the row is a ghost. It is also a concurrency optimization for key-range locking (which is discussed in Chapter 10), along with other locking modes. In addition, ghost records are used to support row-level versioning; that topic also is discussed in Chapter 10.

Ghost records are cleaned up sooner or later, depending on the load on your system, and sometimes they can be cleaned up before you have a chance to inspect them. There is a background thread called the *ghost-cleanup thread*, whose job it is to remove ghost records that are no longer needed to support active transactions, or any other feature. In the code shown here, if you perform the *DELETE* and then wait a minute or two to run *DBCC PAGE*, the ghost record might really disappear. That is why we look at the page number for the table before we run the *DELETE*, so we can execute the *DELETE* and the *DBCC PAGE* with a single click from the query window. To guarantee that the ghost record is not cleaned up, we can put the *DELETE* into a user transaction and not commit or roll back the transaction before examining the page. The ghost-cleanup thread does not clean up ghost records that are part of an active transaction. Alternatively, we can use the undocumented trace flag 661 to disable ghost cleanup to ensure consistent results when running tests such as in this script. As usual, keep in mind that undocumented trace flags are not guaranteed to continue to work in any future release or service pack, and no support is available for them. Also, be sure to turn off the trace flag when you're done with your testing. You can also force SQL Server to clean up the ghost records. The procedure *sp_clean_db_free_space* will remove all ghost records from an entire database (as long as they are not part of an uncommitted transaction) and the procedure *sp_clean_db_file_free_space* will do the same for a single file of a database.

The following example builds the same table used in the previous *DELETE* example, but this time, the table has a primary key declared, which means a clustered index is built. The data is the leaf level of the clustered index, so when the row is removed, it is marked as a ghost:

```
USE AdventureWorks2008;
GO
DROP TABLE smallrows;
GO
CREATE TABLE smallrows
(
    a int IDENTITY PRIMARY KEY,
    b char(10)
);
GO
INSERT INTO smallrows
    VALUES ('row 1');
INSERT INTO smallrows
    VALUES ('row 2');
INSERT INTO smallrows
    VALUES ('row 3');
INSERT INTO smallrows
    VALUES ('row 4');
INSERT INTO smallrows
    VALUES ('row 5');
GO
TRUNCATE TABLE sp_tablepages;
INSERT INTO sp_tablepages
    EXEC ('DBCC IND (AdventureWorks2008, smallrows, -1)' );
SELECT PageFID, PagePID
FROM sp_tablepages
WHERE PageType = 1;

Results:
PageFID PagePID
------- -----------
1       4568

DELETE FROM smallrows
WHERE a = 3;
GO
DBCC TRACEON(3604);
DBCC PAGE(AdventureWorks2008, 1, 4544, 1);
GO
```

Here is the output from *DBCC PAGE*:

```
PAGE HEADER:
Page @0x064AE000
m_pageId = (1:4568)              m_headerVersion = 1              m_type = 1
m_typeFlagBits = 0x4             m_level = 0                      m_flagBits = 0x8000
m_objId (AllocUnitId.idObj) = 172    m_indexId (AllocUnitId.idInd) = 256
```

Metadata: AllocUnitId = 72057594049200128
Metadata: PartitionId = 72057594043105280                    Metadata:
    IndexId = 1
Metadata: ObjectId = 1179867270      m_prevPage = (0:0)      m_nextPage = (0:0)
pminlen = 18                         m_slotCnt = 5           m_freeCnt = 7981
m_freeData = 201                     m_reservedCnt = 0       m_lsn = (233:499:2)
m_xactReserved = 0                   m_xdesId = (0:18856)    m_ghostRecCnt = 1
m_tornBits = 0


DATA:
Slot 0, Offset 0x60, Length 21, DumpStyle BYTE
Record Type = PRIMARY_RECORD       Record Attributes =  NULL_BITMAP
Memory Dump @0x61B6C060
00000000:   10001200 01000000 726f7720 31202020 †........row 1
00000010:   20200200 fc††††††††††††††††††††††††††  ...

Slot 1, Offset 0x75, Length 21, DumpStyle BYTE
Record Type = PRIMARY_RECORD       Record Attributes =  NULL_BITMAP
Memory Dump @0x61B6C075
00000000:   10001200 02000000 726f7720 32202020 †........row 2
00000010:   20200200 fc††††††††††††††††††††††††††  ...

Slot 2, Offset 0x8a, Length 21, DumpStyle BYTE
Record Type = GHOST_DATA_RECORD       Record Attributes =  NULL_BITMAP
Memory Dump @0x61B6C08A
00000000:   1c001200 03000000 726f7720 33202020 †........row 3
00000010:   20200200 fc††††††††††††††††††††††††††  ...

Slot 3, Offset 0x9f, Length 21, DumpStyle BYTE
Record Type = PRIMARY_RECORD       Record Attributes =  NULL_BITMAP
Memory Dump @0x61B6C09F
00000000:   10001200 04000000 726f7720 34202020 †........row 4
00000010:   20200200 fc††††††††††††††††††††††††††  ...

Slot 4, Offset 0xb4, Length 21, DumpStyle BYTE
Record Type = PRIMARY_RECORD       Record Attributes =  NULL_BITMAP
Memory Dump @0x61B6C0B4
00000000:   10001200 05000000 726f7720 35202020 †........row 5
00000010:   20200200 fc††††††††††††††††††††††††††  ...

OFFSET TABLE:
Row - Offset
4 (0x4) - 180 (0xb4)
3 (0x3) - 159 (0x9f)
2 (0x2) - 138 (0x8a)
1 (0x1) - 117 (0x75)
0 (0x0) - 96 (0x60)

Note that the row still shows up in the page itself (using *DBCC PAGE* style 1) because the table has a clustered index. Also, you can experiment using different output styles to see how both a heap and a clustered index work with ghosted records, but you still see empty slots, GHOST_DATA_RECORD types, or both for clarification. The header information for the row shows that this is really a ghost record. The slot array at the bottom of the page shows that the row at slot 2 is still at the same offset and that all rows are in the same location as before the deletion. In addition, the page header gives us a value (*m_ghostRecCnt*) for the number of ghost records in the page. To see the total count of ghost records in a table, you can look at the *sys.dm_db_index_physical_stats* function.

> **More Info**  A detailed discussion of the ghost cleanup mechanism and an examination of the transaction logging involved are available at Paul Randal's blog—see the blog post at *http://www.SQLskills.com/BLOGS/PAUL/post/Inside-the-Storage-Engine-Ghost-cleanup-in-depth.aspx.*

### Deleting Rows in the Non-Leaf Levels of an Index

When you delete a row from a table, all nonclustered indexes must be maintained because every nonclustered index has a pointer to the row that's now gone. Rows in index non-leaf pages aren't ghosted when deleted, but just as with heap pages, the space isn't compacted until new index rows need space in that page.

### Reclaiming Pages

When the last row is deleted from a data page, the entire page is deallocated by the ghost cleanup background thread. The exception is if the table is a heap, as we discussed earlier. (If the page is the only one remaining in the table, it isn't deallocated. A table always contains at least one page, even if it's empty.) Deallocation of a data page results in the deletion of the row in the index page that pointed to the deallocated data page. Non-leaf index pages are deallocated if an index row is deleted (which, again, for an update might occur as part of a *DELETE/INSERT* strategy), leaving only one entry in the index page. That entry is moved to its neighboring page if there is space, and then the empty page is deallocated.

The discussion so far has focused on the page manipulation necessary for deleting a single row. If multiple rows are deleted in a single *DELETE* operation, you must be aware of some other issues. Because the issues of modifying multiple rows in a single query are the same for *INSERT*s, *UPDATE*s, and *DELETE*s, we discuss this issue in its own section, later in this chapter.

## Updating Rows

SQL Server updates rows in multiple ways, automatically and invisibly choosing the fastest update strategy for the specific operation. In determining the strategy, SQL Server evaluates the number of rows affected, how the rows are accessed (via a scan or an index retrieval, and via which index), and whether changes to the index keys occur. Updates can happen either in place, by just changing one column's value to a new value in the original row, or as a *DELETE* followed by an *INSERT*. In addition, updates can be managed by the query processor or by the storage engine. In this section, we examine only whether the update happens in place or whether SQL Server treats it as two separate operations: delete the old row and insert a new row. The question of whether the update is controlled by the query processor or the storage engine is actually relevant to all data modification operations (not just updates), so we look at that in a separate section.

## Moving Rows

What happens if a table row has to move to a new location? In SQL Server 2008, this can happen because a row with variable-length columns is updated to a new, larger size so that it no longer fits on the original page. It can also happen when the clustered or nonclustered index column(s) change because rows are logically ordered by the index key. For example, if we have a clustered index on *lastname*, a row with a *lastname* value of *Abbot* is stored near the beginning of the table. If the *lastname* value is then updated to *Zappa*, this row has to move to near the end of the table.

Earlier in this chapter, we looked at the structure of indexes and saw that the leaf level of nonclustered indexes contains a row locator, or bookmark, for every single row in the table. If the table has a clustered index, that row locator is the clustering key for that row. So if—and only if—the clustered index key is being updated, modifications are required in every nonclustered index (with the possible exception of filtered nonclustered indexes). Keep this in mind when you decide on which columns to build your clustered index. It's a great idea to cluster on a nonvolatile column, such as an identity.

If a row moves because it no longer fits on the original page, it still has the same row locator (in other words, the clustering key for the row stays the same), and no nonclustered indexes have to be modified. This is true even if the table is moved to a new physical location (filegroup or partitioning scheme). Nonclustered indexes are updated only if the clustering key changes, and moving the physical location of a table row does not change its clustering key.

In our discussion of index internals, you also saw that if a table has no clustered index (in other words, if it's a heap), the row locator stored in the nonclustered index is actually the physical location of the row. In SQL Server 2008, if a row in a heap moves to a new page, the row leaves a forwarding pointer in the original location. The nonclustered indexes won't need to be changed; they still refer to the original location, and from there, they are directed to the new location. In this case, if the table moves to a new location (filegroup or partitioning scheme), the nonclustered indexes are updated, as the physical location of all records in the heap must change, thus invalidating the prior row locators in the nonclustered indexes.

Let's look at an example. We have created a table a lot like the one we created for doing inserts, but this table has a third column of variable length. After we populate the table with five rows, which fill the page, we update one of the rows to make its third column much longer. The row no longer fits on the original page and has to move. We can then load the output from *DBCC IND* into the *sp_tablepages* table to get the page numbers used by the table:

```
USE AdventureWorks2008;
GO
DROP TABLE bigrows;
GO
CREATE TABLE bigrows
(   a int IDENTITY ,
    b varchar(1600),
    c varchar(1600));
GO
```

```
INSERT INTO bigrows
    VALUES (REPLICATE('a', 1600), '');
INSERT INTO bigrows
    VALUES (REPLICATE('b', 1600), '');
INSERT INTO bigrows
    VALUES (REPLICATE('c', 1600), '');
INSERT INTO bigrows
    VALUES (REPLICATE('d', 1600), '');
INSERT INTO bigrows
    VALUES (REPLICATE('e', 1600), '');
GO
UPDATE bigrows
SET c = REPLICATE('x', 1600)
WHERE a = 3;
GO

TRUNCATE TABLE sp_tablepages;
INSERT INTO sp_tablepages
    EXEC ('DBCC IND (AdventureWorks2008, bigrows, -1)' );
SELECT PageFID, PagePID
FROM sp_tablepages
WHERE PageType = 1;

RESULTS:
PageFID PagePID
------- -----------

1       2252
1       4586


DBCC TRACEON(3604);
GO
DBCC PAGE(AdventureWorks2008, 1, 2252, 1);
GO
```

We won't show you the entire output from the *DBCC PAGE* command, but we'll show you what appears in the slot where the row with *a = 3* formerly appeared:

```
Slot 2, Offset 0x1feb, Length 9, DumpStyle BYTE
Record Type = FORWARDING_STUB        Record Attributes =
Memory Dump @0x61ADDFEB
00000000:    04ea1100 00010000 00†††††††††††††††††††††.........
```

The value of 4 in the first byte means that this is just a forwarding stub. The 0011ea in the next 3 bytes is the page number to which the row has been moved. Because this is a hexadecimal value, we need to convert it to 4,586 decimal. The next group of 4 bytes tells us that the page is at slot 0, file 1. If you then use *DBCC PAGE* to look at that page 4,586, you can see what the forwarded record looks like.

## Managing Forwarding Pointers

Forwarding pointers allow you to modify data in a heap without worrying about having to make drastic changes to the nonclustered indexes. If a row that has been forwarded must move again, the original forwarding pointer is updated to point to the new location. You never end up with a forwarding pointer pointing to another forwarding pointer. In addition, if the forwarded row shrinks enough to fit in its original place, the record might move back to its original place, if there is still room on that page, and the forwarding pointer would be eliminated.

A future version of SQL Server might include some mechanism for performing a physical reorganization of the data in a heap, which would get rid of forwarding pointers. Note that forwarding pointers exist only in heaps, and that the ALTER TABLE option to reorganize a table won't do anything to heaps. You can defragment a nonclustered index on a heap, but not the table itself. Currently, when a forwarding pointer is created, it stays there forever—with only a few exceptions. The first exception is the case we already mentioned, in which a row shrinks and returns to its original location. The second exception is when the entire database shrinks. The bookmarks are actually reassigned when a file is shrunk. The shrink process never generates forwarding pointers. For pages that were removed because of the shrink process, any forwarded rows or stubs they contain are effectively "unforwarded." Other cases in which the forwarding pointers are removed are the obvious ones: if the forwarded row is deleted or if a clustered index is built on the table so that it is no longer a heap.

To get a count of forwarded records in a table, you can look at the output from the *sys.dm_db_ index_physical_stats* function.

## Updating in Place

In SQL Server 2008, updating a row in place is the rule rather than the exception. This means that the row stays in exactly the same location on the same page and only the bytes affected are changed. In addition, the log contains a single record for each update in-place operation unless the table has an update trigger on it or is marked for replication. In these cases, the update still happens in place, but the log contains a *DELETE* record followed by an *INSERT* record if any of the index key columns are updated.

In cases where a row can't be updated in place, the cost of a not-in-place update is minimal because of the way the nonclustered indexes are stored and because of the use of forwarding pointers. In fact, you can have an update not in place, for which the row stays on the original page. Updates happen in place if a heap is being updated (and there is enough space on the page) or if a table with a clustered index is updated without any change to the clustering keys. You can also get an update in place if the clustering key changes but the row does not need to move at all. For example, if you have a clustered index on a *lastname* column containing consecutive key values of *Able*, *Becker*, and *Charlie*, you might want to update *Becker* to *Baker*. Because the row stays in the same location even after the clustered index key changes, SQL Server performs this as an update in place. On the other hand, if you update *Able* to *Buchner*, the update cannot occur in place, but the new row might stay on the same page.

## Updating Not in Place

If your update can't happen in place because you're updating clustering keys, the update occurs as a *DELETE* followed by an *INSERT*. In some cases, you get a hybrid update: some of the rows are updated in place and some aren't. If you're updating index keys, SQL Server builds a list of all the rows that need to change as both a *DELETE* and an *INSERT* operation. This list is stored in memory, if it's small enough, and is written to *tempdb* if necessary. This list is then sorted by key value and operator (*DELETE* or *INSERT*). If the index whose keys are changing isn't unique, the *DELETE* and *INSERT* steps are then applied to the table. If the index is unique, an additional step is carried out to collapse *DELETE* and *INSERT* operations on the same key into a single *UPDATE* operation.

## Table-Level vs. Index-Level Data Modification

We've been discussing only the placement and index manipulation necessary for modifying either a single row or a few rows with no more than a single index. If you are modifying multiple rows in a single operation (*INSERT, UPDATE,* or *DELETE*) or by using *BCP* or the *BULK INSERT* command and the table has multiple indexes, you must be aware of some other issues. SQL Server 2008 offers two strategies for maintaining all the indexes that belong to a table: table-level modification and index-level modification. The Query Optimizer chooses between them based on its estimate of the anticipated execution costs for each strategy.

Table-level modification is sometimes called *row-at-a-time*, and index-level modification is sometimes called *index-at-a-time*. In table-level modification, all indexes are maintained for each row as that row is modified. If the update stream isn't sorted in any way, SQL Server has to do a lot of random index accesses, one access per index per update row. If the update stream is sorted, it can't be sorted in more than one order, so nonrandom index accesses can occur for at most one index.

In index-level modifications, SQL Server gathers all the rows to be modified and sorts them for each index. In other words, there are as many sort operations as there are indexes. Then, for each index, the updates are merged into the index, and each index page is never accessed more than once, even if multiple updates pertain to a single index leaf page.

Clearly, if the update is small—say, less than a handful of rows—and the table and its indexes are sizable, the Query Optimizer usually considers table-level modification the best choice. Most OLTP operations use table-level modification. On the other hand, if the update is relatively large, table-level modifications require a lot of random I/O operations and might even read and write each leaf page in each index multiple times. In that case, index-level modification offers much better performance. The amount of logging required is the same for both strategies.

You can determine whether your updates were done at the table level or the index level by inspecting the query execution plan. If SQL Server performs the update at the index level, you see a plan produced that contains an *UPDATE* operator for each of the affected indexes. If SQL Server performs the update at the table level, you see only a single *UPDATE* operator in the plan.

# Logging

Standard *INSERT, UPDATE,* and *DELETE* statements are always logged to ensure atomicity, and you can't disable logging of these operations. The modification must be known to be safely on disk in the transaction log (write-ahead logging) before the commit of the statement or transaction can be acknowledged to the calling application. Page allocations and deallocations, including those done by *TRUNCATE TABLE,* are also logged. As we saw in Chapter 4, "Logging and Recovery," certain operations can be minimally logged when your database is in the *BULK_LOGGED* recovery mode, but even then, information about allocations and deallocations is written to the log, along with the fact that a minimally logged operation has been executed.

# Locking

Any data modification must always be protected with some form of exclusive lock. For the most part, SQL Server makes all the locking decisions internally; a user or programmer doesn't need to request a particular kind of lock. Chapter 10 explains the different types of locks and their compatibility. However, because locking is closely tied to data modification, you should always be aware of the following points:

- Every type of data modification performed in SQL Server requires some form of exclusive lock. For most data modification operations, SQL Server considers row locking as the default, but if many locks are required, SQL Server can lock pages or even the whole table.

- Update locks can be used to signal the intention to do an update, and they are important for avoiding deadlock conditions. But ultimately, the update operation requires that an exclusive lock be performed. The update lock serializes access to ensure that an exclusive lock can be acquired, but the update lock isn't sufficient by itself.

- Exclusive locks must always be held until the end of a transaction in case the transaction needs to be undone (unlike shared locks, which can be released as soon as the scan moves off the page, such as when the *READ COMMITTED* isolation is in effect).

- If a full table scan must be employed to find qualifying rows for an *UPDATE* or a *DELETE,* SQL Server has to inspect every row to determine the row to modify. Other processes that need to find individual rows are blocked even if they ultimately modify different rows. Without inspecting the row, SQL Server has no way of knowing whether the row qualifies for the modification. If you're modifying only a subset of rows in the table, as determined by a WHERE clause, be sure that you have indexes available to allow SQL Server to access the needed rows directly so it doesn't have to scan every row in the table.

# Fragmentation

*Fragmentation* is a general term used to describe various effects that can occur in indexes because of data modifications. There are two general types of fragmentation: internal and external.

Internal fragmentation (often called *physical fragmentation* or *page density*) is where there is wasted space on index pages, both at the leaf and non-leaf levels. This can occur because of any or all of the following:

- Page splits (described earlier) leaving empty space on the page that was split and the newly allocated page

- *DELETE* operations that leave pages less than full

- Row sizes that contribute to under-full pages (for instance, a fixed-width, 5,000-byte data record in a clustered index leads to 3,000 wasted bytes per clustered index data page)

Internal fragmentation means the index is taking more space than necessary, leading to increased disk space usage, more pages to read to process the data, and more memory used to hold the pages in the buffer pool. Sometimes internal fragmentation can be advantageous, as it allows more rows to be inserted on pages without *causing* page splits. Deliberate internal fragmentation can be achieved using the FILLFACTOR and PAD_INDEX options, which are described in the next section.

External fragmentation (often called *logical fragmentation* or *extent fragmentation*) is where the pages or extents comprising the leaf level of a clustered or nonclustered index are not in the most efficient order. The most efficient order is where the logical order of the pages and extents (as defined by the index keys, following the next-page pointers from the page headers) is the same as the physical order of the pages and extents within the data file(s). In other words, the index leaf-level page that has the row with the next index key is also the next physically contiguous page in the data file. This is separate from fragmentation at the *file-system* level, where the actual data files may be comprised of several physical sections.

External fragmentation is caused by page splits and reduces the efficiency of ordered scans of part of a clustered or nonclustered index. The more external fragmentation there is, the less likely it is that the storage engine can perform efficient prereading of the pages necessary for the scan.

The methods of detecting and removing fragmentation are discussed in the next section.

# Managing Index Structures

SQL Server maintains your indexes automatically, in terms of making sure the correct rows are there. As you add new rows, it automatically inserts them into the correct position in a table with a clustered index, and it adds new leaf-level rows to your nonclustered indexes that point to the new data rows. When you remove rows, SQL Server automatically deletes the corresponding leaf-level rows from your nonclustered indexes.

So, although your indexes continue to contain all the correct index rows in the B-tree to help SQL Server find the rows you are looking for, you might still occasionally need to perform maintenance operations on your indexes, especially to deal with fragmentation in its various forms. In addition, several properties of indexes can be changed.

## Dropping Indexes

One of the biggest differences between managing indexes created using the *CREATE INDEX* command and indexes that support constraints is in how you can drop the index. The *DROP INDEX* command allows you to drop only indexes that were built with the *CREATE INDEX* command. To drop indexes that support constraints, you must use *ALTER TABLE* to drop the constraint. In addition, to drop a PRIMARY KEY or UNIQUE constraint that has any FOREIGN KEY constraints referencing it, you must first drop the FOREIGN KEY constraint. This can leave you with a window of vulnerability if your goal is to drop indexes and immediately rebuild them, perhaps with a new *fillfactor*. Although the FOREIGN KEY constraint is gone, an *INSERT* statement can add a row to the table that violates your referential integrity.

One way to avoid this problem is to use *ALTER INDEX*, which allows you to drop and rebuild one or all of your indexes on a table in a single statement, without requiring the auxiliary step of removing FOREIGN KEY constraints. Alternatively, you can use the *CREATE INDEX* command with the DROP_EXISTING option if you want to rebuild existing indexes without having to drop and re-create them in two steps. Although you can normally use *CREATE INDEX* with DROP_EXISTING to redefine the properties of an index—such as the key columns or included columns, or whether the index is unique—if you use *CREATE INDEX* with DROP_EXISTING to rebuild an index that supports a constraint, you cannot make these kinds of changes. The index must be re-created with the same columns, in the same order, and the same values for uniqueness and clustering.

## *ALTER INDEX*

SQL Server 2005 introduced the *ALTER INDEX* command to allow you to use a single command to invoke various kinds of index changes that in previous versions required an eclectic collection of different commands, including *sp_indexoption*, *UPDATE STATISTICS*, *DBCC DBREINDEX*, and *DBCC INDEXDEFRAG*. Instead of having individual commands or procedures for each different index maintenance activity, they all can be done by using *ALTER INDEX*. For a complete description of all the options to *ALTER INDEX*, see the *SQL Server Books Online* topic "ALTER INDEX."

Basically, you can make four types of changes using *ALTER INDEX*, three of which have corresponding options that you can specify when you create an index using *CREATE INDEX*.

### Rebuilding an Index

Rebuilding the index replaces the *DBCC DBREINDEX* command and can be thought of as replacing the DROP_EXISTING option to the *CREATE INDEX* command. However, this option allows indexes to be moved or partitioned, too. A new option allows indexes to be rebuilt online, in the same way you can create indexes online (as we mentioned in the section entitled "Index Creation Options," earlier in this chapter). We discuss online index building and rebuilding shortly.

## Disabling an Index

Disabling an index makes it completely unavailable, so it can't be used for finding rows for any operations. Disabling the index also means that it won't be maintained as changes to the data are made. You can disable one index or all indexes with a single command. There is no ENABLE option. Because no maintenance is performed while an index is disabled, indexes must be completely rebuilt to make them useful again. Re-enabling, which can take place either online or offline, is done with the REBUILD option to *ALTER INDEX*. This feature was introduced mainly for the internal purposes of SQL Server when applying upgrades and service packs, but there are a few interesting uses for disabling an index. First, you can use it if you want to ignore the index temporarily for troubleshooting purposes. Second, instead of dropping nonclustered indexes before loading data, you can disable them. However, you cannot disable the clustered index. If you disable the clustered index on a table, the table's data will be unavailable because the leaf level of the clustered index *is* the data. Disabling the clustered index essentially disables the table. However, if your data is going to be loaded in clustered index order (for an ever-increasing clustering key) such that all new data goes to the end of the table, then disabling the nonclustered indexes can help to improve load performance. Once the data has been loaded, then you can rebuild the nonclustered indexes without having to supply the entire index definition. All the metadata has been saved while the index was disabled.

## Changing Index Options

Most of the options that you can specify during a *CREATE INDEX* operation can also be specified with the *ALTER INDEX* command. These options are ALLOW_ROW_LOCKS, ALLOW_PAGE_LOCKS, IGNORE_DUP_KEY, FILLFACTOR, PAD_INDEX, STATISTICS _NORECOMPUTE, MAXP_DOP, and SORT_IN_TEMPDB. IGNORE_DUP_KEY was described in the section entitled "Index Creation Options," earlier in this chapter.

**FILLFACTOR and PAD_INDEX**    FILLFACTOR is probably the most commonly used of these options and lets you reserve some space on each leaf page of an index. In a clustered index, because the leaf level contains the data, you can use FILLFACTOR to control how much space to leave in the table itself. By reserving free space, you can later avoid the need to split pages to make room for a new entry. An important fact about FILLFACTOR is that the value is not maintained; it indicates only how much space is reserved with the existing data at the time the index is built or rebuilt. If you need to, you can use the *ALTER INDEX* command to rebuild the index and reestablish the original FILLFACTOR specified. If you don't specify a new FILLFACTOR when using *ALTER INDEX*, the previously used FILLFACTOR is used.

FILLFACTOR should always be specified on an index-by-index basis. If FILLFACTOR isn't specified, the serverwide default is used. The value is set for the server via the *sp_configure* procedure, with the *fillfactor* option. This configuration value is 0 by default (and is the same as 100), which means that leaf pages of indexes are made as full as possible. It is a best practice *not* to change this serverwide setting. FILLFACTOR applies only to the index's leaf pages.

In specialized and high-use situations, you might want to reserve space in the intermediate index pages to avoid page splits there, too. You can do this by specifying the PAD_INDEX option, which instructs SQL Server to use the same FILLFACTOR value at all levels of the index. Just as for FILLFACTOR, PAD_INDEX is applicable only when an index is created (or re-created).

When you create a table that includes PRIMARY KEY or UNIQUE constraints, you can specify whether the associated index is clustered or nonclustered, and you can also specify the *fillfactor*. Because the *fillfactor* applies only at the time the index is created, and because there is no data when you first create the table, it might seem that specifying the *fillfactor* at that time is completely useless. However, if you decide to rebuild your indexes after the table is populated and if no new *fillfactor* is specified, the original value is used. You can also specify a *fillfactor* when you use *ALTER TABLE* to add a PRIMARY KEY or UNIQUE constraint to a table; if the table already has data in it, the *fillfactor* value is applied when you build the index to support the new constraint.

**DROP_EXISTING**   The DROP_EXISTING option specifies that a given index should be dropped and rebuilt as a single transaction. This option is particularly useful when you rebuild clustered indexes. Normally, when a developer drops a clustered index, SQL Server must rebuild every nonclustered index to change its bookmarks to RIDs instead of the clustering keys. Then, if a developer builds (or rebuilds) a clustered index, SQL Server must again rebuild all nonclustered indexes to update the bookmarks. The DROP_EXISTING option of the *CREATE INDEX* command allows a clustered index to be rebuilt without having to rebuild the nonclustered indexes twice. If you are creating the index on exactly the same keys that it had previously, the nonclustered indexes do not need to be rebuilt at all. If you are changing the key definition, the nonclustered indexes are rebuilt only once, after the clustered index is rebuilt. Instead of using the DROP_EXISTING option to rebuild an existing index, you can use the *ALTER INDEX* command.

**SORT_IN_TEMPDB**   The SORT_IN_TEMPDB option allows you to control where SQL Server performs the sort operation on the key values needed to build an index. The default is that SQL Server uses space from the filegroup on which the index is to be created. While the index is being built, SQL Server scans the data pages to find the key values and then builds leaf-level index rows in internal sort buffers. When these sort buffers are filled, they are written to disk. If the SORT_IN_TEMPDB option is specified, the sort buffers are allocated from *tempdb*, so much less space is needed in the source database. If you don't specify SORT_IN_TEMPDB, not only does your source database require enough free space for the sort buffers and a copy of the index (or the data, if a clustered index is being built), but the disk heads for the database need to move back and forth between the base table pages and the work area where the sort buffers are stored. If, instead, your *CREATE INDEX* command includes the SORT_IN_TEMPDB option, performance can be greatly improved if your *tempdb* database is on a separate physical disk from the database you're working with. You can optimize head movement because two separate heads read the base table pages and manage the sort buffers. You can speed up index creation even more if your *tempdb* database is on a faster disk than your user database and you use the SORT_IN_TEMPDB option.

## Reorganizing an Index

Reorganizing an index is the only change that doesn't have a corresponding option in the *CREATE INDEX* command. The reason for this is that when you create an index, there is nothing to reorganize. The REORGANIZE option replaces the *DBCC INDEXDEFRAG* command and removes some of the fragmentation from an index, but it is not guaranteed to remove all the fragmentation, just as *DBCC INDEXDEFRAG* may not remove all the fragmentation (in spite of its name). Before we discuss removing fragmentation, we must first discuss detecting fragmentation, which we do in the next section.

## Detecting Fragmentation

As we've already seen in numerous examples, the output of *sys.dm_db_index_physical_stats* returns a row for each level of an index. However, when a table is partitioned, it effectively treats each partition as a table, so this DMV actually returns a row for each level of each partition of each index. For a small index with only in-row data (no row-overflow or LOB pages) and only the one default partition, we might get only two or three rows back (one for each index level). But if there are multiple partitions and additional allocation units for the row-overflow and LOB data, we might see many more rows. For example, a clustered index on a table containing row-overflow data, built on 11 partitions and being two levels deep, have 33 rows (2 levels × 11 partitions + 11 partitions for the *row_overflow* allocation units) in the fragmentation report returned by *sys.dm_db_index_ physical_stats*.

The section entitled "Tools for Analyzing Indexes," earlier in this chapter, has a comprehensive discussion of the input parameters and the output results, but the following columns give fragmentation information that is not obvious:

- *Forwarded_record_count*   Forwarded records (discussed in the section entitled "Data Modification Internals," earlier in this chapter) are possible only in a heap and occur when a row with variable-length columns increases in size due to updates so that it no longer fits in its original location. If a table has lots of forwarded records, scanning the table can be very inefficient.

- *Ghost_Record_Count and version_ghost_record_count*   Ghost records are rows that physically still exist on a page but logically have been removed, as discussed in the section entitled "Data Modification Internals." Background processes in SQL Server clean up ghost records, but until that happens, no new records can be inserted in their place. So if there are lots of ghost records, your table has the drawback of lots of internal fragmentation (that is, the table is spread out over more pages and takes longer to scan) with none of the advantages (there is no room on the pages to insert new rows to avoid external fragmentation). A subset of ghost records is measured by *version_ghost_record_count*. This value reports the number of rows that have been retained by an outstanding Snapshot isolation transaction. These are not cleaned up until all relevant transactions have been committed or rolled back. Snapshot isolation is discussed in Chapter 10.

# Removing Fragmentation

If fragmentation becomes too severe and is affecting query performance, you have several options for removing it. You might also wonder how severe is too severe. First of all, fragmentation is not always a bad thing. The biggest performance penalty from having fragmented data arises when your application needs to perform an ordered scan on the data. The more the logical order differs from the physical order, the greater the cost of scanning the data. If, on the other hand, your application needs only one or a few rows of data, it doesn't matter whether the table or index data is in logical order or is physically contiguous, or whether it is spread all over the disk in totally random locations. If you have a good index to find the rows you are interested in, SQL Server can find one or a few rows very efficiently, wherever they happen to be physically located.

If you are doing ordered scans of an index (such as table scans on a table with a clustered index, or a leaf-level scan of a nonclustered index), it is frequently recommended that if your *avg_fragmentation_in_percent* value is between 5 and 20, you should reorganize your index to remove the fragmentation. As we see shortly, reorganizing an index (also called *defragging*) compacts the leaf-level pages back to their originally specified fillfactor and then rearranges the pages in the leaf level to correct the logical fragmentation, using the same pages that the index originally occupied. No new pages are allocated, so this is a much more space-efficient operation than rebuilding the index.

If the *avg_fragmentation_in_percent* value is greater than 30, you should consider completely rebuilding your index. Rebuilding an index means that a whole new set of pages is allocated for the index. This removes almost all fragmentation, but it is not guaranteed to eliminate it completely. If the free space in the database is itself fragmented, you might not be able to allocate enough contiguous space to remove all gaps between extents. In addition, if other work is going on that needs to allocate new extents while your index is being rebuilt, the extents allocated to the two processes can end up being interleaved.

Defragmentation is designed to remove logical fragmentation from the leaf level of an index while keeping the index online and as available as possible. When defragmenting an index, SQL Server acquires an Intent-Exclusive lock on the index B-tree. Exclusive page locks are taken on individual pages only while those pages are being manipulated, as we see later in this chapter when we describe the defragmentation algorithm. Defragmentation in SQL Server 2008 is initiated using the *ALTER INDEX* command. The general form of the command to remove fragmentation is as follows:

```
ALTER INDEX { index_name | ALL }
    ON <object>
      REORGANIZE
            [ PARTITION = partition_number ]
            [ WITH ( LOB_COMPACTION = { ON | OFF } ) ]
```

*ALTER INDEX* with the REORGANIZE option offers enhanced functionality compared to *DBCC INDEXDEFRAG* in SQL Server 2000. It supports partitioned indexes, so you can choose to defragment just one particular partition (the default is to defragment all the partitions), and it allows you to control whether the LOB data is affected by the defragmenting.

As mentioned earlier, every index is created with a specific fillfactor. The initial fillfactor value is stored with the index metadata, so when defragmenting is requested, SQL Server can inspect this value. During defragmentation, SQL Server attempts to reestablish the initial fillfactor if it is greater than the current fillfactor on a leaf-level page. Defragmentation is designed to compact data, and this can be done by putting more rows per page and increasing the fullness percentage of each page. SQL Server might end up then removing pages from the index after the defragmentation. If the current fillfactor is greater than the initial fillfactor, SQL Server cannot *reduce* the fullness level of a page by moving rows out of it. The compaction algorithm inspects adjacent pages (in logical order) to see if there is room to move rows from the second page to the first. From SQL Server 2005 onwards, the process is even more efficient by looking at a sliding window of eight logically consecutive pages. It determines whether enough rows can be moved around within the eight pages to allow a single page to be emptied and removed, and moves rows only if this is the case.

As mentioned earlier, SQL Server 2005 also introduced the option to compact your LOB pages. The default is ON. Reorganizing a specified clustered index compacts all LOB columns that are contained in the clustered index before it compacts the leaf pages. Reorganizing a nonclustered index compacts all LOB columns that are non-key (*INCLUDEd*) columns in the index.

In SQL Server 2000, the only way a user can compact LOBs in a table is to unload and reload the LOB data. LOB compaction in SQL Server 2005 onwards finds low-density extents—those that are used at less than 75 percent. It moves pages out of these low-density uniform extents and places the data from them in available space in other uniform extents already allocated to the LOB allocation unit. This functionality allows much better use of disk space, which can be wasted with low-density LOB extents. No new extents are allocated, either during this compaction phase or during the next phase.

The second phase of the reorganization operation actually moves data to new pages in the in-row allocation unit with the goal of having the logical order of data match the physical order. The index is kept online because only two pages at a time are processed in an operation similar to a heapsort or smoothsort (the details of which are beyond the scope of this book). The following example is a simplification of the actual process of reorganization. Consider an index on a column of *datetime* data. Monday's data logically precedes Tuesday's data, which precedes Wednesday's data, which precedes Thursday's data, and so on. If, however, Monday's data is on page 88, Tuesday's is on page 50, Wednesday's is on page 100, and Thursday's is on page 77, the physical and logical ordering doesn't match in the slightest, and we have logical fragmentation. When defragmenting an index, SQL Server determines the first physical page belonging to the leaf level (page 50, in our case) and the first logical page in the leaf level (page 88, which holds Monday's data) and swaps the data on those two pages using one additional new page as a temporary storage area. After this swap, the first logical page with Monday's data is on page 50, the lowest numbered physical page. After each page swap, all locks and latches are released and the key of the last page moved is saved. The next iteration of the algorithm uses the saved key to find the next logical page—Tuesday's data, which is now on page 88. The next physical page is 77, which holds Thursday's data. So another swap is made to place Tuesday's data on page 77 and Thursday's on page 88. This process continues until no more swaps need to be made. Note that no defragmenting is done for pages on mixed extents.

You need to be aware of some restrictions on using the REORGANIZE option. Certainly, if the index is disabled it cannot be defragmented. Also, because the process of removing fragmentation needs to work on individual pages, you get an error if you try to reorganize an index that has the option ALLOW_PAGE_LOCKS set to OFF. Reorganization cannot happen if a concurrent online index is built on the same index or if another process is concurrently reorganizing the same index.

You can observe the progress of each index's reorganization in the *sys.dm_exec_requests* DMV in the *percent_complete* column. The value in this column reports the percentage completed in one index's reorganization. If you are reorganizing multiple indexes in the same command, you might see the value go up and down as each index is defragmented in turn.

## Rebuilding an Index

You can completely rebuild an index in several ways. You can use a simple combination of *DROP INDEX* followed by *CREATE INDEX*, but this method is probably the least preferable. In particular, if you are rebuilding a clustered index in this way, all the nonclustered indexes must be rebuilt when you drop the clustered index. This nonclustered index rebuilding is necessary to change the row locators in the leaf level from the clustered key values to row IDs. Then, when you rebuild the clustered index, all the nonclustered indexes must be rebuilt again. In addition, if the index supports a PRIMARY KEY or UNIQUE constraint, you can't use the *DROP INDEX* command at all—unless you first drop all the FOREIGN KEYs. Although this is possible, it is not preferable.

Better solutions are to use the *ALTER INDEX* command or to use the DROP_EXISTING clause along with *CREATE INDEX*. As an example, here are both methods for rebuilding the *PK_TransactionHistory_TransactionID* index on the *Production.TransactionHistory* table:

```
ALTER INDEX PK_TransactionHistory_TransactionID
        ON Production.TransactionHistory REBUILD;

CREATE UNIQUE CLUSTERED INDEX PK_TransactionHistory_TransactionID
        ON Production.TransactionHistory
            (TransactionDate, TransactionID)
        WITH DROP_EXISTING;
```

Although the *CREATE* method requires knowing the index schema, it is actually more powerful and offers more options that you can specify. You can change the columns that make up the index, change the uniqueness property, or change a nonclustered index to clustered, as long as there isn't already a clustered index on the table. You can also specify a new filegroup or a partition scheme to use when rebuilding. Note that if you do change the clustered index key properties, all nonclustered indexes must be rebuilt, but only once (not twice, as would happen if we were to execute *DROP INDEX* followed by *CREATE INDEX*).

When using the *ALTER INDEX* command to rebuild a clustered index, the nonclustered indexes never need to be rebuilt just as a side effect because you can't change the index definition at all. However, you can specify ALL instead of an index name and request that all indexes be rebuilt. Another advantage of the *ALTER INDEX* method is that you can specify just a single partition to be rebuilt—if, for example, the fragmentation report from *sys.dm_db_index_physical_stats* shows fragmentation in just one partition or a subset of the partitions.

## Online Index Building

The default behavior of either method of rebuilding an index is that SQL Server takes an exclusive lock on the index, so it is completely unavailable while the index is being rebuilt. If the index is clustered, the entire table is unavailable; if the index is nonclustered, there is a shared lock on the table, which means no modifications can be made but other processes can *SELECT* from the table. Of course, they cannot take advantage of the index you're rebuilding, so the query might not perform as well as it should.

SQL Server 2005 introduced the option to rebuild one or all indexes online. The ONLINE option is available with both *ALTER INDEX* and *CREATE INDEX*, with or without the DROP_EXISTING option. Here's the syntax for building the preceding index, but doing it online:

```
ALTER INDEX PK_TransactionHistory_TransactionID
        ON Production.TransactionHistory REBUILD WITH (ONLINE = ON);
```

The online build works by maintaining two copies of the index simultaneously: the original (the source) and the new one (the target). The target is used only for writing any changes made while the rebuild is going on. All reading is done from the source, and modifications are applied to the source as well. SQL Server row-level versioning is used, so anyone retrieving information from the index can read consistent data. Figure 6-3 (taken from *SQL Server Books Online*) illustrates the source and target, and it shows three phases that the build process goes through. For each phase, the illustration describes what kind of access is allowed, what is happening in the source and target tables, and what locks are applied.

The actual processes might differ slightly depending on whether the index is being built initially or being rebuilt and whether the index is clustered or nonclustered.

Here are the steps involved in rebuilding a nonclustered index:

1. A Shared lock (S-lock) is taken on the index, which prevents any data modification queries, and an Intent-Shared lock (IS-lock) is taken on the table.

2. The index is created with the same structures as the original and marked as write-only.

3. The Shared lock is released on the index, leaving only the Intent-Shared lock on the table.

4. A versioned scan (discussed in detail in Chapter 10) is started on the original index, which means modifications made during the scan are ignored. The scanned data is copied to the target.

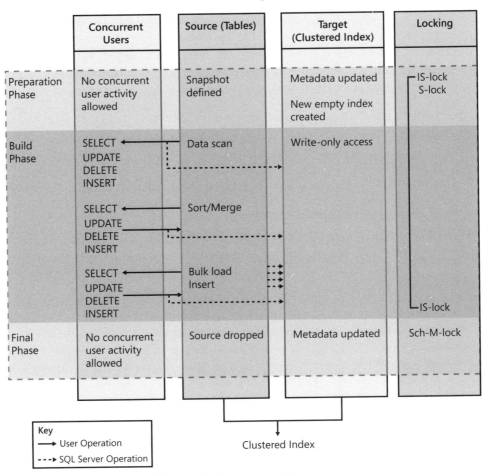

| Concurrent Users | Source (Tables) | Target (Clustered Index) | Locking |
|---|---|---|---|
| **Preparation Phase**<br>No concurrent user activity allowed | Snapshot defined | Metadata updated<br><br>New empty index created | IS-lock<br>S-lock |
| **Build Phase**<br>SELECT<br>UPDATE<br>DELETE<br>INSERT | Data scan | Write-only access | |
| SELECT<br>UPDATE<br>DELETE<br>INSERT | Sort/Merge | | |
| SELECT<br>UPDATE<br>DELETE<br>INSERT | Bulk load<br>Insert | | IS-lock |
| **Final Phase**<br>No concurrent user activity allowed | Source dropped | Metadata updated | Sch-M-lock |

Key
→ User Operation
---▸ SQL Server Operation

Clustered Index

**FIGURE 6-3** The structures and phases of online index building

5. All subsequent modifications write to both the source and the target. Reads use only the source.

6. The scan of the source and copy to the target continues while normal operations are performed. SQL Server uses a proprietary method for reconciling obvious problems such as a record being deleted before the scan has inserted it into the new index.

7. The scan completes.

8. A Schema-Modification lock (Sch-M-lock)—the strictest of all types of locks—is taken to make the table completely unavailable.

9. The source index is dropped, metadata is updated, and the target index is made to be read-write.

10. The Schema-Modification lock is released.

Building a new nonclustered index involves exactly the same steps except there is no target index so the versioned scan is done on the base table, and write operations need to maintain only the target index rather than both indexes. A clustered index rebuild works exactly like a nonclustered rebuild, so long as there is no schema change (a change of index keys or uniqueness property).

For a build of new clustered index, or a rebuild of a clustered index with a schema change, there are a few more differences. First, an intermediate mapping index is used to translate between the source and target physical structures. In addition, all existing nonclustered indexes are rebuilt one at a time after a new base table has been built. For example, creating a clustered index on a heap with two nonclustered indexes involves the following steps:

1. Create a new write-only clustered index.

2. Create a new nonclustered index based on the new clustered index.

3. Create another new nonclustered index based on the new clustered index.

4. Drop the heap and the two original nonclustered indexes.

Before the operation is completed, SQL Server will be maintaining six structures at once. Online index building is not really considered a performance enhancement because an index can actually be built faster offline, and all these structures do not need to be maintained simultaneously. Online index building is an availability feature—you can rebuild indexes to remove all fragmentation or reestablish a fillfactor even if your data must be fully available at all times.

> **Note** There are two exceptions to being able to perform online index operations:
>
> ❑ If the index contains a LOB column, online index operations are not available. This means that if the table contains a LOB column, the clustered index cannot be rebuilt online. Online operations are prevented only if a nonclustered index specifically includes a LOB column.
>
> ❑ A single partition of a clustered or nonclustered index cannot be rebuilt online.

# Summary

In this chapter, we have discussed index concepts, index internals, special index structures, data modifications, and index management. We covered many best practices along the way and, although performance tuning wasn't our primary goal, the more you know about how indexes work internally, the more optimal structures you can create. In addition, by understanding how SQL Server organizes indexes on disk, you can be more adept at troubleshooting problems and managing changes within your database.

# Chapter 7
# Special Storage

*Kalen Delaney*

In Chapter 5, "Tables," and Chapter 6, "Indexes: Internals and Management," we discussed the storage of "regular rows" for both data and index information. I told you in Chapter 5 that regular rows are in a format called *FixedVar*. SQL Server provides ways of storing data in another format called *Column Descriptor (CD)*. It also can store special values in either the FixedVar or CD format that don't fit on the regular 8-KB pages. In this chapter, I'll describe data that exceeds the normal row size limitations and is stored as either row-overflow or Large Object (LOB) data. I'll tell you about two additional methods for storing data on the actual data pages, introduced in Microsoft SQL Server 2008, one that uses a new type of complex column with a regular data row (sparse columns), and one that uses the new CD format (compressed data). I'll also discuss filestream data, a new feature in SQL Server 2008, which allows you to access data from operating system files as if it were part of your relational tables.

Finally, I will discuss the ability of SQL Server to separate data into partitions. Although this doesn't change the format of data in the rows on or the pages, it does change the metadata that keeps track of what space is allocated to which objects.

## Large Object Storage

SQL Server 2008 has two special formats for storing data that doesn't fit on the regular 8-KB data page. These formats allow you to have rows that exceed the maximum row size of 8,060 bytes. As discussed previously, this maximum row size value includes several bytes of overhead stored with the row on the physical pages, so the total size of all the table's defined columns must be slightly less than this amount. In fact, the error message that you get if you try to create a table with more bytes than the allowable maximum is very specific. If you execute the following *CREATE TABLE* statement with column definitions that add up to exactly 8,060 bytes, you'll get the error message shown here:

```
USE test;
CREATE TABLE dbo.bigrows_fixed
(    a char(3000),
     b char(3000),
     c char(2000),
     d char(60) ) ;

Msg 1701, Level 16, State 1, Line 1
Creating or altering table 'bigrows' failed because the minimum row size would be 8067,
including 7 bytes of internal overhead. This exceeds the maximum allowable table row size of
8060 bytes.
```

In this message, you can see the number of overhead bytes (7) that SQL Server wants to store with the row itself. There is also an additional 2 bytes for the row-offset bytes at the end of the page, but those bytes are not included in this total here.

## Restricted-Length Large Object Data (Row-Overflow Data)

One way to exceed this size limit of 8,060 bytes is to use variable-length columns because for variable-length data, SQL Server 2005 and SQL Server 2008 can store the columns in special row-overflow pages, so long as all the fixed-length columns fit into the regular in-row size limit. So let's take a look at a table with all variable-length columns. Note that although my example uses columns that are all *varchar*, columns of other data types can also be stored on row-overflow data pages. These other data types include *varbinary*, *nvarchar*, and *sqlvariant* columns, as well as columns that use the CLR user-defined data types. The following code creates a table with rows that have a maximum defined length that is much longer than 8,060 bytes:

```
USE test;
CREATE TABLE dbo.bigrows
  (a varchar(3000),
   b varchar(3000),
   c varchar(3000),
   d varchar(3000) );
```

In fact, if you run this *CREATE TABLE* statement in SQL Server 7.0, you get an error, and the table is not created at all. In SQL Server 2000, the table is created but you get a warning that inserts or updates might fail if the row size exceeds the maximum.

With SQL Server 2005 and SQL Server 2008, not only can the preceding *dbo.bigrows* table be created, but you can insert a row with column sizes that add up to more than 8,060 bytes with a simple *INSERT*, as shown here:

```
INSERT INTO dbo.bigrows
    SELECT REPLICATE('e', 2100), REPLICATE('f', 2100),
     REPLICATE('g', 2100),  REPLICATE('h', 2100);
```

To determine whether SQL Server is storing any data in row-overflow data pages for a particular table, you can run the following allocation query from Chapter 5:

```
SELECT object_name(object_id) AS name,
    partition_id, partition_number AS pnum,  rows,
    allocation_unit_id AS au_id, type_desc as page_type_desc,
    total_pages AS pages
FROM sys.partitions p  JOIN sys.allocation_units a
   ON p.partition_id = a.container_id
WHERE object_id=object_id('dbo.bigrows');
```

This query should return output similar to that shown here:

```
name     partition_id      pnum rows au_id              page_type_desc    pages
----     ----------------- ---- ---- ----------------   ---------------   -----
bigrows 72057594039238656 1    1    72057594043957248  IN_ROW_DATA       2
bigrows 72057594039238656 1    1    72057594044022784  ROW_OVERFLOW_DATA 2
```

You can see that there are two pages for the one row of regular in-row data and two pages for the one row of row-overflow data. Alternatively, you can use the command *DBCC IND(test, bigrows, -1)* and see the four pages individually. Looking at only four pages with *DBCC IND* is not too awkward, but once a table starts growing and contains hundreds or thousands of pages (or even more), the output of *DBCC IND* can be very difficult to work with, as *DBCC IND* returns one row per page. Chapter 6 provided you a script to build a table called *sp_tablepages*, which can be used to capture your *DBCC IND* output into a table, and then it is much easier to find just the rows you're interested in, to count the rows, to group them by page type, or to display just a subset of the columns. To populate this table with the information about the *bigrows* table, I can run the following *INSERT* statement:

```
INSERT INTO sp_tablepages
    EXEC ('DBCC IND (test, bigrows, -1)');
```

Once the table is populated, you can select only the columns of interest, as follows:

```
SELECT PageFID, PagePID, ObjectID, PartitionID, IAM_chain_type, PageType
FROM sp_tablepages;
```

You should see the four rows shown, one for each page, as follows:

```
PageFID PagePID  ObjectID  PartitionID        IAM_chain_type   PageType
------- -------- --------- -----------------  ---------------  --------
1       2252     85575343  72057594039238656  Row-overflow data 3
1       2251     85575343  72057594039238656  Row-overflow data 10
1       2254     85575343  72057594039238656  In-row data       1
1       2253     85575343  72057594039238656  In-row data       10
```

Two pages are for the row-overflow data, and two are for the in-row data. As you saw in Chapter 6, the *PageType* values have the following meanings:

- *PageType* = 1, Data page.
- *PageType* = 2, Index page.
- *PageType* = 3, LOB or row-overflow page, TEXT_MIXED.
- *PageType* = 4, LOB or row-overflow page, TEXT_DATA.
- *PageType* = 10, IAM page.

I'll tell you more about the different types of LOB pages in the section entitled "Unrestricted-Length Large Object Data," later in this chapter.

We can see that there is one data page and one IAM page for the in-row data, and one data page and one IAM page for the row-overflow data. With the results from *DBCC IND*, we could then look at the page contents with *DBCC PAGE*. On the data page for the in-row data, we would see three of the four *varchar* column values, and the fourth column would be stored on the data page for the row-overflow data. If you run *DBCC PAGE* for the data page storing the in-row data (page 1:2254 in my example), you'll notice that it isn't necessarily the fourth column in the column order that is stored off the row. I won't show you the entire contents of the rows because the single row fills almost the entire page. When I look at the in-row data page using *DBCC PAGE*, I see the column with *e*, the column with *g*, and the column with *h*, and it is the column with *f* that has moved to the new row. In the place of that column, we can see the bytes shown here:

```
65020000 00010000 00290000 00340800 00cc0800 00010000 0067
```

I have included the last byte with *e* (ASCII code hexadecimal 65) and the first byte with *g* (ASCII code hexadecimal 67), and in between, there are 24 other bytes. Bytes 16 through 23 (the 17th through the 24th bytes) of those 24 bytes are treated as an 8-byte numeric value: cc08000001000000. We need to reverse the byte order and break it into a 2-byte hex value for the slot number, a 2-byte hex value for the file number, and a 4-byte hex value for the page number. So the file number is 0x0000 for slot 0 because this overflowing column is the first (and only) data on the row-overflow page. We have 0x0001, or 1, for the file number, and 0x000008cc, or 2252, for the page number. These are the same file and page numbers that we saw using *DBCC IND*.

The first 16 bytes in the row have the meanings indicated in Table 7-1.

**TABLE 7-1  The First 16 Bytes of a Row-Overflow Pointer**

| Bytes | Hex Value | Decimal Value | Meaning |
|---|---|---|---|
| 0 | 0x02 | 2 | Type of special field:<br>1 = LOB<br>2 = overflow |
| 1–2 | 0x0000 | 0 | Level in the B-tree (always 0 for overflow) |
| 3 | 0x00 | 0 | Unused |
| 4–7 | 0x00000001 | 1 | Sequence: a value used by optimistic concurrency control for cursors that increases every time a LOB or overflow column is updated |
| 8–11 | 0x00000029 | 2686976 | Timestamp: a random value used by *DBCC CHECKTABLE* that remains unchanged during the lifetime of each LOB or overflow column |
| 12–15 | 0x00000834 | 2100 | Length |

SQL Server stores variable-length columns on row-overflow pages only under certain conditions. The determining factor is the length of the row itself. It doesn't matter how full the regular page is into which SQL Server is trying to insert the new row. SQL Server constructs the row normally, and stores some of its columns on overflow pages only if the row itself needs more than 8,060 bytes.

Each column in the table is either completely on the row or completely off the row. This means that a 4,000-byte variable-length column cannot have half its bytes on the regular data page and half on a row-overflow page. If a row is less than 8,060 bytes and there is no room on the page where SQL Server is trying to insert it, normal page splitting algorithms (described in Chapter 6) are applied.

One row can span many row-overflow pages if it contains many large variable-length columns. For example, you can create the table *dbo.hugerows* and insert a single row into it as follows:

```
CREATE TABLE dbo.hugerows
  (a varchar(3000),
   b varchar(8000),
   c varchar(8000),
   d varchar(8000));

INSERT INTO dbo.hugerows
    SELECT REPLICATE('a', 3000), REPLICATE('b', 8000),
        REPLICATE('c', 8000),  REPLICATE('d', 8000);
```

Now if I run the allocation query shown previously, substituting *hugerows* for *bigrows*, I get the results shown here:

| name | partition_id | pnum | rows | au_id | page_type_desc | pages |
|------|-------------|------|------|-------|----------------|-------|
| hugerows | 72057594039304192 | 1 | 1 | 72057594044088320 | IN_ROW_DATA | 2 |
| hugerows | 72057594039304192 | 1 | 1 | 72057594044153856 | ROW_OVERFLOW_DATA | 4 |

There are four pages for the row-overflow information, one for the row-overflow IAM page, and three for the columns that didn't fit in the regular row. The number of large variable-length columns that a table can have is not unlimited, although it is quite large. There is a limit of 1,024 columns in any table. (The 1,024-column limit can be exceeded when you are using sparse columns, which is discussed later in this chapter.) But another limit is reached before that. When a column has to be moved off a regular page onto a row-overflow page, SQL Server keeps a pointer to the row-overflow information as part of the original row, which we saw in the DBCC output before is 24 bytes, and the row still needs 2 bytes in the column-offset array for each variable-length column, whether or not the variable-length column is stored in the row. So it turns out that 308 is the maximum number of overflowing columns we can have, and such a row needs 8,008 bytes just for the 26 overhead bytes for each overflowing column in the row.

> **Note**  Just because SQL Server can store lots of large columns on row-overflow pages doesn't mean it's always a good idea to do so. This capability does allow you more flexibility in the organization of your tables, but you might pay a heavy performance price if many additional pages need to be accessed for every row of data. Row-overflow pages are intended to be a solution in the situation where most rows fit completely on your data pages and you have row-overflow data only occasionally. Using row-overflow pages, SQL Server can handle the extra data effectively, without requiring a redesign of your table.

In some cases, if a large variable-length column shrinks, it can be moved back to the regular row. However, for efficiency reasons, if the decrease is just a few bytes, SQL Server does not bother checking. Only when a column stored in a row-overflow page is reduced by more than 1,000 bytes does SQL Server even consider checking to see whether the column can now fit on the regular data page. You can observe this behavior if you previously created the *dbo.bigrows* table for the previous example and inserted only the one row with 2,100 characters in each column.

The following update reduces the size of the first column by 500 bytes, reducing the row size to 7,900 bytes, which should all fit on one data page:

```
UPDATE bigrows
SET a = replicate('a', 1600);
```

However, if you run the allocation query again, you'll still see two row-overflow pages: one for the row-overflow data and one for the IAM page. Now reduce the size of the first column by more than 1,000 bytes and run the allocation query once more:

```
UPDATE bigrows
SET a = 'aaaaa';
```

You should see only three pages for the table now, because there is no longer a row-overflow data page. The IAM page for the row-overflow data pages has not been removed, but you no longer have a data page for row-overflow data.

Keep in mind that row-overflow data storage applies only to columns of variable-length data, which are defined as no longer than the normal variable-length maximum of 8,000 bytes per column. In addition, to store a variable-length column on a row-overflow page, you must meet the following conditions:

- All the fixed-length columns, including overhead bytes, must add up to no more than 8,060 bytes. (The pointer to each row-overflow column adds 24 bytes of overhead to the row.)

- The actual length of the variable-length column must be more than 24 bytes.

- The column must not be part of the clustered index key.

If you have single columns that might need to store more than 8,000 bytes, you should use either LOB (*text*, *image*, or *ntext*) columns or use the *MAX* data types.

## Unrestricted-Length Large Object Data

If a table contains the older LOB data types (*text*, *ntext*, or *image* types), by default the actual data is not stored on the regular data pages. Like row-overflow data, LOB data is stored in its own set of pages, and the allocation query shows you pages for LOB data as well as pages for regular in-row data and row-overflow data. For LOB columns, SQL Server stores a 16-byte pointer in the data row that indicates where the actual data can be found. Although the default behavior is to store all the LOB data off the data row, SQL Server allows you to change the storage mechanism by setting a table option to allow LOB data to be stored in the data row itself if it is small enough. Note that there is no database or server setting to control storing small LOB columns on the data pages; it is managed as a table option.

By default no LOB data is stored in the data row. Instead, the data row contains only a 16-byte pointer to a page (or the first of a set of pages) where the data can be found. These pages are 8 KB in size, like any other page in SQL Server, and individual *text*, *ntext*, and *image* pages aren't limited to storing data for only one occurrence of a *text*, *ntext*, or *image* column. A *text*, *ntext*, or *image* page can hold data from multiple columns and from multiple rows; the page can even have a mix of *text*, *ntext*, and *image* data. However, one *text* or *image* page can hold only *text* or *image* data from a single table. (Even more specifically, one *text* or *image* page can hold only *text* or *image* data from a single partition of a table, which will become clear when I discuss partitioning metadata at the end of this chapter.)

The collection of 8-KB pages that make up a LOB column aren't necessarily located next to each other. The pages are logically organized in a B-tree structure, so operations starting in the middle of the LOB string are very efficient. The structure of the B-tree varies slightly depending on whether the amount of data is less than or more than 32 KB. (See Figure 7-1 for the general structure.) B-trees were discussed in detail when describing indexes in Chapter 6.

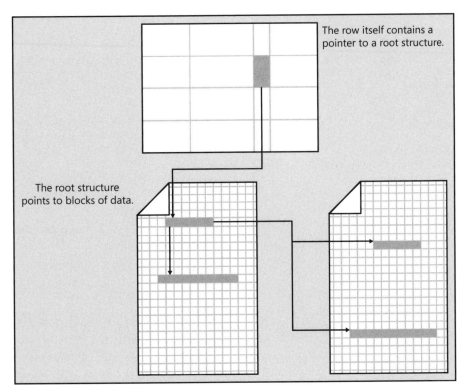

**FIGURE 7-1** A text column pointing to a B-tree that contains the blocks of data

If the amount of LOB data is less than 32 KB, the text pointer in the data row points to an 84-byte text root structure. This forms the root node of the B-tree structure. The root node points to the blocks of *text, ntext,* or *image* data. Although the data for LOB columns is arranged logically in a B-tree, both the root node and the individual blocks of data are spread physically throughout LOB pages for the table. They're placed wherever space is available. The size of each block of data is determined by the size written by an application. Small blocks of data are combined to fill a page. If the amount of data is less than 64 bytes, it's all stored in the root structure.

If the amount of data for one occurrence of a LOB column exceeds 32 KB, SQL Server starts building intermediate nodes between the data blocks and the root node. The root structure and the data blocks are interleaved throughout the *text* and *image* pages. The intermediate nodes, however, are stored in pages that aren't shared between occurrences of *text* or *image* columns. Each page storing intermediate nodes contains only intermediate nodes for one *text* or *image* column in one data row.

SQL Server can store the LOB root and the actual LOB data on two different types of pages. One of these, referred to as TEXT_MIXED, allows LOB data from multiple rows to share the same pages. However, once your text data gets larger than about 40 KB, SQL Server starts devoting whole pages to a single LOB value. These pages are referred to as TEXT_DATA pages.

You can see this behavior by creating a table with a *text* column, inserting a value of less than 40 KB and then a value of greater than 40 KB, and examining the output of *DBCC IND*. The following script uses the *sp_tablepages* table created previously:

```
IF EXISTS (SELECT * FROM sys.tables
                        WHERE name = 'textdata')
    DROP TABLE textdata;
GO
CREATE TABLE textdata
 (bigcol text);
GO
INSERT INTO textdata
    SELECT REPLICATE(convert(varchar(MAX), 'a'), 38000);
GO
TRUNCATE TABLE sp_tablepages;
GO
INSERT INTO sp_tablepages
  EXEC('DBCC IND(test, textdata, -1)');
GO
SELECT PageFID, PagePID, ObjectID, IAM_chain_type, PageType
FROM sp_tablepages;
GO
INSERT INTO textdata
    SELECT REPLICATE(convert(varchar(MAX), 'a'), 41000);
GO
TRUNCATE TABLE sp_tablepages;
GO
INSERT INTO sp_tablepages
  EXEC('DBCC IND(test, textdata, -1)');
GO
SELECT PageFID, PagePID, ObjectID, IAM_chain_type, PageType
FROM sp_tablepages;
```

The first time that you select from *sp_tablepages*, you should have *PageType* values of 1, 3, and 10. The second time, once we have inserted data greater than 40 KB in size, we should also see *PageType* values of 4. *PageType* 3 indicates a TEXT_MIXED page, and *PageType* 4 indicates a TEXT_DATA page.

## LOB Data Stored in the Data Row

If you store all your LOB data type values outside your regular data pages, SQL Server needs to perform additional page reads every time you access that data, just as it does for row-overflow pages. In some cases, you might notice a performance improvement by allowing some of the LOB data to be stored in the data row. You can enable a table option called *text in row* for a particular table by setting the option to 'ON' (including the quote marks) or by specifying a maximum number of bytes to be stored in the data row. The following command enables up to 500 bytes of LOB data to be stored with the regular row data in a table called *employee*:

```
EXEC sp_tableoption employee, 'text in row', 500;
```

Note that the value is in bytes, not characters. For *ntext* data, each character needs 2 bytes so that any *ntext* column is stored in the data row if it is less than or equal to 250 characters. Once you enable the *text in row* option, you never get just the 16-byte pointer for the LOB data in the row, as is the case when the option is not 'ON'. If the data in the LOB field is more than the specified maximum, the row holds the root structure containing pointers to the separate chunks of LOB data. The minimum size of a root structure is 24 bytes, and the possible range of values that *text in row* can be set to is 24 to 7,000 bytes. (If you specify the option 'ON' instead of a specific number, SQL Server assumes the default value of 256 bytes.)

To disable the *text in row* option, you can set the value to either 'OFF' or 0. To determine whether a table has the *text in row* property enabled, you can inspect the *sys.tables* catalog view as follows:

```
SELECT name, text_in_row_limit
FROM sys.tables
WHERE name = 'employee';
```

This *text_in_row_limit* value indicates the maximum number of bytes allowed for storing LOB data in a data row. If a 0 is returned, the *text in row* option is disabled.

Let's create a table very similar to the one we created to look at row structures, but we'll change the *varchar(250)* column to the *text* data type. We'll use almost the same *INSERT* statement to insert one row into the table:

```
CREATE TABLE HasText
(
Col1 char(3)      NOT NULL,
Col2 varchar(5)   NOT NULL,
Col3 text         NOT NULL,
Col4 varchar(20)  NOT NULL
);

INSERT HasText VALUES
    ('AAA', 'BBB', REPLICATE('X', 250), 'CCC');
```

Now let's find the basic information for this table using the allocation query and also look at the *DBCC IND* values for this table:

```
SELECT convert(char(7), object_name(object_id))  AS name,
    partition_id, partition_number AS pnum,  rows,
    allocation_unit_id AS au_id, convert(char(17), type_desc) as page_type_desc,
    total_pages AS pages
FROM sys.partitions p  JOIN sys.allocation_units a
  ON p.partition_id = a.container_id
WHERE object_id=object_id('dbo.HasText');

DBCC IND (test, HasText, -1);
```

```
name      partition_id       pnum rows  au_id               page_type_desc   pages
-------   ----------------   ---- ----- ----------------   ---------------   -----
HasText 72057594039435264 1   1     72057594044350464 IN_ROW_DATA       2
HasText 72057594039435264 1   1     72057594044416000 LOB_DATA          2


PageFID  PagePID  ObjectID   PartitionID         IAM_chain_type    PageType
-------  -------  --------   ----------------   --------------    --------
1        2197     133575514  72057594039435264   LOB data          3
1        2198     133575514  72057594039435264   LOB data          10
1        2199     133575514  72057594039435264   In-row data       1
1        2200     133575514  72057594039435264   In-row data       10
```

You can see two LOB pages (the LOB data page and the LOB IAM page) and two pages for the in-row data (again, the data page and the IAM page). The data page for the in-row data is 2199, and the LOB data is on page 2197. Figure 7-2 shows the output from running *DBCC PAGE* on page 2199. The row structure is very similar to the row structure shown in Chapter 5, in Figure 5-10, except for the text field itself. Bytes 21 to 36 are the 16-byte text pointer, and you can see the value 9508 starting at offset 29. When we reverse the bytes, it becomes 0x0895, or 2197 decimal, which is the page containing the text data, as we saw in the *DBCC IND* output.

```
DATA:


Slot 0, Offset 0x60, Length 40, DumpStyle BYTE

Record Type = PRIMARY_RECORD        Record Attributes =  NULL_BITMAP VARIABLE_COLUMNS
Record Size = 40
Memory Dump @0x625BC060

00000000:   30000700 41414104 00600300 15002580 †0...AAA..`....%.
00000010:   28004242 420000e1 07000000 00950800 †(.BBB..á.,...?..
00000020:   00010001 00434343 ††††††††††††††††††.....CCC
```

**FIGURE 7-2** A row containing a text pointer

Now let's enable text data in the row, for up to 500 bytes:

```
EXEC sp_tableoption HasText, 'text in row', 500;
```

Enabling this option does not force the text data to be moved into the row. We have to update the text value to actually force the data movement:

```
UPDATE HasText
SET col3 =  REPLICATE('Z', 250);
```

If you run *DBCC PAGE* on the original data page, you see that the text column of 250 *z*'s is now in the data row and that the row is practically identical in structure to the row containing *varchar* data that we saw in Figure 5-10.

Although enabling *text in row* does not move the data immediately, disabling the option does. If you turn off *text in row*, the LOB data moves immediately back onto its own pages, so you must make sure you don't turn this off for a large table during heavy operations.

A final issue when working with LOB data and the *text in row* option is dealing with the situation where *text in row* is enabled but the LOB is longer than the maximum configured length for some rows. If you change the maximum length for *text in row* to 50 for the *HasText* table we've been working with, this also forces the LOB data for all rows with more than 50 bytes of LOB data to be moved off the page immediately, just as when you disable the option completely:

```
EXEC sp_tableoption HasText, 'text in row', 50;
```

However, setting the limit to a smaller value is different than disabling the option in two ways. First, some of the rows might still have LOB data that is under the limit, and for those rows, the LOB data is stored completely in the data row. Second, if the LOB data doesn't fit, the information stored in the data row itself is not simply the 16-byte pointer, as it would be if *text in row* were turned off. Instead, for LOB data that doesn't fit in the defined size, the row contains a root structure for a B-tree that points to chunks of the LOB data. So long as the *text in row* option is not 'OFF' (or 0), SQL Server never stores the simple 16-byte LOB pointer in the row. It stores either the LOB data itself, if it fits, or the root structure for the LOB data B-tree.

A root structure is at least 24 bytes long (which is why 24 is the minimum size for the *text in row* limit) and the meaning of the bytes is similar to the meaning of the 24 bytes in the row-overflow pointer. The main difference is that no length is stored in bytes 12–15. Instead, bytes 12–23 constitute a link to a chunk of LOB data on a separate page. If multiple LOB chucks are accessed via the root, multiple sets of 12 bytes can be here, each pointing to LOB data on a separate page.

As indicated previously, when you first enable *text in row*, no data movement occurs until the text data is actually updated. The same is true if the limit is increased—that is, even if the new limit is large enough to accommodate the LOB data that was stored outside the row, the LOB data is not moved onto the row automatically. You must update the actual LOB data first.

Another point to keep in mind is that even if the amount of LOB data is less than the limit, the data is not necessarily stored in the row. You're still limited to a maximum row size of

8,060 bytes for a single row on a data page, so the amount of LOB data that can be stored in the actual data row might be reduced if the amount of non-LOB data is large. In addition, if a variable-length column needs to grow, it might push LOB data off the page so as not to exceed the 8,060-byte limit. Growth of variable-length columns always has priority over storing LOB data in the row. If no variable-length *char* fields need to grow during an update operation, SQL Server checks for growth of in-row LOB data, in column offset order. If one LOB needs to grow, others might be pushed off the row.

Finally, you should be aware that SQL Server logs all movement of LOB data, which means that reducing the limit of or turning OFF the *text in row* option can be a very time-consuming operation for a large table.

Although large data columns using the LOB data types can be stored and managed very efficiently, using them in your tables can be problematic. Data stored as *text*, *ntext*, or *image* cannot always be manipulated using the normal data manipulation commands, and in many cases, you need to resort to using the operations *readtext*, *writetext*, and *updatetext*, which require dealing with byte offsets and data-length values. Prior to SQL Server 2005, you had to decide whether to limit your columns to a maximum of 8,000 bytes or deal with your large data columns using different operators than you used for your shorter columns. SQL Server 2005 and SQL Server 2008 provide a solution that gives you the best of both worlds, as we'll see in the next section.

## Storage of MAX-Length Data

SQL Server 2005 and SQL Server 2008 give us the option of defining a variable-length field using the MAX specifier. Although this functionality is frequently described by referring only to *varchar(MAX)*, the MAX specifier can also be used with *nvarchar* and *varbinary*. You can indicate the MAX specifier instead of an actual size when you define a column, variable, or parameter using one of these types. By using the MAX specifier, you leave it up to SQL Server to determine whether to store the value as a regular *varchar*, *nvarchar*, or *varbinary* value or as a LOB. In general, if the actual length is 8,000 bytes or less, the value is treated as if it were one of the regular variable-length data types, including possibly overflowing onto row-overflow pages. However, if the *varchar(MAX)* column does need to spill off the page, the extra pages required are considered LOB pages and show the *IAM_chain_type* LOB when examined using *DBCC IND*. If the actual length is greater than 8,000 bytes, SQL Server stores and treats the value exactly as if it were *text*, *ntext*, or *image*. Because variable-length columns with the MAX specifier are treated either as regular variable-length columns or as LOB columns, no special discussion of their storage is needed.

The size of values specified with MAX can reach the maximum size supported by LOB data, which is currently 2 GB. By using the MAX specifier, though, you are indicating that the maximum size should be the maximum the system supports. If you upgrade a table with a *varchar(MAX)* column to a later version of SQL Server in the future, the MAX length will be whatever the new maximum is in the new version.

**Tip**  Because the MAX data types can store LOB data as well as regular row data, it is recommended that you use these data types in future development in place of the *text, ntext,* or *image* types, which Microsoft has indicated will be removed in a future version.

**Note**  Although the acronym *LOB* can be expanded to mean "Large Object," I will be using these two terms to mean two different things. I will use *LOB* only when I want to refer to the data using the special storage format shown in Figure 7-1. I will use the term *large object* when referring to any of the methods for storing data that might be too large for a regular data page. This includes row-overflow columns, the actual LOB data types, the MAX data types, and filestream data.

## Appending Data into a LOB Column

In the storage engine, each LOB column is broken into fragments of a maximum size of 8,040 bytes each. When you append data to a large object, SQL Server finds the append point and looks at the current fragment where the new data will be added. It calculates the size of the new fragment (including the newly appended data). If the size is more than 8,040 bytes, SQL Server allocates new large object pages until a fragment is left that is less than 8,040 bytes, and then it finds a page that has enough space for the remaining bytes.

When SQL Server allocates pages for LOB data, it has two allocation strategies:

1. For data that is less than 64 KB in size, it randomly allocates a page. This page comes from an extent that is part of the large object IAM, but the pages are not guaranteed to be continuous.

2. For data that is more than 64 KB in size, it uses an append-only page allocator that allocates one extent at a time and writes the pages continuously in the extent.

So from a performance standpoint, it is beneficial to write fragments of 64 KB at a time. It might be beneficial to allocate 1 MB in advance if you know that the size will be 1 MB. However, you need to take into account the space required for the transaction log as well. If you a create a 1-MB fragment first with any random contents, SQL Server logs the 1 MB, and then all the changes are logged as well. When you perform large object data updates, no new pages need to be allocated, but the changes still need to be logged.

So long as the large object values are small, they can be in the data page. In this case, some preallocation might be a good idea so that the large object data doesn't become too fragmented. A general recommendation might be that if the amount of data to be inserted into a large object column in a single operation is relatively small, that you insert a large object value of the final expected value, and then replace substrings of that initial value as needed. For larger sizes, try to append or insert in chunks of 8 * 8,040 bytes. This allocates a whole extent each time, and 8,040 bytes are stored on each page.

If you do find that your large object data is becoming fragmented, there is an option to ALTER INDEX REORGANIZE to defragment your large object data. In fact, this option (WITH LOB_ COMPACTION) is on by default, so you just need to make sure that you don't set it to 'OFF'.

# Filestream Data

Although the flexible methods that SQL Server uses to store large object data in the database give you many advantages over data stored in the file system, they also have many disadvantages. Some of the benefits of storing large objects in your database include the following:

- Transactional consistency of your large object data can be guaranteed.
- Your backup and restore operations include the large object data, allowing you integrated, point-in-time recovery of your large objects.
- All data can be stored using a single storage and query environment.

Some of the disadvantages of storing large objects in your database include the following:

- Large objects can take a very large number of buffers in cache.
- Updating large objects can cause extensive database fragmentation.
- Database files can become extremely large.

SQL Server 2008 allows you to manage file system objects as if they were part of your database to provide the benefits of having large objects in the database while minimizing the disadvantages. The data stored in the file system is referred to as *filestream* data. As you start evaluating whether filestream data is beneficial for your applications, you must consider both the benefits and the drawbacks. Some of the benefits of filestream data include the following:

- The large object data is stored in the file system but rooted in the database as a 48-byte file pointer value in the column containing the filestream data.
- The large object data is kept transactionally consistent with structured data.
- The large object data is accessible through both Transact-SQL (T-SQL) and the NTFS streaming APIs, which can provide great performance benefits.
- The large object size is limited only by the NTFS volume size, not the old 2-GB limit for LOB data.

Some of the drawbacks of using filestream data include the following:

- Database mirroring cannot be used on databases containing filestream data.
- Database snapshots cannot include the filestream filegroups, so the filestream data is unavailable. A *SELECT* statement in a database snapshot that requests a filestream column generates an error.
- Filestream data can't be encrypted natively by SQL Server.

# Enabling Filestream Data for SQL Server

The capability to access filestream data must be enabled both outside and inside your SQL Server 2008 instance, which I mentioned in Chapter 1, "SQL Server 2008 Architecture and Configuration," when discussing configuration. Through the SQL Server Configuration Manager, you must enable T-SQL access to filestream data, and if that has been enabled, you can also enable file I/O streaming access. If file I/O streaming access is allowed, you can allow remote clients to have access to the streaming data if you want. Once the SQL Server Configuration Manager is opened, make sure you have selected SQL Server Services in the left pane. In the right pane, right-click the SQL instance that you want to configure and select Properties from the drop-down menu. The Properties dialog box has four tabs, including one labeled *FILESTREAM*. You can see the details of the *FILESTREAM* tab of the SQL Server Properties dialog box in Figure 7-3.

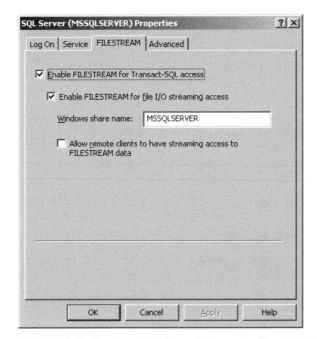

**FIGURE 7-3** Configuring a SQL Server instance to allow *FILESTREAM* access

After the server instance has been configured, you need to use *sp_configure* to set your SQL Server instance to the level of filestream access that you require. Three values are possible. A value of 0 means that no filestream access is allowed, a value of 1 means that you can use T-SQL to access filestream data, and a value of 2 means that you can use both T-SQL and the Win32 API for filestream access. As with all configuration options, don't forget to run the *RECONFIGURE* command after changing a setting, as shown here:

```
EXEC sp_configure 'filestream access level', 1;
RECONFIGURE;
```

## Creating a Filestream-Enabled Database

To store filestream data, a database must have at least one filegroup that has been created to allow filestream data. When creating a database, a filegroup that allows filestream data is specified differently than a filegroup containing row data in several different ways:

- There can be only one file in the filestream filegroup.

- The path specified for the filestream filegroup must exist only up to the last folder name. The last folder name must not exist but will be created when SQL Server creates the database.

- The *size, maxsize,* and *filegrowth* properties do not apply to filestream filegroups.

- If there is no filestream-containing filegroup specified as DEFAULT, the first filestream-containing filegroup listed is the default. (Therefore, there is one default filegroup for row data and one default filegroup for filestream data.)

Look at the following code, which creates a database with two filestream-containing filegroups. The path C:\Data2 must exist, but it must not contain either the *filestream1* or the *filestream2* folders:

```
CREATE DATABASE MyFilestreamDB
ON
PRIMARY ( NAME = Rowdata1,
    FILENAME = 'c:\Data2\Rowdata1.mdf'),
FILEGROUP FileStreamGroup1 CONTAINS FILESTREAM DEFAULT( NAME = FSData1,
    FILENAME = 'c:\Data2\filestream1'),
FILEGROUP FileStreamGroup2 CONTAINS FILESTREAM ( NAME = FSData2,
    FILENAME = 'c:\Data2\filestream2')
LOG ON  ( NAME = FSDBLOG,
    FILENAME = 'c:\Data2\FSDB_log.ldf');
```

When the above *MyFilestreamDB* database is created, SQL Server creates the two folders, *filestream1* and *filestream2*, in the C:\Data2 directory. These folders are referred to as the filestream *containers.* Initially, each container contains an empty folder called *$FSLOG* and a header file called *filestream.hdr.* As tables are created to use filestream space in a container, a folder for each partition or each table containing filestream data is created in the container.

An existing database can be altered to have a filestream filegroup added, and then a subsequent *ALTER DATABASE* command can add a file to the filestream filegroup. Note that you cannot add filestream filegroups to the *master, model,* and *tempdb* databases.

## Creating a Table to Hold Filestream Data

To specify that a column is to contain filestream data, it must be defined as type *varbinary(MAX)* with a *FILESTREAM* property. The database containing the table must have at least one filegroup defined for *FILESTREAM.* Your table creation statement can specify which filegroup its filestream data is stored in, and if none is specified, the default filestream filegroup is used. Finally, any table that has filestream columns must have a column of the *uniqueidentifier* data type with the *ROWGUIDCOL* attribute specified. This column must not allow NULL values and must be guaranteed to be unique by specifying either the UNIQUE or PRIMARY KEY single-column constraint. The *ROWGUIDCOL* column acts as a key that the *FILESTREAM* agent can use to locate the actual row in the table to check permissions, obtain the physical path to the file, and possibly lock the row if required.

Now let's look at the files that are created within the container. When created in the *MyFilestreamDB* database, the table here adds several folders to the container for the *FileStreamGroup1* container:

```
CREATE TABLE MyFilestreamDB.dbo.Records
(
        [Id] [uniqueidentifier] ROWGUIDCOL NOT NULL UNIQUE,
        [SerialNumber] INTEGER UNIQUE,
        [Chart_Primary] VARBINARY(MAX) FILESTREAM NULL,
        [Chart_Secondary] VARBINARY(MAX) FILESTREAM NULL)
FILESTREAM_ON FileStreamGroup1;
```

Because this table is created on *FileStreamGroup1*, the *filestream1* container is used. One subfolder is created within *filestream1* for each table or partition created in the *FileStreamGroup1* filegroup, and those file names will be GUIDs. Each of those files has a subfolder for each column within the table or partition, which holds filestream data, and again, the names of those folders will be GUIDs. Figure 7-4 shows the structure of my files on disk right after the *MyFilestreamDB.dbo.Records* table is created. The *filestream2* folder only has the $FSLOG subfolder, and no subfolders for any tables. The *filestream1* folder has a GUID-named subfolder for the *dbo.Records* table, and within that, a GUID-named subfolder for each of the two *FILESTREAM* columns in the table. There are still no files except for the original *filestream.hdr* file.

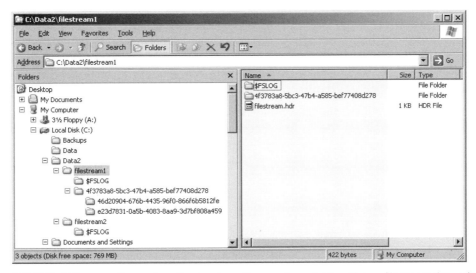

**FIGURE 7-4** The operating system file structure after creating a table with two filestream data columns

Files are not added until we actually insert filestream data into the table.

> **Warning** When the table is dropped, the folders, subfolders, and the files they contain are *not* removed from the file system immediately. They are removed by a Garbage Collection thread, which fires at regular intervals and also when the SQL Server service stops and restarts. You can delete the files manually, but be careful. You can delete folders for a column or table that still exists in the database even while the database is online. Subsequent access to that table generates an error message containing the text "Path not found." You might think that SQL Server should prevent any file that is part of the database from being deleted; but to absolutely prevent the file deletions, SQL Server has to hold open file handles for every single file in all the filestream containers for the entire database, and for large tables, that would not be practical.

## Manipulating Filestream Data

Filestream data can be manipulated either using T-SQL or the Win32 API. When using T-SQL, the data can be processed exactly as if it were *varbinary(MAX)*. Using the Win32 API requires that you first obtain the file path and current transaction context. You can then open a WIN32 handle and use that handle to read and write the large object data. All the examples in this section use T-SQL. You can get the details of Win32 manipulation from *SQL Server Books Online*.

As you add data to the table, files are added to the subfolders for each column. *INSERT* operations that fail with a run-time error (for example, due to a uniqueness violation) still create a file for each of the filestream columns in the row. Although the row is never accessible, it still uses file system space.

### Inserting Filestream Data

Data can be inserted using normal T-SQL *INSERT* statements. Filestream data must be inserted using the *varbinary(MAX)* data type, but any string data can be converted in the *INSERT* statement. The following statement adds one row to the *dbo.Records* table created previously, which has two filestream columns. The first filestream column gets a 90,000-byte character string converted to *varbinary(MAX)* and the second filestream column gets an empty binary string. Note that we first convert the nine-character string *Base Data* to *varchar(MAX)* because a normal string value cannot be more than 8,000 bytes. The *REPLICATE* function returns the same data type as its first parameter, so I want that first parameter to be unambiguously a large object. Replicating the 9-byte string 10,000 times results in a 90,000-byte string, which is then converted to *varbinary(MAX)*:

```
USE MyFileStreamDB
INSERT INTO dbo.Records
    SELECT newid (), 24,
      CAST (REPLICATE (CONVERT(varchar(MAX), 'Base Data'), 10000)
                    AS varbinary(max)),
    0x;
```

Note that a value of 0x is an empty binary string, which is not the same as a NULL. Every row that has a non-NULL value in a *FILESTREAM* column has a file, even for zero-length values.

Figure 7-5 shows you what your file system would look like after running the previous code to create a database with two filestream containers and create a table with two *FILESTREAM* columns, and then inserting one row into that table. In the left pane, you can see the two filestream containers (*filestream1* and *filestream2*).

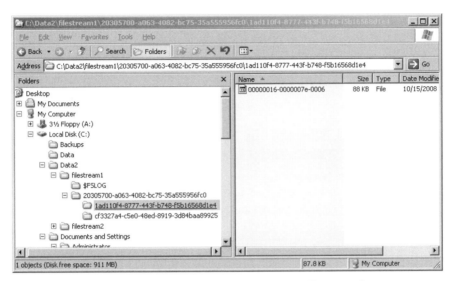

**FIGURE 7-5** The operating system file structure after inserting filestream data

The *filestream1* container has a folder with a GUID name for the *dbo.Records* table that I created, and that folder container has two folders with GUID names, for the two columns in that table. The right pane shows you the file containing the actual data inserted into one of the columns.

## Updating Filestream Data

When an *UPDATE* statement is used to modify a filestream column, the file containing the data is modified and the file increases or decreases in size as appropriate. Specifically, setting the column to an empty, zero-length value causes the file to have a size of zero. Also, in this first release, the T-SQL "chunked update," specified with the .WRITE clause, is not supported. It is recommended that you use file system streaming access for manipulation (both inserts and updates) of your filestream data. Updates to *FILESTREAM* data are always performed as a *DELETE* followed by an *INSERT*, so you see a new row in the directory for the column(s) updated.

When a filestream cell is set to NULL, the filestream file associated with that cell is deleted when the Garbage Collection thread runs. (I'll tell you about Garbage Collection later in this chapter.)

## Deleting Filestream Data

When a row is deleted through the use of a *DELETE* or a *TRUNCATE TABLE* statement, any *FILESTREAM* file associated with the row is deleted. However, the delete of the file is not synchronous with the deletion of the row. The file is deleted by the *FILESTREAM* Garbage Collection thread. This is also true for *DELETE*s that are generated as part of an *UPDATE*. A new row is added, but the old one is not physically removed until Garbage Collection runs.

> **Note** The OUTPUT clause for data manipulation operations (*INSERT, UPDATE, DELETE,* and *MERGE*) is supported the same way as it is for column modifications. However, you need to be careful if you are using the OUTPUT clause to insert into a table with a *varbinary(MAX)* column instead without the filestream specifier. If the filestream data is larger than 2 GB, the insert of filestream data into the table may result in a run-time error.

## Filestream Data and Transactions

Filestream data manipulation is fully transactional. But you need to be aware that when you are manipulating *FILESTREAM* data, not all isolation levels are supported. In addition, some isolation levels are supported for T-SQL access but not for filesystem access. Table 7-2 indicates which isolation levels are available in which access mode.

**TABLE 7-2 Isolation Levels Supported with Filestream Data Manipulation**

| Isolation Level | T-SQL Access | Filesystem Access |
| --- | --- | --- |
| Read uncommitted | Supported | Not supported |
| Read committed | Supported | Supported |
| Repeatable read | Supported | Not supported |
| Serializable | Supported | Not supported |
| Read committed snapshot | Supported | Not supported |
| Snapshot | Supported | Not supported |

If two processes trying to access the same *FILESTREAM* datafile are in incompatible modes, the filesystem APIs fail with an ERROR_SHARING_VIOLATION message instead of just blocking, as would happen when using T-SQL. As with all data access, readers and writers within the same transaction can never get a conflict on the same file but unlike non-*FILESTREAM* access, two write operations within the same transaction can end up conflicting with each other when accessing the same file, unless the file handle has been previously closed. You can read much more about transactions, isolation levels, and conflicts in Chapter 10, "Transactions and Concurrency."

## Logging Filestream Changes

As mentioned previously, each *FILESTREAM* filegroup has a $FSLOG folder that keeps track of all filestream activity that touches that filegroup. The data in this folder is used when you perform transaction log backup and restore operations in the database (which include the *FILESTREAM* filegroup) and also during the recovery process.

The $FSLOG folder primarily keeps track of new information added to the filestream filegroup. A file gets added to the log folder to reflect each of the following:

■ A new table containing filestream data is created.

■ A *FILESTREAM* column is defined.

■ A new row is inserted containing non-NULL data in the *FILESTREAM* column.

■ A *FILESTREAM* value is updated.

■ A *COMMIT* occurs.

Here are some examples:

■ If you create a table containing two filestream columns, four files are added to the $FSLOG folder—one for the table, two for the columns, and one for the implied *COMMIT*.

■ If you insert a single row containing filestream data in an autocommit transaction, two files will be added to the $FSLOG folder—one for the *INSERT* and one for the *COMMIT*.

■ If you insert five rows in an explicit transaction, six files are added to the $FSLOG folder.

Files are not added to the $FSLOG folder when data is deleted or when a table is truncated or dropped. However, the SQL Server transaction log keeps track of these operations, and a new metadata table contains information about the data that has been removed.

## Garbage Collection for Filestream Data

The filestream data can be viewed as serving as the live user data, as well as the log of changes to that data, and as row versions for snapshot operations (discussed in Chapter 10). SQL Server needs to make sure that the filestream data files are not removed if there is any possibility they might be needed for any backup or recovery needs. In particular, for log backups, all new filestream content must be backed up since the transaction log does not contain the actual filestream data, and only the filestream data has the redo information for the actual *FILESTREAM* contents. In general, if your database is not in the SIMPLE recovery mode, you need to back up the log twice before the Garbage Collector can remove unneeded data files from your *FILESTREAM* folders. Let's look at an example. We'll start with a clean slate, by dropping and re-creating the *MyFilestreamDB* database. A *DROP DATABASE* statement immediately removes all the folders and files because now there is no chance we're going to do any subsequent log backups. The script given here re-creates the database and creates a table with just a single *FILESTREAM* column. Finally, the script inserts three rows into the table and backs up the database. If you inspect the *filestream1* container, you see that the folder for the columns contains three files for the three rows:

```
USE master;
GO
DROP DATABASE MyFilestreamDB;
GO
CREATE DATABASE  MyFilestreamDB  ON  PRIMARY
    (NAME = N'Rowdata1', FILENAME = N'c:\data\Rowdata1.mdf' , SIZE = 2304KB ,
     MAXSIZE = UNLIMITED, FILEGROWTH = 1024KB ),
```

```
      FILEGROUP  FileStreamGroup1  CONTAINS FILESTREAM  DEFAULT
         (NAME = N'FSData1', FILENAME = N'c:\data\filestream1' ),
      FILEGROUP  FileStreamGroup2  CONTAINS FILESTREAM
         (NAME = N'FSData2', FILENAME = N'c:\data\filestream2' )
      LOG ON
         (NAME = N'FSDBLOG', FILENAME = N'c:\data\FSDB_log.ldf' , SIZE = 1024KB ,
          MAXSIZE = 2048GB , FILEGROWTH = 10%);
      GO
      USE MyFilestreamDB;
      GO
      CREATE TABLE dbo.Records
      (
              Id [uniqueidentifier] ROWGUIDCOL NOT NULL UNIQUE,
              SerialNumber INTEGER UNIQUE,
              Chart_Primary VARBINARY(MAX) FILESTREAM NULL
      )
      FILESTREAM_ON FileStreamGroup1;
      GO
      INSERT INTO dbo.Records
          VALUES (newid(), 1,
                    CAST (REPLICATE (CONVERT(varchar(MAX), 'Base Data'),
                            10000) as varbinary(max))),
                 (newid(), 2,
                    CAST (REPLICATE (CONVERT(varchar(MAX), 'New Data'),
                            10000) as    varbinary(max))),
                 (newid(), 3, 0x);
      GO
      BACKUP DATABASE MyFileStreamDB to disk = 'C:\backups\FBDB.bak';
      GO
```

Now delete one of the rows, as follows:

```
DELETE dbo.Records
WHERE SerialNumber = 2;
GO
```

Now inspect the files on disk, and you still see three files.

Back up the log and run a checkpoint. Note that in a real system, enough changes would probably be made to your data that your database's log would get full enough to trigger an automatic *CHECKPOINT*. However, during testing, I'm not putting much into the log at all, so I have to force the *CHECKPOINT*:

```
BACKUP LOG  MyFileStreamDB to disk = 'C:\backups\FBDB_log.bak';
CHECKPOINT;
```

Now if you check the *FILESTREAM* data files, you still see three rows. Wait five seconds for Garbage Collection, and you'll still see three rows. We need to back up the log and then force another *CHECKPOINT*:

```
BACKUP LOG  MyFileStreamDB to disk = 'C:\backups\FBDB_log.bak';
CHECKPOINT;
```

Now within five seconds, you should see one of the files disappear. The reason that we need to back up the log twice before the physical file is available for garbage collection is to make sure that the file space is not reused by other filestream operations while it still might be needed for restore purposes.

You can run some additional tests of your own. For example, if you try dropping the *dbo.Records* table, notice that you again have to perform two log backups and *CHECKPOINTs* before SQL Server removes the folders for the table and the column.

## Metadata for Filestream Data

Within your SQL Server tables, the storage required for filestream is not particularly complex. In the row itself, each filestream column contains a file pointer that is 48 bytes in size. Even if you look at a data page with the *DBCC PAGE* command, there is not much more information about the file that is available. However, SQL Server does provide a new function to translate the file pointer to a path name. The function is actually a method applied to the column name in the table. So the following code returns a UNC name for the file containing the actual column's data in the row I inserted previously:

```
SELECT Chart_Primary, Chart_Primary.PathName()
FROM dbo.Records
WHERE SerialNumber = 24;
GO
```

The UNC value returned looks like this:

```
\\<server_name>\<share_name>\v1\<db_name>\<object_schema>\<table_name>\<column_name>\<GUID>
```

Keep in mind the following points about using the *PathName* function:

■ The function name is case-sensitive, even on a server that is not case-sensitive, so it always must be entered as *PathName*.

■ The default *share_name* is the service name for your SQL Server instance. (So for the default instance, it is MSSQLSERVER.) Using the SQL Server Configuration Manager, you can right-click your SQL Server instance and choose Properties. The *FILESTREAM* tab of the SQL Server Properties dialog box allows you to change the *share_name* to another value of your choosing.

■ The *PathName* function can take an optional parameter of 0, 1, or 2, with 0 being the default. The parameter controls only how the *server_name* value is returned; all other values in the UNC string are unaffected. Table 7-3 shows the meanings of the different values.

**TABLE 7-3 Parameter Values for the *PathName* Function**

| Value | Description |
| --- | --- |
| 0 | Returns the server name converted to BIOS format; for example: \\SERVERNAME\ MSSQLSERVER\v1\MyFilestream\dbo\Records\Chart_Primary\ A73F19F7-38EA-4AB0-BB89-E6C545DBD3F9 |
| 1 | Returns the server name without conversion; for example: \\ServerName\MSSQLSERVER\ v1\MyFilestream\Dbo\Records\ Chart_Primary\ A73F19F7-38EA-4AB0-BB89-E6C545DBD3F9 |
| 2 | Returns the complete server path; for example: \\ServerName.MyDomain.com\ MSSQLSERVER\v1\MyFilestream\Dbo\Records\ Chart_Primary\A73F19F7-38EA-4AB0-BB89-E6C545DBD3F9 |

Some of the metadata added in SQL Server 2005 has been enhanced to give you information about your filestream data:

- ***sys.database_files*** returns a row for each of your filestream files. These files have a *type* value of 2 and a *type_desc* value of *FILESTREAM*.

- ***sys.filegroups*** returns a row for each of your filestream filegroups. These files have a *type* value of FD and a *type_desc* value of *FILESTREAM_DATA_FILEGROUP*.

- ***sys.data_spaces*** returns one row for each data space, which is either a filegroup or a partition scheme. Filegroups holding filestream data are indicated by the type FD.

- ***sys.tables*** has a value in the column for *filestream_data_space_id*, which is the data space ID for either the filestream filegroup or the partition scheme that the filestream data uses. Tables with no filestream data have NULL in this column.

- ***sys.columns*** has a value of 1 in the *is_filestream* column for columns with the filestream attribute.

The older metadata, such as the system procedure *sp_helpdb* <database_name> or *sp_help* <object_name>, does not show any information about filestream data.

I mentioned previously that rows or objects that are deleted do not generate files in the $FSLOG folder, but data about the removed data is stored in a system table. No metadata view allows you to see this table; you can observe it only by using the dedicated administrator connection (DAC). You can look in a view called *sys.internal_tables* for an object with *TOMBSTONE* in its name. Then using the DAC, you can look at the data inside the *TOMBSTONE* table. If you rerun the above script but don't back up the log, you can use the following script:

```
USE MyFilestreamDB;
GO
SELECT name FROM sys.internal_tables
WHERE name like '%tombstone%';

-- I see the table named: filestream_tombstone_2073058421
-- Reconnect using DAC, which puts us in the master database
USE MyFileStreamDB;
GO
SELECT * FROM sys.filestream_tombstone_2073058421;
GO
```

If this table is empty, then the log in SQL Server and the $FSLOG are in sync, and all unneeded files have been removed from the *FILESTREAM* containers on disk.

## Performance Considerations for Filestream Data

Although a thorough discussion of performance tuning and troubleshooting is beyond the scope of this book, I want to provide you with some basic information about setting up your system to get high performance from filestream data. Paul Randal, one of the co-authors of this book, has written a white paper on *FILESTREAM* that you can access on the MSDN site at *http://msdn.microsoft.com/en-us/library/cc949109.aspx.* (This white paper is also available on this book's companion Web site, *http://www.SQLServerInternals.com/companion.*) In this section, I'll just briefly mention some of the main points Paul makes regarding what you can do to get good performance. All these suggestions are explained in much more detail in the white paper.

- Make sure you're storing the right-sized data in the right way. Jim Gray (et al.) published a research paper a couple of years ago called "To BLOB or Not To BLOB: Large Object Storage in a Database or a Filesystem?" To summarize the findings, large object data smaller than 256 KB should be stored in a database, and data that is 1 MB or larger should be stored in the file system. For data between these two values, the answer depends on other factors and you should test your application thoroughly. The key point here is that you won't get good performance if you store lots of relatively small large objects using *FILESTREAM*.

- Use an appropriate RAID level for the NTFS volume that hosts the *FILESTREAM* data container. For example, don't use RAID-5 for a write-intensive workload.

- Use an appropriate disk technology. SCSI is usually faster than SATA/IDE because SCSI drives usually have higher rotational speeds, so they have lower latency and seek times. However, SCSI drives are also more expensive.

- Whichever disk technology you choose, if it is SATA, ensure that it supports NCQ, and if SCSI, ensure that it supports CTQ. Both of these allow the drives to process multiple, interleaved I/Os concurrently.

- Separate the data containers from each other, and separate the containers from other database data and log files. This avoids contention for the disk heads.

- Defragment the NTFS volume if needed before setting up *FILESTREAM*, and defragment periodically to maintain good scan performance.

- Turn off 8.3 name generation on the NTFS volume using the command-line *fsutil* utility. This is an order-N algorithm that has to check that the new name generated doesn't collide with any existing names in the directory. Note, however, that this slows insert and update performance down a lot.

- Turn off tracking of last access time using *fsutil*.

- Set the NTFS cluster size appropriately. For larger objects greater than 1 MB in size, use a cluster size of 64 KB to help reduce fragmentation.

- A partial update of *FILESTREAM* data creates a new file. Batch lots of small updates into one large update to reduce churn.

- When streaming the data back to the client, use an SMB buffer size of approximately 60 KB or multiples thereof. This helps keep the buffers from getting overly fragmented, because Transmission Control Protocol/Internet Protocol (TCP/IP) buffers are 64 KB.

Taking these suggestions into consideration and performing thorough testing of your application can give you great performance when working with very large data objects.

# Sparse Columns

In this section, we'll look at another special storage format, added in SQL Server 2008. Sparse columns are ordinary columns that have an optimized storage format for NULL values. Sparse columns reduce the space requirements for NULL values, allowing you to have many more columns in your table definition, so long as most of them are NULL. The cost of using sparse columns is that there will be more overhead to store and retrieve non-NULL values.

Sparse columns are intended to be used for tables storing data describing entities with many possible attributes, where most of the attributes will be NULL for most rows. For example, a content management system like Microsoft Windows SharePoint Services may need to keep track of many different types of data in a single table. Different properties apply to different subsets of rows in the table. So for each row, only a small subset of the columns is populated with values. Another way of looking at it is that for any particular property, only a subset of rows has a value for that property. The sparse columns in SQL Server 2008 allow us to store a very large number of possible columns for a single row. For this reason, the SPARSE column feature is sometimes also referred to as the *wide-table* feature.

## Management of Sparse Columns

It is recommended that you don't consider defining a column as SPARSE unless at least 90 percent of the rows in the table are expected to have NULL values for that column. This is not an enforced limit, however, and you can define almost any column as SPARSE. Sparse columns save space on NULL values.

This new SQL Server 2008 feature allows you to have far more columns that you ever could before. The limit is now 30,000 columns in a table, with no more than 1,024 of them being non-sparse. (Computed columns are considered non-sparse.) Obviously, not all 30,000 columns could have values in them. The number of populated columns you can have depends on the bytes of data in the row. Sparse columns optimize the storage size for NULL values, which take no space at all for sparse columns, unlike non-sparse columns, which do need space even for NULLs. (As we saw in Chapter 5, a fixed-length NULL column always uses the whole column width, and a variable-length NULL column uses at least two bytes in the column offset array.). Although the sparse columns themselves take no space, some fixed overhead is needed to allow for sparse columns in a row. As soon as you define even one column with the SPARSE attribute, SQL Server adds a sparse vector to the end of the row. We'll see the actual structure of this sparse vector in the section entitled "Physical Storage," later in this chapter, but to start with, you should be aware even with sparse columns, the maximum size of a data row (excluding LOB and row-overflow) remains at 8,060, including overhead bytes. Because the sparse vector includes additional overhead, the maximum number of bytes for the rest of the rows decreases. In addition, the size of all fixed-length non-NULL sparse columns in a row is limited to 8,019 bytes.

## Table Creation

Creating a table with sparse columns is very straightforward, as you can just add the attribute SPARSE to any column of any data type except *text, ntext, image, geography, geometry, timestamp,* or any user-defined data type. In addition, sparse columns cannot include the *IDENTITY, ROWGUIDCOL,* or *FILESTREAM* attributes. A sparse column cannot be part of a clustered index or part of the primary key. Tables containing sparse columns cannot be compressed, either at the row level or the page level. (I'll discuss compression in detail in the next section.) There are also a few other restrictions, particularly if you are partitioning a table with sparse columns, so you should check the documentation for full details. The examples in this section are necessarily very simple because it would be impractical to print code examples with enough columns to make sparse columns really useful. The following example shows the creation of two very similar tables, one that doesn't allow sparse columns and another that does. I attempt to insert the same rows into each table. Because a row allowing sparse columns has a smaller maximum length, it fails when trying to insert a row that the table with no sparse columns has no problem with:

```
USE test;
GO
CREATE TABLE test_nosparse
(
  col1 int,
  col2 char(8000),
  col3 varchar(8000)
);
GO
INSERT INTO test_nosparse
        SELECT null, null, null;
INSERT INTO test_nosparse
        SELECT 1, 'a', 'b';
GO
```

These two rows can be inserted with no error. Now, build the second table:

```
CREATE TABLE test_sparse
(
 col1 int SPARSE,
 col2 char(8000) SPARSE,
 col3 varchar(8000) SPARSE
);
GO
```

```
INSERT INTO test_sparse
        SELECT NULL, NULL, NULL;
INSERT INTO test_sparse
        SELECT 1, 'a', 'b';
GO
```

The second *INSERT* statement generates the following error:

```
Msg 576, Level 16, State 5, Line 2
Cannot create a row that has sparse data of size 8042 which is greater than the allowable
maximum sparse data size of 8019.
```

Although the second row inserted into the *test_sparse* table looks just like a row that was inserted successfully into the *test_nosparse* table, internally it is not. The total of the sparse columns is 4 bytes for the *int,* plus 8,000 bytes for the *char,* and 24 bytes for the row-overflow pointer, which is greater than the 8,019-byte limit.

## Altering a Table

Tables can be altered to convert a non-sparse column into a sparse column, or vice versa. Be careful, however, because if you are altering a very large row in a table with no sparse columns, changing one column to be sparse reduces the number of bytes of data that are allowed on a page. This can result in an error being thrown in cases where an existing column is converted into a sparse column. For example, the following code creates a table with large rows, but my *INSERT* statements, with or without NULLs, are accepted. However, when we try to make one of the columns SPARSE, even a relatively small column like the 8-byte *datetime* column, the extra overhead makes the existing rows too large and the *ALTER* fails:

```
IF EXISTS (SELECT * FROM sys.tables WHERE name = 'test_nosparse_alter')
                DROP TABLE test_nosparse_alter;
GO
CREATE TABLE test_nosparse_alter
(
c1 int,
c2 char(4020) ,
c3 char(4020) ,
c4 datetime
);
GO
INSERT INTO test_nosparse_alter SELECT NULL, NULL, NULL, NULL;
INSERT INTO test_nosparse_alter SELECT 1, 1, 'b', GETDATE();
GO
ALTER TABLE test_nosparse_alter
  ALTER COLUMN c4 datetime SPARSE;
```

We receive this error:

```
Msg 1701, Level 16, State 1, Line 2
Creating or altering table 'test_nosparse_alter' failed because the minimum row size would
be 8075, including 23 bytes of internal overhead. This exceeds the maximum allowable table
row size of 8060 bytes.
```

In general, sparse columns can be treated just like any other column, with only a few restrictions. In addition to the restrictions mentioned previously on the data types that cannot be defined as SPARSE, there are also the following limitations to keep in mind:

- A sparse column cannot have a default value.

- A sparse column cannot be bound to a rule.

- Although a computed column can refer to a sparse column, a computed column cannot be marked as SPARSE.

- A sparse column cannot be part of a clustered index or a unique primary key index. However, both persisted and nonpersisted computed columns that refer to sparse columns can be part of a clustered key.

- A sparse column cannot be used as a partition key of a clustered index or heap. However, a sparse column can be used as the partition key of a nonclustered index.

Note that except for the requirement that sparse columns cannot be part of the clustered index or primary key, there aren't any other restrictions on building indexes on sparse columns. However, if you are using sparse columns the way they are intended to be used, and the vast majority of your rows have NULL for the sparse columns, any regular index on a sparse column is very inefficient and may have limited usefulness. Sparse columns are really intended to be used with filtered indexes, which are discussed in Chapter 6.

## Column Sets and Sparse Column Manipulation

If sparse columns are used as intended, only a few columns in each row have values, and your INSERT and UPDATE statements are relatively straightforward. For INSERT statements, you can specify a column list and then specify values only for those few columns in the column list. For UPDATE statements, there are only a few columns in each row whose values can be manipulated. The only time you need to be concerned about how to deal with a potentially very large list of columns is if you are selecting data without listing individual columns (that is, using a SELECT *). Good developers know that using SELECT * is never a good idea, but SQL Server needs a way of dealing with a result set with potentially thousands (or tens of thousands) of columns. The mechanism provided to help deal with SELECT * is a construct called a COLUMN_SET. A COLUMN_SET is an untyped XML representation that combines multiple columns of a table into a structured output. You can think of a COLUMN_SET as a nonpersisted computed column because the COLUMN_SET is not physically stored in the table. In this release of SQL Server, the only possible COLUMN_SET contains all the sparse columns in the table. Future versions may allow us to define other COLUMN_SET variations.

A table can only have one COLUMN_SET defined, and once a table has a COLUMN_SET defined, SELECT * no longer returns individual sparse columns. Instead, it returns an XML fragment containing all the non-NULL values for the sparse columns. Let's look at an example.

The following code builds a table containing an identity column, 25 sparse columns, and a column set:

```
USE test;
GO
IF EXISTS (SELECT * FROM sys.tables WHERE name = 'lots_of_sparse_columns')
                DROP TABLE lots_of_sparse_columns;
GO
CREATE TABLE lots_of_sparse_columns
(ID int IDENTITY,
 col1 int SPARSE,
 col2 int SPARSE,
 col3 int SPARSE,
 col4 int SPARSE,
 col5 int SPARSE,
 col6 int SPARSE,
 col7 int SPARSE,
 col8 int SPARSE,
 col9 int SPARSE,
 col10 int SPARSE,
 col11 int SPARSE,
 col12 int SPARSE,
 col13 int SPARSE,
 col14 int SPARSE,
 col15 int SPARSE,
 col16 int SPARSE,
 col17 int SPARSE,
 col18 int SPARSE,
 col19 int SPARSE,
 col20 int SPARSE,
 col21 int SPARSE,
 col22 int SPARSE,
 col23 int SPARSE,
 col24 int SPARSE,
 col25 int SPARSE,
 sparse_column_set XML COLUMN_SET FOR ALL_SPARSE_COLUMNS);
GO
```

Next, I insert values into 3 of the 25 columns, specifying individual column names:

```
INSERT INTO lots_of_sparse_columns (col4, col7, col12)  SELECT 4,6,11;
```

You can also insert directly into the COLUMN_SET, specifying values for columns in an XML fragment. Being able to update the COLUMN_SET is another feature that differentiates COLUMN_SETs from computed columns:

```
INSERT INTO lots_of_sparse_columns (sparse_column_set)
                SELECT '<col8>42</col8><col17>0</col17><col22>30000</col22>';
```

Here are the results when I run *SELECT* * from this table:

```
SELECT * FROM lots_of_sparse_columns;
Results:
ID      sparse_column_set
------- --------------------------------------------------
1       <col4>4</col4><col7>6</col7><col12>11</col12>
2       <col8>42</col8><col17>0</col17><col22>30000</col22>
```

We can still select from individual columns, either instead of or in addition to selecting the entire COLUMN_SET. So the following *SELECT* statements are both valid:

```
SELECT ID, col10, col15, col20
    FROM lots_of_sparse_columns;
SELECT *, col11
    FROM lots_of_sparse_columns;
```

Keep the following points in mind if you decide to use sparse columns in your tables:

- Once defined, the COLUMN_SET cannot be altered. To change a COLUMN_SET, you must drop and re-create the COLUMN_SET column.

- A COLUMN_SET can be added to a table that does not include any sparse columns. If sparse columns are later added to the table, they appear in the column set.

- A COLUMN_SET is optional and is not required to use sparse columns.

- Constraints or default values cannot be defined on a COLUMN_SET.

- Distributed queries are not supported on tables that contain COLUMN_SETs.

- Replication does not support COLUMN_SETs.

- The Change Data Capture feature does not support COLUMN_SETs.

- A COLUMN_SET cannot be part of any kind of index. This includes XML indexes, full-text indexes, and indexed views. A COLUMN_SET cannot be added as an included column in any index.

- A COLUMN_SET cannot be used in the filter expression of a filtered index or filtered statistics.

- When a view includes a COLUMN_SET, the COLUMN_SET appears in the view as an XML column.

- XML data has a size limit of 2 GB. If the combined data of all the non-NULL sparse columns in a row exceeds this limit, the operation produces an error.

- Copying all columns from a table with a COLUMN_SET (using either *SELECT * INTO* or *INSERT INTO SELECT **) does not copy the individual sparse columns. Only the COLUMN_SET, as data type XML, is copied.

Now let's look at how sparse columns are actually stored.

## Physical Storage

At a high level, you can think of sparse columns as being stored much as they are displayed using the COLUMN_SET; that is, as a set of (column-name, value) pairs. So if there is no value for a particular column, it is not listed and no space at all is required. If there is a value for a column, not only does SQL Server need to store the value, but it needs to store information about which column has that value. So non-NULL sparse columns take more space than their NULL counterparts. To see the difference graphically, you can compare Tables 7-4 and 7-5.

Table 7-4 represents a table with non-sparse columns. You can see a lot of wasted space when most of the columns are NULL. Table 7-5 shows what the same table looks like if all the columns except the ID are defined as SPARSE. All that is stored are the names of all the non-NULL columns and their values.

**TABLE 7-4** **Representation of a Table Defined with Non-SPARSE Columns, with Many NULL Values**

| ID | sc1 | sc2 | sc3 | sc4 | sc5 | sc6 | sc7 | sc8 | sc9 |
|----|-----|-----|-----|-----|-----|-----|-----|-----|-----|
| 1  | 1   |     |     |     |     |     |     |     | 9   |
| 2  |     | 2   |     | 4   |     |     |     |     |     |
| 3  |     |     |     |     |     | 6   | 7   |     |     |
| 4  | 1   |     |     |     | 5   |     |     |     |     |
| 5  |     |     |     | 4   |     |     |     | 8   |     |
| 6  |     |     | 3   |     |     |     |     |     | 9   |
| 7  |     |     |     |     | 5   |     | 7   |     |     |
| 8  |     | 2   |     |     |     |     |     | 8   |     |
| 9  |     |     | 3   |     |     | 6   |     |     |     |

**TABLE 7-5** **Representation of a Table Defined with SPARSE Columns, with Many NULL Values**

| ID | \<sparse columns> |
|----|-------------------|
| 1  | (sc1,sc9)(1,9)    |
| 2  | (sc2,sc4)(2,4)    |
| 3  | (sc6,sc7)(6,7)    |
| 4  | (sc1,sc5)(1,5)    |
| 5  | (sc4,sc8)(4,8)    |
| 6  | (sc3,sc9)(3,9)    |
| 7  | (sc5,sc7)(5,7)    |
| 8  | (sc2,sc8)(2,8)    |
| 9  | (sc3,sc6)(3,6)    |

SQL Server keeps track of the physical storage of SPARSE columns with a structure within a row called a *sparse vector*. Sparse vectors are present only in the data records of a base table that has at least one sparse column declared and each data record of these tables contains a sparse vector.

A sparse vector is stored as a special variable-length column at the end of a data record. It is a special system column, and there is no metadata about this column in *sys.columns* or any other view. The sparse vector is stored as the last variable-length column in the row. The only thing after the sparse vector would be versioning information, used primarily with Snapshot isolation, as is discussed in Chapter 10. There is no bit in the NULL bitmap for the sparse vector column (if a sparse vector exists, it is never NULL), but the count in the row of the number of variables columns includes the sparse vector. You may want to revisit Figure 5-10 in Chapter 5 at this time to familiarize yourself with the general structure of data rows.

Table 7-6 lists the meaning of the bytes in the sparse vector.

**TABLE 7-6  Bytes in a Sparse Vector**

| Name | Number of Bytes | Meaning |
| --- | --- | --- |
| Complex Column Header | 2 | A value of 05 indicates that the complex column is a sparse vector. |
| Sparse Column Count | 2 | Number of sparse columns. |
| Column ID Set | 2 * the number of sparse columns | Two bytes for the column ID of each column in the table with a value stored in the sparse vector. |
| Column Offset Table | 2 * the number of sparse columns | Two bytes for the offset of the ending position of each sparse column. |
| Sparse Data | Depends on actual values | Data |

Let's look at the bytes of a row containing SPARSE columns. First, build a table containing two sparse columns, and populate it with three rows:

```
USE test;
GO
IF EXISTS (SELECT * FROM sys.tables WHERE name = 'sparse_bits')
                DROP TABLE sparse_bits;
GO
CREATE TABLE sparse_bits
(
c1 int IDENTITY,
c2 varchar(4),
c3 char(4) SPARSE,
c4 varchar(4) SPARSE
);
GO
INSERT INTO sparse_bits SELECT 'aaaa', 'bbbb', 'cccc';
INSERT INTO sparse_bits SELECT 'dddd', null, 'eeee';
INSERT INTO sparse_bits SELECT 'ffff', null, 'gg';
GO
```

Now we can use *DBCC IND* to find the page number for the data page storing these three rows and then use *DBCC PAGE* to look at the bytes on the page:

```
DBCC IND(test, sparse_bits, -1);
GO
-- The output indicated that the data page for my table was on page 289;
DBCC TRACEON(3604);
DBCC PAGE(test, 1, 289, 1);
```

I won't show you the entire page output, but only the output for the first row (spread over three lines of output):

```
00000000:   30000800 01000000 02000002 00150029 †0..............)
00000010:   80616161 61050002 00030004 00100014 †.aaaa...........
00000020:   00626262 62636363 63††††††††††††††††††.bbbbcccc
```

The grayed bytes are the sparse vector. I can find it easily because it starts right after the last non-sparse variable-length column, which contained *aaaa,* or 61616161, and continues to the end of the row. Figure 7-6 translates the sparse vector according to the meanings given in Table 7-6. Don't forget that you need to byte-swap numeric fields before translating. For example, the first two bytes are 05 00, which need to be swapped to get the hex value 0x0005. Then you can convert it to decimal.

Byte offsets within the sparse vector:

Values after byte swapping the numeric values:

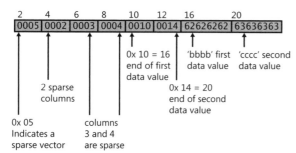

**FIGURE 7-6** Interpretation of the actual bytes in a sparse vector for a row in the *sparse_bits* table

You can apply the same analysis to the bytes in the other two rows on the page. Here are some things to note:

■ No information about columns with NULL values appears in the sparse vector.

■ Within the sparse vector, there is no difference in storage between fixed-length and variable-length strings. However, that doesn't mean you should use the two interchangeably. A SPARSE *varchar* column that doesn't fit in the 8,060 bytes can be stored as row-overflow data; a SPARSE *char* column cannot be.

■ Because only two bytes are used to store the number of sparse columns, this sets the limit on the maximum number of sparse columns.

■ The two bytes for the complex column header indicate that there might be other possibilities for complex columns. At this time, the only other type of complex column that can be stored is one storing a back-pointer, as SQL Server does when it creates a forwarded record. (I discussed forwarded records when discussing updates to heaps in Chapter 5.)

## Metadata

Very little extra metadata is needed to support SPARSE columns. The catalog view *sys.columns* contains the following two columns to keep track of SPARSE columns in your tables. Each of these columns has only two possible values, 0 or 1:

- *is_sparse*
- *is_column_set*

Corresponding to these column properties in *sys.columns,* the property function *COLUMNPROPERTY()* also has the following two properties related to SPARSE columns:

- *IsSparse*
- *IsColumnSet*

If I want to inspect all the tables I had created with "sparse" in their name and determine which of their columns were SPARSE, which were column sets, and which were neither, I could run the following query:

```
SELECT OBJECT_NAME(object_id) as 'Table', name as 'Column', is_sparse, is_column_set
FROM sys.columns
WHERE OBJECT_NAME(object_id) like '%sparse%';
```

If I want to see just the table and column names for all COLUMN_SET columns, I could run the following query:

```
SELECT OBJECT_NAME(object_id) as 'Table', name as 'Column'
FROM sys.columns
WHERE COLUMNPROPERTY(object_id, name, 'IsColumnSet') = 1;
```

## Storage Savings with Sparse Columns

The SPARSE column feature is designed to save you considerable space when most of your values are NULL. In fact, as mentioned previously, columns that are not NULL but are defined as SPARSE take up more space than if they weren't defined as SPARSE because the sparse vector has to store a couple of extra bytes to keep track of them. To start to see the space differences, you can run the following script, which creates four tables with relatively short, fixed-length columns. Two have sparse columns and two don't. Rows are inserted into each of the tables in a loop, which inserts 100,000 rows. One table with sparse columns is populated with rows with NULL values, and the other is populated with rows that are not NULL. One of the tables with no sparse columns is populated with rows with NULL values, and the other is populated with rows that are not NULL:

```
USE test;
GO
SET NOCOUNT ON;
GO
```

```
IF EXISTS (SELECT * FROM sys.tables
                        WHERE name = 'sparse_nonulls_size')
                DROP TABLE sparse_nonulls_size;
GO
CREATE TABLE sparse_nonulls_size
(col1 int IDENTITY,
 col2 datetime SPARSE,
 col3 char(10) SPARSE
 );
GO
IF EXISTS (SELECT * FROM sys.tables
                        WHERE name = 'nonsparse_nonulls_size')
                DROP TABLE nonsparse_nonulls_size;
GO
CREATE TABLE nonsparse_nonulls_size
(col1 int IDENTITY,
 col2 datetime,
 col3 char(10)
 );
GO
IF EXISTS (SELECT * FROM sys.tables
                        WHERE name = 'sparse_nulls_size')
                DROP TABLE sparse_nulls_size;
GO
CREATE TABLE sparse_nulls_size
(col1 int IDENTITY,
 col2 datetime SPARSE,
 col3 char(10) SPARSE
 );
GO
IF EXISTS (SELECT * FROM sys.tables
                        WHERE name = 'nonsparse_nulls_size')
                DROP TABLE nonsparse_nulls_size;
GO
CREATE TABLE nonsparse_nulls_size
(col1 int IDENTITY,
 col2 datetime,
 col3 char(10)
 );
GO
DECLARE @num int
SET @num = 1
WHILE @num < 100000
BEGIN
  INSERT INTO sparse_nonulls_size
        SELECT GETDATE(), 'my message';
  INSERT INTO nonsparse_nonulls_size
        SELECT GETDATE(), 'my message';
  INSERT INTO sparse_nulls_size
        SELECT NULL, NULL;
  INSERT INTO nonsparse_nulls_size
        SELECT NULL, NULL;
  SET @num = @num + 1;
END;
GO
```

Now look at the number of pages in each table. The following metadata query looks at the number of data pages in the *sys.allocation_units* view for each of the four tables:

```
SELECT object_name(object_id) as 'table with 100K rows', data_pages
FROM sys.allocation_units au
    JOIN sys.partitions p
        ON p.partition_id = au.container_id
WHERE object_name(object_id) LIKE '%sparse%size';
```

And here are my results:

```
table with 100K rows     data_pages
----------------------   ----------
sparse_nonulls_size      610
nonsparse_nonulls_size   402
sparse_nulls_size        169
nonsparse_nulls_size     402
```

Note that the smallest number of pages is required when the table has sparse columns that are NULL. If the table has no sparse columns, the space usage is the same whether the columns have NULLs or not because the data was defined as fixed length. This space requirement is more than twice as much as needed for the sparse columns with NULL. The worst case is if the columns have been defined as SPARSE but there are no NULL values.

Of course, the previous examples are edge cases, where *all* the data is either NULL or non-NULL, and it is all of fixed-length data types. So although we can say that SPARSE columns require more storage space for non-NULL values than is required for identical data that is not declared as SPARSE, the actual space savings depends on the data types and the percentage of rows that are NULL. Table 7-7 is reprinted from *SQL Server Books Online* and shows the space usage for each data type. The *NULL Percentage* column indicates what percent of the data must be NULL to achieve a net space savings of 40 percent. Table 7-7 shows the savings for various data types in SQL Server 2008.

**TABLE 7-7  Storage Requirements for SPARSE Columns**

| Data Type | Storage Bytes When Not SPARSE | Storage Bytes When SPARSE and Not NULL | NULL Percentage |
|---|---|---|---|
| **Fixed-Length Data Types** | | | |
| bit | 0.125 | 4.125 | 98 percent |
| tinyint | 1 | 5 | 86 percent |
| smallint | 2 | 6 | 76 percent |
| int | 4 | 8 | 64 percent |
| bigint | 8 | 12 | 52 percent |
| real | 4 | 8 | 64 percent |
| float | 8 | 12 | 52 percent |

**TABLE 7-7  Storage Requirements for SPARSE Columns**

| Data Type | Storage Bytes When Not SPARSE | Storage Bytes When SPARSE and Not NULL | NULL Percentage |
|---|---|---|---|
| **Fixed-Length Data Types** | | | |
| smallmoney | 4 | 8 | 64 percent |
| money | 8 | 12 | 52 percent |
| smalldatetime | 4 | 8 | 64 percent |
| datetime | 8 | 12 | 52 percent |
| uniqueidentifier | 16 | 20 | 43 percent |
| date | 3 | 7 | 69 percent |
| **Precision-Dependent–Length Data Types** | | | |
| datetime2(0) | 6 | 10 | 57 percent |
| datetime2(7) | 8 | 12 | 52 percent |
| time(0) | 3 | 7 | 69 percent |
| time(7) | 5 | 9 | 60 percent |
| datetimeoffset(0) | 8 | 12 | 52 percent |
| datetimeoffset (7) | 10 | 14 | 49 percent |
| decimal/numeric(1,s) | 5 | 9 | 60 percent |
| decimal/numeric(38,s) | 17 | 21 | 42 percent |
| **Data-Dependent–Length Data Types** | | | |
| sql_variant | Varies | | |
| varchar or char | 4+avg. data | 2+avg. data | 60 percent |
| nvarchar or nchar | 4+avg. data | 2+avg. data | 60 percent |
| varbinary or binary | 4+avg. data | 2+avg. data | 60 percent |
| xml | 4+avg. data | 2+avg. data | 60 percent |
| hierarchyId | 4+avg. data | 2+avg. data | 60 percent |

The general recommendation is that you should consider using SPARSE columns when you anticipate that it provides a space savings of at least 20 to 40 percent.

# Data Compression

SQL Server 2008 provides the capability of data compression, a new feature that is available in Enterprise edition only. Compression can reduce the size of your tables by exploiting inefficiencies that exist in the actual data. These inefficiencies can be grouped into two general categories. The first category relates to storage of individual data values when they are stored in columns defined using the maximum possible size. For example, a table may need to define a *quantity* column as *int*, because occasionally you may be storing values larger than 32,767, which is the maximum *smallint* value. However, *int* columns always need four bytes, and if most of your *quantity* values are less than 100, they could be stored in *tinyint* columns, which need only 1 byte of storage. The Row Compression feature of SQL Server can compress individual columns of data to use only the minimum amount of space required.

The second type of inefficiency in the data storage occurs when the data on a page contains duplicate values or common prefixes across columns and rows. This inefficiency can be minimized by storing the repeating values only once and then referencing those values from other columns. The Page Compression feature of SQL Server can compress the data on a page by maintaining entries containing common prefixes or repeating values. Note that when you choose to apply page compression to a table or index, SQL Server always also applies row compression.

## Vardecimal

SQL Server 2005 SP2 introduced a simple from of compression, which could be applied only to columns defined using the *decimal* data type. (Keep in mind that the data type numeric is completely equivalent to *decimal*, and anytime I mention *decimal*, it also means *numeric*.) In SQL Server 2005, the option has to be enabled at both the database level (using the procedure *sp_db_vardecimal_storage_format*) and at the table level (using the procedure *sp_tableoption*). In SQL Server 2008, all user databases are enabled automatically for the vardecimal storage format, so vardecimal must only be enabled for individual tables. Like data compression in SQL Server 2008, which we'll look at in detail in this section, the vardecimal storage format is available only in SQL Server Enterprise edition.

In SQL Server 2005, once both of these stored procedures have been run, *decimal* data in the tables enabled for vardecimal will be stored differently. Instead of being treated as fixed-length data, *decimal* columns are stored in the variable section of the row and use only the number of bytes required. (We looked at the difference between fixed-length data and variable-length data storage in Chapter 5.) In addition to all the partitions of the table using the vardecimal format for all *decimal* data, all indexes on the table use the vardecimal format automatically.

*Decimal* data values are defined with a precision of between 1 and 38, and depending on the defined precision, they use between 5 and 17 bytes. Fixed-length *decimal* data uses the same number of bytes for every row, even if the actual data could fit into far fewer bytes. When a table is not using the vardecimal storage format, every entry in the table consumes the same number of bytes for each defined decimal column, even if the value of a row is 0, NULL, or some value that could be expressed in a smaller number of bytes, such as the number 3. When vardecimal storage format is enabled for a table, the *decimal* columns in each row use the minimum amount of space required to store the specified value. Of course, as we saw in Chapter 5, every variable-length column has 2 bytes of additional overhead associated with it, but when storing very small values in a column defined as *decimal* with a large precision, the space saving can more than make up for those additional 2 bytes. For vardecimal storage, both NULLs and zeros are stored as zero-length data and use only the 2 bytes of overhead.

Although SQL Server 2008 supports the vardecimal format, it is recommended that you use row compression when you want to reduce the storage space required by your data rows. Both the table option and the database option for enabling vardecimal storage have been deprecated.

# Row Compression

You can think of row compression as an extension of the vardecimal storage format. There can be many situations in which SQL Server uses more space than is necessary to store data values, and without SQL Server 2008 Enterprise Edition, the only control you have is to use a variable-length data type. Any fixed-length data types always uses the same amount of space in every row of a table, even if space is wasted. For example, you may declare a column as type *int* because occasionally you may need to store values greater than 32,000. An *int* needs 4 bytes of space, no matter what number is stored, even if the column is NULL. Only character and binary data can be stored in variable-length columns (and, of course, decimal, once that option is enabled). Row compression allows integer values to use only the amount of storage space required, with the minimum being 1 byte. A value of 100 needs only a single byte for storage, and a value of 1,000 needs 2 bytes. There is an optimization that allows zero and NULL to use no storage space for the data itself. We'll see the details about this later in this section.

## Enabling Row Compression

Compression can be enabled when creating a table or index, or using the *ALTER TABLE* or *ALTER INDEX* command. In addition, if the table or index is partitioned, you can choose to just compress a subset of the partitions. (We'll look at partitioning later in this chapter.)

The following script creates two copies of the *dbo.Employees* table in the *AdventureWorks2008* database. When storing row-compressed data, SQL Server treats values that can be stored in 8 bytes or fewer (that is, short columns) differently than it stores data that needs more than 8 bytes (long columns). For this reason, my script updates one of the rows in the new tables so that none of the columns contains more than 8 bytes. The *Employees_rowcompressed* table is then enabled for row compression, and the *Employees_uncompressed* table is left uncompressed. A metadata query examining pages allocated to each table is executed against each of the tables so that you can compare the sizes before and after row compression:

```
USE AdventureWorks2008;
GO
IF EXISTS (SELECT * FROM sys.tables
        WHERE name = 'Employees_uncompressed')
           DROP TABLE Employees_uncompressed;
GO
SELECT e.BusinessEntityID, NationalIDNumber, JobTitle,
        BirthDate, MaritalStatus, VacationHours,
        FirstName, LastName
  INTO Employees_uncompressed
```

```
       FROM HumanResources.Employee e
        JOIN Person.Person p
            ON e.BusinessEntityID = p.BusinessEntityID;
GO
UPDATE Employees_uncompressed
SET NationalIDNumber = '1111',
        JobTitle = 'Boss',
        LastName = 'Gato'
WHERE FirstName = 'Ken'
AND LastName = 'Sánchez';
GO
ALTER TABLE dbo.Employees_uncompressed
    ADD CONSTRAINT EmployeeUn_ID
        PRIMARY KEY (BusinessEntityID);
GO
SELECT OBJECT_NAME(object_id) as name,
        rows, data_pages, data_compression_desc
FROM sys.partitions p JOIN sys.allocation_units au
        ON p.partition_id = au.container_id
WHERE object_id = object_id('dbo.Employees_uncompressed');

IF EXISTS (SELECT * FROM sys.tables
        WHERE name = 'Employees_rowcompressed')
            DROP TABLE Employees_rowcompressed;
GO
SELECT BusinessEntityID, NationalIDNumber, JobTitle,
        BirthDate, MaritalStatus, VacationHours,
        FirstName, LastName
  INTO Employees_rowcompressed
  FROM dbo.Employees_uncompressed
GO
ALTER TABLE dbo.Employees_rowcompressed
    ADD CONSTRAINT EmployeeR_ID
        PRIMARY KEY (BusinessEntityID);
GO
ALTER TABLE dbo.Employees_rowcompressed
REBUILD WITH (DATA_COMPRESSION = ROW);
GO
SELECT OBJECT_NAME(object_id) as name,
        rows, data_pages, data_compression_desc
FROM sys.partitions p JOIN sys.allocation_units au
        ON p.partition_id = au.container_id
WHERE object_id = object_id('dbo.Employees_rowcompressed');
GO
```

I'll refer to the *dbo.Employees_rowcompressed* table again later in this section, or you can examine it on your own as I discuss the details of compressed row storage.

Now we'll start looking at the details of row compression, but keep these points in mind:

- Row compression is available only in SQL Server 2008 Enterprise and Developer editions.

- Row compression does not change the maximum row size of a table or index.

- Row compression cannot be enabled on a table with any columns defined as SPARSE.

- If a table or index has been partitioned, row compression can be enabled on all the partitions or on a subset of the partitions.

## New Row Format

In Chapter 5, we looked at the format for storing rows that has been used since SQL Server 7.0 and is still used in SQL Server 2008 if you have not enabled compression. That format is referred to as *FixedVar* format because it has a fixed-length data section separate from a variable-length data section. A completely new row format is introduced in SQL Server 2008 for storing compressed rows, and this format is referred to as *CD* format. CD stands for "column descriptor," and that term refers to the fact that every column has description information contained in the row itself. You might want to re-examine Figure 5-10 in Chapter 5 as a reminder of what the FixedVar format looks like, and compare it to the new CD format. Figure 7-7 shows an abstraction of the CD format. It's difficult to be as specific as Figure 5-10 is because except for the Header, the number of bytes in each region is completely dependent on the data in the row.

| Header | CD Region | Short Data Region | Long Data Region | Special Information |
|--------|-----------|-------------------|------------------|---------------------|

**FIGURE 7-7** General structure of a CD record

I'll describe each of these sections in detail.

**Header**    The row header is always a single byte and roughly corresponds to what I called Status Bits A in Chapter 5. The bits have the following meanings:

**Bit 0**    Indicates the type of record; it's 1 for the new CD record format.

**Bit 1**    Indicates that the row contains versioning information.

**Bits 2 through 4**    Taken as a three-bit value, these bits indicate what kind of information is stored in the row. The possible values are the following:

- 000—primary record

- 001—ghost empty record

- 010—forwarding record

- 011—ghost data record

- 100—forwarded record

- 101—ghost forwarded record

- 110—index record

- 111—ghost index record

**Bit 5**   Indicates that the row contains a long data region (with values greater than 8 bytes in length).

**Bit 6 - 7**   Not used in SQL Server 2008.

**The CD Region**   The CD region is composed of two parts. The first part is either 1 or 2 bytes, indicating the number of short columns. If the most significant bit of the first byte is set to 0, then it is a 1-byte field with a maximum value of 127. If there are more than 127 columns, then the most significant bit is 1, and SQL Server uses 2 bytes to represent the number of columns, which can be up to 32,767.

Following the 1 or 2 bytes for the number of columns is the CD array. The CD array uses four bits for each column in the table, to represent information about the length of the column. Four bits can have 16 different possible values, but in SQL Server 2008, only 13 of them are used:

- 0 (0x0) indicates that the corresponding column is NULL

- 1 (0x1) indicates that the corresponding column is a 0-byte short value.

- 2 (0x2) indicates that the corresponding column is a 1-byte short value.

- 3 (0x3) indicates that the corresponding column is a 2-byte short value.

- 4 (0x4) indicates that the corresponding column is a 3-byte short value.

- 5 (0x5) indicates that the corresponding column is a 4-byte short value.

- 6 (0x6) indicates that the corresponding column is a 5-byte short value.

- 7 (0x7) indicates that the corresponding column is a 6-byte short value.

- 8 (0x8) indicates that the corresponding column is a 7-byte short value.

- 9 (0x9) indicates that the corresponding column is an 8-byte short value.

- 10 (0xa) indicates that the corresponding column is long data value and uses no space in the short data region.

- 11 (0xb) is used for columns of type bit with the value of 1. The corresponding column takes no space in the short data region.

- 12 (0xc) indicates that the corresponding column is a 1-byte symbol, representing a value in the page dictionary. (I'll talk about the dictionary in the section entitled "Page Compression," later in this chapter).

**The Short Data Region**   The short data region doesn't need to store the length of each of the short data values because that information is available in the CD region. However, if there are hundreds of columns in the table, it can be expensive to access the last columns. To minimize this cost, columns are grouped into clusters of 30 columns each and at the beginning of the short data region, there is an area called the short data cluster array. Each array entry is a single-byte integer and indicates the sum of the sizes of all the data in the previous cluster in the short data region, so that the value is basically a pointer to the first column of the cluster. The first cluster of short data starts right after the cluster array, so no cluster offset is needed for it. There may not be 30 data columns in a cluster, however, because only columns with a length less than or equal to 8 bytes are stored in the short data region.

As an example, consider a row with 64 columns, and columns 5, 10, 15, 20, 25, 30, 40, 50, and 60 are long data, and the others are short. The CD region contains the following:

- A single byte containing 64, the number of columns, in the CD region.

- A CD array of 4 * 64 bits, or 32 bytes, containing information about the length of each column. There are 55 entries with values indicating an actual data length for the short data, and 8 entries of 0xa, indicating long data.

- The short data region contains the following.

  - A short data cluster offset array containing the two values, each containing the length of a short data cluster. In this example, the first cluster, which is all the short data in the first 30 columns, has a length of 92, so the 92 in the offset array indicates that the second cluster starts 92 bytes after the first. The number of clusters can be calculated as (Number of columns − 1) /30. The maximum value for any entry in the cluster array is 240, if all 30 columns were short data of 8 bytes in length.

  - All the short data values.

Figure 7-8 illustrates the CD region and the short data region with sample data for the row described previously. The CD array is shown in its entirety, with a symbol indicating the length of each of the 64 values. So the array can fit on a page of this book, the actual data values are not shown. The first cluster has 24 values in the short data region (6 are long values), the second cluster has 27 (3 are long) and the third cluster has the remaining 4 columns (all short). I'll discuss the storage of the long values next.

| CD Region | | Short Data Region | | | |
|---|---|---|---|---|---|
| Number of columns | CD array --64 4-bit values ('a' indicates long column) | Length of short data in each 30-column cluster (N–1)/30 values | | Three clusters of actual data | |
| N = 64 | 3285a4358a6543a3456a6666a5463a 254372644a745269277a463495736a 5433 | 92 | 106 | 24 values | 27 values | 4 values |

**FIGURE 7-8** The CD region and short data region in a CD record

To locate the entry for a short column value in the short data region, the short data cluster array is first examined to determine the start address of the containing cluster for the column in the short data region.

**The Long Data Region**    Any data in the row longer than 8 bytes is stored in the long data region. This includes complex columns, which do not contain actual data but rather contain information necessary to locate data stored off the row. This can include large object data and row overflow data pointers. Unlike short data, where the length can be stored simply in the CD array, long data needs an actual offset value to allow SQL Server to determine the location of each value. This offset array looks very similar to the offset array I talked about in Chapter 5 for the FixedVar records.

The long data region is composed of three parts: an offset array, a long data cluster array, and the long data.

The offset array is composed of the following:

- A 1-byte header. In SQL Server 2008, only the first two bits are used. Bit 0 indicates if the long data region contains any 2-byte offset values, and in SQL Server 2008, this value is always 1, as all offsets are always 2 bytes. Bit 1 indicates if the long data region contains any complex columns.

- A 2-byte value indicating the number of offsets to follow. The most significant bit in the first byte of the offset value is used to indicate whether the corresponding entry in the long data region is a complex column or not. The rest of the bits/bytes in the array entry store the ending offset value for the corresponding entry in the long data region.

The long data cluster array is similar to the cluster array for the short data and is used to limit the cost of finding columns near the end of a long list of columns. It has one entry for each 30-column cluster (except the last one). Because we already have the offset of each long data column stored in the offset array, the cluster array just needs to keep track of how many of the long data values are in each cluster. Each value is a one-byte integer representing the number of long data columns in that cluster. Just as for the short data cluster, the number of entries in the cluster array can be computed as (Number of columns in the table – 1)/ 30.

Figure 7-9 illustrates the long data region for the row described previously, with 64 columns, 9 of which are long. I have not actually included values for the offsets due to space considerations. The long data cluster array has two entries indicating that 6 of the values are in the first cluster and 2 are in the second. The remaining values are in the last cluster.

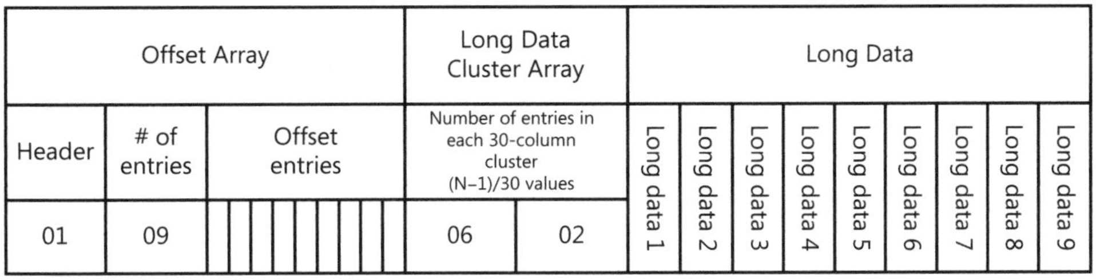

| Offset Array | | | Long Data Cluster Array | Long Data | | | | | | | | |
|---|---|---|---|---|---|---|---|---|---|---|---|---|
| Header | # of entries | Offset entries | Number of entries in each 30-column cluster (N–1)/30 values | Long data 1 | Long data 2 | Long data 3 | Long data 4 | Long data 5 | Long data 6 | Long data 7 | Long data 8 | Long data 9 |
| 01 | 09 | | 06 | 02 | | | | | | | | |

**FIGURE 7-9** The long data region of a CD record

**Special Information**  The end of the row contains three optional pieces of information. The existence of any or all of this information is indicated by bits in the 1-byte header at the very beginning of the row. The three special areas are the following:

- *Forwarding Pointer*  This value is used when a heap contains a forwarding stub that points to a new location to which the original row has been moved. Forwarding pointers were discussed in Chapter 5. The forwarding pointer contains three header bytes and an 8-byte Row ID.

- *Back Pointer*  This value is used in a row that has been forwarded to indicate the original location of the row. It is stored as an 8-byte Row ID.

- *Versioning Info*  When a row is modified under Snapshot isolation, SQL Server adds 14 bytes of versioning information to the row. Row versioning and Snapshot isolation is discussed in Chapter 10.

Now let's look at the actual bytes in two of the rows in the *dbo.Employees_rowcompressed* table created previously. The *DBCC PAGE* command has been enhanced to give additional information about compressed rows and pages. In particular, before the bytes for the row are shown, *DBCC PAGE* will display the CD array. For the first row returned on the first page in the *dbo.Employees_rowcompressed* table, all the columns contain short data. The row has the following data values:

| BusinessEntityID | NationalIDNumber | JobTitle | BirthDate | MaritalStatus | VacationHours | FirstName | LastName |
|---|---|---|---|---|---|---|---|
| 1 | 1111 | Boss | 1959-03-02 | S | 99 | Ken | Gato |

For short data, the CD array contains the actual length of each of the columns, and we can see the following information for the first row in the *DBCC PAGE* output:

```
CD array entry = Column 1 (cluster 0, CD array offset 0): 0x02 (ONE_BYTE_SHORT)
CD array entry = Column 2 (cluster 0, CD array offset 0): 0x09 (EIGHT_BYTE_SHORT)
CD array entry = Column 3 (cluster 0, CD array offset 1): 0x09 (EIGHT_BYTE_SHORT)
CD array entry = Column 4 (cluster 0, CD array offset 1): 0x04 (THREE_BYTE_SHORT)
CD array entry = Column 5 (cluster 0, CD array offset 2): 0x03 (TWO_BYTE_SHORT)
CD array entry = Column 6 (cluster 0, CD array offset 2): 0x02 (ONE_BYTE_SHORT)
CD array entry = Column 7 (cluster 0, CD array offset 3): 0x07 (SIX_BYTE_SHORT)
CD array entry = Column 8 (cluster 0, CD array offset 3): 0x09 (EIGHT_BYTE_SHORT)
```

So the first column has a CD code of 0x02, which indicates a 1-byte value, and, as we see in the data row, is the integer 1. The second column contains an 8-byte value and is the Unicode string 1111. I'll leave it to you to inspect the code for the remaining columns.

Figure 7-10 shows the *DBCC PAGE* output for the row contents, and I have indicated the meaning of the different bytes.

```
Record Memory Dump for first row from DBCC PAGE:

01089249 23978131 00310031 00310042 †..'I#−.1.1.1.B
006f0073 007300c4 e90a5300 e34b0065 †.o.s.s.Äé.S.āK.e
006e0047 00610074 006f00††††††††††††.n.G.a.t.o.
```

Row expansion with byte swapping:

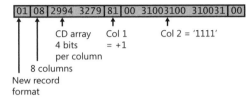

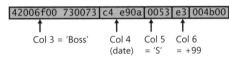

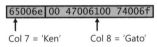

**FIGURE 7-10** A compressed row with eight short data columns

The second row returned on the first page has a few long columns in the following data values:

| Bus... | National | DNumber | JobTitle | BirthDate | Marital... | Vacation... | FirstName | LastName |
|--------|----------|---------|----------|-----------|------------|-------------|-----------|----------|
| 2 | 245797967 | | Vice President of Engineering | 1961-09-01 | S | 1 | Terri | Duffy |

The CD array for this row looks like the following:

```
CD array entry = Column 1 (cluster 0, CD array offset 0): 0x02 (ONE_BYTE_SHORT)
CD array entry = Column 2 (cluster 0, CD array offset 0): 0x0a (LONG)
CD array entry = Column 3 (cluster 0, CD array offset 1): 0x0a (LONG)
CD array entry = Column 4 (cluster 0, CD array offset 1): 0x04 (THREE_BYTE_SHORT)
CD array entry = Column 5 (cluster 0, CD array offset 2): 0x03 (TWO_BYTE_SHORT)
CD array entry = Column 6 (cluster 0, CD array offset 2): 0x02 (ONE_BYTE_SHORT)
CD array entry = Column 7 (cluster 0, CD array offset 3): 0x0a (LONG)
CD array entry = Column 8 (cluster 0, CD array offset 3): 0x0a (LONG)
```

Note that four of the eight columns are long data values.

Figure 7-11 shows the bytes that *DBCC PAGE* returns for this second data row.

```
Record Memory Dump
6294C08B:     2108a24a 23aa8256 ed0a5300 81010400 †!.¢J#ª,ví.S.....
6294C09B:     12004c00 56006000 32003400 35003700 †..L.V.`.2.4.5.7.
6294C0AB:     39003700 39003600 37005600 69006300 †9.7.9.6.7.V.i.c.
6294C0BB:     65002000 50007200 65007300 69006400 †e. .P.r.e.s.i.d.
6294C0CB:     65006e00 74002000 6f006600 20004500 †e.n.t. .o.f. .E.
6294C0DB:     6e006700 69006e00 65006500 72006900 †n.g.i.n.e.e.r.i.
6294C0EB:     6e006700 54006500 72007200 69004400 †n.g.T.e.r.r.i.D.
```

**FIGURE 7-11** A compressed row with four short data columns and four long

I have highlighted the bytes in the long data region. Here are some things to notice in the first part of the row, before the long data region:

- The first byte in the row is 0x21, indicating that not only is this row in the new CD record format, but also that the row contains a long data region.

- The second byte indicates there are eight columns in the table, just as for the first row.

- The following 8 bytes for the CD array has four values of a, which indicate a long value not included in the short data region.

- The short data values are listed in order after the CD array and are as follows:

  - The *BusinessEntityID* is 1 byte, with the value 0x82, or +2
  - The *Birthdate* is 3 bytes
  - The *MaritalStatus* is 1 byte, with the value 0x0053, or 'S'
  - The *VacationHours* is 1 byte, with the value 0x81, or +1

The Long Data Region Offset Array is 10 bytes long, with the following interpretation:

- The first byte is 0x01, which indicates that the row-offset positions are 2 bytes long.

- The second byte is 0x04, which indicates there are four columns in the long data region.

- The next 8 bytes are the 2-byte offsets for each of the four values. Note that the offset refers to position the column ends with the Long Data area itself.

  - The first 2-byte offset is 0x0012, or 18. This indicates that the first long value is 18 bytes long. (It is Unicode string of 9 characters, 245797967, which would need 18 bytes.)

  - The second 2-byte offset is 0x004c, or 76, which indicates that the second long value ends 58 bytes after the first. The second value is *Vice President of Engineering*, which is a 29-byte Unicode string.

  - The third 2-byte offset is 0x0056, or 86, which indicates the third value, *Terri*, is 10 bytes long.

  - The fourth 2-byte offset is 0x0060, or 96, which indicates the fourth value, *Duffy*, is 10 bytes long.

Because there are fewer than 30 columns, there is no Long Data Cluster Array, and the data values are stored immediately after the Long Data Region Offset Array.

Due to space constraints, I won't show you the details of a row with multiple column clusters (that is, more than 30 columns), but hopefully you have enough information to start exploring such rows on your own.

## Page Compression

In addition to storing rows in a compressed format to minimize the space required, SQL Server 2008 can compress whole pages by isolating and reusing repeating patterns of bytes on the page.

Unlike row compression, page compression is applied only once a page is full, and if SQL Server determines that compressing the page saves a meaningful amount of space. (I'll elaborate on what that amount is later in this section.) You should keep the following points in mind when planning for page compression:

- Page compression is available only in the SQL Server 2008 Enterprise and Developer editions.

- Page compression always includes row compression. (That is, if you enable page compression for a table, row compression is automatically enabled.)

- When compressing a B-tree, only the leaf level can be page-compressed. For performance reasons, the node levels are left uncompressed.

- If a table or index has been partitioned, page compression can be enabled on all the partitions, or a subset of the partitions.

- Page compression is not maintained as new rows are added. The page compression algorithm must be reapplied to an entire page and is done only when SQL Server determines that doing so brings benefits. Again, we'll see details about this later in this section.

The code here makes another copy of the *dbo.Employees* table and applies page compression to it. It then captures the page location and linkage information from *DBCC IND*, for the three tables: *dbo.Employees_uncompressed, dbo.Employees_rowcompressed,* and *dbo. Employees_pagecompressed.* The code then uses the captured information to report on the number of data pages in each of the three tables:

```
IF EXISTS (SELECT * FROM sys.tables
        WHERE name = 'Employees_pagecompressed')
                DROP TABLE Employees_pagecompressed;
GO
SELECT BusinessEntityID, NationalIDNumber, JobTitle,
        BirthDate, MaritalStatus, VacationHours,
        FirstName, LastName
  INTO Employees_pagecompressed
  FROM dbo.Employees_uncompressed
GO
ALTER TABLE dbo.Employees_pagecompressed
   ADD CONSTRAINT EmployeeP_ID
      PRIMARY KEY (BusinessEntityID);
GO
ALTER TABLE dbo.Employees_pagecompressed
REBUILD WITH (DATA_COMPRESSION = PAGE);
GO
SELECT OBJECT_NAME(object_id) as name,
                rows, data_pages, data_compression_desc
```

```
FROM sys.partitions p JOIN sys.allocation_units au
                ON p.partition_id = au.container_id
WHERE object_id = object_id('dbo.Employees_pagecompressed');
GO

TRUNCATE TABLE sp_table_pages;
GO
INSERT INTO sp_tablepages
    EXEC ('DBCC IND(AdventureWorks2008, Employees_pagecompressed, -1)');
INSERT INTO sp_tablepages
    EXEC ('DBCC IND(AdventureWorks2008, Employees_rowcompressed, -1)');
INSERT INTO sp_tablepages
    EXEC ('DBCC IND(AdventureWorks2008, Employees_uncompressed, -1)');
GO
SELECT OBJECT_NAME(ObjectID), count(*) as NumPages
FROM sp_tablepages
WHERE pagetype = 1
GROUP BY OBJECT_NAME(ObjectID);
GO
```

If you run this script, note in the output that row compression did not reduce the size of this small table, but page compression shrank the table from five data pages to three.

SQL Server can perform two different operations to try to compress a page using common values: *column prefix compression* and *dictionary compression*.

## Column Prefix Compression

As the name implies, column prefix compression works on columns of data in the table being compressed, but it looks only at the column values on a single page. For each column, SQL Server chooses a common prefix that can be used to reduce the storage space required for values in that column. The longest value in the column that contains that prefix is chosen as the *anchor value*. Each column is then stored not as the actual data value but as a delta from the anchor value. An example is probably needed to clarify this. Suppose that we have the following character values in a column of the table to be page-compressed:

```
DEEM
DEE
FFF
DEED
DEE
DAN
```

SQL Server might note that DEE is a useful common prefix, so *DEED* is chosen as the anchor value. Each column would be stored as the difference between its value and the anchor value. This difference is stored as a two-part value: the number of characters from the anchor to use, and the additional characters to append. So *DEEM* is stored as <3><M>, meaning the value uses the first three characters from the common prefix and appends a single character, *M*, to it. *DEED* is stored as an empty string (but not null) to indicate it matched the prefix exactly. *DEE* is stored as <3>, with the second part empty, because there are no additional characters to be appended. The list of column values is replaced by the values shown here:

```
DEEM -> <3><M>
DEE  -> <3><>
FFF  -> <><FFF>
DEED -> <><>
DEE  -> <3><>
DAN  -> <1><AN>
```

Keep in mind that the compressed row is stored in the CD record format, so the CD array value has a special encoding to indicate the value is actually NULL. If the replacement value is <><>, and the encoding doesn't indicate NULL, then the value matches the prefix exactly.

SQL Server applies the prefix detection and value replacement algorithm to every column and creates a new row called an *anchor record* to store the anchor values for each column. If no useful prefix can be found, the value in the anchor record is NULL, and then all the values in the column are stored just as they are.

Figure 7-12 shows an image of six rows in a table prior to page compression, and then shows the six rows after the anchor record has been created and the substitutions have been made for the actual data values.

| Original Data | | |
|---|---|---|
| ABCD | DEEM | ABC |
| ABD | DEE | DEE |
| ABC | FFF | GHI |
| AAN | DEED | HHH |
| NULL | DEE | KLM |
| ADE | DAN | NOP |

| Data After Column Prefix Compression | | |
|---|---|---|
| Anchor Record | | |
| ABCD | DEED | NULL |
| <><> | <3><M> | ABC |
| <2><D> | <3><> | DEE |
| <3><> | <><FFF> | GHI |
| <1><AN> | <><> | HHH |
| NULL | <3><> | KLM |
| <1><DE> | <1><AN> | NOP |

**FIGURE 7-12** Before and after column prefix compression

## Dictionary Compression

After prefix compression has been applied to every column individually, the second phase of page compression looks at all values on the page to find duplicates in any column of any row, even if they have been encoded to reflect prefix usage. You can see in the bottom part of Figure 7-11 that two of the values occur multiple times: <3><> occurs three times and <1><AN> occurs twice. The process of detecting duplicate values is datatype-agnostic, so values in completely different columns could be the same in their binary representation. For example, a 1-byte character is represented in hex as 0x54, and it would be seen as a duplicate of the 1-byte integer 84, which is also represented in hex as 0x54. The dictionary is stored as a set of symbols, each of which corresponds to a duplicated value on the data page. Once the symbols and data values have been determined, each occurrence of one of the duplicated values is replaced by the symbol. SQL Server recognizes that the value actually stored in the column is a symbol and not a data value by examining the encoding in the CD array. Values which have been replaced by symbols have a CD array value of 0xc. Figure 7-13 shows the data from Figure 7-12 after replacing the five values with symbols.

| Dictionary of Symbols:<br>[S1] = <1><AN>  [S2] = <3><> | | |
|---|---|---|
| <><> | <3><M> | ABC |
| <2><D> | [S2] | DEE |
| [S2] | <><FFF> | GHI |
| [S1] | <><> | HHH |
| NULL | [S2] | KLM |
| <1><DE> | [S1] | NOP |

**FIGURE 7-13** A page compressed with dictionary compression

Not every page in a compressed table has both an anchor record for prefixes and a dictionary. If there are no useful prefix values, the page might just have a dictionary. If no values repeat often enough that replacing them with symbols saves space, the page might just have an anchor record. And, of course, there may be pages that have neither an anchor record nor a dictionary, if there are no patterns at all in the data on the page.

## Physical Storage

There is only one main structural change to a page when it is page-compressed. SQL Server adds a hidden row right after the page header (at byte offset 96, or 0x60) called the *compression information (CI) record*. The structure of the CI record is shown in Figure 7-14.

| Header | PageModCount | Offsets | Anchor Record | Dictionary |
|---|---|---|---|---|

**FIGURE 7-14** Structure of a CI record

The CI record does not have an entry in the slot array for the page, but it is always at the same location. In addition, a bit in the page header indicates that the page is page-compressed, so SQL Server looks for the CI record. If you use *DBCC PAGE* to dump a page, the page header information contains a value called *m_typeFlagBits*. If this value is 0x80, the page is compressed.

The following script can be run if you have already created the table called *sp_tablepages*, described earlier in this chapter. This script captures the *DBCC IND* information from the tables created in this section: *Employees_uncompressed, Employees_rowcompressed,* and *Employees_pagecompressed*. The script then displays the first data page number for each of the tables. You can use this information to examine the page with *DBCC PAGE*. Note that only the page for *Employees_pagecompressed* has the *m_typeFlagBits* value set to 0x80:

```
USE AdventureWorks2008;
GO
TRUNCATE TABLE sp_tablepages;
GO
INSERT INTO sp_tablepages
    EXEC ('DBCC IND(AdventureWorks2008, Employees_pagecompressed, -1)');
GO
INSERT INTO sp_tablepages
    EXEC ('DBCC IND(AdventureWorks2008, Employees_rowcompressed, -1)');
GO
INSERT INTO sp_tablepages
    EXEC ('DBCC IND(AdventureWorks2008, Employees_uncompressed, -1)');
GO
SELECT OBJECT_NAME(ObjectID), PageFID, PagePID
FROM sp_tablepages
WHERE pagetype = 1
  AND PrevPagePID = 0;
GO
DBCC TRACEON(3604);
GO
```

Using *DBCC PAGE* to look at a page-compressed page does provide information about the contents of the CI record, and we'll look at some of that information after we examine what each of the sections means, which is discussed next.

**Header**   The header is a 1-byte value keeping track of information about the CI. Bit 0 indicates the version, which in SQL Server 2008 is always 0. Bit 1 indicates whether the CI has an anchor record, and bit 2 indicates whether the CI has a dictionary. The rest of the bits are unused.

*PageModCount*    The *PageModCount* value keeps track of the changes to this particular page and is used when determining whether the compression on the page should be reevaluated, and a new CI record built. I'll talk more about how this value is used in the next section, when I discuss page compression analysis.

**Offsets**    The offsets contain values to help SQL Server find the dictionary. It contains a value indicating the page offset for the end of the anchor record and a value indicating the page offset for the end of the CI record itself.

**Anchor Record**    The anchor record looks exactly like a regular CD record on the page, including the record header, the CD array, and both a short data area and a long data area. The values stored in the data area are the common prefix values for each column, some of which might be NULL.

**Dictionary**    The dictionary area is composed of three sections. The first is a 2-byte field containing a numeric value representing the number of entries in the dictionary. The second section is an offset array of 2-byte entries, indicating the end offset of each dictionary entry relative to the start of the dictionary data section. The third section contains the actual dictionary data entries.

Remember that each dictionary entry is a byte string that is replaced in the regular data rows by a symbol. The symbol is simply an integer value from 0 to N. In addition, remember that the byte strings are datatype-independent; that is, they are just bytes. After SQL Server determines what recurring values are stored in the dictionary, it sorts the list first by data length, then by data value, and then assigns the symbols in order. So suppose that the values to be stored in the dictionary are these:

```
0x 53 51 4C
0x FF F8
0x DA 15 43 77 64
0x 34 F3 B6 22 CD
0x 12 34 56
```

Table 7-8 shows the sorted dictionary, along with the length and symbol for each entry.

**TABLE 7-8 Values in a Page Compression Dictionary**

| Value | Length | Symbol |
|---|---|---|
| 0x FF F8 | 2 bytes | 0 |
| 0x 12 34 56 | 3 bytes | 1 |
| 0x 53 51 4C | 3 bytes | 2 |
| 0x 34 F3 B6 22 CD | 4 bytes | 3 |
| 0x DA 15 43 77 64 | 4 bytes | 4 |

The dictionary area would then look like Figure 7-15.

| Header | Offsets | Dictionary |
|--------|---------|------------|
| 5 | 02 00 | 0x FF F8 |
| | 05 00 | 0x 12 34 56 |
| | 08 00 | 0x 53 51 4C |
| | 0D 00 | 0x 34 F3 B6 22 CD |
| | 12 00 | 0x DA 15 43 77 64 |

**FIGURE 7-15** The dictionary area in a Compression Information Record

Note that the dictionary never actually stores the symbol values. They are stored only in the data records that need to use the dictionary. Because they are simply integers, they can be used as an index into the offset list to find the appropriate dictionary replacement value. For example, if a row on the page contains the dictionary symbol [2], SQL Server looks in the offset list for the third entry, which in Figure 7-14 ends at offset 0800 from the start of the dictionary. SQL Server then finds the value that ends at that byte, which is 0x 53 51 4C. If this byte string was stored in a *char* or *varchar* column (that is, a single-byte character string), it would correspond to the character string *SQL*.

I illustrated earlier in this chapter that the *DBCC PAGE* output shows you the CD array for compressed rows. For compressed pages, *DBCC PAGE* shows the CI record and details about the anchor record within it. In addition, with format 3, *DBCC PAGE* shows details about the dictionary entries. When I captured the *DBCC PAGE* in format 3 for the first page of my *Employees_pagecompressed* table and copied it to a Microsoft Office Word document, it needed 261 pages. Needless to say, I will not show you all that output. Even when I just copied the CI record information, it took 7 pages, which is still too much to show in this book. I'll leave it to you to explore the output of *DBCC PAGE* for the tables with compressed pages.

## Page Compression Analysis

In this section, I discuss some of the details regarding how SQL Server determines whether to compress a page or not and what values it uses for the anchor record and the dictionary. Row compression is always performed when requested, but page compression depends on the amount of space that can be saved. However, the actual work of compressing the rows has to wait until page compression has been performed. Because both types of page compression, prefix substitution and dictionary symbol substitution, replace the actual data values with encodings, the row cannot be compressed until SQL Server determines what encodings are going to replace the actual data.

When page compression is first enabled for a table or partition, SQL Server goes through every full page to determine the possible space savings. (Any pages that are not full are not considered for compression.) This compression analysis actually creates the anchor record, modifies all the columns to reflect the anchor values, and generates the dictionary. Then it compresses each row. If the new compressed page can hold at least five more rows, or 25 percent more rows than the current page (whichever is larger), then the compressed page replaces the uncompressed page. If compressing the page does not result in this much savings, the compressed page is discarded.

When determining what values to use for the anchor record on a compressed page, SQL Server needs to look at every byte in every row, one column at a time. As it scans the column, it also keeps track of possible dictionary entries (which can be used in multiple columns). The anchor record values can be determined for each column in a single pass; that is, by the time all the bytes in all the rows for the first column are examined once, SQL Server has determined the anchor record value for that column or it has determined that no anchor record value will save sufficient space.

As SQL Server examines each column, it collects a list of possible dictionary entries. As we've discussed, the dictionary contains values that occur enough times on the page so that replacing them with a symbol is cost-effective in terms of space. For each possible dictionary entry, SQL Server keeps track of the value, its size, and the count of occurrences. If (size_of_data_value $-1$) * (count$-1$) $-2$ is greater than zero, it means the dictionary replacement saves space, and the value is considered eligible for the dictionary. In general, SQL Server tries to keep no more than 300 entries in the dictionary, so if more dictionary entries are possible, they are sorted by count during the analysis and only the most frequently occurring values are used in the dictionary.

## Rebuilding the CI Record

If a table is enabled for either page or row compression, new rows are always compressed before they are inserted into the table. However, the CI record containing the anchor record and the dictionary is rebuilt on an all-or-nothing basis; that is, SQL Server does not just add some new entry to the dictionary when new rows are inserted. SQL Server evaluates whether to rebuild the CI record when the page has been changed a sufficient number of times. It keeps track of changes to each page in the *PageModCount* field of the CI record, and that value is updated every time a row is inserted, updated, or deleted. If a full page is encountered during a data modification operation, SQL Server examines the *PageModCount* value. If the *PageModCount* value is greater than 25, or if the value *PageModCount/<number of rows on the page>* is greater than 25 percent, SQL Server applies the compression analysis as it does when it first compresses a page. Only if it is determined that recompressing the page makes room for at least five more rows (or 25 percent more rows than the current page) does the new compressed page replace the old page.

There are some important differences between compression of pages in a B-tree and compression of pages in a heap.

**Compression of B-tree Pages** For B-trees, only the leaf level is page-compressed. When inserting a new row into a B-tree, if the compressed row fits on the page, it is inserted, and nothing more is done. If it doesn't fit, SQL Server tries to recompress the page, according to the conditions described in the preceding section. If the recompression succeeded, it means that the CI record changed, so the new row must be recompressed and then SQL Server tries to insert it into the page. Again, if it fits, it is simply inserted. If the new compressed row doesn't fit on the page, even after possibly recompressing the page, the page needs to be split. When splitting a compressed page, the CI record is copied to a new page, exactly as is, except that the *PageModCount* value is set to 25. This means that the first time the page gets full, it gets a full analysis to determine if it should be recompressed. B-tree pages are also checked for possible recompression during index rebuilds (either online or offline) and during shrink operations.

**Compression of Heap Pages** Pages in a heap are checked for possible compression only during rebuild and shrink operations. (Note that SQL Server 2008 provides an option to rebuild a table and specify a compression level for just this reason.) Also, if you drop a clustered index on a table so that it becomes a heap, SQL Server runs compression analysis on any full pages. To make sure that the *RowID* values stay the same, heaps are not recompressed during normal data modification operations. Although the *PageModCount* value is maintained, SQL Server never tries to recompress a page based on the *PageModCount* value.

## Compression Metadata

There is not an enormous amount of metadata information relating to data compression. The catalog view *sys.partitions* has a *data_compression* column and a *data_compression_desc* column. The *data_compression* column has possible values of 0, 1, and 2, corresponding to *data_compression_desc* values of NONE, ROW, and PAGE. Keep in mind that although row compression is always performed, page compression is not. Even if *sys.partitions* indicates that a table or partition is page-compressed, that just means that page compression is enabled. Each page is analyzed individually, and if a page is not full, or if compression would not save enough space, the page is not compressed.

You can also inspect the dynamic management function *sys.dm_db_index_operational_stats*. This table-valued function returns the following compression-related columns:

- *page_compression_attempt_count* The number of pages that were evaluated for PAGE-level compression for specific partitions of a table, index, or indexed view. Includes pages that were not compressed because significant savings could not be achieved.

- **page_compression_success_count** The number of data pages that were compressed by using PAGE compression for specific partitions of a table, index, or indexed view.

SQL Server 2008 also provides a stored procedure called *sp_estimate_data_compression_savings*, which can give you some idea of whether compression provides a large space savings or not.

This procedure samples up to 5,000 pages of the table and creates an equivalent table with the sampled pages in *tempdb*. Using this temporary table, SQL Server can estimate the new table size for the requested compression state (NONE, ROW, or PAGE). Compression can be evaluated for whole tables or parts of tables. This includes heaps, clustered indexes, nonclustered indexes, indexed views, and table and index partitions.

Keep in mind that the result is only an estimate and your actual savings can vary widely based on the fillfactor and the size of the rows. If the procedure indicates that you can reduce your row size by 40 percent, you might not actually get a 40-percent space savings for the whole table. For example, if you have a row that is 8,000 bytes long and you reduce its size by 40 percent, you still can fit only one row on a data page and your table still needs the same number of pages.

You may get results from running *sp_estimate_data_compression_savings* that indicate that the table will grow. This can happen when many rows in the table use almost the whole maximum size of the data types, and the addition of the overhead needed for the compression information is more than the savings from compression.

If the table is already compressed, you can use this procedure to estimate the size of the table (or index) if it were to be uncompressed.

## Performance Issues

The main motivation for compressing your data is to save space with extremely large tables, such as data warehouse fact tables. A second goal is to increase performance when scanning a table for reporting purposes, because far fewer pages need to be read. You need to keep in mind that compression comes at a cost: there is a tradeoff between the space savings and the extra CPU overhead to compress the data for storage and then uncompress the data when it needs to be used. On a CPU-bound system, you may find that compressing your data can actually slow down your system considerably.

Page compression provides the most benefit for systems that are I/O-bound, with tables for which the data is written once and then read repeatedly, as in the situations I mentioned in the previous paragraph: data warehousing and reporting. For environments with heavy read and write activity, such as OLTP applications, you might want to consider enabling row compression only and avoid the costs of analyzing the pages and rebuilding the CI record. In this case, the CPU overhead is minimal. In fact, row compression is highly optimized so that it is visible only at the storage engine layer. The relational engine (query processor) doesn't need to deal with compressed rows at all. The relational engine sends uncompressed rows to the storage engine, which compresses them if required. When returning rows to the relational engine, the storage engine waits as long as it can before uncompressing them. In the storage engine, comparisons can be done on compressed data, as internal conversions can convert a data type to its compressed form before comparing to data in the table. In addition, only columns requested by the relational engine need to be uncompressed, as opposed to uncompressing an entire row.

**Compression and Logging**   In general, SQL Server logs only uncompressed data because the log needs to be read in an uncompressed format. This means that logging changes to compressed records has a greater performance impact because each row needs to be uncompressed and decoded (from the anchor record and dictionary) prior to writing to the log. This is another reason why compression gives you more benefit on primarily read-only systems, where logging is minimal.

SQL Server writes compressed data to the log in a few situations. The most common situation is when a page is split. SQL Server writes the compressed rows as it logs the data movement during the split operation.

**Compression and the Version Store**   I will be discussing the version store in Chapter 10, when I talk about Snapshot isolation, but I want to mention briefly here how the version store interacts with compression. SQL Server can write compressed rows to the version store and the version store processing can traverse older versions in their compressed form. However, the version store does not support page compression, so the rows in the version store cannot contain encodings of the anchor record prefixes and the page dictionary. So anytime any row from a compressed page needs to be versioned, the page must be uncompressed first.

The version store is used for both varieties of Snapshot isolation (full snapshot and read-committed snapshot) and is also used for storing the before-and-after images of changed data when triggers are fired. (These images are visible in the logical tables *inserted* and *deleted*.) You should keep this in mind when evaluating the costs of compression. Snapshot isolation has lots of overhead already, and adding page compression into the mix affects performance even more.

## Backup Compression

I mentioned backup compression briefly in Chapter 1, when discussing configuration options. I believe it bears repeating that the algorithm used for compressing backups is very different than the database compression algorithms discussed in this chapter. Backup compression uses an algorithm very similar to zipping, where it is just looking for patterns in the data. Even after tables and indexes have been compressed using the data compression techniques, they still can be compressed further using the backup compression algorithms.

Page compression looks only for prefix patterns, and it can still leave other patterns that are not compressed, including common suffixes. Page compression eliminates redundant strings, but there still are plenty of strings in most cases that are not redundant, and string data compresses very well using zip-type algorithms.

In addition, there is a fair amount of space in a database that constitutes overhead, such as unallocated slots on pages and unallocated pages in allocated extents. Depending on whether Instant File Initialization was used, and what was on the disk previously if it was, the background data can actually compress very well.

So making a compressed backup of a database that has many compressed tables and indexes can provide additional space savings for the backup set.

# Table and Index Partitioning

As we've already seen when looking at the metadata for table and index storage, partitioning is an integral feature of SQL Server space organization. Figure 5-7 in Chapter 5 illustrated the relationship between tables and indexes (hobts), partitions, and allocation units. Tables and indexes that are built without any reference to partitions are considered to be stored on a single partition. One of the more useful metadata objects for retrieving information about data storage is the dynamic management view called *sys.dm_db_partition_stats*, which combines information found in *sys.partitions*, *sys.allocation_units*, and *sys.indexes*.

A partitioned object is one that is split internally into separate physical units that can be stored in different locations. Partitioning is invisible to the users and programmers, who can use T-SQL code to select from a partitioned table exactly the same way they select from a nonpartitioned table. Creating large objects on multiple partitions improves the manageability and maintainability of your database system and can greatly enhance the performance of activities such as purging historic data and loading large amounts of data. In SQL Server 2000, partitioning was available only by manually creating a view that combines multiple tables. That functionality is referred to as *partitioned* views. The SQL Server 2005 and SQL Server 2008 built-in partitioning of tables and indexes has many advantages over partitioned views, including improved execution plans and fewer prerequisites for implementation.

In this section, we focus primarily on physical storage of partitioned objects and the partitioning metadata. In Chapter 8, "The Query Optimizer," we'll examine query plans involving partitioned tables and partitioned indexes.

## Partition Functions and Partition Schemes

To understand the partitioning metadata, we need a little background into how partitions are defined. I will use an example based on the SQL Server samples. You can find my script, called *Partition.sql,* on the companion Web site. This script defines two tables: *TransactionHistory* and *TransactionHistoryArchive*, along with a clustered index and two nonclustered indexes on each. Both tables are partitioned on the *TransactionDate* column, with each month of data in a separate partition. Initially, there are 12 partitions in *TransactionHistory* and 2 in *TransactionHistoryArchive*.

Before you create a partitioned table or index, you must define a partition function. A partition function is used to define the partition boundaries logically. When a partition function is created, you must specify whether or not the partition will use a LEFT- or RIGHT-based boundary point. Simply put, this defines whether the boundary value itself is part of the left-hand or right-hand partition. Another way to consider this is to ask this question: Is it an upper boundary of one partition (in which case it goes to the LEFT), or a lower boundary point of the next partition (in which case it goes to the RIGHT)? The number of partitions created by a partition function with *n* boundaries will be *n*+1. Here is the partition function that we are using for this example:

```
CREATE PARTITION FUNCTION [TransactionRangePF1] (datetime)
AS RANGE RIGHT FOR VALUES ('20081001', '20081101', '20081201',
              '20090101', '20090201', '20090301', '20090401',
              '20090501', '20090601', '20090701', '20090801');
```

Note that the table name is not mentioned in the function definition because the partition function is not tied to any particular table. The function *TransactionRangePF1* divides the data into 12 partitions because there are 11 *datetime* boundaries. The keyword *RIGHT* specifies that any value that equals one of the boundary points goes into the partition to the right of the endpoint. So for this function, all values less than October 1, 2008, go in the first partition, and values greater than or equal to October 1, 2008, and less than November 1, 2008, go in the second partition. I could have also specified *LEFT* (which is the default), in which case the value equal to the endpoint goes in the partition to the left. After you define the partition function, you define a partition scheme, which lists a set of filegroups onto which each range of data is placed. Here is the partition schema for my example:

```
CREATE PARTITION SCHEME [TransactionsPS1]
AS PARTITION [TransactionRangePF1]
TO ([PRIMARY], [PRIMARY], [PRIMARY]
, [PRIMARY], [PRIMARY], [PRIMARY]
, [PRIMARY], [PRIMARY], [PRIMARY]
, [PRIMARY], [PRIMARY], [PRIMARY]);
GO
```

To avoid having to create 12 files and filegroups, I have put all the partitions on the PRIMARY filegroup, but for the full benefit of partitioning, you should probably have each partition on its own filegroup. The *CREATE PARTITION SCHEME* command must list at least as many filegroups as there are partitions, but there can be one more. If one extra filegroup is listed, it is considered the "next used" filegroup. If the partition function splits, the new boundary point is added in the filegroup used next. If you do not specify an extra filegroup at the time you create the partition scheme, you can alter the partition scheme to set the next-used filegroup prior to modifying the function.

As you've seen, the listed filegroups do not have to be unique. In fact, if you want to have all the partitions on the same filegroup, as I do here, there is a shortcut syntax:

```
CREATE PARTITION SCHEME [TransactionsPS1]
AS PARTITION [TransactionRangePF1]
ALL TO ([PRIMARY]);
GO
```

Note that putting all the partitions on the same filegroup is usually just done for the purpose of testing your code.

Additional filegroups are used in order as more partitions are added, which can happen when a partition function is altered to split an existing range into two. If you do not specify extra filegroups at the time you create the partition scheme, you can alter the partition scheme to add another filegroup.

The partition function and partition scheme for a second table are shown here:

```
CREATE PARTITION FUNCTION [TransactionArchivePF2] (datetime)
AS RANGE RIGHT FOR VALUES ('20080901');
GO

CREATE PARTITION SCHEME [TransactionArchivePS2]
AS PARTITION [TransactionArchivePF2]
TO ([PRIMARY], [PRIMARY]);
GO
```

My script then creates two tables and loads data into them. I will not include all the details here. To partition a table, you must specify a partition scheme in the *CREATE TABLE* statement. I create a table called *TransactionArchive* that includes this line as the last part of the *CREATE TABLE* statement as follows:

```
ON [TransactionsPS1] (TransactionDate)
```

My second table, *TransactionArchiveHistory*, is created using the *TransactionsPS1* partitioning scheme.

My script then loads data into the two tables, and because the partition scheme has already been defined, each row is placed in the appropriate partition as the data is loaded. After the tables are loaded, we can examine the metadata.

## Metadata for Partitioning

Figure 7-16 shows most of the catalog views for retrieving information about partitions. Along the left and bottom edges, you can see the *sys.tables*, *sys.indexes*, *sys.partitions*, and *sys.allocation_units* catalog views that I've discussed previously in this chapter.

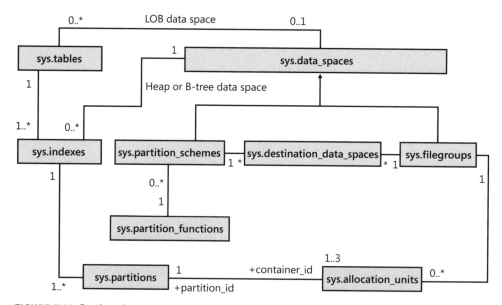

**FIGURE 7-16** Catalog views containing metadata for partitioning and data storage

In some of my queries, I am using the undocumented *sys.system_internals_allocation_units* view instead of *sys.allocation_units* to retrieve page address information. Here, I'll describe the most relevant columns of each of these views:

- **sys.data_spaces**  has a primary key called *data_space_id,* which is either a partition ID or a filegroup ID, and there is one row for each filegroup and one row for each partition scheme. One of the columns in *sys.data_spaces* specifies to which type of data space the row refers. If the row refers to a partition scheme, *data_space_id* can be joined with *sys.partition_schemes.data_space_id.* If the row refers to a filegroup, *data_space_id* can be joined with *sys.filegroups.data_space_id.* The *sys.indexes* view also has a *data_space_id* column to indicate how each heap or B-tree stored in *sys.indexes* is stored. So, if we know that a table is partitioned, we can directly join it with *sys.partition_schemes* without going through *sys.data_spaces.* Alternatively, you can use the following query to determine whether a table is partitioned by replacing *Production.TransactionHistoryArchive* with the name of the table in which you're interested:

```
SELECT DISTINCT object_name(object_id) as TableName,
          ISNULL(ps.name, 'Not partitioned') as PartitionScheme
    FROM (sys.indexes i LEFT  JOIN sys.partition_schemes ps
              ON (i.data_space_id = ps.data_space_id))
    WHERE (i.object_id = object_id('Production.TransactionHistoryArchive'))
          AND   (i.index_id IN (0,1));
```

- **sys.partition_schemes**  has one row for each partition scheme. In addition to the *data_space_id* and the name of the partition scheme, it has a *function_id* column to join with *sys.partition_functions.*

- **sys.destination_data_spaces**  is a linking table because *sys.partition_schemes* and *sys.filegroups* are in a many-to-many relationship with each other. For each partition scheme, there is one row for each partition. The partition number is in the *destination_id* column, and the filegroup ID is stored in the *data_space_id* column.

- **sys.partition_functions**  contains one row for each partition function, and its primary key *function_id* is a foreign key in *sys.partition_schemes.*

- **sys.partition_range_values**  (not shown) has one row for each endpoint of each partition function. Its *function_id* column can be joined with *sys.partition_functions,* and its *boundary_id* column can join with either *partition_id* in *sys.partitions* or with *destination_id* in *sys.destination_data_spaces.*

These views have other columns that I haven't mentioned, and there are additional views that provide information, such as the columns and their data types that the partitioning is based on. However, the preceding information should be sufficient to understand Figure 7-15 and the view shown in the next block of code. This view returns information about each partition of each partitioned table. The WHERE clause filters out partitioned indexes (other than the clustered index), but you can change that condition if you desire. When selecting from the view, you can add your own WHERE clause to find information about just the table you're interested in:

```
CREATE VIEW Partition_Info AS
SELECT OBJECT_NAME(i.object_id) as Object_Name,
        p.partition_number, fg.name AS Filegroup_Name, rows, au.total_pages,
        CASE boundary_value_on_right
                  WHEN 1 THEN 'less than'
                  ELSE 'less than or equal to' END as 'comparison', value
FROM sys.partitions p JOIN sys.indexes i
    ON p.object_id = i.object_id and p.index_id = i.index_id
      JOIN sys.partition_schemes ps
              ON ps.data_space_id = i.data_space_id
      JOIN sys.partition_functions f
                ON f.function_id = ps.function_id
      LEFT JOIN  sys.partition_range_values rv
 ON f.function_id = rv.function_id
                  AND p.partition_number = rv.boundary_id
      JOIN sys.destination_data_spaces dds
            ON dds.partition_scheme_id = ps.data_space_id
                AND dds.destination_id = p.partition_number
      JOIN sys.filegroups fg
              ON dds.data_space_id = fg.data_space_id
      JOIN (SELECT container_id, sum(total_pages) as total_pages
                FROM sys.allocation_units
                GROUP BY container_id) AS au
            ON au.container_id = p.partition_id
  WHERE i.index_id <2;
```

The LEFT JOIN operator is needed to get all the partitions because the *sys.partition_range_values* view has a row only for each boundary value, not for each partition. LEFT JOIN gives the last partition with a boundary value of NULL, which means that the value of the last partition has no upper limit. A derived table groups together all the rows in *sys.allocation_units* for a partition, so the space used for all the types of storage (in-row, row-overflow, and LOB) is aggregated into a single value. This query uses the preceding view to get information about my *TransactionHistory* table's partitions:

```
SELECT * FROM Partition_Info
WHERE Object_Name = 'TransactionHistory';
```

Here are my results:

| Object_Name | Partition _number | Filegroup _Name | Rows | Total_ pages | Comparison | Value |
|---|---|---|---|---|---|---|
| *TransactionHistory* | 1 | PRIMARY | 11155 | 209 | Less than | 2008-10-01 |
| *TransactionHistory* | 2 | PRIMARY | 9339 | 177 | Less than | 2008-11-01 |
| *TransactionHistory* | 3 | PRIMARY | 10169 | 185 | Less than | 2008-12-01 |
| *TransactionHistory* | 4 | PRIMARY | 12181 | 225 | Less than | 2009-01-01 |
| *TransactionHistory* | 5 | PRIMARY | 9558 | 177 | Less than | 2009-02-01 |

| Object_Name | Partition _number | Filegroup _Name | Rows | Total_ pages | Comparison | Value |
|---|---|---|---|---|---|---|
| *TransactionHistory* | 6 | PRIMARY | 10217 | 193 | Less than | 2009-03-01 |
| *TransactionHistory* | 7 | PRIMARY | 10703 | 201 | Less than | 2009-04-01 |
| *TransactionHistory* | 8 | PRIMARY | 10640 | 193 | Less than | 2009-05-01 |
| *TransactionHistory* | 9 | PRIMARY | 12508 | 225 | Less than | 2009-06-01 |
| *TransactionHistory* | 10 | PRIMARY | 12585 | 233 | Less than | 2009-07-01 |
| *TransactionHistory* | 11 | PRIMARY | 3380 | 73 | Less than | 2009-08-01 |
| *TransactionHistory* | 12 | PRIMARY | 1008 | 33 | Less than | NULL |

This view contains details about the boundary point of each partition, as well as the filegroup that each partition is stored on, the number of rows in each partition, and the amount of space used. Note that although the comparison indicates that the values in the partitioning column for the rows in a particular partition are less than the specified value, you should assume that it also means that the values are greater than or equal to the specified value in the preceding partition. However, this view doesn't provide information about where in the particular filegroup the data is located. We'll look at a metadata query that gives us location information in the next section.

**Note** If a partitioned table contains filestream data, it is recommended that the filestream data be partitioned using the same partition function as the non-filestream data. Because the regular data and the filestream data are on separate filegroups, the filestream data needs its own partition scheme. However, the partition scheme for the filestream data can use the same partition function to make sure the same partitioning is used for both filestream and non-filestream data.

## The Sliding Window Benefits of Partitioning

One of the main benefits of partitioning your data is that you can move data from one partition to another as a metadata-only operation. The data itself doesn't have to move. As I mentioned, this is not intended to be a complete how-to guide to SQL Server 2008 partitioning; rather, it is a description of the internal storage of partitioning information. However, to show the internals of rearranging partitions, we need to look at some additional partitioning operations.

The main operation you use when working with partitions is the SWITCH option to the *ALTER TABLE* command. This option allows you to

- Assign a table as a partition to an already-existing partitioned table
- Switch a partition from one partitioned table to another
- Reassign a partition to form a single table

In all these operations, no data is moved. Rather, the metadata is updated in the *sys.partitions* and *sys.system_internals_allocation_units* views to indicate that a given allocation unit now is part of a different partition. Let's look at an example. The following query returns information about each allocation unit in the first two partitions of my *TransactionHistory* and *TransactionHistoryArchive* tables, including the number of rows, the number of pages, the type of data in the allocation unit, and the page where the allocation unit starts:

```
SELECT convert(char(25),object_name(object_id)) AS name,
    rows, convert(char(15),type_desc) as page_type_desc,
    total_pages AS pages, first_page, index_id, partition_number
FROM sys.partitions p JOIN sys.system_internals_allocation_units a
    ON p.partition_id = a.container_id
WHERE (object_id=object_id('[Production].[TransactionHistory]')
    OR object_id=object_id('[Production].[TransactionHistoryArchive]'))
    AND index_id = 1 AND partition_number <= 2;
```

Here is the data I get back. (I left out the *page_type_desc* because all the rows are of type IN_ROW_DATA.)

| name | rows | pages | first_page | index_id | partition_number |
|------|------|-------|------------|----------|------------------|
| TransactionHistory | 11155 | 209 | 0xD81B00000100 | 1 | 1 |
| TransactionHistory | 9339 | 177 | 0xA82200000100 | 1 | 2 |
| TransactionHistoryArchive | 89253 | 1553 | 0x981B00000100 | 1 | 1 |
| TransactionHistoryArchive | 0 | 0 | 0x000000000000 | 1 | 2 |

Now let's move one of my partitions. My ultimate goal is to add a new partition to *TransactionHistory* to store a new month's worth of data and to move the oldest month's data into *TransactionHistoryArchive*. The partition function used by my *TransactionHistory* table divides the data into 12 partitions, and the last one contains all dates greater than or equal to August 1, 2009. I'm going to alter the partition function to put a new boundary point in for September 1, 2009, so the last partition is split. Before doing that, I must ensure that the partition scheme using this function knows what filegroup to use for the newly created partition. With this command, some data movement occurs and all data from the last partition of any tables using this partition scheme is moved to a new allocation unit. Please refer to *SQL Server Books Online* for complete details about each of the following commands:

```
ALTER PARTITION SCHEME TransactionsPS1
NEXT USED [PRIMARY];
GO

ALTER PARTITION FUNCTION TransactionRangePF1()
SPLIT RANGE ('20090901');
GO
```

Next, I'll do something similar for the function and partition scheme used by *TransactionHistoryArchive*. In this case, I'll add a new boundary point for October 1, 2008:

```
ALTER PARTITION SCHEME TransactionArchivePS2
NEXT USED [PRIMARY];
GO

ALTER PARTITION FUNCTION TransactionArchivePF2()
SPLIT RANGE ('20081001');
GO
```

I want to move all data from *TransactionHistory* with dates earlier than October 1, 2008, to the second partition of *TransactionHistoryArchive*. However, the first partition of *TransactionHistory* technically has no lower limit; it includes everything earlier than October 1, 2008. The second partition of *TransactionHistoryArchive* does have a lower limit, which is the first boundary point, or September 1, 2008. To SWITCH a partition from one table to another, I have to guarantee that all the data to be moved meets the requirements for the new location. So I add a CHECK constraint that guarantees that no data in *TransactionHistory* is earlier than September 1, 2008. After adding the CHECK constraint, I run the *ALTER TABLE* command with the SWITCH option to move the data in partition 1 of *TransactionHistory* to partition 2 of *TransactionHistoryArchive*. (For testing purposes, you could try leaving out the next step that adds the constraint and try just executing the *ALTER TABLE/SWITCH* command. You get an error message. After that, you can add the constraint and run the *ALTER TABLE/SWITCH* command again.)

```
ALTER TABLE [Production].[TransactionHistory]
ADD CONSTRAINT [CK_TransactionHistory_DateRange]
CHECK ([TransactionDate] >= '20080901');
GO
ALTER TABLE [Production].[TransactionHistory]
SWITCH PARTITION 1
TO [Production].[TransactionHistoryArchive] PARTITION 2;
GO
```

Now we run the metadata query that examines the size and location of the first two partitions of each table as follows:

```
SELECT convert(char(25),object_name(object_id)) AS name,
    rows, convert(char(15),type_desc) as page_type_desc,
    total_pages AS pages, first_page, index_id, partition_number
FROM sys.partitions p JOIN sys.system_internals_allocation_units a
    ON p.partition_id = a.container_id
WHERE (object_id=object_id('[Production].[TransactionHistory]')
   OR object_id=object_id('[Production].[TransactionHistoryArchive]'))
  AND index_id = 1 AND partition_number <= 2;
```

```
RESULTS:
name                    rows    pages     first_page       index_id   partition_number
--------------------    ------- --------- --------------   ---------- ----------------
TransactionHistory      0       0         0x000000000000   1          1
TransactionHistory      9339    177       0xA82200000100   1          2
TransactionHistoryAr    89253   1553      0x981B00000100   1          1
TransactionHistoryAr    11155   209       0xD81B00000100   1          2
```

You'll notice that the second partition of *TransactionHistoryArchive* now has exactly the same information that the first partition of *TransactionHistory* had in the first result set. It has the same number of rows (11,155), the same number of pages (209), and the same starting page (0xD81B00000100, or file 1, page 7,128). No data was moved; the only change was that the allocation unit starting at file 1, page 7,128 is not recorded as belonging to the second partition of the *TransactionHistoryArchive* table.

Although my partitioning script created the indexes for my partitioned tables using the same partition scheme used for the tables themselves, this is not always necessary. An index for a partitioned table can be partitioned using the same partition scheme or a different one. If you do not specify a partition scheme or filegroup when you build an index on a partitioned table, the index is placed in the same partition scheme as the underlying table, using the same partitioning column. Indexes built on the same partition scheme as the base table are called *aligned indexes*.

However, an internal storage component is associated with automatically aligned indexes. As previously mentioned, if you build an index on a partitioned table and do not specify a filegroup or partitioning scheme on which to place the index, SQL Server creates the index using the same partitioning scheme that the table uses. However, if the partitioning column is not part of the index definition, SQL Server adds the partitioning column as an extra included column in the index. If the index is clustered, adding an included column is not necessary because the clustered index already contains all the columns. Another case in which SQL Server does not add an included column automatically is when you create a unique index, either clustered or nonclustered. Because unique partitioned indexes require that the partitioning column is contained in the unique key, a unique index for which you have not explicitly included the partitioning key is not partitioned automatically.

## Summary

In this chapter, we looked at how SQL Server 2008 stores data that doesn't use the normal FixedVar record format and data that doesn't fit into the normal 8-KB data page.

I discussed row-overflow and large object data, which is stored on its own separate pages, and filestream data, which is stored outside SQL Server, in files in the filesystem.

Some of the new storage capabilities in SQL Server 2008 require that we look at row storage in a completely different way. Sparse columns allow us to have very wide tables of up to 30,000 columns, so long as most of those columns are NULL in most rows. Each row in a table containing sparse columns has a special descriptor field that provides information about which columns are non-NULL for that particular row.

I also described a completely new row storage format used with compressed data. Data can be compressed at either the row level or the page level, and the rows and pages themselves describe the data that is contained therein. This type of row format is referred to as the CD format.

Finally we looked at partitioning of tables and indexes. Although partitioning doesn't really require a special format for your rows and pages, it does require accessing the metadata in a special way.

# Chapter 8

# The Query Optimizer

*Conor Cunningham*

The Query Optimizer in Microsoft SQL Server 2008 determines the query plan to be executed for a given SQL statement. Because the Query Optimizer does not have a lot of exposed features, it is not as widely understood as some of the other components in the SQL Server Engine. This chapter describes the Query Optimizer and how it works. After reading this chapter, you should understand the high-level optimizer architecture and should be able to reason about why a particular plan was selected by the Query Optimizer. By extension, you should be able to troubleshoot problem query plans in the case when the Query Optimizer may not select the desired query plan and how to affect that selection.

This chapter is split into two sections. The first section explains the basic mechanisms of the Query Optimizer. This includes the high-level structures that are used and how this defines the set of alternatives considered for each plan. The second section discusses specific areas in the Query Optimizer and how they fit into this framework. For example, it discusses topics like "How do indexes get selected?", "How do statistics get used?", and "How do I understand update plans?"

## Overview

The basic compilation "pipeline" for a single query appears in Figure 8-1.

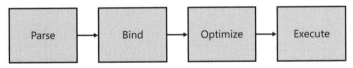

**FIGURE 8-1** Query processor pipeline

When a query is compiled, the SQL statement is first *parsed* into an equivalent tree representation. For queries with valid SQL syntax, the next stage performs a series of validation steps on the query, generally called *binding,* where the columns and tables in the tree are compared to database metadata to make sure that those columns and tables exist and are visible to the current user. This stage also performs semantic checks on the query to make sure it is valid, such as making sure that the columns bound to a *GROUP BY* operation are valid. Once the query tree has been bound and is determined to be a valid query, the Query Optimizer takes the query and starts evaluating different possible query plans. The Query Optimizer performs this search and then selects the query plan to be executed and returns it to the system to execute. The *execution* component runs the query plan and returns the results of the query.

The SQL Server 2008 Query Optimizer has a number of additional features that extend this diagram to make it more useful for database developers and DBAs. For example, query plans are cached because they are expensive to produce and are often used repeatedly. Old query plans are recompiled if the underlying data has changed sufficiently. SQL Server also supports the T-SQL language, which means that batches of multiple statements can be processed in one request to the SQL Server Engine. The Query Optimizer does not consider batch compilation or workload analysis, so this chapter focuses on what happens in a single query's compilation.

## Tree Format

When you submit a SQL query to the query processor, the SQL string is parsed into a tree representation. Each node in the tree represents a query operation to be performed. For example, each table in the FROM clause has its own operator. A WHERE clause is also represented in a separate operator. Joins are represented with operators that have one input for each table. For example, the query *SELECT * FROM Customers C INNER JOIN Orders O on C.cid = O.cid WHERE O.date = '2008-11-06'* might be represented internally, as seen in Figure 8-2.

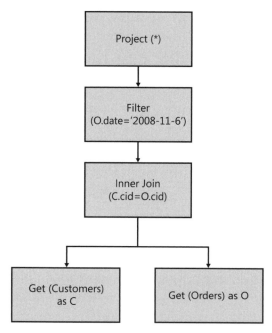

**FIGURE 8-2** Query tree format example

The query processor actually uses different tree formats throughout the compilation process. For example, one job that the Query Optimizer performs is to convert a tree from a logical description of the desired result, as seen previously, to a plan with real physical operators that can be executed. Perhaps the most obvious place where this selection happens is when the Query Optimizer selects a join algorithm, converting a logical join (for example, *INNER JOIN*) into a physical join (a hash join, merge join, or nested loops join). Most of the tree formats are pretty close to each other. In many of the examples in this chapter, optimizer output trees are used to describe specific optimizations performed by the Query Optimizer in earlier, internal tree formats.

# What Is Optimization?

So far, we have discussed only the basic transformation from a logical query tree into an equivalent physical query plan. Another major job of the Query Optimizer is to find an *efficient* query plan. There are usually many ways to evaluate a given query, and often some plans are much slower than others. The speed difference between these two plans is so significant that selecting the wrong query plan can cause a database application to perform so slowly that it appears broken to the user. Therefore, it is very important that the Query Optimizer select an efficient plan.

At first, it might seem that there would be an "obvious" best plan for every SQL query, and the Query Optimizer should just select it as quickly as it can. Unfortunately, query optimization is actually a much more difficult problem. Consider the following SQL query:

```
SELECT * FROM A
INNER JOIN B ON (A.a = B.b)
INNER JOIN C ON (A.a = C.c)
INNER JOIN D ON (A.a = D.d)
INNER JOIN E ON (A.a = E.e)
INNER JOIN F ON (A.a = F.f)
INNER JOIN G ON (A.a = G.g)
INNER JOIN H ON (A.a = H.h)
```

This query has many possible implementation plans because inner joins can be computed in different orders. Actually, if you add more tables into this query using this same pattern, the query would have so many possible plan choices that it isn't feasible to consider them all. Because inner joins can be evaluated in any order (ABCD…, ABDC…, ACBD…, …) and in different topologies [(A join B) join (B join C)], the number of possible query plans for this query is actually greater than $N!$ [$N \times (N-1) \times (N-2) \times$ …]. As the number of tables in a query increases, the set of alternatives to consider quickly grows to be larger than what can be computed on any computer. The storage of all the possible query plans also becomes a problem. In 32-bit Intel x86-based machines, SQL Server usually has about 1.6 GB of memory that could be used to compile a query, and it may not be possible to store every possible alternative in memory. Even if a computer could store all these alternatives, the user may not want to wait that long to enumerate all those possible choices. The Query Optimizer solves this problem using heuristics and statistics to guide those heuristics, and this chapter describes these concepts.

Many people believe that it is the job of the Query Optimizer to select the absolute best query plan for a given query. You can now see that the scope of the problem makes this impossible—if you can't consider every plan shape, it is difficult to prove that a plan is optimal. However, it *is* possible for the Query Optimizer to find a "good enough" plan quickly, and often this is the optimally performing plan or very close to it.

# How the Query Optimizer Explores Query Plans

The Query Optimizer uses a framework to search and compare many different possible plan alternatives efficiently. This framework allows SQL Server to consider complex, non-obvious ways to implement a given query. Keeping track of all these different alternatives to find a plan to run efficiently is not easy. The search framework of SQL Server contains several components that help it perform its job efficiently and reliably. Although largely internal, these components are described in this section to give you a better idea about how a query is optimized and to better design your applications to take advantage of its capabilities.

## Rules

The Query Optimizer is a search framework. From a given query tree, the Query Optimizer considers transformations of that tree from the current state to a different, equivalent state that is also stored in memory. In the framework used in SQL Server, the transformations are done via *rules*. These rules are very similar to the mathematical theorems you likely learned in school. For example, we know that *A INNER JOIN B* is equivalent to *B INNER JOIN A* because both queries return the same result for all possible table data sets. This is a form of commutativity (which, in regular integer arithmetic, means that (1+2) is equivalent to (2+1), meaning that this operation can be performed in any order and yield the same result (or, in the case of databases, return the same set of rows). Rules are matched to tree patterns and are then applied if they are suitable to generate new alternatives (which then may also lead to more rule matching). These rules form the basis of how the Query Optimizer works, and they also help encode some of the heuristics necessary to perform the search in a reasonable amount of time.

The Query Optimizer has different kinds of rules. Rules that heuristically rewrite a query tree into a new shape are called *substitution rules*. Rules that consider mathematical equivalences are called *exploration rules*. These rules generate new tree shapes but cannot be directly executed. Rules that convert logical trees into physical trees to be executed are called *implementation rules*. The best of these generated physical alternatives is eventually output by the Query Optimizer as the final query execution plan.

**More Info**  This chapter contains many examples of query execution plans, used to illustrate the Query Optimizer's behavior. If you would like more background information on how to interpret query execution plans, and what the various operators mean, you can refer to Chapter 3 in *Inside Microsoft SQL Server 2005: Query Tuning and Optimization* (Microsoft Press, 2007). Other than some minor visual changes in the way graphical query plans are displayed in SQL Server 2008, almost all the content in that chapter is applicable to SQL Server 2008. We have made this chapter available for you on the companion Web site (*http://www.SQLServerInternals.com/companion*).

# Properties

The search framework collects information about the query tree in a format that can make it easier for rules to work. These are called *properties,* and they collect information from sub-trees to help make decisions about what rules can be processed at a higher point in a tree. For example, one property used in SQL Server is the set of columns that make up a unique key on the data. Consider the following query:

```
SELECT col1, col2, MAX(col3) FROM Table1 GROUP BY col1, col2;
```

This query is represented internally as a tree, as seen in Figure 8-3.

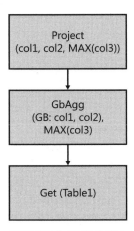

**FIGURE 8-3** GROUP BY tree example

If the columns (*col1, col2*) make up a unique key on table *groupby,* then it is not necessary to do grouping at all—each group has exactly one row. The *MAX()* of a set of size one is the element itself. So, it is possible to write a rule that removes the *groupby* from the query tree completely. You can see this rule in action in Figure 8-4.

```
CREATE TABLE groupby (col1 int, col2 int, col3 int);
ALTER TABLE groupby ADD CONSTRAINT unique1 UNIQUE(col1, col2);
SELECT col1, col2, MAX(col3) FROM groupby GROUP BY col1, col2;
```

**FIGURE 8-4** Query plan with aggregate operation removed

If you look at the final query plan, you can see that the Query Optimizer performs no grouping operation even though the query has a *GROUP BY* in it. The properties collected during optimization enable this rule to perform a tree transformation to make the resulting query plan complete more quickly.

SQL Server also collects many properties during optimization. As is done in most modern compilers, the Query Optimizer collects domain constraint information about each column referenced in the query. The Query Optimizer collects information from predicates, join conditions, partitioning information, and check constraints to reason about how all these predicates can be used to optimize the query. One useful application of this scalar property is in *contradiction detection*. The Query Optimizer can determine if the query is written in such a way as to never return any rows at all. When the Query Optimizer detects a contradiction, it actually rewrites the query to remove the portion of the query containing the contradiction. Figure 8-5 contains an example of a contradiction detected during optimization.

```
CREATE TABLE DomainTable(col1 int);
GO
SELECT *
FROM DomainTable D1
INNER JOIN DomainTable D2
ON D1.col1=D2.col1
WHERE D1.col1 > 5 AND D2.col1 < 0;
```

```
  SELECT              Constant Scan
Cost: 0 %            Cost: 100 %
```

**FIGURE 8-5** Query plan simplified via contradiction

The final query plan does not actually even reference the table at all—it is replaced with a special Constant Scan operator that does not access the storage engine and, in this case, returns zero rows. This means that the query runs faster, takes less memory, and does not need to acquire locks against the resources referenced in the section containing the contradiction when being executed.

**Note** In this chapter, I have tried to create examples that you can run so you can see for yourself how the system operates based on experiments. Unfortunately, in some cases, different features interact in a way that makes it difficult for me to show you how exactly one feature operates in isolation. In this example, I added a join to avoid another optimization, called *trivial plan,* that sometimes overrides contradiction detection. Because features change from release to release, I ask that you use these examples only to explore the current state of the Query Optimizer—there are no guarantees about how the internals of the Query Optimizer work from release to release, so you should not attempt to build detailed knowledge of the Query Optimizer into your application.

Like rules, there are both logical and physical properties. Logical properties cover things like the output column set, key columns, and whether a column can output any nulls or not. These apply to all equivalent logical and all physical plan fragments. When an exploration rule is evaluated, the resulting query tree shares the same logical properties as the original tree used by the rule. Physical properties are specific to a single plan, and each plan operator has a set of physical properties associated with it. One common physical property is whether the result is sorted. This property would influence whether the Query Optimizer looks for an index to deliver that desired sort. Another physical property is the set of columns from a table that a query can read. This drives decisions such as whether a secondary index is sufficient to return all the needed columns in a query or whether each matching row also needs a base table lookup as well.

## Storage of Alternatives—The "Memo"

Earlier in this chapter, I mentioned that the storage of all the alternatives considered during optimization could be large for some queries. The Query Optimizer contains a mechanism to avoid storing duplicate information, thus saving memory (and time) during the compilation process. The structure is called the *Memo*, and one of its purposes is to find previously explored sub-trees and avoid reoptimizing those areas of the plan. It lives for the life of one optimization.

The Memo works by storing equivalent trees in *groups*. If you were to execute each sub-tree in a group, every alternative in that sub-tree would return the same logical result. Conceptually, each operator from the original query tree starts in its own group, meaning that groups reference other groups instead of referencing other operators directly while stored in the Memo. This model is used to avoid storing trees more than once during query optimization, and it enables the Query Optimizer to avoid searching the same possible plan alternatives more than once as well.

In addition to storing equivalent alternatives, groups also store properties structures. Alternatives that are rooted in the same group have equivalent logical and scalar properties. Logical properties are actually called *group properties* in SQL Server, even when not being stored in the Memo. So, every alternative in a group should all have the same output columns, key columns, possible partitionings, and so on. Computing these properties is expensive, so this structure also helps to avoid unnecessary work during optimization.

All considered plans are stored in the Memo. For large queries, the Memo may contain many thousands of groups and many alternatives within each group. Combined, this represents a huge number of alternatives. Although most queries do not consume large amounts of memory during optimization, it is possible that large data warehouse queries could consume all memory on a machine during optimization. If the Query Optimizer is about to run out of memory while searching the set of plans, it contains logic to pick a "good enough" query plan instead of running out of memory.

When the Query Optimizer has finished searching for a plan, it goes through the Memo, starting at the root, to select the best alternative from each group that satisfies the requirements for the query. These operators are assembled into the final query plan and are then transformed into a format that can be understood by the query execution component in SQL Server. This final tree transformation does contain a small number of run-time optimization rewrites, but it is very close to the showplan output generated for the query plan.

An example of how the Memo works is shown during the examination of the Query Optimizer's architecture and pipeline, later in this chapter.

## Operators

SQL Server 2008 has around 40 logical operators and even more physical operators. Some operators are extremely common, such as Join or Filter. Others are harder to find, such as Segment, Sequence Project, and UDX. Operators in SQL Server 2008 follow the model seen in Figure 8-6.

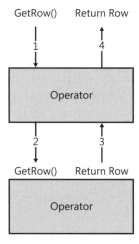

**FIGURE 8-6** SQL Server operator data flow model

Every operator in SQL Server works by requesting rows from one or more children and then producing rows to return to the caller. The caller can be another operator or can be sent to the user if it is the uppermost operator in the query tree. Each operator returns one row at a time, meaning that the caller must call for each row. The uniformity in this design allows operators to be combined in many different ways. It allows new operators to be added to the system without major changes to the Query Optimizer, such as the property framework, that help the Query Optimizer select a query plan.

To make sure that everyone gets the most of this chapter, I'll cover a few of the more rare and exotic operators so that I can reference them later in the chapter, as well as to give you an idea how your query is represented in the system.

### Compute Scalar—Project

The Compute Scalar, called a *Project* in the Query Optimizer, is a simple operator that attempts to declare a set of columns, compute some value, or perhaps restrict columns from other operators in the query tree. These correspond to the *SELECT* list in the SQL language. These are actually not overly interesting operations to the Query Optimizer—there is not much that the Query Optimizer needs to do with them. The Query Optimizer ends up moving them around the query tree during optimization, trying to separate them from the rest of the Query Optimizer logic that deals with join order, index selection, and other optimizations.

## Compute Sequence—Sequence Project

Compute Sequence is known as a *Sequence Project* in the Query Optimizer, and this operator is somewhat similar to a Compute Scalar in that it computes a new value to be added into the output stream. The key difference is that this works on an ordered stream and contains state that is preserved from row to row. Ranking functions use this operator, for example. This is implemented using a different physical operation and it imposes additional restrictions on how the Query Optimizer can reorder this expression. This operator is usually seen in the ranking and windowing functions.

## Semi-Join

The term *semi-join* comes from the academic database literature, and it is used to describe an operator that performs a join but returns only values from one of its inputs. The query processor uses this internal mechanism to handle most subqueries. SQL Server represents subqueries in this manner because it makes it easier to reason about the set of possible transformations for the query and because the run-time implementation of a semi-join and a regular join are similar. Contrary to popular belief, a subquery is not always executed and cached in a temporary table. It is treated much like a regular join. In fact, the Query Optimizer has transformation rules that can transform regular joins to semi-joins.

One common misconception is that it is inherently incorrect to use subqueries. Like most generalizations, this is not true. Often a subquery is the most natural way to represent what you want in SQL, and that is why it is part of the SQL language. Sometimes, a subquery is blamed for a poorly indexed table, missing statistics, or a predicate that is written in a way that is too obtuse for the Query Optimizer to reason about using its domain constraint property framework. Like everything in life, it is possible to have too many subqueries in a system, especially if they are duplicated many times in the same query. So, if your company's development practices say, "No subqueries," then examine your system a little closely—these are blamed for many other problems that might lie right under the surface.

Listing 8-1 is an example of where a subquery would be appropriate. Let's say that we need to ask a sales tracking system for a store to show me each customer who has made an order in the last 30 days so that we can send them a thank-you e-mail. Figures 8-7, 8-8, and 8-9 show the query plans for the three different approaches to try to submit queries to answer this question.

**LISTING 8-1** Common Errors in Writing Subquery Plans

```
CREATE TABLE Customers(custid int IDENTITY, name NVARCHAR(100));
CREATE TABLE Orders (orderid INT IDENTITY, custid INT, orderdate DATE, amount MONEY);
INSERT INTO Customers(name) VALUES ('Conor Cunningham');
INSERT INTO Customers(name) VALUES ('Paul Randal');
INSERT INTO Orders(custid, orderdate, amount) VALUES (1, '2008-08-12', 49.23);
INSERT INTO Orders(custid, orderdate, amount) VALUES (1, '2008-08-14', 65.00);
INSERT INTO Orders(custid, orderdate, amount) VALUES (2, '2008-08-12', 123.44);
```

```
-- Let's find out customers who have ordered something in the last month

-- Semantically wrong way to ask the question - returns duplicate names (See Figure 8-7)
SELECT name FROM Customers C INNER JOIN Orders O ON C.custid = O.custid WHERE
DATEDIFF("m", O.orderdate, '2008-08-30') < 1

-- and then people try to "fix" by adding a distinct (See Figure 8-8)
SELECT DISTINCT name
FROM
Customers C
INNER JOIN
Orders O
ON C.custid = O.custid
WHERE DATEDIFF("m", O.orderdate, '2008-08-30') < 1;
-- this happens to work, but it is fragile, hard to modify, and it is usually not done
properly.

-- the subquery way to write the query returns one row for each matching Customer
SELECT name
FROM Customers C
WHERE
EXISTS (
SELECT 1
FROM Orders O
WHERE C.custid = O.custid AND DATEDIFF("m", O.orderdate, '2008-08-30') < 1
);
-- note that the subquery plan has a cheaper estimated cost result
-- and should be faster to run on larger systems
```

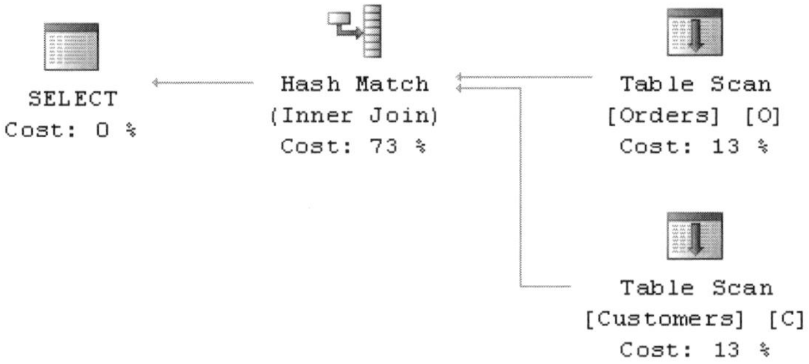

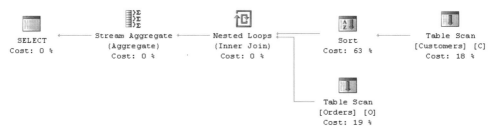

```
SELECT          Hash Match          Table Scan
Cost: 0 %       (Inner Join)        [Orders] [O]
                Cost: 73 %          Cost: 13 %


                                    Table Scan
                                    [Customers] [C]
                                    Cost: 13 %
```

**FIGURE 8-7** Plan for query using *INNER JOIN* instead of subquery

```
SELECT      Stream Aggregate    Nested Loops        Sort        Table Scan
Cost: 0 %   (Aggregate)         (Inner Join)        Cost: 63 %  [Customers] [C]
            Cost: 0 %           Cost: 0 %                       Cost: 18 %


                                            Table Scan
                                            [Orders] [O]
                                            Cost: 19 %
```

**FIGURE 8-8** Plan for query using *DISTINCT* and *INNER JOIN* instead of subquery

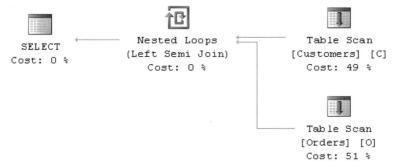

**FIGURE 8-9** Plan for query using subquery

In this last query plan, the matching rows from the *Customers* table are kept and directly returned to the user through the Left Semi-Join operator.

> **Note** The Left and Right Semi-Join have to do with which child's rows are preserved in the operation. Unfortunately for anyone confused as to the meaning of these operators, the plan representation in SQL Server Management Studio and in previous tools is transposed. The "left" child is the top child and the "right" child is the bottom child in the transposed form.

## Apply

*CROSS APPLY* and *OUTER APPLY* were added to SQL Server 2005, and they represent a special kind of subquery where a value from the left input is passed as a parameter to the right child. This is sometimes called a *correlated nested loops join,* and it represents passing a parameter to a subquery. The most common application for this feature is to do an index lookup join, as seen in Listing 8-2 and Figure 8-10.

**LISTING 8-2** Example of *APPLY* Query

```
CREATE TABLE idx1(col1 INT PRIMARY KEY, col2 INT);
CREATE TABLE idx2(col1 INT PRIMARY KEY, col2 INT);
GO
SELECT *
FROM idx1
CROSS APPLY (
    SELECT *
    FROM idx2
    WHERE idx1.col1=idx2.col1
) AS a;
```

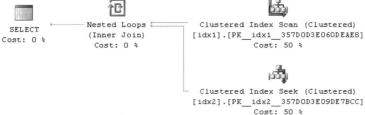

**FIGURE 8-10** *APPLY* query plan

This query is logically equivalent to an *INNER JOIN*, and Figure 8-11 demonstrates that the resulting query plan is identical in SQL Server 2008.

```
SELECT * FROM idx1 INNER JOIN idx2
ON idx1.col1=idx2.col1;
```

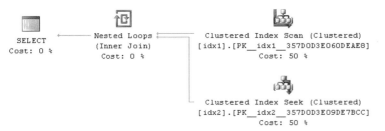

FIGURE 8-11 *INNER JOIN* query generates a nested loop and seek plan

In both cases, a value from the outer table is referenced as an argument to the seek on the inner table. Notice that a standard inner join is also able to generate a seek, which means that the Query Optimizer considers turning a JOIN into an APPLY as part of the optimization process. Although the example I have done here is so simple that you would not need to write the query in the way that I did, there are more complex scenarios where this syntax is useful. First, there is a common pattern for dynamic management views (DMVs, including an example in the section entitled "Plan Hinting," later in this chapter) where a value is passed to a management function using a cross apply. Second, there may be rare, very complex cases when the Query Optimizer's rule engine cannot rewrite a simple inner join to get an index seek. In those cases, rewriting the query to use *CROSS APPLY* is useful to pass a parameter down past an opaque operator manually. The semantics of a query can change as a result of a rewrite like this, so be very sure that you understand the semantics of your query when considering a rewrite like this.

The Apply operator is almost like a function call in a procedural language. For each row from the outer (left) side, some logic on the inner (right) side is evaluated and zero or more rows are returned for that invocation of the right sub-tree. The Query Optimizer can sometimes remove the correlation and convert an Apply into a more general join, and in those cases other joins can sometimes be reordered to explore different plan choices.

## Spools

SQL Server has a number of different, specialized spools. Each one is highly tuned for some scenario. Conceptually, they all do the same thing—they read all the rows from the input, store it in memory or spill it to disk, and then allow operators to read the rows from this cache. Spools exist to make a copy of the rows, and this can be important for transactional consistency in some update plans and to improve performance by caching a complex subexpression to be used multiple times in a query.

The most exotic spool operation is called a *common subexpression spool*. This spool has the ability to be written once and then read by multiple, different children in the query. This is currently the only operator that can have multiple parents in the final query plan. This spool shows up multiple times in the showplan output and it is actually the *same* operator. Common subexpression spools have only one client at a time. So, the first instance populates the spool, and each later reference reads from this spool in sequence. The first reference has children, while later references appear in the query plan as leaves of the query tree.

Common subexpression spools are used most frequently in wide update plans, described later in this chapter. However, they are also used in windowed aggregate functions. These are special aggregates that do not have to collapse the rows like a regular aggregate computation. Listing 8-3 and Figure 8-12 demonstrate how a common subexpression spool is used to store the intermediate query input and then use it multiple times as inputs to other parts of the query tree. The initial table spool reads values from *window1*, and the later branches in the tree supply the spooled rows to multiple branches.

**LISTING 8-3** Aggregate with OVER Clause Uses Common Subexpression Spool

```
CREATE TABLE window1(col1 INT, col2 INT);
GO
DECLARE @i INT=0;
WHILE @i<100
BEGIN
INSERT INTO window1(col1, col2) VALUES (@i/10, rand()*1000);
SET @i+=1;
END;

SELECT col1, SUM(col2) OVER(PARTITION BY col1) FROM window1;
```

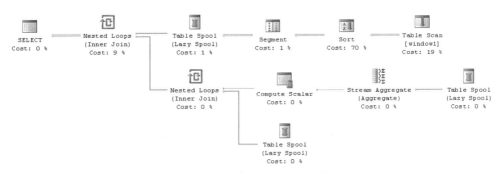

**FIGURE 8-12** Query plan containing common subexpression spool

## Exchange

The Exchange operator is used to represent parallelism in query plans. This can be seen in the showplan as a Gather Streams, Repartition Streams, or Distribute Streams operation, based on whether it is collecting rows from threads or distributing rows to threads, respectively. Several row distribution algorithms exist, and each operator has a preferred algorithm based on its context in a query. In SQL Server, parallelism exists in zones where the system tries to speed up by using additional CPUs. Figure 8-13 demonstrates a query where multiple threads scan a table in parallel.

```
    SELECT              Parallelism           Table Scan
    Cost: 0 %         (Gather Streams)        [exchange]
                          Cost: 0 %           Cost: 100 %
```

**FIGURE 8-13** Exchange operator in query plan

 **More Info** Other SQL Server 2008 operators are described online at *http://technet.microsoft.com/ en-us/library/ms191158.aspx.*

# Optimizer Architecture

The Query Optimizer contains many optimization phases that each performs different functions. The different phases help the Query Optimizer perform the highest-value operations earliest in the optimization process.

The major phases in the optimization of a query, as shown in Figure 8-14, are as follows:

- Simplification
- Trivial plan
- Auto-stats create/update
- Exploration/implementation (phases)
- Convert to executable plan

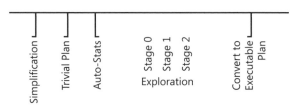

**FIGURE 8-14** Query Optimizer pipeline

## Before Optimization

The SQL Server query processor performs several steps before the actual optimization process begins. These transformations help shape the tree into a form about which it can be easily reasoned. View expansion is one major preoptimization activity. When a query is compiled that references a view, the text of the view is read from the server's metadata and parsed as well. One consequence of this design choice is that a query that references a view many times gets this view expanded many times before it is optimized. Coalescing adjacent *UNION* operations is another preoptimization transformation that is performed to simplify the tree. This converts the syntactic two-child form of *UNION [ALL]*, *INTERSECT [ALL]*, and *EXCEPT [ALL]* into a single operator that can have more than two children. This rewrite simplifies the tree structure and makes it easier for the Query Optimizer to write rules to affect *UNION*s. For example, grouping *UNION* operations makes the task of removing duplicate rows easier and more efficient.

## Simplification

Early in optimization, the tree is normalized in the Simplification phase to convert the tree from a form linked closely to the user syntax into one that helps later processing. For example, the Query Optimizer detects semantic contradictions in the query and removes them by rewriting the query into a simpler form. In addition, the rewrites performed in this section make subsequent operations such as index matching, computed column matching, and statistics generation easier to perform correctly.

The Simplification phase performs a number of other tree rewrites as well. These activities include

- Grouping joins together and picking an initial join order, based on cardinality data for each table

- Finding contradictions in queries that can allow portions of a query not to be executed

- Performing the necessary work to rewrite *SELECT* lists to match computed columns.

A contradiction detection example was shown earlier in this chapter in Figure 8-5.

## Trivial Plan/Auto-Parameterization

The main optimization path in SQL Server is a very powerful cost-based model of the execution time of a query. As databases and queries over those databases have become larger and more complex, this model has allowed SQL Server to solve bigger and bigger business problems. The fixed startup cost for running this model can be expensive for applications that are not trying to perform complex operations. Making a single path that spans from the smallest to the largest queries can be challenging, as the requirements and specifications are vastly different.

To be able to satisfy small query applications well, a fast path was added to SQL Server to identify queries where cost-based optimization was not needed. Generally, this code identifies cases where a query does not have any cost-based choices to make. This means that there is only one plan to execute or there is an obvious best plan that can be identified. In these cases, the Query Optimizer directly generates the best plan and returns it to the system to be executed. For example, the query *SELECT col1 FROM Table1* for a table without any indexes has a straightforward best plan choice—read the rows from the base table heap and return them to the user, as seen in Figure 8-15.

```
CREATE TABLE Table1 (col1 INT, col2 INT);
SELECT col1 FROM Table1;
```

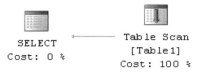

```
   SELECT        ←————————   Table Scan
  Cost: 0 %                   [Table1]
                           Cost: 100 %
```

**FIGURE 8-15** Trivial plan example—table scan

The SQL Server query processor actually takes this concept one step further. When simple queries are compiled and optimized, the query processor attempts to turn these queries into a parameterized query. If the plan is determined to be trivial, the parameterized query is turned into an executable plan. Then, future queries that have the same shape except for constants in well-known locations in the query just run the existing compiled query and avoid going through the Query Optimizer at all. This speeds up applications with small queries on SQL Server significantly.

```
SELECT col1 FROM Table1 WHERE col2 = 5;
SELECT col1 FROM Table1 WHERE col2 = 6;
```

If you look at the text of these queries in the procedure cache in Listing 8-4, you see that there is actually only one query plan, and it is parameterized.

**LISTING 8-4** Automatically Parameterized Query Text

```
SELECT text
    FROM sys.dm_exec_query_stats AS qs
    CROSS APPLY sys.dm_exec_sql_text(qs.sql_handle) AS st
WHERE st.text LIKE '%Table1%';

-----------------------------------------
(@1 tinyint)SELECT [col1] FROM [Table1] WHERE [col2]=@1
```

If you examine the XML plan for this query plan, you see that there is an indication that this query was a trivial plan. The other choice is full, meaning that cost-based optimization was performed):

```
... <StmtSimple ... StatementOptmLevel="TRIVIAL"> ...
```

(XML plan output is verbose, so I have omitted most of it for space. The bold code shows the choice the Query Optimizer made.)

## Limitations

The trivial plan optimization was introduced in SQL Server 7.0. While each version of SQL Server has slightly different rules, all versions have queries that skip the trivial plan stage completely and only perform regular optimization activities. Using more complex features can disqualify a query from being considered trivial because they always have a cost-based plan choice or are too difficult to identify as trivial or not. Examples of query features that cause a query not to be considered trivial include Distributed Query, Bulk Insert, XPath queries, queries with joins or subqueries, and queries with hints, some cursor queries, and queries over tables containing filtered indexes.

SQL Server 2005 added another feature, called *forced parameterization*, to auto-parameterize queries more aggressively. This feature parameterizes all constants, ignoring cost-based considerations. This feature is most useful for an application where the SQL is generated (and you cannot make it generate parameterized queries) and the resulting query plans are almost always identical (or the plans perform similarly even if they differ). Specifically, it is worth considering when the application queries cannot be changed by the DBA in charge of the server.

The benefit of this feature is that it can reduce compilations, compilation time, and the number of plans in the procedure cache. All these things *can* improve system performance. On the other hand, this feature can reduce performance when different parameter values would cause different plans to be selected. These values are used in the Query Optimizer's cardinality and property framework to make decisions about how many rows will be returned from each possible plan choice, and forced parameterization blocks these optimizations. So if you think that your application would benefit from using forced parameterization, perform some experiments and see whether the application works better. Chapter 9, "Plan Caching and Recompliation," goes into more detail on the various parameterization options.

## The Memo—Exploring Multiple Plans Efficiently

The core structure of the Query Optimizer is the Memo. This structure helps store the result of all the rules that are run in the Query Optimizer, and it also helps guide the search of possible plans to find a good plan quickly and avoid searching a sub-tree more than once. This speeds up the compilation process and reduces the memory requirements. In effect, this allows the Query Optimizer to run more advanced optimizations compared to other optimizers without a similar mechanism. Although this structure is internal to the Query Optimizer, this section describes its basic operations so that you can better understand the way that the Query Optimizer selects a plan.

The Memo stores operators from a query tree and uses logical pointers to represent the edges of that tree. If we consider the query *SELECT * FROM (A INNER JOIN B ON A.a=B.b) AS D INNER JOIN C ON D.c=C.c,* this can be drawn as a tree, as seen in Figure 8-16.

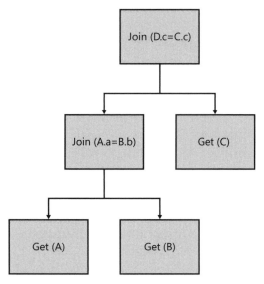

**FIGURE 8-16**  Tree of a three-table join

The same query stored in the Memo can be seen in Figure 8-17.

```
(Root) Group 4:
          0 Join 3 2
Group 3:
          0 Join 0 1
Group 2:
          0 Table C
Group 1:
          0 Table B
Group 0:
          0 Table A
```

**FIGURE 8-17**  Initial Memo layout for a three-table join

The Memo is made up a series of *groups*. When the Memo is first populated, each operator is put into its own group. The references between operators are changed to be references to other groups in the Memo. In this model, it is possible to store multiple alternatives that yield the same result in the same group in the Memo. With this change, it is possible to search for the best sub-tree independently of what exists in higher-level groups in the Memo. Logical properties are stored within each memo group, and every additional entry in a group can share the property structure for that group with the initial alternative.

One type of alternative explored by the Query Optimizer is *join associativity*. [(A join B) join C)] is equivalent to [A join (B join C)]. After this transformation is considered by the Query Optimizer, Figure 8-18 describes the updated Memo structure. (The bold sections are new.)

```
Group 5:
        0 Join 1 2
(Root) Group 4:
        1 Join 0 5
        0 Join 3 2
Group 3:
        0 Join 0 1
Group 2:
        0 Table C
Group 1:
        0 Table B
Group 0:
        0 Table A
```

**FIGURE 8-18** Three-table Memo after the join associativity rule has been applied

Notice how the new alternative fits into a structure. (B join C) that has not been previously seen in the Memo, so a new group is created that then references the existing groups for B and C. This representation saves a lot of memory when considering multiple possible query plans, and it makes it possible for the Query Optimizer to know if it has previously considered a section of the search space so that it can avoid doing that work again. (A join C) would be another valid alternative, though it is not shown.

Rules are the mechanisms that allow the Memo to explore new alternatives during the optimization process. The join associativity example is implemented as an optimization rule that matches a specific pattern and then creates a new alternative that is equivalent to the first one (returns the same result for that portion of the query). The result of a rule, by definition, can go into the same group as the root of the original pattern.

An optimization search pass is split into two parts. In the first part of the search, exploration rules match logical trees and generate new, equivalent alternative logical trees that are inserted into the Memo. Implementation rules run next, generating physical trees from the logical trees. Once a physical tree has been generated, it is evaluated by the costing component to determine the cost for this query tree. The resulting cost is stored in the Memo for that alternative. When all physical alternatives and their costs are generated for all groups in the Memo, the Query Optimizer finds the one query tree in the Memo that has the lowest cost and copies that into a stand-alone tree. The selected physical tree is very close to the showplan form of the tree.

The optimization process is optimized further by using multiple search passes, separating the rules based on cost and how likely they are to be useful. There are three phases, and each phase runs a set of exploration and implementation rules. The phases are configured to make small queries optimize quickly and to make more expensive queries consider more aggressive rewrite rules that may take longer to compile. For example, index matching is performed in the first phase, whereas the matching of index view is generally not performed until a later stage. The Query Optimizer can quit optimization at the end of a phase if a sufficiently good plan has been found. This calculation is done by comparing the estimated cost of the best plan found so far against the actual time spent optimizing so far. If the current best plan is still very expensive, then another phase is run to try to find a better plan. This model allows the Query Optimizer to generate plans efficiently for a wide range of workloads.

### Convert to Executable Plan

At the end of the search, the Query Optimizer has selected a single plan to be returned to the system. This plan is copied from the Memo into a separate tree format that can be stored in the Procedure Cache. During this process, a few small, physical rewrites are performed. Finally, the plan is copied into a new piece of contiguous memory and is stored in the procedure cache.

# Statistics, Cardinality Estimation, and Costing

The Query Optimizer uses a model with estimated costs of each operator to determine which plan to choose. The costs are based on statistical information used to estimate the number of rows processed in each operator. By default, statistics are generated automatically during the optimization process to help generate these cardinality estimates. The Query Optimizer also determines which columns need statistics on each table.

Once a set of columns is identified as needing statistics, the Query Optimizer attempts to find a preexisting statistics object for that column. If it doesn't find one, the system samples the table data to create a new statistics object. If one already existed, it is examined to determine if the sample was recent enough to be useful for the compilation of the current query. If it is considered out of date, a new sample is used to rebuild the statistics object. This process continues for each column where statistics are needed.

Both auto-create and auto-update statistics are enabled by default. In practice, most people leave these flags enabled and get good behavior from the Query Optimizer. However, it is possible to disable the creation and update behavior of statistics:

```
ALTER DATABASE ... SET AUTO_CREATE_STATISTICS {ON | OFF }
ALTER DATABASE ... SET AUTO_UPDATE_STATISTICS {ON | OFF }
```

These commands modify the behavior for auto-create and auto-update statistics, respectively, for all tables in a database. If automatic creation or updating of statistics is disabled, the Query Optimizer returns a warning in the showplan output when compiling a query where it thinks it needs this information. In this mode of operation, it would be the responsibility of the DBA to keep the statistics objects up to date in the system.

It is also possible to control the auto-update behavior of individual statistics objects using hints on specific operations:

```
CREATE INDEX ... WITH (STATISTICS_NORECOMPUTE = ON)
CREATE STATISTICS ... WITH (NORECOMPUTE)
```

While these settings are usually left enabled, some reasons for disabling creating or updating statistics include the following:

- The database has a maintenance window when the DBA has decided to update statistics explicitly instead of having these objects update automatically during the day. This is often because the DBA has reason to believe that the Query Optimizer may choose a poor plan if the statistics are changed.

- The database table is very large, and the time to update the statistics automatically is too high.

- The database table has many unique values, and the sample rate used to generate statistics is not high enough to capture all the statistical information needed to generate a good query plan. The DBA likely uses a maintenance window to update statistics manually at a higher sample rate than the default (which varies based the size of the table).

- The database application has a short query timeout defined and does not want automatic statistics to cause a query to take noticeably longer than average to compile because it could cause that timeout to abort the query.

This last scenario manifests in a subtle manner that can break your applications. If a query in an OLTP application was set with a small timeout of a few seconds, this is generally sufficient to compile all queries (even with automatic statistics). However, as the database table grows, the time to sample the table to create or update statistics grows. Eventually, the total time to perform this operation reaches the query timeout. Because each query is compiled as part of a user transaction, a timeout forces the transaction to abort and roll back. When the next query against that table was compiled, the timeout is hit again and the whole query roll backs. This unfortunately caused applications to fail unexpectedly, and often this would happen after an application was deployed because it was just some timing threshold based on database size.

To address this functionality, SQL Server 2005 introduced a feature called *asynchronous statistics update (ALTER DATABASE . . . SET AUTO_UPDATE_STATISTICS_ASYNC {ON | OFF)*. This allows the statistics update operation to be performed on a background thread in a different transaction context. The benefit of this model is that it avoids the repeating rollback issue. The original query continues and uses out-of-date statistical information to compile the query and return it to be executed. When the statistics are updated, plans based on those statistics objects are invalidated and are recompiled on their next use.

## Statistics Design

Statistics are stored in the system metadata. They are composed primarily of a histogram (a representation of the data distribution for a column). Do not get this confused: sometimes people say *statistics* when they mean *histogram*. Other elements in the statistics object include some header information (including the number of rows sampled when the object was created), trie trees (a representation of the data distribution for string columns), and density information (which tracks information about average data distributions across one or more columns).

Statistics can be created over most, but not all, data types in SQL Server 2008. As a general rule, data types that support comparisons (such as >, =, and so on) support the creation of statistics. The Query Optimizer doesn't need to reason about distributions if these are not comparable in the language. Examples of data types where statistics are not supported include old-style BLOBs (such as *image, text,* and *ntext*) and some of the newer user-defined data type (UDT)–based types when they are not byte-order comparable.

In addition, SQL Server supports statistics on computed columns. This allows the Query Optimizer to make cardinality estimates over expressions, such as *col1 + col2*, or some of the more complex types, such as the geography type, where the primary use case is to run a function on the UDT instead of comparing the UDT directly.

Listing 8-5 creates statistics on a persisted computed column created on a function of an otherwise non-comparable UDT. When this UDT method is used in later queries, the Query Optimizer can use this statistic to estimate cardinality more accurately.

**LISTING 8-5** *DBCC SHOW_STATISTICS* over a Persisted Computed Column

```
CREATE TABLE geog(col1 INT IDENTITY, col2 GEOGRAPHY);
INSERT INTO geog(col2) VALUES (NULL);
INSERT INTO geog(col2) VALUES (GEOGRAPHY::Parse('LINESTRING(0 0, 0 10, 10 10, 10 0, 0 0)'));
ALTER TABLE geog ADD col3 AS col2.STStartPoint().ToString() PERSISTED;
CREATE STATISTICS s2 ON geog(col3);
DBCC SHOW_STATISTICS('geog', 's2');
```

Statistics can be enumerated by querying the system metadata using the following code, and the results are shown in Figure 8-19.

```
SELECT o.name AS tablename, s.name AS statname
FROM sys.stats s INNER JOIN sys.objects o ON s.object_id = o.object_id;
```

| | tablename | statname |
|---|---|---|
| 86 | Customers | _WA_Sys_00000001_00551192 |
| 87 | Customers | _WA_Sys_00000002_00551192 |
| 88 | Orders | _WA_Sys_00000003_014935... |
| 89 | Orders | _WA_Sys_00000002_014935... |
| 90 | idx1 | PK__idx1__357D0D3E060DE... |
| 91 | idx2 | PK__idx2__357D0D3E09DE7... |
| 92 | idx2 | i1 |
| 93 | geog | s2 |
| 94 | queue_me... | queue_clustered_index |
| 95 | queue_me... | queue_secondary_index |
| 96 | queue_me... | queue_clustered_index |
| 97 | queue_me... | queue_secondary_index |
| 98 | queue_me... | queue_clustered_index |

**FIGURE 8-19** Query output listing statistics objects

Once identified, the statistics object can be viewed using the *DBCC SHOW_STATISTICS* command, as shown in Figure 8-20.

DBCC SHOW_STATISTICS(exchange,_WA_Sys_00000004_4C0144E4)

Results | Messages

| Name | Updated | Rows | Rows Sampled | Steps | Density | Average key length | String Index | Filter Expression | Unfiltered Rows |
|---|---|---|---|---|---|---|---|---|---|
| 1 | _WA_Sys_00000004_4C0144E4 | Nov 27 2008 9:49AM | 60000 | 8264 | 185 | 0.703127 | 4 | NO | NULL | 60000 |

| All density | Average Length | Columns |
|---|---|---|
| 1 | 0.0001049208 | 4 | col4 |

| | RANGE_HI_KEY | RANGE_ROWS | EQ_ROWS | DISTINCT_RANGE_ROWS | AVG_RANGE_ROWS |
|---|---|---|---|---|---|
| 1 | 0 | 0 | 1 | 0 | 1 |
| 2 | 23 | 102.4228 | 28.55033 | 22 | 4.65558 |
| 3 | 80 | 321.9001 | 20.53245 | 52 | 6.17722 |
| 4 | 119 | 263.3728 | 20.53245 | 38 | 6.930864 |
| 5 | 161 | 226.7933 | 20.53245 | 41 | 5.531543 |
| 6 | 192 | 204.8455 | 20.53245 | 30 | 6.828184 |
| 7 | 229 | 146.3182 | 20.53245 | 29 | 5.028785 |
| 8 | 268 | 219.4774 | 20.53245 | 38 | 5.77572 |
| 9 | 319 | 314.5842 | 20.53245 | 50 | 6.291684 |
| 10 | 357 | 234.1092 | 28.55033 | 34 | 6.80407 |
| 11 | 396 | 182.8978 | 20.53245 | 38 | 4.819702 |
| 12 | 423 | 190.2137 | 28.55033 | 26 | 7.315912 |
| 13 | 467 | 197.5296 | 28.55033 | 33 | 6.052347 |
| 14 | 521 | 336.5319 | 20.53245 | 53 | 6.349659 |
| 15 | 567 | 314.5842 | 20.53245 | 45 | 6.99076 |
| 16 | 621 | 270.6887 | 20.53245 | 50 | 5.377159 |
| 17 | 672 | 256.0569 | 35.93245 | 45 | 5.68644 |
| 18 | 699 | 139.0023 | 20.53245 | 22 | 6.31407 |
| 19 | 743 | 204.8455 | 28.55033 | 38 | 5.398066 |
| 20 | 780 | 182.8978 | 11.53645 | 36 | 5.080494 |
| 21 | 828 | 292.6365 | 20.53245 | 47 | 6.226308 |
| 22 | 867 | 197.5296 | 20.53245 | 36 | 5.46 |
| 23 | 911 | 219.4774 | 28.55033 | 38 | 5.783642 |
| 24 | 938 | 131.6864 | 20.53245 | 26 | 5.152974 |
| 25 | 1001 | 270.6887 | 20.53245 | 50 | 5.377159 |

**FIGURE 8-20** *DBCC SHOW_STATISTICS* output

Once the Query Optimizer has determined that it needs to either create a new statistics object or update an existing one that is out of date, the system creates an internal query to generate a new statistics object. Figure 8-21 demonstrates the query that builds the statistics object in the SQL Server Profiler output.

Showplan All For Query Compile                                          Micr

```
StmtText                                                               StmtId
--------                                                               ------
Stream Aggregate(DEFINE:([Expr1004]=STATMAN([s1].[dbo].[trace].[col1])))  0
  |--Sort(ORDER BY:([s1].[dbo].[trace].[col1] ASC))                       0
     |--Table Scan(OBJECT:([s1].[dbo].[trace]))                           0
```

**FIGURE 8-21** SQL Profiler showplan output for histogram generation

**Note** *STATMAN* is a special internal aggregate function that works like other aggregate functions in the system—many rows are consumed by a streaming group by operator and are passed to the *STATMAN* aggregate. It generates a BLOB that stores the histogram, density information, and any trie trees created during this operation. When finished, the statistics blob is stored in the database metadata and is used by queries (including the one that issued the command originally, except in the case of asynchronous statistics update).

The Optimizer samples database pages to generate statistics, including all rows from each sampled page. For small tables, all pages are sampled (meaning all rows are considered when building the histogram). For larger tables, a smaller and smaller percentage of pages are sampled. To keep the histogram a reasonable size, it is limited to 200 total steps. If it examines more than 200 unique values while building the histogram, the Query Optimizer uses logic to try to reduce the number of steps based on an algorithm that preserves as much distribution information as possible. Because histograms are most useful for capturing the non-uniform data distributions of a system, this means that it tries to preserve the information that captures the most frequent values and how much more frequent they are than the least frequent values in the data.

## Density/Frequency Information

In addition to a histogram, the Query Optimizer also keeps track of the number of unique values for a set of columns. When combined with the total number of rows viewed when creating the table, this can calculate the average number of duplicate values in the column. This information, called the *density information,* is stored in the histogram. Density is calculated by the formula *1/frequency,* with *frequency* being the average number of duplicates for each value in a table. This information is also returned when one calls *DBCC SHOW_STATISTICS.* For multicolumn statistics, the *statistics* object stores density information for each combination of columns (in the order that they were specified in the *CREATE STATISTICS* statement) in the *statistics* object. This stores information about the number of duplicate *sets* of values.

In Listing 8-6, we will create a two-column table with 30,000 rows.

**LISTING 8-6** Multicolumn Statistics

```
CREATE TABLE MULTIDENSITY (col1 INT, col2 INT);
go
DECLARE @i INT;
SET @i=0;
WHILE @i < 10000
BEGIN
        INSERT INTO MULTIDENSITY(col1, col2) VALUES (@i, @i+1);
        INSERT INTO MULTIDENSITY(col1, col2) VALUES (@i, @i+2);
        INSERT INTO MULTIDENSITY(col1, col2) VALUES (@i, @i+3);
        set @i+=1;
END;
GO
-- create multi-column density information
CREATE STATISTICS s1 ON MULTIDENSITY(col1, col2);
GO
```

In *col1*, there are 10,000 unique values, each duplicated three times. In *col2*, there are actually 10,002 unique values. For the multicolumn density, each set of (*col1, col2*) in the table is unique. Figure 8-22 shows the data stored for the multicolumn statistics object.

```
DBCC SHOW_STATISTICS ('MULTIDENSITY', 's1')
```

| | Name | Updated | Rows | Rows Sampled | Steps | Density |
|---|---|---|---|---|---|---|
| 1 | s1 | Nov 27 2008 10:16AM | 30000 | 30000 | 3 | 0.3333333 |

| | All density | Average Length | Columns |
|---|---|---|---|
| 1 | 0.0001 | 4 | col1 |
| 2 | 3.333333E-05 | 8 | col1, col2 |

**FIGURE 8-22** Multicolumn density information in the *statistics* object

The density information for *col1* is 0.0001. 1/0.0001 = 10,000, which is the number of unique values of *col1*. The density information for (*col1, col2*) is about 0.00003 (the numbers are stored as floating point and are imprecise).

Let's examine the cardinality estimates for the *GROUP BY* operation using *GROUP BY* lists that match the density information in Figure 8-23. The actual and estimated cardinalities match up exactly for this query.

```
SET STATISTICS PROFILE ON
SELECT COUNT(*) AS CNT FROM MULTIDENSITY GROUP BY col1
```

| | Rows | Executes | StmtText | EstimateRows |
|---|---|---|---|---|
| 1 | 10000 | 1 | SELECT COUNT(*) AS CNT FROM MULTIDENSITY GROUP ... | 10000 |
| 2 | 0 | 0 | \|--Compute Scalar(DEFINE:([Expr1004]=CONVERT_IMPLICIT(i... | 10000 |
| 3 | 10000 | 1 | \|--Hash Match(Aggregate, HASH:([s1].[dbo].[MULTIDENSI... | 10000 |
| 4 | 30000 | 1 | \|--Table Scan(OBJECT:([s1].[dbo].[MULTIDENSITY])) | 30000 |

**FIGURE 8-23** *STATISTICS PROFILE* output for the hash aggregate

**Note**  I have reordered the columns from the *STATISTICS PROFILE* output to show the *EstimateRows* column for the Hash Match implementing the *GROUP BY* operation.

For a query grouping over both columns, you can see that the estimate matches up with the value seen in the density calculation. The *STATISTICS PROFILE* output in Figure 8-24 shows that this changes the estimate to 30,000 rows.

```
SET STATISTICS PROFILE ON
SELECT COUNT(*) AS CNT FROM MULTIDENSITY GROUP BY col1, col2
```

| Rows | Executes | StmtText | EstimateRows |
|---|---|---|---|
| 30000 | 1 | SELECT COUNT(*) AS CNT FROM MULTIDENSITY GROUP ... | 30000 |
| 0 | 0 | \|--Compute Scalar(DEFINE:([Expr1004]=CONVERT_IMPLICIT(i... | 30000 |
| 30000 | 1 | \|--Hash Match(Aggregate, HASH:([s1].[dbo].[MULTIDENSI... | 30000 |
| 30000 | 1 | \|--Table Scan(OBJECT:([s1].[dbo].[MULTIDENSITY])) | 30000 |

**FIGURE 8-24** The *STATISTICS PROFILE* output for a two-column aggregate

The Query Optimizer actually has to perform an additional step when calculating the output cardinality for an operator. Because statistics are usually created before the compilation of the query that uses them and are often only samples of the data, the values stored in the statistics object do not usually match the exact count of rows at the time the query is compiled. So the Query Optimizer uses these two values to calculate the fraction of rows that should qualify in the operation. This is then scaled to the actual number of values in the table at the time that the query is compiled.

The Query Optimizer does not expose exactly how each part of the cardinality estimate is computed. However, if you find that a query has estimates that vary widely from what actually happens when you run the query, statistics profile can help you identify if the Query Optimizer has bad information. You may need to update statistics to capture new data in the table, create statistics with a higher sample rate, or otherwise make sure that the information used during compilation is accurate. Although SQL Server does this automatically in most cases, this is often a good way to find and fix problems with poor plan selection.

## Filtered Statistics

As part of the Filtered Index feature added in SQL Server 2008, the Filtered Statistics feature was also added. This means that the *statistics* object is created over a subset of the rows in a table based on a filter predicate. Creating a filtered index auto-creates a matching filtered *statistics* object that matches the behavior of nonfiltered indexes. This information is exposed through the *sys.stats* metadata view shown in Figure 8-25.

```
SELECT * FROM SYS.STATS
```

| | object_id | name | stats_id | auto_created | user_created | no_recompute | has_filter | filter_definition |
|---|---|---|---|---|---|---|---|---|
| 95 | 26157... | s1 | 2 | 0 | 1 | 0 | 0 | NULL |
| 96 | 26157... | _WA_Sys_00000002_0F975522 | 3 | 1 | 0 | 0 | 0 | NULL |
| 97 | 26157... | s3 | 4 | 0 | 1 | 0 | 1 | ([col2]>(5)) |
| 98 | 19930... | queue_clustered_index | 1 | 0 | 0 | 0 | 0 | NULL |

**FIGURE 8-25** The *filter_definition* expression in SQL Server 2008 Statistics

Filtered statistics are used in a manner that is similar to traditional statistics—the set of columns on which distributions are needed is determined early in query compilation. The set of filter predicates defined on the table for the query must be a subset of the *filter_definition* of the statistics object for the statistic to be considered. If multiple such statistics exist, the one with the tightest bounds is used.

Filtered statistics can avoid a common problem in cardinality estimation where estimates become skewed due to data correlation between columns. For example, if you create a table called *CARS*, you might have a column called *MAKE* and a column called *MODEL*. For example, the following table shows that multiple models of cars are made by Ford.

| CAR_ID | MAKE | MODEL |
|---|---|---|
| 1 | Ford | F-150 |
| 2 | Ford | Taurus |
| 3 | BMW | M3 |

In addition, let's assume that you want to run a query like this:

```
SELECT * FROM CARS WHERE MAKE='Ford' AND MODEL='F-150';
```

When the query processor tries to estimate the selectivity for each condition in an AND clause, it usually assumes that each condition is *independent*. This allows the selectivity of each predicate to be multiplied together to form the total selectivity for the complete WHERE clause. For this example, it would be:

2/3 * 1/3 = 2/9

The actual selectivity is really 1/3 for this query, because every F-150 is a Ford. This kind of estimation error can be large in some data sets. Detecting statistical correlations like this is a very computationally expensive problem, so the default behavior is to assume independence even though that may introduce some amount of error into the cardinality estimation process.

Filtered Statistics solves this problem by capturing the conditional probability for the *MODEL* column when the *MAKE* value is *Ford*. While using this solution requires a lot of *statistics* objects, it can be effective to fix the most important cases in an application where cardinality estimation error is causing poorly performing plans to be chosen by the Query Optimizer, especially when the WHERE clause has a relatively small number of distinct values.

In additional to the Independence assumption, the Query Optimizer contains other assumptions that are used to both simplify the estimation process and to be consistent in how estimates are made across all operators. Another assumption in the Query Optimizer is the *Uniformity* assumption. This means that if a range of values is being considered but they are not known, then they are assumed to be uniformly distributed over the range in which they exist. For example, if a query has an IN list with different parameters for each value, the values of the parameters are assumed not to be grouped. The final assumption in the Query Optimizer is the *Containment* assumption. This says that if a range of values is being joined with another range of values, then the default assumption is that that query is being asked because those ranges overlap and qualify rows. Without this assumption, many common queries would be underestimated and poor plans would be chosen.

## String Statistics

SQL Server 2005 introduced a feature to improve cardinality estimation for strings called *String Statistics* or *Trie Trees*. SQL Server histograms can have up to 200 steps, or unique values, to store information about the overall distribution of a table. While this works well for many numeric types, the string data types often have many more unique values as well as numerous functions that depend more heavily on a deeper statistical understanding of the type, such as *LIKE*. Two hundred unique values is often not sufficient to provide accurate cardinality estimates for strings, and storing lots of strings outside of the table can use a lot of space. Trie trees were created to store a sample of the strings in a column in a space-efficient manner.

The trie tree is not documented, but generally trie trees work as follows:

If we have a column containing the following values:

```
ABC
AAA
ABCDEF
ADAD
BBB
```

The trie tree for this structure is shown in Figure 8-26.

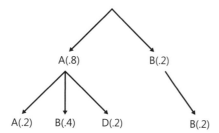

**FIGURE 8-26** Example of a trie tree

SQL Server actually stores a *sample* of the strings in the column, and even this is bound to take up not too much space. SQL Server also has some idea of the relative frequency for each substring listed in the trie tree. Overall, this provides the ability to store far more than 200 unique substrings worth of frequency information.

## Cardinality Estimation Details

During optimization, each operator in the query is evaluated to estimate the number of rows that are processed by that operator. This helps the Query Optimizer make proper tradeoffs based on the costs of different query plans. This process is done bottom-up, with the base table cardinalities and statistics being used as input to tree nodes above it. This process continues all the way up the query tree, and the estimated number of rows returned from a query in showplan information is based on this calculation.

Listing 8-7 contains a sample used to explain how the cardinality derivation process works.

**LISTING 8-7** Cardinality Estimation Sample

```
CREATE TABLE Table3(col1 INT, col2 INT, col3 INT);
GO
SET NOCOUNT ON;
BEGIN TRANSACTION;
DECLARE @i INT=0;
WHILE @i< 10000
BEGIN
INSERT INTO Table3(col1, col2, col3) VALUES (@i, @i,@i % 50);
SET @i+=1;
END;
COMMIT TRANSACTION;
GO
SELECT col1, col2 FROM Table3 WHERE col3 < 10;
```

This query is represented in the query processor using the tree shown in Figure 8-27.

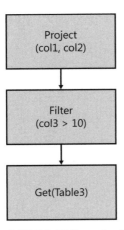

**FIGURE 8-27** Example of a logical query tree for cardinality estimation

For this query, the Filter operator requests statistics on each column participating in the predicate (*col3* in this query). The request is passed down to *Table3,* where an appropriate *statistics* object is created or updated. That *statistics* object is then passed to the filter to determine the *selectivity* of the operator. *Selectivity* is the fraction of rows that are expected to be qualified by the predicate and then returned to the user. Selectivity is used (instead of merely counting the number of matching values in a statistics histogram) to scale the estimate from the sample to the current row count properly, as the current row count may differ from when the *statistics* object was created and the *statistics* object may be over only a sample of the rows.

Once the selectivity for an operator is computed, it is multiplied by the current number of rows for the query. The selectivity of this filter operation is based on the histogram loaded for column *col3*. This can be seen in Figure 8-28.

| | Name | Updated | Rows | Rows Sampled | Steps | Density | Average key length | String Index | Filter Expression | Unfiltered Rows |
|---|---|---|---|---|---|---|---|---|---|---|
| 1 | _WA_Sys_00000003_108B795B | Nov 27 2008 10:30AM | 10000 | 10000 | 50 | 0 | 4 | NO | NULL | 10000 |

| | All density | Average Length | Columns |
|---|---|---|---|
| 1 | 0.02 | 4 | col3 |

| | RANGE_HI_KEY | RANGE_ROWS | EQ_ROWS | DISTINCT_RANGE_ROWS | AVG_RANGE_ROWS |
|---|---|---|---|---|---|
| 1 | 0 | 0 | 200 | 0 | 1 |
| 2 | 1 | 0 | 200 | 0 | 1 |
| 3 | 2 | 0 | 200 | 0 | 1 |
| 4 | 3 | 0 | 200 | 0 | 1 |
| 5 | 4 | 0 | 200 | 0 | 1 |
| 6 | 5 | 0 | 200 | 0 | 1 |
| 7 | 6 | 0 | 200 | 0 | 1 |
| 8 | 7 | 0 | 200 | 0 | 1 |
| 9 | 8 | 0 | 200 | 0 | 1 |
| 10 | 9 | 0 | 200 | 0 | 1 |
| 11 | 10 | 0 | 200 | 0 | 1 |

**FIGURE 8-28** Using a histogram to estimate cardinality

I've used a synthetic data distribution for this example to make it easier to follow the computations. Because I've created a distribution on *col3* that is uniformly distributed from 0 to 49, there are 10/50 values less than 10, or 20 percent of the rows. Therefore, the selectivity of this filter in the query is 0.2. So the calculation of the number of rows resulting from the filter is:

(# rows in operator below) * (selectivity of this operator)

10000 * 0.2 = 2000 rows

We can validate this computation by looking at the showplan information for the query shown in Figure 8-29.

| ⊟ **Misc** | |
|---|---|
| ⊞ Defined Values | [s1].[dbo].[Table3].col1, [s1].[dbo].[Table] |
| Description | Scan rows from a table. |
| Estimated CPU Cost | 0.0110785 |
| Estimated I/O Cost | 0.0232035 |
| Estimated Number of Executions | 1 |
| Estimated Number of Rows | 2000 |
| Estimated Operator Cost | 0.034282 (100%) |

**FIGURE 8-29** Operator row estimate for cardinality example

The estimate for the operator is taken by looking at the histogram, counting the number of sampled rows matching the criteria (in this case, we have 10 histogram steps with 200 equal rows for values that match the filter condition). Then, the number of qualifying rows (2,000) is normalized against the number of rows sampled when the histogram was created (10,000) to create the selectivity for the operator (0.2). This is then multiplied by the current number of rows in the table (10,000) to get the estimated query output cardinality. The cardinality estimation process is continued for any other filter conditions and the results are usually just multiplied to estimate the total selectivity for each condition.

One other interesting aspect of the histogram is *RANGE_ROWS, DISTINCT_RANGE_ROWS*, and *AVG_RANGE_ROWS*. Because histograms are limited to 200 steps, some values being queried may not be represented in the histogram steps. These values are represented in the *RANGE* values, and they are counts of rows between the step values. For query conditions that do not match one of the equal (EQ) rows in the histogram, values in the range are assumed to be uniformly distributed over the domain between the two bounding histogram steps. The fraction is determined from this assumption and used to generate the selectivity, as in the previous examples.

Although most operators work using a mechanism similar to Filter, some other operators need additional mechanisms to make good cardinality estimates. For example, *GROUP BY* actually doesn't try to determine which slices of a histogram should be used to estimate the selectivity of the operator. Instead, it needs to determine the number of unique values over a set of columns, as can be seen in Figure 8-30. This information can be estimated by looking at the histogram, but there is another mechanism in the *statistics* object to help perform this calculation quickly. The *density* information is stored in the histogram in the second result set, and in this case, it is 0.02 for *col3*.

```
SELECT COUNT(*) FROM Table3 GROUP BY col3;
```

| ⊟ **Misc** | |
|---|---|
| Build Residual | [s1].[dbo].[Table3].[col3] = [s1].[dbo].[Tab |
| ⊞ Defined Values | [Expr1007] = Scalar Operator(COUNT(*)) |
| Description | Use each row from the top input to build a |
| Estimated CPU Cost | 0.0834958 |
| Estimated I/O Cost | 0 |
| Estimated Number of Executions | 1 |

**FIGURE 8-30** *GROUP BY cardinality estimate*

This is a representation of the average number of duplicates for any value in the table. In other words, this tells us how to compute the number of groups using the total number of rows. For this simple *GROUP BY* query, the estimate of rows is (1/0.02)*(10,000/10,000) = 50, which matches the number of groups we would expect from our creation script:

```
GROUP BY Selectivity = (1/density)
GROUP BY Card. Estimate = (Input operator) * (selectivity)
```

When a multicolumn statistics object is created, it computes density information for the sets of columns being evaluated in the order of the *statistics* object. So a *statistics* object created on (*col1*, *col2*, *col3*) has density information stored for ((*col1*), (*col1*, *col2*), and (*col1*, *col2*, *col3*)). This can be used to compute the cardinality estimate for a query over that table doing *GROUP BY col1*, *GROUP BY col1*, *col2*, or *GROUP BY col1*, *col2*, *col3*.

We can see this computation in the results of *DBCC SHOW_STATISTICS* in Figure 8-31.

```
CREATE TABLE Table4(col1 int, col2 int, col3 int)
GO
DECLARE @i int=0
WHILE @i< 10000
BEGIN
INSERT INTO Table4(col1, col2, col3) VALUES (@i % 5, @i % 10,@i % 50);
SET @i+=1
END
CREATE STATISTICS s1 on Table4(col1, col2, col3)
DBCC SHOW_STATISTICS (Table4, s1)
```

| | All density | Average Length | Columns |
|---|---|---|---|
| 1 | 0.2 | 4 | col1 |
| 2 | 0.1 | 8 | col1, col2 |
| 3 | 0.02 | 12 | col1, col2, col3 |

**FIGURE 8-31** Multicolumn density information

> **Note** SQL Server does not automatically create statistics for multicolumn cases like this except in index creation, so we need to create the statistics object manually for this example.

Multicolumn density information is important because it captures correlation data between columns in the same table. By default, if every column were assumed to be completely independent, then one would expect a large number of different groups to be returned because each column added to the grouping columns would add more and more uniqueness (and less and less selectivity for the *GROUP BY* operator). However, in this case, we see that the selectivity of the *GROUP BY* is the same as in our previous example—50 groups. The data captured in the multicolumn density can be used to get this cardinality estimation to be more accurate.

If I create a similar table with random data in the first two columns, the density looks quite different, as shown in Figure 8-32.

| | All density | Average Length | Columns |
|---|---|---|---|
| 1 | 0.01 | 4 | col1 |
| 2 | 0.0001579031 | 8 | col1, col2 |
| 3 | 0.0001009387 | 12 | col1, col2, col3 |

**FIGURE 8-32** Multicolumn density for random data distribution

This would imply that every combination of *col1*, *col2*, and *col3* are actually unique in that case. By examining the various inputs into the cardinality estimation process, it is possible to determine whether the plan used reasonable information during the compilation process.

There are many, many more details to cardinality estimation than can be covered in this chapter. Most of the details change somewhat from release to release, and most of the details are not exposed or documented enough to make it useful to try to follow the exact computation. It is still very useful to understand the statistics and cardinality estimation mechanism so that you can perform plan debugging and hinting (explained later in this chapter).

## Limitations

The cardinality estimation of SQL Server is usually very good. Unfortunately, it is very difficult to make a model that is perfect for every query for all applications. While most of these are internal details, some of them are interesting to know about so that you can understand that the calculations explained earlier in this section do not work perfectly in every query.

- **Multiple predicates in an operator**  The selectivities of multiple predicates are multiplied during cardinality estimation to determine the resulting estimate for the whole operator. This means that the predicates are assumed to be statistically independent. In practice, most data has some statistical dependencies between columns. As the number of predicates in the query increases, the Query Optimizer actually does not directly multiply all the selectivities and assumes that these different predicates are related. So the selectivity of an operator with many predicates may be greater than you might expect.

- **Deep Query Trees**   The process of tree-based cardinality estimation is good, but it also means that any errors lower in the query tree are magnified as the calculation proceeds higher up the query tree to more and more operators. Eventually, the error introduced in all these computations overwhelms the value of using histograms to compute cardinality estimates. As a result, very deep query trees eventually stop using histograms for the higher portions of the query tree and may use simpler heuristics to make cardinality estimates to avoid assuming information on data that is very likely to be invalid.

- **Less common operators**   The Query Optimizer has many operators. Most of the common operators have extremely deep support developed over multiple versions of the product. Some of the lesser-used operators, however, don't necessarily have the same depth of support for every single scenario. So if you are using an infrequent operator or one that has only recently been introduced, it may not provide cardinality estimates that are as good as the most core operators. In these cases, it is worth double-checking the estimates using *SET STATISTICS PROFILE ON* to see if the estimates are close to what is expected. In many cases where the estimates are incorrect, the impact is often mitigated because specialized operators do not always have many plan choices and the impact of an error in cardinality estimation may be reduced.

## Costing

The process of estimating cardinality is done using the logical query trees. *Costing* is the process of determining how much time each potential plan choice will take to run, and it is done separately for each physical plan considered. Given that the Query Optimizer considers multiple different physical plans that return the same results, this makes sense. Costing is the component that picks between hash joins and loops joins or between one join order and another.

The idea behind costing is actually quite simple. Using the cardinality estimates and some additional information about the average and maximum width of each column in a table, it is able to determine how many rows fit on each database page. This value is then translated into a number of disk reads that a query requires to complete. The total costs for each operator are then added to determine the total query cost, and the Query Optimizer is able to select the fastest (lowest-cost) query plan from the set of considered plans during optimization.

In practice, costing is not this simple. There is a cost difference between sequential I/Os, where disk blocks are stored sequentially on disk and therefore do not require waiting to move the disk head to a new track or even waiting for a complete rotation of the disk platter, and random I/Os, where neither of these conditions are guaranteed to be true. In addition, some queries are large enough that the data can be read into memory and read multiple times during a query. These additional reads are often going to be able to read the page from the memory-based page buffer pool, avoiding the need to read from disk at all. Even further, some queries may take more memory than is available in the server for the query—in this case, the costing component needs to determine that some pages get evicted from the buffer pool and must be reread, either randomly or sequentially. The Optimizer uses logic to consider all these conditions, and the process of determining the actual cost for an operator can take awhile to calculate. All these considerations help make sure that SQL Server does the best job possible to select a good query plan for each query.

To make the Query Optimizer more consistent, the development team used several assumptions when creating the costing model. First, a query is assumed to start with a cold cache. This means that the query processor assumes that each initial I/O for a query requires reading from disk. In a very small number of cases (usually small, OLTP queries), this may cause the Query Optimizer to pick a slightly slower plan that optimizes for the number of initial I/Os required to complete the query. The cold-cache assumption is a simplification that allows the query processor to generate plans more consistently, but it is a (small) difference between the mathematical model used to compare plans and reality. Second, random I/Os are assumed to be evenly dispersed over the set of pages in a table or index. If a non-indexed based table (a heap) has 100 disk pages and the query is doing 100 random bookmark-based lookups into the heap, the Query Optimizer assumes that 100 random I/Os occur in the query because it assumes that each target row is on a separate page. Like the statistical column correlation example earlier in the chapter, this assumption also does not always hold. The actual set of rows could be clustered physically on the same pages (perhaps they were all inserted at the same time and thus ended up on adjacent pages), and it may only require five I/Os to read the rows of interest. In this case, the Query Optimizer would overcost this query. This also rarely happens, but it is valuable to understand that the mathematical model used for costing is just that—a model. In the rare cases when the model does not work properly, query hints can be used to help force a different query plan.

The Query Optimizer has other assumptions built into its costing model. One assumption relates to how the client reads the query results. Costing assumes every query reads every row in the query result. However, some clients read only a few rows and then close the query. For example, if you are using an application that shows you pages of rows on a screen at a time, then that application may read 40 rows even though the original query may have returned 10,000 rows. If the Query Optimizer knows the number of rows that the user will consume, then it can optimize for the number in the plan selection process to pick a faster plan. Typically, this causes the Query Optimizer to switch from using operators such as hash join (which has a larger startup cost at the beginning of a query) to nested loops joins (which have a lower startup cost but a higher per-row cost).

SQL Server exposes a hint called FAST N for just this case. If a user typically only reads a subset of the rows in a query, then it can pass OPTION (FAST N) to the query to tell the Query Optimizer to cost the query for returning N rows instead of the whole result set. Listing 8-8 contains an example to demonstrate the FAST N hint, which selects a hash join without the FAST N hint. Figure 8-33 shows that a loop join is picked when the hint is applied.

**LISTING 8-8** FAST N Example

```
CREATE TABLE A(col1 INT);
CREATE CLUSTERED INDEX i1 ON A(col1);
GO
SET NOCOUNT ON;
BEGIN TRANSACTION;
DECLARE @i INT=0;
WHILE @i < 10000
BEGIN
INSERT INTO A(col1) VALUES (@i);
SET @i+=1;
END;
COMMIT TRANSACTION;
GO
SELECT A1.* FROM A as A1 INNER JOIN A as A2 ON A1.col1=A2.col1;
SELECT A1.* FROM A as A1 INNER JOIN A as A2 ON A1.col1=A2.col1 OPTION (FAST 1);
```

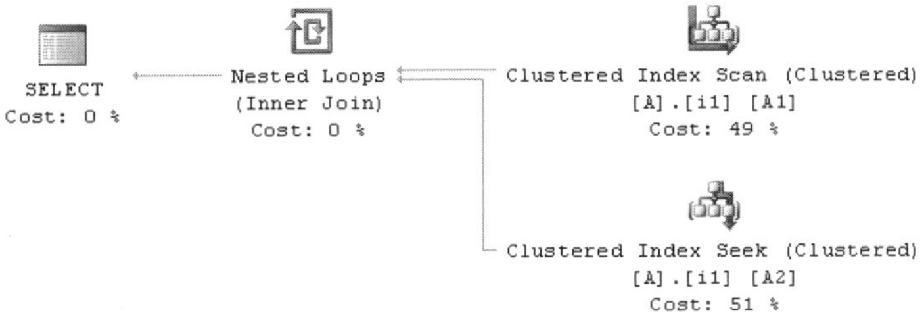

**FIGURE 8-33** Loops join plan (with FAST 1 hint)

# Index Selection

Index selection is one of the most important aspects of query optimization. The basic idea behind index matching is to take predicates from a WHERE clause, join condition, or other limiting operation in a query and to convert that operation that can be performed against an index. Two basic operations can be performed against an index:

- Seek (for a single value or a range of values on the index key)
- Scan the index (forwards or backwards)

For Seek, the initial operation starts at the root of a B+ tree and navigates down the tree to a desired location in the index based on the index keys. Once completed, the query processor can iterate over all rows that match the predicate or until the last value in the range is found. Because leaves in a B+ tree are linked in SQL Server, it is possible to scan rows in order using this structure once the intermediate B+ tree nodes have been traversed.

The job of the Query Optimizer is to figure out which predicates can be applied to the index to return rows as quickly as possible. Some predicates can be applied to an index, while others cannot. For example, the query SELECT col1, PKcol FROM MyTable WHERE col1=2 has one predicate in the form of <column> = <constant>. This pattern can be matched to a seek operation if there is an index on that column. The resulting alternative that is generated is to perform a seek against the nonclustered index and to return the rows that match, if any. Figure 8-34 demonstrates a basic seek plan generated by the Query Optimizer.

```
CREATE TABLE idxtest2(col2 INT, col3 INT, col4 INT);
CREATE INDEX i2 ON idxtest2(col2, col3);

SELECT col2, col3 FROM idxtest2 WHERE col2=5
```

```
                        Index Seek (NonClustered)
  SELECT                      [idxtest2].[i2]
  Cost: 0 %                    Cost: 100 %
```

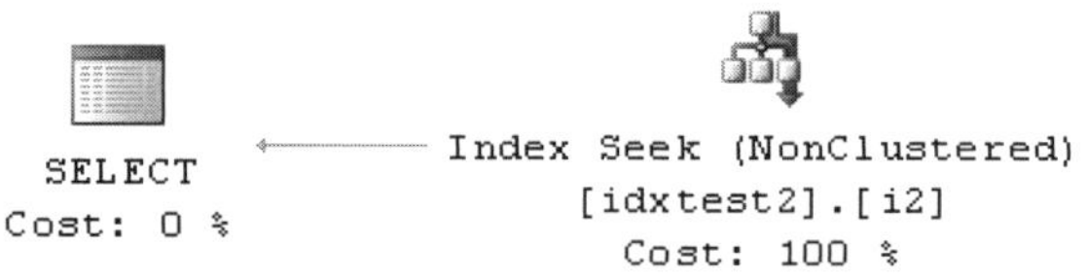

**FIGURE 8-34** Index seek plan

The Query Optimizer can also apply compound predicates against multicolumn indexes as long as the operation can be converted into starting and ending index keys. Figure 8-35 shows a multicolumn seek plan, and you can see the predicates used if you look at the properties for this operator in Management Studio.

```
Query 1: Query cost (relative to the batch): 100%
SELECT col2, col3 FROM idxtest2 WHERE col2=5 AND col3 = 10

                      Index Seek (NonClustered)
  SELECT                    [idxtest2].[i2]
  Cost: 0 %                   Cost: 100 %
```

**FIGURE 8-35** Multicolumn index seek plan

Predicates that can be converted into an index operation are often called *sarg*able, or "Search-ARGument-able." This means that the form of the predicate can be converted into an index operation. Predicates that cannot ever match or do not match the selected index are called *non-sargable predicates*. Predicates that are non-sargable would be applied after any index seek or range scan operations so that the query can return rows that match all predicates. Making things somewhat confusing is that SQL Server usually evaluates non-sargable predicates within the seek/scan operator in the query tree. This is a performance optimization—if this were not done, the series of steps performed would be as follows:

1. Seek Operator: Seek to a key in an index's B+ tree.

2. Latch the page.

3. Read the row.

4. Release the latch on the page.

5. Return the row to the filter operator.

6. Filter: evaluate the non-sargable predicate against the row. If it qualifies, pass the row to the parent operator. Otherwise, go to step 2 to get the next candidate row.

This is slower than optimal because returning the row to a different operator requires loading in a different set of instructions and data to the CPU. By keeping the logic in one place, the overall CPU cost of evaluating the query goes down. The actual operation in SQL Server looks like this:

1. Seek Operator: Seek to a key in an index's B+ tree.

2. Latch the page.

3. Read the row.

4. Apply the non-sargable predicate filter. If the row does not pass the filter, go to step 3. Otherwise, continue to step 5.

5. Release the latch on the page.

6. Return the row.

This is called *pushing non-sargable predicates* (the predicate is pushed from the filter into the seek/scan). It is a physical optimization, but it can show up in queries that process many rows.

Not all predicates can be evaluated in the seek/scan operator. Because the latch operation prevents other users from even looking at a page in the system, this optimization is reserved for predicates that are very cheap to perform. This is called *non-pushable, non-sargable predicates*. Examples include:

- Predicates on large objects (including *varbinary(max), varchar(max), nvarchar(max)*)

- CLR functions

- Some T-SQL functions

Predicate sargability is an important consideration in database application design. One reason systems can perform poorly is that the application against the database is written in such a way as to make predicates non-sargable. In many cases, this is avoidable if the issue is identified early enough, and fixing this one issue can sometimes increase database application performance by an order of magnitude.

SQL Server considers many formulations when trying to apply indexes against sargable predicates in a query. For AND conditions (WHERE *col1*=5 AND *col2*=6 AND . . .), SQL Server tries to do the following:

1. Given a list of required seek equality columns, seek inequality columns, and columns needed to satisfy the query but without predicates, first attempt to find an index that exactly matches the request. If such an index exists, use it.

2. Try to find a set of indexes to satisfy the equality conditions and perform an inner join for all such indexes.

**3.** If step 2 did not cover all required columns, consider joins with any other indexes based on the set of columns in the indexes included so far in the solution.

**4.** Finally, perform a join back to the base table to get any remaining columns.

In all cases, the costs of each solution are considered and the solution is only returned if it is believed to be least-cost. So, a solution that joins many indexes together will only be used if it is believed to be cheaper than a scan of all rows in the base table. Second, this algorithm is performed locally in the query tree. Even if the Query Optimizer generates a specific alternative using this process, it may not ultimately be part of the final query plan. Costing is used to determine the cheapest, complete query plan. So, this is not a rule-based mechanism for selecting indexes. It is a heuristic that is part of a broader costing infrastructure to help choose efficient query plans.

## Filtered Indexes

SQL Server 2008 introduces the ability to create indexes with simple predicates that restrict the set of rows included in the index. On first glance, this feature is a subset of the functionality already contained in indexed views. Nevertheless, there are good reasons for this feature to exist. First, indexed views are more expensive to use and maintain. Second, the matching capability of the Indexed View feature is not supported in all editions of SQL Server. Third, a number of different SQL Server users had scenarios that were just slightly more complex than the regular index feature and therefore, they were not really interested in moving to a full indexed view solution. So, although indexed views are still a very useful feature, they tend to be more useful for the more classical relational query precomputation scenarios.

Filtered Indexes are created using a new WHERE clause on a *CREATE INDEX* statement.

Listing 8-9 demonstrates how to create an index and how it can be used in a query. Figures 8-36 and 8-37 show the resulting query plans for a query where the filtered index is covering and when it is not, respectively.

**LISTING 8-9** Filtered Index Example

```
CREATE TABLE testfilter1(col1 INT, col2 INT);
go
DECLARE @i INT=0;
SET NOCOUNT ON;
BEGIN TRANSACTION;
WHILE @i < 40000
BEGIN
INSERT INTO testfilter1(col1, col2) VALUES (rand()*1000, rand()*1000);
SET @i+=1;
END;
COMMIT TRANSACTION;
go

CREATE INDEX i1 ON testfilter1(col2) WHERE col2 > 800;

SELECT col2 FROM testfilter1 WHERE col2 > 800;
SELECT col2 FROM testfilter1 WHERE col2 > 799;
```

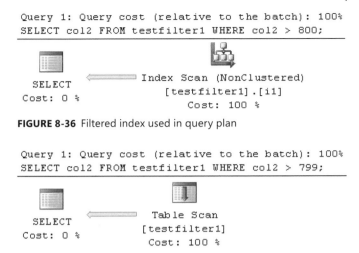

```
Query 1: Query cost (relative to the batch): 100%
SELECT col2 FROM testfilter1 WHERE col2 > 800;
```

**FIGURE 8-36** Filtered index used in query plan

```
Query 1: Query cost (relative to the batch): 100%
SELECT col2 FROM testfilter1 WHERE col2 > 799;
```

**FIGURE 8-37** Filtered index not used due to noncovering filter condition

The cost of the first select query is 0.0141293, whereas the second query has an estimated cost of 0.112467. The filtered index benefits from having fewer rows and is also narrower than the base table, so it has fewer pages as well. When you know specific constraints that are used on queries with large tables where space is an issue, this kind of index can be quite useful.

SQL Server imposes a number of restrictions on the scalar constructs that can be used to formulate the filter in the *CREATE INDEX* command. These are largely based on what the Query Optimizer's domain property framework can use easily when matching indexes. As a result, some of the more complex pieces of the system are not supported in this release because there is no way to match these indexes efficiently.

Several scenarios can be handled by filtered indexes:

- Not all data fits easily into the relational database model with a small, fixed set of columns that are set for every row. Often, some fields are used only occasionally, resulting in many NULL entries for that column. A traditional index stores a lot of NULLs and wastes a lot of storage space. Updates to the table have to maintain this index for every row.

- If you are querying a table with a small number of distinct values and are using a multicolumn predicate where some of the elements are fixed, you can create a filtered index to speed up this specific query. This might be useful for a regular report run only for your boss—it speeds up a small set of queries while not slowing down updates as much for everyone else.

- As shown in the original example, the index can be used when there is a known query condition on an expensive query on a large table.

## Indexed Views

Traditional, non-indexed views have been used for goals such as simplifying SQL queries, abstracting data models from user models, and enforcing user security. From an optimization perspective, SQL Server does not do much with these views because they are expanded, or in-lined, before optimization begins. This gives the Query Optimizer opportunities to optimize queries globally, but it also makes it difficult for the Query Optimizer to consider plans that perform the view evaluation first, then process the rest of the query. Arbitrary tree matching is a computationally complex problem, and the feature set of views is too large to perform this operation efficiently.

> **Note** Matching of indexed views is supported only in SQL Server 2008 Enterprise Edition.

The Indexed Views feature allows SQL Server to expose some of the benefits of view materialization while retaining the benefits of global reasoning about query operations. SQL Server exposes a *CREATE INDEX* command on views that creates a materialized form of the query result. The resulting structure is physically identical to a table with a clustered index. Nonclustered indexes also are supported on this structure. The Query Optimizer can use this structure to return results more efficiently to the user. The Query Optimizer contains logic to use this index both in cases when the original query text referenced the view explicitly as well as in cases when the user submits a query that uses the same components as the view (in any equivalent order). Actually, the query processor expands indexed views early in the query pipeline and always uses the same matching code for both cases. The WITH(NOEXPAND) hint tells the query processor not to expand the view definition. Listing 8-10 contains an example with three different paths to get SQL Server to match the view. The plans for the matches are visible in Figures 8-38, 8-39, and 8-40.

**LISTING 8-10** Indexed View Matching Examples

```
-- Create two tables for use in our indexed view
CREATE TABLE table1(id INT PRIMARY KEY, submitdate DATETIME, comment NVARCHAR(200));
CREATE TABLE table2(id INT PRIMARY KEY IDENTITY, commentid INT, product NVARCHAR(200));
GO
-- submit some data into each table
INSERT INTO table1(id, submitdate, comment) VALUES (1, '2008-08-21', 'Conor Loves Indexed
Views');
INSERT INTO table2(commentid, product) VALUES (1, 'SQL Server 2008');
GO
-- create a view over the two tables
CREATE VIEW dbo.v1 WITH SCHEMABINDING AS
SELECT t1.id, t1.submitdate, t1.comment, t2.product FROM dbo.table1 t1 INNER JOIN dbo.table2
t2 ON t1.id=t2.commentid;
go
-- indexed the view
CREATE UNIQUE CLUSTERED INDEX i1 ON v1(id);

-- query the view directly --> matches
SELECT * FROM dbo.v1;
-- query the statement used in the view definition --> matches as well
```

```
SELECT t1.id, t1.submitdate, t1.comment, t2.product
FROM dbo.table1 t1 INNER JOIN dbo.table2 t2
    ON t1.id=t2.commentid;
-- query a logically equivalent statement used in the view definition that
-- is written differently --> matches as well
SELECT t1.id, t1.submitdate, t1.comment, t2.product
FROM dbo.table2 t2 INNER JOIN dbo.table1 t1 ON t2.commentid=t1.id;
```

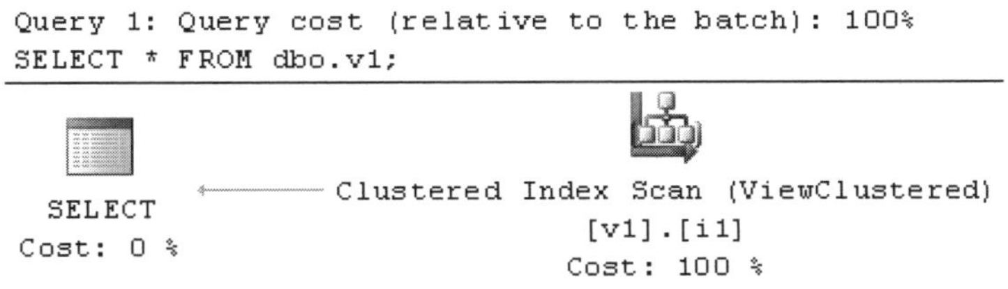

```
Query 1: Query cost (relative to the batch): 100%
SELECT * FROM dbo.v1;
```

SELECT
Cost: 0 %

Clustered Index Scan (ViewClustered)
[v1].[i1]
Cost: 100 %

**FIGURE 8-38** A direct reference match of an indexed view

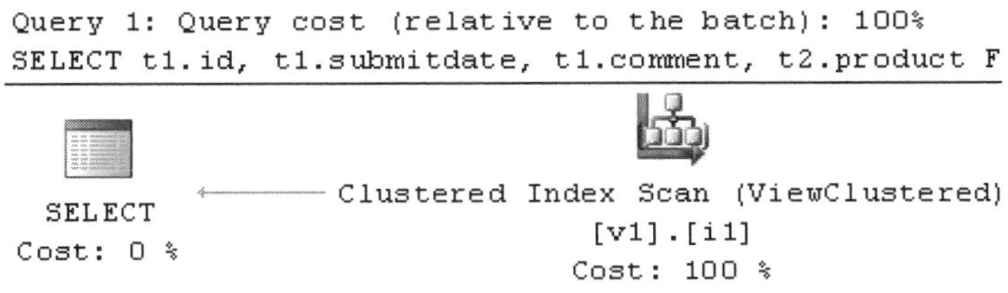

```
Query 1: Query cost (relative to the batch): 100%
SELECT t1.id, t1.submitdate, t1.comment, t2.product F
```

SELECT
Cost: 0 %

Clustered Index Scan (ViewClustered)
[v1].[i1]
Cost: 100 %

**FIGURE 8-39** An Indexed View match when the query is a match to the view definition

```
Query 1: Query cost (relative to the batch): 100%
SELECT t1.id, t1.submitdate, t1.comment, t2.product F
```

SELECT
Cost: 0 %

Clustered Index Scan (ViewClustered)
[v1].[i1]
Cost: 100 %

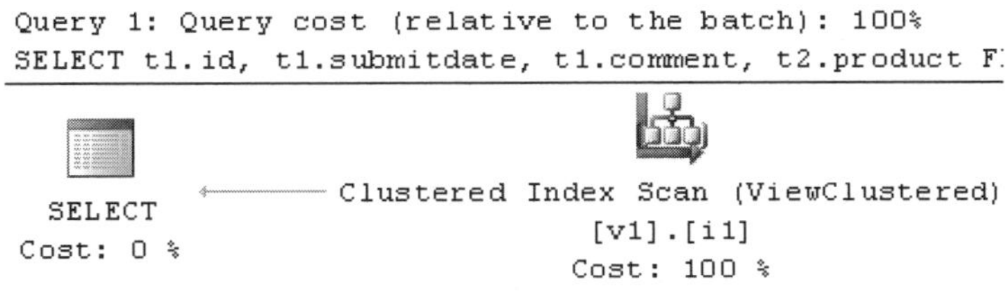

**FIGURE 8-40** An Indexed View match when the query is not an exact match to the view definition

There are cases when the Query Optimizer does not match the view. First, remember that indexed views are inserted into the Memo and evaluated against other plan choices. While they are often the best plan choice, this is not always the case. In Listing 8-11, the Query Optimizer can detect logical contradictions between the view definition and the query that references the view. Figure 8-41 shows the query plan that directly references the base table instead of the view.

**LISTING 8-11** Example When an Index View Is Not Matched

```
CREATE TABLE table3(col1 INT PRIMARY KEY IDENTITY, col2 INT);
INSERT INTO table3(col2) VALUES (10);
INSERT INTO table3(col2) VALUES (20);
INSERT INTO table3(col2) VALUES (30);
GO
-- create a view that returns values of col2 > 20
CREATE VIEW dbo.v2 WITH SCHEMABINDING AS
SELECT t3.col1, t3.col2 FROM dbo.table3 t3 WHERE t3.col2 > 20;
```

```
GO
-- materialize the view
CREATE UNIQUE CLUSTERED INDEX i1 ON v2(col1);
GO


-- now query the view and filter the results to have col2 values equal to 10.
-- The optimizer can detect this is a contradition and avoid matching the indexed view
-- (the trivial plan feature can "block" this optimization)
SELECT * FROM dbo.v2 WHERE col2 = CONVERT(INT, 10);
```

```
Query 1: Query cost (relative to the batch): 100%
SELECT * FROM dbo.v2 WHERE col2 = CONVERT(INT, 10);
```

```
                          Clustered Index Scan (Clustered)
    SELECT                [table3].[PK__table3__357D0D3E595B4...
    Cost: 0 %                        Cost: 100 %
```

**FIGURE 8-41** A query plan when Indexed View is not matched

**Note** The predicate in this example is *[v1].[dbo].[table3].[col2] as [t3].[col2]=[@1] AND [v1].[dbo].[table3].[col2] as [t3].[col2]>(20)*. While I have tried to make the examples in this chapter as simple as possible, the Query Optimizer uses logic here to detect that I have made this query example too simple. As a result, it has treated it like a trivial plan and auto-parameterized it for use by all future queries like this one that vary only by the constant (10). Although the intricacies of trivial plan are not formally documented and are subject to change each release, Figure 8-42 shows what could happen when you modify the query slightly to avoid the trivial plan feature (in my case, I used a query hint, but that is not shown in the code).

```
Query 1: Query cost (relative to the batch): 100%
SELECT * FROM dbo.v2 WHERE col2 = CONVERT(INT, 10)
```

```
    SELECT              Constant Scan
    Cost: 0 %           Cost: 100 %
```

**FIGURE 8-42** A Constant Scan plan due to non-trivial plan contradiction detection

This is a zero-row scan because the Query Optimizer recognizes that *col2* = 10 and *col2* > 20 never return rows. This query plan doesn't even try to scan *table3* or *v2*.

**Tip** Unfortunately, there are also some cases where the Query Optimizer does not recognize an indexed view even when it would be a good plan choice. Often, these cases deal with complex interactions between high-level features within the query processor (such as computed column matching and the algorithm to explore join orders). Although SQL Server does provide some information through warnings and showplans that can help you see the behaviors of the system at this level, it requires a lot of internal knowledge to understand fully. If you happen to find yourself in a case where you believe that the indexed view should match but does not, then consider the WITH (NOEXPAND) hint to force the query processor to pick that indexed view. This usually is enough to get the plan to include the indexed view.

SQL Server also supports matching indexed views in cases beyond exact matches of the query text to the view definition. It also supports using an indexed view for inexact matches where the definition of the view is broader than the query submitted by the user. SQL Server then applies residual filters, projections (columns in the select list), and even aggregates to use the view as a partial precomputation of the query result.

Listing 8-12 demonstrates view matching for both filter and projection residuals. It creates a view that has more rows and more columns than our final query, but the indexed view is still matched by the Query Optimizer. The resulting query plan is shown in Figure 8-43.

**LISTING 8-12** Indexed View Matching Example (A Subset of Rows and Columns)

```
-- base table
CREATE TABLE basetbl1 (col1 INT, col2 INT, col3 BINARY(4000));
CREATE UNIQUE CLUSTERED INDEX i1 ON basetbl1(col1);
GO
-- populate base table
SET NOCOUNT ON;
DECLARE @i INT =0;
WHILE @i < 50000
BEGIN
INSERT INTO basetbl1(col1, col2) VALUES (@i, 50000-@i);
SET @i+=1;
END;
GO
-- create a view over the 2 integer columns
CREATE VIEW dbo.v2 WITH SCHEMABINDING AS
SELECT col1, col2 FROM dbo.basetbl1;
GO
-- index that on col2 (base table is only indexed on col1)
CREATE UNIQUE CLUSTERED INDEX iv1 on dbo.v2(col2);

-- the indexed view still matches for both a restricted
-- column set and a restricted row set
SELECT col1 FROM dbo.basetbl1 WHERE col2 > 2500;
```

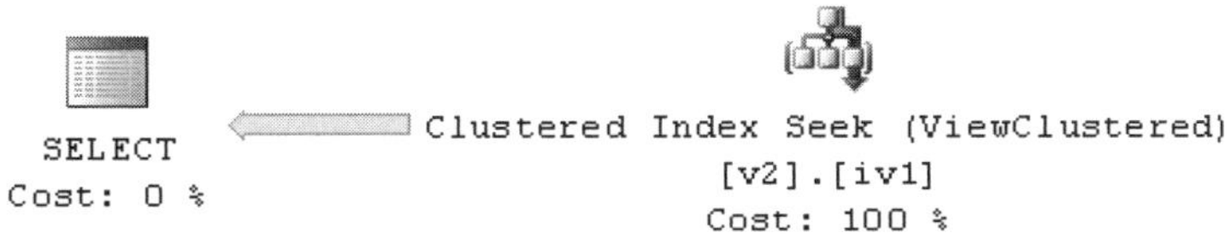

**FIGURE 8-43** An indexed view matched for a subset of rows and columns

The projection is not explicitly listed as a separate Compute Scalar operator in this query because SQL Server 2008 has special logic to remove projections that do not compute an expression. The filter operator in the index matching code is translated into an index seek against the view. If we modify the query to compute an expression, Figure 8-44 demonstrates the residual Compute Scalar added to the plan:

```
SELECT col1 + 1 FROM dbo.basetbl1 WHERE col2 > 2500 AND col1 > 10;
```

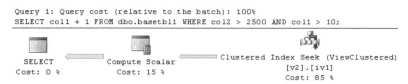

```
Query 1: Query cost (relative to the batch): 100%
SELECT col1 + 1 FROM dbo.basetbl1 WHERE col2 > 2500 AND col1 > 10;
```

**FIGURE 8-44** Compute Scalar, only needed when computing new values

Like all options considered by the Query Optimizer, indexed view alternatives are generated and stored in the Memo and are compared using costing equations against other possible plans. Alternatives including partial matches cost the residual operations as well, and this means that an indexed-view plan can be generated but not picked when the Query Optimizer considers other plans to have lower costs.

Indexed views are maintained as part of the update processing for tables on which the view is based. This makes sure that the view provides a consistent result if it is selected by the Query Optimizer for any query plan. Some query operations are incompatible with this design guarantee. As a result, SQL Server places some restrictions on the set of supported constructs in indexed views to make sure that the view can be created, matched, and updated as efficiently as possible. The description of the restrictions in *SQL Server Books Online* is very long and detailed, and this can make it very difficult to understand the higher-level rules.

For updating indexed views, the core question behind the restrictions is "Can the query processor compute the necessary changes to the Indexed View clustered and nonclustered indexes without having to recompute the whole indexed view?" If so, the query processor can perform these changes efficiently as part of the maintenance of the base tables that are referenced in the view. This property is relatively easy for filters, projections (compute scalar), and inner joins on keys. Operators that destroy or create data are more difficult to maintain, so often these are restricted from use in indexed views.

How indexed views are represented in update plans is discussed in the section entitled "Updates," later in this chapter.

# Partitioned Tables

As SQL Server is used to store more and more data, management of very large databases becomes a bigger concern for DBAs. First, the time to perform operations like an index rebuild grows with the data size, and eventually this can affect system availability. Second, the size of large tables makes performing operations difficult because the system is often strained for resources, such as temp space, log space, and physical memory. Table and index partitioning can help you manage large databases better and minimize downtime.

Physically, partitioned tables and indexes are really *N* tables or indexes that store a fraction of the rows. When comparing this to their nonpartitioned equivalents, the difference in the plan is often that the partitioned case requires iterating over a list of tables or a list of indexes to return all the rows. In SQL Server 2005, this was represented using an APPLY operator, which is essentially a nested loops join. In the 2005 representation, a special table of partition IDs was passed in as parameters to the query execution component in a join to iterate over each partition. While this works well in most cases, there are some important scenarios that didn't work well with this model. For example, there is a restriction in parallel query plans that requires that the parallel table or index scan feature (where multiple threads read rows from a table at once to improve performance) did not work on the inner side of a nested loops join, and this was not possible to fix before SQL Server 2005 shipped. Unfortunately, this is the majority case for table partitioning. In addition, the APPLY representation enabled join collocation, where two tables partitioned in the same way can be joined very efficiently. Unfortunately, this turned out to be less common in practice than was foreseen when the feature was originally designed. For reasons like this, the representation was refined further in the 2008 version of the product.

SQL Server 2008 represents partitioning in most cases by storing the partitions within the operator that accesses the partitioned table or index. This provides a number of benefits, like enabling parallel scans to work properly. It also removed a number of other differences between partitioned and nonpartitioned cases in the Query Optimizer that manifested themselves as missed performance optimizations. Hopefully this makes it easier to deploy partitioning in applications that started out nonpartitioned.

Listing 8-13 contains the example to show this new design. Figure 8-45 contains the resulting query plan for SQL Server 2008 over partitioned tables.

**LISTING 8-13** SQL Server 2008 Partitioning Example—No Apply Needed

```
CREATE PARTITION FUNCTION pf2008(date) AS RANGE RIGHT
        FOR VALUES ('2008-10-01', '2008-11-01', '2008-12-01');
CREATE PARTITION SCHEME ps2008 AS PARTITION pf2008 ALL TO ([PRIMARY]);

CREATE TABLE ptnsales(saledate DATE, salesperson INT, amount MONEY) ON ps2008(saledate);
INSERT INTO ptnsales (saledate, salesperson, amount) VALUES ('2008-10-20', 1, 250.00);
INSERT INTO ptnsales (saledate, salesperson, amount) VALUES ('2008-11-05', 2, 129.00);
INSERT INTO ptnsales (saledate, salesperson, amount) VALUES ('2008-12-23', 2, 98.00);
INSERT INTO ptnsales (saledate, salesperson, amount) VALUES ('2008-10-3', 1, 450.00);

SELECT * FROM ptnsales WHERE (saledate) NOT BETWEEN '2008-11-01' AND '2008-11-30';
```

```
Query 1: Query cost (relative to the batch): 100%
SELECT * FROM ptnsales WHERE (saledate) NOT BETWEEN '2008-11-01' AND '2008-11-30';
```

```
   SELECT          ←———      Table Scan
   Cost: 0 %                 [ptnsales]
                             Cost: 100 %
```

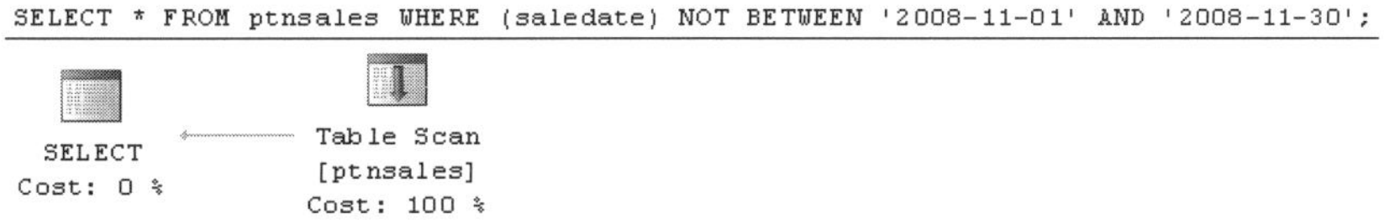

**FIGURE 8-45** Query plan for the new SQL Server 2008 partitioning model

You can see that the base case doesn't require an extra join with a Constant Scan. This makes the query plans look like the nonpartitioned cases more often, which should make it easier to understand the query plans.

One benefit of this model is that it is now possible to get parallel scans over partitioned tables. The following example creates a large partitioned table and then performs a *COUNT(\*)* operation that generates a parallel scan. In SQL Server, some aggregate functions can be split into two parts, with one part executed in the same thread as the table. This can speed up execution time in large queries and minimize the number of rows that need to be passed from thread to thread. Listing 8-14 demonstrates how SQL Server 2008 now generates parallel scans over partitioned tables to compute aggregates. Figure 8-46 contains the resulting query plan.

**LISTING 8-14** Partitioned Parallel Scan Example—SQL Server 2008

```
CREATE PARTITION FUNCTION pfparallel(INT) AS RANGE RIGHT FOR VALUES (100, 200, 300);
CREATE PARTITION SCHEME psparallel AS PARTITION pfparallel ALL TO ([PRIMARY]);
GO
CREATE TABLE testscan(randomnum INT, value INT, data BINARY(3000)) ON psparallel(randomnum);
GO
SET NOCOUNT ON;
BEGIN TRANSACTION;
DECLARE @i INT=0;
WHILE @i < 100000
BEGIN
INSERT INTO testscan(randomnum, value) VALUES (rand()*400, @i);
SET @i+=1;
END;
COMMIT TRANSACTION;
GO
-- now let's demonstrate a parallel scan over a partitioned table in SQL Server 2008
SELECT COUNT(*) FROM testscan;
```

```
Query 1: Query cost (relative to the batch): 100%
SELECT COUNT(*) FROM testscan;
```

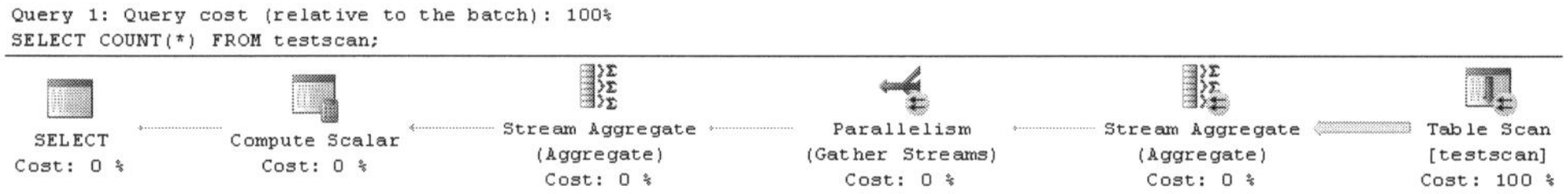

**FIGURE 8-46** Parallel scan on partitioned tables in SQL Server 2008

SQL Server 2005 had limitations on how parallel queries could be executed against partitioned tables. The use of the APPLY operator to scan each partition interacted poorly with some other restrictions in the system to allow SQL Server 2005 to run only one thread per partition. Although this allowed the query to run in parallel when scanning many partitions, this model did not work well when the query accessed a single partition. When accessing a single partition, only one thread could access the partition, essentially ignoring the Parallel Scan feature. Unfortunately, one of the core reasons for SQL Server range partitioning is to access the most current partition in a date range. In addition, the APPLY model also made it difficult to handle partition skew (where one partition is much larger than others) efficiently. While SQL Server 2005 would consider the size of the largest partition when costing a query using this pattern, it still has one thread finishing later than the other threads.

The Query Optimizer has improved the end-to-end experience in partitioned table plan generation. The ability to represent partitioned table access in the same manner as nonpartitioned access guarantees that the performance differences between partitioned and nonpartitioned tables are minimized. Specifically, the set of considered parallel plan options is much more consistent. The query execution component can dynamically adjust between using one thread per partition and using multiple threads per partition, which should allocate threads to finish processing a query more efficiently.

In SQL Server 2008, join collocation is still represented using the apply/nested loops join, but other cases use the traditional representation. This works with other features within the query processor to guarantee that they behave the same as nonpartitioned tables. The following example builds upon the last example to demonstrate that joining two tables with the same partitioning scheme can be done using the collocated join technique. The scenarios for this remain the same as in SQL Server 2005—cases when you want to join two partitioned tables or indexes together. Often, this would be a fact table and a large dimension table index that is partitioned in the same manner as the fact table. Figure 8-47 shows a per-partitioned join example when the original SQL Server 2005 partitioning logic is still visible.

```
-- SQL Server 2008 join collocation still uses the constant scan + apply model
SELECT * FROM testscan t1 INNER JOIN testscan t2 ON t1.randomnum=t2.randomnum;
```

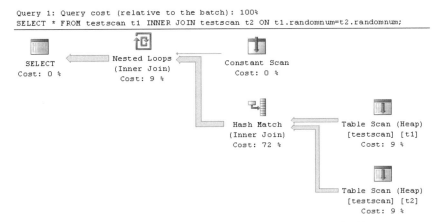

**FIGURE 8-47** Query plan for a per-partition join against a partitioned table

The partitioned table implementation in SQL Server 2008 does have a quirk that is worth noting because it may surprise you at first. If you look closely at the showplan output in Figure 8-48 for this last query plan, you may notice that this partitioned table heap scan has a seek predicate.

| | |
|---|---|
| ⊞ Output List | [s1].[dbo].[testscan].randomnum, [s1].[dbo].[testscan].value, [s1].[dbo].[testscan].data |
| Parallel | False |
| Partitioned | True |
| Physical Operation | Table Scan |
| Scan Direction | FORWARD |
| ⊞ Seek Predicates | Seek Keys[1]: Prefix: PtnId1001 = Scalar Operator([Expr1008]) |
| TableCardinality | 100000 |

**FIGURE 8-48** Seek predicate for partitioned heaps

Although SQL Server 2005 exposed the partition ID within the query plan, SQL Server 2008 largely hides that from view. It is still in the query plan, but it is much more closely tied to indexing in most cases. Every partitioned access structure in SQL Server 2008 is modeled as an index where the first column is the partitioning column. Because the partitioning ID (derived from the partitioning key) is needed to perform seeks anyway, this actually matches the effective behavior seen in SQL Server 2005. The only quirk is that partitioned heaps now appear to have an index. You can see this in the properties from the previous example.

## Partition-Aligned Index Views

SQL Server 2008 now allows for partition-aligned index views that can survive across *SWITCH* operations. In SQL Server 2005, these views had to be dropped before a *SWITCH* could be performed, and this hampered the ability to keep a system running as a production system while the indexed views were disabled and rebuilt. Now, partitioned tables, especially in large data warehouses, have a way to maintain a database while keeping it fully available.

# Data Warehousing

SQL Server contains a number of special optimizations that speed the execution of Data Warehouse queries. A *data warehouse* is a large database that usually has one large fact table and a number of smaller dimension tables that contain detail information referenced by the fact table. These are typically called *star schema* or *snowflake schema* (*snowflake* applies to dimension tables that reference other dimension tables). These kinds of schemas are often used to store large amounts of raw data which is then processed to help discover information to help a company learn something about its business.

Data warehouses often try to make each row in the fact table as small as possible because the table is so large. Large data, such as strings, is moved to dimension tables to reduce in-row space. Fact tables are usually so large that the use of nonclustered indexes is limited because of the large storage requirements to store these structures. Dimension tables are often indexed. This pattern does not match a typical transaction processing system, where each table is accessed based on the queries used against the system.

When optimizing queries against data warehouses, it is important not to scan the fact table more than necessary because this is usually the largest single contributor to execution time. SQL Server can recognize star and snowflake schemas and apply special optimizations to improve query performance. First, SQL Server orders joins differently in data warehouses to try to perform as many limiting operations against the dimension tables as is possible *before* a scan of the fact table is performed. This can even include performing full cross products between dimension tables so that scans of the fact table can be eliminated.

SQL Server 2008 also contains improvements to bitmap operators which help reduce data movement across threads in parallel queries. The bitmap can be used to reduce each row to a single bit. Because two bitmaps can be intersected or unioned efficiently, this model allows SQL Server to join two tables simply by performing a bitmap operation. This allows each dimension table to be queried to identify qualifying rows, creating a bitmap that is then sent to the thread(s) scanning the fact table. These bitmaps are applied using a probe filter applied as a non-sargable predicate to the fact table. This is somewhat like a special on-the-fly index, created just for data warehouse queries of this pattern.

One limitation in SQL Server that still affects large tables, such as the fact table in a data warehouse configuration, is that there can only be 200 steps in a histogram. Very large tables often have more than 200 steps of interesting data distribution data, so sometimes queries may be overestimated or underestimated as a result of this limitation, even with full-scan statistics. Luckily, filtered statistics can be used to alleviate this problem somewhat—it is possible to create filtered statistics for the range that defines a partition and then have that be used to estimate cardinality. As many queries on partitioned tables are over the current partition in a date range, this covers a reasonable number of the scenarios that were not covered as well in SQL Server 2005.

# Updates

Updates are an interesting area within query processing. In addition to many of the challenges faced while optimizing traditional *SELECT* queries, update optimization also considers physical optimizations such as how many indexes need to be touched for each row, whether to process the updates one index at a time or all at once, and how to avoid unnecessary locking deadlocks while processing changes as quickly as possible. The Optimizer contains a number of features that are specific to updates that help make queries complete as quickly as possible. In this section, we discuss a number of these optimizations.

In this section, the term *update processing* actually includes all top-level commands that change data. This includes *INSERT, UPDATE, DELETE,* and (as of SQL Server 2008) *MERGE.* As you see in this section, SQL Server treats these commands almost identically. Every update query in SQL Server is composed of the same basic operations:

- Determines what rows are changed (inserted, updated, deleted, merged)
- Calculates the new values for any changed columns
- Applies the change to the table and any nonclustered index structures.

Figure 8-49 shows how *INSERT* works using this pattern.

```
CREATE TABLE update1 (col1 INT PRIMARY KEY IDENTITY, col2 INT, col3 INT);
INSERT INTO update1 (col2, col3) VALUES (2, 3);
```

```
Query 1: Query cost (relative to the batch): 100%
INSERT INTO update1 (col2, col3) VALUES (2, 3);
```

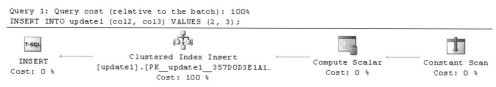

FIGURE 8-49 Basic *INSERT* query plan

The *INSERT* query has an operator called a *Constant Scan*. A Constant Scan is a special operator in the relational algebra that generates rows without reading them from a table. If you are inserting a row into a table, it doesn't really have an existing table, so this operator creates a row for the insert operator to process. The *Compute Scalar* operation evaluates the values to be inserted. In our example, these are constants, but they could be arbitrary scalar expressions or scalar subqueries. Finally, the insert operator physically updates the primary key-clustered index.

Figure 8-50 shows how *UPDATE* plans are represented.

```
UPDATE update1 SET col2 = 5;
```

```
Query 1: Query cost (relative to the batch): 100%
UPDATE update1 SET col2 = 5;
```

FIGURE 8-50 *UPDATE* query plan

The *UPDATE* query reads values from the clustered index, performs a *Top* operation, and then updates the same clustered index. The *Top* operation is actually a placeholder for processing *ROWCOUNT,* and it does nothing unless you have executed a *SET ROWCOUNT N* operation in your session. Also note that in the example, the *UPDATE* command does not modify the key of the clustered index, so the row in the index does not need to be moved within an index. Finally, there does not appear to be an operator to calculate the new value 5 for *col2*. This is obviously not true—it is handled, but there is a physical optimization to collapse this command into the Update operator for processing. If you examine the properties of the Update operator (as seen in Figure 8-50), you see that the query has also been auto-parameterized and the target value is supplied directly into the Update. Figure 8-51 shows the *DELETE* query plan pattern.

```
DELETE FROM update1 WHERE col3 = 10;
```

The *DELETE* query is very similar to the *UPDATE* query—the only real difference is that the row is deleted at the end. The only material difference is that the WHERE clause is used as a condition to the source table's seek operation.

```
Query 1: Query cost (relative to the batch): 100%
DELETE FROM update1 WHERE col3 = 10;
```

FIGURE 8-51 *DELETE* query plan

SQL Server generates different plans based on the physical layout of tables, indexes, and other secondary structures. For example, if we consider a very similar example that does not have a primary key-clustered index, we can see that the resulting plan shape changes in Figure 8-52.

```
CREATE TABLE update2 (col1 INT , col2 INT, col3 INT);
INSERT INTO update2 (col2, col3) VALUES (2, 3);
```

```
Query 1: Query cost (relative to the batch): 100%
INSERT INTO update2 (col2, col3) VALUES (2, 3);
```

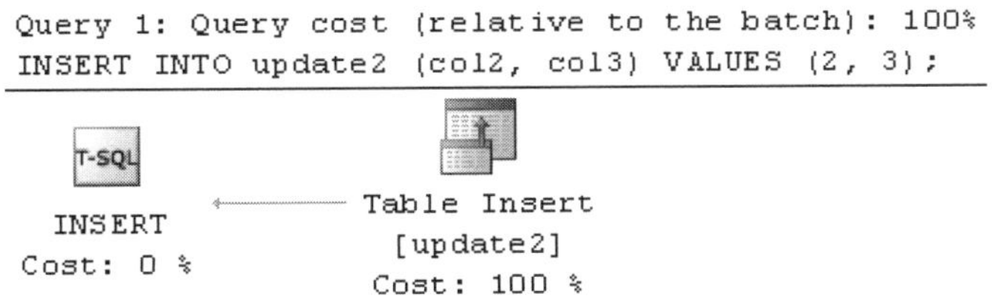

**FIGURE 8-52** Simple *INSERT* query plan

When the table is a heap (it has no clustered index), a special optimization occurs that can collapse the operations into a smaller form. This is called a *simple update* (the word *update* is used generically to refer to insert, update, delete, and merge plans), and it is obviously faster. This is a single operator that does all the work to insert into a heap, but it does not support every feature in Updates.

Figure 8-53 shows how inserts work against tables with multiple indexes.

```
CREATE TABLE update3 (col1 INT , col2 INT, col3 INT);
CREATE INDEX i1 ON update3(col1);
CREATE INDEX i2 ON update3(col2);
CREATE INDEX i3 ON update3(col3);

INSERT INTO update3(col1, col2, col3) VALUES (1, 2, 3);
```

```
Query 1: Query cost (relative to the batch): 100%
INSERT INTO update3(col1, col2, col3) VALUES (1, 2, 3);
```

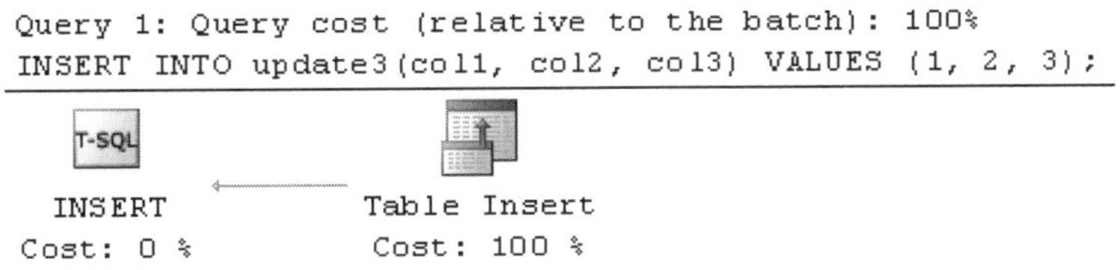

**FIGURE 8-53** All-in-one *INSERT* query plan

This query needs to update all the indexes because a new row has been created. However, Figure 8-53 demonstrates that the plan has only the one operator. If you look at the properties for this operator in Management Studio, as shown in Figure 8-54, you can see that it actually updates all indexes in one operator.

| ⊟ Object | [s1].[dbo].[update3], [s1].[dbo].[update3].[i1] |
|---|---|
| ⊞ [1] | [s1].[dbo].[update3] |
| ⊞ [2] | [s1].[dbo].[update3].[i1] |
| ⊞ [3] | [s1].[dbo].[update3].[i2] |
| ⊞ [4] | [s1].[dbo].[update3].[i3] |

**FIGURE 8-54** Multiple indexes updated by a single operator

This is another one of the physical optimizations that are done to improve the performance of common update scenarios. This kind of insert is called an *all-in-one* or a *per-row* insert.

Using the same table, we can try an *UPDATE* command to update some, but not all, of the indexes. Figure 8-55 contains the resulting query plan.

```
UPDATE update3 SET col2=5, col3=5;
```

```
Query 1: Query cost (relative to the batch): 100%
UPDATE update3 SET col2=5, col3=5;
```

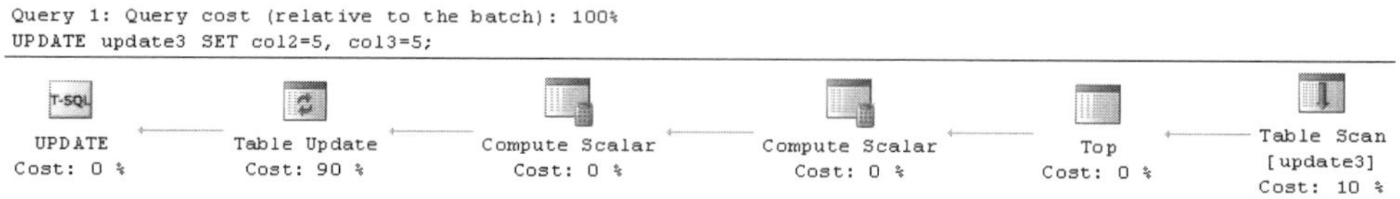

FIGURE 8-55  A query plan that modifies only some of the indexes on a table

Well, now things are getting a bit more complex. The query scans the heap in the Table Scan operator, performs the *ROWCOUNT Top*, then two Compute Scalars, and then a Table Update. If you examine the properties for the Table Update, you see that it lists only indexes *i2* and *i3*, because the Query Optimizer can statically determine that *i1* will not be changed by this command. One of the Compute Scalars calculates the new values for the columns. The other is yet another physical optimization that helps compute whether each row needs to modify each and every index. SQL Server contains logic to handle non-updating updates. In this case, the user calls for an update but actually submits the existing value for the row. The Query Optimizer can recognize this case and avoid some internal steps, such as logging changes, when a value is updated to the same value. Because a number of prepackaged SQL applications and tools allow users to retrieve a row, modify some columns, then write a complete update for all columns back to the database (not just the columns that changed), this actually turned out to be a needed and useful way to speed up queries. This optimization is not always applied—SQL Server uses logic to make an educated guess as to how likely and useful this optimization is, but it does reduce write traffic and log traffic in the cases when it applies.

## Halloween Protection

*Halloween Protection* describes a feature of relational databases that is used to provide correctness in update plans. The need for the solution is best described by explaining what happens in a naive implementation of an update plan. One simple way to perform an update is to have an operator that iterates through a B+ tree index and updates each value that satisfies the filter. This works fine so long as one assigns a value to a constant or to a value that does not apply to the filter. If one is not careful, the iterator can see rows that have already been processed earlier in the scan because the previous update moved the row ahead of the cursor iterating through the B+ tree.

Not every query needs to worry about this problem, but it is an issue for some shapes of query plans. The typical protection against this problem is to scan all the rows into a buffer, then process the rows from the buffer. In SQL Server, this is usually implemented using a Spool or a Sort operator, each of which has certain guarantees about reading all input rows before producing output rows to the next operator in the query tree. SQL Server also can use a special form of the Compute Scalar operator to provide Halloween Protection in certain limited cases, but the showplan has no public information to indicate that this is happening (other than an extra Compute Scalar being in the plan). In all cases, the copy protects against seeing the same row twice.

## Split/Sort/Collapse

SQL Server contains a physical optimization called *Split/Sort/Collapse,* which is used to make wide update plans more efficient. The feature examines all the change rows to be changed in a batch and determines the net effect that these changes would have on an index. Unnecessary changes are avoided, which can reduce the I/O requirements to complete the query. This change also allows a single, linear pass to be made to apply changes to each index, which is more efficient than a series of random I/Os. Figure 8-56 contains the resulting query plan.

```
CREATE TABLE update5(col1 INT PRIMARY KEY);
INSERT INTO update5(col1) VALUES (1), (2), (3);
UPDATE update5 SET col1=col1+1;
```

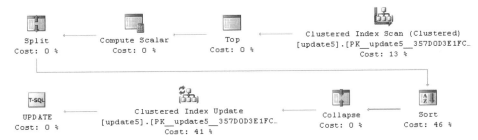

**FIGURE 8-56** Split/Sort/Collapse *UPDATE* query plan

This query is modifying a clustered index that has three rows with values 1, 2, and 3. After this query, we would expect the rows to have the values 2, 3, and 4. Instead of modifying three rows, it is possible to determine that we can just delete 1 and insert 4 to make the changes to this query. For our trivial example, we can avoid the modification of one row, but for larger tables, this savings can be substantial.

This optimization is implemented using an internal column called the *action column.* It contains a value to represent whether each row is an *INSERT, UPDATE, DELETE,* or *MERGE.* The action column is used by the Update operator to determine what change should be applied to the index. Although the showplan shows different names for this Update operator based on the submitted query, it is the same operator internally and is modified by the action column. Unfortunately, you can't see the values of this column because it is only a construct within the query processor.

The action column is also used by the query processor to help determine the net changes to be applied to an index. It also is used by the Split/Sort/Collapse logic to determine the next change to the index. Let's walk through what happens in each step. Before the split, the row data is shown in Table 8-1.

**TABLE 8-1** Pre-Split Update Data Representation

| Action | Old Value | New Value |
|--------|-----------|-----------|
| UPDATE | 1 | 2 |
| UPDATE | 2 | 3 |
| UPDATE | 3 | 4 |

Split converts each UPDATE into one DELETE and one INSERT. Immediately after the split, the rows now appear as shown in Table 8-2.

**TABLE 8-2** Post-Split Data Representation

| Action | Value |
|--------|-------|
| DELETE | 1 |
| INSERT | 2 |
| DELETE | 2 |
| INSERT | 3 |
| DELETE | 3 |
| INSERT | 4 |

The Sort sorts on (value, action), where DELETE sorts before INSERT. After the sort, the rows appear as seen in Table 8-3.

**TABLE 8-3** Post-Sort Data Representation

| Action | Value |
|--------|-------|
| DELETE | 1 |
| DELETE | 2 |
| INSERT | 2 |
| DELETE | 3 |
| INSERT | 3 |
| INSERT | 4 |

The Collapse operator looks for (DELETE, INSERT) pairs for the same value and removes them. In this example, it replaces the DELETE and INSERT rows with UPDATE for the rows with the values 2 and 3. The UPDATE reduces the number of B+ tree maintenance operations necessary, and the storage engine is instrumented not to log anything for B+ tree updates to the same value (locks are still taken, however, for correctness). The final form of the rows after the collapse is Table 8-4.

**TABLE 8-4** **Post-Collapse Data Representation**

| Action | Value |
|--------|-------|
| *DELETE* | 1 |
| *UPDATE* | 2 |
| *UPDATE* | 3 |
| *INSERT* | 4 |

The result is the net change that needs to be made to the index. Technically, each index also contains a primary key reference or heap row identifier, and even the rows missing from Table 8-5 are actually updated to fix the reference to the heap or clustered index. Log traffic is still reduced from the regular update path, and the I/O ordering benefits are also gained.

While the Split/Sort/Collapse logic is a performance optimization, it also helps avoid false failures when modifying a unique index (such as this primary key). If the original plan were to be executed without Split/Sort/Collapse, it would try to change the row with value 1 to 2. This would conflict with the existing row that has value 2 in the index. Although this could be avoided for this query by iterating over the rows backwards, it is not always possible to pick a single scan order to avoid this issue. Split/Sort/Collapse allows SQL Server to support queries such as this example without returning an error.

## Merge

SQL Server 2008 introduces a new type of update operation called *MERGE*. *MERGE* is a hybrid of the other update operations and can be used to perform conditional changes to a table. The business value of this operation is that it can collapse multiple T-SQL operations into a single query. This simplifies the code that you have to write to modify tables, improves performance, and really helps operations against large tables that could be so large as to make multistep operations effectively too slow to be useful.

Now that you have seen how the other update operations are handled, you might have figured out that *MERGE* is actually not a difficult extension of the action column techniques used in the other operations. Like the other queries, the source data is scanned, filtered, and modified. However, in the case of *MERGE*, the set of rows to be changed is then joined with the target source to determine what should be done with each row. Based on this join, the action column for each row is modified to tell the *STREAM UPDATE* operation what to do with each row.

In Listing 8-15, an existing table is going to be updated with new data, some of which might already exist in the table. Therefore, *MERGE* is used to determine only the set of rows that are missing. Figure 8-57 contains the resulting *MERGE* query plan.

**LISTING 8-15** A *MERGE* Example

```
CREATE TABLE AnimalsInMyYard(sightingdate DATE, Animal NVARCHAR(200));
GO
INSERT INTO AnimalsInMyYard(sightingdate, Animal) VALUES ('2008-08-12', 'Deer');
INSERT INTO AnimalsInMyYard(sightingdate, Animal) VALUES ('2008-08-12', 'Hummingbird');
INSERT INTO AnimalsInMyYard(sightingdate, Animal) VALUES ('2008-08-13', 'Gecko');
GO
CREATE TABLE NewSightings(sightingdate DATE, Animal NVARCHAR(200));
GO
INSERT INTO NewSightings(sightingdate, Animal) VALUES ('2008-08-13', 'Gecko');
INSERT INTO NewSightings(sightingdate, Animal) VALUES ('2008-08-13', 'Robin');
INSERT INTO NewSightings(sightingdate, Animal) VALUES ('2008-08-13', 'Dog');
GO

-- insert values we have not yet seen - do nothing otherwise
MERGE AnimalsInMyYard A USING NewSightings N
    ON (A.sightingdate = N.sightingdate AND A.Animal = N.Animal)
WHEN NOT MATCHED
    THEN INSERT (sightingdate, Animal) VALUES (sightingdate, Animal);
```

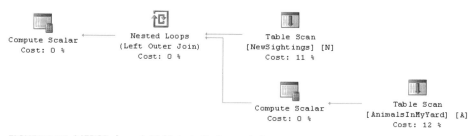

```
Query 1: Query cost (relative to the batch): 100%
MERGE AnimalsInMyYard A USING NewSightings N ON (A.sightingdate = N.sightingdate AND
    A.Animal = N.Animal) WHEN NOT MATCHED THEN INSERT (sightingdate, Animal)
        VALUES (sightingdate, Animal);
```

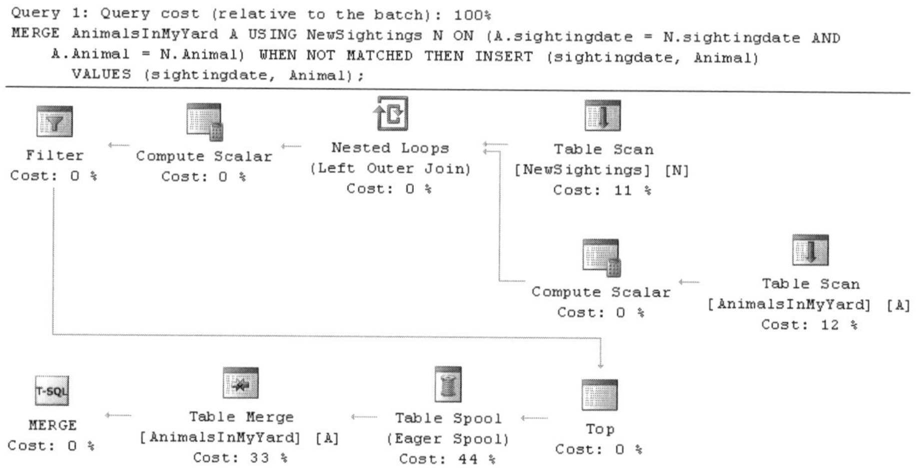

**FIGURE 8-57** Merge query plan

As *MERGE* plans tend to get a bit large, I'll split this into pieces and discuss each portion of the query plan. The first part of the plan can be seen in Figure 8-58.

**FIGURE 8-58** *MERGE* plan—initial join to find preexisting rows

First, the source table *NewSightings* is read, and the query processor performs a probe into the target table *AnimalsInMyYard* to see if the row is already there. The Compute Scalar underneath the Left Outer Join exists merely to add a column that is 1 if the value was matched and, due to the nature of how Left Outer Joins work, returns a value of NULL if there is no matching row to match the source table row. The Compute Scalar above the join generates the *Action* column:

```
[Action1008] = Scalar Operator(ForceOrder(CASE WHEN [TrgPrb1006] IS NOT NULL THEN NULL ELSE
(4) END))
```

Table Merge                 Table Spool           Top              Filter
[AnimalsInMyYard] [A]      (Eager Spool)       Cost: 0 %         Cost: 0 %
    Cost: 33 %              Cost: 44 %

**FIGURE 8-59** *MERGE* plan—Update, Halloween protection spool, and row filter

In the upper half of this plan (shown in Figure 8-59), the filter eliminates rows that have a null action (Predicate: [Action1008] IS NOT NULL), as this *MERGE* statement only has one action (It is possible to have multiple operations within a single *MERGE* statement). The Spool provides Halloween Protection, which means that it consumes all rows from its inputs before attempting to write values back into the *AnimalsInMyYard* table. Table *MERGE* is really just an *Update* operation, but the showplan output has been changed to avoid confusion.

## Wide Update Plans

SQL Server also has special optimization logic to speed the execution of large batch changes to a table. If a large percentage of a table is being changed by a query, SQL Server can create a plan that avoids modifying each B+ tree with many individual updates. Instead, it can generate a per-index plan that determines all the rows that need to be changed, sorts them into the order of the index, and then applies the changes in a single pass through the index. This approach can be noticeably more efficient than updating each row individually. These plans are called *per index* or *wide update* plans, as you see in their plan shape.

The following example demonstrates a wide update plan. Figure 8-60 contains the resulting plan.

```
CREATE TABLE dbo.update6(col1 INT PRIMARY KEY, col2 INT, col3 INT);
CREATE INDEX i1 ON update6(col2);
GO
CREATE VIEW v1 WITH SCHEMABINDING AS SELECT col1, col2 FROM dbo.update6;
GO
CREATE UNIQUE CLUSTERED INDEX i1 ON v1(col1);
UPDATE update6 SET col1=col1 + 1;
```

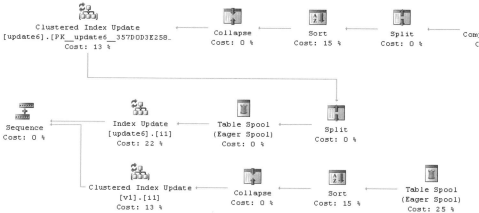

**FIGURE 8-60** Wide update query plan (truncated)

Because this is complicated, let's split the plan into smaller sections so that it can fit on the printed page and not be as overwhelming.

Figure 8-61 contains the first portion of the query plan, and it works just like the previous example—the set of net changes are applied to the clustered index. This set is a superset of all the nonclustered indexes because a clustered index includes all columns.

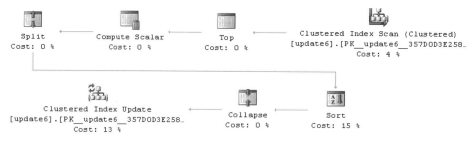

**FIGURE 8-61** Clustered index update section of wide update plan

Figure 8-62 contains the next part of the query plan. The section of the first branch above the clustered index update does a number of things. The spool in this plan is a common subexpression spool (described earlier in the chapter). This is a way of broadcasting the rows to allow each index to use this data as input. The Sequence operator does not change or modify data—it is designed to process the first input first, the second input second, and so on. This drives the processing of the rows in a wide update plan. Finally, because there can be multiple clients of this set of rows that each perform Split/Sort/Collapse, SQL Server has an optimization to perform the split once instead of *N* times by doing it on the first branch.

**FIGURE 8-62** Updated rows are split and stored in a multiread spool

Finally, the second branch reads the previous spooled and split rows, sorts them for this index, collapses them, and performs the net change to this index. Figure 8-63 contains this portion of the plan. If the query had additional indexes to update, they could be applied as additional branches in the query that would be processed in order.

**FIGURE 8-63** One nonclustered index branch in a wide update plan

> **Note** Wide update plans are the most general and fully functional form of update plan in SQL Server, and architecturally any plan can be executed as a wide plan in SQL Server. Some features, such as indexed views and query notifications, are updated using only wide update plans. Because some optimizations available in SQL Server are limited to more traditional feature sets, be aware that using some features forces SQL Server to use wide update plans. In most cases, this does not matter to your application, but it could matter in systems with small amounts of data that perform many updates.

## Non-Updating Updates

*UPDATE* operations have a number of special optimizations to improve performance for common scenarios. For example, a common programming paradigm for updating a row against a database is as follows:

1. Run a *SELECT* query that retrieves a row from the database and copies the values into the client or mid-tier layer, such as:

   ```
   SELECT col1, col2, col3, ... FROM Table WHERE primarykey = <constant>
   ```

2. Allow the user to update some columns selectively.

3. When the client is finished modifying the row, attempt to write the values back to the server with a query like this:

   ```
   UPDATE Table SET col1=@p1, col2=@p2, col3=@p3 ... WHERE primarykey = constant AND col1
   = originalcol1value AND col2 = originalcol2value AND col3 = originalcol3value AND ...
   ```

This pattern provides a functional but not optimal concurrency control without requiring the server to hold locks on the base table. In addition, the database programmer generally implements only one *UPDATE* query that can handle any set of modified columns and just passes in the original values in the SET list to avoid having to deal with many query plans.

SQL Server has update logic that can determine the set of indexes to maintain based on the columns in the SET list of an *UPDATE*. By default, however, the pattern described here would cause SQL Server to update all indexes for each *UPDATE*, even if only one column value actually changed. To avoid this problem, SQL Server implements a feature called *Non-Updating Updates*, which can dynamically detect unchanged values and avoid updates to unchanged indexes. While the query plan still reference each index, it is possible to avoid the cost to write unneeded values.

This optimization is not performed in all cases—some logic is used to try to apply it to scenarios where it seems most likely to improve performance. This optimization is transparent to the user, though you can see it as additional filters in some query plans.

# Sparse Column Updates

SQL Server 2008 introduced a new feature called *sparse columns* that supports creating more columns in a table than were previously supported, as well as creating rows that were technically greater than the size of a database page. The primary use case for the feature is flexible-schema systems where users can create columns dynamically. Often these columns are mostly NULL but have some set of rows where a value is defined. This pattern is also largely independent for each sparse column, meaning that a given row potentially has a few but usually not many non-NULL sparse column values.

Sparse columns are stored in a complex column in a regular data row, as described in Chapter 7, "Special Storage." When working with the sparse column data, SQL Server must interpret the complex columns to determine which columns actually have values. To modify sparse columns, rows are read, new values are computed, and then rows are written. The main difference is that sparse columns require a bit more work to read and modify.

# Partitioned Updates

Updating partitioned tables is somewhat more complicated than nonpartitioned equivalents. Instead of a single physical table (heap) or B+ tree, the query processor has to handle one heap or B+ tree *per partition*. It needs to figure out where each row belongs, and rows can move between partitions in some update plans. In addition, each index can be partitioned using a separate partition function. Even indexed views can be partitioned, and they too can be partitioned differently than the other access paths associated with a table. Luckily, partitioned update plans SQL Server 2008 are an extension of the update plan shapes already discussed in this chapter. So this section discusses only how those plans are different when using partitioning.

In the description of *SELECT* plans over partitioned tables earlier in this chapter, you may recall that the partitioning ID was represented within the query processor as a virtual leading column on every access method (heap or index). Partitioned table updates also use this representation, which makes the plans look a lot like the plans to update indexes. This leading column also appears in some of the other operators used in update plans, such as the Split/Sort/Collapse operators. The following examples demonstrate how partitioning fits into these plans.

In the first example, we create a partitioned table and then insert a single row into it. The plan can be seen in Figure 8-64.

```
CREATE PARTITION FUNCTION pfinsert(INT) AS RANGE RIGHT FOR VALUES (100, 200, 300);
CREATE PARTITION SCHEME psinsert AS PARTITION pfinsert ALL TO ([PRIMARY]);
go
CREATE TABLE testinsert(ptncol INT, col2 INT) ON psinsert(ptncol);
go
INSERT INTO testinsert(ptncol, col2) VALUES (1, 2);
```

```
Query 1: Query cost (relative to the batch): 100%
INSERT INTO testinsert(ptncol, col2) VALUES (1, 2);
```

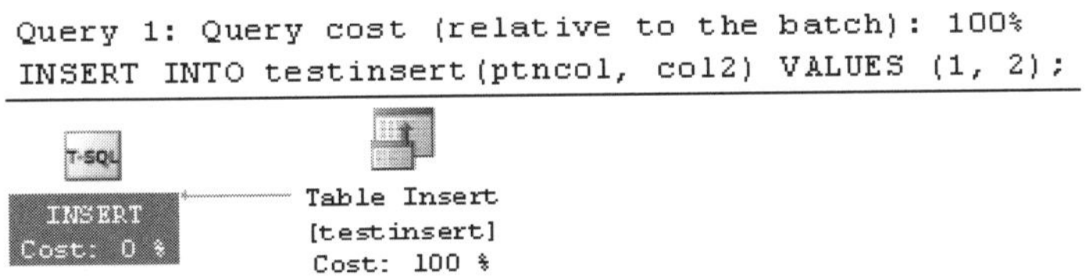

**FIGURE 8-64** Partitioned insert—single partition

Looking at the query plan, this matches the behavior one would expect from a nonpartitioned table. It has a single operator that just inserts into the table. Underneath the covers, however, the Query Execution operator has to determine which partition needs to be updated, load that partition, and set the appropriate value. Looking at the properties for the *INSERT* operator, we can see (in Figure 8-65) the partitioning-specific logic that makes this happen. First, *Expr1005* is computed to determine the target partition to use, and you can see the partition boundaries passed to an internal function called *RangePartitionNew*. In the *Predicate* section, the extra *Expr1005* computed value is used to set the *PtnId1001* column, which is the virtual partition ID column that is exposed in the system to support partitioning. The rest of the *Predicate* list supports setting values for the regular columns *ptncol* and *col2*.

| ⊟ **Misc** | |
|---|---|
| ⊞ Defined Values | [Expr1005] = Scalar Operator(RangePartitionNew([@1],(1),(100),(200),(300))) |
| Description | Insert input rows into the table specified in Argument field. |
| Estimated CPU Cost | 0.000001 |
| Estimated I/O Cost | 0.01 |
| Estimated Number of Executi | 1 |
| Estimated Number of Rows | 1 |
| Estimated Operator Cost | 0.0100022 (100%) |
| Estimated Rebinds | 0 |
| Estimated Rewinds | 0 |
| Estimated Row Size | 9 B |
| Estimated Subtree Cost | 0.0100022 |
| Logical Operation | Insert |
| Node ID | 0 |
| ⊞ Object | [s1].[dbo].[testinsert] |
| ⊞ Output List | |
| Parallel | False |
| Partitioned | True |
| Physical Operation | Table Insert |
| Predicate | [s1].[dbo].[testinsert].[ptncol] = [@1],[s1].[dbo].[testinsert].[col2] = [@2],[PtnId1001] = RaiseIfNullInsert([Expr1005] |

**FIGURE 8-65** Partition selection computation in the query plan

The query processor can load the partition necessary to modify each row dynamically. If we insert multiple rows in a single statement, we can see in Figure 8-66 how the query processor supports updating each row properly.

```
INSERT INTO testinsert(ptncol, col2) VALUES (5, 10),(105,25);
```

FIGURE 8-66  Dynamic partition computation in insert plans

This query attempts to insert two rows, and the query plan represents this using the Constant Scan operator. The Compute Scalar operator runs the partitioning function to determine the target partition of each row, as seen in Figure 8-67.

FIGURE 8-67  Range partitioning computation in showplan output

Furthermore, the Table Insert operator uses this computed scalar (as shown in Figure 8-68) and, for each row, changes to the right partition if necessary.

Predicate
 ScalarOperator      Scalar Operator([s1].[dbo].[testinsert].[ptncol] = [Union1005],[s1].[dbo].[testinsert].[col2] = [Union1006],[PtnId100
   Item
   ScalarString      [s1].[dbo].[testinsert].[ptncol] = [Union1005],[s1].[dbo].[testinsert].[col2] = [Union1006],[PtnId1001] = [Expr1007]

FIGURE 8-68  Insert uses a range partition to determine insert target partition

> **Note**  Compute Scalar exists in this two-row plan and not in the first example for reasons connected purely to implementation; these factors are not necessary to understand the plans or materially affect the performance of the plans when they are run.

Changing partitions can be a somewhat expensive operation, especially when many of the rows in the table are being changed in a single statement. The Split/Sort/Collapse logic can also be used to reduce the number of partition switches that happen, improving run-time performance. In the following example, a large number of rows are inserted into the partitioned table, and the Query Optimizer chooses to sort on the virtual partition ID column before inserting to reduce the number of partition switches at run time. Figure 8-69 shows the Sort optimization in the query plan.

```
INSERT INTO testinsert SELECT * FROM #nonptn;
```

Query 1: Query cost (relative to the batch): 100%
INSERT INTO testinsert SELECT * FROM #nonptn;

| T-SQL INSERT Cost: 0 % | Table Insert [testinsert] Cost: 21 % | Sort Cost: 75 % | Top Cost: 0 % | Compute Scalar Cost: 0 % | Table Scan [#nonptn] Cost: 4 % |

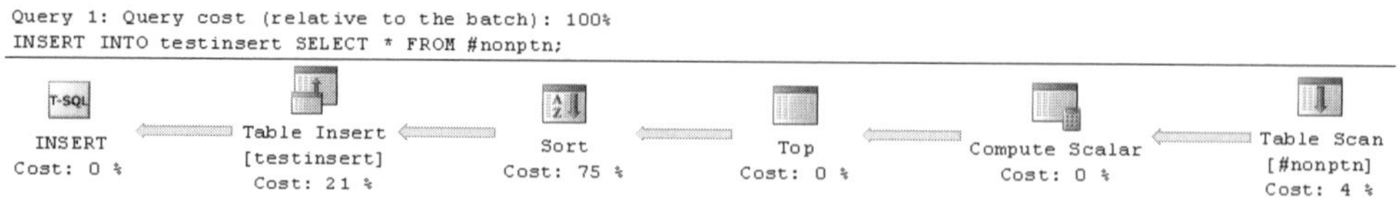

FIGURE 8-69  Sort optimization to reduce partition switching

The sort has an ordering requirement, as defined in Figure 8-70, which is derived from the call to the partitioning function in the Compute Scalar earlier in the plan, just like the previous example.

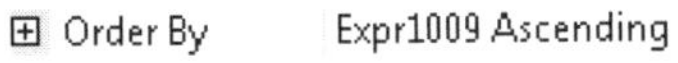

⊞ Order By      Expr1009 Ascending

**FIGURE 8-70** Ordering requirement for partitioned insert sort optimization

Updates to partitioned tables are more complex because they can move rows. However, they follow the same principles as updates. The key property to understand is that the query processor must read each row, determine the change to that row, compute the target partition for that row, and then perform the change. This may include deleting the partition from one B+ tree and inserting it into another. This matches closely with the Split/Sort/Collapse idea for batch updates, but for partitioned updates, it can happen even for smaller changes.

## Locking

SQL Server contains a number of tricks and optimizations to improve the overall performance and throughput of updates within the system. While much of the Query Optimizer is agnostic to locking, several targeted features and locking modes in Updates improve concurrency (and avoid deadlock errors). One special locking mode is called a U (for Update) lock. This is a special lock type that is compatible with other S (shared) locks but incompatible with other U locks. In many of the plan shapes used in *Update* queries, SQL Server has two different operators accessing the same access method. The first one is the source table, and it is only reading. The second is the update itself. If only a shared (S) lock were taken in the read operator, multiple users could run queries at the same time, both acquire S locks for a row and then deadlock because neither could upgrade the lock to an exclusive (X) lock when the update operator later saw the row. To prevent this, the U lock is compatible with other S locks but not with other U locks. This prevents other potential writers from reading a row, which then avoids the deadlock.

Listing 8-16 demonstrates how to examine the locking behavior of an update query plan. Figure 8-71 contains the query plan used in this example, and Figure 8-72 contains the locking output from *sp_lock*.

**LISTING 8-16** Update Locking Example

```
CREATE TABLE lock(col1 INT, col2 INT);
CREATE INDEX i2 ON lock(col2);
INSERT INTO lock (col1, col2) VALUES (1, 2);
INSERT INTO lock (col1, col2) VALUES (10, 3);

SET TRANSACTION ISOLATION LEVEL REPEATABLE READ;
BEGIN TRANSACTION;
UPDATE lock SET col1 = 5 WHERE col1 > 5;
EXEC sp_lock;
ROLLBACK;
```

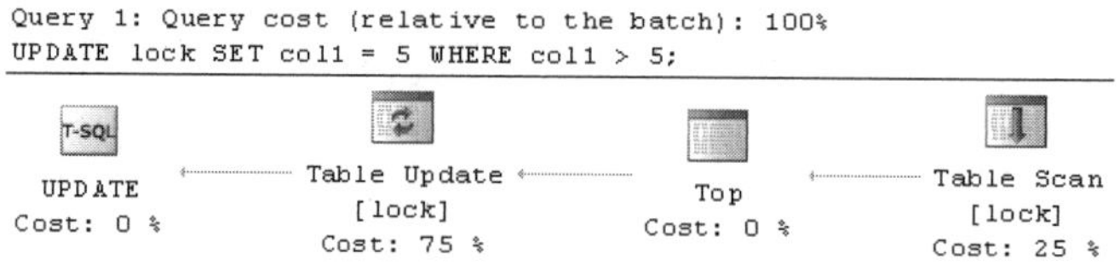

```
Query 1: Query cost (relative to the batch): 100%
UPDATE lock SET col1 = 5 WHERE col1 > 5;
```

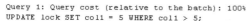

UPDATE          Table Update          Top          Table Scan
Cost: 0 %          [lock]                    Cost: 0 %          [lock]
                  Cost: 75 %                                   Cost: 25 %

**FIGURE 8-71** An update plan used in the locking example

| | spid | dbid | ObjId | IndId | Type | Resource | Mode | Status |
|---|---|---|---|---|---|---|---|---|
| 1 | 52 | 21 | 0 | 0 | DB | | S | GRANT |
| 2 | 52 | 1 | 1131151075 | 0 | TAB | | IS | GRANT |
| 3 | 52 | 21 | 693577509 | 0 | PAG | 1:75676 | IX | GRANT |
| 4 | 52 | 21 | 693577509 | 0 | RID | 1:75676:1 | X | GRANT |
| 5 | 52 | 21 | 693577509 | 0 | TAB | | IX | GRANT |

**FIGURE 8-72** The sp_lock output for the update plan

Using a higher isolation mode with a user-controlled (non-auto-commit) transaction allows you to examine the final locking state of each object in the query. In this case, you can see that the row (*Resource 1:69641:1*) was locked with an X lock. This lock started as a U lock and was promoted to an X lock by the *UPDATE*.

We can run a slightly different query that shows that the locks vary based on the query plan selected. Figure 8-73 contains a seek-based update plan. In the second example, the U lock is taken by the nonclustered index, whereas the base table contains the X lock. So, this U lock protection works only when going through the same access paths because it is taken on the first access path in the query plan. Figure 8-74 shows the locking behavior of this query.

```
BEGIN TRANSACTION;
UPDATE lock SET col1 = 5 WHERE col2 > 2;
EXEC sp_lock;
```

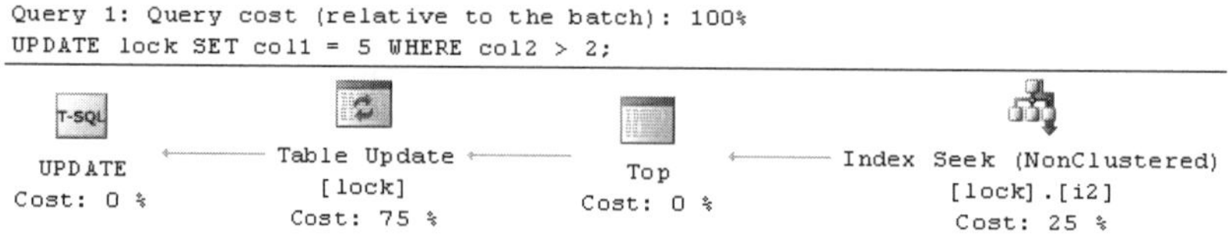

```
Query 1: Query cost (relative to the batch): 100%
UPDATE lock SET col1 = 5 WHERE col2 > 2;
```

UPDATE          Table Update          Top          Index Seek (NonClustered)
Cost: 0 %          [lock]                    Cost: 0 %          [lock].[i2]
                  Cost: 75 %                                   Cost: 25 %

**FIGURE 8-73** Locking behavior of an update plan with a seek

| | spid | dbid | ObjId | IndId | Type | Resource | Mode | Status |
|---|---|---|---|---|---|---|---|---|
| 1 | 52 | 21 | 0 | 0 | DB | | S | GRANT |
| 2 | 52 | 21 | 693577509 | 2 | KEY | (a0004dc87aeb) | U | GRANT |
| 3 | 52 | 1 | 1131151075 | 0 | TAB | | IS | GRANT |
| 4 | 52 | 21 | 693577509 | 2 | PAG | 1:75678 | IU | GRANT |
| 5 | 52 | 21 | 693577509 | 0 | PAG | 1:75676 | IX | GRANT |
| 6 | 52 | 21 | 693577509 | 0 | RID | 1:75676:1 | X | GRANT |
| 7 | 52 | 21 | 693577509 | 0 | TAB | | IX | GRANT |

**FIGURE 8-74** The sp_lock output for a seek-based update plan

### Partition-Level Lock Escalation

Locking behavior is usually not the domain of the Query Optimizer. Although the Query Optimizer does try to generate plans that minimize locking conflicts, it is largely agnostic to the locking interactions of plans, for better or worse. The Query Optimizer uses a lot of logic to implement partitioning, including logic to prune unnecessary partitions from query plans so that they are not touched. One great addition in the SQL Server 2008 product is *partition-level lock escalation*. This feature allows the database to avoid lock escalation to the table-level for partitioned tables. When combined with pruning, this provides a powerful way to improve application concurrency, especially when queries over large, partitioned tables can take a long time to execute. The functionality can be enabled using the following command:

```
ALTER TABLE TableName SET (LOCK_ESCALATION = AUTO);
```

Locking is discussed in detail in Chapter 10, "Transactions and Concurrency."

# Distributed Query

SQL Server includes a feature called *Distributed Query*, which accesses data on different SQL Server instances, other database source, and non-database tabular data such as Microsoft Office Excel files or comma-separated text files. Distributed Query is based on the OLE DB interfaces, and most OLE DB providers are feature-rich enough to be used by the Distributed Query feature. Because multiple sources can be referenced within a single query, it is an effective mechanism to interact with data from multiple sources without writing a lot of special-case code.

Distributed Query supports several distinct use cases. First, Distributed Query is useful to move data from one source to another. Although it is not a complete extract, transform, and load (ETL) tool like SQL Server Integration Services, it is often a very easy way to copy a table from one server instance to another. For example, if a company's financial reporting group wanted a copy of the sales figures for each month, it would be possible to write a query to copy the data from the SQL Server instance servicing the Sales team to another instance in the Financial Reporting group. Another application of Distributed Query is to integrate nontraditional sources into a SQL Server query. As there are OLE DB providers for non-database data such as Active Directory Domain Services, Microsoft Exchange Server, and a number of third-party sources, it is possible to write queries to gather information from those sources and to then use the power of the SQL language to ask rich questions of that data that may not be supported by the source of that data. Distributed Query can also be used for reporting. Because multiple sources can be queried in a single query, you can use this to gather data into a single source and generate reports (which can be surfaced through Reporting Services, if desired). Finally, Distributed Query can be used for scale-out scenarios. SQL Server supports a special *UNION ALL* view called a *Distributed Partitioned View (DPV)*. This view stitches together distinct portions of a single range that are each stored on a different SQL Server instance. Exceptionally large tables can be stored on different servers and queries can be directed to access only the subset necessary to satisfy a particular query. The Distributed Query feature covers a number of scenarios and can help make solving those scenarios much easier.

Distributed Query is implemented within the Query Optimizer's plan-searching framework. With the exception of pass-through queries, which are not modified during optimization, distributed queries initially are represented using the same operators as regular queries. Each base table represented in the Query Optimizer tree contains metadata collected from the remote source using OLE DB metadata interfaces such as OLE DB schema rowsets. The information collected is very similar to the information that the query processor collects for local tables, including column information, index information, and statistics. One additional piece of collected information includes information about what SQL grammar constructs the remote source supports, which are used later in optimization. Once metadata is collected, the Query Optimizer derives special property information for each operator that manipulates remote data. This property determines whether it is possible to generate a SQL statement to represent the whole query sub-tree that can be sent directly to the remote data source. Some operators can be remoted easily, like Filter and Project. Others can be performed only locally, such as the streaming table-valued function operator used to implement portions of the XQuery feature in SQL Server. SQL Server performs exploration rules to transform query trees into forms that might allow the server to remote larger trees. For example, SQL Server attempts to group all remote tables from the same source together in a single sub-tree and splitting aggregates into local forms that can be remoted. During this process, some of the more advanced rules in SQL Server are disabled if they are known to generate alternatives that prevent sub-tree remoting. While SQL Server does not maintain specific costing models for each remote source, the feature is designed to remote large sub-trees to that source in the hopes of moving the least amount of data between servers. This usually provides a close-to-optimal query plan.

In this example, we create a linked server to point to a remote SQL Server instance. Then, we use the four-part name syntax to generate a query that can be completely remoted to the remote source (shown in Figure 8-75).

```
EXEC sp_addlinkedserver 'remote', N'SQL Server';
go
SELECT * FROM remote.Northwind.dbo.customers WHERE ContactName = 'Marie Bertrand';
```

| SELECT | Compute Scalar | Remote Query |
|--------|----------------|--------------|
| Cost: 0 % | Cost: 0 % | Cost: 100 % |

**FIGURE 8-75** A fully remoted Distributed Query

As you can see, this relatively simple query was essentially completely remoted by the Query Optimizer. The properties information for the Remote Query node contains the query text that is executed on the remote server. The results are brought back to the local server and returned to the user.

The generated query, shown here, is somewhat more verbose than the text submitted originally, but this is necessary to ensure that the semantics of the remoted query match the local query text exactly:

```
SELECT "Tbl1002"."CustomerID" "Col1004","Tbl1002"."CompanyName" "Col1005",
"Tbl1002"."ContactName" "Col1006","Tbl1002"."ContactTitle" "Col1007","Tbl1002"."Address"
"Col1008","Tbl1002"."City" "Col1009","Tbl1002"."Region" "Col1010","Tbl1002".
"PostalCode" "Col1011","Tbl1002"."Country" "Col1012","Tbl1002"."Phone"
"Col1013","Tbl1002"."Fax" "Col1014" FROM "Northwind"."dbo"."customers" "Tbl1002" WHERE
"Tbl1002"."ContactName"=N'Marie Bertrand';
```

Because the OLE DB model has a rich, cursor-based update model, it is possible to use SQL Server to update remote data sources using regular *UPDATE* statements. These plans look identical to the local plans discussed in this chapter, except that the top-level Update operation is specific to the remote source. Because the storage engine model in SQL Server is originally based on the OLE DB interfaces, the mechanisms for performing local and remote updates are actually very similar. In the case when a whole update query can be remoted (because the property information for every operator determines that the remote source can support an *UPDATE* statement that is semantically equivalent to performing the operation locally through the exposed OLE DB interfaces), SQL Server can and will generate complete remote *INSERT, UPDATE,* and *DELETE* statements to be performed on the remote server. You should examine any query that you think can be completely remoted to make sure that it actually can—in some cases there may be a specific grammar construct or intrinsic function that is not necessary in the query that blocks it from being completely remoted.

The Distributed Query feature was introduced in SQL Server 7.0, and there are some limitations with the feature that you should consider when designing scenarios that use it. First, the feature relies on the remote providers to supply very detailed cardinality and statistical information to SQL Server so that it can use this knowledge to compare different query plans. As most OLE DB providers do not provide much statistical information, this can limit the quality of query plans generated by the Query Optimizer. In addition, OLE DB is not being actively extended by Microsoft, and therefore some providers are not actively maintained. Also, not every feature in SQL Server is supported via the remote query mechanism, such as some XML and UDT-based functionality. SQL Server 2008 does not have a native mechanism to support querying managed adaptors written for the CLR run time. Finally, the costing model used within SQL Server is good for general use but sometimes generates a plan that is substantially slower than optimal. Unfortunately, the impact of not remoting a query in the Distributed Query feature is larger than in the local case because there is just more work to be done to move rows from a remote source. Care should be taken when using the feature to test out the functionality before you put it into production. It might be useful to pregenerate pass-through queries for common, expensive queries to make sure that they are always remoted properly.

# Extended Indexes

SQL Server contains a number of special indexes to support specific use cases. Full-text indexes support document storage, querying, and retrieval. XML indexes are used to support XQuery operations on XML data stored in the database. Spatial indexes, added in SQL Server 2008, support queries over spatial data. These indexes are usually better suited for their specific domain than a B+ tree index, but they are often specific to a particular set of use cases. While the Query Optimizer contains support for each of these, they are not conceptually different from B+ tree indexes.

## Full-Text Indexes

In SQL Server 2008, full-text indexes have moved from being a completely external construct to being a mostly internal index type. Specific keywords in SQL grammar tell the system to pick the index implicitly, and this is done before the Optimization process begins. Information about full-text-index generations and other details of the index is abstracted from the Query Optimizer to simplify the maintenance of this index and to avoid recompiles to account for each new index generation.

## XML Indexes

XML indexes are somewhat unlike other indexes in that it is actually stored more similarly to an indexed view. It uses the same physical storage as a clustered index, and it also has secondary indexes on various columns. However, this is not matched by the Query Optimizer. Like full-text indexes, XQuery constructs are very specific in the syntax, and they are taken to imply that the operation should always use this index if it exists.

An XML index essentially takes each attribute and value in an XML document and shreds it into its own row. In addition to these values, other columns are added to this structure to store information such as the attribute for a value and its relative location in the document (its path from the root node). This information makes specific XQuery constructs significantly faster when the index is used.

Within the query tree representation, XML is represented using a number of nontraditional operators. One of these is the Streaming Table-Valued Function (STVF), which is used for other functionality, including SQL Server's Dynamic Management Objects. This construct allows an XML BLOB to be split into pieces, each returned in one row.

## Spatial Indexes

Spatial indexes are new in SQL Server 2008, and these indexes are matched in the Query Optimizer. Spatial indexes decompose a space and allow points to be indexed. The primary model of a spatial index is to divide areas of the space into regions and then use bounding boxes for each region. Within the plan, an STVF generates candidates, based on the encoding function, close to the requested point(s) and the results are used in the rest of the query. Figure 8-76 contains an example spatial index query plan.

```
CREATE TABLE geo(col1 INT PRIMARY KEY, point GEOGRAPHY);
CREATE SPATIAL INDEX spaidx ON geo(point);
SELECT * FROM geo WITH (INDEX=spaidx)
    WHERE geo.point.STEquals('POINT(24.0 24.0)')=1;
```

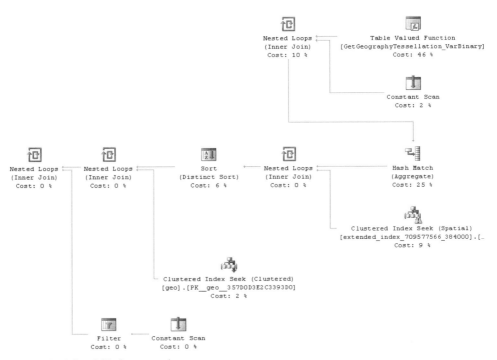

**FIGURE 8-76** Spatial index example

The spatial index uses more operators in the plan than just the STVF. The first Constant Scan and Hash Match help reduce duplicates due to the hierarchy encoding. The first loops join retrieves values from the index structure. The sort is needed to find duplicate base rows (perhaps there is more than one point for a single database row). The second loops join retrieves any other requested columns from the base table. Finally, the last loops join applies the CLR function as a residual predicate.

# Plan Hinting

There is a lot of misinformation about query hints, and often the misuse of hints can cause the creation of global policies for or against the use of hints in queries. One of the goals of this chapter is to give DBAs and developers the tools they need to have a different kind of conversation about the design, implementation, and maintenance of SQL Server applications. This section explains query hints and when to use them.

Early in the chapter, I discussed some of the problems that face the engineering team for a Query Optimizer. The complexity of some of the algorithms involved in optimizing SQL queries is high enough that it is effectively impossible to explore every possible query plan for every query that can be sent to the system. Latency restrictions in statistics gathering and mathematical modeling issues in cardinality estimation also place some limits on the powers of the Query Optimizer, given the current computational powers of processors today. The reality is that there are some queries for which the Query Optimizer cannot generate a perfect plan.

That being said, the Query Optimizer actually does an amazing job on most queries. Many years of very smart thinking has gone into the development of this component, and the result is a system that almost always finds a very good query plan very quickly. This is accomplished through a number of smart algorithms, heuristics, and an understanding of common scenarios. Each release of the product gets better and can handle more and more scenarios.

When people ask me about hints, I first ask them about their application. Many people don't realize that the design of the application has a huge impact on whether hints are appropriate or necessary. If your database schema has a classic, third-normal form set of data tables and your queries are all written using an understanding of the American National Standards Institute (ANSI) SQL grammar, then your odds are very good that SQL Server will do a reasonable job on your query without any modification. As you push the system and stress the design in different directions, you can find areas where the algorithms and heuristics in the product start to not work as well. For example, if you have huge variations in data distribution or you have an application that relies on the statistical correlation of column values to select a great plan, then sometimes you may not get a join order that is near optimal for your query. So before you consider hints, make sure that you can understand how your application is designed, specifically around what kinds of things make your application not look like a common database application.

If you have identified a poorly performing query that is important to your application and you have an idea why the Query Optimizer could be having trouble, then that would be an appropriate time to consider whether a hint will help this application. I usually tell people not to use a hint unless there is a good reason, which means that the standard behavior of the system is unacceptable for your business and there is a better plan choice that is acceptable. So, if you know that a particular join order or index selection yields deadlocks with the other queries in your system, then you should consider using a hint—locking is not a factor in how the Query Optimizer optimizes queries, and each query is effectively optimized independently of the others in the system.

Now, some database development teams may impose rules such as "No hints," or "Always force this index on this table when doing a *SELECT*." This doesn't mean that they are wrong—often there is a very good reason for these kinds of rules to exist. I urge you to read through this chapter and make sure that you have a conversation with your DBA about the reasons for each rule. When you are building a new feature and changing a database application, it may be completely appropriate to use a hint or to alter these development practices. The goal of this section is to help you understand the purpose of each hint. I hope that this lets you see the situations when it might be appropriate to use a hint (and when it might not be appropriate).

Query and table hints are, in almost all cases, actually requirements given by the query author to the Query Optimizer when generating a query plan. So, if a hint cannot be satisfied, the Query Optimizer actually returns an error and does not return a plan at all. Locking hints are an exception—these are sometimes ignored to preserve the correctness of data manipulation operations necessary for the system to work properly. The name is somewhat misleading, but this behavior allows you to modify the query and know that you had an impact on the query generation process.

## Debugging Plan Issues

Determining when to use a hint requires an understanding of the workings of the Query Optimizer, how it might not be making a correct decision, and then an understanding of how the hint might change the plan generation process to address the problem. For more than half of the problems that Microsoft typically sees in support calls about query plans, issues with incorrect cardinality estimates are the primary cause of a poor plan choice. In other words, a better cardinality estimate would yield a plan choice that is acceptable. In other cases, more complex issues around costing, physical data layout, lock escalation, memory contention, or other issues were factors in the performance degradation. This section explains how to identify cardinality estimation errors and then use hints to correct poor plan choices, as these are usually something that can be fixed without buying new hardware or otherwise altering the host machine.

The primary tool to identify cardinality estimation errors is the statistics profile output in SQL Server. When enabled, this mode generates the *actual* cardinalities for each query operator in the plan. These can be compared against the Query Optimizer's estimated cardinalities to find any differences. As cardinality estimation is performed from the bottom of the tree upwards (right to left in the showplan's graphical display), errors propagate. Usually, the location of the lowest error indicates where to consider hints.

Other tools exist to track down performance issues with query plans. Setting statistics time on is a great way to determine run-time information for a query. SQL Profiler is a great tool for tracking deadlocks and other system-wide issues that can be captured by tracing. *DBCC MEMORYSTATUS* is an excellent tool to find out what components in the system are causing memory pressure within SQL Server. Most of these tools fall outside of the scope of this chapter, though these tools can be helpful for some plan issues. It is recommended that cardinality issues be researched first when there are concerns about plan quality, as this is probably the most common issue.

In Figure 8-77, we run a query against one of the catalog views to see how each operator's estimated and actual cardinalities match up.

```
SET STATISTICS PROFILE ON;
SELECT * FROM sys.objects;
```

| | Rows | Executes | StmtText | EstimateRows | EstimateExecutions |
|---|---|---|---|---|---|
| 1 | 91 | 1 | SELECT * FROM sys.objects; | 91 | NULL |
| 2 | 91 | 1 | \|-Nested Loops(Left Outer Join, OUTER REFEREN... | 91 | 1 |
| 3 | 91 | 1 | \|-Nested Loops(Left Outer Join, OUTER REFER... | 91 | 1 |
| 4 | 91 | 1 | \| \|-Filter(WHERE:(has_access('CO',[s1].[sys].[sy... | 91 | 1 |
| 5 | 0 | 0 | \| \| \|-Compute Scalar(DEFINE:([Expr1006]=CO... | 91 | 1 |
| 6 | 91 | 1 | \| \| \|-Clustered Index Scan(OBJECT:([s1].[sys]... | 91 | 1 |
| 7 | 0 | 91 | \| \|-Clustered Index Seek(OBJECT:([s1].[sys].[sys... | 1 | 91 |
| 8 | 91 | 91 | \|-Clustered Index Seek(OBJECT:([mssqlsystemres... | 1 | 91 |

**FIGURE 8-77** Statistics profile ouput

> **Note** The *EstimateRows* and *EstimateExecutions* columns have been moved from the actual output order for display in the screenshot. While the estimation for this query is actually perfect, it is common for estimates to vary from the actual cardinalities, especially as queries get more complex. Usually, you'd like them to be close enough that the plan choice won't change, which is almost always less than an order of magnitude off by the top of the tree. Also, note that the *EstimateRows* number is the average per-execution, whereas *Rows* is merely total rows. You can divide *Rows* by *Executes* to get the numbers to be comparable.

If an error is found by looking at the statistics profile output, this can help identify a place where the Query Optimizer has used bad information to make a decision. Usually, updating statistics with fullscan can help isolate whether this is an issue with out-of-date or undersampled statistics. If the Query Optimizer makes a poor decision even with up-to-date statistics, then this might mean that there is an out-of-model condition with the Query Optimizer. For example, if there is a strong data correlation between two columns in a query, this could cause errors in the cardinalities seen in the query. Once an out-of-model condition is identified as being the cause of a poor plan choice, hints are the mechanism to correct the plan choice and to use a better query plan.

This section describes how most of the query or table hints fit within the context of the Query Optimizer's architecture, including situations where it might be appropriate to use hints.

## {HASH | ORDER} GROUP

SQL Server has two possible implementations for *GROUP BY* (and *DISTINCT*). It can be implemented by sorting the rows and then using the fact that rows in the same group are now adjacent physically. It can also hash each group into a different memory location. When one of these options is specified, it is implemented by turning off the implementation rule for the other physical operator. Note that this applies to all *GROUP BY* operations within a query, including those from views included in the query.

Many data warehouse queries have a common pattern of a number of joins followed by an aggregate operation. If the estimates for the number of rows returned in the joins section is in error, the estimated size for the aggregate operation can be substantially incorrect. If it is underestimated, then a sort and a stream aggregate may be chosen. As memory is allocated to each operator based on the estimated cardinality estimates, an underestimation could cause the sort to spill to disk. In a case like this, hinting a hash algorithm might be a good option. Similarly, if memory is scarce or there are more distinct grouping values than expected, then perhaps using a stream aggregate would be more appropriate. This hint is a good way to affect system performance, especially in larger queries and in situations when many queries are being run at once on a system.

## {MERGE | HASH | CONCAT } UNION

Many people incorrectly use *UNION* in queries when they likely want to use *UNION ALL*, perhaps because it is shorter. *UNION ALL* is actually a faster operation, in general, because it takes rows from each input and simply returns them all. *UNION* actually has to compare rows from each side and make sure that no duplicates are returned. Essentially, *UNION* performs a *UNION ALL* and then a *GROUP BY* operation over all output columns. In some cases, the Query Optimizer can determine that the output columns contain a key that is unique over both inputs and can convert the *UNION* to a *UNION ALL*, but in general, it is worth making sure that you are actually asking the right query. These three hints apply only to *UNION*.

Now, assuming that you have the right operation, you can pick among three join patterns, and these hints let you specify which one to use. This example shows the MERGE UNION hint.

```
CREATE TABLE t1 (col1 INT);
CREATE TABLE t2 (col1 INT);
go
INSERT INTO t1(col1) VALUES (1), (2);
INSERT INTO t2(col1) VALUES (1);

SELECT * FROM t1
UNION
SELECT * FROM t2
OPTION (MERGE UNION);
```

As you can see, each hint forces a different query plan pattern. MERGE UNION is useful when there are common input sizes. CONCAT UNION is best at low-cardinality plans (one sort). HASH UNION works best when there is a small input that can be used to make a hash table against which the other inputs can be compared.

*UNION* hinting is done for roughly the same reasons as *GROUP BY* hinting—both operations are commonly used near the top of a query definition, and they have the potential to suffer if there is error in cardinality estimation in a query with many joins. Typically, one either hints to the HASH operator to address cardinality underestimation or hints to the CONCAT operator to address overestimation.

## FORCE ORDER, {LOOP | MERGE | HASH } JOIN

Join order and algorithm hints are common techniques to fix poor plan choices. When estimating the number of rows that qualify a join, the best algorithm depends on factors such as the cardinality of the inputs, the histograms over those inputs (which are used to make estimates about how many rows qualify the join condition), the available memory to store data in memory such as hash tables, and what indexes are available (which can speed up loops join scenarios). If the cardinality or histograms are not representative of the input, then a poor join order or algorithm can result. In addition, there can be correlations in data across joins that are extremely difficult to model with current technologies (even filtered statistics in SQL Server 2008 work only within a single table).

> **Tip** If the statistics profile output demonstrates that the cardinality estimates were substantially incorrect, the join order can be forced by rewriting the query into the order you would like to see the tables in the output plan. This modifies how the Query Optimizer sets the initial join order and then disables rules that reorder joins. Once hinted, you should time the new query and make sure that the plan is faster than the original. In addition, as your data changes, you need to reexamine these hints regularly to make sure that the plan you have forced is still appropriate—you are essentially saying "I know better than the Query Optimizer," which is the equivalent of performing all the maintenance on your own car.

Places where I have seen these hints be appropriate in the past are the following:

- Small, OLTP-like queries where locking is a concern.

- Larger data-warehouse systems with many joins, complex data correlations, and enough of a fixed query pattern that you can reason about the join order in ways that make sense for all queries. For example: "I am happy if I access dimension tables in this order first, then the fact table and everything is a hash join."

- Systems that extend beyond traditional relational application design and using some engine feature enough to change query performance materially. Examples might include using SQL as a document store with Full-Text or XQuery components that are mixed with traditional relational components or using Distributed Queries against a remote provider that does not surface statistical information to SQL Server's query processor.

Unfortunately, no semi-join specific implementation hints are exposed in SQL Server 2008, although they can be indirectly affected by the other join hints.

## INDEX=<indexname> | <indexid>

The INDEX=<indexname> | <indexid> hint has been in the product for many releases and is very effective in forcing the Query Optimizer to use a specific index when compiling a plan. The primary scenario where this is interesting is an OLTP application where you wish to force a plan to avoid scans of any type. Remember that the Query Optimizer tries to generate a plan using only this index first, but it also adds joins to additional indexes for a table if the index you have forced is not covering for the query (meaning that it has all the columns contained in the index key, the table's primary key, or listed as an INCLUDED column). One would generally have a query filter predicate that could be used to generate a seek against the index, but this hint is also valid for index scans if you use indexes to narrow row widths to improve query execution time. A second scenario where this would be useful is a plan developed on one server for use on another, such as a test to deployment server or an ISV that creates a plan for an application and then ships this application to their customers to deploy on their own SQL Server instance.

# FORCESEEK

This hint was added in SQL Server 2008. It tells the Query Optimizer that it needs to generate a seek predicate when using an index. There are a few cases when the Query Optimizer can determine that a scan of an index is better than a seek when compiling the query. For example, if a query is compiled while the table is almost empty, the storage engine may store all the existing rows in one page in an index. In this case, a scan is faster than a seek, in terms of I/O, because the storage engine supports scanning from the leaf nodes of a B+ tree, which would avoid one extra page of I/O. This condition might be ephemeral, given that newly created tables are often populated soon after. The hint is effective in avoiding such a scenario if you know that perhaps the table won't have enough rows to trigger a recompile or that the performance impact of this condition would be detrimental enough to the system to warrant the hint.

The other scenario where such a hint is interesting is to avoid locks in OLTP applications. This hint precludes an index scan, so it can be effective if you have a high-scale OLTP application where locking is a concern in scaling and concurrency. The hint avoids the possibility of the plan taking more locks than desired. Because the Query Optimizer does not explicitly reason about locking in plan selection (it does not prefer a plan that has fewer locks, but it might prefer a plan that it things will perform faster that also happens to take fewer locks). Care should be taken in hinting high-scale applications only when necessary, as a poor hint can cause the system to behave substantially worse than an unhinted plan.

# FAST <number_rows>

The Query Optimizer assumes that the user will read every row produced by a query. Although this is often true, some user scenarios, such as manually paging through results, do not follow this pattern—in these cases, the client reads some small number of rows and then closes the query result. Often a similar query is submitted in the near future to retrieve another batch of rows from the server. In the costing component, this assumption affects the plan choice. For example, hash joins are more efficient for larger result sets but have a higher startup cost (to build a hash table for one side of a join). Nested loops joins have no startup cost but a somewhat higher per-row cost. So, when a client wants only a few rows but does not specify a query that returns only a few rows, the latency of the first row may be slower due to the startup costs for stop-and-go operators like hash joins, spools, and sorts.

The FAST <number_rows> hint supplies the costing infrastructure with a hint from the user about how many rows the user will want to read from a query. Internally, this is called a *row goal*, and simply provides an input into the costing formulas to help specify what point on the costing function is appropriate for the user's query.

The *TOP()* syntax in SQL Server introduces a row goal as well. Note that if you supply *TOP(@param)*, then the Query Optimizer may not have a good value to sniff from the T-SQL context. In this scenario, you would want to use the OPTIMIZE FOR hint (described later in this section).

## MAXDOP <N>

MAXDOP stands for maximum degree of parallelism, which describes the preferred degree of fan-out to be used when this query is run (in SKUs that support parallel query plans). For expensive queries, the Query Optimizer attempts to use multiple threads to reduce the run time of a query. Within the costing functions, this means that some portions of the costs of a query are divided over multiple processor cores, reducing the overall cost compared to an otherwise identical serial plan. Very complex queries can actually have multiple zones of parallelism, meaning that each zone can have up to MAXDOP threads assigned to it during execution.

Large queries can consume a nontrivial fraction of the resources available to the system. A parallel query can consume memory and threads, blocking other queries that want to begin execution. In some cases, it is beneficial to the overall health of the system to reduce the degree of parallelism for one or more queries to lower the resources required to run a long-running query. This helps workloads that do not use the resource governor to manage resources. Often a server that services mixed workloads would be a good candidate for considering this hint, when needed.

## OPTIMIZE FOR

The Query Optimizer uses scalar values within the query text to help estimate the cardinality for each operator in the query. This ultimately helps choose the lowest-cost plan, as cardinality is a major input into the costing functions. Parameterized queries can make this process more difficult because parameters can change from one execution to the next. Given that SQL Server automatically parameterizes queries as well, this design choice affects more queries than one would expect. When estimating cardinality for parameterized queries, the Query Optimizer usually uses a less accurate estimate of the average number of distinct values in the column or it sniffs the parameter value from the context (usually only on recompile, unfortunately).

This sniffed value is used for cardinality estimation and plan selection, but it is not used to simplify the query or otherwise depend on the specific parameter value. So, parameter sniffing can help pick a plan that is good for a specific case. Because most data sets have nonuniform column distributions, the value sniffed can affect the run time of the query plan. If a value representing the common distribution is picked, this might work very well in the average case and less optimally in the outlier case (a value with substantially more instances than the average case). If the outlier is used to sniff the value, then the plan picked might perform noticeably worse than it would have if the average case value had been sniffed. This can be a problem due to the plan caching policy in SQL Server—a parameterized query is kept in the cache even though the values change from execution to execution. When a recompile happens, only the information from that specific context is used to recompile.

The OPTIMIZE FOR hint allows the query author to specify the actual values to use during compilation. This can be used to tell the Query Optimizer, "This is a common value that I expect to see at run time," and this can provide more plan predictability on parameterized queries. This hint works for both the initial compilation and for recompiles. While specifying a common value is usually the best approach, test out this hint to make sure that it gives the desired behavior.

In Listing 8-17, the OPTIMIZE FOR hint is used to force the query plan to account for an average value in the optimization of the query. (Note: I am only demonstrating that the plans change, not that these two plans perform differently. This technique can be used on arbitrarily complex queries to hint plans.) Note that when the value of 23 is used to compile the query (as shown in Figure 8-79), a different index is picked than when it is not (shown in Figure 8-78) because 23 is a very common value and it is not as selective as the predicate on *col2*. Parameter values can cause index changes, join order changes, and other more complex changes to your query plan—testing forced parameters is highly recommended.

**LISTING 8-17** Parameter Sniffing Example

```
CREATE TABLE param1(col1 INT, col2 INT);
go
SET NOCOUNT ON;
BEGIN TRANSACTION;
DECLARE @a INT=0;
WHILE @a < 10000
BEGIN
INSERT INTO param1(col1, col2) VALUES (@a, @a);
SET @a+=1;
END;
COMMIT TRANSACTION;
go
CREATE INDEX i1 ON param1(col1);
go
CREATE INDEX i2 ON param1(col2);
go
DECLARE @b INT;
DECLARE @c INT;
SELECT * FROM param1 WHERE col1=@b AND col2=@c;
```

Query 1: Query cost (relative to the batch): 100%
DECLARE @b INT; DECLARE @c INT; SELECT * FROM param1 WHERE col1=@b AND col2=@c;
SELECT
Cost: 0 %
Nested Loops
(Inner Join)
Cost: 0 %
Index Seek (NonClustered)
[param1].[i1]
Cost: 50 %
RID Lookup (Heap)
[param1]
Cost: 50 %

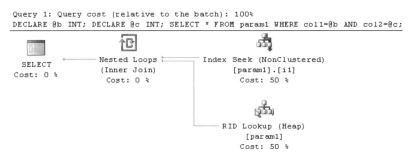

**FIGURE 8-78** Non-sniffed parameters use index i1

```
SELECT * FROM param1 WHERE col1=23 AND col2=5;
```

Query 1: Query cost (relative to the batch): 100%
SELECT * FROM param1 WHERE col1=23 AND col2=5;
SELECT
Cost: 0 %
Nested Loops
(Inner Join)
Cost: 0 %
Index Seek (NonClustered)
[param1].[i1]
Cost: 50 %
RID Lookup (Heap)
[param1]
Cost: 50 %

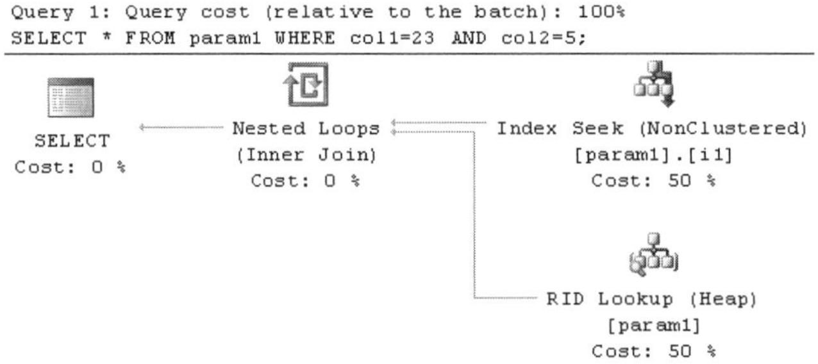

**FIGURE 8-79** Sniffed parameters use i2

```
DECLARE @b INT;
DECLARE @c INT;
SELECT * FROM param1 WHERE col1=@b AND col2=@c
OPTION (OPTIMIZE FOR (@b=22));
```

Using the OPTIMIZE FOR hint instructs the Query Optimizer to use a known common value when generating the plan so that it works for a wide range of parameter values.

## PARAMETERIZATION {SIMPLE | FORCED}

SIMPLE parameterization is the model that has existed in SQL Server for many releases. This corresponds to the concept of the trivial plan explained in this chapter. FORCED parameterization always replaces most literals in the query with parameters. As the plan quality can suffer, using FORCED should be done with care and an understanding of the global behavior of your application. Usually, FORCED mode should be used only in an OLTP system with many almost equivalent queries that (almost) always yield the same query plan. Essentially, you are betting that the plans will not change between possible parameter values. If all the queries are very small, the risk of this bet is smaller. The reasoning for this hint is that some OLTP systems with ad-hoc queries spent a large fraction of their time compiling the same (or similar) queries repeatedly. When possible, this is a good case to consider adding parameters into your application's queries.

# NOEXPAND

By default, the query processor expands view definitions when parsing and binding the query tree. While the Query Optimizer usually matches the indexed views during optimization (as well as portions of any query even when the indexed view was not specified), there are some cases where the internal queries are rewritten such that it is not possible to match indexed views anymore. The NOEXPAND hint forces the query processor to force the use of the indexed view in the final query plan. In many cases, this can speed up the execution of the query plan because the indexed view often pre-computes an expensive portion of a query. However, this is not always true—the Query Optimizer may be able to find a better plan using the information from the fully expanded query tree.

# USE PLAN

The USE PLAN *N'xml plan'* hint directs the Query Optimizer to try to generate a plan that looks like the plan in the supplied XML string. The Query Optimizer has been instrumented to use the shape of this plan as a series of hints to guide the optimization process to get the desired plan shape. Note that this does not guarantee that the _exact_ same plan is selected, but it will usually be identical or very close.

The common use of this hint is a DBA or database developer who wishes to fix a plan regression in the Query Optimizer. If a baseline of good/expected query plans is saved when the application is developed or first deployed, these can be used later to force a query plan to change back to what was expected if the Query Optimizer later determines to change to a different plan that is not performing well. This could be necessary to force a join order to avoid locking deadlocks or merely to get the right physical plan shape and algorithms to be chosen. In some scenarios, the Query Optimizer does not have enough information to make a good decision about a portion of the query plan (for example, the join order) and it can lead to a suboptimal plan choice. DBAs should use this option with care—forcing the original query plan may actually degrade performance further because the plan was likely created for different data volumes and distributions. Try out a plan hint on a test database before deploying it, when possible.

Although this feature was added in SQL Server 2005, the feature has been improved in SQL Server 2008 with the inclusion of scripting support through Management Studio and the ability to hint more types of queries. For example, *INSERT/DELETE/UPDATE/MERGE* queries are now supported in USE PLAN hints, which can be very useful in forcing specific update plans that avoid deadlocks in stress scenarios.

While SQL Server 2008 supports additional query types, some are not supported with this feature. These include:

- Dynamic, Keyset, and Fast Forward cursors
- Queries containing remote tables

- Full-text Queries

- DDL commands, including *CREATE INDEX* and *ALTER PARTITION FUNCTION,* which manipulate data

In the context of rules, properties, and the Memo, the USE PLAN hint is used by the Query Optimizer to control both the initial shape of the query tree (for example, the initial join order after the tree is normalized early in Optimization) as well as the rules that are enabled to run for each group in the Memo. In the case of join orders, the Query Optimizer enables only join order transformations that led to the configuration specified in the plan hint. Physical implementation rules are also hinted, meaning that a hash aggregate in the XML plan hint requires that the implementation rule for hash aggregation be enabled and that the stream aggregation rule be disabled.

The following example demonstrates how to retrieve a plan hint from SQL Server and then apply it as a hint to a subsequent compilation to guarantee the query plan:

```
CREATE TABLE customers(id INT, name NVARCHAR(100));
CREATE TABLE orders(orderid INT, customerid INT, amount MONEY);
go
SET SHOWPLAN_XML ON;
go
SELECT * FROM customers c INNER JOIN orders o ON c.id = o.customerid;
```

The *SELECT* statement returns a single row and single column of text of XML that contains the XML plan for the query. It is too large to print in the book, but it starts with

```
<ShowPlanXML xmlns="http://schemas.microsoft.com/sqlserver/2004/07/showplan" Version="1.0"
...
```

Once we have copied the XML, it is necessary to escape single quotes before we can use it in the USE PLAN hint. Usually, I copy the XML into an editor and then search for single quotes and replace them with double quotes. Then we can copy the XML into the query using the OPTION (USE PLAN '<xml .../>') hint. (The hint was again shortened for space.)

```
SET SHOWPLAN_XML OFF;
SELECT  * FROM customers  c INNER JOIN orders o ON c.id = o.customerid
OPTION (USE PLAN '<ShowPlanXML xmlns="http://schemas.microsoft.com/sqlserver/2004/07/
showplan" Version="1.0" ...');
```

This technique makes it possible to force one query plan in scenarios when you can manipulate the query submitted to the server. The names used in the XML plan format are logical (table names instead of *object_id*), so it should be possible to take a USE PLAN hint from one table and use it on another with the same physical schema (columns, indexes, and so on) with only minor modifications. A very straightforward way to copy a plan from one table to another table with the same structure, or from one database or SQL Server instance to another is to create a *plan guide* incorporating the USE PLAN hint. Plan Guides are discussed in Chapter 9.

# Summary

The Query Optimizer is a complex component with many internal features. While it is not always possible to know exactly why the Query Optimizer chose a specific plan, knowing a little about the Query Optimizer's design can help a DBA or database developer examine any query plan and diagnose any problems. Knowing how the Query Optimizer works can also help reinforce good database design methodologies that can improve the quality of your application and reduce problems in deployment.

This chapter explains the mechanisms used in query processing and optimization, including trees, rules, properties, and the Memo framework. These ideas are used through different stages of optimization to try to find a reasonable plan quickly. The examples throughout the chapter demonstrate many of the operators and how they are used to implement the SQL queries submitted by the user. Finally, the use of the statistics profile output can help identify poorly optimized queries and to use statistics and hints to get the Query Optimizer to select a better plan.

# Chapter 9
# Plan Caching and Recompilation

*Kalen Delaney*

We've now looked at the query optimization process and the details of query execution in Microsoft SQL Server. Because query optimization can be a complex and time-consuming process, SQL Server frequently and beneficially reuses plans that have already been generated and saved in the plan cache, rather than producing a completely new plan. However, in some cases, a previously created plan may not be ideal for the current query execution, and we might achieve better performance by creating a new plan.

In this chapter, we look at the SQL Server 2008 plan cache and how it is organized. Most of the discussion is relevant to SQL Server 2005 as well, and I will tell you when a behavior or feature is specific to SQL Server 2008. I will tell you about what kinds of plans are saved, and under what conditions SQL Server might decide to reuse them. We look at what might cause an existing plan to be re-created. We also look at the metadata that describes the contents of plan cache. Finally, I describe the ways that you can encourage SQL Server to use an existing plan when it might otherwise create a new one, and how you can force SQL Server to create a new plan when you need to know that the most up-to-date plan is available.

## The Plan Cache

It's important to understand that the plan cache in SQL Server 2008 is not actually a separate area of memory. Releases prior to SQL Server 7 had two effective configuration values to control the size of the plan cache, which was then called the *procedure cache*. One value specified a fixed size for the total usable memory in SQL Server; the other specified a percentage of that memory (after fixed needs were satisfied) to be used exclusively for storing procedure plans. Also, in releases prior to SQL Server 7, query plans for adhoc SQL statements were never stored in cache, only the plans for stored procedures. That is why it was called procedure cache in older versions. In SQL Server 2008, the total size of memory is by default dynamic, and the space used for query plans is also very fluid.

### Plan Cache Metadata

In the first part of this chapter, I explore the different mechanisms by which a plan can be reused, and to observe this plan reuse (or non-reuse), we need to look at only a couple of different metadata objects. There are actually about a dozen different metadata views and functions that give us information about the contents of plan cache, and that doesn't include the metadata that gives us information about memory usage by the plan cache. Later in the chapter, we look at more details available in the plan cache metadata, but for now, we are using just one view and one function. The view is *sys.dm_exec_cached_plans*, which contains one row for each plan in cache, and we look at the columns *usecounts, cacheobjtype,* and *objtype*. The value in *usecounts* allows us to see how many times a plan has been reused. The possible values for *cacheobjtype* and *objtype* are described in the next section. We also use the value in the column *plan_handle* as the parameter when we use the CROSS APPLY operator to join the *sys.dm_exec_cached_plans* view with the table-valued function (TVF) *sys.dm_exec_sql_text*. This is the query we use, which we refer to as the *usecount query:*

```
SELECT usecounts, cacheobjtype, objtype, [text]
FROM sys.dm_exec_cached_plans P
    CROSS APPLY sys.dm_exec_sql_text(plan_handle)
WHERE cacheobjtype = 'Compiled Plan'
    AND [text] NOT LIKE '%dm_exec_cached_plans%';
```

## Clearing Plan Cache

Because SQL Server 2008 has the potential to cache almost every query, the number of plans in cache can become quite large. There is a very efficient mechanism, described later in the chapter, for finding a plan in cache. There is not a direct performance penalty for having lots of cached plans, aside from the memory usage. However, if you have many very similar queries, the lookup time for SQL Server to find the right plan can sometimes be excessive. In addition, from a testing and troubleshooting standpoint, having lots of plans to look at can sometimes make it difficult to find just the plan in which we're currently interested. SQL Server provides a mechanism for clearing out all the plans in cache, and you probably want to do that occasionally on your test servers to keep the cache size manageable and easy to examine. You can use any of the following commands:

- **DBCC FREEPROCCACHE**   This command removes all cached plans from memory. SQL Server 2008 added the capability to add parameters to this command, to allow SQL Server to remove a specific plan from cache, all plans with the same *sql_handle* value, or all plans in a specific resource governor resource pool. I discuss the use of this procedure later in this chapter, when I discuss examining the contents of the plan cache.

- **DBCC FREESYSTEMCACHE**   This command clears out all SQL Server memory caches, in addition to the plan caches. I talk a bit more about the different memory caches in the section entitled "Cache Stores," later in this chapter.

- **DBCC FLUSHPROCINDB (<dbid>)**   This command allows you to specify a particular database ID, and then clears all plans from that particular database. Note that the *usecount* query that we use in this section does not return database ID information, but the *sys.dm_exec_sql_text* function has that information available, so dbid could be added to the *usecount* query.

**Tip** It is, of course, recommended that you don't use these commands on your production servers because it could affect the performance of your running applications. Usually, you want to keep plans in cache.

# Caching Mechanisms

SQL Server can avoid compilations of previously executed queries by using four mechanisms to make plan caching accessible in a wide set of situations:

- Adhoc query caching

- Autoparameterization

- Prepared queries, using either *sp_executesql* or the prepare and execute method invoked through your API

- Stored procedures or other compiled objects (triggers, TVFs, etc.)

To determine which mechanism is being used for each plan in cache, we need to look at the values in the *cacheobjtype* and *objtype* columns in the *sys.dm_exec_cached_plans* view. The *cacheobjtype* column can have one of six possible values:

- *Compiled Plan*

- *Compiled Plan Stub*

- *Parse Tree*

- *Extended Proc*

- *CLR Compiled Func*

- *CLR Compiled Proc*

In this section, the only values we are looking at are *Compiled Plan* and *Compiled Plan Stub*. Notice that I filter the *usecount* query to limit the results to rows with one of these values.

There are 11 different possible values for the *objtype* column:

- *Proc* (Stored procedure)

- *Prepared* (Prepared statement)

- *Adhoc* (Adhoc query)

- *ReplProc* (Replication-filter-procedure)

- *Trigger*

- *View*

- *Default (*Default constraint or default object)
- *UsrTab* (User table)
- *SysTab* (System table)
- *Check* (CHECK constraint)
- *Rule* (Rule object)

We are mainly examining the first three values, but many caching details that apply to stored procedures also apply to replication filter procedures and triggers.

## Adhoc Query Caching

If the caching metadata indicates a *cacheobjtype* value of *Compiled Plan* and an *objtype* value of *Adhoc*, the plan is considered to be an adhoc plan. Prior to SQL Server 2005, adhoc plans were cached occasionally, but it was not something on which you could depend. However, even when SQL Server caches your adhoc queries, you might not be able to depend on their reuse. When SQL Server caches the plan from an adhoc query, the cached plan is reused only if a subsequent batch matches exactly. This feature requires no extra work to use, but it is limited to *exact* textual matches. For example, if the following three queries are executed in the *Northwind2* database (which can be found on the companion Web site, *http://www.SQLServerInternals.com/companion*), the first and third queries use the same plan, but the second one needs to generate a new plan:

```
SELECT * FROM Orders WHERE CustomerID = 'HANAR';
SELECT * FROM Orders WHERE CustomerID = 'CHOPS';
SELECT * FROM Orders WHERE CustomerID = 'HANAR';
```

You can verify this by first clearing out the plan cache and then running the three queries in separate batches. Then run the *usecount* query referred to previously:

```
USE Northwind2;
DBCC FREEPROCCACHE;
GO
SELECT * FROM Orders WHERE CustomerID = 'HANAR';
GO
SELECT * FROM Orders WHERE CustomerID = 'CHOPS';
GO
SELECT * FROM Orders WHERE CustomerID = 'HANAR';
GO
SELECT usecounts, cacheobjtype, objtype, [text]
FROM sys.dm_exec_cached_plans P
    CROSS APPLY sys.dm_exec_sql_text (plan_handle)
WHERE cacheobjtype = 'Compiled Plan'
    AND [text] NOT LIKE '%dm_exec_cached_plans%';
```

You should get two rows back because the NOT LIKE condition filters out the row for the *usecount* query itself. The two rows are shown here and indicate that one plan was used only once, and the other was used twice:

| usecounts | cacheobjtype | objtype | text |
|-----------|--------------|---------|------|
| 1 | Compiled Plan | Adhoc | SELECT * FROM Orders WHERE CustomerID = 'CHOPS' |
| 2 | Compiled Plan | Adhoc | SELECT * FROM Orders WHERE CustomerID = 'HANAR' |

> **Note** The results shown in this section are obtained with the Optimize for Ad Hoc Workloads configuration option set to 0, which is the default value when you install SQL Server. I discuss this new SQL Server 2008 option later in this chapter.

The results show that with a change of the *CustomerID* value, the same plan cannot be reused. However, to take advantage of reuse of adhoc query plans, you need to make sure that not only are the same *CustomerID* values used in the queries, but also that the queries are identical, character for character. If one query has a new line or an extra space that another one doesn't have, they are not treated the same. If one query contains a comment that the other doesn't have, they are not identical. In addition, if one query uses a different case for either identifiers or keywords, even in a database with a case-insensitive collation, the queries are not the same. If you run the code here, you see that none of the queries can reuse the same plan:

```
USE Northwind2;
DBCC FREEPROCCACHE;
GO
SELECT * FROM orders WHERE customerID = 'HANAR';
GO
-- Try it again
SELECT * FROM orders WHERE customerID = 'HANAR';
GO
SELECT * FROM orders
WHERE customerID = 'HANAR';
GO
SELECT * FROM Orders WHERE CustomerID = 'HANAR';
GO
select * from orders where customerid = 'HANAR';
GO
SELECT usecounts, cacheobjtype, objtype, [text]
FROM sys.dm_exec_cached_plans P
    CROSS APPLY sys.dm_exec_sql_text (plan_handle)
WHERE cacheobjtype = 'Compiled Plan'
    AND [text] NOT LIKE '%dm_exec_cached_plans%';
```

Your results should show five rows in *sys.dm_exec_cached_plans*, each with a *usecounts* value of 1.

> **Note** The *SELECT* statements are all in their own batch, separated by GO. If there were no GOs, there would just be one batch, and each batch has its own plan containing the execution plan for each individual query within the batch. For reuse of adhoc query plans, the entire batch must be identical.

There are a few special kinds of statements that are always considered to be adhoc. These constructs include the following:

- A statement used with EXEC, as in EXEC('SELECT FirstName, LastName, Title FROM Employees WHERE EmployeeID = 6')

- A statement submitted using *sp_executesql*, if no parameters are supplied

Queries that you submit via your application with *sp_prepare* and *sp_prepexec* are not considered to be adhoc.

## Optimizing for Adhoc Workloads

If most of your queries are adhoc and never be reused, it might seem like a waste of memory to cache their execution plans. Later in this chapter, I talk about how the maximum size of plan cache is determined. It is true that having tens of thousands of cached plans for adhoc queries that have little likelihood of reuse is probably not the best use of SQL Server's memory. For this reason, SQL Server 2008 added a configuration option that you can enable in those cases where you expect most of your queries to be adhoc. Once this option is enabled, SQL Server caches only a stub of your query plan the first time any adhoc query is compiled, and only after a second compilation is the stub replaced with the full plan.

### Controlling the Optimize for Ad Hoc Workloads setting

Enabling the Optimize for Ad Hoc Workloads option is very straightforward, as shown in the following code:

```
EXEC sp_configure 'optimize for ad hoc workloads', 1;
RECONFIGURE;
```

You can also enable this option using SQL Server Management Studio, in the Advanced page of the Server Properties dialog box, as shown in Figure 9-1.

### The Compiled Plan Stub

The stub that SQL Server caches when Optimize for Ad Hoc Workloads is enabled is only about 300 bytes in size and does not contain any part of a query execution plan. It is basically only a placeholder to keep track of whether a particular query has been seen compiled previously. The stub contains the full cache key and a pointer to the actual query

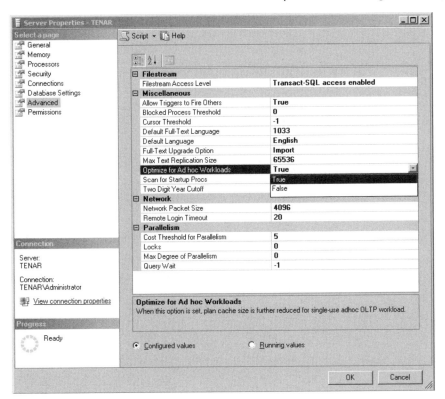

**FIGURE 9-1** Using the Server Properties dialog box in Management Studio to enable the Optimize for Ad Hoc Workloads option

text, which is stored in the SQL Manager cache. I discuss cache keys and the SQL Manager in the section entitled "Plan Cache Internals," later in this chapter. The *usecounts* value in the cache metadata is always 1 for compiled plan stubs because they are never reused.

When a query or batch that generated a compiled plan stub is recompiled, the stub is replaced with the full compiled plan. Initially, the *usecounts* value is set to 1 because there is no guarantee that the previous query had exactly the same execution plan. All that is known is that the query itself is the same. I will execute some of the same queries I used in the previous section after enabling the Optimize for Ad Hoc Workloads option, and we see what the *usecounts* query shows us. I need to modify my *usecounts* query slightly, and instead of looking for rows that have a *cacheobjtype* value of *Compiled Plan*, I look for *cacheobjtype* values that start with *Compiled Plan*:

```
EXEC sp_configure 'optimize for ad hoc workloads', 1;
RECONFIGURE;
GO
USE Northwind2;
DBCC FREEPROCCACHE;
GO
```

```
SELECT * FROM Orders WHERE CustomerID = 'HANAR';
GO
SELECT usecounts, cacheobjtype, objtype, [text]
FROM sys.dm_exec_cached_plans P
        CROSS APPLY sys.dm_exec_sql_text (plan_handle)
WHERE cacheobjtype LIKE 'Compiled Plan%'
        AND [text] NOT LIKE '%dm_exec_cached_plans%';
GO
SELECT * FROM Orders WHERE CustomerID = 'HANAR';
GO
SELECT usecounts, cacheobjtype, objtype, [text]
FROM sys.dm_exec_cached_plans P
        CROSS APPLY sys.dm_exec_sql_text (plan_handle)
WHERE cacheobjtype LIKE 'Compiled Plan%'
        AND [text] NOT LIKE '%dm_exec_cached_plans%';
GO
```

The first execution of the *usecounts* query returns the following:

| usecounts | cacheobjtype | objtype | text |
| --- | --- | --- | --- |
| 1 | Compiled Plan Stub | Adhoc | SELECT * FROM Orders WHERE CustomerID = 'HANAR' |

The second execution shows the replacement of the stub with the compiled plan:

| usecounts | cacheobjtype | objtype | text |
| --- | --- | --- | --- |
| 1 | Compiled Plan | Adhoc | SELECT * FROM Orders WHERE CustomerID = 'HANAR' |

The stub is generated when the plan is compiled, not when it is executed, so you would see this same behavior if you examined the query plan only twice with one of the SHOWPLAN options, without ever executing the query.

If the Optimize for Ad Hoc Workloads option is set to 1 and then is set back to 0 after Compiled Plan Stubs are placed in the plan cache, the stubs are not immediately removed from cache. As when the option was set to 1, any resubmission of the same adhoc T-SQL batch replaces the stub with the compiled plan, and then no further stubs are created.

Even with this new SQL Server 2008 mechanism for improving the caching behavior when your workloads use primarily adhoc queries, this does not mean that adhoc workloads are a good idea. There are times that you have no control over the kind of queries being submitted to your SQL Server, and in that case, you might find this option beneficial. However, if you and your developers have control over the how your queries are submitted, I recommend that you consider another options, such as Prepared Queries or stored procedures, which is discussed later in this chapter.

If you are running my sample queries as you are reading, you might want to turn off the Optimize for Ad Hoc Workloads option at this point:

```
EXEC sp_configure 'optimize for ad hoc workloads', 0;
RECONFIGURE;
GO
```

## Simple Parameterization

For certain queries, SQL Server can decide to treat one or more of the constants as parameters. When this happens, subsequent queries that follow the same basic template can use the same plan. For example, these two queries run in the *Northwind2* database can use the same plan:

```
SELECT FirstName, LastName, Title FROM Employees
WHERE EmployeeID = 6;
SELECT FirstName, LastName, Title FROM Employees
WHERE EmployeeID = 2;
```

Internally, SQL Server parameterizes these queries as follows:

```
SELECT FirstName, LastName, Title FROM Employees
WHERE EmployeeID = @1
```

You can observe this behavior by running the following code and observing the output of the *usecount* query:

```
USE Northwind2
GO
DBCC FREEPROCCACHE;
GO
SELECT FirstName, LastName, Title FROM Employees WHERE EmployeeID = 6;
GO
SELECT FirstName, LastName, Title FROM Employees WHERE EmployeeID = 2;
GO
SELECT usecounts, cacheobjtype, objtype, [text]
FROM sys.dm_exec_cached_plans P
    CROSS APPLY sys.dm_exec_sql_text (plan_handle)
WHERE cacheobjtype = 'Compiled Plan'
    AND [text] NOT LIKE '%dm_exec_cached_plans%';
GO
```

You should get three rows returned, similar to the following:

| usecounts | cacheobjtype | objtype | text |
|---|---|---|---|
| 1 | Compiled Plan | Adhoc | SELECT FirstName, LastName, Title FROM Employees WHERE EmployeeID = 2; |
| 1 | Compiled Plan | Adhoc | SELECT FirstName, LastName, Title FROM Employees WHERE EmployeeID = 6; |
| 2 | Compiled Plan | Prepared | (@1 tinyint)SELECT [FirstName], [LastName], [Title] FROM [Employees] WHERE [EmployeeID] = @1 |

You should notice that the two individual queries with their distinct constants get cached as adhoc queries. However, these are only considered *shell* queries and are cached only to make it easier to find the parameterized version of the query if the exact same query with the same constant is reused later. These shell queries do not contain the full execution plan but only a pointer to the full plan in the corresponding prepared plan.

> **Tip** Do not confuse a shell query with a plan stub. A shell query contains the complete text of the query, and uses at least 16 KB of memory. Shell queries are created only for those plans that SQL Server thinks are parameterizable. A plan stub, as mentioned previously, only uses about 200 bytes of memory, and is created only for unparameterizable, adhoc queries, and only when the Optimize for Ad Hoc Workloads option is set to 1.

In the output shown previously, the third row returned from *sys.dm_exec_cached_plans* has an *objtype* value of *Prepared*. (The order of the returned rows is not guaranteed. You should have two rows with a *cacheobjtype* value of *Adhoc* and one row with a *cacheobjtype* value of *Prepared*.) The query plan is associated with the prepared plan, and you can observe that the plan was used twice. In addition, the text for that *Prepared* row shows a parameter in place of a constant.

By default, SQL Server is very conservative about deciding when to parameterize automatically. SQL Server automatically parameterizes queries only if the query template is considered to be *safe*. A template is safe if the plan selected does not change even if the actual parameter values change. This ensures that the parameterization won't degrade a query's performance. The *employees* table used in the previous queries has a unique index, so any query that has an equality comparison on *employeeID* is guaranteed to never find more than one row. A plan using a seek on that unique index can be useful no matter what actual value is used.

However, consider a query that has either an inequality comparison or an equality comparison on a nonunique column. In those situations, some actual values may return many rows, and others return no rows, or only one. A nonclustered index seek might be a good choice when only a few rows are returned, but it might be a terrible choice when many rows are returned. So a query for which there is more than one possible best plan, depending on the value used in the query, is not considered safe, and it is not parameterized. By default, the only way for SQL Server to reuse a plan for such a query is to use the adhoc plan caching described in the previous section (which does not happen if the constant values in the query are different).

In addition to requiring that there only be one possible plan for a query template, there are many query constructs that normally disallow simple parameterization. Such constructs include any statements with the following elements:

- *JOIN*
- *BULK INSERT*
- *IN* lists
- *UNION*
- *INTO*

- *FOR BROWSE*

- *OPTION* <query hints>

- *DISTINCT*

- *TOP*

- *WAITFOR* statements

- *GROUP BY, HAVING, COMPUTE*

- Full-text predicates

- Subqueries

- FROM clause of a *SELECT* statement has a table-valued method or full-text table or *OPENROWSET* or *OPENXML* or *OPENQUERY* or *OPENDATASOURCE*

- Comparison predicate of the form EXPR <> a non-null constant

Simple parameterization is also disallowed for data modification statements that use the following constructs:

- *DELETE/UPDATE* with a FROM clause

- *UPDATE* with a SET clause that has variables

## Forced Parameterization

If your application uses many similar queries that you know benefit from the same plan but are not autoparameterized, either because SQL Server doesn't consider the plans safe or because they use one of the disallowed constructs, SQL Server 2008 provides an alternative. A database option called PARAMETERIZATION FORCED can be enabled with the following command:

```
ALTER DATABASE <database_name> SET PARAMETERIZATION FORCED;
```

Once this option is enabled, SQL Server treats constants as parameters, with only a very few exceptions. These exceptions, as listed in *SQL Server Books Online,* include the following:

- *INSERT . . . EXECUTE* statements.

- Statements inside the bodies of stored procedures, triggers, or user-defined functions. SQL Server already reuses query plans for these routines.

- Prepared statements that have already been parameterized on the client-side application.

- Statements that contain XQuery method calls, in which the method appears in a context in which its arguments would typically be parameterized, such as a WHERE clause. If the method appears in a context in which its arguments would not be parameterized, the rest of the statement is parameterized.

- Statements inside a T-SQL cursor. (*SELECT* statements inside API cursors are parameterized.)

- Deprecated query constructs.

- Any statement that is run in the context of ANSI_PADDING or ANSI_NULLS set to OFF.

- Statements that contain more than 2,097 literals.

- Statements that reference variables, such as WHERE  T.col2  >=  @p.

- Statements that contain the RECOMPILE query hint.

- Statements that contain a COMPUTE clause.

- Statements that contain a WHERE CURRENT OF clause.

You need to be careful when setting this option on for the entire database because assuming that all constants should be treated as parameters during optimization and then reusing existing plans frequently gives very poor performance. An alternative that allows only selected queries to be autoparameterized is to use plan guides, which are discussed at the end of this chapter. In addition, plan guides can also be used to override forced parameterization for selected queries, if the database has been set to PARAMETERIZATION FORCED.

## Drawbacks of Simple Parameterization

A feature of autoparameterization that you might have noticed in the output from the *usecount* query shown previously is that SQL Server makes its own decision as to the data type of the parameter, which might not be the data type you think should be used. In the earlier example, looking at the *employees* table, SQL Server chose to assume a parameter of type *tinyint*. If we rerun the batch and use a value that doesn't fit into the *tinyint* range (that is, a value less than 0 or larger than 255), SQL Server cannot use the same autoparameterized query. The batch below autoparameterizes both *SELECT* statements, but it is not able to use the same plan for both queries. The output from the *usecount* query should show two adhoc shell queries, and two prepared queries. One prepared query has a parameter of type *tinyint,* and the other is *smallint.* As strange as it may seem, even if you switch the order of the queries and use the bigger value first, you get two prepared queries with two different parameter data types:

```
USE Northwind2;
GO
DBCC FREEPROCCACHE;
GO
SELECT FirstName, LastName, Title FROM Employees WHERE EmployeeID = 6;
GO
SELECT FirstName, LastName, Title FROM Employees WHERE EmployeeID = 622;
GO
SELECT usecounts, cacheobjtype, objtype, [text]
FROM sys.dm_exec_cached_plans P
    CROSS APPLY sys.dm_exec_sql_text (plan_handle)
WHERE cacheobjtype = 'Compiled Plan'
    AND [text] NOT LIKE '%dm_exec_cached_plans%';
GO
```

The only way to force SQL Server to use the same data type for both queries is to enable PARAMETERIZATION FORCED for the database.

As mentioned, simple parameterization is not always appropriate, which is why SQL Server is so conservative in choosing to use it. Consider the following example. The *BigOrders* table in the *Northwind2* database has 4,150 rows and 105 pages, so we might expect that a table scan reading 105 pages would be the worst possible performance for any query accessing the *BigOrders* table. There is a nonclustered nonunique index on the *CustomerID* column. If we enable forced parameterization for the *Northwind2* database, the plan used for the first *SELECT* is also used for the second *SELECT*, even though the constants are different. The first query returns 5 rows and the second returns 155. Normally, a nonclustered index seek would be chosen for the first *SELECT* and a clustered index scan for the second because the number of qualifying rows exceeds the number of pages in the table. However, with PARAMETERIZATION FORCED, that's not what we get, as you can see when you run the following code:

```
USE Northwind2;
GO
ALTER DATABASE Northwind2 SET PARAMETERIZATION FORCED;
GO
SET STATISTICS IO ON;
GO
DBCC FREEPROCCACHE;
GO
SELECT * FROM BigOrders WHERE CustomerID = 'CENTC'
GO
SELECT * FROM BigOrders WHERE CustomerID = 'SAVEA'
GO
SELECT usecounts, cacheobjtype, objtype, [text]
FROM sys.dm_exec_cached_plans P
    CROSS APPLY sys.dm_exec_sql_text (plan_handle)
WHERE cacheobjtype = 'Compiled Plan'
    AND [text] NOT LIKE '%dm_exec_cached_plans%';
GO
ALTER DATABASE Northwind2 SET PARAMETERIZATION SIMPLE;
GO
```

When we run this code, we see that the first *SELECT* required 12 logical reads and the second required 312, almost three times as many reads as would have been required if scanning the table. The output of the *usecount* query, shown here, shows that forced parameterization was applied and the parameterized prepared plan was used twice:

| usecounts | cacheobjtype | objtype | text |
|---|---|---|---|
| 1 | Compiled Plan | Adhoc | SELECT * FROM BigOrders WHERE CustomerID = 'SAVEA' |
| 1 | Compiled Plan | Adhoc | SELECT * FROM BigOrders WHERE CustomerID = 'CENTC' |
| 2 | Compiled Plan | Prepared | (@0 varchar(8000))select * from BigOrders where CustomerID = @0 |

In this example, forcing SQL Server to treat the constant as a parameter is not a good thing, and the batch sets the database back to PARAMETERIZATION SIMPLE (the default) as the last step. Note also that while we are using PARAMETERIZATION FORCED, the data type chosen for the parameterized query is the largest possible regular character data type.

So what can you do if you have many queries that should not be parameterized and many others that should be? As we've seen, the SQL Server query processor is much more conservative about deciding whether a template is safe than an application can be. SQL Server guesses which values are really parameters, whereas your application developers should actually know. Rather than rely on SQL Server to parameterize your queries automatically, you can use one of the prepared query mechanisms to mark values as parameters when they are known.

The SQL Server Performance Monitor includes an object called *SQLServer:SQL Statistics* that has several counters dealing with automatic parameterization. You can monitor these counters to determine whether there are many unsafe or failed automatic parameterization attempts. If these numbers are high, you can inspect your applications for situations in which the application developers can take responsibility for explicitly marking the parameters.

## Prepared Queries

As we saw previously, a query that is parameterized by SQL Server shows an *objtype* of *Prepared* in the cached plan metadata. There are two other constructs that have prepared plans. Both of these constructs allow the programmer to take control over which values are parameters and which aren't. In addition, unlike with simple parameterization, the programmer also determines the data type that be used for the parameters. One construct is the SQL Server stored procedure *sp_executesql*, which is called from within a T-SQL batch, and the other is to use the prepare and execute method from the client application.

### The *sp_executesql* Procedure

The stored procedure *sp_executesql* is halfway between adhoc caching and stored procedures. Using *sp_executesql* requires that you identify the parameters and their data types, but it doesn't require all the persistent object management needed for stored procedures and other programmed objects.

Here's the general syntax for the procedure:

```
sp_executesql @batch_text, @batch_parameter_definitions,
   param1,...paramN
```

Repeated calls with the same values for *@batch_text* and *@batch_parameter_definitions* use the same cached plan, with the new parameter values specified. The plan is reused so long as the plan has not been removed from cache and is still valid. The section entitled "Causes of Recompilation," later in this chapter, discusses those situations in which SQL Server determines that a plan is no longer valid. The same cached plan can be used for all the following queries:

```
EXEC sp_executesql N'SELECT FirstName, LastName, Title
    FROM Employees
    WHERE EmployeeID = @p', N'@p tinyint', 6;
EXEC sp_executesql N'SELECT FirstName, LastName, Title
    FROM Employees
    WHERE EmployeeID = @p', N'@p tinyint', 2;
EXEC sp_executesql N'SELECT FirstName, LastName, Title
    FROM Employees
    WHERE EmployeeID = @p', N'@p tinyint', 6;
```

Just like forcing autoparameterization, using *sp_executesql* to force reuse of a plan is not always appropriate. If we take the same example used earlier when we set the database to PARAMETERIZATION FORCED, we can see that using *sp_executesql* is just as inappropriate.

```
USE Northwind2;
GO
SET STATISTICS IO ON;
GO
DBCC FREEPROCCACHE;
GO
EXEC sp_executesql N'SELECT * FROM BigOrders
    WHERE CustomerID = @p', N'@p nvarchar(10)', 'CENTC';
GO
EXEC sp_executesql N'SELECT * FROM BigOrders
    WHERE CustomerID = @p', N'@p nvarchar(10)', 'SAVEA';
GO
SELECT usecounts, cacheobjtype, objtype, [text]
FROM sys.dm_exec_cached_plans P
    CROSS APPLY sys.dm_exec_sql_text (plan_handle)
WHERE cacheobjtype = 'Compiled Plan'
    AND [text] NOT LIKE '%dm_exec_cached_plans%';
GO
SET STATISTICS IO OFF;
GO
```

Again, we can see that the first *SELECT* required 12 logical reads and the second required 312. The output of the *usecount* query, seen here, shows the parameterized query being used twice. Note that with *sp_executesql*, we do not have any entries for the adhoc (unparameterized) shell queries.

| usecounts | cacheobjtype | objtype | text |
| --- | --- | --- | --- |
| 2 | Compiled Plan | Prepared | (@p nvarchar(10))SELECT * FROM BigOrders WHERE CustomerID = @p |

## The Prepare and Execute Method

This last mechanism is like *sp_executesql* in that parameters to the batch are identified by the application, but there are some key differences. The prepare and execute method does not require the full text of the batch to be sent at each execution. Rather, the full text is sent once at prepare time; a handle that can be used to invoke the batch at execute time is returned. ODBC and OLE DB expose this functionality via *SQLPrepare/SQLExecute* and *ICommandPrepare*. You can also use this mechanism via ODBC and OLE DB when cursors are involved. When you use these functions, SQL Server is informed that this batch is meant to be used repeatedly.

### Caching Prepared Queries

If your queries have been parameterized at the client using the prepare and execute method, the metadata shows you prepared queries, just as for queries that are parameterized at the server, either automatically or by using *sp_executesql*. However, queries that are not parameterized (either under simple or forced parameterization) do not have any corresponding adhoc shell queries in cache, containing the unparameterized actual values; they have only the prepared plans. There is no guaranteed way to detect whether a prepared plan was prepared by SQL Server using simple or forced parameterization or by the developer through client-side parameterization. If you see a corresponding shell query, you can know that the query was parameterized by SQL Server, but the opposite is not always true. Because the shell queries have zero cost, they are among the first candidates to be removed when SQL Server is under memory pressure. So a lack of a shell query might just mean that adhoc plan was already removed from cache, not that there never was a shell query.

## Compiled Objects

When looking at the metadata in *sys.dm_exec_cached_plans*, we've seen compiled plans with *objtype* values of *Adhoc* and *Prepared*. The third *objtype* value that we will be discussing is *Proc*, and you will see this type used when executing stored procedures, user-defined scalar functions, and multistatement TVFs. With these objects, you have full control over what values are parameters and what their data types are when executing these objects.

### Stored Procedures

Stored procedures and user-defined scalar functions are treated almost identically. The metadata indicates that a compiled plan with an *objtype* value of *Proc* is cached and can be reused repeatedly. By default, the cached plan is reused for all successive executions, and as we've seen with the *sp_executesql*, this is not always desirable. However, unlike the plans cached and reused with *sp_executesql*, you have an option with stored procedures and user-defined scalar functions to force recompilation when the object is executed. In addition, for stored procedures, you can create the object so that a new plan is created every single time it is executed.

To force recompilation for a single execution, you can use the EXECUTE . . . WITH RECOMPILE option. Here is an example in the *Northwind2* database of forcing recompilation for a stored procedure:

```
USE Northwind2;
GO
CREATE PROCEDURE P_Customers
  @cust nvarchar(10)
AS
  SELECT RowNum, CustomerID, OrderDate, ShipCountry
  FROM BigOrders
WHERE CustomerID = @cust;
GO
```

```
DBCC FREEPROCCACHE;
GO
SET STATISTICS IO ON;
GO
EXEC P_Customers 'CENTC';
GO
EXEC P_Customers 'SAVEA';
GO
EXEC P_Customers 'SAVEA' WITH RECOMPILE;
```

If you look at the output from STATISTICS IO, you see that the second execution used a suboptimal plan that required more pages to be read than would be needed by a table scan. This is the situation that you may have seen referred to as *parameter sniffing*. SQL Server is basing the plan for the procedure on the first actual parameter, in this case, *CENTC,* and then subsequent executions assume the same or a similar parameter is used. The third execution uses the WITH RECOMPILE option to force SQL Server to come up with a new plan, and you should see that the number of logical page reads is equal to the number of pages in the table.

If you look at the results from running the *usecounts* query, shown here, you should see that the cached plan for the *P_Customers* procedure has a *usecounts* value of 2, instead of 3.

| usecounts | cacheobjtype | objtype | text |
|---|---|---|---|
| 2 | Compiled Plan | Proc | CREATE PROCEDURE P_Customers @cust nvarchar(10) AS SELECT RowNum, CustomerID, OrderDate, ShipCountry FROM BigOrders WHERE CustomerID = @cust |

The plan developed for a procedure executed with the WITH RECOMPILE option is considered valid only for the current execution; it is never kept in cache for reuse.

## Functions

User-defined scalar functions can behave exactly the same way as procedures. If you execute them using the *EXECUTE* statement instead of as part of an expression, you can also force recompilation. Here is an example of a function that masks part of a Social Security number. We create it in the *pubs* sample database because the *authors* table contains a Social Security number in the *au_id* column:

```
USE pubs;
GO
CREATE FUNCTION dbo.fnMaskSSN (@ssn char(11))
RETURNS char(11)
AS
BEGIN
  SELECT @SSN = 'xxx-xx-' + right (@ssn,4);
  RETURN @SSN;
END;
GO
```

```
DBCC FREEPROCCACHE;
GO

DECLARE @mask char(11);
EXEC @mask = dbo.fnMaskSSN '123-45-6789';
SELECT @mask;
GO
DECLARE @mask char(11);
EXEC @mask = dbo.fnMaskSSN '123-66-1111';
SELECT @mask;
GO
DECLARE @mask char(11);
EXEC @mask = dbo.fnMaskSSN '123-66-1111' WITH RECOMPILE;
SELECT @mask;
GO
```

If you run the *usecounts* query, you should notice the cached plan for the function has an *objtype* of *Proc* and has a *usecounts* value of 2. If a scalar function is used within an expression, as in the example here, there is no way to request recompilation:

```
SELECT dbo.fnMaskSSN(au_id), au_lname, au_fname, au_id  FROM authors;
```

TVFs may or may not be treated like procedures depending on how you define them. You can define a TVF as an inline function or as a multistatement function. Neither method allows you to force recompilation when the function is called. Here are two functions that do the same thing:

```
USE Northwind2;
GO
CREATE FUNCTION Fnc_Inline_Customers (@cust nvarchar(10))
RETURNS TABLE
AS
 RETURN
 (SELECT RowNum, CustomerID, OrderDate, ShipCountry
 FROM BigOrders
 WHERE CustomerID = @cust);
GO

CREATE FUNCTION Fnc_Multi_Customers (@cust nvarchar(10))
RETURNS @T TABLE (RowNum int, CustomerID nchar(10), OrderDate datetime,
 ShipCountry nvarchar(30))
AS
BEGIN
 INSERT INTO @T
  SELECT RowNum, CustomerID, OrderDate, ShipCountry
  FROM BigOrders
  WHERE CustomerID = @cust
  RETURN
END;
GO
```

Here are the calls to the functions:

```
DBCC FREEPROCCACHE
GO
```

```
SELECT * FROM Fnc_Multi_Customers('CENTC');
GO
SELECT * FROM Fnc_Inline_Customers('CENTC');
GO
SELECT * FROM Fnc_Multi_Customers('SAVEA');
GO
SELECT * FROM Fnc_Inline_Customers('SAVEA');
GO
```

If you run the *usecounts* query, you see that only the multistatement function has its plan reused. The inline function is actually treated like a view, and the only way the plan can be reused would be if the exact same query were reexecuted; that is, if the same *SELECT* statement called the function with the exact same parameter.

# Causes of Recompilation

Up to this point, we've been discussing the situations in which SQL Server automatically reuses a plan, and the situation in which a plan may be reused inappropriately so that you need to force recompilation. However, there are also situations in which an existing plan is not reused because of changes to the underlying objects or the execution environment. The reasons for these unexpected recompilations fall into one of two different categories, which we call *correctness-based recompiles* and *optimality-based recompiles*.

## Correctness-Based Recompiles

SQL Server may choose to recompile a plan if it has a reason to suspect that the existing plan may no longer be correct. This can happen when there are explicit changes to the underlying objects, such as changing a data type or dropping an index. Obviously, any existing plan that referenced the column assuming its former data type or that accessed data using the now nonexistent index would not be correct. Correctness-based recompiles fall into two general categories: schema changes and environmental changes. The following changes mark an object's schema as changed:

- Adding or dropping columns to or from a table or view

- Adding or dropping constraints, defaults, or rules to or from a table

- Adding an index to a table or an indexed view

- Dropping an index defined on a table or an indexed view if the index is used by the plan

- Dropping a statistic defined on a table that causes a correctness-related recompilation of any query plans that use that table

- Adding or dropping a trigger from a table

In addition, running the procedure *sp_recompile* on a table or view changes the modification date for the object, which you can observe in the *modify_date* column in *sys.objects*. This makes SQL Server determine that a schema change has occurred so that recompilation takes place at the next execution of any stored procedure, function, or trigger that accesses the table or view. Running *sp_recompile* on a procedure, trigger, or function clears all the plans for the executable object out of cache to guarantee that the next time it is executed, it will be recompiled.

Other correctness-based recompiles are invoked when the environment changes by changing one of a list of SET options. Changes in certain SET options can cause a query to return different results, so when one of these values changes, SQL Server wants to make sure a plan is used that was created in a similar environment. SQL Server keeps track of which SET options are set when a plan is executed, and you have access to a bitmap of these SET options using the DMF called *sys.dm_exec_plan_attributes*. This function is called by passing in a plan handle value that you can obtain from the *sys.dm_exec_cached_plans* view and returns one row for each of a list of plan attributes. You need to make sure you include *plan_handle* in the list of columns to be retrieved, not just the few columns we used earlier in the *usecounts* query. Here's an example of retrieving all the plan attributes when we supply a *plan_handle* value. Table 9-1 shows the results of running this code:

```
SELECT * FROM sys.dm_exec_plan_attributes
(0x06001200CF0B831CB821AA05000000000000000000000000)
```

Later in the chapter, when we explore cache management and caching internals, you learn about some of these values in which the meaning is not obvious and I also go into more detail about the metadata that keeps track of your plans. To get the attributes to be returned in a row along with each *plan_handle*, you can use the PIVOT operator and list each of the attributes that you want to turn into a column. In this next query, we want to retrieve the *set_options*, the *object_id,* and the *sql_handle* from the list of attributes:

```
SELECT plan_handle, pvt.set_options, pvt.object_id, pvt.sql_handle
FROM (SELECT plan_handle, epa.attribute, epa.value
        FROM sys.dm_exec_cached_plans
            OUTER APPLY sys.dm_exec_plan_attributes(plan_handle) AS epa
        WHERE cacheobjtype = 'Compiled Plan'
    ) AS ecpa
PIVOT (MAX(ecpa.value) FOR ecpa.attribute
    IN ("set_options", "object_id", "sql_handle")) AS pvt;
```

We get a value of 4347 for *set_options* which is equivalent to the bit string 1000011111011. To see which bit refers to which SET options, we could change one option and then see how the bits have changed. For example, if we clear the plan cache and change ANSI_NULLS to OFF, the *set_options* value change to 4315, or binary 1000011011011. The difference is the sixth bit from the right, which has a value of 32, the difference between 4347 and 4315. If we didn't clear the plan cache, we would end up with two plans for the same batch, one for each *set_options* value.

**TABLE 9-1 Attributes Corresponding to a Particular *plan_handle***

| Attribute | Value | is_cache_key |
|---|---|---|
| set_options | 4347 | 1 |
| objectid | 478350287 | 1 |
| dbid | 18 | 1 |
| dbid_execute | 0 | 1 |
| user_id | -2 | 1 |
| language_id | 0 | 1 |
| date_format | 1 | 1 |
| date_first | 7 | 1 |
| Compat_level | 100 | 1 |
| status | 0 | 1 |
| required_cursor_options | 0 | 1 |
| acceptable_cursor_options | 0 | 1 |
| merge_action_type | 0 | 1 |
| is_replication_specific | 0 | 1 |
| optional_spid | 0 | 1 |
| optional_clr_trigger_dbid | 0 | 1 |
| optional_clr_trigger_objid | 0 | 1 |
| inuse_exec_context | 0 | 0 |
| free_exec_context | 1 | 0 |
| hits_exec_context | 0 | 0 |
| misses_exec_context | 0 | 0 |
| removed_exec_context | 0 | 0 |
| inuse_cursors | 0 | 0 |
| free_cursors | 0 | 0 |
| hits_cursors | 0 | 0 |
| misses_cursors | 0 | 0 |
| removed_cursors | 0 | 0 |
| sql_handle | 0x02000000CF0B831CBBE70632EC8A 8F7828AD6E6 | 0 |

Not all changes to SET options cause a recompile, although many of them do. The following is a list of the SET options that cause a recompile when changed:

- ANSI_NULL_DFLT_OFF

- ANSI_NULL_DFLT_ON

- ANSI_NULLS

- ANSI_PADDING

- ANSI_WARNINGS
- ARITHABORT
- CONCAT_NULL_YIELDS_NULL
- DATEFIRST
- DATEFORMAT
- FORCEPLAN
- LANGUAGE
- NO_BROWSETABLE
- NUMERIC_ROUNDABORT
- QUOTED_IDENTIFIER

Two of the SET options in this list have a special behavior in relationship to objects, including stored procedures, functions, views, and triggers. The SET option settings for ANSI_NULLS and QUOTED_IDENTIFIER are actually saved along with the object definition and the procedure or function always executes with the SET values as they were when the object was first created. You can determine what values these two SET options had for your objects by selecting from the *OBJECTPROPERTY* function, as shown:

```
SELECT OBJECTPROPERTY(object_id('<object name>'), 'ExecIsQuotedIdentOn');
SELECT OBJECTPROPERTY(object_id('<object name>'), 'ExecIsAnsiNullsOn');
```

A returned value of 0 means the SET option is OFF, a value of 1 means the option is ON, and a value of *NULL* means that you typed something incorrectly or that you don't have appropriate permissions. However, even though changing the value of either of these options does not cause any difference in execution of the objects, SQL Server may still recompile the statement that accesses the object. The only objects for which recompilation is avoided is for cached plans with an *objtype* value of *Proc*, namely stored procedures and multistatement TVFs. For these compiled objects, the *usecounts* query shows you the same plan being reused and does not show additional plans with different *set_options* values. Inline TVFs and views create new plans if these options are changed, and the *set_options* value indicates a different bitmap. However, the behavior of the underlying *SELECT* statement does not change.

## Optimality-Based Recompiles

SQL Server may also choose to recompile a plan if it has reason to suspect that the existing plan is no longer optimal. The primary reasons for suspecting a nonoptimal plan deal with changes to the underlying data. If any of the statistics used to generate the query plan have been updated since the plan was created, or if any of the statistics are considered stale, SQL Server recompiles the query plan.

**Updated Statistics**   Statistics can be updated either manually or automatically. Manual updates happen when someone runs *sp_updatestats* or the *UPDATE STATISTICS* command. Automatic updates happen when SQL Server determines that existing statistics are out of date or stale, and these updates happen only when the database has the option AUTO_UPDATE_STATISTICS or AUTO_UPDATE_STATISTICS_ASYNC set to ON. This could happen if another batch had tried to use one of the same tables or indexes used in the current plan, detected the statistics were stale, and initiated an *UPDATE STATISTICS* operation.

**Stale Statistics**   SQL Server detects out-of-date statistics when it is first compiling a batch that has no plan in cache. It also detects stale statistics for existing plans. Figure 9-2 shows a flowchart of the steps involved in finding an existing plan and checking to see if recompilation

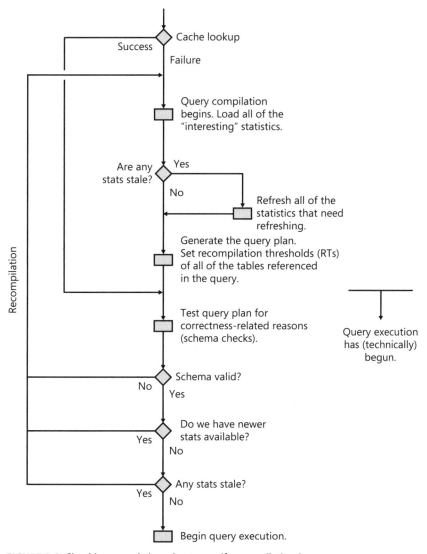

**FIGURE 9-2** Checking an existing plan to see if recompilation is necessary

is required. You can see that SQL Server checks for stale statistics after checking to see if there already are updated statistics available. If there are stale statistics, the statistics are updated, and then a recompile begins on the batch. If AUTO_UPDATE_STATISTICS_ASYNC is ON for the database, SQL Server does not wait for the update of statistics to complete; it just recompiles based on the stale statistics.

Statistics are considered to be stale if a sufficient number of modifications have occurred on the column supporting the statistics. Each table has a recompilation threshold (RT) that determines how many changes can take place before any statistics on that table are marked as stale. The RT values for all the tables referenced in a batch are stored with the query plans of that batch.

The RT values depend on the type of table, that is, whether it is permanent or temporary, and on the current number of rows in the table at the time a plan is compiled. The exact algorithms for determining the RT values are subject to change with each service pack, so I show you the algorithm for the RTM release of SQL Server 2008. The formulas used in the various service packs will be similar to this, but are not guaranteed to be exactly the same. $N$ indicates the cardinality of the table.

- For both permanent and temporary tables, if $N$ is less or equal to 500, the RT value is 500. This means that for a relatively small table, you must make at least 500 changes to trigger recompilation. For larger tables, at least 500 changes must be made, plus 20 percent of the number of rows.

- For temporary tables, the algorithm is the same, with one exception. If the table is very small or empty ($N$ is less than six prior to any data modification operations), all we need are six changes to trigger a recompile. This means that a procedure that creates a temporary table, which is empty when created, and then inserts six or more rows into that table, will have to be recompiled as soon as the temporary table is accessed.

  You can get around this frequent recompilation of batches that create temporary tables by using the KEEP PLAN query hint. Use of this hint changes the recompilation thresholds for temporary tables and makes them identical to those for permanent tables. So if changes to temporary tables are causing many recompilations, and you suspect that the recompilations are affecting overall system performance, you can use this hint and see if there is a performance improvement. The hint can be specified as shown in this query:

  ```
  SELECT <column list>
  FROM dbo.PermTable A INNER JOIN #TempTable B ON A.col1 = B.col2
  WHERE <filter conditions>
  OPTION (KEEP PLAN)
  ```

- For table variables, there is no RT value. This means that you will not get recompilations caused by changes in the number of rows in a table variable.

**Modification Counters**   The RT values discussed here are the number of changes required for SQL Server to recognize that statistics are stale. In versions of SQL Server prior to SQL

Server 2005, the *sysindexes* system table keeps track of the number of changes that had actually occurred in a table in a column called *rowmodctr*. These counters keep track of any changes in any row of the table or index, even if the change was to a column that was not involved in any index or useful statistics. SQL Server 2008 now uses a set of Column Modification Counters or *colmodctr* values, with a separate count being maintained for each column in a table, except for computed nonpersisted columns. These counters are not transactional, which means that if a transaction starts, inserts thousands of rows into a table, and then is rolled back, the changes to the modification counters are *not* rolled back. Unlike the *rowmodctr* values in *sysindexes*, the *colmodctr* values are not visible to the user. They are only available internally to the Query Optimizer.

**Tracking Changes to Tables and Indexed Views Using *colmodctr* Values**   The *colmodctr* values that SQL Server keeps track of are continually modified as the table data changes. Table 9-2 describes when and how the *colmodctr* values are modified based on changes to your data, including *INSERT, UPDATE, DELETE, BULK INSERT,* and *TRUNCATE TABLE* operations. Although we are only mentioning table modifications specifically, keep in mind the same *colmodctr* values are kept track of for indexed views.

**TABLE 9-2 Factors Affecting Changes to the Internal *colmodctr* Values**

| Statement | Changes to *colmodctr* Values |
| --- | --- |
| *INSERT* | All *colmodctr* values increased by 1 for each row inserted. |
| *DELETE* | All *colmodctr* values increased by 1 for each row deleted. |
| *UPDATE* | If the update is to nonkey columns: *colmodctr* values for modified columns are increased by 1 for each row updated. If the update is to key columns: *colmodctr* values are increased by 2 for *all* the columns in the table, for each row updated. |
| *BULK INSERT* | Treated like *N INSERT* operations. All *colmodctr* values increased by *N* where *N* is the number of rows bulk inserted. |
| *TRUNCATE TABLE* | Treated like *N DELETE* operations. All *colmodctr* values increased by *N* where *N* is the table's cardinality. |

## Skipping the Recompilation Step

There are several situations in which SQL Server bypasses recompiling a statement for plan optimality reasons. These include the following:

- When the plan is a trivial plan. A trivial plan is one for which there are no alternative plans, based on the tables referenced by the query, and the indexes (or lack of indexes) on those tables. In these cases, where there really is only one way to process a query, any recompilation would be a waste of resources, no matter how much the statistics had changed. Keep in mind that there is no assurance that a query will continue to have a trivial plan just because it originally had a trivial plan. If new indexes have been added since the query was last compiled, there may now be multiple possible ways to process the query.

- If the query contains the OPTION hint KEEPFIXED PLAN, SQL Server will not recompile the plan for any optimality-related reasons.

- If automatic updates of statistics for indexes and statistics defined on a table or indexed view are disabled, all plan optimality-related recompilations caused by those indexes or statistics will stop.

> **Caution**  Turning off the auto-statistics feature is usually not a good idea because the Query Optimizer would no longer be sensitive to data changes in those objects, and suboptimal query plans could easily result. You can consider using this technique only as a last resort after exhausting all of the other alternative ways to avoid recompilation. Make sure you thoroughly test your applications after changing the auto-statistics options to verify that you are not hurting performance in other areas.

- If all the tables referenced in the query are read-only, SQL Server will not recompile the plan.

## Multiple Recompilations

In the previous discussion of unplanned recompilation, we primarily described situations in which a cached plan would be recompiled prior to execution. However, even if SQL Server calculates that it can reuse an existing plan, there may be cases where stale statistics or schema changes are discovered after the batch begins execution, and then a recompile occurs after execution starts. Each batch or stored procedure can contain multiple query plans, one for each optimizable statement. Before SQL Server begins executing any of the individual query plans, it checks for correctness and optimality of that plan. If one of the checks fails, the corresponding statement is compiled *again*, and a possibly different query plan is produced.

In some cases, query plans may be recompiled even if the plan for the batch was not cached. For example, if a batch contains a literal larger than 8 KB, it is never cached. However, if this batch creates a temporary table, and then inserts multiple rows into that table, the insertion of the seventh row causes a recompilation because of passing the recompilation threshold for temporary tables. Because of the large literal, the batch was not cached, but the currently executing plan needs to be recompiled.

In SQL Server 2000, when a batch was recompiled, *all* the statements in the batch were recompiled, not just the one that initiated the recompilation. SQL Server 2005 introduced statement-level recompilation, which means that only the statement that causes the recompilation has a new plan created, not the entire batch. This means that SQL Server spends less CPU time and memory during recompilations.

## Removing Plans from Cache

In addition to needing to recompile a plan based on schema or statistics changes, SQL Server needs to compile plans for batches if all previous plans have been removed from the plan cache. Plans are removed from cache based on memory pressure, which we talk about in the section entitled "Cache Size Management," later in this chapter. However, other operations can cause plans to be removed from cache. Some of these operations remove all the plans from a particular database, and others remove all the plans for the entire SQL Server instance.

The following operations flush the entire plan cache so that all batches submitted afterwards will need a fresh plan. Note that although some of these operations affect only a single database, the entire plan cache is cleared.

- Upgrading any database to SQL Server 2008
- Running the *DBCC FREEPROCCACHE* or *DBCC FREESYSTEMCACHE* commands
- Changing any of the following configuration options:
  - cross db ownership chaining
  - index create memory
  - cost threshold for parallelism
  - max degree of parallelism
  - max text repl size
  - min memory per query
  - min server memory
  - max server memory
  - query governor cost limit
  - query wait
  - remote query timeout
  - user options

The following operations clear all plans associated with a particular database:

- Running the *DBCC FLUSHPROCINDB* command
- Detaching a database
- Closing or opening an auto-close database
- Modifying a collation for a database using the *ALTER DATABASE . . . COLLATE* command
- Altering a database with any of the following commands:
  - *ALTER DATABASE . . . MODIFY_NAME*
  - *ALTER DATABASE . . . MODIFY FILEGROUP*
  - *ALTER DATABASE . . . SET ONLINE*
  - *ALTER DATABASE . . . SET OFFLINE*
  - *ALTER DATABASE . . . SET EMERGENCY*

       ❏ *ALTER DATABASE . . . SET READ_ONLY*

       ❏ *ALTER DATABASE . . . SET READ_WRITE*

       ❏ *ALTER DATABASE . . . COLLATE*

■ Dropping a database

Clearing a single plan from cache can be done in a couple of different ways. First, you can create a plan guide that exactly matches the SQL text for the cached plan, and then all plans with that text will be removed automatically. SQL Server 2008 provides an easy way of creating a plan guide from plan cache. We look at plan guides in detail later in the chapter. The second method of removing a single plan from cache is new in SQL Server 2008 and uses new options for *DBCC FREEPROCCACHE*. The syntax is illustrated in the following code:

```
DBCC FREEPROCCACHE [ ( { plan_handle | sql_handle | pool_name } ) ] [ WITH NO_INFOMSGS ]
```

This command now allows you to specify one of three parameters to indicate which plan or plans you want to remove from cache:

■ *plan_handle*   By specifying a *plan_handle*, you can remove the plan with that handle from cache. (The *plan_handle* is guaranteed to be unique for all currently existing plans.)

■ *sql_handle*   By specifying a *sql_handle*, you can remove the plans with that handle from cache. You can have multiple plans for the same SQL text if any of the cache key values are changed, such as SET options. The following code illustrates this:

```
USE Northwind2;
GO
DBCC FREEPROCCACHE;
GO
SET ANSI_NULLS ON
GO
SELECT * FROM orders WHERE customerid = 'HANAR';
GO
SELECT * FROM Orders WHERE CustomerID = 'CENTC';
GO
SET ANSI_NULLS OFF
GO
SELECT * FROM orders WHERE customerid = 'HANAR';
GO
SET ANSI_NULLS ON
GO

-- Now examine the sys.dm_exec_query_stats view and notice two different rows for the
-- query searching for 'HANAR'
SELECT execution_count, text, sql_handle, query_plan
FROM sys.dm_exec_query_stats
   CROSS APPLY sys.dm_exec_sql_text(sql_handle) AS TXT
      CROSS APPLY sys.dm_exec_query_plan(plan_handle)AS PLN;
GO
```

```
-- The two rows containing 'HANAR' should have the same value for sql_handle;
-- Copy that sql_handle value and paste into the command below:
DBCC FREEPROCCACHE(0x02000000CECDF507D9D4D70720F581172A42506136AA80BA);
GO
-- If you examine sys.dm_exec_query_stats again, you see the rows for this query
-- have been removed
SELECT execution_count, text, sql_handle, query_plan
FROM sys.dm_exec_query_stats
    CROSS APPLY sys.dm_exec_sql_text(sql_handle) AS TXT
        CROSS APPLY sys.dm_exec_query_plan(plan_handle)AS PLN;
GO
```

- *pool_name*   By specifying the name of a Resource Governor pool, you can clear all the plans in cache that are associated with queries that were assigned to workload group using the specified resource pool. (The Resource Governor, workload groups, and resource pools were discussed in Chapter 1, "SQL Server 2008 Architecture and Configuration.")

# Plan Cache Internals

Knowing when and how plans are reused or recompiled can help you design high-performing applications. The more you understand about optimal query plans, and how different actual values and cardinalities require different plans, the more you can determine when recompilation is a useful thing. When you are getting unnecessary recompiles, or when SQL Server is not recompiling when you think it should, your troubleshooting efforts will be easier the more you know about how plans are managed internally. In this section, we explore the internal organization of the plan cache, the metadata available, how SQL Server finds a plan in cache, plan cache sizing, and the plan eviction policy.

## Cache Stores

The plan cache in SQL Server is made up of four separate memory areas, called *cache stores*. There are actually other stores in its memory, which can be seen in the DMV called *sys.dm_os_memory_cache_counters*, but only four that contain query plans. The names in parentheses below are the values that can be seen in the *type* column of *sys.dm_os_memory_cache_counters*:

- **Object Plans** *(CACHESTORE_OBJCP)*   Object Plans include plans for stored procedures, functions, and triggers.

- **SQL Plans** *(CACHESTORE_SQLCP)*   SQL Plans include the plans for adhoc cached plans, autoparameterized plans, and prepared plans. The memory clerk that manages the SQLCP cache store is also used for the SQL Manager, which manages all the T-SQL text used in your adhoc queries.

- **Bound Trees** *(CACHESTORE_PHDR)*    Bound Trees are the structures produced by the algebrizer in SQL Server for views, constraints, and defaults.

- **Extended Stored Procedures** *(CACHESTORE_XPROC)*    Extended Procs (Xprocs) are predefined system procedures, like *sp_executesql* and *sp_tracecreate,* that are defined using a dynamic link library (DLL), not using T-SQL statements. The cached structure contains only the function name and the DLL name in which the procedure is implemented.

Each plan cache store contains a hash table to keep track of all the plans in that particular store. Each bucket in the hash table contains zero, one, or more cached plans. When determining which bucket to use, SQL Server uses a very straightforward hash algorithm. The hash key is computed as (*object_id * database_id*) mod (hash table size). For plans that are associated with adhoc or prepared plans, the *object_id* is an internal hash of the batch text. The DMV *sys.dm_os_memory_cache_hash_tables* contains information about each hash table, including its size. You can query this view to retrieve the number of buckets for each of the plan cache stores using the following query:

```
SELECT type as 'plan cache store', buckets_count
FROM sys.dm_os_memory_cache_hash_tables
WHERE type IN ('CACHESTORE_OBJCP', 'CACHESTORE_SQLCP',
    'CACHESTORE_PHDR', 'CACHESTORE_XPROC');
```

You should notice that the Bound Trees store has about 10 percent of the number of hash buckets of the stores for Object Plans and SQL Plans. (On a 64-bit system, the number of buckets for the Object Plan and SQL Plan stores is about 40,000 and on a 32-bit system, the number is about 10,000.) The number of buckets for the Extended Stored Procedures store is always set to 127 entries. We will not be discussing Bound Trees and Extended Stored Procedures further. The rest of the chapter dealing with caching of plans is concerned only with Object Plans and SQL Plans.

To find the size of the stores themselves, you can use the view *sys.dm_os_memory_objects.* The following query returns the size of all the cache stores holding plans, plus the size of the SQL Manager, which stores the T-SQL text of all the adhoc and prepared queries:

```
SELECT type AS Store, SUM(pages_allocated_count) AS Pages_used
FROM sys.dm_os_memory_objects
WHERE type IN ('MEMOBJ_CACHESTOREOBJCP', 'MEMOBJ_CACHESTORESQLCP',
    'MEMOBJ_CACHESTOREXPROC', 'MEMOBJ_SQLMGR')
GROUP BY type
```

Finding a plan in cache is a two-step process. The hash key described previously leads SQL Server to the bucket in which a plan might be found, but if there are multiple entries in the bucket, SQL Server needs more information to determine if the exact plan it is looking for can be found. For this second step, it needs a cache key, which is a combination of several attributes of the plan. Earlier, we looked at the DMF *sys.dm_exec_plan_attributes,* to which we could pass a *plan_handle.* The results obtained were a list of attributes for a particular plan, and a Boolean value indicating whether that particular value was part of the cache key. Table 9-1 included 17 attributes that comprise the cache key, and SQL Server needs to make sure all 17 values match before determining that it has found a matching plan in cache. In addition to the 17 values found in *sys.dm_exec_plan_attributes*, the column *sys.dm_exec_cached_plans.pool_id* is also part of the cache key for any plan.

## Compiled Plans

There are two main types of plans in the Object and SQL plan cache stores: compiled plans and execution plans. Compiled plans are the type of object we have been looking at up to this point when examining the *sys.dm_exec_cached_plans* view. We have already discussed the three main *objtype* values that can correspond to a compiled plan: *Adhoc, Prepared,* and *Proc.* Compiled plans can be stored in either the Object Store or the SQL Store depending on which of those three *objtype* values they have. The compiled plans are considered valuable memory objects, since they can be costly to re-create. SQL Server attempts to keep them in cache. When SQL Server experiences heavy memory pressure, the policies used to remove cache objects ensure that our compiled plans are not the first objects to be removed.

A compiled plan is generated for an entire batch, not just for a single statement. For a multistatement batch, you can think of the compiled plan as an array of plans, with each element of the array containing a query plan for an individual statement. Compiled plans can be shared between multiple sessions or users. However, you should be aware that not every user executing the same plan will get the same results, even if there is no change to the underlying data. Unless the compiled plan is an adhoc plan, each user has his or her own parameters and local variables, and the batch may build temporary tables or worktables specific to that user. The information specific to one particular execution of a compiled plan is stored in another structure called the *executable plan*.

## Execution Contexts

Executable plans, or execution contexts, are considered to be dependent on compiled plans and do not show up in the *sys.dm_exec_cached_plans* view. Executable plans are run-time objects created when a compiled plan is executed. Just as for compiled plans, executable plans can be Object Plans, stored in the Object Store, or SQL Plans, stored in the SQL Store. Each executable plan exists in the same cache store as the compiled plan on which it depends. Executable plans contain the particular run-time information for one execution of a compiled plan, and include the actual run-time parameters, any local variable information, object IDs for objects created at run time, the user ID, and information about the currently executing statement in the batch.

When SQL Server starts executing a compiled plan, it generates an executable plan from that compiled plan. Each individual statement in a compiled plan gets its own executable plan, which you can think of as a run-time query plan. Unlike compiled plans, executable plans are for a single session. For example, if 100 users are executing the same batch simultaneously, there will be 100 executable plans for the same compiled plan. Executable plans can be regenerated from their associated compiled plan, and they are relatively inexpensive to create. Later in this section, we look at the *sys.dm_exec_cached_plan_dependent_objects* view, which contains information about your executable plans. Note that Compiled Plan Stubs, generated when the Optimize for Ad Hoc Workloads configuration option is set to 1, do not have associated execution contexts.

## Plan Cache Metadata

We have already looked at some of the information in the *sys.dm_exec_cached_plans* DMV when we looked at *usecount* information to determine whether or not our plans were being reused. In this section, we look at some of the other metadata objects and discuss the meaning of some of the data contained in the metadata.

## Handles

The *sys.dm_exec_cached_plans* view contains a value called a *plan_handle* for every compiled plan. The *plan_handle* is a hash value that SQL Server derives from the compiled plan of the entire batch, and it is guaranteed to be unique for every currently existing compiled plan. (The *plan_handle* values can be reused over time.) The *plan_handle* can be used as an identifier for a compiled plan. The *plan_handle* remains the same even if individual statements in the batch are recompiled because of the correctness or optimality reasons discussed earlier.

As mentioned, the compiled plans are stored in the two cache stores, depending on whether the plan is an Object Plan or a SQL Plan. The actual SQL Text of the batch or object is stored in another cache called the *SQL Manager Cache (SQLMGR)*. The T-SQL Text associated with each batch is stored in its entirety, including all the comments. The T-SQL Text cached in the SQLMGR cache can be retrieved using a data value called the *sql_handle*. The *sql_handle* contains a hash of the entire batch text, and because it is unique for every batch, the *sql_handle* can serve as an identifier for the batch text in the SQLMGR cache.

Any specific T-SQL batch always has the same *sql_handle*, but it may not always have the same *plan_handle*. If any of the values in the cache key change, we get a new *plan_handle* in plan cache. Refer back to Table 9-1 to see which plan attributes make up the cache keys. The relationship between *sql_handle* and *plan_handle*, therefore, is 1:N.

We've seen that *plan_handle* values can be obtained easily from the *sys.dm_exec_cached_plans* view. We can get the *sql_handle* value that corresponds to a particular *plan_handle* from the *sys.dm_exec_plan_attributes* function that we looked at earlier. Here is the same query we discussed earlier to return attribute information and pivot it so that three of the attributes are returned in the same row as the *plan_handle* value:

```
SELECT plan_handle, pvt.set_options, pvt.object_id, pvt.sql_handle
FROM (SELECT plan_handle, epa.attribute, epa.value
    FROM sys.dm_exec_cached_plans
        OUTER APPLY sys.dm_exec_plan_attributes(plan_handle) AS epa
```

```
    WHERE cacheobjtype = 'Compiled Plan'
    ) AS ecpa
PIVOT (MAX(ecpa.value) FOR ecpa.attribute
    IN ("set_options", "object_id", "sql_handle")) AS pvt;
```

The *sys.dm_exec_query_stats* view contains both *plan_handle* and *sql_handle* values, as well as information about how often each plan was executed and how much work was involved in the execution. The value for *sql_handle* is very cryptic, and it's sometimes difficult to determine which of our queries each *sql_handle* corresponds to. To get that information, we can use another function.

## sys.dm_exec_sql_text

The function *sys.dm_exec_sql_text* can take either a *sql_handle* or a *plan_handle* as a parameter, and it returns the SQL Text that corresponds to the handle. Any sensitive information that might be contained in the SQL Text, like passwords, are blocked when the SQL is returned. The text column in the functions output contains the entire SQL batch text for adhoc, prepared, and autoparameterized queries, and for objects like triggers, procedures, and functions, it gives the full object definition.

Viewing the SQL Text from *sys.dm_exec_sql_text* is useful in quickly identifying identical batches that may have different compiled plans because of several factors, like SET option differences. As an example, consider the following code, which executes two identical batches. This example is similar to the one we saw previously when I discussed using *DBCC FREEPROCCACHE* with a *sql_handle*, but this time, we see the *sql_handle* and *plan_handle* values. The only difference between the two consecutive executions is that the value of the SET option QUOTED _IDENTIFIER has changed. It is OFF in the first execution and ON in the second. After executing both batches, we examine the *sys.dm_exec_query_stats* view:

```
USE Northwind2;
DBCC FREEPROCCACHE;
SET QUOTED_IDENTIFIER OFF;
GO
-- this is an example of the relationship between
-- sql_handle and plan_handle
SELECT LastName, FirstName, Country
FROM Employees
WHERE Country <> 'USA';
GO
SET QUOTED_IDENTIFIER ON;
GO
-- this is an example of the relationship between
-- sql_handle and plan_handle
SELECT LastName, FirstName, Country
FROM Employees
WHERE Country <> 'USA';
GO
SELECT st.text, qs. sql_handle, qs.plan_handle
FROM sys.dm_exec_query_stats qs
    CROSS APPLY sys.dm_exec_sql_text(sql_handle) st;
GO
```

You should see two rows with the same text string and *sql_handle*, but with different *plan_handle* values, as shown here. (In our output, the difference between the two *plan_handle* values is only a single digit so it may be hard to see, but in other cases, the difference may be more obvious.)

| text | sql_handle | plan_handle |
|---|---|---|
| -- this is an example of the -- relationship between -- sql_handle and plan_handle SELECT LastName, FirstName, Country FROM Employees WHERE Country <> 'USA' | 0x0200000012330 B0EEA82077439354E7A 5B12E1B7E37A1361 | 0x0600120012330B0EB82 18705000000000000000 00000000 |
| -- this is an example of the -- relationship between -- sql_handle and plan_handle SELECT LastName, FirstName, Country FROM Employees WHERE Country <> 'USA' | 0x0200000012330 B0EEA82077439354E7A 5B12E1B7E37A1361 | 0x0600120012330B0EB82 18605000000000000000 00000000 |

We can see that we have two plans corresponding to the same batch text, and this example should make clear the importance of making sure that all the SET options that affect plan caching should be the same when the same queries are executed repeatedly. You should verify whatever changes your programming interface makes to your SET options to make sure you don't end up with different plans unintentionally. Not all interfaces use the same defaults for the SET option values. For example, the OSQL interface uses the ODBC driver, which sets QUOTED_IDENTIFIER to OFF for every connection, whereas Management Studio uses ADO.NET, which sets QUOTED_IDENTIFIER to ON. Executing the same batches from these two different clients results in multiple plans in cache.

## sys.dm_exec_query_plan

The function *sys.dm_exec_query_plan* is a table-valued function that takes a *plan_handle* as a parameter and returns the associated query plan in XML format. If the plan is for an object, the TVF includes the database ID, object ID, procedure number, and encryption state of the object. If the plan is for an adhoc or prepared query, these additional values are NULL. If the *plan_handle* corresponds to a *Compiled Plan Stub*, the query plan will also be NULL. I have used this function in some of the preceding examples.

## sys.dm_exec_text_query_plan

The function *sys.dm_exec_text_query_plan* is a table-valued function that takes a *plan_handle* as a parameter and returns the same basic information as *sys.dm_exec_query_plan*. The differences between the two functions are as follows:

- *sys.dm_exec_text_query_plan* can take optional input parameters to specify the start and end offset of statements with a batch.

- The output of *sys.dm_exec_text_query_plan* returns the plan as text data, instead of XML data.

- The XML output for the query plan returned by *sys.dm_exec_query_plan* is limited to 128 levels of nested elements. If the plan exceeds that, a NULL is returned. The text output for the query plan returned by *sys.dm_exec_text_query_plan* is not limited in size.

## sys.dm_exec_cached_plans

The *sys.dm_exec_cached_plans* view is the one we use most often for troubleshooting query plan recompilation issues. It's the one I used in the first section to illustrate the plan reuse behavior of adhoc plans compared to autoparameterized and prepared plans. This view has one row per cached plan, and in addition to the *plan_handle* and *usecounts*, which we've looked at already, this DMV has other useful information about the cached plans, including the following:

- *size_in_byte*   The number of bytes consumed by this cache object
- *cacheobjtype*   The type of the cache object; that is, if it's a Compiled Plan, or a Parse Tree or an Extended Proc
- *memory_object_address*   The memory address of the cache object, which can be used to get the memory breakdown of the cache object

Although this DMV does not have the SQL Text associated with each compiled plan, we've seen that we can find it by passing the *plan_handle* to the *sys.dm_exec_sql_text* function. We can use the query below to retrieve the *text*, *usecounts*, and *size_in_bytes* of the compiled plan and *cacheobjtype* for all the plans in cache. The results are returned in order of frequency, with the batch having the most use showing up first:

```
SELECT st.text, cp.plan_handle, cp.usecounts, cp.size_in_bytes,
  cp.cacheobjtype, cp.objtype
FROM sys.dm_exec_cached_plans cp
  CROSS APPLY sys.dm_exec_sql_text(cp.plan_handle) st
ORDER BY cp.usecounts DESC;
```

## sys.dm_exec_cached_plan_dependent_objects

The *sys.dm_exec_cached_plan_dependent_objects* function returns one row for every dependent object of a compiled plan when you pass a valid *plan_handle* in as a parameter. If the *plan_handle* is not that of a compiled plan, the function returns NULL. Dependent objects include executable plans, as discussed previously, as well as plans for cursors used by the compiled plan. The example shown here uses *sys.dm_exec_cached_plan_dependent_objects*, as well as *sys.dm_exec_cached_plans*, to retrieve the dependent objects for all compiled plans, the *plan_handle*, and their *usecounts*. It also calls the *sys.dm_exec_sql_text* function to return the associated T-SQL batch:

```
SELECT text, plan_handle, d.usecounts, d.cacheobjtype
FROM sys.dm_exec_cached_plans
CROSS APPLY sys.dm_exec_sql_text(plan_handle)
CROSS APPLY
  sys.dm_exec_cached_plan_dependent_objects(plan_handle) d;
```

### sys.dm_exec_requests

The *sys.dm_exec_requests* view returns one row for every currently executing request within your SQL Server instance and is useful for many purposes in addition to tracking down plan cache information. This DMV contains the *sql_handle* and the *plan_handle* for the current statement, as well as resource usage information for each request. For troubleshooting purposes, you can use this view to help identify long-running queries. Keep in mind that the *sql_handle* points to the T-SQL for the entire batch. However, the *sys.dm_exec_requests* view contains the *statement_start_offset* and *statement_end_offset* columns, which indicate the position within the entire batch where the currently executing statement can be found. The offsets start at 0, and an offset of –1 indicates the end of the batch. The statement offsets can be used in combination with the *sql_handle* passed to *sys.dm_exec_sql_text* to extract the query text from the entire batch text, as demonstrated in the following code. This query returns the 10 longest-running queries currently executing:

```
SELECT TOP 10 SUBSTRING(text, (statement_start_offset/2) + 1,
   ((CASE statement_end_offset
        WHEN -1
           THEN DATALENGTH(text)
        ELSE statement_end_offset
   END - statement_start_offset)/2) + 1) AS query_text, *
FROM sys.dm_exec_requests
   CROSS APPLY sys.dm_exec_sql_text(sql_handle)
ORDER BY total_elapsed_time DESC;
```

Note that including the '*' in the *SELECT* list indicates that this query should return *all* of the columns from the *sys.dm_exec_requests* view. You should replace the '*' with the columns that you are particularly interested in, such as *start_time, blocking_session_id,* and so on.

### sys.dm_exec_query_stats

Just as the text returned from the *sql_handle* is the text for the entire batch, the compiled plans that are returned are for the entire batch. For optimum troubleshooting, we can use *sys.dm_exec_query_stats* to return performance information for individual queries within a batch. This view returns performance statistics for queries, aggregated across all executions of the same query. This view also returns both a *sql_handle* and a *plan_handle,* as well as the start and end offsets like we saw in *sys.dm_exec_requests*. The following query returns the top 10 queries by total CPU time, to help you identify the most expensive queries on your SQL Server instance:

```
SELECT TOP 10 SUBSTRING(text, (statement_start_offset/2) + 1,
   ((CASE statement_end_offset
        WHEN -1
           THEN DATALENGTH(text)
        ELSE statement_end_offset
   END - statement_start_offset)/2) + 1) AS query_text, *
```

```
FROM sys.dm_exec_query_stats
   CROSS APPLY sys.dm_exec_sql_text(sql_handle)
   CROSS APPLY sys.dm_exec_query_plan(plan_handle)
ORDER BY total_elapsed_time/execution_count DESC;
```

This view has one row per query statement within a batch, and when a plan is removed from cache, the corresponding rows and the accumulated statistics for that statement are removed from this view. In addition to the *plan_handle, sql_handle,* and performance information, this view contains two new columns in SQL Server 2008, which can help you identify similar queries with different plans.

- **query_hash**   This value is a hash of the query text and can be used to identify similar queries with the plan cache. Queries that differ only in the values of constants have the same *query_hash* value.

- **query_plan_hash**   This value is a hash of the query execution plan and can be used to identify similar plans based on logical and physical operators and a subset of the operator attributes. To look for cases where you might not want to implement forced parameterization, you can search for queries that have similar *query_hash* values but different *query_plan_hash* values.

There are two main differences between *sys.dm_exec_cached_plans* and *sys.dm_exec_query_stats.* First, *sys.dm_exec_cached_plans* has one row for each batch that has been compiled and cached, whereas *sys.dm_exec_query_stats* has one row for each statement. Second, *sys.dm_exec_query_stats* contains summary information aggregating all the executions of a particular statement. The *sys.dm_exec_query_stats* returns a tremendous amount of performance information for each query, including the number of times it was executed, and the cumulative I/O, CPU, and duration information. Keep in mind that this view is updated only when a query is completed, so you might need to retrieve information multiple times if there is currently a large workload on your server.

## Cache Size Management

We've already talked about plan reuse and how SQL Server finds a plan in cache. In this section, we look at how SQL Server manages the size of plan cache and how it determines which plans to remove if there is no room left in cache. Earlier, I discussed a few situations in which plans would be removed from cache. These situations included global operations like running *DBCC FREEPROCCACHE* to clear all plans from cache, as well as changes to a single procedure, such as *ALTER PROCEDURE,* which would drop all plans for that procedure from cache. In most other situations, plans are removed from cache only when memory pressure is detected. The algorithm that SQL Server uses to determine when and how plans should be removed from cache is called the *eviction policy.* Each cache store can have its own eviction policy, but we are discussing only the policies for the Object Plan store and the SQL Plan store.

Determining which plans to evict is based on the cost of the plan, which is discussed in the next section. When eviction starts is based on memory pressure. When SQL Server detects memory pressure, zero-cost plans are removed from cache and the cost of all other plans is reduced by half. As discussed in Chapter 1, there are two types of memory pressure, and both types lead to removal of plans from cache. These two types of memory pressure are referred to as *local* and *global memory pressure*.

When discussing memory pressure, we refer to the term *visible memory*. Visible memory is the directly addressable physical memory available to the SQL Server buffer pool. On a 32-bit SQL Server instance, the maximum value for the visible memory is either 2 GB or 3 GB, depending on whether you have the */3 GB* flag set in your boot.ini file. Memory with addresses greater than 2 GB or 3 GB is available only indirectly, through *AWE-mapped-memory*. On a 64-bit SQL Server instance, visible memory has no special meaning, as all the memory is directly addressable. In any of the discussion that follows, if we refer to visible target memory greater than 3 GB, keep in mind that is only possible on a 64-bit SQL Server instance. The term *target memory* refers to the maximum amount of memory that can be committed to the SQL Server process. Target memory refers to the physical memory committed to the buffer pool and is the lesser of the value you have configured for max server memory and the total amount of physical memory available to the operating system. So *visible target memory* is the visible portion of the target memory. Query plans can be stored only in the non-AWE-mapped memory, which is why the concept of visible memory is important. You can see a value for visible memory, specified as the number of 8-KB buffers, in the *bpool_visible* column in the *sys.dm_os_sys_info* DMV. This view also contains values for *bpool_committed* and *bpool_commit_target*.

SQL Server defines a cache store pressure limit value, which varies depending on the version you're running and the amount of visible target memory. We explain shortly how this value is used. The formula for determining the plan cache pressure limit changed in SQL Server 2005 SP2. Table 9-3 shows how to determine the plan cache pressure limit in SQL Server 2000 and 2005, and indicates the change in SP2, which reduced the pressure limit with higher amounts of memory. SQL Server 2008 RTM uses the same formulas that were added in SQL Server 2005 SP2. Be aware that these formulas may be subject to change again in future service packs.

**TABLE 9-3 Determining the Plan Cache Pressure Limit**

| SQL Server Version | Cache Pressure Limit |
| --- | --- |
| SQL Server 2005 RTM & SP1 | 75 percent of visible target memory from 0 to 8 GB + 50 percent of visible target memory from 8 GB to 64 GB + 25 percent of visible target memory > 64 GB |
| SQL Server 2005 SP2 and SP3, SQL Server 2008 RTM | 75 percent of visible target memory from 0 to 4 GB + 10 percent of visible target memory from 4 GB to 64 GB + 5 percent of visible target memory > 64 GB |
| SQL Server 2000 | 4 GB upper cap on the plan cache |

As an example, assume we are on SQL Server 2005 SP1 on a 64-bit SQL Server instance with 28 GB of target memory. The plan cache pressure limit would be 75 percent of 8 GB plus 50 percent of the target memory over 8 GB (or 50 percent of 20 GB), which is 6 GB + 10 GB, or 16 GB.

On a 64-bit SQL Server 2008 RTM instance with 28 GB of target memory, the plan cache pressure limit would be 75 percent of 4 GB plus 10 percent of the target memory over 4 GB (or 10 percent of 24 GB), which is 3 GB + 2.4 GB, or 5.4 GB.

## Local Memory Pressure

If any single cache store grows too big, it indicates local memory pressure and SQL Server starts removing entries from only that store. This behavior prevents one store from using too much of the total system memory.

If a cache store reaches 75 percent of the plan cache pressure limit, described in Table 9-3, in single-page allocations or 50 percent of the plan cache pressure limit in multipage allocations, internal memory pressure is triggered and plans are removed from cache. For example, in the situation described previously, we computed the plan cache pressure limit to be 5.4 GB. If any cache store exceeds 75 percent of that value, or 4.05 GB in single-page allocations, internal memory pressure is triggered. If adding a particular plan to cache causes the cache store to exceed the limit, the removal of other plans from cache happens on the same thread as the one adding the new plan, which can cause the response time of the new query to be increased.

In addition to memory pressure occurring when the total amount of memory reaches a particular limit, SQL Server also indicates memory pressure when the number of plans in a store exceeds four times the hash table size for that store, regardless of the actual size of the plans. As I mentioned previously when describing the cache stores, there are either about 10,000 or 40,000 buckets in these hash tables, for 32-bit and 64-bit systems, respectively. That means memory pressure can be triggered when either the SQL Store or the Object Store has more than 40,000 or 160,000 entries. The first query shown here is one we saw earlier, and it can be used to determine the number of buckets in the hash tables for the Object Store and the SQL Store, and the second query returns the number of entries in each of those stores:

```
SELECT type as 'plan cache store', buckets_count
FROM sys.dm_os_memory_cache_hash_tables
WHERE type IN ('CACHESTORE_OBJCP', 'CACHESTORE_SQLCP');
GO
SELECT type, count(*) total_entries
FROM sys.dm_os_memory_cache_entries
WHERE type IN ('CACHESTORE_SQLCP', 'CACHESTORE_OBJCP')
GROUP BY type;
GO
```

Prior to SQL Server 2008, internal memory pressure was rarely triggered due to the number of entries in the hash tables but was almost always initiated by the size of the plans in the cache store. However, in SQL Server 2008, if you have enabled Optimize for Ad Hoc Workloads, the actual entries in the SQL cache store may be quite small (each *Compiled Plan Stub* is about 300 bytes) so the number of entries can grow to exceed the limit before the size of the store gets too large. If Optimize for Ad Hoc Workloads is not on, the size of the entries in cache is much larger, with a minimum size of 24 KB for each plan. To see the size of all the plans in a cache store, you need to examine *sys.dm_exec_cached_plans*, as shown here:

```
SELECT objtype, count(*) AS 'number of plans',
      SUM(size_in_bytes)/(1024.0 * 1024.0 * 1024.0)
            AS size_in_gb_single_use_plans
FROM sys.dm_exec_cached_plans
GROUP BY objtype;
```

Remember that the adhoc and prepared plans are both stored in the SQL cache store, so to monitor the size of that store, you have to add those two values together.

### Global Memory Pressure

Global memory pressure applies to memory used by all the cache stores together, and can be either external or internal. External global pressure occurs when the operating system determines that the SQL Server process needs to reduce its physical memory consumption because of competing needs from other processes on the server. All cache stores are reduced in size when this occurs.

Internal global memory pressure can occur when virtual address space is low. Internal global memory pressure can also occur when the memory broker predicts that all cache stores combined will use more than 80 percent of the plan cache pressure limit. Again, all cache stores will have entries removed when this occurs.

As mentioned, when SQL Server detects memory pressure, all zero-cost plans are removed from cache and the cost of all other plans is reduced by half. Any particular cycle updates the cost of at most 16 entries for every cache store. When an updated entry has a zero-cost value, it can be removed. There is no mechanism to free entries that are currently in use. However, unused dependent objects for an in-use compiled plan can be removed. Dependent objects include the executable plans and cursors, and up to half of the memory for these objects can be removed when memory pressure exists. Remember that dependent objects are inexpensive to re-create, especially compared to compiled plans.

 **More Info**  For more information on memory management and memory pressure, see Chapter 1.

## Costing of Cache Entries

The decision of what plans to evict from cache is based on their cost. For adhoc plans, the cost is considered to be zero, but it is increased by 1 every time the plan is reused. For other types of plans, the cost is a measure of the resources required to produce the plan. When one of these plans is reused, the cost is reset to the original cost. For non-adhoc queries, the cost is measured in units called *ticks,* with a maximum of 31. The cost is based on three factors: I/O, context switches, and memory. Each has its own maximum within the 31-tick total:

- I/O: each I/O costs 1 tick, with a maximum of 19

- Context switches: 1 tick each, with a maximum of 8

- Memory: 1 tick per 16 pages, with a maximum of 4

When not under memory pressure, costs are not decreased until the total size of all plans cached reaches 50 percent of the buffer pool size. At that point, the next plan access decrement the cost in ticks of all plans by 1. Once memory pressure is encountered, then SQL Server starts a dedicated resource monitor thread to decrement the cost of either plan objects in one particular cache (for local pressure) or all plan cache objects (for global pressure).

The *sys.dm_os_memory_cache_entries* DMV can show you the current and original cost of any cache entry, as well as the components that make up that cost:

```
SELECT text, objtype, refcounts, usecounts, size_in_bytes,
    disk_ios_count, context_switches_count,
    pages_allocated_count, original_cost, current_cost
FROM sys.dm_exec_cached_plans p
    CROSS APPLY sys.dm_exec_sql_text(plan_handle)
    JOIN sys.dm_os_memory_cache_entries e
    ON p.memory_object_address = e.memory_object_address
WHERE cacheobjtype = 'Compiled Plan'
    AND type in ('CACHESTORE_SQLCP', 'CACHESTORE_OBJCP')
ORDER BY objtype desc, usecounts DESC;
```

Note that we can find the specific entry in *sys.dm_os_memory_cache_entries* that corresponds to a particular plan in *sys.dm_exec_cached_plans* by joining on the *memory_object_address* column.

# Objects in Plan Cache: The Big Picture

In addition to the DMVs and DMFs discussed so far, there is another metadata object called *syscacheobjects* that is really just a pseudotable. Prior to SQL Server 2005, there were no Dynamic Management Objects, but we did have about half a dozen of these pseudotables, including *sysprocesses* and *syslockinfo,* which took no space on disk and were materialized only when someone executed a query to access them, in a similar manner to the way that Dynamic Management Objects work. These objects are still available in SQL Server 2008. In SQL Server 2000, the pseudotables are available only in the *master* database, or by using a full object qualification when referencing them. In SQL Server 2008, you can access *syscacheobjects* from any database using only the *sys* schema as a qualification, so we refer to the object using its schema. Table 9-4 lists some of the more useful columns in the *sys.syscacheobjects* object.

**TABLE 9-4 Useful Columns in the *sys.syscacheobjects* View**

| Column Name | Description |
|---|---|
| *bucketid* | The bucket ID for this plan in an internal hash table; the bucket ID helps SQL Server locate the plan more quickly. Two rows with the same bucket ID refer to the same object (for example, the same procedure or trigger). |
| *cacheobjtype* | Type of object in cache: *Compiled Plan, Parse Tree,* and so on. |
| *objtype* | Type of object: *Adhoc, Prepared, Proc,* and so on. |
| *objid* | One of the main keys used for looking up an object in cache. This is the object ID stored in *sysobjects* for database objects (procedures, views, triggers, and so on). For cache objects, such as *Adhoc* or *Prepared, objid* is an internally generated value. |
| *dbid* | Database ID in which the cache object was compiled. |
| *uid* | The creator of the plan (for adhoc query plans and prepared plans). |
| *refcounts* | Number of other cache objects that reference this cache object. |
| *usecounts* | Number of times this cache object has been used since its creation. |
| *pagesused* | Number of memory pages consumed by the cache object. |
| *setopts* | SET option settings that affect a compiled plan. Changes to values in this column indicate that users have modified SET options. |
| *langid* | Language ID of the connection that created the cache object. |
| *dateformat* | Date format of the connection that created the cache object. |
| *sql* | Module definition or first 3,900 characters of the batch submitted. |

In SQL Server 2000, the *syscacheobjects* pseudotable also includes entries for executable plans. That is, the *cacheobjtype* column could have a value of *Executable Plan.* In SQL Server 2008, because executable plans are considered dependent objects and are stored completely separately from the compiled plans, they are no longer available through the *sys.syscacheobjects* view. To access the executable plans, you need to select directly from the *sys.dm_exec_ cached_plan_dependent_objects* function, and pass in a *plan_handle* as a parameter.

As an alternative to the *sys.syscacheobjects* view, which is a compatibility view and is not guaranteed to exist in future versions, you can create your own view that retrieves the same information from the SQL Server Dynamic Management Objects. The script creates a view called *sp_cacheobjects* in the *master* database. Remember that any objects with a name starting with *sp_*, created in the *master* database, can be accessed from any database without having to qualify the object name fully. Besides being able to access the *sp_cacheobjects* view from anywhere, another benefit of creating your own object is that you can customize it. For example, it would be relatively straightforward to do one more OUTER APPLY, to join this view with the *sys.dm_exec_query_plan* function, to get the XML plan for each of the plans in cache.

```
USE master
GO
CREATE VIEW sp_cacheobjects
    (bucketid, cacheobjtype, objtype, objid, dbid, dbidexec, uid,
```

```
        refcounts, usecounts, pagesused, setopts, langid, dateformat,
        status, lasttime, maxexectime, avgexectime, lastreads,
        lastwrites, sqlbytes, sql)
AS
    SELECT pvt.bucketid,
        CONVERT(nvarchar(18), pvt.cacheobjtype) AS cacheobjtype,
        pvt.objtype,
        CONVERT(int, pvt.objectid) AS object_id,
        CONVERT(smallint, pvt.dbid) AS dbid,
        CONVERT(smallint, pvt.dbid_execute) AS execute_dbid,
        CONVERT(smallint, pvt.user_id) AS user_id,
        pvt.refcounts, pvt.usecounts,
        pvt.size_in_bytes / 8192 AS size_in_bytes,
        CONVERT(int, pvt.set_options) AS setopts,
        CONVERT(smallint, pvt.language_id) AS langid,
        CONVERT(smallint, pvt.date_format) AS date_format,
        CONVERT(int, pvt.status) AS status,
        CONVERT(bigint, 0),
        CONVERT(bigint, 0),
        CONVERT(bigint, 0),
        CONVERT(bigint, 0),
        CONVERT(bigint, 0),
        CONVERT(int, LEN(CONVERT(nvarchar(max), fgs.text)) * 2),
        CONVERT(nvarchar(3900), fgs.text)
FROM (SELECT ecp.*, epa.attribute, epa.value
  FROM sys.dm_exec_cached_plans ecp
    OUTER APPLY
      sys.dm_exec_plan_attributes(ecp.plan_handle) epa) AS ecpa
PIVOT (MAX(ecpa.value) for ecpa.attribute IN
    ("set_options", "objectid", "dbid",
    "dbid_execute", "user_id", "language_id",
    "date_format", "status")) AS pvt
OUTER APPLY sys.dm_exec_sql_text(pvt.plan_handle) fgs;
```

You might notice that several of the output columns are hardcoded to a value of 0. For the most part, these are columns for data that is no longer maintained in SQL Server 2005 or SQL Server 2008. In particular, these are columns that report on performance information for cached plans. In SQL Server 2000, this performance data was maintained for each batch. In later versions, it is maintained on a statement level and available through *sys.dm_exec_query_stats*. To be compatible with the *sys.syscacheobjects* view, the new view must return something in those column positions. If you choose to customize this view, you could choose to remove those columns.

# Multiple Plans in Cache

SQL Server tries to limit the number of plans for a query or a procedure. Because plans are reentrant, this is easy to accomplish. You should be aware of some situations that cause multiple query plans for the same procedure to be saved in cache. The most likely situation is a difference in certain SET options, as discussed previously.

One other connection issue can affect whether a plan can be reused. If an owner name must be resolved implicitly, a plan cannot be reused. For example, suppose user *sue* issues the following *SELECT* statement:

```
SELECT * FROM Orders;
```

SQL Server first tries to resolve the object by looking for an object called *Orders* in the default schema for the user *sue*, and if no such object can be found, it looks for an object called *Orders* in the *dbo* schema. If user *dan* executes the exact same query, the object can be resolved in a completely different way (to a table in the default schema of the user *dan*), so *sue* and *dan* could not share the plan generated for this query. Because there is a possible ambiguity when using the unqualified object name, the query processor does not assume that an existing plan can be reused. However, the situation is different if *sue* issues this command:

```
SELECT * FROM dbo.Orders;
```

Now there's no ambiguity. Anyone executing this exact query always references the same object. In *the sys.syscacheobjects* view, the column *uid* indicates the user ID for the connection in which the plan was generated. For adhoc queries, only another connection with the same *user ID* value can use the same plan. The one exception is if the *user ID* value is recorded as –2 in *syscacheobjects*, which indicates that the query submitted does not depend on implicit name resolution and can be shared among different users. This is the preferred method.

> **Tip**  It is strongly recommended that objects are always qualified with their containing schema name, so that you never need to rely on implicit resolutions and the reuse of plan cache can be more effective.

# When to Use Stored Procedures and Other Caching Mechanisms

Keep the following guidelines in mind when you are deciding whether to use stored procedures or one of the other query mechanisms:

- **Stored procedures**  These objects should be used when multiple connections are executing batches in which the parameters are known. They are also useful when you need to have control over when a block of code is to be recompiled.

- **Adhoc caching**  This option is beneficial only in limited scenarios. It is not dependable enough for you to design an application expecting this behavior to correctly control reuse of appropriate plans.

- **Simple or forced parameterization**  This option can be useful for applications that cannot be easily modified. However, it is preferable when you initially design your applications that you use methods that explicitly allow you to declare what your parameters and what their data types are, such as the two suggestions below.

- **The *sp_executesql* procedure**   This procedure can be useful when the same batch might be used multiple times and when the parameters are known.

- **The prepare and execute methods**   These methods are useful when multiple users are executing batches in which the parameters are known, or when a single user will definitely use the same batch multiple times.

# Troubleshooting Plan Cache Issues

To start addressing problems with plan cache usage and management, you must determine that existing problems are actually caused by plan caching issues. Performance problems caused by misuse or mismanagement of plan cache, or inappropriate recompilation, can manifest themselves as simply a decrease in throughput or an increase in query response time. Problems with caching can also show up as out-of-memory errors or connection time-out errors, which can be caused by all sorts of different conditions.

## Wait Statistics Indicating Plan Cache Problems

To determine that plan caching behavior is causing problems, one of the first things to look at is your wait statistics in SQL Server. Wait statistics are covered in more detail in Chapter 10, "Transactions and Concurrency," but here, I tell you about some of the primary wait types that can indicate problems with your plan cache.

Wait statistics are displayed when you query the *sys.dm_os_wait_stats* view. The query here lists all the resources that your SQL Server service might have to wait for, and it displays the resources with the longest waiting list:

```
SELECT *
FROM sys.dm_os_wait_stats
ORDER BY waiting_tasks_count DESC;
```

You should be aware that the values shown in this view are cumulative, so if you need to see the resources being waited on during a specific time period, you have to poll the view at the beginning and end of the period. If you see relatively large wait times for any of the following resources, or if these resources are near the top of the list returned from the previous query, you should investigate your plan cache usage:

- **CMEMTHREAD waits**   This wait type indicates that there is contention on the memory object from which cache descriptors are allocated. A very high rate of insertion of entries into the plan cache can cause contention problems. Similarly, contention can also occur when entries are removed from cache and the resource monitor thread is blocked. There is only one thread-safe memory object from which descriptors are allocated, and as we've seen, there is only a single cache store for adhoc compiled plans.

Consider the same procedure being called dozens or hundreds of times. Remember that SQL Server will cache the adhoc shell query that includes the actual parameter for each individual call to the procedure, even though there may be only one cached plan for the procedure itself. As SQL Server starts experiencing memory pressure, the work to insert the entry for each individual call to the procedure can begin to cause excessive waits resulting in a drop in throughput or even out-of-memory errors.

SQL Server 2005 SP2 added some enhancements to caching behavior to alleviate some of the flooding of cache that could occur when the same procedure or parameterized query was called repeatedly with different parameters. In all releases after SQL Server 2005 SP2, zero-cost batches that contain *SET* statements or transaction control are not cached at all. The only exception is for those batches that contain only *SET* and transaction control statements. This is not that much of a loss, as plans for batches containing *SET* statements can never be reused in any case. Also, as of SQL Server 2005 SP2, the memory object from which cache descriptors are allocated has been partitioned across all the CPUs to alleviate contention on the memory object which should reduce CMEMTHREAD waits.

- **SOS_RESERVEDMEMBLOCKLIST waits**   This wait type can indicate the presence of cached plans for queries with a large number of parameters, or with a large number of values specified in an IN clause. These types of queries require that SQL Server allocate in larger units, called *multipage allocations*. You can look at the *sys.dm_os_memory_cache_counters* view to see the amount of memory allocated in the multipage units:

```
SELECT name, type, single_pages_kb, multi_pages_kb,
    single_pages_in_use_kb, multi_pages_in_use_kb
FROM sys.dm_os_memory_cache_counters
WHERE type = 'CACHESTORE_SQLCP' OR type = 'CACHESTORE_OBJCP';
```

Clearing out plan cache with *DBCC FREEPROCCACHE* can alleviate problems caused by too many multipage allocations, at least until the queries are reexecuted and the plans are cached again. In addition, the cache management changes in SQL Server 2005 SP2 can also reduce the waits on SOS_RESERVEDMEMBLOCKLIST. You can also consider rewriting the application to use alternatives to long parameters or long IN lists. In particular, long IN lists can almost always be improved by creating a table of the values in the IN list and joining with that table.

- **RESOURCE_SEMAPHORE_QUERY_COMPILE waits**   This wait type indicates that there are a large number of concurrent compilations. To prevent inefficient use of query memory, SQL Server 2008 limits the number of concurrent compile operations that need extra memory. If you notice a high value for RESOURCE_SEMAPHORE_QUERY_COMPILE waits, you can examine the entries in the plan cache through the *sys.dm_exec_cached_plans* view, as shown here:

```
SELECT usecounts, cacheobjtype, objtype, bucketid, text
FROM sys.dm_exec_cached_plans
    CROSS APPLY sys.dm_exec_sql_text(plan_handle)
WHERE cacheobjtype = 'Compiled Plan'
ORDER BY objtype;
```

If there are no results with the *objtype* value of *Prepared*, it means that SQL Server is not automatically parameterizing your queries. You can try altering the database to PARAMETERIZATION FORCED in this case, but this option affects the entire database, including queries that might not benefit from parameterization. To force SQL Server to parameterize just certain queries, plan guides can be used. I discuss plan guides in the next section.

Keep in mind that caching is done on a per-batch level. If you try to force parameterization using *sp_executesql* or prepare and execute, all the statements in the batch must be parameterized for the plan to be reusable. If a batch has some parameterized statements and some using constants, each execution of the batch with different constants is considered distinct, and there is no value to the parameterization in only part of the batch.

## Other Caching Issues

In addition to looking at the wait types that can indicate problems with caching, there are some other coding behaviors that can have a negative impact on plan reuse:

- **Verify parameter types, both for prepared queries and autoparameterization**   With prepared queries, you actually specify the parameter data type, so it's easier to make sure you are always using the same type. When SQL Server parameterizes, it makes its own decisions as to data type. If you look at the parameterized form of your queries of type *Prepared,* you see the data type that SQL Server assumed. We saw earlier in the chapter that a value of 12345 is assumed to be a different data type than 12, and two queries that are identical except for these specific values are never able to share the same autoparameterized plan.

    If the parameter passed is numeric, SQL Server determines the data type based on the precision and scale. A value of 8.4 has a data type of *numeric* (2, 1), and 8.44 has a data type of *numeric* (3, 2). For *varchar* data type, server side parameterization is not so dependent on the length of the actual value. Take a look at these two queries in the *Northwind2* database:

    ```
    SELECT * FROM Customers
    WHERE CompanyName = 'Around the Horn';
    GO
    SELECT * FROM Customers
    WHERE CompanyName = 'Rattlesnake Canyon Grocery';
    GO
    ```

    Both of these queries be autoparameterized to the following:

    ```
    (@0 varchar(8000))SELECT * FROM Customers WHERE CompanyName = @0
    ```

- **Monitor plan cache size and data cache size**   In general, as more queries are run, the amount of memory used for data page caching should increase along with the amount of memory used for plan caching. However, as we saw previously when discussing plan cache size, in SQL Server 2005 prior to SP2, the maximum limit for plan caching could grow to be up to 80 percent of the total buffer pool before memory pressure would start forcing plans to be evicted. This can result in severe performance degradation for those queries that depend on good data caching behavior. For any amount of memory greater than 4 GB, versions after SQL Server 2005 SP1 change the size limit that plan caching can grow to before memory pressure is indicated. One of the easiest places to get a comparison of the pages used for plan caching and the pages used for data caching is the performance counters. Take a look at the following counters: SQL Server: Plan Cache/Cache Pages(_Total) and SQLServer: BufferManager/Database pages.

# Handling Problems with Compilation and Recompilation

There are tools for detecting excessive compiles and recompiles. You can use either System Monitor or one of the tracing or event monitoring tools described in Chapter 2, "Change Tracking, Tracing, and Extended Events," to detect compilations and recompilations. Keep in mind that compiling and recompiling are not the same thing. Recompiling is performed when an existing module or statement is determined to be no longer valid or no longer optimal. All recompiles are considered compiles, but not vice versa. For example, when there is no plan in cache, or when executing a procedure using the WITH RECOMPILE option or executing a procedure that was created with the WITH RECOMPILE option, SQL Server considers it a compile but not a recompile.

If these tools indicate that you have excessive compilation or recompilation, you can consider the following actions:

- If the recompile is caused by a change in a SET option, the SQL Trace text data for T-SQL statements immediately preceding the recompile event can indicate which SET option changed. It's best to change SET options when a connection is first made and avoid changing them after you have started submitting statements on that connection, or inside a store procedure.

- Recompilation thresholds for temporary tables are lower than for normal tables, as we discussed earlier in this chapter. If the recompiles on a temporary table are caused by statistics changes, a trace has a data value in the *EventSubclass* column that indicates that statistics changed for an operation on a temporary table. You can consider changing the temporary tables to table variables, for which statistics are not maintained. Because no statistics are maintained, changes in statistics cannot induce recompilation. However, lack of statistics can result in suboptimal plans for these queries. Your own testing can determine if the benefit of table variables is worth the cost. Another alternative is to use the KEEP PLAN query hint, which sets the recompile threshold for temporary tables to be the same as for permanent tables.

- To avoid all recompilations that are caused by changes in statistics, whether on a permanent or a temporary table, you can specify the KEEPFIXED PLAN query hint. With this hint, recompilations can happen only because of correctness-related reasons, as described earlier. An example might be when a recompilation occurs if the schema of a table that is referenced by a statement changes, or if a table is marked for recompile by using the *sp_recompile* stored procedure.

- Another way to prevent recompiles caused by statistics changes is by turning off the automatic updates of statistics for indexes and columns. Note, however, that turning off the Autostatistics feature is usually not a good idea. If you do, the Query Optimizer is no longer sensitive to data changes and is likely to come up with a suboptimal plan. This method should be considered only as a last resort after exhausting all other options.

- All T-SQL code should use two-part object names (for example, *Inventory.ProductList*) to indicate exactly what object is being referenced, which can help avoid recompilation.

- Do not use DDL within conditional constructs such as *IF* statements.

- Check to see if the stored procedure was created with the WITH RECOMPILE option. In many cases, only one or two statements within a stored procedure might benefit from recompilation on every execution, and we can use the RECOMPILE query hint for just those statements. This is much better than using the WITH RECOMPILE option for the entire procedure, which means every statement in the procedure is recompiled every time the procedure is executed.

# Plan Guides and Optimization Hints

In Chapter 8, "The Query Optimizer," we looked at many different execution plans and discussed what it meant for a query to be optimized. In this chapter, we looked at situations in which SQL Server reuses a plan when it might have been best to come up with a new one, and we've seen situations in which SQL Server does not reuse a plan even if there is a perfectly good one in cache already. One way to encourage plan reuse that has already been discussed in this chapter is to enable the PARAMETERIZATION FORCED database option. In other situations, where we just can't get the optimizer to reuse a plan, we can use optimizer hints. Optimizer hints can also be used to force SQL Server to come up with a new plan in those cases in which it might be using an existing plan. There are dozens of hints that can be used in your T-SQL code to affect the plan that SQL Server comes up with, and some of them were discussed in Chapter 8. In this section, I specifically describe only those hints that affect recompilation, as well as the mother of all hints, USE PLAN, which was added in SQL Server 2005. Finally, we discuss a SQL Server feature called *plan guides*.

## Optimization Hints

All the hints that we are telling you about in this section are referred to in *SQL Server Books Online* as Query Hints, to distinguish them from Table Hints, which are specified in the FROM clause after a table name, and Join Hints, which are specified in the JOIN clause before the word *JOIN*. However, we frequently refer to query hints as *option hints* because they are specified in a special clause called the *OPTION clause*, which is used just for specifying this type of hint. An OPTION clause, if included in a query, is always the last clause of any T-SQL statement, as you can see in the code examples in the subsequent sections.

**RECOMPILE**   The RECOMPILE hint forces SQL Server to recompile a query. It is particularly useful when only a single statement within a batch needs to be recompiled. You know that SQL Server compiles your T-SQL batches as a unit, determining the execution plan for each statement in the batch, and it doesn't execute any statements until the entire batch is compiled. This means that if the batch contains a variable declaration and assignment, the assignment doesn't actually take place during the compilation phase. When the following batch is optimized, SQL Server doesn't have a specific value for the variable:

```
USE Northwind2;
DECLARE @custID nchar(10);
SET @custID = 'LAZYK';
SELECT * FROM Orders WHERE CustomerID = @custID;
```

The plan for the *SELECT* statement will show that SQL Server is scanning the entire clustered index because during optimization, SQL Server had no idea what value it was going to be searching for and couldn't use the histogram in the index statistics to get a good estimate of the number of rows. If we had replaced the variable with the constant LAZYK, SQL Server could have determined that only a very few rows would qualify and would have chosen to use the nonclustered index on *customerID*. The RECOMPILE hint can be very useful here because it tells the optimizer to come up with a new plan for the single *SELECT* statement right before that statement is executed, which is after the *SET* statement has executed:

```
USE Northwind2;
DECLARE @custID nchar(10);
SET @custID = 'LAZYK';
SELECT * FROM Orders WHERE CustomerID = @custID
OPTION (RECOMPILE);
```

> **Note** A variable is not the same as a parameter, even though they are written the same way. Because a procedure is compiled only when it is being executed, SQL Server always uses a specific parameter value. Problems arise when the previously compiled plan is then used for different parameters. However, for a local variable, the value is never known when the statements using the variable are compiled unless the RECOMPILE hint is used.

**OPTIMIZE FOR**    The OPTIMIZE FOR hint tells the optimizer to optimize the query as if a particular value has been used for a variable or parameter. Execution uses the real value. Keep in mind that the OPTIMIZE FOR hint does not force a query to be recompiled. It only instructs SQL Server to assume a variable or parameter has a particular value in those cases in which SQL Server has already determined that the query needs optimization. As the OPTIMIZE FOR hint was discussed in Chapter 8, we won't say any more about it here.

**KEEP PLAN**    The KEEP PLAN hint relaxes the recompile threshold for a query, particularly for queries accessing temporary tables. As we saw earlier in this chapter, a query accessing a temporary table can be recompiled when as few as six changes have been made to the table. If the query uses the KEEP PLAN hint, the recompilation threshold for temporary tables is changed to be the same as for permanent tables.

**KEEPFIXED PLAN**    The KEEPFIXED PLAN hint inhibits all recompiles because of optimality issues. With this hint, queries are recompiled only when forced, or if the schema of the underlying tables is changed, as described in the section entitled "Correctness-Based Recompiles," earlier in this chapter.

**PARAMETERIZATION**   The PARAMETERIZATION hint overrides the PARAMETERIZATION option for a database. If the database is set to PARAMETERIZATION FORCED, individual queries using the PARAMETERIZATION hint can avoid that and be parameterized only if they meet the strict list of conditions. Alternatively, if the database is set to PARAMETERIZATION SIMPLE, individual queries can be parameterized on a case-by-case basis. Note however that the PARAMETERIZATION hint can only be used in conjunction with plan guides, which we discuss shortly.

**USE PLAN**   The USE PLAN hint was discussed in Chapter 8, as a way to force SQL Server to use a plan that you might not be able to specify using the other hints. The plan specified must be in XML format and can be obtained from a query that uses the desired plan by using the option SET SHOWPLAN_XML ON. Because USE PLAN hints contain a complete XML document in the query hint, they are best used within plan guides, which are discussed in the next section.

## Purpose of Plan Guides

Although it is recommended in most cases that you allow the Query Optimizer to determine the best plan for each of your queries, there are times when the Query Optimizer just can't come up with the best plan and you may find that the only way to get reasonable performance is to use a hint. This is usually a straightforward change to your applications, once you have verified that the desired hint is really going to make a difference. However, in some environments, you have no control over the application code. In cases when the actual SQL queries are embedded in inaccessible vendor code or when modifying vendor code would break your licensing agreement or invalidate your support guarantees, you might not be able to simply add a hint onto the misbehaving query.

Plan guides, introduced in SQL Server 2005, provide a solution by giving you a mechanism to add hints to a query without changing the query itself. Basically, a plan guide tells the Optimizer that if it tries to optimize a query having a particular format, it should add a specified hint to the query. SQL Server supports three kinds of plan guides: SQL, Object, and Template, which we explore shortly.

Plan guides are available in the Standard, Enterprise, Evaluation, and Developer editions of SQL Server. If you detach a database containing plan guides from a supported edition and attach the database to an unsupported edition, such as Workgroup or Express, SQL Server does not use any plan guides. However the metadata containing information about plan guides is still available.

## Types of Plan Guides

The three types of plan types can be created using the *sp_create_plan_guide* procedure. The general form of the *sp_create_plan_guide* procedure is as follows:

```
sp_create_plan_guide 'plan_guide_name', 'statement_text',
    'type_of_plan_guide', 'object_name_or_batch_text',
    'parameter_list', 'hints'
```

We discuss each of the types of plan guides, and then we look at the mechanisms for working with plan guides and the metadata that keeps track of information about them.

**Object Plan Guides**   A plan guide of type *object* indicates that you are interested in a T-SQL statement appearing in the context of a SQL Server object, which can be a stored procedure, a user-defined function, or a trigger in the database in which the plan guide is created. As an example, suppose we have a stored procedure called *Sales.GetOrdersByCountry* that takes a country as a parameter, and after some error checking and other validation, it returns a set of rows for the orders placed by customers in the specified country. Suppose further that our testing has determined that a parameter value of *US* gives us the best plan. Here is an example of a plan guide that tells SQL Server to use the OPTIMIZE FOR hint whenever the specified statement is found in the *Sales.GetOrdersByCountry* procedure:

```
EXEC sp_create_plan_guide
    @name = N'plan_US_Country',
    @stmt =
       N'SELECT SalesOrderID, OrderDate, h.CustomerID, h.TerritoryID
            FROM Sales.SalesOrderHeader AS h
            INNER JOIN Sales.Customer AS c
               ON h.CustomerID = c.CustomerID
            INNER JOIN Sales.SalesTerritory AS t
               ON c.TerritoryID = t.TerritoryID
            WHERE t.CountryRegionCode = @Country',
@type = N'OBJECT',
@module_or_batch = N'Sales.GetOrdersByCountry',
@params = NULL,
@hints = N'OPTION (OPTIMIZE FOR (@Country = N''US''))';
```

Once this plan is created in the *AdventureWorks2008* database, every time the *Sales. GetOrdersByCountry* procedure is compiled, the statement indicated in the plan is optimized as if the actual parameter passed was the string 'US'. No other statements in the procedure are affected by this plan, and if the specified query occurs outside of the *Sales.GetOrdersByCountry* procedure, the plan guide is not invoked. (The companion Web site, which contains all the code used in all the book examples, also contains a script to build the *Sales.GetOrdersByCountry* procedure.)

**SQL Plan Guides**   A plan guide of type *SQL* indicates you are interested in a particular SQL statement, either as a stand-alone statement, or in a particular batch. T-SQL statements that are sent to SQL Server by CLR objects or extended stored procedures, or that are part of dynamic SQL invoked with the EXEC (*sql_string*) construct, are processed as batches on SQL Server. To use them in a plan guide, their type should be set to *SQL*. For a stand-alone statement, the *@module_or_batch* parameter to *sp_create_plan_guide* should be set to NULL, so that SQL Server assumes that the batch and the statement have the same value. If the statement you are interested in is in a larger batch, the entire batch text needs to be specified in the *@module_or_batch* parameter. If a batch is specified for a SQL plan guide, the text of the batch needs to be exactly the same as it appears in the application. The rules aren't quite as strict as those for adhoc query plan reuse, discussed earlier in this chapter, but they are close. Make sure you use the same case, the same whitespace, and the other characteristics that your application does.

Here is an example of a plan guide that tells SQL Server to use only one CPU (no parallelization) when a particular query is executed as a stand-alone query:

```
EXEC sp_create_plan_guide
@name = N'plan_SalesOrderHeader_DOP1',
@stmt = N'SELECT TOP 10 *
        FROM Sales.SalesOrderHeader
        ORDER BY OrderDate DESC',
@type = N'SQL',
@module_or_batch = NULL,
@params = NULL,
@hints = N'OPTION (MAXDOP 1)';
```

Once this plan is created in the *AdventureWorks2008* database, every time the specified statement is encountered in a batch by itself, it has a plan created that uses only a single CPU. If the specified query occurs as part of a larger batch, the plan guide is not invoked.

**Template Plan Guides**   A plan guide of type *Template* can use only the PARAMETERIZATION FORCED or PARAMETERIZATION SIMPLE hints to override the PARAMETERIZATION database setting. Template guides are a bit trickier to work with because you have to have SQL Server construct a template of your query in the same format that it will be in once it is parameterized. This isn't hard because SQL Server supplies us with a special procedure called *sp_get_query_template*, but to use template guides, you need to perform several prerequisite steps. If you take a look at the two plan guide examples given previously, you see that the parameter called *@params* was NULL for both OBJECT and SQL plan guides. You only specify a value for *@params* with a TEMPLATE plan guide.

To see an example of using a template guide and forcing parameterization, first clear your procedure cache, and then execute these two queries in the *AdventureWorks2008* database:

```
DBCC FREEPROCCACHE;
GO
SELECT * FROM AdventureWorks2008.Sales.SalesOrderHeader AS h
INNER JOIN AdventureWorks2008.Sales.SalesOrderDetail AS d
   ON h.SalesOrderID = d.SalesOrderID
WHERE h.SalesOrderID = 45639;
GO
SELECT * FROM AdventureWorks2008.Sales.SalesOrderHeader AS h
INNER JOIN AdventureWorks2008.Sales.SalesOrderDetail AS d
   ON h.SalesOrderID = d.SalesOrderID
WHERE h.SalesOrderID = 45640;
```

These queries are very similar, and the plans for both are identical, but because the query is considered too complex, SQL Server does not autoparameterize them. If, after executing both queries, you look at the plan cache, you see only adhoc queries. If you've created the *sp_cacheobjects* view described earlier in the chapter, you could use that; otherwise, replace *sp_cacheobjects* with *sys.syscacheobjects:*

```
SELECT objtype, dbid, usecounts, sql
FROM sp_cacheobjects
WHERE cacheobjtype = 'Compiled Plan';
```

To create a plan guide to force statements of this type to be parameterized, we first need to call the procedure *sp_get_query_template* and pass two variables as output parameters. One parameter holds the parameterized version of the query, and the other holds the parameter list and the parameter data types. The following code then *SELECTs* these two output parameters so you can see their contents. Of course, you can remove this *SELECT* from your own code. Finally, we call the *sp_create_plan_guide* procedure, which instructs the optimizer to use PARAMETERIZATION FORCED anytime it sees a query that matches this specific template. In other words, anytime a query that parameterizes to the same form as the query here, it uses the same plan already cached:

```
DECLARE @sample_statement nvarchar(max);
DECLARE @paramlist nvarchar(max);
EXEC sp_get_query_template
    N'SELECT * FROM AdventureWorks2008.Sales.SalesOrderHeader AS h
      INNER JOIN AdventureWorks2008.Sales.SalesOrderDetail AS d
        ON h.SalesOrderID = d.SalesOrderID
      WHERE h.SalesOrderID = 45639;',
    @sample_statement OUTPUT,
    @paramlist OUTPUT
SELECT @paramlist as parameters, @sample_statement as statement
EXEC sp_create_plan_guide @name = N'Template_Plan',
    @stmt = @sample_statement,
    @type = N'TEMPLATE',
    @module_or_batch = NULL,
    @params = @paramlist,
    @hints = N'OPTION(PARAMETERIZATION FORCED)';
```

After creating the plan guide, run the same two statements as shown previously, and then examine the plan cache:

```
DBCC FREEPROCCACHE;
GO
SELECT * FROM AdventureWorks2008.Sales.SalesOrderHeader AS h
INNER JOIN AdventureWorks2008.Sales.SalesOrderDetail AS d
    ON h.SalesOrderID = d.SalesOrderID
WHERE h.SalesOrderID = 45639;
GO
SELECT * FROM AdventureWorks2008.Sales.SalesOrderHeader AS h
INNER JOIN AdventureWorks2008.Sales.SalesOrderDetail AS d
    ON h.SalesOrderID = d.SalesOrderID
WHERE h.SalesOrderID = 45640;
GO
SELECT objtype, dbid, usecounts, sql
FROM sp_cacheobjects
WHERE cacheobjtype = 'Compiled Plan';
```

You should now see a prepared plan with the following parameterized form:

```
(@0 int)select * from AdventureWorks2008.Sales.SalesOrderHeader as h
   inner join AdventureWorks2008.Sales.SalesOrderDetail as d
   on h.SalesOrderID = d.SalesOrderID
   where h.SalesOrderID = @0
```

## Managing Plan Guides

In addition to the *sp_create_plan_guide* and *sp_get_query_template* procedures, the other basic procedure for working with plan guides is *sp_control_plan_guide*. This procedure allows you to DROP, DISABLE, or ENABLE a plan guide using the following basic syntax:

```
sp_control_plan_guide '<control_option>' [, '<plan_guide_name>']
```

There are six possible *control_option* values: DISABLE, DISABLE ALL, ENABLE, ENABLE ALL, DROP, and DROP ALL. The *plan_guide_name* parameter is optional because with any of the *ALL control_option* values, no *plan_guide_name* value is supplied. Plan guides are local to a particular database, so the DISABLE ALL, ENABLE ALL, and DROP ALL values apply to all plan guides for the current database. In addition, plan guides behave like schema-bound views in a way; the stored procedures, triggers, and functions referred to in any Object plan guide in a database cannot be altered or dropped. So for our example Object plan guide, so long as the plan guide exists, the *AdventureWorks2008.Sales.GetOrdersByCountry* procedure cannot be altered or dropped. This is true whether the plan guide is disabled or enabled, and it remains true until all plan guides referencing those objects are dropped with *sp_control_plan_guide*.

The metadata view that contains information about plan guides in a particular database is *sys.plan_guides*. This view contains all the information supplied in the *sp_create_plan_guide* procedure plus additional information such as the creation date and last modification date of each plan guide. Using the information in this view, you can reconstruct the plan guide definition manually if necessary. In addition, Management Studio allows you to script your plan guide definitions from the Object Explorer tree.

## Plan Guide Considerations

For SQL Server to determine that there is an appropriate plan guide to use, the statement text in the plan guide must match the query being compiled. This must be an exact character-for-character match, including case, whitespace, and comments, just as when SQL Server is determining whether it can reuse adhoc query plans, as we discussed earlier in the chapter. If your statement text is close, but not quite an exact match, this can lead to a situation that is very difficult to troubleshoot. When matching a SQL template, whether the definition also contains a batch that the statement must be part of, SQL Server does allow more leeway in the definition of the batch. In particular, keyword case, whitespace, and comments are ignored.

To make sure your plan guides use the exact text that is submitted by your applications, you can run a trace using SQL Server Profiler and capture the *SQL:BatchCompleted* and *RPC:Completed* events. After the relevant batch (the one you want to create a plan guide for) shows up in the top window of your Profiler output, you can right-click the event and select Extract Event Data to save the SQL Text of the batch to a text file. It is not sufficient to copy and paste from the lower window in the Profiler because the output there can introduce extra line breaks.

To verify that your plan guide was used, you can look at the XML plan for the query. If you can run the query directly, you can use the option SET SHOWPLAN_XML ON, or you can capture the showplan XML through a trace. An XML plan has two specific items, indicating that the query used a plan guide. These items are *PlanGuideDB* and *PlanGuideName*. If the plan guide was a template plan guide, the XML plan also has the items *TemplatePlanGuideDB* and *TemplatePlanGuideName*.

When a query is submitted for processing, if there are any plan guides in the database at all, SQL Server first checks to see if the statement matches a SQL plan guide or Object plan guide. The query string is hashed to make it faster to find any matching strings in the database's existing plan guides. If no matching SQL or Object plan guides are found, SQL Server then checks for a TEMPLATE plan guide. If it finds a TEMPLATE guide, it then tries to match the resulting parameterized query to a SQL plan guide. This gives you the possibility of applying additional hints to your queries using forced parameterization. Figure 9-3, copied from *SQL Server Books Online,* shows the process that SQL Server uses to check for applicable plan guides.

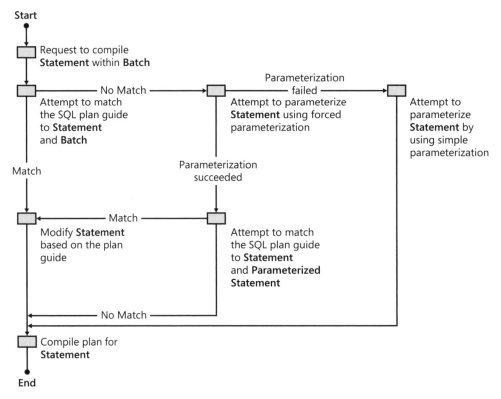

**FIGURE 9-3** Checking for applicable plan guides

The key steps are the following, which follow the flowchart from the top left, take the top branch to the right, the middle branch down, and then right at the center, to the point where the statement is modified based on the plan guide and its hints:

1. For a specific statement within the batch, SQL Server tries to match the statement to a SQL-based plan guide, whose *@module_or_batch* argument matches that of the incoming batch text, including any constant literal values, and whose *@stmt* argument also matches the statement in the batch. If this kind of plan guide exists and the match succeeds, the statement text is modified to include the query hints specified in the plan guide. The statement is then compiled using the specified hints.

2. If a plan guide is not matched to the statement in step 1, SQL Server tries to parameterize the statement by using forced parameterization. In this step, parameterization can fail for any one of the following reasons:

   ❑ The statement is already parameterized or contains local variables.

   ❑ The PARAMETERIZATION SIMPLE database SET option is applied (the default setting), and there is no plan guide of type TEMPLATE that applies to the statement and specifies the PARAMETERIZATION FORCED query hint.

   ❑ A plan guide of type TEMPLATE exists that applies to the statement and specifies the PARAMETERIZATION SIMPLE query hint.

Let's look at an example that involves the distribution of data in the *SpecialOfferID* column in the *Sales.SalesOrderDetail* table in the *AdventureWorks2008* database. There are 12 different *SpecialOfferID* values, and most of them occur only a few hundred times (out of the 121317 rows in the *Sales.SalesOrderDetail*) at most, as the following script and output illustrates:

```
USE AdventureWorks2008
GO
SELECT SpecialOfferID, COUNT(*) as Total
FROM Sales.SalesOrderDetail
GROUP BY SpecialOfferID;

RESULTS:
SpecialOfferID  Total
--------------  -----------
1               115884
2               3428
3               606
4               80
5               2
7               137
8               98
9               61
11              84
13              524
14              244
16              169
```

As there are 1238 pages in the table, for most of the values, a nonclustered index on *SpecialOfferID* could be useful, so here is the code to build one:

```
CREATE INDEX Detail_SpecialOfferIndex ON Sales.SalesOrderDetail(SpecialOfferID);
```

We assume that very few queries actually search for a *SpecialOfferID* value of 1 or 2, and 99 percent of the time the queries are looking for the less popular values. We would like the Query Optimizer to autoparameterize queries that access the *Sales.SalesOrderDetail* table, specifying one particular value for *SpecialOfferID*. So we create a template plan guide to autoparameterize queries of this form:

```
SELECT * FROM Sales.SalesOrderDetail  WHERE SpecialOfferID = 4;
```

However, we want to make sure that the initial parameter that determines the plan is not one of the values that might use a Clustered Index scan, namely the values 1 or 2. So we can take the autoparameterized query produced by the *sp_get_query_template* procedure, and use it first to create a template plan guide, and then to create a SQL plan guide with the OPTIMIZE FOR hint. The hint forces SQL Server to assume a specific value of 4 every time the query needs to be reoptimized:

```
USE AdventureWorks2008;
-- Get plan template and create plan Guide
DECLARE @stmt nvarchar(max);
DECLARE @params nvarchar(max);
EXEC sp_get_query_template
    N'SELECT * FROM Sales.SalesOrderDetail WHERE SpecialOfferID = 4',
    @stmt OUTPUT,
    @params OUTPUT
--SELECT @stmt as statement -- show the value when debugging
--SELECT @params as parameters -- show the value when debugging

EXEC sp_create_plan_guide N'Template_Plan_for SpecialOfferID',
    @stmt,
    N'TEMPLATE',
    NULL,
    @params,
    N'OPTION (PARAMETERIZATION FORCED)';

EXEC sp_create_plan_guide
    @name = N'Force_Value_for_Prepared_Plan',
    @stmt = @stmt,
    @type = N'SQL',
    @module_or_batch = NULL,
    @params = @params,
    @hints = N'OPTION (OPTIMIZE FOR (@0 = 4))';
GO
```

You can verify that the plan is being autoparameterized and optimized for a value that uses a nonclustered index on SpecialOfferID by running a few tests as follows:

```
DBCC FREEPROCCACHE;
SET STATISTICS IO ON;
SELECT * FROM Sales.SalesOrderDetail
```

```
WHERE SpecialOfferID = 3;
GO
SELECT * FROM Sales.SalesOrderDetail
WHERE SpecialOfferID = 4;
GO
SELECT * FROM Sales.SalesOrderDetail
WHERE SpecialOfferID = 5;
GO
```

You should note in the STATISTICS IO output that each execution uses a different number of reads because it is finding a different number of rows through the nonclustered index. You can also verify that SQL Server is using the prepared plan by examining the STATISTICS XML output. If you set that option to ON, and run the query looking for a value of 5, you should have a node in your XML document that looks very much like this:

```
<ParameterList>
<ColumnReference Column="@0"       ParameterCompiledValue="(4)"
        ParameterRuntimeValue="(5)" />
</ParameterList>
```

Plan guides are not intended to speed up query compilation time. Not only does SQL Server first have to determine if there is a plan guide that could be a potential match for the query being compiled, but the plan enforced by the plan guide has to be one that the Query Optimizer would have come up with on its own. To know that the forced plan is valid, the Query Optimizer has to go through most of the process of optimization. The benefit of plan guides is to reduce execution time for those queries in which the Query Optimizer is not coming up with the best plan on its own.

The main plan guide enhancements in SQL Server 2008 have to do with making plan guides more usable. SQL Server 2008 contains SMO and Management Studio support, including scripting of plan guides as part of scripting out a database. Once a plan guide is scripted, it can be copied to other SQL Server instances running the same queries.

## Plan Guide Validation

One limitation of the SQL Server 2005 implementation of plan guides was that it was possible to change the physical design of a table (for example, dropping an index) in a way that could invalidate a plan guide and any queries using that plan guide would fail whenever they were executed. SQL Server 2008 can detect cases when changing the table design would break a plan guide. It can now recompile the query without the plan guide and to notify the administrator through trace events. In addition, there is a new system function that can be used to validate plan guides. This function can be used to detect physical database design changes that break existing plan guides and allow you to roll back the breaking transaction before it can break the system.

To validate all of the existing plan guides in a system, you can use the *sys.fn_validate_plan_guide* function:

```
SELECT * FROM sys.plan_guides pg
CROSS APPLY
(SELECT * FROM sys.fn_validate_plan_guide(pg.plan_guide_id)) v;
```

The function returns nothing for valid plan guides. When the guide would generate an error, it returns a row. So you can incorporate this into any schema changes in the system:

```
BEGIN TRANSACTION;
DROP INDEX t2.myindex;
IF EXISTS(
SELECT * FROM sys.plan_guides pg
CROSS APPLY
   (SELECT * FROM sys.fn_validate_plan_guide(pg.plan_guide_id)) v
)
ROLLBACK TRANSACTION
ELSE
COMMIT TRANSACTION;
```

## Freezing a Plan from Plan Cache

SQL Server 2008 added a new stored procedure to allow you to create a plan guide automatically from a plan that has already been cached. The procedure *sp_create_plan_guide_from_handle* requires a *plan_handle* and a plan guide name as parameters and creates a plan guide using the execution plan stored in cache for that *plan_handle* value. The capability is called *plan freezing* because it allows you to make sure that a well-performing plan is reused every time the associated query is executed. Suppose that we have found that the plan just executed for the following query performs extremely well, and we'd like to make sure that plan is the one used on subsequent executions:

```
SELECT City, StateProvinceID, PostalCode FROM Person.Address ORDER BY PostalCode DESC;
```

I can find the corresponding plan in cache by searching for a text value that matches the query:

```
SELECT plan_handle
FROM sys.dm_exec_query_stats AS qs CROSS APPLY sys.dm_exec_sql_text(qs.sql_handle) AS st
WHERE st.text LIKE N'SELECT City,%';
```

Once I have that *plan_handle,* I can pass it as a parameter to the *sp_create_plan_guide_from_handle* procedure as follows:

```
EXEC sp_create_plan_guide_from_handle
    @name = N'Guide1_from_XML_showplan',
    @plan_handle = 0x06000600F19B1E1FC0A14C0A00000000000000000000000
```

There are several situations in which plan guides and plan freezing can be particularly beneficial:

- You can use plan guides to provide a workaround for plan regressions after a server upgrade.

- You can disallow plan changes for critical plans in a well-performing system.

- You can troubleshoot a problematic query by freezing a good plan (assuming a good plan ever is used).

- ISVs can create known good plans for shipping with their applications.

- You can optimize on a test system and then port the plan guide to your production system.

- You can include plan guides in a cloned database.

# Summary

For all the caching mechanisms, reusing a cached plan avoids recompilation and optimization. This saves compilation time, but it means that the same plan is used regardless of the particular parameter values passed in. If the optimal plan for a given parameter value is not the same as the cached plan, the optimal execution time is not achieved. For this reason, SQL Server is very conservative about autoparameterization. When an application uses *sp_executesql*, prepare and execute, or stored procedures, the application developer is responsible for determining what should be parameterized. You should parameterize only constants whose range of values does not drastically affect the optimization choices.

In this chapter, we looked at the caching and reuse of plans generated by the Query Optimizer. SQL Server can cache and reuse plans not only from stored procedures, but also from adhoc and autoparameterized queries. Because generating query plans can be expensive, it helps to understand how and why query plans are reused and when they must be regenerated. Understanding how caching and reusing plans work helps you determine when using the cached plan can be the right choice and when you might need to make sure SQL Server comes up with a new plan to give your queries and applications the best performance.

# Chapter 10
# Transactions and Concurrency

*Kalen Delaney*

*Concurrency* can be defined as the ability of multiple processes to access or change shared data at the same time. The greater the number of concurrent user processes that can be active without interfering with each other, the greater the concurrency of the database system.

Concurrency is reduced when a process that is changing data prevents other processes from reading that data or when a process that is reading data prevents other processes from changing that data. I use the terms *reading* or *accessing* to describe the impact of using the *SELECT* statement on your data. Concurrency is also affected when multiple processes attempt to change the same data simultaneously and they cannot all succeed without sacrificing data consistency. I use the terms *modifying, changing,* or *writing* to describe the impact of using the *INSERT, UPDATE, MERGE,* or *DELETE* statements on your data. (Note that *MERGE* is a new data modification statement in SQL Server 2008, and you can think of it as a combination of *INSERT, UPDATE,* and *DELETE*.)

In general, database systems can take two approaches to managing concurrent data access: optimistic or pessimistic. Microsoft SQL Server 2008 supports both approaches. Pessimistic concurrency was the only concurrency model available before SQL Server 2005. As of SQL Server 2005, you specify which model to use by using two database options and a SET option called TRANSACTION ISOLATION LEVEL.

After I describe the basic differences between the two models, we look at the five possible isolation levels in SQL Server 2008, as well as the internals of how SQL Server controls concurrent access using each model. We look at how to control the isolation level, and we look at the metadata that shows you what SQL Server is doing.

## Concurrency Models

In either concurrency model, a conflict can occur if two processes try to modify the same data at the same time. The difference between the two models lies in whether conflicts can be avoided before they occur or can be dealt with in some manner after they occur.

### Pessimistic Concurrency

With pessimistic concurrency, the default behavior is for SQL Server to acquire locks to block access to data that another process is using. Pessimistic concurrency assumes that enough data modification operations are in the system that any given read operation is likely affected by a data modification made by another user. In other words, the system behaves pessimistically and assumes that a conflict will occur. Pessimistic concurrency avoids conflicts by acquiring locks on data that is being read, so no other processes can modify that data. It also acquires locks on data being modified, so no other processes can access that data for either reading or modifying. In other words, readers block writers and writers block readers in a pessimistic concurrency environment.

## Optimistic Concurrency

Optimistic concurrency assumes that there are sufficiently few conflicting data modification operations in the system that any single transaction is unlikely to modify data that another transaction is modifying. The default behavior of optimistic concurrency is to use row versioning to allow data readers to see the state of the data before the modification occurs. Older versions of data rows are saved, so a process reading data can see the data as it was when the process started reading and not be affected by any changes being made to that data. A process that modifies the data is unaffected by processes reading the data because the reader is accessing a saved version of the data rows. In other words, readers do not block writers and writers do not block readers. Writers can and will block writers, however, and this is what causes conflicts. SQL Server generates an error message when a conflict occurs, but it is up to the application to respond to that error.

# Transaction Processing

No matter what concurrency model you're working with, an understanding of transactions is crucial. A transaction is the basic unit of work in SQL Server. Typically, it consists of several SQL commands that read and update the database, but the update is not considered final until a *COMMIT* command is issued (at least for an explicit transaction). In general, when I talk about a modification operation or a read operation, I am talking about the transaction that performs the data modification or the read, which is not necessarily a single SQL statement. When I say that writers will block readers, I mean that so long as the transaction that performed the write operation is active, no other process can read the modified data.

The concept of a transaction is fundamental to understanding concurrency control. The mechanics of transaction control from a programming perspective are beyond the scope of this book, but I discuss basic transaction properties. I also go into detail about the transaction isolation levels because that has a direct impact on how SQL Server manages the data being accessed in your transactions.

An implicit transaction is any individual *INSERT*, *UPDATE*, *DELETE*, or *MERGE* statement. (You can also consider *SELECT* statements to be implicit transactions, although SQL Server does not write to the log when *SELECT* statements are processed.) No matter how many rows are affected, the statement must exhibit all the ACID properties of a transaction, which I tell you about in the next section. An explicit transaction is one whose beginning is marked with a *BEGIN TRAN* statement and whose end is marked by a *COMMIT TRAN* or *ROLLBACK TRAN* statement. Most of the examples I present use explicit transactions because it is the only way to show the state of SQL Server in the middle of a transaction. For example, many types of locks are held for only the duration of the transaction. I can begin a transaction, perform some operations, look around in the metadata to see what locks are being held, and then end the transaction. When the transaction ends, the locks are released; I can no longer look at them.

## ACID Properties

Transaction processing guarantees the consistency and recoverability of SQL Server databases. It ensures that all transactions are performed as a single unit of work—even in the presence of a hardware or general system failure. Such transactions are referred to as having the ACID properties, with *ACID* standing for *atomicity, consistency, isolation,* and *durability.* In addition to guaranteeing that explicit multistatement transactions maintain the ACID properties, SQL Server guarantees that an implicit transaction also maintains the ACID properties.

Here's an example in pseudocode of an explicit ACID transaction:

```
BEGIN TRANSACTION DEBIT_CREDIT
Debit savings account $1000
Credit checking account $1000
COMMIT TRANSACTION DEBIT_CREDIT
```

Now let's take a closer look at each of the ACID properties.

### Atomicity

SQL Server guarantees the atomicity of its transactions. *Atomicity* means that each transaction is treated as all or nothing—it either commits or aborts. If a transaction commits, all its effects remain. If it aborts, all its effects are undone. In the preceding DEBIT_CREDIT example, if the savings account debit is reflected in the database but the checking account credit isn't, funds essentially disappear from the database—that is, funds are subtracted from the savings account but never added to the checking account. If the reverse occurs (if the checking account is credited and the savings account is not debited), the customer's checking account mysteriously increases in value without a corresponding customer cash deposit or account transfer. Because of the atomicity feature of SQL Server, both the debit and credit must be completed or else neither event is completed.

### Consistency

The consistency property ensures that a transaction won't allow the system to arrive at an incorrect logical state—the data must always be logically correct. Constraints and rules are honored even in the event of a system failure. In the DEBIT_CREDIT example, the logical rule is that money can't be created or destroyed: a corresponding, counterbalancing entry must be made for each entry. (Consistency is implied by, and in most situations redundant with, atomicity, isolation, and durability.)

## Isolation

Isolation separates concurrent transactions from the updates of other incomplete transactions. In the DEBIT_CREDIT example, another transaction can't see the work in progress while the transaction is being carried out. For example, if another transaction reads the balance of the savings account after the debit occurs, and then the DEBIT_CREDIT transaction is aborted, the other transaction is working from a balance that never logically existed.

SQL Server accomplishes isolation among transactions automatically. It locks data or creates row versions to allow multiple concurrent users to work with data while preventing side effects that can distort the results and make them different from what would be expected if users were to serialize their requests (that is, if requests were queued and serviced one at a time). This serializability feature is one of the isolation levels that SQL Server supports. SQL Server supports multiple isolation levels so that you can choose the appropriate tradeoff between how much data to lock, how long to hold locks, and whether to allow users access to prior versions of row data. This tradeoff is known as concurrency vs. consistency.

## Durability

After a transaction commits, the durability property of SQL Server ensures that the effects of the transaction persist even if a system failure occurs. If a system failure occurs while a transaction is in progress, the transaction is completely undone, leaving no partial effects on the data. For example, if a power outage occurs in the middle of a transaction before the transaction is committed, the entire transaction is rolled back when the system is restarted. If the power fails immediately after the acknowledgment of the commit is sent to the calling application, the transaction is guaranteed to exist in the database. Write-ahead logging and automatic rollback and roll-forward of transactions during the recovery phase of SQL Server startup ensure durability.

# Transaction Dependencies

In addition to supporting all four ACID properties, a transaction might exhibit several other behaviors. Some people call these behaviors "dependency problems" or "consistency problems," but I don't necessarily think of them as problems. They are merely possible behaviors, and except for lost updates, which are never considered desirable, you can determine which of these behaviors you want to allow and which you want to avoid. Your choice of isolation level determines which of these behaviors is allowed.

## Lost Updates

Lost updates occur when two processes read the same data and both manipulate the data, changing its value, and then both try to update the original data to the new value. The second process might overwrite the first update completely. For example, suppose that two clerks in a receiving room are receiving parts and adding the new shipments to the inventory database. Clerk A and Clerk B both receive shipments of widgets. They both check the current inventory and see that 25 widgets are currently in stock. Clerk A's shipment has 50 widgets, so he adds 50 to 25 and updates the current value to 75. Clerk B's shipment has 20 widgets, so she adds 20 to the value of 25 that she originally read and updates the current value to 45, completely overriding the 50 new widgets that Clerk A processed. Clerk A's update is lost.

Lost updates are only one of the behaviors described here that you probably want to avoid in all cases.

## Dirty Reads

Dirty reads occur when a process reads uncommitted data. If one process has changed data but not yet committed the change, another process reading the data will read it in an inconsistent state. For example, say that Clerk A has updated the old value of 25 widgets to 75, but before he commits, a salesperson looks at the current value of 75 and commits to sending 60 widgets to a customer the following day. If Clerk A then realizes that the widgets are defective and sends them back to the manufacturer, the salesperson has done a dirty read and taken action based on uncommitted data.

By default, dirty reads are not allowed. Keep in mind that the process updating the data has no control over whether another process can read its data before the first process is committed. It's up to the process reading the data to decide whether it wants to read data that is not guaranteed to be committed.

## Nonrepeatable Reads

A read is nonrepeatable if a process might get different values when reading the same data in two separate reads within the same transaction. This can happen when another process changes the data in between the reads that the first process is doing. In the receiving room example, suppose that a manager comes in to do a spot check of the current inventory. She walks up to each clerk, asking the total number of widgets received today and adding the numbers on her calculator. When she's done, she wants to double-check the result, so she goes back to the first clerk. However, if Clerk A received more widgets between the manager's first and second inquiries, the total is different and the reads are nonrepeatable. Nonrepeatable reads are also called *inconsistent analysis*.

## Phantoms

Phantoms occur when membership in a set changes. It can happen only when a query with a predicate—such as WHERE count_of_widgets < 10—is involved. A phantom occurs if two *SELECT* operations using the same predicate in the same transaction return a different number of rows. For example, let's say that our manager is still doing spot checks of inventory. This time, she goes around the receiving room and notes which clerks have fewer than 10 widgets. After she completes the list, she goes back around to offer advice to everyone with a low total. However, if during her first walkthrough, a clerk with fewer than 10 widgets returned from a break but was not spotted by the manager, that clerk is not on the manager's list even though he meets the criteria in the predicate. This additional clerk (or row) is considered to be a phantom.

The behavior of your transactions depends on the isolation level. As mentioned earlier, you can decide which of the behaviors described previously to allow by setting an appropriate isolation level using the command *SET TRANSACTION ISOLATION LEVEL* <isolation_level>. Your concurrency model (optimistic or pessimistic) determines how the isolation level is implemented—or, more specifically, how SQL Server guarantees that the behaviors you don't want will not occur.

## Isolation Levels

SQL Server 2008 supports five isolation levels that control the behavior of your read operations. Three of them are available only with pessimistic concurrency, one is available only with optimistic concurrency, and one is available with either. We look at these levels now, but a complete understanding of isolation levels also requires an understanding of locking and row versioning. In my descriptions of the isolation levels, I mention the locks or row versions that support that level, but keep in mind that locking and row versioning are discussed in detail later in the chapter.

### Read Uncommitted

In Read Uncommitted isolation, all the behaviors described previously, except lost updates, are possible. Your queries can read uncommitted data, and both nonrepeatable reads and phantoms are possible. Read Uncommitted isolation is implemented by allowing your read operations to not take any locks, and because SQL Server isn't trying to acquire locks, it won't be blocked by conflicting locks acquired by other processes. Your process is able to read data that another process has modified but not yet committed.

In addition to reading individual values that are not yet committed, the Read Uncommitted isolation level introduces other undesirable behaviors. When using this isolation level and scanning an entire table, SQL Server can decide to do an allocation order scan (in page-number order), instead of a logical order scan (which would follow the page pointers). If there are concurrent operations by other processes that change data and move rows to a new location in the table, your allocation order scan can end up reading the same row twice. This can happen when you've read a row before it is updated, and then the update moves the row to a higher page number than your scan encounters later. In addition, performing an allocation order scan under Read Uncommitted can cause you to miss a row completely. This can happen when a row on a high page number that hasn't been read yet is updated and moved to a lower page number that has already been read.

Although this scenario isn't usually the ideal option, with Read Uncommitted, you can't get stuck waiting for a lock, and your read operations don't acquire any locks that might affect other processes that are reading or writing data.

When using Read Uncommitted, you give up the assurance of strongly consistent data in favor of high concurrency in the system without users locking each other out. So when should you choose Read Uncommitted? Clearly, you don't want to use it for financial transactions in which every number must balance. But it might be fine for certain decision-support analyses—for example, when you look at sales trends—for which complete precision isn't necessary and the tradeoff in higher concurrency makes it worthwhile. Read Uncommitted isolation is a pessimistic solution to the problem of too much blocking activity because it just ignores the locks and does not provide you with transactional consistency.

## Read Committed

SQL Server 2008 supports two varieties of Read Committed isolation, which is the default isolation level. This isolation level can be either optimistic or pessimistic, depending on the database setting READ_COMMITTED_SNAPSHOT. Because the default for the database option is off, the default for this isolation level is to use pessimistic concurrency control. Unless indicated otherwise, when I refer to the Read Committed isolation level, I am referring to both variations of this isolation level. I refer to the pessimistic implementation as Read Committed (locking), and I refer to the optimistic implementation as Read Committed (snapshot).

Read Committed isolation ensures that an operation never reads data that another application has changed but not yet committed. (That is, it never reads data that logically never existed.) With Read Committed (locking), if another transaction is updating data and consequently has exclusive locks on data rows, your transaction must wait for those locks to be released before you can use that data (whether you're reading or modifying). Also, your transaction must put share locks (at a minimum) on the data that are visited, which means that data might be unavailable to others to use. A share lock doesn't prevent others from reading the data, but it makes them wait to update the data. By default, share locks can be released after the data has been processed—they don't have to be held for the duration of the transaction, or even for the duration of the statement. (That is, if shared row locks are acquired, each row lock can be released as soon as the row is processed, even though the statement might need to process many more rows.)

Read Committed (snapshot) also ensures that an operation never reads uncommitted data, but not by forcing other processes to wait. In Read Committed (snapshot), every time a row is updated, SQL Server generates a version of the changed row with its previous committed values. The data being changed is still locked, but other processes can see the previous versions of the data as it was before the update operation began.

## Repeatable Read

Repeatable Read is a pessimistic isolation level. It adds to the properties of Committed Read by ensuring that if a transaction revisits data or a query is reissued, the data does not change. In other words, issuing the same query twice within a transaction cannot pick up any changes to data values made by another user's transaction because no changes can be made by other transactions. However, the Repeatable Read isolation level does allow phantom rows to appear.

Preventing nonrepeatable reads is a desirable safeguard in some cases. But there's no free lunch. The cost of this extra safeguard is that all the shared locks in a transaction must be held until the completion (*COMMIT* or *ROLLBACK*) of the transaction. (Exclusive locks must always be held until the end of a transaction, no matter what the isolation level or concurrency model, so that a transaction can be rolled back if necessary. If the locks were released sooner, it might be impossible to undo the work because other concurrent transactions might have used the same data and changed the value.) No other user can modify the data visited by your transaction as long as your transaction is open. Obviously, this can seriously reduce concurrency and degrade performance. If transactions are not kept short or if applications are not written to be aware of such potential lock contention issues, SQL Server can appear to stop responding when a process is waiting for locks to be released.

> **Note** You can control how long SQL Server waits for a lock to be released by using the session option LOCK_TIMEOUT. It is a SET option, so the behavior can be controlled only for an individual session. There is no way to set a LOCK_TIMEOUT value for SQL Server as a whole. You can read about LOCK_TIMEOUT in *SQL Server Books Online.*

## Snapshot

Snapshot isolation (sometimes referred to as SI) is an optimistic isolation level. Like Read Committed (snapshot), it allows processes to read older versions of committed data if the current version is locked. The difference between Snapshot and Read Committed (snapshot) has to do with how old the older versions have to be. (We see the details in the section entitled "Row Versioning," later in this chapter.) Although the behaviors prevented by Snapshot isolation are the same as those prevented by Serializable, Snapshot is not truly a Serializable isolation level. With Snapshot isolation, it is possible to have two transactions executing simultaneously that give us a result that is not possible in any serial execution. Table 10-1 shows an example of two simultaneous transactions. If they run in parallel, they end up switching the price of two books in the *titles* table in the *pubs* database. However, there is no serial execution that would end up switching the values, whether we run Transaction 1 and then Transaction 2, or run Transaction 2 and then Transaction 1. Either serial order ends up with the two books having the same price.

**TABLE 10-1  Two Simultaneous Transactions in Snapshot Isolation That Cannot Be Run Serially**

| Time | Transaction 1 | Transaction 2 |
|------|---------------|---------------|
| 1 | USE pubs<br>SET TRANSACTION ISOLATION LEVEL<br>SNAPSHOT<br>DECLARE @price money<br>BEGIN TRAN | USE pubs<br>SET TRANSACTION ISOLATION LEVEL<br>SNAPSHOT<br>DECLARE @price money<br>BEGIN TRAN |
| 2 | SELECT @price = price<br>FROM titles<br>WHERE title_id = 'BU1032' | SELECT @price = price<br>FROM titles<br>WHERE title_id = 'PS7777' |
| 3 | UPDATE titles<br>SET price = @price<br>WHERE title_id = 'PS7777' | UPDATE titles<br>SET price = @price<br>WHERE title_id = 'BU1032' |
| 4 | COMMIT TRAN | COMMIT TRAN |

## Serializable

Serializable is also a pessimistic isolation level. The Serializable isolation level adds to the properties of Repeatable Read by ensuring that if a query is reissued, rows were not added in the interim. In other words, phantoms do not appear if the same query is issued twice within a transaction. Serializable is therefore the strongest of the pessimistic isolation levels because it prevents all the possible undesirable behaviors discussed earlier—that is, it does not allow uncommitted reads, nonrepeatable reads, or phantoms, and it also guarantees that your transactions can be run serially.

Preventing phantoms is another desirable safeguard. But once again, there's no free lunch. The cost of this extra safeguard is similar to that of Repeatable Read—all the shared locks in a transaction must be held until the transaction completes. In addition, enforcing the Serializable isolation level requires that you not only lock data that has been read, but also lock data that does not exist! For example, suppose that within a transaction, we issue a *SELECT* statement to read all the customers whose ZIP code is between 98000 and 98100, and on first execution, no rows satisfy that condition. To enforce the Serializable isolation level, we must lock that range of potential rows with ZIP codes between 98000 and 98100 so that if the same query is reissued, there are still no rows that satisfy the condition. SQL Server handles this situation by using a special kind of lock called a *key-range lock*. Key-range locks require that there be an index on the column that defines the range of values. (In this example, that would be the column containing the ZIP codes.) If there is no index on that column, Serializable isolation requires a table lock. I discuss the different types of locks in detail in the section on locking. The Serializable level gets its name from the fact that running multiple serializable transactions at the same time is the equivalent of running them one at a time—that is, serially.

For example, suppose that transactions A, B, and C run simultaneously at the Serializable level and each tries to update the same range of data. If the order in which the transactions acquire locks on the range of data is B, C, and then A, the result obtained by running all three simultaneously is the same as if they were run sequentially in the order B, C, and then A. Serializable does not imply that the order is known in advance. The order is considered a chance event. Even on a single-user system, the order of transactions hitting the queue would be essentially random. If the batch order is important to your application, you should implement it as a pure batch system. Serializable means only that there should be a way to run the transactions serially to get the same result you get when you run them simultaneously. Table 10-1 illustrates a case where two transactions cannot be run serially and get the same result.

Table 10-2 summarizes the behaviors that are possible in each isolation level and notes the concurrency control model that is used to implement each level. You can see that Read Committed and Read Committed (snapshot) are identical in the behaviors they allow, but the behaviors are implemented differently—one is pessimistic (locking), and one is optimistic (row versioning). Serializable and Snapshot also have the same No values for all the behaviors, but one is pessimistic and one is optimistic.

**TABLE 10-2  Behaviors Allowed in Each Isolation Level**

| Isolation Level | Dirty Read | Nonrepeatable Read | Phantom | Concurrency Control |
|---|---|---|---|---|
| Read Uncommitted | Yes | Yes | Yes | Pessimistic |
| Read Committed (locking) | No | Yes | Yes | Pessimistic |
| Read Committed (snapshot) | No | Yes | Yes | Optimistic |
| Repeatable Read | No | No | Yes | Pessimistic |
| Snapshot | No | No | No | Optimistic |
| Serializable | No | No | No | Pessimistic |

# Locking

Locking is a crucial function of any multiuser database system, including SQL Server. Locks are applied in both the pessimistic and optimistic concurrency models, although the way other processes deal with locked data is different in each. The reason I refer to the pessimistic variation of Read Committed isolation as Read Committed (locking) is because locking allows concurrent transactions to maintain consistency. In the pessimistic model, writers always block readers and writers, and readers can block writers. In the optimistic model, the only blocking that occurs is that writers block other writers. But to really understand what these simplified behavior summaries mean, we need to look at the details of SQL Server locking.

## Locking Basics

SQL Server can lock data using several different modes. For example, read operations acquire shared locks, and write operations acquire exclusive locks. Update locks are acquired during the initial portion of an update operation, while SQL Server is searching for the data to update. SQL Server acquires and releases all these types of locks automatically. It also manages compatibility between lock modes, resolves deadlocks, and escalates locks if necessary. It controls locks on tables, on the pages of a table, on index keys, and on individual rows of data. Locks can also be held on system data—data that's private to the database system, such as page headers and indexes.

SQL Server provides two separate locking systems. The first system affects all fully shared data and provides row locks, page locks, and table locks for tables, data pages, Large Object (LOB) pages, and leaf-level index pages. The second system is used internally for index concurrency control, controlling access to internal data structures and retrieving individual rows of data pages. This second system uses latches, which are less resource-intensive than locks and provide performance optimizations. You could use full-blown locks for all locking, but because of their complexity, they would slow down the system if you used them for all internal needs. If you examine locks using the *sp_lock* system stored procedure or a similar mechanism that gets information from the *sys.dm_tran_locks* view, you cannot see latches— you see only information about locks.

Another way to look at the difference between locks and latches is that locks ensure the logical consistency of the data and latches ensure the physical consistency. Latching happens when you place a row physically on a page or move data in other ways, such as compressing the space on a page. SQL Server must guarantee that this data movement can happen without interference.

## Spinlocks

For shorter-term needs, SQL Server achieves mutual exclusion with a spinlock. Spinlocks are used purely for mutual exclusion and never to lock user data. They are even more lightweight than latches, which are lighter than the full locks used for data and index leaf pages. The requester of a spinlock repeats its request if the lock is not immediately available. (That is, the requester "spins" on the lock until it is free.)

Spinlocks are often used as mutexes within SQL Server for resources that are usually not busy. If a resource is busy, the duration of a spinlock is short enough that retrying is better than waiting and then being rescheduled by the operating system, which results in context switching between threads. The savings in context switches more than offsets the cost of spinning as long as you don't have to spin too long. Spinlocks are used for situations in which the wait for a resource is expected to be brief (or if no wait is expected). The *sys.dm_os_tasks* dynamic management view (DMV) shows a status of SPINLOOP for any task that is currently using a spinlock.

## Lock Types for User Data

We examine four aspects of locking user data. First we look at the mode of locking (the type of lock). I already mentioned shared, exclusive, and update locks, and I go into more detail about these modes as well as others. Next we look at the granularity of the lock, which specifies how much data is covered by a single lock. This can be a row, a page, an index key, a range of index keys, an extent, a partition, or an entire table. The third aspect of locking is the duration of the lock. As mentioned earlier, some locks are released as soon as the data has been accessed, and some locks are held until the transaction commits or rolls back. The fourth aspect of locking concerns the ownership of the lock (the scope of the lock). Locks can be owned by a session, a transaction, or a cursor.

# Lock Modes

SQL Server uses several locking modes, including shared locks, exclusive locks, update locks, and intent locks, plus variations on these. It is the mode of the lock that determines whether a concurrently requested lock is compatible with locks that have already been granted. We see the lock compatibility matrix at the end of this section in Figure 10-2.

## Shared Locks

Shared locks are acquired automatically by SQL Server when data is read. Shared locks can be held on a table, a page, an index key, or an individual row. Many processes can hold shared locks on the same data, but no process can acquire an exclusive lock on data that has a shared lock on it (unless the process requesting the exclusive lock is the same process as the one holding the shared lock). Normally, shared locks are released as soon as the data has been read, but you can change this by using query hints or a different transaction isolation level.

## Exclusive Locks

SQL Server automatically acquires exclusive locks on data when the data is modified by an *INSERT, UPDATE,* or *DELETE* operation. Only one process at a time can hold an exclusive lock on a particular data resource; in fact, as you see when we discuss lock compatibility later in this chapter, no locks of any kind can be acquired by a process if another process has the requested data resource exclusively locked. Exclusive locks are held until the end of the transaction. This means the changed data is normally not available to any other process until the current transaction commits or rolls back. Other processes can decide to read exclusively locked data by using query hints.

## Update Locks

Update locks are really not a separate kind of lock; they are a hybrid of shared and exclusive locks. They are acquired when SQL Server executes a data modification operation but first, SQL Server needs to search the table to find the resource that needs to be modified. Using query hints, a process can specifically request update locks, and in that case, the update locks prevent the conversion deadlock situation presented in Figure 10-6 later in this chapter.

Update locks provide compatibility with other current readers of data, allowing the process to later modify data with the assurance that the data hasn't been changed since it was last read. An update lock is not sufficient to allow you to change the data—all modifications require that the data resource being modified have an exclusive lock. An update lock acts as a serialization gate to queue future requests for the exclusive lock. (Many processes can hold shared locks for a resource, but only one process can hold an update lock.) So long as a process holds an update lock on a resource, no other process can acquire an update lock or an exclusive lock for that resource; instead, another process requesting an update or exclusive lock for the same resource must wait. The process holding the update lock can convert it into an exclusive lock on that resource because the update lock prevents lock incompatibility with any other processes. You can think of update locks as "intent-to-update" locks, which is essentially the role they perform. Used alone, update locks are insufficient for updating data—an exclusive lock is still required for actual data modification. Serializing access for the exclusive lock lets you avoid conversion deadlocks. Update locks are held until the end of the transaction or until they are converted to an exclusive lock.

Don't let the name fool you: update locks are not just for *UPDATE* operations. SQL Server uses update locks for any data modification operation that requires a search for the data prior to the actual modification. Such operations include qualified updates and deletes, as well as inserts into a table with a clustered index. In the latter case, SQL Server must first search the data (using the clustered index) to find the correct position at which to insert the new row. While SQL Server is only searching, it uses update locks to protect the data; only after it has found the correct location and begins inserting does it convert the update lock to an exclusive lock.

## Intent Locks

Intent locks are not really a separate mode of locking; they are a qualifier to the modes previously discussed. In other words, you can have intent shared locks, intent exclusive locks, and even intent update locks. Because SQL Server can acquire locks at different levels of granularity, a mechanism is needed to indicate that a component of a resource is already locked. For example, if one process tries to lock a table, SQL Server needs a way to determine whether a row (or a page) of that table is already locked. Intent locks serve this purpose. We discuss them in more detail when we look at lock granularity.

## Special Lock Modes

SQL Server offers three additional lock modes: schema stability locks, schema modification locks, and bulk update locks. When queries are compiled, schema stability locks prevent other processes from acquiring schema modification locks, which are taken when a table's structure is being modified. A bulk update lock is acquired when the *BULK INSERT* command is executed or when the bcp utility is run to load data into a table. In addition, the bulk import operation must request this special lock by using the TABLOCK hint. Alternatively, the table owner can set the table option called *table lock on bulk load* to True, and then any bulk copy *IN* or *BULK INSERT* operation automatically requests a bulk update lock. Requesting this special bulk update table lock does not necessarily mean it is granted. If other processes already hold locks on the table, or if the table has any indexes, a bulk update lock cannot be granted. If multiple connections have requested and received a bulk update lock, they can perform parallel loads into the same table. Unlike exclusive locks, bulk update locks do not conflict with each other, so concurrent inserts by multiple connections is supported.

## Conversion Locks

Conversion locks are never requested directly by SQL Server, but are the result of a conversion from one mode to another. The three types of conversion locks supported by SQL Server 2008 are SIX, SIU, and UIX. The most common of these is the SIX, which occurs if a transaction is holding a shared (S) lock on a resource and later an IX lock is needed. The lock mode is indicated as SIX. For example, suppose that you issue the following batch:

```
SET TRANSACTION ISOLATION LEVEL REPEATABLE READ
BEGIN TRAN
SELECT * FROM bigtable
UPDATE bigtable
    SET col = 0
    WHERE keycolumn = 100
```

If the table is large, the *SELECT* statement acquires a shared table lock. (If the table has only a few rows, SQL Server acquires individual row or key locks.) The *UPDATE* statement then acquires a single exclusive key lock to perform the update of a single row, and the X lock at the key level means an IX lock at the page and table level. The table then shows SIX when viewed through *sys.dm_tran_locks*. Similarly, SIU occurs when a process has a shared lock on a table and an update lock on a row of that table, and UIX occurs when a process has an update lock on the table and an exclusive lock on a row.

Table 10-3 shows most of the lock modes, as well as the abbreviations used in *sys.dm_tran_locks*.

**TABLE 10-3 SQL Server Lock Modes**

| Abbreviation | Lock Mode | Description |
|---|---|---|
| S | Shared | Allows other processes to read but not change the locked resource. |
| X | Exclusive | Prevents another process from modifying or reading data in the locked resource. |
| U | Update | Prevents other processes from acquiring an update or exclusive lock; used when searching for the data to modify. |
| IS | Intent shared | Indicates that a component of this resource is locked with a shared lock. This lock can be acquired only at the table or page level. |
| IU | Intent update | Indicates that a component of this resource is locked with an update lock. This lock can be acquired only at the table or page level. |

**TABLE 10-3** **SQL Server Lock Modes**

| Abbreviation | Lock Mode | Description |
| --- | --- | --- |
| IX | Intent exclusive | Indicates that a component of this resource is locked with an exclusive lock. This lock can be acquired only at the table or page level. |
| SIX | Shared with intent exclusive | Indicates that a resource holding a shared lock also has a component (a page or row) locked with an exclusive lock. |
| SIU | Shared with intent update | Indicates that a resource holding a shared lock also has a component (a page or row) locked with an update lock. |
| UIX | Update with intent exclusive | Indicates that a resource holding an update lock also has a component (a page or row) locked with an exclusive lock. |
| Sch-S | Schema stability | Indicates that a query using this table is being compiled. |
| Sch-M | Schema modification | Indicates that the structure of the table is being changed. |
| BU | Bulk update | Used when a bulk copy operation is copying data into a table and the TABLOCK hint is being applied (either manually or automatically). |

## Key-Range Locks

Additional lock modes—called *key-range locks*—are taken only in the Serializable isolation level for locking ranges of data. Most lock modes can apply to almost any lock resource. For example, shared and exclusive locks can be taken on a table, a page, a row, or a key. Because key-range locks can be taken only on keys, I describe the details of key-range locks later in this chapter in the section on key locks.

## Lock Granularity

SQL Server can lock user data resources (not system resources, which are protected with latches) at the table, page, or row level. (If locks are escalated, SQL Server can also lock a single partition of a table or index.) In addition, SQL Server can lock index keys and ranges of index keys. Figure 10-1 shows the basic lock levels in a table that can be acquired when a resource is first accessed. Keep in mind that if the table has a clustered index, the data rows are at the leaf level of the clustered index and they are locked with key locks instead of row locks.

The *sys.dm_tran_locks* view keeps track of each lock and contains information about the resource, which is locked (such as a row, key, or page), the mode of the lock, and an identifier for the specific resource. Keep in mind that *sys.dm_tran_locks* is only a dynamic view that is used to display the information about the locks that are held. The actual information is stored in internal SQL Server structures that are not visible to us at all. So when I talk about information being in the *sys.dm_tran_locks* view, I am referring to the fact that the information can be seen through that view.

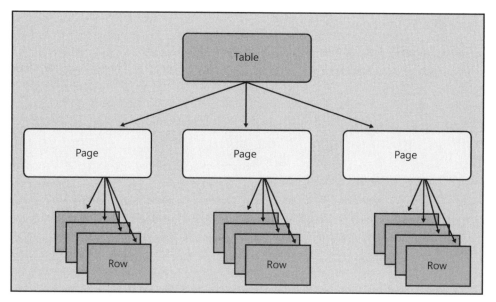

**FIGURE 10-1** Levels of granularity for SQL Server locks on a table

When a process requests a lock, SQL Server compares the lock requested to the resources already listed in *sys.dm_tran_locks* and looks for an exact match on the resource type and identifier. However, if one process has a row exclusively locked in the *Sales.SalesOrderHeader* table, for example, another process might try to get a lock on the entire *Sales.SalesOrderHeader* table. Because these are two different resources, SQL Server does not find an exact match unless additional information is already in *sys.dm_tran_locks*. This is what intent locks are for. The process that has the exclusive lock on a row of the *Sales.SalesOrderHeader* table also has an intent exclusive lock on the page containing the row and another intent exclusive lock on the table containing the row. We can see those locks by first running this code:

```
USE Adventureworks2008;
BEGIN TRAN
UPDATE  Sales.SalesOrderHeader
SET ShipDate = ShipDate + 1
WHERE SalesOrderID = 43666;
```

This statement should affect a single row. Because I have started a transaction and not yet terminated it, the exclusive locks acquired are still held. I can look at those locks using the *sys.dm_tran_locks view:*

```
SELECT resource_type, resource_description,
       resource_associated_entity_id, request_mode, request_status
FROM sys.dm_tran_locks
WHERE resource_associated_entity_id > 0;
```

I give you more details about the data in the section entitled *"sys.dm_tran_locks"* later in this chapter, but for now, just note that the reason for the filter in the WHERE clause is that I am interested only in locks that are actually held on data resources. If you are running a query on a SQL Server instance that others are using, you might have to provide more filters to get just the rows you're interested in. For example, you could include a filter on *request_session_id* to limit the output to locks held by a particular session. Your results should look something like this:

```
resource_type resource_description resource_associated_entity_id request_mode request_status
------------- -------------------- ----------------------------- ------------ --------------
KEY           (92007ad11d1d)       72057594045857792             X            GRANT
PAGE          1:5280               72057594045857792             IX           GRANT
OBJECT                             722101613                     IX           GRANT
```

Note that there are three locks, even though the *UPDATE* statement affected only a single row. For the KEY and the PAGE locks, the *resource_associated_entity_id* is a partition_id. For the OBJECT locks, the *resource_associated_entity_id* is a table. We can verify what table it is by using the following query:

```
SELECT object_name(722101613)
```

The results should tell us that the object is the *Sales.SalesOrderHeader* table. When the second process attempts to acquire an exclusive lock on that table, it finds a conflicting row already in *sys.dm_tran_locks* on the same lock resource (the *Sales.SalesOrderHeader* table), and it is blocked. The *sys.dm_tran_locks* view shows us the following row, indicating a request for an exclusive lock on an object that is unable to be granted. The process requesting the lock is in a WAIT state:

```
resource_type resource_description resource_associated_entity_id request_mode request_status
------------- -------------------- ----------------------------- ------------ --------------
OBJECT                             722101613                     X            WAIT
```

Not all requests for locks on resources that are already locked result in a conflict. A conflict occurs when one process requests a lock on a resource that is already locked by another process in an incompatible lock mode. For example, two processes can each acquire shared locks on the same resource because shared locks are compatible with each other. I discuss lock compatibility in detail later in this chapter.

## Key Locks

SQL Server 2008 supports two kinds of key locks, and which one it uses depends on the isolation level of the current transaction. If the isolation level is Read Committed, Repeatable Read, or Snapshot, SQL Server tries to lock the actual index keys accessed while processing the query. With a table that has a clustered index, the data rows are the leaf level of the index, and you see key locks acquired. If the table is a heap, you might see key locks for the nonclustered indexes and row locks for the actual data.

If the isolation level is Serializable, the situation is different. We want to prevent phantoms, so if we have scanned a range of data within a transaction, we need to lock enough of the table to make sure no one can insert a value into the range that was scanned. For example, we can issue the following query within an explicit transaction in the *AdventureWorks2008* database:

```
BEGIN TRAN
SELECT * FROM Sales.SalesOrderHeader
WHERE CustomerID BETWEEN 100 and 110;
```

When you use Serializable isolation, locks must be acquired to make sure no new rows with *CustomerID* values between 100 and 110 are inserted before the end of the transaction. Much older versions of SQL Server (prior to 7.0) guaranteed this by locking whole pages or even the entire table. In many cases, however, this was too restrictive—more data was locked than the actual WHERE clause indicated, resulting in unnecessary contention. SQL Server 2008 uses the key-range locks mode, which is associated with a particular key value in an index and indicates that all values between that key and the previous one in the index are locked.

The *AdventureWorks2008* database includes an index on the *Person* table with the *LastName* column as the leading column. Assume that we are in TRANSACTION ISOLATION LEVEL SERIALIZABLE and we issue this *SELECT* statement inside a user-defined transaction:

```
SELECT * FROM Person.Person
WHERE LastName BETWEEN 'Freller' AND 'Freund';
```

If *Fredericksen, French,* and *Friedland* are sequential leaf-level index keys in an index on the *LastName* column, the second two of these keys (*French* and *Friedland*) acquire key-range locks (although only one row, for *French,* is returned in the result set). The key-range locks prevent any inserts into the ranges ending with the two key-range locks. No values greater than *Fredericksen* and less than or equal to *French* can be inserted, and no values greater than *French* and less than or equal to *Friedland* can be inserted. Note that the key-range locks imply an open interval starting at the previous sequential key and a closed interval ending at the key on which the lock is placed. These two key-range locks prevent anyone from inserting either *Fremlich* or *Frenkin,* which are in the range specified in the WHERE clause. However, the key-range locks would also prevent anyone from inserting *Freedman* (which is greater than *Fredericksen* and less than *French*), even though *Freedman* is not in the query's specified range. Key-range locks are not perfect, but they do provide much greater concurrency than locking whole pages or tables, while guaranteeing that phantoms are prevented.

There are nine types of key-range locks, and each has a two-part name: the first part indicates the type of lock on the range of data between adjacent index keys, and the second part indicates the type of lock on the key itself. These nine types of key-range locks are described in Table 10-4.

**TABLE 10-4  Types of Key-Range Locks**

| Abbreviation | Description |
| --- | --- |
| RangeS-S | Shared lock on the range between keys; shared lock on the key at the end of the range |
| RangeS-U | Shared lock on the range between keys; update lock on the key at the end of the range |
| RangeIn-Null | Exclusive lock to prevent inserts on the range between keys; no lock on the keys themselves |
| RangeX-X | Exclusive lock on the range between keys; exclusive lock on the key at the end of the range |
| RangeIn-S | Conversion lock created by S and RangeIn_Null lock |
| RangeIn-U | Conversion lock created by U and RangeIn_Null lock |
| RangeIn-X | Conversion of X and RangeIn_Null lock |
| RangeX-S | Conversion of RangeIn_Null and RangeS_S lock |
| RangeX-U | Conversion of RangeIn_Null and RangeS_U lock |

Many of these lock modes are very rare or transient, so you do not see them very often in *sys.dm_tran_locks*. For example, the RangeIn-Null lock is acquired when SQL Server attempts to insert into the range between keys in a session using Serializable isolation. This type of lock is not often seen because it is typically very transient. It is held only until the correct location for insertion is found, and then the lock is converted into an X lock. However, if one transaction scans a range of data using the Serializable isolation level and then another transaction tries to insert into that range, the second transaction has a lock request with a WAIT status with the RangeIn-Null mode. You can observe this by looking at the status column in *sys.dm_tran_locks*, which we discuss in more detail later in the chapter.

## Additional Lock Resources

In addition to locks on objects, pages, keys, and rows, a few other resources can be locked by SQL Server. Locks can be taken on extents—units of disk space that are 64 KB in size (eight pages of 8 KB each). This kind of locking occurs automatically when a table or an index needs to grow and a new extent must be allocated. You can think of an extent lock as another type of special-purpose latch, but it does show up in *sys.dm_tran_locks*. Extents can have both shared extent and exclusive extent locks.

When you examine the contents of *sys.dm_tran_locks*, you should notice that most processes hold a lock on at least one database (*resource_type* = DATABASE). In fact, any process holding locks in any database other than *master* or *tempdb* has a lock for that database resource. These database locks are always shared locks if the process is just using the database. SQL Server checks for these database locks when determining whether a database is in use, and then it can determine whether the database can be dropped, restored, altered, or closed. Because few changes can be made to *master* and *tempdb* and they cannot be dropped or closed, DATABASE locks are unnecessary. In addition, *tempdb* is never restored, and to restore the *master* database, the entire server must be started in single-user mode, so again, DATABASE locks are unnecessary. When attempting to perform one of these operations, SQL Server requests an exclusive database lock, and if any other processes have a shared lock on the database, the request blocks. Generally, you don't need to be concerned with extent or database locks, but you see them if you are perusing *sys.dm_tran_locks*.

You might occasionally see locks on ALLOCATION_UNIT resources. Although all table and index structures contain one or more ALLOCATION_UNITs, when these locks occur, it means SQL Server is dealing with one of these resources that is no longer tied to a particular object. For example, when you drop or rebuild large tables or indexes, the actual page deallocation is deferred until after the transaction commits. Deferred drop operations do not release allocated space immediately, and they introduce additional overhead costs, so a deferred drop is done only on tables or indexes that use more than 128 extents. If the table or index uses 128 or fewer extents, dropping, truncating, and rebuilding are not deferred operations. During the first phase of a deferred operation, the existing allocation units used by the table or index are marked for deallocation and locked until the transaction commits. This is where you see ALLOCATION_UNIT locks in *sys.dm_tran_locks*. You can also look in the *sys.allocation_units* view to find allocation units with a *type_desc* value of DROPPED to see how much space is being used by the allocation units that are not available for reuse but are not currently part of any object. The actual physical dropping of the allocation unit's space occurs after the transaction commits.

Finally, you occasionally have locks on individual partitions, which are indicated in the lock metadata as HOBT locks. This can happen only when locks are escalated, and only if you have specified that escalation to the partition level is allowed (and, of course, only when the table or index has been partitioned). We look at how you can specify that you want partition-level locking in the section entitled "Lock Escalation," later in this chapter.

## Identifying Lock Resources

When SQL Server tries to determine whether a requested lock can be granted, it checks the *sys.dm_tran_locks* view to determine whether a matching lock with a conflicting lock mode already exists. It compares locks by looking at the database ID (*resource_database_ID),* the values in the *resource_description* and *resource_associated_entity_id* columns, and the type of resource locked. SQL Server knows nothing about the meaning of the resource description. It simply compares the strings identifying the lock resources to look for a match. If it finds a match with a *request_status* value of GRANT, it knows the resource is already locked; it then uses the lock compatibility matrix to determine whether the current lock is compatible with the one being requested. Table 10-5 shows many of the possible lock resources that are displayed in the first column of the *sys.dm_tran_locks* view and the information in the *resource_description* column, which is used to define the actual resource locked.

**TABLE 10-5  Lockable Resources in SQL Server**

| Resource_Type | Resource_Description | Example |
|---|---|---|
| DATABASE | None; the database is always indicated in the *resource_database_ID* column for every locked resource. | 12 |
| OBJECT | The object ID (which can be any database object, not necessarily a table) is reported in the *resource_associated_entity_id* column. | 69575286 |
| HOBT | *hobt_id* is reported in the *resource_associated_entity_id* column. Used only when partition locking has been enabled for a table. | 72057594038779904 |
| EXTENT | File number:page number of the first page of the extent. | 1:96 |
| PAGE | File number:page number of the actual table or index page. | 1:104 |
| KEY | A hashed value derived from all the key components and the locator. For a nonclustered index on a heap, where columns *c1* and *c2* are indexed, the hash will contain contributions from *c1, c2,* and the *RID*. | ac0001a10a00 |
| ROW | File number:page number:slot number of the actual row. | 1:161:3 |

Note that key locks and key-range locks have identical resource descriptions because key range is considered a mode of locking, not a locking resource. When you look at output from the *sys.dm_tran_locks* view, you see that you can distinguish between these types of locks by the value in the lock mode column.

Another type of lockable resource is METADATA. More than any other resource, METADATA resources are divided into multiple subtypes, which are described in the *resource_subtype* column of *sys.dm_tran_locks*. You might see dozens of subtypes of METADATA resources, but most of them are beyond the scope of this book. For some, however, even though *SQL Server Books Online* describes them as "for internal use only," it is pretty obvious what they refer to. For example, when you change properties of a database, you can see a *resource_type* of METADATA and a *resource_subtype* of DATABASE. The value in the *resource_description* column of that row is *database_id =<ID>*, indicating the ID of the database whose metadata is currently locked.

## Associated Entity ID

For locked resources that are part of a larger entity, the *resource_associated_entity_id* column in *sys.dm_tran_locks* displays the ID of that associated entity in the database. This can be an object ID, a partition ID, or an allocation unit ID, depending on the resource type. Of course, for some resources, such as DATABASE and EXTENT, there is no *resource_associated_entity_id*. An *object ID* value is given in this column for OBJECT resources, and an allocation unit ID is given for ALLOCATION_UNIT resources. A partition ID is provided for resource types PAGE, KEY, and RID.

There is no simple function to convert a partition ID value to an object name; you have to actually select from the *sys.partitions* view. The following query translates all the *resource_associated_entity_id* values for locks in the current database by joining *sys.dm_tran_locks* to *sys.partitions*. For OBJECT resources, the *object_name* function is applied to the *resource_associated_entity_id* column. For PAGE, KEY, and RID resources, I use the *object_name* function with the *object_id* value from the *sys.partitions* view. For other resources for which there is no *resource_associated_entity_id*, the code just returns n/a. Because the code references the *sys.partitions* view, which occurs in each database, this code is filtered to return only lock information for resources in the current database. The output is organized to reflect the information returned by the *sp_lock* procedure, but you can add any additional filters or columns that you need. I will use this query in many examples later in this chapter, so I create a VIEW based on the *SELECT* and call it *DBlocks*:

```
CREATE VIEW DBlocks AS
SELECT request_session_id as spid,
    db_name(resource_database_id) as dbname,
    CASE
  WHEN resource_type = 'OBJECT' THEN
        object_name(resource_associated_entity_id)
     WHEN resource_associated_entity_id = 0 THEN 'n/a'
   ELSE object_name(p.object_id)
    END as entity_name, index_id,
      resource_type as resource,
      resource_description as description,
      request_mode as mode, request_status as status
FROM sys.dm_tran_locks t LEFT JOIN sys.partitions p
  ON p.partition_id = t.resource_associated_entity_id
WHERE resource_database_id = db_id();
```

# Lock Duration

The length of time that a lock is held depends primarily on the mode of the lock and the transaction isolation level in effect. The default isolation level for SQL Server is Read Committed. At this level, shared locks are released as soon as SQL Server has read and processed the locked data. In Snapshot isolation, the behavior is the same—shared locks are released as soon as SQL Server has read the data. If your transaction isolation level is Repeatable Read or Serializable, shared locks have the same duration as exclusive locks; that is, they are not released until the transaction is over. In any isolation level, an exclusive lock is held until the end of the transaction, whether the transaction is committed or rolled back. An update lock is also held until the end of the transaction unless it has been promoted to an exclusive lock, in which case the exclusive lock, as is always the case with exclusive locks, remains for the duration of the transaction.

In addition to changing your transaction isolation level, you can control the lock duration by using query hints. I discuss query hints for locking, briefly, later in this chapter.

# Lock Ownership

Lock duration is also directly affected by the lock ownership. Lock ownership has nothing to do with the process that requested the lock, but you can think of it as the "scope" of the lock. There are four types of lock owners, or lock scopes: transactions, cursors, transaction_ workspaces, and sessions. The lock owner can be viewed through the *request_owner_type* column in the *sys.dm_tran_locks* view.

Most of our locking discussion deals with locks with a lock owner of TRANSACTION. As we've seen, these locks can have two different durations depending on the isolation level and lock mode. The duration of shared locks in Read Committed isolation is only as long as the locked data is being read. The duration of all other locks owned by a transaction is until the end of the transaction.

A lock with a *request_ownertype* value of CURSOR must be requested explicitly when the cursor is declared. If a cursor is opened using a locking mode of SCROLL_LOCKS, a cursor lock is held on every row fetched until the next row is fetched or the cursor is closed. Even if the transaction commits before the next fetch, the cursor lock is not released.

In SQL Server 2008, locks owned by a session must also be requested explicitly and apply only to APPLICATION locks. A session lock is requested using the *sp_getapplock* procedure. Its duration is until the session disconnects or the lock is released explicitly.

Transaction_workspace locks are acquired every time a database is accessed, and the resource associated with these locks is always a database. A workspace holds database locks for sessions that are enlisted into a common environment. Usually, there is one workspace per session, so all DATABASE locks acquired in the session are kept in the same workspace object. In the case of distributed transactions, multiple sessions are enlisted into the same workspace, so they share the database locks.

Every process acquires a DATABASE lock with an owner of SHARED_TRANSACTION_ WORKSPACE on any database when the process issues the *USE* command. The exception is any processes that use *master* or *tempdb*, in which case no DATABASE lock is taken. That lock isn't released until another *USE* command is issued or until the process is disconnected. If a process attempts to *ALTER, RESTORE,* or *DROP* the database, the DATABASE lock acquired has an owner of EXCLUSIVE_TRANSACTION_WORKSPACE. SHARED_TRANSACTION_ WORKSPACE and EXCLUSIVE_TRANSACTION_WORKSPACE locks are maintained by the same workspace and are just two different lists in one workspace. The use of two different owner names is misleading in this case.

# Viewing Locks

To see the locks currently outstanding in the system, as well as those that are being waited for, the best source of information is the *sys.dm_tran_locks* view. I've shown you some queries from this view in previous sections, and in this section, I show you a few more and explain what more of the output columns mean. This view replaces the *sp_lock* procedure. Although calling a procedure might require less typing than querying the *sys.dm_tran_locks* view, the view is much more flexible. Not only are there many more columns of information providing details about your locks, but as a view, *sys.dm_tran_locks* can be queried to select just the columns you want, or only the rows that meet your criteria. It can be joined with other views and aggregated to get summary information about how many locks of each kind are being held.

## sys.dm_tran_locks

All the columns (with the exception of the last column called *lock_owner_address*) in *sys.dm_tran_locks* start with one of two prefixes. The columns whose names begin with *resource_* describe the resource on which the lock request is being made. The columns whose names begin with *request_* describe the process requesting the lock. Two requests operate on the same resource only if all the *resource_* columns are the same.

***resource_* Columns**  I've mentioned most of the *resource_* columns already, but I referred only briefly to the *resource_subtype* column. Not all resources have subtypes, and some have many. The METADATA resource type, for example, has over 40 subtypes.

Table 10-6 lists all the subtypes for resource types other than METADATA.

**TABLE 10-6  Subtype Resources**

| Resource Type | Resource Subtypes | Description |
| --- | --- | --- |
| DATABASE | BULKOP_BACKUP_DB | Used for synchronization of database backups with bulk operations |
| | BULKOP_BACKUP_LOG | Used for synchronization of database log backups with bulk operations |
| | DDL | Used to synchronize Data Definition Language (DDL) operations with File Group operations (such as *DROP*) |
| | STARTUP | Used for database startup synchronization |
| TABLE | UPDSTATS | Used for synchronization of statistics updates on a table |
| | COMPILE | Used for synchronization of stored procedure compiles |
| | INDEX_OPERATION | Used for synchronization of index operations |
| HOBT | INDEX_REORGANIZE | Used for synchronization of heap or index reorganization operations |
| | BULK_OPERATION | Used for heap-optimized bulk load operations with concurrent scan, in the Snapshot, Read Uncommitted, and Read Committed SI levels |
| ALLOCATION_UNIT | PAGE_COUNT | Used for synchronization of allocation unit page count statistics during deferred drop operations |

As previously mentioned, most METADATA subtypes are documented as being for INTERNAL USE ONLY, but their meaning is often pretty obvious. Each type of metadata can be locked separately as changes are made. Here is a partial list of the METADATA subtypes:

- INDEXSTATS
- STATS
- SCHEMA
- DATABASE_PRINCIPAL
- DB_PRINCIPAL_SID
- USER_TYPE
- DATA_SPACE
- PARTITION_FUNCTION
- DATABASE
- SERVER_PRINCIPAL
- SERVER

Most of the other METADATA subtypes not listed here refer to elements of SQL Server 2008 that are not discussed in this book, including CLR routines, XML, certificates, full-text search, and notification services.

***request_* Columns***    I've also mentioned a couple of the most important *request_* columns in *sys.dm_tran_locks*, including *request_mode* (the type of lock requested), *request_owner_type* (the scope of the lock requested), and *request_session_id*. Here are some of the others:

- ***request_type***    In SQL Server 2008, the only type of resource request tracked in *sys. dm_tran_locks* is for a LOCK. Future versions may include other types of resources that can be requested.

- ***request_status***    Status can be one of three values: GRANT, CONVERT, or WAIT. A status of CONVERT indicates that the requestor has already been granted a request for the same resource in a different mode and is currently waiting for an upgrade (convert) from the current lock mode to be granted. (For example, SQL Server can convert a U lock to X.) A status of WAIT indicates that the requestor does not currently hold a granted request on the resource.

- ***request_reference_count***    This value is a rough count of number of times the same requestor has requested this resource and applies only to resources that are not automatically released at the end of a transaction. A granted resource is no longer considered to be held by a requestor if this field decreases to 0 and *request_lifetime* is also 0.

- ***request_lifetime***    This value is a code that indicates when the lock on the resource is released.

- **request_session_id**   This value is the ID of the session that has requested the lock. The owning session ID can change for distributed and bound transactions. A value of –2 indicates that the request belongs to an orphaned DTC transaction. A value of –3 indicates that the request belongs to a deferred recovery transaction. (These are transactions whose rollback has been deferred at recovery because the rollback could not be completed successfully.)

- **request_exec_context_id**   This value is the execution context ID of the process that currently owns this request. A value greater than 0 indicates that this is a subthread used to execute a parallel query.

- **request_request_id**   This value is the request ID (batch ID) of the process that currently owns this request. This column is populated only for the requests coming in from a client application using Multiple Active Result Sets (MARS).

- **request_owner_id**   This value is currently used only for requests with an owner of TRANSACTION, and the owner ID is the transaction ID. This column can be joined with the *transaction_id* column in the *sys.dm_tran_active_transactions* view.

- **request_owner_guid**   This value is currently used only by DTC transactions when it corresponds to the DTC GUID for that transaction.

- **lock_owner_address**   This value is the memory address of the internal data structure that is used to track this request. This column can be joined with the *resource_address* column in *sys.dm_os_waiting_tasks* if this request is in the WAIT or CONVERT state.

## Locking Examples

The following examples show what many of the lock types and modes discussed earlier look like when reported using the *DBlocks* view that I described previously.

### Example 1: *SELECT* with Default Isolation Level

**SQL BATCH**

```
USE Adventureworks2008;
SET TRANSACTION ISOLATION LEVEL READ COMMITTED;
BEGIN TRAN
SELECT * FROM Production.Product
WHERE Name = 'Reflector';
SELECT * FROM DBlocks WHERE spid = @@spid;
COMMIT TRAN
```

**RESULTS FROM *DBlocks***

| spid | dbname | entity_name | index_id | resource | description | mode | status |
|------|--------|-------------|----------|----------|-------------|------|--------|
| 60 | Adventureworks2008 | n/a | NULL | DATABASE | | S | GRANT |
| 60 | AdventureWorks2008 | DBlocks | NULL | OBJECT | | IS | GRANT |

There are no locks on the data in the *Production.Product* table because the batch was performing only *SELECT* operations that acquired shared locks. By default, the shared locks are released as soon as the data has been read, so by the time the *SELECT* from the view is executed, the locks are no longer held. There is only the ever-present DATABASE lock, and an OBJECT lock on the view.

## Example 2: *SELECT* with Repeatable Read Isolation Level

### SQL BATCH

```
USE AdventureWorks2008;
SET TRANSACTION ISOLATION LEVEL REPEATABLE READ;
BEGIN TRAN
SELECT * FROM Production.Product
WHERE Name LIKE 'Racing Socks%';
SELECT * FROM DBlocks
WHERE spid = @@spid
AND entity_name = 'Product';
COMMIT TRAN
```

### RESULTS FROM *DBlocks*

| spid | dbname | entity_name | index_id | resource | description | mode | status |
|------|--------|-------------|----------|----------|-------------|------|--------|
| 54 | AdventureWorks2008 | Product | NULL | OBJECT | | IS | GRANT |
| 54 | AdventureWorks2008 | Product | 1 | PAGE | 1:16897 | IS | GRANT |
| 54 | AdventureWorks2008 | Product | 1 | KEY | (6b00b8eeda30) | S | GRANT |
| 54 | AdventureWorks2008 | Product | 1 | KEY | (6a00dd896688) | S | GRANT |
| 54 | AdventureWorks2008 | Product | 3 | KEY | (9502d56a217e) | S | GRANT |
| 54 | AdventureWorks2008 | Product | 3 | PAGE | 1:1767 | IS | GRANT |
| 54 | AdventureWorks2008 | Product | 3 | KEY | (9602945b3a67) | S | GRANT |

This time, I filtered out the database lock and the locks on the view and the rowset, just to keep the focus on the data locks. Because the *Production.Product* table has a clustered index, the rows of data are all index rows in the leaf level. The locks on the two individual data rows returned are listed as key locks. There are also two key locks at the leaf level of the nonclustered index on the table used to find the relevant rows. In the *Production.Product* table, that nonclustered index is on the *Name* column. You can tell the clustered and nonclustered indexes apart by the value in the *index_id* column: the data rows (the leaf rows of the clustered index) have an *index_id* value of 1, and the nonclustered index rows have an *index_id* value of 3. (For nonclustered indexes, the *index_id* value can be anything between 2 and 250 or between 356 and 1005.) Because the transaction isolation level is Repeatable Read, the shared locks are held until the transaction is finished. Note that the index rows have shared (S) locks, and the data and index pages, as well as the table itself, have intent shared (IS) locks.

## Example 3: *SELECT* with Serializable Isolation Level

### SQL BATCH

```
USE AdventureWorks2008 ;
SET TRANSACTION ISOLATION LEVEL SERIALIZABLE;
BEGIN TRAN
SELECT * FROM Production.Product
WHERE Name LIKE 'Racing Socks%';
```

```
SELECT * FROM DBlocks
WHERE spid = @@spid
AND entity_name = 'Product';
COMMIT TRAN
```

**RESULTS FROM** *DBlocks*

| spid | dbname | entity_name | index_id | resource | description | mode | status |
|------|--------|-------------|----------|----------|-------------|------|--------|
| 54 | AdventureWorks2008 | Product | NULL | OBJECT | | IS | GRANT |
| 54 | AdventureWorks2008 | Product | 1 | PAGE | 1:16897 | IS | GRANT |
| 54 | AdventureWorks2008 | Product | 1 | KEY | (6b00b8eeda30) | S | GRANT |
| 54 | AdventureWorks2008 | Product | 1 | KEY | (6a00dd896688) | S | GRANT |
| 54 | AdventureWorks2008 | Product | 3 | KEY | (9502d56a217e) | RangeS-S | GRANT |
| 54 | AdventureWorks2008 | Product | 3 | PAGE | 1:1767 | IS | GRANT |
| 54 | AdventureWorks2008 | Product | 3 | KEY | (23027a50f6db) | RangeS-S | GRANT |
| 54 | AdventureWorks2008 | Product | 3 | KEY | (9602945b3a67) | RangeS-S | GRANT |

The locks held with the Serializable isolation level are almost identical to those held with the Repeatable Read isolation level. The main difference is in the mode of the lock. The two-part mode RangeS-S indicates a key-range lock in addition to the lock on the key itself. The first part (RangeS) is the lock on the range of keys between (and including) the key holding the lock and the previous key in the index. The key-range locks prevent other transactions from inserting new rows into the table that meet the condition of this query; that is, no new rows with a product name starting with *Racing Socks* can be inserted. The key-range locks are held on ranges in the nonclustered index on *Name* (*index_id* = 3) because that is the index used to find the qualifying rows. There are three key locks in the nonclustered index because three different ranges need to be locked. The two *Racing Socks* rows are *Racing Socks, L* and *Racing Socks, M*. SQL Server must lock the range from the key preceding the first *Racing Socks* row in the index up to the first *Racing Socks*. It must lock the range between the two rows starting with *Racing Socks*, and it must lock the range from the second *Racing Socks* to the next key in the index. (So actually nothing could be inserted between *Racing Socks* and the previous key, *Pinch Bolt,* or between *Racing Socks* and the next key, *Rear Brakes*. For example, we could not insert a product with the name *Portkey* or *Racing Tights*.)

## Example 4: Update Operations

**SQL BATCH**

```
USE AdventureWorks2008;
SET TRANSACTION ISOLATION LEVEL READ COMMITTED;
BEGIN TRAN
UPDATE Production.Product
SET ListPrice = ListPrice * 0.6
WHERE Name LIKE 'Racing Socks%';
SELECT * FROM DBlocks
WHERE spid = @@spid
AND entity_name = 'Product';
COMMIT TRAN
```

**RESULTS FROM** *DBlocks*

| spid | dbname | entity_name | index_id | resource | description | mode | status |
|------|--------|-------------|----------|----------|-------------|------|--------|
| 54 | AdventureWorks2008 | Product | NULL | OBJECT | | IX | GRANT |
| 54 | AdventureWorks2008 | Product | 1 | PAGE | 1:16897 | IX | GRANT |
| 54 | AdventureWorks2008 | Product | 1 | KEY | (6b00b8eeda30) | X | GRANT |
| 54 | AdventureWorks2008 | Product | 1 | KEY | (6a00dd8966 88) | X | GRANT |

The two rows in the leaf level of the clustered index are locked with X locks. The page and the table are then locked with IX locks. I mentioned earlier that SQL Server actually acquires update locks while it looks for the rows to update. However, these are converted to X locks when the actual update is performed, and by the time we look at the *DBLocks* view, the update locks are gone. Unless you actually force update locks with a query hint, you might never see them in the lock report from *DBLocks* or by direct inspection of *sys.dm_tran_locks*.

## Example 5: Update with Serializable Isolation Level Using an Index

**SQL BATCH**

```
USE AdventureWorks2008;
SET TRANSACTION ISOLATION LEVEL SERIALIZABLE;
BEGIN TRAN
UPDATE Production.Product
SET ListPrice = ListPrice * 0.6
WHERE Name LIKE 'Racing Socks%';
SELECT * FROM DBlocks
WHERE spid = @@spid
AND entity_name = 'Product';
COMMIT TRAN
```

**RESULTS FROM** *DBlocks*

| spid | dbname | entity_name | index_id | resource | description | mode | status |
|------|--------|-------------|----------|----------|-------------|------|--------|
| 54 | AdventureWorks2008 | Product | NULL | OBJECT | | IX | GRANT |
| 54 | AdventureWorks2008 | Product | 1 | PAGE | 1:16897 | IX | GRANT |
| 54 | AdventureWorks2008 | Product | 1 | KEY | (6a00dd896688) | X | GRANT |
| 54 | AdventureWorks2008 | Product | 1 | KEY | (6b00b8eeda30) | X | GRANT |
| 54 | AdventureWorks2008 | Product | 3 | KEY | (9502d56a217e) | RangeS-U | GRANT |
| 54 | AdventureWorks2008 | Product | 3 | PAGE | 1:1767 | IU | GRANT |
| 54 | AdventureWorks2008 | Product | 3 | KEY | (23027a50f6db) | RangeS-U | GRANT |
| 54 | AdventureWorks2008 | Product | 3 | KEY | (9602945b3a67) | RangeS-U | GRANT |

Again, notice that the key-range locks are on the nonclustered index used to find the relevant rows. The range interval itself needs only a shared lock to prevent insertions, but the searched keys have U locks so no other process can attempt to update them. The keys in the table itself (*index_id* = 1) obtain the exclusive lock when the actual modification is made.

Now let's look at an *UPDATE* operation with the same isolation level when no index can be used for the search.

## Example 6: Update with Serializable Isolation Not Using an Index

**SQL BATCH**

```
USE AdventureWorks2008;
SET TRANSACTION ISOLATION LEVEL SERIALIZABLE;
BEGIN TRAN
UPDATE Production.Product
SET ListPrice = ListPrice * 0.6
WHERE Color = 'White';
SELECT * FROM DBlocks
WHERE spid = @@spid
AND entity_name = 'Product';
COMMIT TRAN
```

**RESULTS FROM *DBlocks* (Abbreviated)**

| spid | dbname | entity_name | index_id | resource | description | mode | status |
|------|--------|-------------|----------|----------|-------------|------|--------|
| 54 | AdventureWorks2008 | Product | NULL | OBJECT |  | IX | GRANT |
| 54 | AdventureWorks2008 | Product | 1 | KEY | (7900ac71caca) | RangeS-U | GRANT |
| 54 | AdventureWorks2008 | Product | 1 | KEY | (6100dc0e675f) | RangeS-U | GRANT |
| 54 | AdventureWorks2008 | Product | 1 | KEY | (5700a1a9278a) | RangeS-U | GRANT |
| 54 | AdventureWorks2008 | Product | 1 | PAGE | 1:16898 | IU | GRANT |
| 54 | AdventureWorks2008 | Product | 1 | PAGE | 1:16899 | IU | GRANT |
| 54 | AdventureWorks2008 | Product | 1 | PAGE | 1:16896 | IU | GRANT |
| 54 | AdventureWorks2008 | Product | 1 | PAGE | 1:16897 | IX | GRANT |
| 54 | AdventureWorks2008 | Product | 1 | PAGE | 1:16900 | IU | GRANT |
| 54 | AdventureWorks2008 | Product | 1 | PAGE | 1:16901 | IU | GRANT |
| 54 | AdventureWorks2008 | Product | 1 | KEY | (5600c4ce9b32) | RangeS-U | GRANT |
| 54 | AdventureWorks2008 | Product | 1 | KEY | (7300c89177a5) | RangeS-U | GRANT |
| 54 | AdventureWorks2008 | Product | 1 | KEY | (7f00702ea1ef) | RangeS-U | GRANT |
| 54 | AdventureWorks2008 | Product | 1 | KEY | (6b00b8eeda30) | RangeX-X | GRANT |
| 54 | AdventureWorks2008 | Product | 1 | KEY | (c500b9eaac9c) | RangeX-X | GRANT |
| 54 | AdventureWorks2008 | Product | 1 | KEY | (c6005745198e) | RangeX-X | GRANT |
| 54 | AdventureWorks2008 | Product | 1 | KEY | (6a00dd896688) | RangeX-X | GRANT |

The locks here are similar to those in the previous example except that all the locks are on the table itself (*index_id* = 1). A clustered index scan (on the entire table) had to be done, so all keys initially received the RangeS-U lock, and when four rows were eventually modified, the locks on those keys were converted to RangeX-X locks. You can see all the RangeX-X locks, but not all the RangeS-U locks are shown for space reasons (the table has 504 rows).

## Example 7: Creating a Table

**SQL BATCH**

```
USE AdventureWorks2008;
SET TRANSACTION ISOLATION LEVEL READ COMMITTED;
BEGIN TRAN
SELECT *
INTO newProducts
FROM Production.Product
WHERE ListPrice between 1 and 10;
SELECT * FROM DBlocks
WHERE spid = @@spid;
COMMIT TRAN
```

**RESULTS FROM** *DBlocks* **(Abbreviated)**

| spid | dbname | entity_name | index_id | resource | description | mode | status |
|------|--------|-------------|----------|----------|-------------|------|--------|
| 54 | AdventureWorks2008 | n/a | NULL | DATABASE | | NULL | GRANT |
| 54 | AdventureWorks2008 | n/a | NULL | DATABASE | | NULL | GRANT |
| 54 | AdventureWorks2008 | n/a | NULL | DATABASE | | S | GRANT |
| 54 | AdventureWorks2008 | n/a | NULL | METADATA | user_type_id = 258 | Sch-S | GRANT |
| 54 | AdventureWorks2008 | n/a | NULL | METADATA | data_space_id = 1 | Sch-S | GRANT |
| 54 | AdventureWorks2008 | n/a | NULL | DATABASE | | S | GRANT |
| 54 | AdventureWorks2008 | n/a | NULL | METADATA | $seq_type = 0, objec | Sch-M | GRANT |
| 54 | AdventureWorks2008 | n/a | NULL | METADATA | user_type_id = 260 | Sch-S | GRANT |
| 54 | AdventureWorks2008 | sysrowsetcol | NULL | OBJECT | | IX | GRANT |
| 54 | AdventureWorks2008 | sysrowsets | NULL | OBJECT | | IX | GRANT |
| 54 | AdventureWorks2008 | sysallocunit | NULL | OBJECT | | IX | GRANT |
| 54 | AdventureWorks2008 | syshobtcolum | NULL | OBJECT | | IX | GRANT |
| 54 | AdventureWorks2008 | syshobts | NULL | OBJECT | | IX | GRANT |
| 54 | AdventureWorks2008 | sysserefs | NULL | OBJECT | | IX | GRANT |
| 54 | AdventureWorks2008 | sysschobjs | NULL | OBJECT | | IX | GRANT |
| 54 | AdventureWorks2008 | syscolpars | NULL | OBJECT | | IX | GRANT |
| 54 | AdventureWorks2008 | sysidxstats | NULL | OBJECT | | IX | GRANT |
| 54 | AdventureWorks2008 | sysrowsetcol | 1 | KEY | (15004f6b3486) | X | GRANT |
| 54 | AdventureWorks2008 | sysrowsetcol | 1 | KEY | (0a00862c4e8e) | X | GRANT |
| 54 | AdventureWorks2008 | sysrowsets | 1 | KEY | (000000aaec7b) | X | GRANT |
| 54 | AdventureWorks2008 | sysallocunit | 1 | KEY | (00001f2dcf47) | X | GRANT |
| 54 | AdventureWorks2008 | syshobtcolum | 1 | KEY | (1900f7d4e2cc) | X | GRANT |
| 54 | AdventureWorks2008 | syshobts | 1 | KEY | (000000aaec7b) | X | GRANT |
| 54 | AdventureWorks2008 | NULL | NULL | RID | 1:6707:1 | X | GRANT |
| 54 | AdventureWorks2008 | DBlocks | NULL | OBJECT | | IS | GRANT |
| 54 | AdventureWorks2008 | newProducts | NULL | OBJECT | | Sch-M | GRANT |
| 54 | AdventureWorks2008 | sysserefs | 1 | KEY | (010025fabf73) | X | GRANT |
| 54 | AdventureWorks2008 | sysschobjs | 1 | KEY | (3b0042322c99) | X | GRANT |
| 54 | AdventureWorks2008 | syscolpars | 1 | KEY | (4200c1eb801c) | X | GRANT |
| 54 | AdventureWorks2008 | syscolpars | 1 | KEY | (4e00092bfbc3) | X | GRANT |
| 54 | AdventureWorks2008 | sysidxstats | 1 | KEY | (3b0006e110a6) | X | GRANT |
| 54 | AdventureWorks2008 | sysschobjs | 2 | KEY | (9202706f3e6c) | X | GRANT |
| 54 | AdventureWorks2008 | syscolpars | 2 | KEY | (6c0151be80af) | X | GRANT |
| 54 | AdventureWorks2008 | syscolpars | 2 | KEY | (2c03557a0b9d) | X | GRANT |
| 54 | AdventureWorks2008 | sysidxstats | 2 | KEY | (3c00f3332a43) | X | GRANT |
| 54 | AdventureWorks2008 | sysschobjs | 3 | KEY | (9202d42ddd4d) | X | GRANT |
| 54 | AdventureWorks2008 | sysschobjs | 4 | KEY | (3c0040d00163) | X | GRANT |
| 54 | AdventureWorks2008 | newProducts | 0 | PAGE | 1:6707 | X | GRANT |
| 54 | AdventureWorks2008 | newProducts | 0 | HOBT | | Sch-M | GRANT |

Very few of these locks are actually acquired on elements of the *newProducts* table. In the *entity_name* column, you can see that most of the objects are undocumented, and normally invisible, system table names. As the new table is created, SQL Server acquires locks on nine different system tables to record information about this new table. In addition, notice the schema modification (Sch-M) lock and other metadata locks on the new table.

The final example looks at the locks held when there is no clustered index on the table and the data rows are being updated.

### Example 8: Row Locks

**SQL BATCH**

```
USE AdventureWorks2008;
SET TRANSACTION ISOLATION LEVEL READ COMMITTED
BEGIN TRAN
UPDATE newProducts
SET ListPrice = 5.99
WHERE name = 'Road Bottle Cage';
SELECT * FROM DBlocks
WHERE spid = @@spid
AND entity_name = 'newProducts';
COMMIT TRAN
```

**RESULTS FROM** *DBlocks*

| spid | dbname | entity_name | index_id | resource | description | mode | status |
|------|--------|-------------|----------|----------|-------------|------|--------|
| 54 | AdventureWorks2008 | newProducts | NULL | OBJECT | | IX | GRANT |
| 54 | AdventureWorks2008 | newProducts | 0 | PAGE | 1:6708 | IX | GRANT |
| 54 | AdventureWorks2008 | newProducts | 0 | RID | 1:6708:5 | X | GRANT |

There are no indexes on the *newProducts* table, so the lock on the actual row meeting our criteria is an exclusive (X) lock on the row (RID). For RID locks, the description actually reports the specific row in the form *File number:Page number:Slot number*. As expected, IX locks are taken on the page and the table.

# Lock Compatibility

Two locks are compatible if one lock can be granted while another lock on the same resource is held by a different process. If a lock requested for a resource is not compatible with a lock currently being held, the requesting connection must wait for the lock. For example, if a shared page lock exists on a page, another process requesting a shared page lock for the same page is granted the lock because the two lock types are compatible. But a process that requests an exclusive lock for the same page is not granted the lock because an exclusive lock is not compatible with the shared lock already held. Figure 10-2 summarizes the compatibility of locks in SQL Server 2008. Along the top are all the lock modes that a process might already hold. Along the left edge are the lock modes that another process might request.

At the point where the held lock and requested lock meet, there can be three possible values. *N* indicates that there is no conflict, *C* indicates that there will be a conflict and the requesting process will have to wait, and *I* indicates an invalid combination that could never occur. All the *I* values in the chart involve range locks, which can be applied only to KEY resources, so any type of lock that can never be applied to KEY resources indicates an invalid comparison.

|       | NL | SCH-S | SCH-M | S | U | X | IS | IU | IX | SIU | SIX | UIX | BU | RS-S | RS-U | RI-N | RI-S | RI-U | RI-X | RX-S | RX-U | RX-X |
|-------|----|-------|-------|---|---|---|----|----|----|-----|-----|-----|----|------|------|------|------|------|------|------|------|------|
| NL    | N  | N     | N     | N | N | N | N  | N  | N  | N   | N   | N   | N  | N    | N    | N    | N    | N    | N    | N    | N    | N    |
| SCH-S | N  | N     | C     | N | N | N | N  | N  | N  | N   | N   | N   | N  | I    | I    | I    | I    | I    | I    | I    | I    | I    |
| SCH-M | N  | C     | C     | C | C | C | C  | C  | C  | C   | C   | C   | C  | I    | I    | I    | I    | I    | I    | I    | I    | I    |
| S     | N  | N     | C     | N | N | C | N  | N  | C  | N   | C   | C   | C  | N    | N    | N    | N    | N    | C    | N    | N    | C    |
| U     | N  | N     | C     | N | C | C | N  | C  | C  | C   | C   | C   | C  | N    | C    | N    | N    | C    | C    | N    | C    | C    |
| X     | N  | N     | C     | C | C | C | C  | C  | C  | C   | C   | C   | C  | N    | C    | N    | C    | C    | C    | C    | C    | C    |
| IS    | N  | N     | C     | N | N | C | N  | N  | N  | N   | N   | N   | C  | I    | I    | I    | I    | I    | I    | I    | I    | I    |
| IU    | N  | N     | C     | N | C | C | N  | N  | N  | N   | N   | C   | C  | I    | I    | I    | I    | I    | I    | I    | I    | I    |
| IX    | N  | N     | C     | C | C | C | N  | N  | C  | C   | C   | C   | C  | I    | I    | I    | I    | I    | I    | I    | I    | I    |
| SIU   | N  | N     | C     | N | C | C | N  | N  | C  | N   | C   | C   | C  | I    | I    | I    | I    | I    | I    | I    | I    | I    |
| SIX   | N  | N     | C     | C | C | C | N  | N  | C  | C   | C   | C   | C  | I    | I    | I    | I    | I    | I    | I    | I    | I    |
| UIX   | N  | N     | C     | C | C | C | N  | C  | C  | C   | C   | C   | C  | I    | I    | I    | I    | I    | I    | I    | I    | I    |
| BU    | N  | N     | C     | C | C | C | C  | C  | C  | C   | C   | C   | N  | I    | I    | I    | I    | I    | I    | I    | I    | I    |
| RS-S  | N  | I     | I     | N | N | C | I  | I  | I  | I   | I   | I   | I  | N    | N    | C    | C    | C    | C    | C    | C    | C    |
| RS-U  | N  | I     | I     | N | C | C | I  | I  | I  | I   | I   | I   | I  | N    | C    | C    | C    | C    | C    | C    | C    | C    |
| RI-N  | N  | I     | I     | N | N | N | I  | I  | I  | I   | I   | I   | I  | C    | C    | N    | N    | N    | N    | C    | C    | C    |
| RI-S  | N  | I     | I     | N | N | C | I  | I  | I  | I   | I   | I   | I  | C    | C    | N    | N    | N    | C    | C    | C    | C    |
| RI-U  | N  | I     | I     | N | C | C | I  | I  | I  | I   | I   | I   | I  | C    | C    | N    | N    | C    | C    | C    | C    | C    |
| RI-X  | N  | I     | I     | C | C | C | I  | I  | I  | I   | I   | I   | I  | C    | C    | N    | C    | C    | C    | C    | C    | C    |
| RX-S  | N  | I     | I     | N | N | C | I  | I  | I  | I   | I   | I   | I  | C    | C    | C    | C    | C    | C    | C    | C    | C    |
| RX-U  | N  | I     | I     | N | C | C | I  | I  | I  | I   | I   | I   | I  | C    | C    | C    | C    | C    | C    | C    | C    | C    |
| RX-X  | N  | I     | I     | C | C | C | I  | I  | I  | I   | I   | I   | I  | C    | C    | C    | C    | C    | C    | C    | C    | C    |

**FIGURE 10-2** SQL Server lock compatibility matrix

Lock compatibility comes into play between locks on different resources, such as table locks and page locks. A table and a page obviously represent an implicit hierarchy because a table is made up of multiple pages. If an exclusive page lock is held on one page of a table, another process cannot get even a shared table lock for that table. This hierarchy is protected using intent locks. A process acquiring an exclusive page lock, update page lock, or intent exclusive page lock first acquires an intent exclusive lock on the table. This intent exclusive table lock prevents another process from acquiring the shared table lock on that table. (Remember that intent exclusive locks and shared locks on the same resource are not compatible.)

Similarly, a process acquiring a shared row lock must first acquire an intent shared lock for the table, which prevents another process from acquiring an exclusive table lock. Or if the exclusive table lock already exists, the intent shared lock is not granted and the shared page lock has to wait until the exclusive table lock is released. Without intent locks, process A can lock a page in a table with an exclusive page lock and process B can place an exclusive table lock on the same table and hence think that it has a right to modify the entire table, including the page that process A has exclusively locked.

> **Note**  Obviously, lock compatibility is an issue only when the locks affect the same object. For example, two or more processes each can hold exclusive page locks simultaneously so long as the locks are on different pages or different tables.

Even if two locks are compatible, the requester of the second lock might still have to wait if an incompatible lock is waiting. For example, suppose that process A holds a shared page lock. Process B requests an exclusive page lock and must wait because the shared page lock and the exclusive page lock are not compatible. Process C requests a shared page lock that is compatible with the shared page already granted to process A. However, the shared page lock cannot be granted immediately. Process C must wait for its shared page lock because process B is ahead of it in the lock queue with a request (exclusive page) that is not compatible.

By examining the compatibility of locks not only with processes granted locks, but also processes waiting, SQL Server prevents lock starvation, which can result when requests for shared locks keep overlapping so that the request for the exclusive lock can never be granted.

# Internal Locking Architecture

Locks are not on-disk structures. You won't find a lock field directly on a data page or a table header, and the metadata that keeps track of locks is never written to disk. Locks are internal memory structures—they consume part of the memory used for SQL Server. A lock is identified by *lock resource,* which is a description of the resource that is locked (a row, index key, page, or table). To keep track of the database, the type of lock, and the information describing the locked resource, each lock requires 64 bytes of memory on a 32-bit system and 128 bytes of memory on a 64-bit system. This 64-byte or 128-byte structure is called a *lock block.*

Each process holding a lock also must have a *lock owner,* which represents the relationship between a lock and the entity that is requesting or holding the lock. The lock owner requires 32 bytes of memory on a 32-bit system and 64 bytes of memory on a 64-bit system. This 32-byte or 64-byte structure is called a *lock owner block.* A single transaction can have multiple lock owner blocks; a scrollable cursor sometimes uses several. Also, one lock can have many lock owner blocks, as is the case with a shared lock. As mentioned, the lock owner represents a relationship between a lock and an entity, and the relationship can be granted, waiting, or in a state called *waiting-to-convert.*

The lock manager maintains a lock hash table. Lock resources, contained within a lock block, are hashed to determine a target hash slot in the hash table. All lock blocks that hash to the same slot are chained together from one entry in the hash table. Each lock block contains a 15-byte field that describes the locked resource. The lock block also contains pointers to lists of lock owner blocks. There is a separate list for lock owners in each of the three states. Figure 10-3 shows the general lock architecture.

The number of slots in the hash table is based on the system's physical memory, as shown in Table 10-7. There is an upper limit of $2^{31}$ slots. All instances of SQL Server on the same machine have a hash table with the same number of slots. Each entry in the lock hash table is 16 bytes in size and consists of a pointer to a list of lock blocks and a spinlock to guarantee serialized access to the same slot.

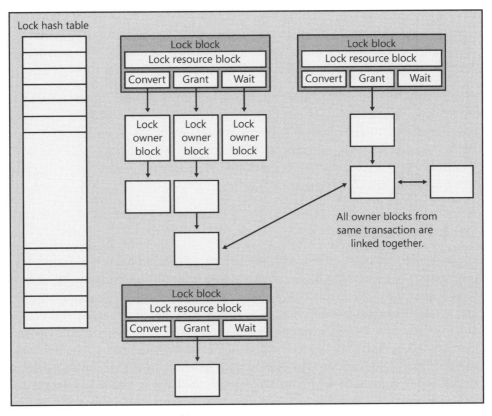

**FIGURE 10-3** SQL Server locking architecture

**TABLE 10-7** **Number of Slots in the Internal Lock Hash Table**

| Physical Memory (MB) | Number of Slots | Memory Used |
|---|---|---|
| < 32 | $2^{14}$ = 16384 | 128 KB |
| >= 32 and < 64 | $2^{15}$ = 32768 | 256 KB |
| >= 64 and < 128 | $2^{16}$ = 65536 | 512 KB |
| >= 128 and < 512 | $2^{18}$ = 262144 | 2048 KB |
| >= 512 and < 1024 | $2^{19}$ = 524288 | 4096 KB |
| >= 1024 and < 4096 | $2^{21}$ = 2097152 | 16384 KB |
| >= 4096 and < 8192 | $2^{22}$ = 4194304 | 32768 KB |
| >= 8192 and < 16384 | $2^{23}$ = 8388608 | 65536 KB |
| >= 16384 | $2^{25}$ = 33554432 | 262144 KB |

The lock manager allocates in advance a number of lock blocks and lock owner blocks at server startup. On NUMA configurations, these lock and lock owner blocks are divided among all NUMA nodes. So when a lock request is made, local lock blocks are used. If the number of locks has been set by *sp_configure*, it allocates that configured number of lock blocks and the same number of lock owner blocks. If the number is not fixed (0 means auto-tune), it allocates 2,500 lock blocks for your SQL Server instance. It allocates twice as many (2 * # lock blocks) of the lock owner blocks. At their maximum, the static allocations can't consume more than 25 percent of the committed buffer pool size.

When a request for a lock is made and no free lock blocks remain, the lock manager dynamically allocates new lock blocks instead of denying the lock request. The lock manager cooperates with the global memory manager to negotiate for server allocated memory. When necessary, the lock manager can free the dynamically allocated lock blocks. The lock manager is limited to 60 percent of the buffer manager's committed target size allocation to lock blocks and lock owner blocks.

## Lock Partitioning

For large systems, locks on frequently referenced objects can become a performance bottleneck. The process of acquiring and releasing locks can cause contention on the internal locking resources. Lock partitioning enhances locking performance by splitting a single lock resource into multiple lock resources. For systems with 16 or more CPUs, SQL Server automatically splits certain locks into multiple lock resources, one per CPU. This is called *lock partitioning,* and there is no way for a user to control this process. (Do not confuse lock partitioning with partition locks, which are discussed in the section entitled "Lock Escalation," later in this chapter.) An informational message is sent to the error log whenever lock partitioning is active. The error message is "Lock partitioning is enabled. This is an informational message only. No user action is required." Lock partitioning applies only to full object locks (for example, tables and views) in the following lock modes: S, U, X, and SCH-M. All other modes (NL, SCH_S, IS, IU, and IX) are acquired on a single CPU. SQL Server assigns a default lock partition to every transaction when the transaction starts. During the life of that transaction, all lock requests that are spread over all the partitions use the partition assigned to that transaction. By this method, access to lock resources of the same object by different transactions is distributed across different partitions.

The *resource_lock_partition* column in *sys.dm_tran_locks* indicates which lock partition a particular lock is on, so you can see multiple locks for the exact same resource with different *resource_lock_partition* values. For systems with fewer than 16 CPUs, for which lock partitioning is never used, the *resource_lock_partition* value is always 0.

For example, consider a transaction acquiring an IS lock in REPEATABLE READ isolation, so that the IS lock is held for the duration of the transaction. The IS lock is acquired on the transaction's default partition—for example, partition 4. If another transaction tries to acquire an X lock on the same table, the X lock must be acquired on ALL partitions. SQL Server successfully acquires the X lock on partitions 0 to 3, but it blocks when attempting to acquire an X lock on partition 4. On partition IDs 5 to 15, which have not yet acquired the X lock for this table, other transactions can continue to acquire any locks that do not cause blocking.

With lock partitioning, SQL Server distributes the load of checking for locks across multiple spinlocks, and most accesses to any given spinlock are from the same CPU (and practically always from the same node), which means the spinlock should not spin often.

## Lock Blocks

The lock block is the key structure in SQL Server's locking architecture, shown earlier in Figure 10-3. A lock block contains the following information:

- Lock resource information containing the lock resource name and details about the lock.

- Pointers to connect the lock blocks to the lock hash table.

- Pointers to lists of lock owner blocks for locks on this resource that have been granted. Four *grant lists* are maintained to minimize the amount of time it takes to find a granted lock.

- A pointer to a list of lock owner blocks for locks on this resource that are waiting to be converted to another lock mode. This is called the *convert list*.

- A pointer to a list of lock owner blocks for locks that have been requested on this resource but have not yet been granted. This is called the *wait list*.

The lock resource uniquely identifies the data being locked. Its structure is shown in Figure 10-4. Each "row" in the figure represents 4 bytes, or 32 bits.

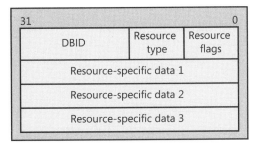

**FIGURE 10-4** The structure of a lock resource

The meanings of the fields shown in Figure 10-4 are described in Table 10-8. The value in the *resource type* byte is one of the locking resources described earlier in Table 10-5. The number in parentheses after the resource type is the code number for the resource type (which we see in the *syslockinfo* table a little later in the chapter). The meaning of the values in the three data fields varies depending on the type of resource being described. SR indicates a subresource (which I describe shortly).

**TABLE 10-8 Fields in the Lock Resource Block**

| Resource Type | Resource Content | | |
| --- | --- | --- | --- |
| | Data 1 | Data 2 | Data 3 |
| Database (2) | SR | 0 | 0 |
| File (3) | File ID | 0 | 0 |
| Index (4) | Object ID | SR | Index ID |
| Table (5) | Object ID | SR | 0 |
| Page (6) | Page number | | 0 |
| Key (7) | Partition ID | Hashed key | |
| Extent (8) | Extent ID | | 0 |
| RID (9) | RID | | 0 |

The following are some of the possible SR (SubResource) values. If the lock is on a Database resource, SR indicates one of the following:

- Full database lock
- Bulk operation lock

If the lock is on a Table resource, SR indicates one of the following:

- Full table lock (default)
- Update statistics lock
- Compile lock

If the lock is on an Index resource, SR indicates one of the following:

- Full index lock (default)
- Index ID lock
- Index name lock

## Lock Owner Blocks

Each lock owned or waited for by a session is represented in a lock owner block. Lists of lock owner blocks form the grant, convert, and wait lists that hang off the lock blocks. Each lock owner block for a granted lock is linked with all other lock owner blocks for the same transaction or session so they can be freed as appropriate when the transaction or session ends.

## *syslockinfo* Table

Although the recommended way of retrieving information about locks is through the *sys.dm_tran_locks* view, there is another metadata object called *syslockinfo* that provides internal information about locks. Prior to the introduction of the DMVs in SQL Server 2005, *syslockinfo* was the only internal metadata available for examining locking information.

In fact, the stored procedure *sp_lock* is still defined to retrieve information from *syslockinfo* instead of from *sys.dm_tran_locks*. I will not go into full detail about *syslockinfo* because almost all the information from that table is available, in a much more readable form, in the *sys.dm_tran_locks* view. However, *syslockinfo* is available in the *master* database for you to take a look at. One column, however, is of particular interest—the *rsc_bin* column, which contains a 16-byte description of a locked resource.

You can analyze the *syslockinfo.rsc_bin* field as the resource block. Let's look at an example. I select a single row from the *Person* table in *AdventureWorks2008* using the REPEATABLE READ isolation level, so my shared locks continue to be held for the duration of the transaction. I then look at the *rsc_bin* column in *syslockinfo* for key locks, page locks, and table locks:

```
USE AdventureWorks2008
GO
SET TRANSACTION ISOLATION LEVEL REPEATABLE READ
GO
BEGIN TRAN
SELECT * FROM Person.Person
WHERE BusinessEntityID = 249;
GO
SELECT rsc_bin, rsc_type
FROM master..syslockinfo
WHERE rsc_type IN (5,6,7);
GO
```

Here are the three rows in the result set:

```
rsc_bin                              rsc_type
----------------------------------   --------
0x805EFA590000000000000000007000500  5
0x19050000010000000000000007000600   6
0x710000000001F900CE79D52507000700   7
```

The last 2 bytes in *rsc_bin* are the resource mode, so after byte-swapping, you can see the same value as in the *rsc_type* column—for example, you byte-swap 0500 to 0005 to resource mode 5 (a table lock). The next 2 bytes at the end indicate the database ID, and for all three rows, the value after byte-swapping is 0007, which is the database ID of my *AdventureWorks2008* database.

The rest of the bytes vary depending on the type of resource. For a table, the first 4 bytes represent the object ID. The preceding row for the object lock (*rsc_type* = 5) after byte swapping has a value of 59FA5E80, which is 1509580416 in decimal. I can translate this to an object name as follows:

```
SELECT object_name(1509580416)
```

This shows me the *Person* table.

For a PAGE (*rsc_type* = 6), the first 6 bytes are the page number followed by the file number. After byte-swapping, the file number is 0001, or 1 decimal, and the page number is 00000519, or 9889 in decimal. So the lock is on file 1, page 1305.

Finally, for a KEY (*rsc_type* = 7), the first 6 bytes represent the partition ID but the translation is a bit trickier. We need to add another 2 bytes of zeros to the value after byte-swapping, so we end up with 0100000000710000, which translates to 72057594045333504 in decimal. To see which object this partition belongs to, I can query the *sys.partitions* view:

```
SELECT object_name(object_id)
FROM sys.partitions
WHERE partition_ID = 72057594045333504;
```

Again, the result is that this partition is part of the *Person* table. The next 6 bytes of *rsc_bin* for the KEY resource are F900CE79D525. This is a character field, so no byte-swapping is needed. However, the value is not further decipherable. Key locks have a hash value generated for them, based on all the key columns of the index. Indexes can be quite long, so for almost any possible data type, SQL Server needs a consistent way to keep track of which keys are locked. The hashing function therefore generates a 6-byte hash string to represent the key. Although you can't reverse-engineer this value and determine exactly which index row is locked, you can use it to look for matching entries, just like SQL Server does. If two *rsc_bin* values have the same 6-byte hash string, they are referring to the same lock resource.

In addition to detecting references to the same lock resource, you can determine which specific keys are locked by using the undocumented value *%%lockres%%*, which can return the hash string for any key. Selecting this value, along with data from the table, returns the lock resource for every row in the result set, based on the index used to retrieve the data. Consider the following example, which creates a clustered and nonclustered index on a tiny table and then selects the *%%lockres%%* value for each row, first using the clustered index and then using the nonclustered index:

```
CREATE TABLE lockres (c1 int, c2 int);
GO
INSERT INTO lockres VALUES (1,10);
INSERT INTO lockres VALUES (2,20);
INSERT INTO lockres VALUES (3,30);
GO
CREATE UNIQUE CLUSTERED INDEX lockres_ci ON lockres(c1);
CREATE UNIQUE NONCLUSTERED INDEX lockres_nci ON lockres(c2);
GO
SELECT %%lockres%% AS lock_resource, * FROM lockres WITH (INDEX = lockres_ci);
SELECT %%lockres%% AS lock_resource, * FROM lockres WITH (INDEX = lockres_nci);
GO
```

I get the following results. The first set of rows shows the lock resource for the clustered index keys, and the second set shows the lock resources for the nonclustered index:

```
lock_resource                     c1          c2
-------------------------------- ----------- -----------
(010086470766)                    1           10
(020068e8b274)                    2           20
(03000d8f0ecc)                    3           30
```

| lock_resource | c1 | c2 |
| --- | --- | --- |
| (0a0087c006b1) | 1 | 10 |
| (14002be0c001) | 2 | 20 |
| (1e004f007d6e) | 3 | 30 |

I can use this lock resource to find which row in a table matches a locked resource. For example, if *sys.dm_tran_locks* indicates that a row with the lock resource (010086470766) is holding a lock in the *lockres* table, I could find which row that resource corresponds to with the following query:

```
SELECT * FROM lockres
WHERE %%lockres%% = '(010086470766)'
```

Note that if the table is a heap and I look for the lock resource when scanning the table, the lock resource is the actual row ID (RID). The value returned looks just like the special value *%%physloc%%*, which I told you about in Chapter 5, "Tables":

```
CREATE TABLE lockres_on_heap (c1 int, c2 int);
GO
INSERT INTO lockres_on_heap VALUES (1,10);
INSERT INTO lockres_on_heap VALUES (2,20);
INSERT INTO lockres_on_heap VALUES (3,30);
GO
SELECT %%lockres%% AS lock_resource, * FROM lockres_on_heap;
```

Here are my results:

| lock_resource | c1 | c2 |
| --- | --- | --- |
| 1:169:0 | 1 | 10 |
| 1:169:1 | 2 | 20 |
| 1:169:2 | 3 | 30 |

**Caution** You need to be careful when trying to find the row in a table with a hash string that matches a particular lock resource. These queries have to perform a complete scan of the table to find the row you are interested in, and with a large table, that process can be very expensive.

# Row-Level Locking vs. Page-Level Locking

Although SQL Server 2008 fully supports row-level locking, in some situations, the lock manager decides not to lock individual rows and instead locks pages or the whole table. In other cases, many smaller locks are escalated to a table lock, as I discuss in the upcoming section entitled "Lock Escalation."

Prior to SQL Server 7.0, the smallest unit of data that SQL Server could lock was a page. Even though many people argued that this was unacceptable and it was impossible to maintain good concurrency while locking entire pages, many large and powerful applications were written and deployed using only page-level locking. If they were well designed and tuned, concurrency was not an issue, and some of these applications supported hundreds of active user connections with acceptable response times and throughput. However, with the change in page size from 2 KB to 8 KB for SQL Server 7.0, the issue has become more critical. Locking an entire page means locking four times as much data as in previous versions. Beginning with SQL Server 7.0, the software implements full row-level locking, so any potential problems due to lower concurrency with the larger page size should not be an issue. However, locking isn't free. Resources are required to manage locks. Recall that a lock is an in-memory structure of 64 or 128 bytes (for 32-bit or 64-bit machines, respectively) with another 32 or 64 bytes for each process holding or requesting the lock. If you need a lock for every row and you scan a million rows, you need more than 64 MB of RAM just to hold locks for that one process.

Beyond memory consumption issues, locking is a fairly processing-intensive operation. Managing locks requires substantial bookkeeping. Recall that, internally, SQL Server uses a lightweight mutex called a *spinlock* to guard resources, and it uses latches—also lighter than full-blown locks—to protect non-leaf level index pages. These performance optimizations avoid the overhead of full locking. If a page of data contains 50 rows of data, all of which are used, it is obviously more efficient to issue and manage one lock on the page than to manage 50. That's the obvious benefit of page locking—a reduction in the number of lock structures that must exist and be managed.

Let's say two processes each need to update a few rows of data, and even though the rows are not the same ones, some of them happen to exist on the same page. With page-level locking, one process would have to wait until the page locks of the other process were released. If you use row-level locking instead, the other process does not have to wait. The finer granularity of the locks means that no conflict occurs in the first place because each process is concerned with different rows. That's the obvious benefit of row-level locking. Which of these obvious benefits wins? Well, the decision isn't clear-cut, and it depends on the application and the data. Each type of locking can be shown to be superior for different types of applications and usage.

The *ALTER INDEX* statement lets you manually control the unit of locking within an index with options to disallow page locks or row locks within an index. Because these options are available only for indexes, there is no way to control the locking within the data pages of a heap. (But remember that if a table has a clustered index, the data pages are part of the index and are affected by a value set with *ALTER INDEX*.) The index options are set for each table or index individually. Two options, ALLOW_ROW_LOCKS and ALLOW_PAGE_LOCKS, are both set to ON initially for every table and index. If both of these options are set to OFF for a table, only full table locks are allowed.

As mentioned earlier, during the optimization process, SQL Server determines whether to lock rows, pages, or the entire table initially. The locking of rows (or keys) is heavily favored. The type of locking chosen is based on the number of rows and pages to be scanned, the number of rows on a page, the isolation level in effect, the update activity going on, the number of users on the system needing memory for their own purposes, and so on.

# Lock Escalation

SQL Server automatically escalates row, key, or page locks to coarser table or partition locks as appropriate. This escalation protects system resources—it prevents the system from using too much memory for keeping track of locks—and increases efficiency. For example, after a query acquires many row locks, the lock level can be escalated because it probably makes more sense to acquire and hold a single lock than to hold many row locks. When lock escalation occurs, many locks on smaller units (rows or pages) are released and replaced by one lock on a larger unit. This escalation reduces locking overhead and keeps the system from running out of locks. Because a finite amount of memory is available for the lock structures, escalation is sometimes necessary to make sure the memory for locks stays within reasonable limits.

The default in SQL Server is to escalate to table locks. However, SQL Server 2008 introduces the ability to escalate to a single partition using the *ALTER TABLE* statement. The LOCK_ESCALATION option of *ALTER TABLE* can specify that escalation is always to a table level, or that it can be to either a table or partition level. The LOCK_ESCALATION option can also be used to prevent escalation entirely. Here's an example of altering the *TransactionHistory* table (which you may have created if you ran the partitioning example in Chapter 7, "Special Storage"), so that locks can be escalated to either the table or partition level:

```
ALTER TABLE TransactionHistory
SET (LOCK_ESCALATION = AUTO);
```

Lock escalation occurs in the following situations:

- The number of locks held by a single statement on one object, or on one partition of one object, exceeds a threshold. Currently that threshold is 5,000 locks, but it might change in future service packs. The lock escalation does not occur if the locks are spread over multiple objects in the same statement—for example, 3,000 locks in one index and 3,000 in another.

- Memory taken by lock resources exceeds 40 percent of the non-AWE (32-bit) or regular (64-bit) enabled memory and the locks configuration option is set to 0. (In this case, the lock memory is allocated dynamically as needed, so the 40 percent value is not a constant.) If the locks option is set to a nonzero value, memory reserved for locks is statically allocated when SQL Server starts. Escalation occurs when SQL Server is using more than 40 percent of the reserved lock memory for lock resources.

When the lock escalation is triggered, the attempt might fail if there are conflicting locks. So, for example, if an X lock on a RID needs to be escalated and there are concurrent X locks on the same table or partition held by a different process, the lock escalation attempt fails. However, SQL Server continues to attempt to escalate the lock every time the transaction acquires another 1,250 locks on the same object. If the lock escalation succeeds, SQL Server releases all the row and page locks on the index or the heap.

**Note**  SQL Server never escalates to page locks. The result of a lock escalation is always a table or partition. In addition, multiple partition locks are never escalated to a table lock.

### Controlling Lock Escalation

Lock escalation can potentially lead to blocking of future concurrent access to the index or the heap by other transactions needing row or page locks on the object. SQL Server cannot de-escalate the lock when new requests are made. So lock escalation is not always a good idea for all applications.

SQL Server 2008 also supports disabling lock escalation for a single table using the *ALTER TABLE* statement. Here is an example of disabling lock escalation on the *TransactionHistory* table:

```
ALTER TABLE TransactionHistory
SET (LOCK_ESCALATION = DISABLE);
```

SQL Server 2008 also supports disabling lock escalation using trace flags. Note that these trace flags affect lock escalation on all tables in all databases in a SQL Server instance.

■  Trace flag 1211 completely disables lock escalation. It instructs SQL Server to ignore the memory acquired by the lock manager up to the maximum statically allocated lock memory (specified using the locks configuration option) or 60 percent of the non-AWE (32-bit) or regular (64-bit) dynamically allocated memory. At that time, an out-of-lock memory error is generated. You should exercise extreme caution when using this trace flag as a poorly designed application can exhaust the memory and seriously degrade the performance of your SQL Server instance.

■  Trace flag 1224 also disables lock escalation based on the number of locks acquired, but it allows escalation based on memory consumption. It enables lock escalation when the lock manager acquires 40 percent of the statically allocated memory (as per the locks option) or 40 percent of the non-AWE (32-bit) or regular (64-bit) dynamically allocated memory. You should note that if SQL Server cannot allocate memory for locks due to memory use by other components, the lock escalation can be triggered earlier. As with trace flag 1211, SQL Server generates an out-of-memory error when memory allocated to the lock manager exceeds the total statically allocated memory or 60 percent of non-AWE (32-bit) or regular (64-bit) memory for dynamic allocation.

If both trace flags (1211 and 1224) are set at the same time, trace flag 1211 takes precedence. Remember that these trace flags affect the entire SQL Server instance. In many cases, it is desirable to control the escalation threshold at the object level, so you should consider using the *ALTER TABLE* command when possible.

## Deadlocks

A deadlock occurs when two processes are waiting for a resource and neither process can advance because the other process prevents it from getting the resource. A true deadlock is a Catch-22 in which, without intervention, neither process can ever make progress. When a deadlock occurs, SQL Server intervenes automatically. I refer mainly to deadlocks acquired due to conflicting locks, although deadlocks can also be detected on worker threads, memory, and parallel query resources.

> **Note** A simple wait for a lock is not a deadlock. When the process that's holding the lock completes, the waiting process can acquire the lock. Lock waits are normal, expected, and necessary in multiuser systems.

In SQL Server, two main types of deadlocks can occur: a cycle deadlock and a conversion deadlock. Figure 10-5 shows an example of a cycle deadlock. Process A starts a transaction, acquires an exclusive table lock on the *Product* table, and requests an exclusive table lock on the *PurchaseOrderDetail* table. Simultaneously, process B starts a transaction, acquires an exclusive lock on the *PurchaseOrderDetail* table, and requests an exclusive lock on the *Product* table. The two processes become deadlocked—caught in a "deadly embrace." Each process holds a resource needed by the other process. Neither can progress, and, without intervention, both would be stuck in deadlock forever. You can actually generate the deadlock in SQL Server Management Studio, as follows:

1. Open a query window, and change your database context to the *AdventureWorks2008* database. Execute the following batch for process A:

```
BEGIN TRAN
UPDATE  Production.Product
    SET ListPrice = ListPrice * 0.9
WHERE ProductID  = 922;
```

2. Open a second window, and execute this batch for process B:

```
BEGIN TRAN
UPDATE  Purchasing.PurchaseOrderDetail
    SET OrderQty = OrderQty + 200
    WHERE ProductID  = 922
    AND PurchaseOrderID = 499;
```

3. Go back to the first window, and execute this *UPDATE* statement:

```
UPDATE  Purchasing.PurchaseOrderDetail
    SET OrderQty = OrderQty - 200
    WHERE ProductID  = 922
    AND PurchaseOrderID = 499;
```

At this point, the query should block. It is not deadlocked yet, however. It is waiting for a lock on the *PurchaseOrderDetail* table, and there is no reason to suspect that it won't eventually get that lock.

4. Go back to the second window, and execute this *UPDATE* statement:

```
UPDATE  Production.Product
    SET ListPrice = ListPrice * 1.1
    WHERE ProductID  = 922;
```

At this point, a deadlock occurs. The first connection never gets its requested lock on the *PurchaseOrderDetail* table because the second connection does not give it up until it gets a lock on the *Product* table. Because the first connection already has the lock on the *Product* table, we have a deadlock. One of the processes receives the following error message. (Of course, the actual process ID reported will probably be different.)

```
Msg 1205, Level 13, State 51, Line 1
Transaction (Process ID 57) was deadlocked on lock resources with another process and has
been chosen as the deadlock victim. Rerun the transaction.
```

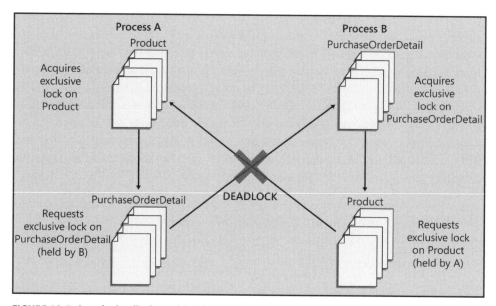

**FIGURE 10-5** A cycle deadlock resulting from two processes, each holding a resource needed by the other

Figure 10-6 shows an example of a conversion deadlock. Process A and process B each hold a shared lock on the same page within a transaction. Each process wants to promote its shared lock to an exclusive lock but cannot do so because of the other process's lock. Again, intervention is required.

SQL Server automatically detects deadlocks and intervenes through the lock manager, which provides deadlock detection for regular locks. In SQL Server 2008, deadlocks can also involve resources other than locks. For example, if process A is holding a lock on *Table1* and is waiting for memory to become available and process B has some memory that it can't release until it acquires a lock on *Table1*, the processes deadlock. When SQL Server detects a deadlock, it terminates one process's batch, rolling back the active transaction and releasing all that process's locks to resolve the deadlock. In addition to deadlocks on lock resources and memory resources, deadlocks can also occur with resources involving worker threads, parallel query execution–related resources, and MARS resources. Latches are not involved in deadlock detection because SQL Server uses deadlock-proof algorithms when it acquires latches.

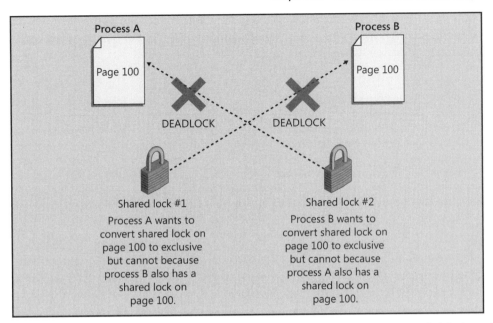

**FIGURE 10-6** A conversion deadlock resulting from two processes wanting to promote their locks on the same resource within a transaction

In SQL Server, a separate thread called LOCK_MONITOR checks the system for deadlocks every five seconds. As deadlocks occur, the deadlock detection interval is reduced and can go as low as 100 milliseconds. In fact, the first few lock requests that cannot be satisfied after a deadlock has been detected will immediately trigger a deadlock search rather than wait for the next deadlock detection interval. If the deadlock frequency declines, the interval can go back to every five seconds.

This LOCK_MONITOR thread checks for deadlocks by inspecting the list of waiting locks for any cycles, which indicate a circular relationship between processes holding locks and processes waiting for locks. SQL Server attempts to choose as the victim the process that would be least expensive to roll back, considering the amount of work the process has already done. That process is killed and error message 1205 is sent to the corresponding client connection. The transaction is rolled back, meaning all its locks are released, so other processes involved in the deadlock can proceed. However, certain operations are marked as golden, or unkillable, and cannot be chosen as the deadlock victim. For example, a process involved in rolling back a transaction cannot be chosen as a deadlock victim because the changes being rolled back could be left in an indeterminate state, causing data corruption.

Using the *SET DEADLOCK_PRIORITY* statement, a process can determine its priority for being chosen as the victim if it is involved in a deadlock. There are 21 different priority levels, from −10 to 10. You can also specify the value *LOW*, which is equivalent to −5, *NORMAL*, which is equivalent to 0, and *HIGH*, which is equivalent to 5. Which session is chosen as the deadlock victim depends on each session's deadlock priority. If the sessions have different deadlock priorities, the session with the lowest deadlock priority is chosen as the deadlock victim. If both sessions have set the same deadlock priority, SQL Server selects as the victim the session that is less expensive to roll back.

> **Note**  The lightweight latches and spinlocks used internally do not have deadlock detection services. Instead, deadlocks on latches and spinlocks are avoided rather than resolved. Avoidance is achieved via strict programming guidelines used by the SQL Server development team. These lightweight locks must be acquired in a hierarchy, and a process must not have to wait for a regular lock while holding a latch or spinlock. For example, one coding rule is that a process holding a spinlock must never directly wait for a lock or call another service that might have to wait for a lock, and a request can never be made for a spinlock that is higher in the acquisition hierarchy. By establishing similar guidelines for your development team for the order in which SQL Server objects are accessed, you can go a long way toward avoiding deadlocks in the first place.

In the example in Figure 10-5, the cycle deadlock could have been avoided if the processes had decided on a protocol beforehand—for example, if they had decided always to access the *Product* table first and the *PurchaseOrderDetail* table second. Then one of the processes gets the initial exclusive lock on the table being accessed first, and the other process waits for the lock to be released. One process waiting for a lock is normal and natural. Remember, waiting is not a deadlock.

You should always try to have a standard protocol for the order in which processes access tables. If you know that the processes might need to update the row after reading it, they should initially request an update lock, not a shared lock. If both processes request an update lock rather than a shared lock, the process that is granted an update lock is assured that the lock can later be promoted to an exclusive lock. The other process requesting an update lock has to wait. The use of an update lock serializes the requests for an exclusive lock. Other processes needing only to read the data can still get their shared locks and read. Because the holder of the update lock is guaranteed an exclusive lock, the deadlock is avoided.

In many systems, deadlocks cannot be completely avoided, but if the application handles the deadlock appropriately, the impact on any users involved, and on the rest of the system, should be minimal. (Appropriate handling implies that when error 1205 occurs, the application resubmits the batch, which most likely succeeds on the second try. Once one process is killed, its transaction is aborted, and its locks are released, the other process involved in the deadlock can finish its work and release its locks, so the environment is not conducive to another deadlock.) Although you might not be able to avoid deadlocks completely, you can minimize their occurrence. For example, you should write your applications so that your processes hold locks for a minimal amount of time; in that way, other processes won't have to wait too long for locks to be released. Although you don't usually invoke locking directly, you can influence locking by keeping transactions as short as possible. For example, don't ask for user input in the middle of a transaction. Instead, get the input first and then quickly perform the transaction.

# Row Versioning

At the beginning of this chapter, I described two concurrency models that SQL Server can use. Pessimistic concurrency uses locking to guarantee the appropriate transactional behavior and avoid problems such as dirty reads, according to the isolation level you are using. Optimistic concurrency uses a new technology called *row versioning* to guarantee your transactions. Starting in SQL Server 2005, optimistic concurrency is available after you enable one or both of the database properties called READ_COMMITTED_SNAPSHOT and ALLOW_SNAPSHOT_ ISOLATION. Exclusive locks can be acquired when you use optimistic concurrency, so you still need to be aware of all issues related to lock modes, lock resources, and lock duration, as well as the resources required to keep track of and manage locks. The difference between optimistic and pessimistic concurrency is that with optimistic concurrency, writers and readers do not block each other. Or, using locking terminology, a process requesting an exclusive lock does not block when the requested resource currently has a shared lock. Conversely, a process requesting a shared lock does not block when the requested resource currently has an exclusive lock.

It is possible to avoid blocking because as soon as one of the new database options is enabled, SQL Server starts using *tempdb* to store copies (versions) of all rows that have changed, and it keeps those copies as long as there are any transactions that might need to access them. The space in *tempdb* used to store previous versions of changed rows is called the *version store*.

## Overview of Row Versioning

In earlier versions of SQL Server, the tradeoff in concurrency solutions is that we can avoid having writers block readers if we are willing to risk inconsistent data—that is, if we use Read Committed isolation. If our results must always be based on committed data, we need to be willing to wait for changes to be committed.

SQL Server 2005 introduced a new isolation level called *Snapshot isolation* and a new nonblocking flavor of Read Committed isolation called *Read Committed Snapshot Isolation (RCSI)*. These row versioning–based isolation levels allow a reader to get to a previously committed value of the row without blocking, so concurrency is increased in the system. For this to work, SQL Server must keep old versions of a row when it is updated or deleted. If multiple updates are made to the same row, multiple older versions of the row might need to be maintained. Because of this, row versioning is sometimes called *multiversion concurrency control*.

To support storing multiple older versions of rows, additional disk space is used from the *tempdb* database. The disk space for the version store must be monitored and managed appropriately, and I point out some of the ways you can do that later in this section. Versioning works by making any transaction that changes data keep the old versions of the data around so that a snapshot of the database (or a part of the database) can be constructed from these old versions.

## Row Versioning Details

When a row in a table or index is updated, the new row is stamped with the transaction sequence number (XSN) of the transaction that is doing the update. The XSN is a monotonically increasing number that is unique within each SQL Server database. The concept of XSN is not the same as Log Sequence Numbers (LSNs), which I discussed in Chapter 4, "Logging and Recovery." I discuss XSNs in more detail later. When updating a row, the previous version is stored in the version store, and the new row contains a pointer to the old row in the version store. Old rows in the version store might contain pointers to even older versions. All the old versions of a particular row are chained in a linked list, and SQL Server might need to follow several pointers in a list to reach the right version. Version rows must be kept in the version store only as long as there are operations that might require them.

In Figure 10-7, the current version of the row is generated by transaction T3, and it is stored in the normal data page. The previous versions of the row, generated by transaction T2 and transaction Tx, are stored in pages in the version store (in *tempdb*).

Row versioning gives SQL Server an optimistic concurrency model to work with when an application requires it or when the concurrency reduction of using the default pessimistic model is unacceptable. Before you switch to the row versioning–based isolation levels, you must carefully consider the tradeoffs of using this new concurrency model. In addition to requiring extra management to monitor the increased use of *tempdb* for the version store, versioning slows the performance of update operations due to the extra work involved in maintaining old versions. Update operations bear this cost, even if there are no current readers of the data. If there are readers using row versioning, they have the extra cost of traversing the link pointers to find the appropriate version of the requested row.

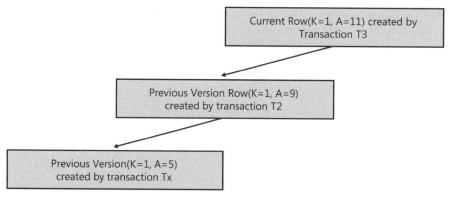

**FIGURE 10-7**  Versions of a row

In addition, because the optimistic concurrency model of Snapshot isolation assumes (optimistically) that not many update conflicts will occur, you should not choose the Snapshot isolation level if you are expecting contention for updating the same data concurrently. Snapshot isolation works well to enable readers not to be blocked by writers, but simultaneous writers are still not allowed. In the default pessimistic model, the first writer will block all subsequent writers, but using Snapshot isolation, subsequent writers could actually receive error messages and the application would need to resubmit the original request. Note that these update conflicts occur only with the full Snapshot isolation, not with the enhanced RCSI.

## Snapshot-Based Isolation Levels

SQL Server 2008 provides two types of snapshot-based isolation, both of which use row versioning to maintain the snapshot. One type, RCSI, is enabled simply by setting a database option. Once enabled, no further changes need to be made. Any transaction that would have operated under the default Read Committed isolation will run under RCSI. The other type, Snapshot isolation must be enabled in two places. You must first enable the database with the ALLOW_SNAPSHOT_ISOLATION option, and then each connection that wants to use SI must set the isolation level using the *SET TRANSACTION ISOLATION LEVEL* command. Let's compare these two types of Snapshot-based isolation.

### Read Committed Snapshot Isolation

RCSI is a statement-level Snapshot-based isolation, which means any queries see the most recent committed values as of the beginning of the statement. For example, let's look at the scenario in Table 10-9. Assume that two transactions are running in the *AdventureWorks2008* database, which has been enabled for RCSI, and that before either transaction starts running, the *ListPrice* value of product 922 is 8.89.

**TABLE 10-9  A *SELECT* Running in RCSI**

| Time | Transaction 1 | Transaction 2 |
|------|---------------|---------------|
| 1 | BEGIN TRAN<br>UPDATE Production.Product<br>SET ListPrice = 10.00<br>WHERE ProductID  = 922; | BEGIN TRAN |
| 2 | | SELECT ListPrice<br>FROM Production.Product<br>WHERE ProductID  = 922;<br>-- **SQL Server returns 8.89** |
| 3 | COMMIT TRAN | |
| 4 | | SELECT ListPrice<br>FROM Production.Product<br>WHERE ProductID  = 922;<br>-- **SQL Server returns 10.00** |
| 5 | | COMMIT TRAN |

We should note that at Time = 2, the change made by Transaction 1 is still uncommitted, so the lock is still held on the row for *ProductID* = 922. However, Transaction 2 does not block on that lock; it has access to an old version of the row with a last committed *ListPrice* value of 8.89. After Transaction 1 has committed and released its lock, Transaction 2 sees the new value of *ListPrice*. This is still Read Committed isolation (just a nonlocking variation), so there is no guarantee that read operations are repeatable.

You can consider RCSI to be just a variation of the default isolation level Read Committed. The same behaviors are allowed and disallowed, as indicated back in Table 10-2.

RCSI is enabled and disabled with the *ALTER DATABASE* command, as shown in this command to enable RCSI in the *AdventureWorks2008* database:

```
ALTER DATABASE AdventureWorks2008
   SET READ_COMMITTED_SNAPSHOT ON;
```

Ironically, although this isolation level is intended to help avoid blocking, if there are any users in the database when the preceding command is executed, the *ALTER* statement blocks it. (The connection issuing the *ALTER* command can be in the database, but no other connections can be.) Until the change is successful, the database continues to operate as if it is not in RCSI mode. The blocking can be avoided by specifying a TERMINATION clause for the *ALTER* command, as discussed in Chapter 3, "Databases and Database Files":

```
ALTER DATABASE AdventureWorks2008
   SET READ_COMMITTED_SNAPSHOT ON WITH NO_WAIT;
```

If there are any users in the database, the preceding *ALTER* fails with the following error:

```
Msg 5070, Level 16, State 2, Line 1
Database state cannot be changed while other users are using
the database 'AdventureWorks2008'
Msg 5069, Level 16, State 1, Line 1
ALTER DATABASE statement failed.
```

You can also specify one of the ROLLBACK termination options, basically to break any current database connections.

The biggest benefit of RCSI is that you can introduce greater concurrency because readers do not block writers and writers do not block readers. However, writers do block writers because the normal locking behavior applies to all *UPDATE*, *DELETE*, and *INSERT* operations. No SET options are required for any session to take advantage of RCSI, so you can reduce the concurrency impact of blocking and deadlocking without any change in your applications.

## Snapshot Isolation

Snapshot isolation requires using a *SET* command in the session, just like for any other change of isolation level (for example, *SET TRANSACTION ISOLATION LEVEL SERIALIZABLE*). For a session-level option to take effect, you must also allow the database to use SI by altering the database:

```
ALTER DATABASE AdventureWorks2008
   SET ALLOW_SNAPSHOT_ISOLATION ON;
```

When altering the database to allow SI, a user in the database does not necessarily block the command from completing. However, if there is an active transaction in the database, the *ALTER* is blocked. This does not mean that there is no effect until the statement completes. Changing the database to allow full SI can be a deferred operation. The database can actually be in one of four states with regard to ALLOW_SNAPSHOT_ISOLATION. It can be ON or OFF, but it can also be IN_TRANSITION_TO_ON or IN_TRANSITION_TO_OFF.

Here is what happens when you *ALTER* a database to ALLOW_SNAPSHOT_ISOLATION:

- SQL Server waits for the completion of all active transactions, and the database status is set to IN_TRANSITION_TO_ON.

- Any new *UPDATE* or *DELETE* transactions start generating versions in the version store.

- New snapshot transactions cannot start because transactions that are already in progress are not storing row versions as the data is changed. New snapshot transactions would have to have committed versions of the data to read. There is no error when you execute the *SET TRANSACTION ISOLATION LEVEL SNAPSHOT* command; the error occurs when you try to *SELECT* data, and you get this message:

```
Msg 3956, Level 16, State 1, Line 1
Snapshot isolation transaction failed to start in database 'AdventureWorks2008'
because the ALTER DATABASE command which enables snapshot isolation for this database
has not finished yet. The database is in transition to pending ON state. You must wait
until the ALTER DATABASE Command completes successfully.
```

- As soon as all transactions that were active when the *ALTER* command began have finished, the *ALTER* can finish and the state change are complete. The database now is in the state ALLOW_SNAPSHOT_ISOLATION.

Taking the database out of ALLOW_SNAPSHOT_ISOLATION mode is similar, and again, there is a transition phase.

- SQL Server waits for the completion of all active transactions, and the database status is set to IN_TRANSITION_TO_OFF.

- New snapshot transactions cannot start.

- Existing snapshot transactions still execute snapshot scans, reading from the version store.

- New transactions continue generating versions.

## Snapshot Isolation Scope

SI gives you a transactionally consistent view of the data. Any rows read are the most recent committed version of the rows as of the beginning of the transaction. (For RCSI, we get the most recent committed version as of the beginning of the statement.) A key point to keep in mind is that the transaction does not start at the *BEGIN TRAN* statement; for the purposes of SI, a transaction starts the first time the transactions accesses any data in the database.

As an example of SI, let's look at a scenario similar to the one in Table 10-9. Table 10-10 shows activities in a database with ALLOW_SNAPSHOT_ISOLATION set to ON. Assume two transactions are running in the *AdventureWorks2008* database and that before either transaction starts, the *ListPrice* value of Product 922 is 10.00.

**TABLE 10-10  A *SELECT* Running in a SNAPSHOT Transaction**

| Time | Transaction 1 | Transaction 2 |
|------|---------------|---------------|
| 1 | BEGIN TRAN | |
| 2 | UPDATE Production.Product<br>SET ListPrice = 12.00<br>WHERE ProductID = 922; | SET TRANSACTION ISOLATION<br>LEVEL SNAPSHOT |
| 3 | | BEGIN TRAN |
| 4 | | SELECT ListPrice<br>FROM Production.Product<br>WHERE ProductID = 922;<br>-- **SQL Server returns 10.00**<br>-- This is the beginning of<br>-- the transaction |
| 5 | COMMIT TRAN | |
| 6 | | SELECT ListPrice<br>FROM Production.Product<br>WHERE ProductID = 922;<br>-- **SQL Server returns 10.00**<br>-- Return the committed<br>-- value as of the beginning<br>-- of the transaction |
| 7 | | COMMIT TRAN |
| | | SELECT ListPrice<br>FROM Production.Product<br>WHERE ProductID = 922;<br>-- **SQL Server returns 12.00** |

Even though Transaction 1 has committed, Transaction 2 continues to return the initial value it read of 10.00 until Transaction 2 completes. Only after Transaction 2 is complete does the connection read a new value for *ListPrice*.

## Viewing Database State

The catalog view *sys.databases* contains several columns that report on the Snapshot isolation state of the database. A database can be enabled for SI and/or RCSI. However, enabling one does not automatically enable or disable the other. Each one has to be enabled or disabled individually using separate *ALTER DATABASE* commands.

The column *snapshot_isolation_state* has possible values of 0 to 4, indicating each of the four possible SI states, and the *snapshot_isolation_state_desc* column spells out the state. Table 10-11 summarizes what each state means.

**TABLE 10-11** **Possible Values for the Database Option ALLOW_SNAPSHOT_ISOLATION**

| Snapshot Isolation State | Description |
|---|---|
| OFF | Snapshot isolation state is disabled in the database. In other words, transactions with Snapshot isolation are not allowed. Database versioning state is initially set to OFF during recovery. If versioning is enabled, versioning state is set to ON after recovery. |
| IN_TRANSITION_TO_ON | The database is in the process of enabling SI. It waits for the completion of all *UPDATE* transactions that were active when the *ALTER DATABASE* command was issued. New *UPDATE* transactions in this database start paying the cost of versioning by generating row versions. Transactions using Snapshot isolation cannot start. |
| ON | SI is enabled. New snapshot transactions can start in this database. Existing snapshot transactions (in another snapshot-enabled session) that start before versioning state is turned ON cannot do a snapshot scan in this database because the snapshot those transactions are interested in is not properly generated by the *UPDATE* transactions. |
| IN_ TRANSITION_TO_OFF | The database is in the process of disabling the SI state and is unable to start new snapshot transactions. *UPDATE* transactions still pay the cost of versioning in this database. Existing snapshot transactions can still do snapshot scans. IN_TRANSITION_TO_OFF does not become OFF until all existing transactions finish. |

The *is_read_committed_snapshot_on* column has a value of 0 or 1. Table 10-12 summarizes what each state means.

**TABLE 10-12** **Possible Values for the Database Option READ_COMMITTED_SNAPSHOT**

| READ_COMMITTED_SNAPSHOT State | Description |
|---|---|
| 0 | READ_COMMITTED_SNAPSHOT is disabled. |
| 1 | READ_COMMITTED_SNAPSHOT is enabled. Any query with Read Committed isolation executes in the nonblocking mode. |

You can see the values of each of these snapshot states for all your databases with the following query:

```
SELECT name, snapshot_isolation_state_desc,
       is_read_committed_snapshot_on , *
FROM sys.databases;
```

## Update Conflicts

One crucial difference between the two optimistic concurrency levels is that SI can potentially result in update conflicts when a process sees the same data for the duration of its transaction and is not blocked simply because another process is changing the same data. Table 10-13 illustrates two processes attempting to update the *Quantity* value of the same row in the *ProductInventory* table in the *AdventureWorks2008* database. Two clerks have each received shipments of ProductID 872 and are trying to update the inventory. The *AdventureWorks2008* database has ALLOW_SNAPSHOT_ISOLATION set to ON, and before either transaction starts, the *Quantity* value of Product 872 is 324.

**TABLE 10-13  An Update Conflict in SNAPSHOT Isolation**

| Time | Transaction 1 | Transaction 2 |
|---|---|---|
| 1 | | SET TRANSACTION ISOLATION LEVEL SNAPSHOT |
| 2 | | BEGIN TRAN |
| 3 | | SELECT Quantity FROM Production.ProductInventory WHERE ProductID = 872; -- **SQL Server returns 324** -- This is the beginning of -- the transaction |
| 4 | BEGIN TRAN UPDATE Production.ProductInventory SET Quantity=Quantity + 200 WHERE ProductID = 872; -- **Quantity is now 524** | |
| 5 | | UPDATE Production.ProductInventory SET Quantity=Quantity + 300 WHERE ProductID = 872; -- **Process will block** |
| 6 | COMMIT TRAN | |
| 7 | | --  Process receives error 3960 |

The conflict happens because Transaction 2 started when the *Quantity* value was 324. When that value was updated by Transaction 1, the row version with 324 was saved in the version store. Transaction 2 continues to read that row for the duration of the transaction. If both *UPDATE* operations were allowed to succeed, we would have a classic lost update situation. Transaction 1 added 200 to the quantity, and then Transaction 2 would add 300 to the original value and save that. The 200 added by Transaction 1 would be completely lost. SQL Server does not allow that.

When Transaction 2 first tries to perform the *UPDATE*, it doesn't get an error immediately—it is simply blocked. Transaction 1 has an exclusive lock on the row, so when Transaction 2 attempts to get an exclusive lock, it is blocked. If Transaction 1 had rolled back its transaction, Transaction 2 would have been able to complete its *UPDATE*. But because Transaction 1 committed, SQL Server detects a conflict and generates the following error:

```
Msg 3960, Level 16, State 2, Line 1
Snapshot isolation transaction aborted due to update conflict. You cannot use snapshot
isolation to access table 'Production.ProductInventory' directly or indirectly in database'
AdventureWorks2008' to update, delete, or insert the row that has been modified or deleted
by another transaction. Retry the transaction or change the isolation level for the
update/delete statement.
```

Conflicts are possible only with SI because that isolation level is transaction-based, not statement-based. If the example in Table 10-13 were executed in a database using RCSI, the *UPDATE* statement executed by Transaction 2 would not use the old value of the data. It would be blocked when trying to read the current *Quantity,* and then when Transaction 1 finished, it would read the new updated *Quantity* as the current value and add 300 to that. Neither update would be lost.

If you choose to work in SI, you need to be aware that conflicts can happen. They can be minimized, but as with deadlocks, you cannot be sure that you will never have conflicts. Your application must be written to handle conflicts appropriately and not assume that the *UPDATE* has succeeded. If conflicts occur occasionally, you might consider it part of the price to be paid for using SI, but if they occur too often, you might need to take extra steps.

You might consider whether SI is really necessary, and if it is, you should determine whether the statement-based RCSI might give you the behavior you need without the cost of detecting and dealing with conflicts. Another solution is to use a query hint called UPDLOCK to make sure no other process updates data before you're ready to update it. In Table 10-13, Transaction 2 could use UPDLOCK on its initial *SELECT* as follows:

```
SELECT Quantity
FROM Production.ProductInventory WITH (UPDLOCK)
WHERE ProductID  = 872;
```

The UPDLOCK hint forces SQL Server to acquire update locks for Transaction 2 on the row that is selected. When Transaction 1 then tries to update that row, it blocks. It is not using SI, so it does not see the previous value of *Quantity.* Transaction 2 can perform its update because Transaction 1 is blocked, and it commits. Transaction 1 can then perform its update on the new value of *Quantity,* and neither update is lost.

I will provide a few more details about locking hints at the end of this chapter.

## Data Definition Language and SNAPSHOT Isolation

When working with SI, you need to be aware that although SQL Server keeps versions of all the changed data, that metadata is not versioned. Therefore, certain DDL statements are not allowed inside a snapshot transaction. The following DDL statements are disallowed in a snapshot transaction:

- *CREATE / ALTER / DROP INDEX*
- *DBCC DBREINDEX*
- *ALTER TABLE*
- *ALTER PARTITION FUNCTION / SCHEME*

On the other hand, the following DDL statements are allowed:

- *CREATE TABLE*
- *CREATE TYPE*
- *CREATE PROC*

Note that the allowable DDL statements are ones that create brand-new objects. In SI, there is no chance that any simultaneous data modifications affect the creation of these objects. Table 10-14 shows a pseudo-code example of a snapshot transaction that includes both *CREATE TABLE* and *CREATE INDEX*.

**TABLE 10-14  DDL Inside a SNAPSHOT Transaction**

| Time | Transaction 1 | Transaction 2 |
|------|---------------|---------------|
| 1 | SET TRANSACTION ISOLATION LEVEL SNAPSHOT; | |
| 2 | BEGIN TRAN | |
| 3 | SELECT count(*) FROM Production.Product; -- This is the beginning of -- the transaction | |
| 4 | | BEGIN TRAN |
| 5 | CREATE TABLE NewProducts ( <column definitions>) -- This DDL is legal | INSERT Production.Product VALUES (9999, .....) <br><br> -- A new row is insert into --   the Product table |
| 6 | | COMMIT TRAN |
| 7 | CREATE INDEX PriceIndex ON Production.Product (ListPrice) -- This DDL will generate an -- error | |

The *CREATE TABLE* statement succeeds even though Transaction 1 is in SI because it is not affected by anything any other process can do. The *CREATE INDEX* statement is a different story. When Transaction 1 started, the new row with ProductID 9999 did not exist. But when the *CREATE INDEX* statement is encountered, the *INSERT* from Transaction 2 has been committed. Should Transaction 1 include the new row in the index? There is actually no way to avoid including the new row, but that would violate the snapshot that Transaction 1 is using, and SQL Server generates an error instead of creating the index.

Another aspect of concurrent DDL to consider is what happens when a statement outside the snapshot transaction changes an object referenced by a snapshot transaction. The DDL is allowed, but you can get an error in the snapshot transaction when this happens. Table 10-15 shows an example.

**TABLE 10-15  Concurrent DDL Outside the SNAPSHOT Transaction**

| Time | Transaction 1 | Transaction 2 |
|---|---|---|
| 1 | `SET TRANSACTION ISOLATION`<br>`LEVEL SNAPSHOT;` | |
| 2 | `BEGIN TRAN` | |
| 3 | `SELECT TOP 10 *`<br>`FROM Production.Product;`<br>`-- This is the start of`<br>`-- the transaction` | |
| 4 | | `BEGIN TRAN`<br>`ALTER TABLE Purchasing.Vendor`<br>`    ADD notes varchar(1000);`<br>`COMMIT TRAN` |
| 5 | `SELECT TOP 10 *`<br>`FROM Production.Product;`<br>`-- Succeeds`<br>`-- The ALTER to a different`<br>`--   table does not affect`<br>`--   this transaction` | |
| 6 | | `BEGIN TRAN`<br>`ALTER TABLE Production.Product`<br>`    ADD LowestPrice money;`<br>`COMMIT TRAN` |
| 7 | `SELECT TOP 10 * FROM Production.`<br>`Product;`<br>`-- ERROR` | |

For the preceding situation, in Transaction 1, the repeated *SELECT* statements should always return the same data from the *Product* table. An external *ALTER TABLE* on a completely different table has no effect on the snapshot transaction, but Transaction 2 then alters the *Product* table to add a new column. Because the metadata representing the former table structure is not versioned, Transaction 1 cannot produce the same results for the third *SELECT*. SQL Server generates this error:

```
Msg 3961, Level 16, State 1, Line 1
Snapshot isolation transaction failed in database 'AdventureWorks2008' because the object
accessed by the statement has been modified by a DDL statement in another concurrent
transaction since the start of this transaction. It is disallowed because the metadata is
not versioned. A concurrent update to metadata can lead to inconsistency if mixed with
snapshot isolation.
```

In this version, any concurrent change to metadata on objects referenced by a snapshot transaction generates this error, even if there is no possibility of anomalies. For example, if Transaction 1 issues a *SELECT count(\*),* which is not affected by the *ALTER TABLE* statement, SQL Server still generates error 3961.

## Summary of Snapshot-Based Isolation Levels

SI and RCSI are similar in the sense that they are based on the versioning of rows in a database. However, there are some key differences in how these options are enabled from an administration perspective and also in how they affect your applications. I have discussed many of these differences already, but for completeness, Table 10-16 lists both the similarities and the differences between the two types of snapshot-based isolation.

**TABLE 10-16  Snapshot vs. Read Committed Snapshot Isolation**

| Snapshot Isolation | Read Committed Snapshot Isolation |
| --- | --- |
| The database must be configured to allow SI, and the session must issue the command *SET TRANSACTION ISOLATION LEVEL SNAPSHOT.* | The database must be configured to use RCSI, and sessions must use the default isolation level. No code changes are required. |
| Enabling SI for a database is an online operation. It allows a DBA to turn on versioning for one particular application such as one that is creating large reports. The DBA can then turn off versioning after the reporting transaction has started to prevent new snapshot transactions from starting. Turning on SI in an existing database is synchronous. When the *ALTER DATABASE* command is given, control does not return to the DBA until all existing update transactions that need to create versions in the current database finish. At this time, ALLOW_SNAPSHOT_ISOLATION is changed to ON. Only then can users start a snapshot transaction in that database. Turning off SI is also synchronous. | Enabling RCSI for a database requires a SHARED_ TRANSACTION_WORKSPACE lock on the database. All users must be kicked out of a database to enable this option. |
| There are no restrictions on active sessions in the database when this database option is enabled. | There should be no other sessions active in the database when you enable this option. |
| If an application runs a snapshot transaction that accesses tables from two databases, the DBA must turn on ALLOW_SNAPSHOT_ ISOLATION in both databases before the application starts a snapshot transaction. | RCSI is really a table-level option, so tables from two different databases, referenced in the same query, can each have their own individual setting. One table might get its data from the version store, while the other table is reading only the current versions of the data. There is no requirement that both databases must have the RCSI option enabled. |
| The IN_TRANSITION versioning states do not persist. Only the ON and OFF states are remembered on disk. | There are no IN_TRANSITION states here. Only ON and OFF states persist. |

**TABLE 10-16** Snapshot vs. Read Committed Snapshot Isolation

| Snapshot Isolation | Read Committed Snapshot Isolation |
| --- | --- |
| When a database is recovered after a server crash, or after your SQL Server instance is shut down, restored, attached, or made ONLINE, all versioning history for that database is lost. If database versioning state is ON, SQL Server can allow new snapshot transactions to access the database, but must prevent previous snapshot transactions from accessing the database. Those previous transactions would need to access data from a point in time before the database recovers. | This is an object-level option; it is not at the transaction level, so it is not applicable. |
| If the database is in the IN_TRANSITION_ TO_ON state, *ALTER DATABASE SET ALLOW_ SNAPSHOT_ ISOLATION OFF* waits for about six seconds and might fail if the database state is still in the IN_TRANSITION_TO_ON state. The DBA can retry the command after the database state changes to ON. | This option can be enabled only when there is no other active session in the database, so there are no transitional states. |
| For read-only databases, versioning is automatically enabled. You still can use *ALTER DATABASE SET ALLOW_SNAPSHOT_ISOLATION ON* for a read-only database. If the database is made read-write later, versioning for the database is still enabled. | As for SI, versioning is enabled automatically for read-only databases. |
| If there are long-running transactions, a DBA might need to wait a long time before the versioning state change can finish. A DBA can cancel the wait, and the versioning state is rolled back and set to the previous one. | This option can be enabled only when there is no other active session in the database, so there are no transitional states. |
| You cannot use *ALTER DATABASE* to change the database versioning state inside a user transaction. | As for SI, you can change the database versioning state inside a user transaction. |
| You can change the versioning state of *tempdb*. The versioning state of *tempdb* is preserved when SQL Server restarts, although the content of *tempdb* is not preserved. | You cannot turn this option ON for *tempdb*. |
| You can change the versioning state of the *master* database. | You cannot change this option for the *master* database. |
| You can change the versioning state of model. If versioning is enabled for model, every new database created will have versioning enabled as well. However, the versioning state of *tempdb* is not automatically enabled if you enable versioning for *model*. | Similar to the behavior for SI, except that there are no implications for *tempdb*. |

**TABLE 10-16** **Snapshot vs. Read Committed Snapshot Isolation**

| Snapshot Isolation | Read Committed Snapshot Isolation |
| --- | --- |
| You can turn this option ON for *msdb*. | You cannot turn on this option ON for *msdb* because this can potentially break the applications built on *msdb* that rely on blocking behavior of Read Committed isolation. |
| A query in a SI transaction sees data that was committed before the start of the transaction, and each statement in the transaction sees the same set of committed changes. | A statement running in RCSI sees everything committed before the start of the statement. Each new statement in the transaction picks up the most recent committed changes. |
| SI can result in update conflicts that might cause a rollback or abort the transaction. | There is no possibility of update conflicts. |

## The Version Store

As soon as a database is enabled for ALLOW_SNAPSHOT_ISOLATION or READ_COMMITTED_SNAPSHOT, all *UPDATE* and *DELETE* operations start generating row versions of the previously committed rows, and they store those versions in the version store on data pages in *tempdb*. Version rows must be kept in the version store only so long as there are snapshot queries that might need them.

SQL Server 2008 provides several DMVs that contain information about active snapshot transactions and the version store. We won't examine all the details of all those DMVs, but we look at some of the crucial ones to help you determine how much use is being made of your version store and what snapshot transactions might be affecting your results. The first DMV we look at, *sys.dm_tran_version_store*, contains information about the actual rows in the version store. Run the following script to make a copy of the *Production.Product* table, and then turn on ALLOW_SNAPSHOT_ISOLATION in the *AdventureWorks2008* database. Finally, verify that the option is ON and that there are currently no rows in the version store. You might need to close any active transactions currently using *AdventureWorks2008*:

```
USE AdventureWorks2008
SELECT * INTO NewProduct
FROM Production.Product;
GO
ALTER DATABASE ADVENTUREWORKS2008 SET ALLOW_SNAPSHOT_ISOLATION ON;
GO
SELECT name, snapshot_isolation_state_desc,
       is_read_committed_snapshot_on
FROM sys.databases
WHERE name= AdventureWorks2008;
GO
SELECT COUNT(*) FROM sys.dm_tran_version_store;
GO
```

As soon as you see that the database option is ON and there are no rows in the version store, you can continue. What I want to illustrate is that as soon as ALLOW_SNAPSHOT_ ISOLATION is enabled, SQL Server starts storing row versions, even if no snapshot transactions need to read those versions. So now run this *UPDATE* statement on the *NewProduct* table and look at the version store again:

```
UPDATE  NewProduct
SET ListPrice = ListPrice * 1.1;
GO
SELECT COUNT(*) FROM sys.dm_tran_version_store;
GO
```

You should see that there are now 504 rows in the version store because there are 504 rows in the *NewProduct* table. The previous version of each row, prior to the update, has been written to the version store in *tempdb*.

> **Note** SQL Server starts generating versions in *tempdb* as soon as a database is enabled for one of the snapshot-based isolation levels. In a heavily updated database, this can affect the behavior of other queries that use *tempdb*, as well as the server itself.

As shown earlier in Figure 10-7, the version store maintains link lists of rows. The current row points to the next older row, which can point to an older row, and so on. The end of the list is the oldest version of that particular row. To support row versioning, a row needs 14 additional bytes of information to keep track of the pointers. Eight bytes are needed for the actual pointer to the file, page, and row in *tempdb*, and 6 bytes are needed to store the XSN to help SQL Server determine which rows are current, or which versioned row is the one that a particular transaction needs to access. I tell you more about the XSN when we look at some of the other snapshot transaction metadata. In addition, one of the bits in the first byte of each data row (the TagA byte) is turned on to indicate that this row has versioning information in it.

Any row inserted or updated when a database is using one of the snapshot-based isolation levels will contain these 14 extra bytes. The following code creates a small table and inserts two rows into it in the *AdventureWorks2008* database, which already has ALLOW_SNAPSHOT_ISOLATION enabled. I then find the page number using *DBCC IND* (it is page 6,709) and use DBCC to look at the rows on the page. The output shows only one of the rows inserted:

```
CREATE TABLE T1 (T1ID char(1), T1name char(10));
GO
INSERT T1 SELECT 'A', 'aaaaaaaaaa';
INSERT T1 SELECT 'B', 'bbbbbbbbbb';
GO
DBCC IND (AdventureWorks2008, 'T1',-1); -- page 6709
DBCC TRACEON (3604);
DBCC PAGE('AdventureWorks2008', 1, 6709, 1);
OUTPUT ROW:
Slot 0, Offset 0x60, Length 32, DumpStyle BYTE
Record Type = PRIMARY_RECORD
Record Attributes =  NULL_BITMAP VERSIONING_INFO
```

```
Memory Dump @0x6207C060
00000000:    50000f00 41616161 61616161 61616102 †P...Aaaaaaaaaaa.
00000010:    00fc0000 00000000 0000020d 00000000 †...............
```

I have highlighted the new header information that indicates this row contains versioning information, and I have also highlighted the 14 bytes of the versioning information. The XSN is all 0's in the row because it was not modified as part of a transaction that Snapshot isolation needs to keep track of. *INSERT* statements create new data that no snapshot transaction needs to see. If I update one of these rows, the previous row is written to the version store and the XSN is reflected in the row versioning information:

```
UPDATE T1 SET T1name = '2222222222' where T1ID = 'A';
GO
DBCC PAGE('AdventureWorks2008', 1, 6709, 1);
GO
OUTPUT ROW:
Slot 0, Offset 0x60, Length 32, DumpStyle BYTE
Record Type = PRIMARY_RECORD
Record Attributes =  NULL_BITMAP VERSIONING_INFO
Memory Dump @0x61C4C060
00000000:    50000f00 41323232 32323232 32323202 †P...A2222222222.
00000010:    00fc1804 00000100 0100590d 00000000 †.........Y.....
```

As mentioned, if your database is enabled for one of the snapshot-based isolation levels, every new row has an additional 14 bytes added to it whether or not that row is ever actually involved in versioning. Every row updated also has the 14 bytes added to it, if they aren't already part of the row, and the update is done as a *DELETE* followed by an *INSERT*. This means that for tables and indexes on full pages, a simple *UPDATE* could result in page splitting.

When a row is deleted in a database enabled for snapshots, a pointer is left on the page as a ghost record to point to the deleted row in the version store. These ghost records are very similar to the ones we saw in Chapter 6, "Indexes: Internals and Management," and they're cleaned up as part of the versioning cleanup process, as I discuss shortly. Here's an example of a ghost record under versioning:

```
DELETE T1 WHERE T1ID = 'B';
DBCC PAGE('AdventureWorks2008 ', 1, 6709, 1);
GO
--Partial Results:
Slot 4, Offset 0x153, Length 15, DumpStyle BYTE

Record Type = GHOST_VERSION_RECORD
Record Attributes =  VERSIONING_INFO
Memory Dump @0x5C0FC153

00000000:    4ef80300 00010000 00210200 000000††††N........!.....
```

The record header indicates that this row is a GHOST_VERSION_RECORD and that it contains versioning information. The actual data, however, is not on the row, but the XSN is, so that snapshot transactions know when this row was deleted and whether they should access the older version of it in their snapshot. The *sys.dm_db_index_physical_stats* DMV that was discussed in Chapter 6 contains the count of ghost records due to versioning (*version_ghost_record_count*) and the count of all ghost records (*ghost_record_count*), which includes the versioning ghosts. If an update is performed as a *DELETE* followed by an *INSERT* (not in place), both the ghost for the old value and the new value must exist simultaneously, increasing the space requirements for the object.

If a database is in a snapshot-based isolation level, all changes to both data and index rows must be versioned. A snapshot query traversing an index still needs access to index rows pointing to the older (versioned) rows. So in the index levels, we might have old values, as ghosts, existing simultaneously with the new value, and the indexes can require more storage space.

The extra 14 bytes of versioning information can be removed if the database is changed to a non-snapshot isolation level. Once the database option is changed, each time a row containing versioning information is updated, the versioning bytes are removed.

## Management of the Version Store

The version store size is managed automatically, and SQL Server maintains a cleanup thread to make sure versioned rows are not kept around longer than needed. For queries running under SI, the row versions must be kept until the end of the transaction. For *SELECT* statements running under RCSI, a particular row version is not needed once the *SELECT* statement has executed and it can be removed.

The regular cleanup function is performed every minute as a background process to reclaim all reusable space from the version store. If *tempdb* actually runs out of free space, the cleanup function is called before SQL Server increases the size of the files. If the disk gets so full that the files cannot grow, SQL Server stops generating versions. If that happens, a snapshot query fails if it needs to read a version that was not generated due to space constraints. Although a full discussion of troubleshooting and monitoring is beyond the scope of this book, I will point out that SQL Server 2008 includes more than a dozen performance counters to monitor *tempdb* and the version store. These include counters to keep track of transactions that use row versioning. The following counters are contained in the SQLServer:Transactions performance object. Additional details and additional counters can be found in *SQL Server Books Online*.

- **Free Space in *tempdb*** This counter monitors the amount of free space in the *tempdb* database. You can observe this value to detect when *tempdb* is running out of space, which might lead to problems keeping all the necessary version rows.

- **Version Store Size** This counter monitors the size in kilobytes of the version store. Monitoring this counter can help determine a useful estimate of the additional space you might need for *tempdb*.

- **Version Generation Rate and Version Cleanup Rate** These counters monitor the rate at which space is acquired and released from the version store, in kilobytes per second.

- **Update Conflict Ratio**   This counter monitors the ratio of update snapshot transactions that have update conflicts. It is the ratio of the number of conflicts compared to the total number of update snapshot transactions.

- **Longest Transaction Running Time**   This counter monitors the longest running time in seconds of any transaction using row versioning. It can be used to determine whether any transaction is running for an unreasonable amount of time, as well as help you determine the maximum size needed in *tempdb* for the version store.

- **Snapshot Transactions**   This counter monitors the total number of active snapshot transactions.

## Snapshot Transaction Metadata

The most important DMVs for observing snapshot transaction behavior are *sys.dm_tran_version_store* (which we briefly looked at earlier in this chapter), *sys.dm_tran_transactions_snapshot,* and *sys.dm_tran_active_snapshot_database_transactions.*

All these views contain a column called *transaction_sequence_num,* which is the XSN that I mentioned earlier. Each transaction is assigned a monotonically increasing XSN value when it starts a snapshot read or when it writes data in a snapshot-enabled database. The XSN is reset to 0 when your SQL Server instance is restarted. Transactions that do not generate version rows and do not use snapshot scans do not receive an XSN.

Another column, *transaction_id,* is also used in some of the snapshot transaction metadata. A transaction ID is a unique identification number assigned to the transaction. It is used primarily to identify the transaction in locking operations. It can also help you identify which transactions are involved in snapshot operations. The transaction ID value is incremented for every transaction across the whole server, including internal system transactions, so whether or not that transaction is involved in any snapshot operations, the current transaction ID value is usually much larger than the current XSN.

You can check current transaction number information using the view *sys.dm_tran_current_transaction*, which returns a single row containing the following columns:

- *transaction_id*   This value displays the transaction ID of the current transaction. If you are selecting from the view inside a user-defined transaction, you should continue to see the same *transaction_id* every time you select from the view. If you are running a *SELECT* from sys.dm_tran_current_transaction outside of transaction, the *SELECT* itself generates a new *transaction_id* value and you see a different value every time you execute the same *SELECT*, even in the same connection.

- *transaction_sequence_num*   This value is the XSN of the current transaction, if it has one. Otherwise, this column returns 0.

- *transaction_is_snapshot*   This value is 1 if the current transaction was started under SNAPSHOT isolation; otherwise, it is 0. (That is, this column is 1 if the current session has set TRANSACTION ISOLATION LEVEL to SNAPSHOT explicitly.)

- *first_snapshot_sequence_num*   When the current transaction started, it took a snapshot of all active transactions, and this value is the lowest XSN of the transactions in the snapshot.

- *last_transaction_sequence_num*   This value is the most recent XSN generated by the system.

- *first_useful_sequence_num*   This value is an XSN representing the upper bound of version store rows that can be cleaned up without affecting any transactions. Any rows with an XSN less than this value are no longer needed.

I now create a simple versioning scenario to illustrate how the values in the snapshot metadata get updated. This is not a complete overview, but it should get you started in exploring the versioning metadata for your own queries. I use the *AdventureWorks2008* database, which has ALLOW_SNAPSHOT_ISOLATION set to ON, and I create a simple table:

```
CREATE TABLE t1
(col1 int primary key, col2 int);
GO
INSERT INTO t1 SELECT 1,10;
INSERT INTO t1 SELECT 2,20;
INSERT INTO t1 SELECT 3,30;
```

We call this session Connection 1. Change the session's isolation level, start a snapshot transaction, and examine some of the metadata:

```
SET TRANSACTION ISOLATION LEVEL SNAPSHOT
GO
BEGIN TRAN
SELECT * FROM t1;
GO
select * from sys.dm_tran_current_transaction;
select * from sys.dm_tran_version_store;
select * from sys.dm_tran_transactions_snapshot;
```

The *sys.dm_tran_current_transaction* view should show you something like this: the current transaction does have an XSN, and the transaction is a snapshot transaction. Also, you can note that the *first_useful_sequence_num* value is the same as this transaction's XSN because no other snapshot transactions are valid now. I refer to this transaction's XSN as XSN1.

The version store should be empty (unless you've done other snapshot tests within the last minute). Also, *sys.dm_tran_transactions_snapshot* should be empty, indicating that there were no snapshot transactions that started when other transactions were in process.

In another connection (Connection 2), run an update and examine some of the metadata for the current transaction:

```
BEGIN TRAN
 UPDATE T1 SET col2 = 100
   WHERE col1 = 1;
SELECT * FROM sys.dm_tran_current_transaction;
```

Note that although this transaction has an XSN because it generates versions, it is not running in SI, so the *transaction_is_snapshot* value is 0. I refer to this transaction's XSN as XSN2.

Now start a third transaction in a Connection 3 to perform another *SELECT*. (Don't worry, this is the last one and we won't be keeping it around.) It is almost identical to the first, but there is an important difference in the metadata results:

```
SET TRANSACTION ISOLATION LEVEL SNAPSHOT
GO
BEGIN TRAN
SELECT * FROM t1;
GO
select * from sys.dm_tran_current_transaction;
select * from sys.dm_tran_transactions_snapshot;
```

In the *sys.dm_tran_current_transaction* view, you see a new XSN for this transaction (XSN3), and you see that the value for *first_snapshot_sequence_num* and *first_useful_sequence_num* are both the same as XSN1. In the *sys.dm_tran_transactions_snapshot* view, you see that this transaction with XSN3 has two rows, indicating the two transactions that were active when this one started. Both XSN1 and XSN2 show up in the *snapshot_sequence_num* column. You can now either commit or roll back this transaction, and then close the connection.

Go back to Connection 2, where you started the *UPDATE*, and commit the transaction.

Now let's go back to the first *SELECT* transaction in Connection 1 and rerun the *SELECT* statement, staying in the same transaction:

```
SELECT * FROM t1;
```

Even though the *UPDATE* in Connection 2 has committed, we still see the original data values because we are running a snapshot transaction. We can examine the *sys.dm_tran_active_snapshot_database_transactions* view with this query:

```
SELECT transaction_sequence_num, commit_sequence_num,
    is_snapshot, session_id,first_snapshot_sequence_num,
    max_version_chain_traversed, elapsed_time_seconds
FROM  sys.dm_tran_active_snapshot_database_transactions;
```

I am not showing you the output here because it is too wide for the page, but there are many columns that you should find interesting. In particular, the *transaction_sequence_num* column contains XSN1, which is the XSN for the current connection. You could actually run the preceding query from any connection; it shows *all* active snapshot transactions in the SQL Server instance, and because it includes the *session_id,* you can join it to *sys.dm_exec_sessions* to get information about the connection that is running the transaction:

```
SELECT transaction_sequence_num, commit_sequence_num,
    is_snapshot, t.session_id,first_snapshot_sequence_num,
    max_version_chain_traversed, elapsed_time_seconds,
    host_name, login_name, transaction_isolation_level
```

```
FROM  sys.dm_tran_active_snapshot_database_transactions t
  JOIN sys.dm_exec_sessions s
    ON t.session_id = s.session_id;
```

Another value to note is in the column called *max_version_chain_traversed*. Although now it should be 1, we can change that. Go back to Connection 2 and run another *UPDATE* statement. Even though the *BEGIN TRAN* and *COMMIT TRAN* are not necessary for a single statement transaction, I am including them to make it clear that this transaction is complete:

```
BEGIN TRAN
 UPDATE T1 SET col2 = 300
   WHERE col1 = 1;
COMMIT TRAN;
```

Examine the version store if desired, to see rows being added:

```
SELECT *
 FROM sys.dm_tran_version_store;
```

When you go back to Connection 1 and run the same *SELECT* inside the original transaction and look again at the *max_version_chain_traversed* column in sys.dm_tran_active_snapshot_database_transactions, you should see that the number keeps growing. Repeated *UPDATE* operations, either in Connection 2 or a new connection, cause the *max_version_chain_traversed* value to just keep increasing, as long as Connection 1 stays in the same transaction. Keep this in mind as an added cost of using Snapshot isolation. As you perform more updates on data needed by snapshot transactions, your read operations take longer because SQL Server must traverse a longer version chain to get the data needed by your transactions.

This is just the tip of the iceberg regarding how the snapshot and transaction metadata can be used to examine the behavior of your snapshot transactions.

## Choosing a Concurrency Model

Pessimistic concurrency is the default in SQL Server 2008 and was the only choice in all versions of SQL Server prior to SQL Server 2005. Transactional behavior is guaranteed by locking, at the cost of greater blocking. When accessing the same data resources, readers can block writers and writers can block readers. Because SQL Server was initially designed and built to use pessimistic concurrency, you should consider using that model unless you can verify that optimistic concurrency really will work better for you and your applications. If you find that the cost of blocking is becoming excessive  you can consider using optimistic concurrency.

In most situations, RCSI is recommended over Snapshot isolation for several reasons:

- RCSI consumes less *tempdb* space than SI.

- RCSI works with distributed transactions; SI does not.

- RCSI does not produce update conflicts.

- RCSI does not require any change in your applications. All that is needed is one change to the database options. Any of your applications written using the default Read Committed isolation level automatically uses RCSI after making the change at the database level.

You can consider using SI in the following situations:

- The probability is low that any of your transactions have to be rolled back because of an update conflict.

- You have reports that need to be generated based on long-running, multistatement queries that must have point-in-time consistency. Snapshot isolation provides the benefit of repeatable reads without being blocked by concurrent modification operations.

Optimistic concurrency does have benefits, but you must also be aware of the costs. To summarize the benefits:

- *SELECT* operations do not acquire shared locks, so readers and writers do not block each other.

- All *SELECT* operations retrieve a consistent snapshot of the data.

- The total number of locks needed is greatly reduced compared to pessimistic concurrency, so less system overhead is used.

- SQL Server needs to perform fewer lock escalations.

- Deadlocks are less likely to occur.

Now let's summarize the other side. When weighing your concurrency options, you must consider the cost of the snapshot-based isolation levels:

- *SELECT* performance can be affected negatively when long-version chains must be scanned. The older the snapshot, the more time it takes to access the required row in an SI transaction.

- Row versioning requires additional resources in *tempdb*.

- Whenever either of the snapshot-based isolation levels are enabled for a database, *UPDATE* and *DELETE* operations must generate row versions. (Although I mentioned earlier that *INSERT* operations do not generate row versions, there are some cases where they might. In particular, if you insert a row into a table with a unique index, if there was an older version of the row with the same key value as the new row and that old row still exists as a ghost, your new row generates a version.)

- Row versioning information increases the size of every affected row by 14 bytes.

- *UPDATE* performance might be slower due to the work involved in maintaining the row versions.

- *UPDATE* operations using SI might have to be rolled back because of conflict detection. Your applications must be programmed to deal with any conflicts that occur.

- The space in *tempdb* must be carefully managed. If there are very long-running transactions, all the versions generated by update transactions during the time must be kept in *tempdb*. If *tempdb* runs out of space, *UPDATE* operations won't fail, but *SELECT* operations that need to read versioned data might fail.

To maintain a production system using SI, you should allocate enough disk space for *tempdb* so that there is always at least 10 percent free space. If the free space falls below this threshold, system performance might suffer because SQL Server expends more resources trying to reclaim space in the version store. The following formula can give you a rough estimate of the size required by version store. For long-running transactions, it might be useful to monitor the generation and cleanup rate using Performance Monitor, to estimate the maximum size needed:

```
[size of common version store] =
2 * [version store data generated per minute]
* [longest running time (minutes) of the transaction]
```

# Controlling Locking

The SQL Server Query Optimizer usually chooses the correct type of lock and the lock mode. You should override this behavior only if thorough testing has shown that a different approach is preferable. Keep in mind that by setting an isolation level, you have an impact on the locks that held, the conflicts that cause blocking, and the duration of your locks. Your isolation level is in effect for an entire session, and you should choose the one that provides the data consistency required by your application. Table-level locking hints can be used to change the default locking behavior only when necessary. Disallowing a locking level can adversely affect concurrency.

## Lock Hints

T-SQL syntax allows you to specify locking hints for individual tables when they are referenced in *SELECT, INSERT, UPDATE*, and *DELETE* statements. The hints tell SQL Server the type of locking or row versioning to use for a particular table in a particular query. Because these hints are specified in a FROM clause, they are called *table-level hints*. *SQL Server Books Online* lists other table-level hints besides locking hints, but the vast majority of them affect locking behavior. They should be used only when you absolutely need finer control over locking at the object level than what is provided by your session's isolation level. The SQL Server locking hints can override the current transaction isolation level for the session. In this section, I will mention only some of the locking hints that you might need to obtain the desired concurrency behavior.

Many of the locking hints work only in the context of a transaction. However, every *INSERT*, *UPDATE*, and *DELETE* statement is automatically in a transaction, so the only concern is when you use a locking hint with a *SELECT* statement. To get the benefit of most of the following hints when used in a *SELECT* query, you must use an explicit transaction, starting with *BEGIN TRAN* and terminating with either *COMMIT TRAN* or *ROLLBACK TRAN*. The lock hint syntax is as follows:

```
SELECT select_list
FROM object [WITH (locking hint)]

DELETE [FROM] object [WITH (locking hint)
[WHERE <search conditions>]

UDPATE object [WITH (locking hint)
SET <set_clause>
[WHERE <search conditions>]

INSERT [INTO] object [WITH (locking hint)
<insert specification>
```

**Tip** Not all the locking hints require the keyword *WITH*, but the syntax without *WITH* will go away in a future version of SQL Server. It is recommended that all hints be specified using *WITH*.

You can specify one of the following keywords for the locking hint:

- **HOLDLOCK**   This hint is equivalent to the SERIALIZABLE hint. Using this hint is similar to specifying *SET TRANSACTION ISOLATION LEVEL SERIALIZABLE*, except that the SET option affects all tables, not only the one specified in this hint.

- **UPDLOCK**   This hint forces SQL Server to take update locks instead of shared locks while reading the table and holds them until the end of the transaction. Taking update locks can be an important technique for eliminating conversion deadlocks.

- **TABLOCK**   This hint forces SQL Server to take a shared lock on the table even if page locks would be taken otherwise. This hint is useful when you know you escalate to a table lock or if you need to get a complete snapshot of a table. You can use this hint with HOLDLOCK if you want the table lock held until the end of the transaction block to operate in Repeatable Read isolation. If you use this hint with a *DELETE* statement on a heap, it allows SQL Server to deallocate the pages as the rows are deleted. (If row or page locks are obtained when deleting from a heap, space will not be deallocated and cannot be reused by other objects.)

- **PAGLOCK**   This hint forces SQL Server to take shared page locks when a single shared table lock might otherwise be taken. (To request an exclusive page lock, you must use the XLOCK hint along with the PAGLOCK hint.)

- **TABLOCKX**   This hint forces SQL Server to take an exclusive lock on the table that is held until the end of the transaction block. (All exclusive locks are held until the end of a transaction, regardless of the isolation level in effect. This hint has the same effect as specifying both the TABLOCK and the XLOCK hints together.)

- **ROWLOCK**   This hint specifies that a shared row lock should be taken when a single shared page or table lock is normally taken.

- **READUNCOMMITTED | REPEATABLEREAD | SERIALIZABLE**   These hints specify that SQL Server should use the same locking mechanisms as when the transaction isolation level is set to the level of the same name. However, the hint controls locking for a single table in a single statement, as opposed to locking all tables in all statements in a transaction.

- **READCOMMITTED**   This hint specifies that *SELECT* operations comply with the rules for the Read Committed isolation level by using either locking or row versioning. If the database option READ_COMMITTED_SNAPSHOT is OFF, SQL Server uses shared locks and releases them as soon as the read operation is completed. If the database option READ_COMMITTED_SNAPSHOT is ON, SQL Server does not acquire locks and uses row versioning.

- **READCOMMITTEDLOCK**   This hint specifies that *SELECT* statements use the locking version of Read Committed isolation (the SQL Server default). No matter what the setting is for the database option READ_COMMITTED_SNAPSHOT, SQL Server acquires shared locks when it reads the data and releases those locks when the read operation is completed.

- **NOLOCK**   This hint allows uncommitted, or dirty, reads. Shared locks are not requested so that the statement does not block when reading data that is holding exclusive locks. In other words, no locking conflict is detected. This hint is equivalent to READUNCOMMITTED.

- **READPAST**   This hint specifies that locked rows are skipped (read past). READPAST applies only to transactions operating at the READ COMMITTED isolation level and reads past row-level locks only.

- **XLOCK**   This hint specifies that SQL Server should take an exclusive lock that is held until the end of the transaction on all data processed by the statement. This lock can be specified with either PAGLOCK or TABLOCK, in which case the exclusive lock applies to the specified resource.

## Setting a Lock Timeout

Setting a LOCK_TIMEOUT also lets you control SQL Server locking behavior. By default, SQL Server does not time out when waiting for a lock; it assumes optimistically that the lock will be released eventually. Most client programming interfaces allow you to set a general timeout limit for the connection so a query is canceled by the client automatically if no response comes back after a specified amount of time. However, the message that comes back when the time period is exceeded does not indicate the cause of the cancellation; it could be because of a lock not being released, it could be because of a slow network, or it could just be a long-running query.

Like other SET options, SET LOCK_TIMEOUT is valid only for your current connection. Its value is expressed in milliseconds and can be accessed by using the system function @@LOCK_TIMEOUT. This example sets the LOCK_TIMEOUT value to five seconds and then retrieves that value for display:

```
SET LOCK_TIMEOUT 5000;
SELECT @@LOCK_TIMEOUT;
```

If your connection exceeds the lock timeout value, you receive the following error message:

```
Server: Msg 1222, Level 16, State 50, Line 1
Lock request time out period exceeded.
```

Setting the LOCK_TIMEOUT value to 0 means that SQL Server does not wait at all for locks. It basically cancels the entire statement and goes on to the next one in the batch. This is not the same as the READPAST hint, which skips individual rows.

The following example illustrates the difference between READPAST, READUNCOMMITTED, and setting LOCK_TIMEOUT to 0. All these techniques let you avoid blocking problems, but the behavior is slightly different in each case.

1. In a new query window, execute the following batch to lock one row in the *HumanResources.Department* table:

```
USE AdventureWorks2008;
BEGIN TRAN;
UPDATE HumanResources.Department
SET ModifiedDate = getdate()
WHERE DepartmentID = 1;
```

2. Open a second connection, and execute the following statements:

```
USE AdventureWorks2008;
SET LOCK_TIMEOUT 0;
SELECT * FROM HumanResources.Department;
SELECT * FROM Sales.SalesPerson;
```

Notice that after error 1222 is received, the second *SELECT* statement is executed, returning all 17 rows from the *SalesPerson* table. The batch is not cancelled when error 1222 is encountered.

**Warning**  Not only is a batch not cancelled when a lock timeout error is encountered, but any active transaction will not be rolled back. If you have two *UPDATE* statements in a transaction and both must succeed if either succeeds, a lock timeout for one of the *UPDATE* statements will still allow the other statement to be processed. You must include error handling in your batch to take appropriate action in the event of an error 1222.

3. Open a third connection, and execute the following statements:

```
USE AdventureWorks2008 ;
SELECT * FROM HumanResources.Department (READPAST);
SELECT * FROM Sales.SalesPerson;
```

SQL Server skips (reads past) only one row, and the remaining 15 rows of *Department* are returned, followed by all the *SalesPerson* rows. The READPAST hint is frequently used in conjunction with a TOP clause, in particular TOP 1, where your table is serving as a work queue. Your *SELECT* must get a row containing an order to be processed, but it really doesn't matter which row. So *SELECT* TOP 1 * FROM <OrderTable> returns the first unlocked row, and you can use that as the row to start processing.

4. Open a fourth connection, and execute the following statements:

```
USE AdventureWorks2008 ;
SELECT * FROM HumanResources.Department (READUNCOMMITTED);
SELECT * FROM Sales.SalesPerson;
```

In this case, SQL Server does not skip anything. It reads all 16 rows from *Department*, but the row for Department 1 shows the dirty data that you changed in step 1. This data has not yet been committed and is subject to being rolled back.

The READUNCOMMITTED hint is probably the least useful because of the availability of row versioning. In fact, anytime you find yourself needing to use this hint, or the equivalent NOLOCK, you should consider whether you can actually afford the cost of one of the snapshot-based isolation levels.

# Summary

SQL Server lets you manage multiple users simultaneously and ensure that transactions observe the properties of the chosen isolation level. Locking guards data and the internal resources that make it possible for a multiuser system to operate like a single-user system. You can choose to have your databases and applications use either optimistic or pessimistic concurrency control. With pessimistic concurrency, the locks acquired by data modification operations block users trying to retrieve data. With optimistic concurrency, the locks are ignored and older committed versions of the data are read instead. In this chapter, we looked at the locking mechanisms in SQL Server, including full locking for data and leaf-level index pages and lightweight locking mechanisms for internally used resources. We also looked at the details of how optimistic concurrency avoids blocking on locks and still has access to data.

It is important to understand the issues of lock compatibility and escalation if you want to design and implement high-concurrency applications. You also need to understand the costs and benefits of the two concurrency models.

# Chapter 11
# DBCC Internals

*Paul Randal*

When anyone mentions consistency checking a Microsoft SQL Server database, the first thing that comes to mind is "DBCC." In SQL Server 7.0, DBCC stood for Database Consistency Checker, but Microsoft changed the definition in the next release, SQL Server 2000, to Database Console Commands. This change reflected the fact that the DBCC command family had grown to do much more than just checking consistency, and also was intended to help dispel the perception that SQL Server databases required regular consistency checking because SQL Server itself caused corruption.

Although SQL Server itself does not cause database corruptions, I/O subsystems (all the software and hardware between the SQL Server buffer pool and the metal oxide of the disk drives) do cause the overwhelmingly vast majority of corruptions. For this reason, the common wisdom is that it is prudent to perform regular consistency checking because all database servers have an I/O subsystem of some sort. The definition of *regular* is a question I am often asked, and it really depends on the situation and how confident you are with the integrity of your I/O subsystem. I would say that in general, performing a consistency check once a week would be acceptable.

*Consistency checking* is the process of examining the physical and logical structure of the database to make sure that there are no corruptions that could prevent the storage engine from being able to process part of the database or could lead to some incorrect behavior. Some simple examples are

- A persisted computed column where the persisted value has been corrupted such that it no longer matches the result of the computation

- A data page where the page ID in the page header is incorrect

- An index where the key order of records is incorrect

The consistency checks in SQL Server have evolved significantly since the SQL Server 7.0 days, when they used to run offline (that is, table locks were required). SQL Server 2000 saw the advent of consistency checks being online by default, with a new, highly efficient mechanism for scanning the database. During SQL Server 2005, the consistency checking and repair code inside the storage engine was significantly rewritten and enhanced. This was done to cope with the plethora of new SQL Server features and rewritten subsystems and to increase the performance, reliability, and functionality of the consistency checks and repairs themselves. SQL Server 2008 added new functionality and further tweaks for performance and scalability.

The most comprehensive way to perform consistency checks on a database is to use the *DBCC CHECKDB* command. The major steps of *DBCC CHECKDB* are as follows:

1. Create a transactionally consistent, static view of the database.

2. Perform low-level consistency checks of the critical system catalogs.

3. Perform allocation consistency checks of the database.

4. Perform consistency checks of each table in the database.

5. So long as no problems were found in the previous steps, the following cross-table consistency checks are performed:

   ❑ Perform consistency checks of Service Broker metadata.

   ❑ Perform consistency checks between various system catalogs.

   ❑ Perform consistency checks of indexed views.

   ❑ Perform consistency checks of XML indexes.

   ❑ Perform consistency checks of spatial indexes.

6. Output results.

Repairs are carried out at various steps if necessary, but only if the user specified a repair option.

In this chapter, I explain how the internals of *DBCC CHECKDB* work in SQL Server 2008, based on the steps I've listed here. For each of the options that can be specified, I'll describe how it affects the behavior of *DBCC CHECKDB*. Finally, I explain how repair works and about the other DBCC consistency-checking commands.

# Getting a Consistent View of the Database

A consistent view of the database is necessary, because *DBCC CHECKDB* must analyze all allocated pages in the database and check the various links between structures on multiple pages. This means that the pages being analyzed (that is, the whole database) cannot change while the consistency checks are running; otherwise *DBCC CHECKDB* reports all kinds of incorrect results. As *DBCC CHECKDB* cannot read all the allocated pages in the database instantaneously, this means the consistent view of the database must be maintained for the duration of the consistency checks. It is also not enough for the database to be simply frozen in time—the consistent view of the database must also be *transactionally* consistent so that there are no uncompleted changes in the view that *DBCC CHECKDB* sees.

Here's an example: consider a transaction to insert a record into a table that has a nonclustered index, with a hypothetical consistency-checking process running concurrently that doesn't enforce a consistent view of the database. The way the query processor works is to insert the table record first and then insert the matching nonclustered index record. Because this hypothetical consistency-checking process doesn't have a consistent view, it might read the record in the table but not that in the nonclustered index, leading to a report that the nonclustered index is out of sync with the table.

How can this happen? As we see later in this chapter, *DBCC CHECKDB* reads the database pages in a special order to enhance performance. Using this mechanism, and continuing this example, it might read the nonclustered index page before the nonclustered index record is inserted but read the table page *after* the table record is inserted. It might then conclude that a corruption exists, but in reality, the problem is that it saw the partial results of an in-flight transaction.

## Obtaining a Consistent View

In SQL Server 7.0, the transactionally consistent view was obtained by taking locks at various levels in the database. This was too detrimental to workload performance, so SQL Server 2000 introduced online consistency checking and removed the need for blocking locks to be held. *DBCC CHECKDB* analyzed the transaction log after scanning the database and essentially ran recovery on its internal view of the database, thus producing a transactionally consistent view of the database.

The SQL Server 2000 solution was too unwieldy for many reasons, so it was replaced in SQL Server 2005 by using a database snapshot, and the mechanism is the same in SQL Server 2008. This means that *DBCC CHECKDB* uses regular storage engine functionality with greatly reduced complexity.

As described earlier in the book in Chapter 3, "Databases and Database Files," a database snapshot is extremely space-efficient, containing only the database pages that have changed since the database snapshot was created. A combination of the database snapshot contents and the unchanged pages in the database give an unchanging, transactionally consistent view of the database.

This is exactly what *DBCC CHECKDB* needs to run online. Creating a database snapshot and then running the consistency-checking algorithms on the database snapshot is conceptually just the same as running the consistency-checking algorithms on a read-only copy of the database.

*DBCC CHECKDB* creates a database snapshot that cannot be accessed by users—it's essentially hidden. This hidden database snapshot is created in a slightly different way from regular database snapshots. A regular database snapshot has one snapshot file corresponding to each data file in the source database, and each file must be explicitly named when the database snapshot is created. *DBCC CHECKDB* doesn't allow any user input to specify the filenames for the hidden database snapshot, so instead it creates an NTFS alternate stream for each existing source database data file. You can think of an alternate stream as a hidden file that can be accessed through the file system path that points at the user-visible file. This mechanism works well and is transparent to the user.

## Disk Space Issues

Sometimes an issue arises when the hidden database snapshot runs out of space. As it is implemented using alternate streams of the existing data files, the database snapshot consumes space from the same location as the existing data files. If there is a heavy update workload on the database being checked, more and more pages are pushed into the database snapshot, causing it to grow. In a situation where there isn't much space in the volumes hosting the database, this can mean the hidden database snapshot runs out of space and *DBCC CHECKDB* stops with an error. An example of this is shown here (the errors may vary depending on the exact point at which the database snapshot runs out of space):

```
DBCC CHECKDB ('SalesDB2') WITH NO_INFOMSGS, ALL_ERRORMSGS;
GO
Msg 1823, Level 16, State 1, Line 5
A database snapshot cannot be created because it failed to start.
Msg 1823, Level 16, State 2, Line 1
A database snapshot cannot be created because it failed to start.
Msg 7928, Level 16, State 1, Line 1
The database snapshot for online checks could not be created. Either the reason is given in
a previous error or one of the underlying volumes does not support sparse files or alternate
streams. Attempting to get exclusive access to run checks offline.
Msg 5128, Level 17, State 2, Line 1
Write to sparse file 'C:\SQLskills\SalesDBData.mdf:MSSQL_DBCC20' failed due to lack of disk
space.
Msg 3313, Level 21, State 2, Line 1
During redoing of a logged operation in database 'SalesDB2', an error occurred at log record
ID (1628:252:1). Typically, the specific failure is previously logged as an error in the
Windows Event Log service. Restore the database from a full backup, or repair the database.
Msg 0, Level 20, State 0, Line 0
A severe error occurred on the current command.  The results, if any, should be discarded.
```

In this case, the solution is to create your own database snapshot, placing the snapshot files on a volume with more disk space, and then to run *DBCC CHECKDB* on that. *DBCC CHECKDB* recognizes that it is already running on a database snapshot and does not attempt to create another one.

If a database snapshot was created by *DBCC CHECKDB*, it is discarded automatically once the consistency-checking algorithms have completed.

As well as creating a database snapshot (if needed), the *FILESTREAM* garbage collection process is suspended while *DBCC CHECKDB* is running. This allows the consistency-checking algorithms to see a transactionally consistent view of the *FILESTREAM* data on any *FILESTREAM* data containers. This is explained in more detail later in this chapter.

## Alternatives to Using a Database Snapshot

A database snapshot is not required under the following conditions:

- The specified database is a database snapshot itself.

- The specified database is read-only, in single-user mode, or in emergency mode.

- The server was started in single-user mode with the –m command-line option.

In these cases, the database is already essentially consistent because there can be no other active connections making changes that would break the consistency checks.

A database snapshot cannot be created under the following conditions:

- The specified database is stored on a non-NTFS file system (in which case, a database snapshot cannot be created because it relies on NTFS sparse-file technology).

- The specified database is *tempdb* (because a database snapshot cannot be created on *tempdb*).

- The TABLOCK option was specified.

If a database snapshot cannot be created for any reason, *DBCC CHECKDB* attempts to use locks to obtain a transactionally consistent view of the database.

First, it obtains a database-level exclusive lock so that it can perform the allocation consistency checks without any changes taking place. This is not possible on *master*, which means that offline consistency checks cannot be run on *master*. It is also not possible on *tempdb*, which means that allocation consistency checks are always skipped for *tempdb* (this was usually the case with SQL Server 2000, too). Instead of waiting for the exclusive lock indefinitely (or whatever the server lock timeout period has been set to), *DBCC CHECKDB* waits for 20 seconds (or the configured lock timeout value for the session) and then exits with the following error:

```
DBCC CHECKDB ('msdb') WITH TABLOCK;
GO
Msg 5030, Level 16, State 12, Line 1
The database could not be exclusively locked to perform the operation.
Msg 7926, Level 16, State 1, Line 1
Check statement aborted. The database could not be checked as a database snapshot could not
be created and the database or table could not be locked. See Books Online for details of
when this behavior is expected and what workarounds exist. Also see previous errors for more
details.
```

If the lock was acquired, after the allocation checks are completed, the exclusive lock is dropped and table-level share locks are acquired while the table-level logical consistency checks are performed. The same time-out applies to these table-level locks.

One way or another, *DBCC CHECKDB* obtains a transactionally consistent view of the database that it's checking. After that, it can start processing the database.

# Processing the Database Efficiently

A database can be thought of as one giant, interconnected structure with all tables linked back to system catalogs, and all system catalogs linked back to the lowest-level allocation metadata stored in *sys.sysallocunits*, which in turn has its first page fixed at page (1:16) in every database. With the addition of the fixed-location allocation bitmaps, such as Page Free Space (PFS) and Global Allocation Map (GAM) pages, the entire database can be represented as a single entity-relationship diagram.

With this thought in mind, one can envisage a consistency-checking algorithm for this metastructure that starts with page (1:16) and the allocation bitmaps and progressively expands into the database-checking linkages between objects and structures as it goes. Whenever a page linkage is found, the link is followed to ensure that the correct page is linked to. Whenever an allocation bitmap has a page marked as, say, an IAM page, that page is checked to make sure it really is an IAM page. This would be a *depth-first* algorithm.

Consider a data page with three data records, with each data record containing a link to two 8,000-byte Large Object (LOB) columns stored off-row. Using the previous algorithm, the sequence of operations to consistency-check the page includes the following:

1. Extract the page ID containing the first LOB column data from record 1.
2. Read that page to make sure it has the correct LOB column data on it.
3. Extract the page ID containing the second LOB column data from record 1.
4. Read that page to make sure it has the correct LOB column data on it.
5. Repeat steps 1–4 as necessary until the whole structure is processed.

As you can see, the algorithm described here is very inefficient. Pages are read as needed and in essentially random order. Pages may be processed multiple times, and the random nature of the page reads means the I/O subsystem cannot be used for read-ahead. In terms of algorithmic complexity, the algorithm would be described as having complexity $O(n^2)$. This can be said as "order $n$-squared," which means that the algorithm takes exponentially longer to run as the number of elements on which it operates increases. In this case, $n$ is the number of pages in the database.

This is not how *DBCC CHECKDB* works in SQL Server 2008 (in fact, from SQL Server 2000 onwards). An $O(n^2)$ algorithm is prohibitively expensive to run on large databases. Instead, *DBCC CHECKDB* uses an algorithm with complexity $O(n*\log(n))$, which provides near-linear scaling. The rest of this section describes the algorithm used.

## Fact Generation

*DBCC CHECKDB* reads all the pages from the objects being consistency-checked in the most efficient way possible—in allocation order (that is, in the order they are stored in the data files) instead of by following page links and reading them in essentially random order. The mechanism for this is described later in this section.

As the pages are read in strict allocation order as much as possible, there is no way to validate all the relationships between pages immediately while they are being processed. Therefore, *DBCC CHECKDB* must remember what it knows about each page so that it can perform the relationship checking at a later stage. It does this by generating bits of information about a page called *facts*.

Continuing the previous example, as part of processing the data page, the following facts are generated:

- Two facts that the first record links to a LOB value (one fact for each LOB value). Each fact contains the following:
    - The page ID and slot ID (that is, the record number) of the data record
    - The page ID and slot ID where the LOB value should be stored (extracted from the text root stored in the data record)
    - The text timestamp of the LOB value (that is, a unique ID that is assigned to that LOB value)
    - The object ID, index ID, partition ID, and allocation unit ID of which the page is part
- Two facts that the second record links to a LOB value.
- Two facts that the third record links to a LOB value.

These facts are known as *parent text* facts.

When each of the text pages containing the actual LOB values is processed, part of the processing generates a fact that the LOB value was encountered. Each fact contains the following:

- The page ID and slot ID of the text record
- The text timestamp of the LOB value
- The object ID, index ID, partition ID, and allocation unit ID of which the page is part

These facts are known as *actual text* facts.

At some later point, the facts are checked against each other (called *aggregation*). So long as there is a matching parent text fact and actual text fact for each LOB value, *DBCC CHECKDB* recognizes that that particular LOB value linkage is free of corruption.

There is one more type of fact apart from actual and parent facts, known as *sibling* facts. These are used when checking index B-tree linkages and describe the linked list that exists at each level of an index B-tree.

The consistency-checking algorithms for the different parts of the database structure use a variety of fact types and fact contents, but the basic algorithm is the same. The fact types used are

- Facts to gather allocation statistics about objects, indexes, partitions, and allocation units
- Facts to track *FILESTREAM* data
- Facts to track IAM chain linkages
- Facts to track IAM page bitmaps for a particular GAM interval
- Facts to track database files
- Facts to track extent allocations and ownership
- Facts to track page allocations and ownership
- Facts to track B-tree linkages
- Facts to track LOB value linkages
- Facts to track forwarding/forwarded records in heaps

Between generation and aggregation, the facts are stored in the query processor in memory used for a sort operation. Sometimes the size of the sort is larger than the memory available to the query processor; as a result, the sort "spills" to disk (into the *tempdb* database), thus generating (possibly significant) physical reads and writes in *tempdb*. Because each fact is essentially a table row, the fact must be split into table columns. Each fact is comprised of five columns:

- **ROWSET_COLUMN_FACT_KEY**   The page ID of a page that the fact describes, or the LSN of a *FILESTREAM* file
- **ROWSET_COLUMN_FACT_TYPE**   The fact type
- **ROWSET_COLUMN_SLOT_ID**   The slot ID of the record the fact describes (if any)
- **ROWSET_COLUMN_COMBINED_ID**   The object, index, partition, and allocation unit IDs of which the page is part
- **ROWSET_COLUMN_FACT_BLOB**   A variable-length column to store any extra data required

If *tempdb* does not have enough space to store the DBCC sort, *DBCC CHECKDB* may fail. If this happens, error 8921 is output, as shown here:

```
Msg 8921, Level 16, State 1, Line 1
Check terminated. A failure was detected while collecting facts. Possibly tempdb out of
space or a system table is inconsistent. Check previous errors.
```

## Using the Query Processor

*DBCC CHECKDB* makes extensive use of the query processor—both to allow easy handling of the facts and also to parallelize the consistency-checking process easily.

The algorithm used to generate facts is as follows:

1. The DBCC code issues a query (using syntax only available within SQL Server) to the query processor, containing a pointer to a rowset and the name of a custom aggregation function.

2. The query processor queries the rowset for a row, essentially calling back into DBCC to get a fact to process.

3. DBCC hands back a single fact as a rowset row (using the column structure described earlier). If there are no facts available, DBCC reads a page and processes it entirely, generating all necessary facts. The facts are stored in thread-local memory as a first-in-first-out (FIFO) queue, and a single fact is handed back to the query processor. One fact is returned from the head of the thread-local fact queue with each subsequent request from the query processor until no more facts are available. Only at that point is another page read and processed to generate facts, populating the fact queue again.

4. The query processor stores the fact internally in sort memory, and possibly in the *tempdb* database as well.

Once all the facts have been generated for the objects being consistency-checked, the query processor completes the sort operation on them and then calls the custom aggregation function that DBCC supplied. The facts are sorted by the fact key and grouped by all columns except the type, so that the aggregation routine gets the facts in the correct order to allow successive facts to be matched easily.

Continuing the previous LOB linkage example, the facts are passed back to the aggregation routine in the following order:

1. Actual text fact for a LOB value (really LOB value 1 from record 1 on the data page)

2. Parent text fact for LOB value 1 in record 1 on the data page

3. Actual text fact for a LOB value (really LOB value 2 in record 1 on the data page)

4. Parent text fact for LOB value 2 in record 1 on the data page

If the facts were not in that order, it would be impossible to match facts without again remembering what had already been seen.

The aggregation algorithm runs as follows:

1. The query processor calls the DBCC custom aggregation function with a single fact.

2. Facts are merged until a fact is passed from the query processor that does not match the facts being merged. For example, the actual and parent facts for LOB value 1 in the previous example are merged. The next fact is for LOB value 2, which is for a different part of the database structure.

3. Once a mismatched fact is encountered, the merged set of facts is aggregated to determine whether any errors are present. Aggregation means that the facts are checked to see whether the right facts exist for the piece of database structure that they describe. For example, a LOB value must have an actual fact (that the value was actually encountered) and a parent fact (that some index or data record links to the LOB value).

4. If errors are present, an entry is made in the list of errors. The entry is generated using the information contained in the aggregated set of facts. Example errors are a LOB value that doesn't have a data or index record pointing to it.

5. The facts are then discarded and a new set of merged facts begins, starting with the mismatched fact that triggered aggregation.

6. The DBCC code then signals to the query processor that it is ready to accept the next fact to merge and aggregate.

Figure 11-1 shows how the query processor and DBCC code interact while *DBCC CHECKDB* is executing.

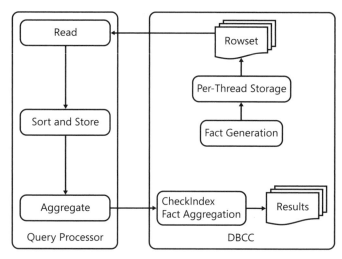

**FIGURE 11-1** Interaction between the query processor and DBCC

These algorithms are kicked off by *DBCC CHECKDB* internally executing a query. The query that *DBCC CHECKDB* runs is shown here:

```
DECLARE @BlobEater VARBINARY(8000);
SELECT @BlobEater = CheckIndex(ROWSET_COLUMN_FACT_BLOB)
FROM <memory address of fact rowset>
GROUP BY ROWSET_COLUMN_FACT_KEY
>> WITH ORDER BY
    ROWSET_COLUMN_FACT_KEY,
    ROWSET_COLUMN_SLOT_ID,
    ROWSET_COLUMN_COMBINED_ID,
    ROWSET_COLUMN_FACT_BLOB
OPTION(ORDER GROUP);
```

This query brings the query processor and the *DBCC CHECKDB* code together to perform the fact-generation, fact-sorting, fact-storing, and fact-aggregation algorithms. The parts of the query are as follows:

- **@BlobEater**   This is a dummy variable with no purpose other than to consume any output from the *CheckIndex* function (there should never be any, but the syntax requires it).

- *CheckIndex (ROWSET_COLUMN_FACT_BLOB)*   This is the custom aggregation function inside *DBCC CHECKDB* that the query processor calls with sorted and grouped facts as part of the overall fact aggregation algorithm.

- **<memory address of fact rowset>**   This is the memory address of the OLEDB rowset that *DBCC CHECKDB* provides to the query processor. The query processor queries this rowset for rows (containing the generated facts) as part of the overall fact generation algorithm.

- *GROUP BY ROWSET_COLUMN_FACT_KEY*   This triggers the aggregation in the query processor.

- **>> WITH ORDER BY <column list>**   This is internal-only syntax that provides ordered aggregation to the aggregation step. As I explained earlier, the *DBCC CHECKDB* aggregation code is based on the assumption that the order of the aggregated stream of facts from the query processor is forced (that is, it requires that the sort order of the keys within each group is the order of the four keys in the query).

- **OPTION(ORDER GROUP)**   This is a Query Optimizer hint that forces stream aggregation. It forces the Query Optimizer to sort on the grouping columns and avoid hash aggregation.

This mechanism is used for the allocation consistency-checking and per-table consistency-checking phases of *DBCC CHECKDB*. By extension, this means the same mechanism is also used by the *DBCC CHECKALLOC*, *DBCC CHECKTABLE*, and *DBCC CHECKFILEGROUP* commands.

If the internal query fails because of a memory shortage, error 8902 is reported. If the internal query fails for any other reason, generic error 8975 is reported. In either case, *DBCC CHECKDB* terminates.

## Batches

During the per-table logical checks phase, *DBCC CHECKDB* usually does not process all tables in the database together, nor does it usually process only a single table at a time. It groups tables into *batches* and runs the fact generation and aggregation algorithms on all tables in that batch. Once all batches have been processed, all tables in the database have been consistency-checked.

The reason that *DBCC CHECKDB* breaks the database into a series of batches is to limit the amount of space that is required in *tempdb* for fact storage. Each fact that is generated takes a certain amount of space, depending on the type of fact and its content. The more complex a schema is, the more facts that must be generated to allow all the aspects of the table's schema to be consistency-checked.

As you can imagine, for a very large database, the amount of space required to store all these facts very quickly exceeds the storage available in *tempdb* if all the tables in the database are consistency-checked in one batch.

The set of tables in a batch is determined while *DBCC CHECKDB* is scanning the metadata about tables at the start of the per-table logical checks phase. Batches always have at least one table (plus all its nonclustered indexes) and the size of each batch is limited by one of the following rules:

- If any repair option is specified, building the batch stops when it contains a single table. This is to guarantee that repairs are ordered correctly.

- When a table is added to a batch and the total number of indexes for all tables in the batch exceeds 512, building the batch stops.

- When a table is added to a batch and the total, worst-case estimation for how much *tempdb* space is required for all facts for all tables in the batch exceeds 32 MB, building the batch stops.

Once a batch has been built, the fact-generation and fact-aggregation algorithms are run on all the tables in the batch. This means that the internal query described earlier is issued once for each batch of tables.

When a batch completes, various deep-dive algorithms may be triggered to find unmatched text timestamp values or unmatched nonclustered index records. At this point, *unchecked assemblies* may also be cleared.

If a table depends on a CLR assembly for the implementation of a CLR user-defined data type (UDT) or computed column and the assembly is subsequently changed using *ALTER ASSEMBLY* with the WITH UNCHECKED DATA option, all tables dependent on the assembly are marked as having unchecked assemblies in the system catalogs. The only mechanism to clear this setting is to run DBCC consistency checks against the affected tables. If no errors are found, the unchecked assembly setting is cleared.

## Reading the Pages to Process

Part of the performance of the fact-generation and fact-aggregation algorithms comes from the fact that the pages that comprise the tables and indexes in the batch are read very efficiently. As I explained earlier, the pages do not have to be read in any specific order, as the facts are aggregated after all relevant pages have been read (and all facts generated).

The fastest way to read a set of pages from a data file is to read them in *allocation order* (the physical order of the pages in the data files). This allows the disk heads to make one sweep across the disk rather than doing all random IOs and incurring excessive disk head seek time overhead.

The pages and extents that comprise each table and index in the batch are tracked by the IAM chains for the various allocation units in the table or index. Once the batch has been built, all these IAM chains are merged into a large bitmap that is managed by a scanning object inside *DBCC CHECKDB*. This bitmap then represents all the pages and extents in *sorted physical order* that comprise all the tables and indexes in the batch.

Using this bitmap, all the necessary pages can be read (nearly) sequentially. The scanning object performs read-ahead on the pages to ensure that the CPU(s) never have to wait for the next page to process to be read into the buffer pool. The read-ahead mechanism is similar to that used in the rest of the storage engine except that it is done in a round-robin fashion among the physical volumes on which the logical data files are created. This is done to try to spread the I/O workload across the physical volumes as such a large amount of I/O is done by *DBCC CHECKDB*.

Whenever the next page is required for processing, a call is made into the scanning object, which then returns a page to the caller. The type of page returned, or the object/index that the page is part of, is completely irrelevant, due to the nature of the fact generation and aggregation algorithms.

It should be noted that sometimes random I/Os are necessary because some rows on the pages being read may have a portion of the row stored on a different (text) page because of the row-overflow feature. *DBCC CHECKDB* materializes an entire row in memory (except off-row LOB columns), which may involve a random I/O to read the row-overflow portion of the row.

## Parallelism

*DBCC CHECKDB* has the ability to run using multiple processor cores in parallel to make more efficient use of the system resources and process the database faster.

It can run the current batch in parallel if all the following conditions are true:

- The SQL Server instance is Enterprise, Enterprise Eval, or Developer.
- There are more than 64 pages comprising all the tables and indexes in the current batch.
- There are no T-SQL-based or CLR-based computed columns in the tables in the batch.
- Parallelism has not been explicitly disabled with trace flag 2528.

If all these conditions are true, *DBCC CHECKDB* signals the query processor that it can be parallelized when it issues the internal query described earlier. The query processor then makes the final determination as to whether to use parallel threads or not. The query processor makes this determination based on the same factors that affect the parallelization of all other queries in SQL Server, such as the following:

- The server's MAXDOP setting

- The projected query cost for parallelism

- The availability of resources on the server at the time the *DBCC CHECKDB* query for the batch is compiled for execution

The determination of whether to parallelize the internal query is performed each time the query is issued, which means that different batches in a single execution of *DBCC CHECKDB* may run with different degrees of parallelism.

The conceptual flow of data when the internal query runs in parallel is shown in Figure 11-2. This diagram illustrates the data flow when the degree of parallelism is 3.

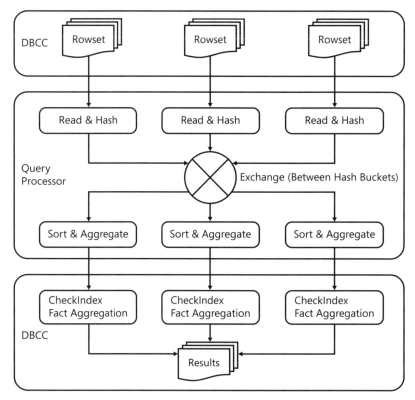

**FIGURE 11-2** Conceptual data flow for the internal query with degree of parallelism = 3

When the internal query runs in parallel, one thread is created for each degree of parallelism. During the fact-generation portion of the algorithm, each thread is responsible for requesting pages to process from the scanning object and completely processing each page. A page is only ever processed by a single thread. During the fact-aggregation portion of the algorithm, each thread is responsible for aggregating a separate, self-contained stream of facts (meaning that all pertinent facts for a particular part of an object's structure must be presented to that one thread—there is no cross-thread fact aggregation).

There is no control over which thread processes which page, so the pages comprising a single object may be processed by multiple threads. This could lead to problems during the fact-aggregation phase if facts that really should aggregate together are actually contained in the sorted and aggregated fact streams for a different thread. For this reason, when the internal query is parallelized, all facts are hashed by their ROWSET_COLUMN_FACT_KEY elements and then passed through an exchange operator into per-thread hash buckets before being sorted. This guarantees that all the facts for a particular part of an object's structure are presented to just one thread.

> **Note**  The *DBCC CHECKTABLE* and *DBCC CHECKFILEGROUP* commands can also use parallelism in this way. *DBCC CHECKALLOC* cannot run in parallel, however.

Parallelism can be disabled for all these DBCC commands using trace flag 2528 if it is determined that the parallelized command places too heavy a workload on the server. Note that disabling parallelism makes the DBCC command take longer to complete.

To allow efficient parallelism and scalability without artificial bottlenecks, all parts of the *DBCC CHECKDB* internals that are multithreading-aware (for example, the scanning object and the progress reporting object) are designed such that access to them from multiple threads do not cause scalability issues up to at least parallelizing across 32 processor cores.

# Primitive System Catalog Consistency Checks

The storage engine in SQL Server 2008 defines three of the system catalogs as being critical to its operations. These tables are

- *sys.sysallocunits*
- *sys.sysrowsets*
- *sys.sysrscols*

In SQL Server 2005, there were two more critical system tables—*sys.syshobts* and *sys.syshobtcolumns*—but these have been folded into the *sys.sysrowsets* and *sys.sysrscols* tables, respectively. Collectively, these are the equivalent of the old *sysindexes, sysobjects,* and *syscolumns* tables. They hold all the base metadata that the storage engine needs to navigate around the table and index structures. *DBCC CHECKDB* also uses them for this purpose, although indirectly through the metadata subsystem in the Relational Engine.

These system catalogs each have a clustered index, and some also have nonclustered indexes. *DBCC CHECKDB* needs to check that the clustered index leaf levels do not have obvious corruptions so that when it calls a metadata function to retrieve some information from one of them, there is a good chance the metadata function will succeed.

The following checks are performed on the leaf level of these three clustered indexes:

- **Each page is read into the buffer pool.** This checks that there are no I/O problems with the page (such as a page checksum failure, invalid page ID, or plain failure of the I/O subsystem to read the page). Error 7985 is reported for any pages that fail this operation.

- **Each page is audited.** Page auditing is explained later in this chapter, but basically, it makes sure the page structure and page header look valid. The page must be a data page and must be allocated to the correct allocation unit. Error 7984 is reported for any page that fails this check.

- **The leaf-level linked-list is checked.** All pages at a level in an index are in a double-linked-list. Once all pages for the leaf level have been read into the buffer pool and audited, the linkage of the pages are checked by following the next-page links through the leaf level and making sure that the previous-page link really does point to the previous page. Error 7986 or 7987 is reported if the linked-list if broken.

- **The leaf-level linked-list is checked for loops.** This is done while the linked-list linkages are checked by having two pointers into the page linked-list—one that advances at every step and one that advances at every second step. If they ever point to the same page before the faster-advancing pointer reaches the right-hand side of the leaf level, there's a loop. It's important that there are no linkage loops; otherwise, a range scan may turn into an infinite loop. I've never seen this occur on a customer system. Error 7988 is reported if a loop is detected.

If any of these checks fail, *DBCC CHECKDB* terminates with an appropriate message, such as the one here:

```
DBCC CHECKDB ('TestDB') WITH NO_INFOMSGS, ALL_ERRORMSGS;
GO
Msg 7985, Level 16, State 2, Line 1
System table pre-checks: Object ID 4. Could not read and latch page (1:65) with latch type
SH. Check statement terminated due to unrepairable error.
DBCC results for 'TestDB'.
Msg 5233, Level 16, State 98, Line 1
Table error: alloc unit ID 262144, page (1:65). The test (IS_OFF (BUF_IOERR, pBUF->bstat))
failed. The values are 12584969 and -4.
CHECKDB found 0 allocation errors and 1 consistency errors not associated with any single
object.
CHECKDB found 0 allocation errors and 1 consistency errors in database 'TestDB'.
```

It terminates because these critical system catalogs are necessary for *DBCC CHECKDB* to check the rest of the database. Note that there is no recommended repair level in the *DBCC CHECKDB* output. These errors cannot be repaired—the only option is to restore from your backups.

If no problems are found, the next stage is to run database-level allocation consistency checks, which is discussed next.

# Allocation Consistency Checks

These checks verify the contents of and relationships between the various structures that track page and extent allocations in the database. The structures involved are as follows:

- PFS pages, which track the allocation status of individual pages within a 64-MB section of a data file (a PFS interval)

- GAM pages, which track the allocation status of all extents within a 4-GB section of a data file (a GAM interval)

- SGAM pages, which track all mixed extents that have at least one page available for allocation with a GAM interval

- IAM pages, which track all pages and extents allocated to an allocation unit from a GAM interval

- IAM chains, which are a linked-list of all IAM pages for an allocation unit (and hence track all pages and extents allocated to the allocation unit from all sections of all data files)

- The storage engine metadata in the three critical system tables, as described previously

The allocation consistency checks are very fast—in fact, magnitudes faster than the per-table and cross-table consistency checks. The reason for this is that the number of database pages that must be read to perform the allocation consistency checks is magnitudes smaller than the number that must be read to perform all the per-table and cross-table consistency checks.

## Collecting Allocation Facts

Before any allocation consistency checks can be run, all the necessary information needs to be collected from the various allocation structures and stored as facts.

For each data file in each online filegroup in the database, the following actions are performed:

- The boot page [page (1:9) in file 1] of the database and the file header page (page 0) in each data file are audited. Error 5250 is reported if this check fails and *DBCC CHECKDB* terminates.

- All PFS pages are read and processed. This provides a bitmap of all the IAM pages in the file, as the PFS page also tracks which pages are IAM pages. This also provides a bitmap of which pages in the file are from mixed extents. Each set of bitmaps collectively takes less space than all the PFS pages in the file because a PFS page stores 8 bits of information for each data file page.

- All GAM pages are read and processed. This provides a bitmap of all the allocated extents in the file.

- All Shared Global Allocation Map (SGAM) pages are read and processed. This provides a bitmap of all mixed extents in the file that have at least one available page.

- The Differential Changed Map (DCM) pages and Minimally Logged Map (ML Map) pages are read while the GAM extent is being processed, just to make sure that they can be read correctly.

  At the start of every GAM interval is a special extent called the *GAM* extent, which contains the GAM and SGAM pages for that GAM interval. It also contains two other pages that track extents in that GAM interval—the DCM and the ML Map pages. The DCM pages track which extents were changed in the GAM interval since the last full database backup. The ML Map pages track which extents were changed in the GAM interval by minimally logged operations since the last transaction log backup.

- All IAM pages are read and processed. This provides

  - ❏ A list of all the mixed pages in the file (pages allocated from mixed extents), and by derivation, a list of all mixed extents in the file (remember that the first IAM page in an IAM chain contains an array—the single-page slot array—to hold up to eight mixed pages for the allocation unit it represents).

  - ❏ A list of all the valid IAM pages in the file. This is necessary because a PFS page may be corrupt and mistakenly have a page marked as an IAM page, or a real IAM page may just be corrupt and unreadable.

  - ❏ A list of all the allocated dedicated extents in the file.

  - ❏ Linkage information for all IAM chains.

  All IAM pages in an IAM chain are linked in a doubly linked list. They also contain a sequence number, starting at 0 for the first IAM page in the chain and increasing by 1 for each IAM page added to the chain.

If any allocation page cannot be read because its header is corrupt, error 8946 is reported (or error 7965 for a corrupt IAM page). This means that a large range of the database is excluded from the consistency checks. The excluded range is reported in error 8998.

After all the per-file information gathering, the storage engine metadata is processed as follows:

1. The page ID of the first IAM page of each IAM chain is stored in the system catalogs (if it wasn't stored somewhere, the storage engine would not know where to find the list of pages and extents allocated to a table or index).

These page IDs are used to generate the parent facts for the first IAM page in each IAM chain. This should match up with an actual fact generated during the per-file steps.

During this phase, all system catalogs are checked to make sure that they are stored in the primary filegroup of the database. Error 8995 is reported if any are not.

2. Information about IAM chains currently waiting to be "deferred-dropped" is stored in an internal queue.

Deferred-drop is an optimization introduced in SQL Server 2005 that prevents a transaction from running out of lock memory while dropping an IAM chain. It is the process by which an IAM chain with more than 128 extents that is dropped (either by dropping and rebuilding an index or dropping and truncating a table) does not have its actual pages and extents deallocated until after the transaction has committed. The IAM chain is unhooked from *sys.sysallocunits* though and hooked into an internal queue.

If *DBCC CHECKDB* didn't scan the internal queue as part of the allocation fact generation process, it might see all kinds of inconsistencies with the various allocation bitmaps.

The allocation facts are passed to the query processor, as described earlier, where they are sorted and grouped together. They are then passed back to *DBCC CHECKDB* so they can be aggregated and any errors found.

## Checking Allocation Facts

The allocation fact-aggregation algorithms perform the following consistency checks:

- Check that each extent in each GAM interval is allocated correctly. The possibilities here are that the extent should be

    - Marked in the GAM page as available for allocation
    - Marked in the SGAM page as a non-full mixed extent
    - Marked in exactly one of the IAM pages that cover the GAM interval
    - Not marked in any of the allocation bitmaps (in which all pages in the extent must be mixed pages, referenced in various IAM pages' single-page slot arrays)

Table 11-1 lists the possible combinations, with illegal states shown along with the resulting error number.

**TABLE 11-1  Possible Combinations of Allocation Bitmaps**

| GAM | SGAM | IAM | Legal | Meaning | Error |
|-----|------|-----|-------|---------|-------|
| 0 | 0 | 0 | Y | Mixed extent with all pages allocated | N/A |
| 0 | 0 | 1 | Y | Dedicated extent allocated to an IAM | N/A |
| 0 | 1 | 0 | Y | Mixed extent with available pages | N/A |
| 0 | 1 | 1 | N | Illegal | 8904 |

**TABLE 11-1 Possible Combinations of Allocation Bitmaps**

| GAM | SGAM | IAM | Legal | Meaning | Error |
|-----|------|-----|-------|---------|-------|
| 1 | 0 | 0 | Y | Extent is not allocated | N/A |
| 1 | 0 | 1 | N | Illegal | 8904 |
| 1 | 1 | 0 | N | Illegal | 8903 |
| 1 | 1 | 1 | N | Illegal | 8904 |

If two IAM pages have the same extent allocated, error 8904 is reported. Error 8904 is always accompanied by error 8913, which gives the second object (or allocation bitmap) that has the extent allocated. If an extent is a mixed extent but none of the mixed pages are seen, error 8905 is reported.

- Check that the PFS byte for each mixed and IAM page is correct. Error 8948 is reported for all pages that fail this check.

- Check that each page marked by a PFS page as being a mixed page appears somewhere in a single-page slot array on an IAM page. Error 8906 is reported for any pages that fail this check, as shown here:

```
Msg 8906, Level 16, State 1, Line 1
Page (1:50139) in database ID 13 is allocated in the SGAM (1:3) and PFS (1:48528), but
was not allocated in any IAM. PFS flags 'MIXED_EXT ALLOCATED 0_PCT_FULL'.
```

- Check that each mixed page is allocated only in a single IAM page's single-page slot array. Error 8910 is reported for any doubly allocated pages.

- Check that the IAM pages in an IAM chain have monotonically increasing sequence numbers. Error 2577 is reported if this check fails.

- Check that no two IAM pages within the same IAM chain map the same GAM interval. Error 8947 is reported when this check fails.

- Check that all IAM pages within an IAM chain belong to the same allocation unit. Error 8959 is reported if this check fails.

- Check that IAM pages map valid portions of data files (for example, not in file ID 0 or 2). Error 8968 is reported if this check fails.

- Check that the linked-list between IAM pages within an IAM chain is correct, including the pointer from the *sys.sysallocunits* catalog to the first IAM page in the IAM chain. Error 8969, 2575, or 2576 is reported if this check fails, depending on which linkage is broken. An example is below:

```
Msg 2576, Level 16, State 1, Line 1
The Index Allocation Map (IAM) page (0:0) is pointed to by the previous pointer
of IAM page (1:79969) in object ID 0, index ID -1, partition ID 0, alloc unit ID
107504789946368 (type Unknown), but it was not detected in the scan.
```

- Check that an IAM page maps a GAM interval somewhere in the same filegroup as itself. Error 8996 is reported for any pages that fail this check.

- Check that all IAM, GAM, and SGAM pages that map the final GAM interval in a file do not have extents marked as allocated that are beyond the physical end of the file. Error 2579 is reported if this check fails.

Once the allocation consistency checks are complete (and any repairs performed if a repair option was specified), the foundation has been laid for the logical consistency checks, discussed next.

# Per-Table Logical Consistency Checks

These checks verify the consistency for all structures in a table and all its indexes. In this section, when I say "a table," I mean "all partitions of the heap or clustered index, all partitions of all nonclustered indexes, and any off-row LOB data." The table could be a regular table, an indexed view, an XML index, a system catalog, a spatial index, a Service Broker queue, or any other database object that is stored internally as a table.

All the tables within a single batch are checked at the same time, using the fact-generation and fact-aggregation algorithms described previously. The first batch contains the critical system tables, and then subsequent batches are built and checked until all tables in the database have been checked.

The consistency checks performed for each table are as follows:

1. Extract and check all the metadata for the table.

2. For each page in the table, do the following:

   ❑ Read and audit the page.

   ❑ Perform page-level consistency checks.

   ❑ Perform record-level consistency checks for all records on the page.

   ❑ For data and index records, perform column-level consistency checks on each column in each record.

3. Perform cross-page consistency checks as follows:

   ❑ Nonclustered index cross-checks.

   ❑ B-tree consistency checks

   ❑ Off-row LOB data consistency checks

   ❑ *FILESTREAM* consistency checks

The remainder of this section explains each step in detail.

## Metadata Consistency Checks

*DBCC CHECKDB* builds an internal cache of most of the metadata that describes each table. This metadata cache is used extensively during the various consistency checks, and it is much faster for *DBCC CHECKDB* to access its own cache than to call continually into the metadata subsystem of the storage engine.

The metadata cache has the following hierarchy of information:

- **Table metadata object**    Holds the metadata describing a table and a linked-list of index metadata objects

- **Index metadata**    Holds the metadata describing each index of a table, including the heap or clustered index, and a linked-list of rowset metadata objects

- **Rowset metadata**    Holds the metadata describing each partition of each index

It is not necessary to list everything that the metadata cache tracks. Instead, I'll list some of the more interesting items that are tracked in each metadata object.

The table metadata cache object includes

- The page and record counts for use in the informational messages in the default output of *DBCC CHECKDB*.

- The count of errors found for the table.

- An expression evaluator that is used to calculate the expected values of persisted and indexed computed columns. This is obtained from the query processor, so long as the CLR has not been disabled for the instance.

- Status information, including whether the table has been found to contain an error.

If the CLR has been disabled, the expression evaluator cannot be created and error 2518 is reported. If the CLR is enabled, but a problem occurs while initializing the expression evaluator, error 2519 is reported. In either case, computed columns and UDTs are not checked.

The index metadata cache object includes

- All metadata concerning any partitioning function that is used for the index, so each record can be checked to ensure that it is in the correct partition.

- Status information, including whether the index has been found to contain an error. For a nonclustered index, if an error has been found, then the nonclustered index cross-checks are not performed.

If the index being considered is on a filegroup other than that specified for *DBCC CHECKFILEGROUP*, it is not included in the checks and error 2594 is reported.

The rowset metadata cache object, the most extensive of the cache objects, includes

- Various column and key counts.

- Metadata to aid in *FILESTREAM* consistency checks.

If a table or index has a rowset (that is, a partition of an index or table) that resides on an offline or invalid filegroup, the table or index is not included in the checks. For an offline filegroup, error 2527 is reported. For an invalid filegroup, error 2522 is reported.

As the rowset metadata cache objects are being constructed, the system catalog page counts for each allocation unit are tested to ensure that they are not negative. This condition could occur in versions of SQL Server prior to SQL Server 2005. If a negative count is found, error 2508 is output, as shown here:

```
Msg 2508, Level 16, State 3, Line 1
The In-row data RSVD page count for object "Receipts", index ID 0, partition ID
49648614572032, alloc unit ID 49648614572032 (type In-row data) is incorrect. Run DBCC
UPDATEUSAGE.
```

In addition, a separate hash table includes every allocation unit ID present in the table with a link to the relevant rowset metadata cache object. This provides a very fast way to find the metadata describing a particular page (because each page has only an allocation unit ID in the page header), rather than having to do a costly search through the metadata cache.

If a specific index was requested to be consistency-checked but the index could not be found in the database metadata, error 2591 is reported.

As this cache is built, it is checked for consistency. If any errors are discovered (for example, mismatches between the various columns counts and arrays), an 8901 or 8930 error is output, depending on the seriousness of the error. An 8901 error prevents a table being checked, but an 8930 error causes *DBCC CHECKDB* to terminate. An example is shown here:

```
Msg 8930, Level 16, State 1, Line 1
Database error: Database 16 has inconsistent metadata. This error cannot be repaired and
prevents further DBCC processing. Please restore from a backup.
```

## Page Audit

All pages read by *DBCC CHECKDB*, no matter what type of page, go through an audit before being processed further. The audit process ensures that the page and the records on it are correct enough that deeper consistency-checking algorithms do not cause problems inside *DBCC CHECKDB*.

*DBCC CHECKDB* does not perform any physical I/Os itself—instead, it uses the buffer pool to read all pages that it processes. In addition to reducing complexity, this allows *DBCC CHECKDB* to use the buffer pool's auditing. Whenever the buffer pool reads a page into memory, the page is checked to ensure that no I/O errors occurred, and then any torn-page or page checksum protection is verified. If any problems are discovered, the usual 823 or 824 error is raised by the buffer pool but is suppressed by *DBCC CHECKDB* and translated into a DBCC-specific error message. These are usually errors 8928 and 8939, as shown here:

```
Msg 8928, Level 16, State 1, Line 1
Object ID 1326627769, index ID 1, partition ID 72057594048872448, alloc unit ID
72057594055557120 (type LOB data): Page (1:69965) could not be processed. See other errors
for details.
Msg 8939, Level 16, State 98, Line 1
Table error: Object ID 1326627769, index ID 1, partition ID 72057594048872448, alloc unit ID
72057594055557120 (type LOB data), page (1:69965). Test (IS_OFF (BUF_IOERR, pBUF->bstat))
failed. Values are 12716041 and -4.
```

If the buffer pool audit fails, the page is not processed any further. Otherwise, the DBCC page audit is performed. This includes the following steps:

1. Check that the page ID in the page header is correct. This check is actually performed by the buffer pool when reading the page and *DBCC CHECKDB* is notified if the check fails. If this check fails while auditing a page from a critical system catalog during the primitive system catalog checks, error 5256 (which does not contain any metadata information) is raised, as shown here:

   ```
   Msg 5256, Level 16, State 1, Line 1
   Table error: alloc unit ID 334184954400421, page (1:2243) contains an incorrect page
   ID in its page header. The PageId in the page header = (0:0).
   ```

   If this check fails in any other circumstance, an 8909 error is raised, as shown here:

   ```
   Msg 8909, Level 16, State 1, Line 1
   Table error: Object ID 0, index ID -1, partition ID 0, alloc unit ID 844424953200640
   (type Unknown), page ID (1:26483) contains an incorrect page ID in its page header.
   The PageId in the page header = (0:0).
   ```

2. Check that the page type is valid for the allocation unit of which it is part. For instance, a data page should not be present in the allocation unit for a nonclustered index. If this check fails, an 8938 error is raised, as shown here:

   ```
   Msg 8938, Level 16, State 1, Line 1|
   Table error: Page (1:4667), Object ID 1877736499, index ID 1, partition ID
   72044394032172426, alloc unit ID 72044394045227020 (type LOB data). Unexpected page
   type 1.
   ```

3. Check that each record on the page has the correct structure and doesn't have any bad pointers (for example, pointing into a different record or into free space). If any record structure audit checks fail, any of errors 8940 through 8944 may be raised, as shown here:

   ```
   Msg 8941, Level 16, State 1, Line 1
   Table error: Object ID 0, index ID -1, partition ID 0, alloc unit ID 72057613244301312
   (type Unknown), page (3:45522). Test (sorted [i].offset >= PAGEHEADSIZE) failed. Slot
   114, offset 0x12 is invalid.
   Msg 8942, Level 16, State 1, Line 1
   ```

```
Table error: Object ID 0, index ID -1, partition ID 0, alloc unit ID 72057613244301312
(type Unknown), page (3:45522). Test (sorted[i].offset >= max) failed. Slot 0, offset
0x72 overlaps with the prior row.
Msg 8944, Level 16, State 12, Line 1
Table error: Object ID 0, index ID -1, partition ID 0, alloc unit ID 72057613244301312
(type Unknown), page (3:45523), row 0. Test (ColumnOffsets <= (nextRec - pRec))
failed. Values are 25 and 17.
```

As part of the page audit process, any page-compression information on the page is validated, including the per-page compression information (CI) record that holds the prefixes (in an anchor record embedded within the CI record) and compression dictionary (an array of offsets plus values). Any corruptions in this record are reported as 5274 errors.

Once the page has passed the audit process, the allocation unit ID in the page header is used to query the metadata hash table described previously to find all the metadata that describes what's stored within the page records. The page is then checked to determine whether it has been changed since the previous full backup was performed. If so, and the relevant differential bitmap has not been set correctly to indicate the change, error 2515 is reported, as shown here:

```
Msg 2515, Level 16, State 1, Line 1
The page (1:24), object ID 60, index ID 1, partition ID 281474980642816, allocation unit ID
281474980642816 (type In-row data) has been modified, but is not marked as modified in the
differential backup bitmap.
```

Once these generic checks have all been performed, the page is processed further according to its type.

## Data and Index Page Processing

Data pages and index pages are processed using the same high-level algorithm, which does the following for each record:

- For records that have off-row LOB data, instantiate the record fully in memory (pulling in any row-overflow columns). For simple records without off-row LOB data, the record is processed directly from the page containing it.

- Check that the record length is correct, taking into account any versioning information appended to the end of the record.

- If the record contains data (that is, isn't a ghost record), loop over all columns in the record and process them.

- Check that there are no antimatter columns in the record, indicating a failed online index operation. Error 5228 or 5229 is output if this check fails, as shown here:

  ```
  Msg 5228, Level 16, State 3, Line 1
  Table error: object ID 2073058421, index ID 0, partition ID 72057594038321152, alloc
  unit ID 72057594042318848 (type "In-row data"), page (3:23345), row 12. DBCC detected
  incomplete cleanup from an online index build operation. (The anti-matter column value
  is 14.)
  ```

■ Check the versioning info for each record, if it exists. If a record has versioning info appended to it, but the page header does not indicate that the page has versioned records on it, error 5260 is output. If a record has versioning info with a NULL version timestamp but a non-NULL version chain pointer, error 5262 is output.

 **Note** The validity of the version store itself is not checked by *DBCC CHECKDB*.

■ Generate all necessary facts from the record and its contents (for example, B-tree linkage facts and LOB linkage facts).

For records that are not stored on heap data pages, the records must be ordered by the defined clustered or nonclustered index keys. As the consistency checks progress through the page, the keys of the previous record are remembered so they can be compared with the current record being processed. If the records are not ordered correctly, error 2511 is output, as shown here:

```
Msg 2511, Level 16, State 1, Line 1
Table error: Object ID 142675606, index ID 1, partition ID 72057594295025664, alloc unit ID
72057594301906944 (type In-row data). Keys out of order on page (1:1124457), slots 59 and 60.
```

For records that are not stored in heap data pages, the records on a page must also have unique key values—that is, no two records can have the same keys. This applies even for indexes that have been defined as non-unique—but only at the relational level. At the storage engine level, every record must be uniquely identifiable. If two records have the same keys, error 2512 is reported, as shown here:

```
Msg 2512, Level 16, State 2, Line 1
Table error: Object ID 4, index ID 1, partition ID 262144, alloc unit ID 262144 (type In-row
data). Duplicate keys on page (1:4224) slot 9 and page (1:4224) slot 10.
```

The consistency checks of the various linkages between pages and records are discussed in the section entitled "Cross-Page Consistency Checks," later in this chapter.

Once all records have been processed, the following counters in the page header are checked:

■ The count of records on the page (the slot count)

■ The count of ghost records on the page

If the record count is incorrect, error 8919 is reported. If the ghost record count is incorrect, error 8927 is reported, as shown here:

```
Msg 8927, Level 16, State 1, Line 1
Object ID 29, index ID 1, partition ID 281474978611200, alloc unit ID 281474978611200 (type
In-row data): The ghosted record count in the header (0) does not match the number of
ghosted records (1) found on page (1:309).
```

For non-leaf B-tree pages, there must be at least one record on the page. If not, error 2574 is reported.

For data pages in a heap, the free space count is checked against the corresponding byte in the relevant PFS page. If the two do not match, error 8914 is reported, as shown here:

```
Msg 8914, Level 16, State 1, Line 3
Incorrect PFS free space information for page (1:2511951) in object ID 357576312, index
ID 0, partition ID 72057594040156160, alloc unit ID 72057594044284928 (type In-row data).
Expected value 100_PCT_FULL, actual value 95_PCT_FULL.
```

# Column Processing

For data and index records, each column is processed according to its type. Many of the checks described in this section result in a generic 2537 ("bad record") error message with some specific text added into the error to identify the exact problem.

For *complex* columns (that is, columns that store LOB or *FILESTREAM* data or links), the column structure is checked as well as being processed to extract the relevant linkage facts. If a corrupt complex column is found, error 8960 is output.

There are also many ways that columns are processed to support cross-page consistency checks. These are discussed in the section entitled "Cross-Page Consistency Checks," later in this chapter.

## Computed Columns

As described earlier, an expression evaluator is compiled for each object that contains computed columns or CLR UDTs. If the expression evaluator cannot be compiled, these columns cannot be consistency checked.

The expression evaluator is called to evaluate persisted computed columns, or computed columns that exist in index records. It returns a value which is then compared against the persisted value in the data or index record. If the NULL status of the two values differs or a byte-comparison of the two values differs, error 2537 is returned.

For UDT columns, the comparison is done within the expression evaluator. It is passed the entire record being checked and returns a value of *True* or *False* depending on the UDT comparison.

It should be noted that the expression evaluator object is not thread-safe. This means that when *DBCC CHECKDB* is running in parallel across multiple processor cores (with one thread per processor core), only one processor core can access and use the expression evaluator at a time. Multiple processor cores can process pages from the same table with computed columns, so all the cores need access to the expression evaluator. There is, of course, internal synchronization to prevent this and inevitably, one or more processor cores may have to wait for access. As is the case with any mutual exclusion mechanism, this could affect the performance of heavily loaded systems with a large number of computed columns or CLR UDTs in the schema.

## NULL and Length Checks

There are three checks performed here:

- Variable-length columns that are NULL must not have a nonzero data length. If this check fails, error 7961 is reported.

- A column that was created as NOT NULL cannot have a NULL value. If this check fails, error 8970 is reported.

- A column cannot be longer than the maximum in-row length as defined by its metadata. If this check fails, error 2537 is reported.

## Data Purity Checks

Data purity checks check whether the value of the column is within any bounds defined for the column's data type. An example is a corrupt *SMALLDATETIME* column value that had a "minutes past midnight" subvalue of 1440 or more into the next day.

As is documented in *SQL Server Books Online,* in versions of SQL Server prior to SQL Server 2005, it was possible to import "out-of-bounds" data values into a database. In SQL Server 2005 and SQL Server 2008, this is no longer possible. SQL Server 2005 introduced the concept of a database being "pure"—in other words, there are no "out-of-bounds" data values in the database.

Pure databases have the data purity checks run by default, and they cannot be disabled. Databases created on SQL Server 2008 are deemed pure from creation. Databases created on SQL Server 2005 are also deemed pure and remain so when upgraded to SQL Server 2008.

Databases that are impure do not have the data purity checks run by default—they must be specifically requested with the WITH DATA_PURITY option. An impure database is one that was created before SQL Server 2005, has been upgraded to SQL Server 2008, and has not had the data purity checks run without errors. Once data purity checks have been run without errors, the database is irrevocably switched to being pure. A database's purity status is stored in the boot page.

Table 11-2 below lists some of the SQL Server data types and the data purity validations that are performed for them.

**TABLE 11-2  Data Purity Checks by Data Type**

| Data Type | Data Purity Checks |
| --- | --- |
| TINYINT | None—all values are valid. |
| SMALLINT | None—all values are valid. |
| INT | None—all values are valid. |
| BIGINT | None—all values are valid. |
| MONEY | None—all values are valid. |
| SMALLMONEY | None—all values are valid. |
| UNIQUEIDENTIFIER | None—all values are valid. |
| TIMESTAMP | None—all values are valid. |
| IMAGE | None—all values are valid. |
| TEXT | Depending on the collation, validates any DBCS byte. |
| NTEXT | Validates that the length is a multiple of 2. |
| BIT | Ensure the value is 0 or 1. |
| REAL or FLOAT | Validates that the floating-point value is not outside the legal range. |
| DATETIME | Validates the fields within the DATETIME structure. For instance, the "days" field must be less than December 31, 9999 and greater than January 1, 1753. |
| SMALLDATETIME | Validates the fields within the SMALLDATETIME structure. For instance, the "minutes" field must be less than 1440 (that is, 60 x 24). |
| DECIMAL or NUMERIC | Validates that the precision of the value is less than or equal to the defined precision, the scale of the value is equal to the defined scale, and the value is legal. |
| BINARY | Validates that the value has the correct length. |
| VARBINARY | Validates that the length is less than or equal to the maximum defined length. |
| VARBINARY(MAX) | None—all values are valid. |
| NCHAR | Validates that the length equals the defined length and that the length is a multiple of 2. |
| NVARCHAR | Validates that the length is less than or equal to the maximum defined length and that the length is a multiple of 2. |
| NVARCHAR(MAX) | Validates that the length is a multiple of 2. |
| CHAR | Validates that the length equals the defined length. Depending on the collation, validates any DBCS byte. |
| VARCHAR | Validates that the length is less than or equal to the maximum defined length. Depending on the collation, validates any DBCS byte. |
| VARCHAR(MAX) | Depending on the collation, validates any DBCS byte. |
| SQLVARIANT | Validates that the SQLVARIANT structure is valid and that the value contained within it is valid for its data type. |
| UDTs | Converts the value to the UDT and performs a byte comparison of the result with the original value. |
| XML | Performs structural validation of the XML value. This is performed by the XML subsystem. |

> **Note** Compressed values (either through row compression, page compression, or *VARDECIMAL*) must be uncompressed before being checked. This can add CPU overhead and extra run time to *DBCC CHECKDB* if a large proportion of the table, filegroup, or database is compressed.

If any column value fails a data purity check, error 2570 is returned, as shown here:

```
Msg 2570, Level 16, State 3, Line 1
Page (1:152), slot 0 in object ID 2073058421, index ID 0, partition ID 72057594038321152,
alloc unit ID 72057594042318848 (type "In-row data"). Column "c1" value is out of range for
data type "datetime".  Update column to a legal value.
```

These errors cannot be repaired and must be dealt with manually. The method for doing this is described in Knowledge Base article 923247 (*http://support.microsoft.com/kb/923247*).

## Partitioning Checks

As described previously, if the table or index being checked is partitioned, the index metadata cache object for it contains all information about the partitioning function used.

Once all column value checks have been completed, every record on the page is tested to ensure that it is in the correct partition. The column used for partitioning is extracted from each record and passed into a helper function within the query processor. The helper function evaluates the partition function and returns the partition ID that the record should be part of. If the partition ID returned does not match the partition ID that the page is part of, errors 8984 and 8988 are output, as shown here:

```
Msg 8984, Level 16, State 1, Line 1
Table error: Object ID 2073058421, index ID 0, partition ID 72057594038452224. A row should
be on partition number 2 but was found in partition number 3. Possible extra or invalid keys
for:
Msg 8988, Level 16, State 1, Line 1
Row (1:162:0) identified by (HEAP RID = (1:162:0)).
```

The 8984 error identifies the partition containing the error and the 8988 error identifies the physical location of the incorrectly partitioned record, along with the index keys that can be used to access the record (or the heap physical RID if the incorrectly partitioned record is part of a partitioned heap).

## Sparse Column Checks

The ability to define a column as SPARSE is a new feature in SQL Server 2008. SPARSE columns that are NULL are not stored in the record at all, not even in the NULL bitmap. This means that NULL values can truly take zero space in a record. When a SPARSE column is non-NULL, it is stored in a special SPARSE column array, which in turn is stored as a variable-length column in the record's variable-length column array. The consistency checking of the SPARSE column array is performed by the query processor and errors reported as for normal column corruptions.

# Text Page Processing

Text pages are used to store LOB values (either actual LOB values that are stored off-row, or non-LOB variable-length columns that have been pushed off-row as row-overflow data). In all error messages involving text records or LOB linkages, the allocation unit type can be *LOB data* or *row-overflow data*.

There are multiple types of text records, used in various ways to construct the loose text-trees that store LOB values. The text records are stored on two types of text pages—either dedicated to a single LOB value or shared between multiple LOB values. Both types of text pages are processed using the same algorithm, which does the following for each text record:

- Instantiates the record and checks it is a valid text record.

- Checks the versioning info for each record, if it exists. If a record has versioning info appended to it but the page header does not indicate that the page has versioned records on it, error 5260 is output. If a record has versioning info with a NULL version timestamp but a non-NULL version chain pointer, error 5262 is output.

- Generates all necessary facts from the record and its contents (that is, LOB linkage facts).

When checking that a text record is valid, multiple types of text records with various structures must be part of that. Apart from regular record format structure checks, the text-specific checks that are performed are as follows:

- Deleted text records that have versioning info must have the correct row size. If this check fails, error 2537 is reported.

- The text record must be at least the minimum size required to hold a text-tree leaf-level node. If this check fails, error 2537 is reported.

- The text record must be on the correct text page type. If this check fails, error 8963 is reported, as shown here:

```
Msg 8963, Level 16, State 1, Line 1
Table error: Object ID 1326627769, index ID 1, partition ID 72057594048872448, alloc
unit ID 72057594022622331 (type LOB data). The off-row data node at page (3:23345),
slot 12, text ID 89622642688 has type 3. It cannot be placed on a page of type 4.
```

- Non-leaf text records must not have more child nodes than are possible to store in their text record type, more child nodes than the size of their child links array, or more child nodes than the maximum permissible text-tree fan-out. If these checks fail, error 2537 is reported.

- The text record must have a valid type. If this check fails, error 8962 is reported.

Errors in text records are usually accompanied by an 8929 error, indicating the data or index record that links to the corrupt text record, as shown here:

```
Msg 8929, Level 16, State 1, Line 1
Object ID 1326627769, index ID 1, partition ID 72057594048872448, alloc unit ID
72057594055622656 (type In-row data): Errors found in off-row data with ID 89622642688 owned
by data record identified by RID = (1:77754:1)
```

The consistency checks of the various linkages between pages and records are discussed in the next section.

Once all records have been processed, the various counters in the page header are checked:

- The count of records on the page (the slot count)
- The count of ghost records on the page

If the record count is incorrect, error 8919 is reported. If the ghost record count is incorrect, error 8927 is reported.

The free space count is checked against the corresponding byte in the relevant PFS page. If the two do not match, error 8914 is reported, as shown here:

```
Msg 8914, Level 16, State 1, Line 1
Incorrect PFS free space information for page (1:35244) in object ID 1683128146, index ID 1,
partition ID 223091033422352, alloc unit ID 81405523118118176 (type LOB data). Exected value
0_PCT_FULL, actual value 100_PCT_FULL
```

## Cross-Page Consistency Checks

As the various data, index, and text pages are being processed, facts are extracted from the records on the pages to support cross-page consistency checks. The various checks performed depend on the schemas present in the database and include

- The linkages between forwarding and forwarded records in heap data pages
- Intra B-tree page and record linkages
- The linkages between data/index records and text records
- Intra text-tree record linkages
- The linkages between data/index records and *FILESTREAM* files
- *FILESTREAM* container structure
- The linkages between base table records and nonclustered index records

These checks are discussed in the remainder of this section.

## Heap Consistency Checks

The cross-page consistency checks for a heap validate the linkages between forwarding and forwarded records. Forwarding/forwarded record pairs occur when a data record in a heap increases in size and the record's current page does not have the space to accommodate the size increase. The record is moved to a new location (becoming a forwarded record) and a small stub record (the forwarding record) is left in the original location to point to the real location of the record.

The forwarded record points back to the forwarding record in case its location ever needs to change again—instead of a chain of forwarding records being created; the original forwarding record is updated to point to the new location.

During regular processing of heap data pages, extra facts are generated from forwarding and forwarded records:

- Forwarding records generate a parent fact.

- Forwarded records generate an actual fact, with a note made of the link back to the forwarding record.

When the facts are aggregated, the following checks are made:

- The forwarded record linked to by a forwarding record must exist. If this check fails, error 8993 is reported, as shown here:

```
Msg 8993, Level 16, State 1, Line 3
Object ID 357576312, forwarding row page (1:2386712), slot 8 points to page
(1:2621015), slot 18. Did not encounter forwarded row. Possible allocation error.
```

- The forwarding record linked back to by a forwarded record must exist. If this check fails, error 8994 is reported, as shown here:

```
Msg 8994, Level 16, State 1, Line 1
Object ID 1967346073, forwarded row page (1:181506), slot 23 should be pointed to by
forwarding row page (1:83535), slot 66. Did not encounter forwarding row. Possible
allocation error.
```

- The forwarded record linked to by a forwarding record must link back to that forwarding record. If this check fails, error 8971 is reported, as shown here:

```
Msg 8971, Level 16, State 1, Line 3
Forwarded row mismatch: Object ID 357576312, partition ID 72057594040156160, alloc
unit ID 72057594044284928 (type In-row data) page (1:3491303), slot 18 points to
forwarded row page (1:2506991), slot 22; the forwarded row points back to page
(1:3423966), slot 1
```

- A forwarded record cannot be linked to by multiple forwarding records. If this check fails, error 8972 is reported, as shown here:

```
Msg 8972, Level 16, State 1, Line 3
Forwarded row referenced by more than one row. Object ID 357576312, partition
ID 72057594040156160, alloc unit ID 72057594044284928 (type In-row data), page
(1:2500650), slot 2 incorrectly points to the forwarded row page (1:4361594), slot 4,
which correctly refers back to page (1:3472293), slot 20.
```

## B-tree Consistency Checks

The cross-page consistency checks for a B-tree validate linkages within a B-tree level, between B-tree levels, and the consistency of key ranges across and between levels.

For pages at the leaf level of an index, page linkage facts are generated from the page headers, plus facts from the first and last records on the page (to give the key range contained on the page). For pages at the non-leaf levels of an index, all these facts are produced plus a fact from every record on the page, containing a pointer to the page at the next level down in the B-tree that record references.

When the facts are aggregated, the following checks are made:

- A page pointed to by the next-page linkage in a page's header must have the same B-tree level. If this check fails, error 2531 is reported.

- The child-page linkage from a non-leaf (parent) page can link only to a page that is one level below it in the B-tree. If this check fails, error 8931 is reported.

- The previous-page linkage must agree with the ordering of child-page links in the parent page. If a parent page has page B following page A, then the previous-page linkage in page B's page header must link to page A. If this check fails, error 8935 is reported, as shown here:

```
Msg 8935, Level 16, State 1, Line 3
Table error: Object ID 1349579846, index ID 1, partition ID 72057594040811520, alloc
unit ID 72057594046382080 (type In-row data). The previous link (1:233719) on page
(1:233832) does not match the previous page (1:275049) that the parent (1:42062), slot
16 expects for this page.
```

- If the next-page linkage in the page header of page A links to page B, the previous-page linkage in the page header of page B must link back to page A. if this check fails, error 8936 is reported, as shown here:

```
Msg 8936, Level 16, State 1, Line 3
Table error: Object ID 1349579846, index ID 1, partition ID 72057594040811520,
alloc unit ID 72057594046382080 (type In-row data). B-tree chain linkage mismatch.
(1:275049)->next = (1:233832), but (1:233832)->Prev = (1:233719).
```

- A page can only be linked to by a single non-leaf page higher in the B-tree (that is, it cannot have two child-page linkages from two "parent" pages). If this check fails, error 8937 is reported, as shown here:

```
Msg 8937, Level 16, State 1, Line 3
Table error: Object ID 1349579846, index ID 1, partition ID 72057594040811520, alloc
unit ID 72057594046382080 (type In-row data). B-tree page (1:148135) has two parent
nodes (1:212962), slot 20 and (1:233839), slot 1.
```

- A page should only be encountered once by the *DBCC CHECKDB* scan. If this check fails, error 8973 is reported.

- A page must be encountered if a child-page linkage on a "parent" page links down to it and a page in the same level has a previous-page link to it. If this check fails, error 8976 is reported, as shown here:

```
Msg 8976, Level 16, State 1, Line 1
Table error: Object ID 2073058421, index ID 1, partition ID 72057594038386688, alloc
unit ID 72057594042384384 (type In-row data). Page (1:158) was not seen in the scan
although its parent (1:154) and previous (1:157) refer to it. Check any previous
errors.
```

- Every page in the B-tree must have a "parent page" with a child-page linkage that links to it. If this check fails, error 8977 is reported, as shown here:

```
Msg 8977, Level 16, State 1, Line 3
Table error: Object ID 1349579846, index ID 1, partition ID 72057594040811520, alloc
unit ID 72057594046382080 (type In-row data). Parent node for page (1:163989) was not
encountered.
```

- Every page in the B-tree must have a previous page with a next-page linkage that links to it. This includes those on the left-hand edge of the B-tree, where a fake linkage fact is created to make the aggregation work. If this check fails, error 8978 is reported, as shown here:

```
Msg 8978, Level 16, State 1, Line 3
Table error: Object ID 1349579846, index ID 1, partition ID 72057594040811520, alloc
unit ID 72057594046382080 (type In-row data). Page (1:238482) is missing a reference
from previous page (1:233835). Possible chain linkage problem.
```

- Every B-tree page must have a "parent" page with a child-page linkage that links to it, and a previous page with a next-page linkage that links to it. This includes those pages on the left-hand edge of the B-tree. When this is not the case, it is often the root page of the B-tree that has the problem, and is caused by a corrupt system catalog entry. This is why this error was created which is really a combination of the two errors above. If this check fails, error 8979 is reported, as shown here:

```
Msg 8979, Level 16, State 1, Line 1
Table error: Object ID 768057822, index ID 8. Page (1:92278) is missing references
from parent (unknown) and previous (page (3:10168)) nodes. Possible bad root entry in
sysindexes.
```

- The page linked to by a child-page linkage in a "parent" page must be encountered as a valid page in the B-tree by the *DBCC CHECKDB* scan. If this check fails, error 8980 is reported, as shown here:

```
Msg 8980, Level 16, State 1, Line 1
Table error: Object ID 421576540, index ID 8. Index node page (1:90702), slot 17
refers to child page (3:10183) and previous child (3:10182), but they were not
encountered.
```

- The page linked to by the next-page linkage in a page's header must be encountered as a valid page in the B-tree by the *DBCC CHECKDB* scan. If this check fails, error 8981 is reported, as shown here:

```
Msg 8981, Level 16, State 1, Line 3
Table error: Object ID 1349579846, index ID 1, partition ID 72057594040811520, alloc
unit ID 72057594046382080 (type In-row data). The next pointer of (1:233838) refers
to page (1:233904). Neither (1:233904) nor its parent were encountered. Possible bad
chain linkage.
```

- The next-page linkage in a page's header must link to a page within the same B-tree. If this check fails, error 8982 is reported.

- A page must be linked to by a "parent" page and previous page from within the same B-tree. If this check fails, error 8926 is reported, as shown here:

```
Msg 8926, Level 16, State 3, Line 1
Table error: Cross object linkage: Parent page (0:1), slot 0 in object 2146106686,
index 1, partition 72057594048806912, AU 72057594053394432 (In-row data), and page
(1:16418)->next in object 366624349, index 1, partition 72057594049593344, AU
72057594054246400 (In-row data), refer to page [1:16768] but are not in the same
object.
```

- The lowest key value on a page must be greater than or equal to the key value in the child-page linkage of the "parent" page in the next level up in the B-tree. If this check fails, error 8933 is reported, as shown here:

```
Msg 8933, Level 16, State 1, Line 3
Table error: Object ID 1349579846, index ID 1, partition ID 72057594040811520, alloc
unit ID 72057594046382080 (type In-row data). The low key value on page (1:148134)
(level 0) is not >= the key value in the parent (1:233839) slot 0.
```

- The highest key value on a page must be less than the key value in the child-page linkage of the "parent" page for the next page at the same level of the B-tree. If this check fails, error 8934 is reported, as shown here:

```
Msg 8934, Level 16, State 3, Line 3
Table error: Object ID 1349579846, index ID 1, partition ID 72057594040811520, alloc
unit ID 72057594046382080 (type In-row data). The high key value on page (1:275049)
(level 0) is not less than the low key value in the parent (0:1), slot 0 of the next
page (1:233832).
```

When a B-tree is corrupt, it is common for many of these errors to occur together for the same B-tree. Also, many of the errors where an expected page was not encountered are accompanied by a 2533 error, as shown here:

```
Msg 2533, Level 16, State 1, Line 1
Table error: Page (3:9947) allocated to object ID 768057822, index ID 4 was not seen. Page
may be invalid or have incorrect object ID information in its header.
Msg 8976, Level 16, State 1, Line 1
Table error: Object ID 768057822, index ID 4. Page (3:9947) was not seen in the scan
although its parent (1:858889) and previous (1:84220) refer to it. Check any previous
errors.
```

If it can be determined that the missing page is allocated to another object, error 2534 is also reported, giving the actual object indicated in the page header.

## LOB Linkage Consistency Checks

As discussed previously, LOB linkage facts are generated from text records and from complex columns in data or index records. This is to allow consistency checking of text trees and of the linkages to off-row LOB columns or row-overflow data values.

At aggregation time, the following checks are performed:

- The text timestamp in a text record must match the text timestamp in the data or index record complex column that links to it. If this check fails, error 8961 is reported, as shown here:

```
Msg 8961, Level 16, State 1, Line 1
Table error: Object ID 434100587, index ID 1, partition ID 72057594146521088, alloc
unit ID 71804568277286912 (type LOB data). The off-row data node at page (1:2487),
slot 0, text ID 3788411843723132928 does not match its reference from page (1:34174),
slot 0.
```

- Every text record must have a link to it from another text record or from a complex column in a data or index record. If this check fails, error 8964 is reported, as shown here:

```
Msg 8964, Level 16, State 1, Line 1
Table error: Object ID 750625717, index ID 0, partition ID 49193006989312, alloc unit
ID 71825312068206592 (type LOB data). The off-row data node at page (1:343), slot 0,
text ID 53411840 is not referenced.
```

It is common for multiple 8964 errors to be reported for text records on the same text page. This can happen if an entire data or index page cannot be processed, and each record on the corrupt page has a complex column linking to a text record on the same text page.

- If a complex column in a data or index record links to a text record, the text record should be encountered by the *DBCC CHECKDB* scan. If this check fails, error 8965 is reported. This commonly happens when a text page cannot be processed for some reason, in which case error 8928 is also reported, as shown here:

```
Msg 8928, Level 16, State 1, Line 1
Object ID 1993058136, index ID 1, partition ID 412092034711552, alloc unit ID
71906736119218176 (type LOB data): Page (1:24301) could not be processed. See other
errors for details.
Msg 8965, Level 16, State 1, Line 1
Table error: Object ID 1993058136, index ID 1, partition ID 412092034711552, alloc
unit ID 71906736119218176 (type LOB data). The off-row data node at page (1:24301),
slot 0, text ID 1606680576 is referenced by page (1:24298), slot 0, but was not seen
in the scan.
```

- A text record can only have one link to it. If this check fails, error 8974 is reported, as shown here:

```
Msg 8974, Level 16, State 1, Line 1
Table error: Object ID 373576369, index ID 1, partition ID
72057594039238656, alloc unit ID 71800601762136064 (type LOB data). The
off-row data node at page (1:13577), slot 13, text ID 31002918912 is
pointed to by page (1:56), slot 3 and by page (1:11416), slot 37.
```

- The LOB linkage from a complex column in a data or index record must link to a text record contained within the same object and index. If this check fails, error 8925 is reported.

These errors commonly occur together, and are usually accompanied by an 8929 error, as shown here:

```
Msg 8961, Level 16, State 1, Line 1
Table error: Object ID 434100587, index ID 1, partition ID 72057594146521088, alloc unit ID
71804568277286912 (type LOB data). The off-row data node at page (1:2487), slot 2, text ID
341442560 does not match its reference from page (1:2487), slot 0.
Msg 8929, Level 16, State 1, Line 1
Object ID 434100587, index ID 1, partition ID 72057594146521088, alloc unit ID
72057594151239680 (type In-row data): Errors found in off-row data with ID 341442560 owned
by data record identified by RID = (1:34174:0)
```

The 8929 error contains the actual data or index record that links to the corrupt text record. This information can be found only by rescanning all data and index records at the end of the batch looking for complex columns that contain a text timestamp matching one in a text record that has been found to be corrupt. It is critical that this rescanning process (known as a *deep-dive*) is performed so that database repairs can remove both records—the corrupt text record, and the record that contains a link to it.

## FILESTREAM Consistency Checks

One of the major new features in SQL Server 2008 is *FILESTREAM* storage—the ability to store LOB values *outside* the database in the NTFS file system. This permits very fast streaming access to the LOB values while maintaining transactional integrity with the relational data stored in the database.

As with any multilocation storage system, link integrity is paramount so that *DBCC CHECKDB* in SQL Server 2008 performs rigorous consistency checking of the *FILESTREAM* storage attached to a database. The *FILESTREAM* storage structure is as follows:

- The top level of the *FILESTREAM* data container is an NTFS directory.

- Each rowset (that is, a partition of a table or index) that contains *FILESTREAM* data has a directory (called a *rowset directory*) in the top level.

- Each column in the partition has as directory (called a *column directory*) in the rowset directory.

- The *FILESTREAM* data values for that column in each record in the partition are stored inside the column directory.

- There is also a *FILESTREAM* log directory (think of it as a transaction log for the *FILESTREAM* storage) stored in the top level of the *FILESTREAM* data container.

If the *FILESTREAM* log directory has been tampered with, the *FILESTREAM* scan fails and causes *DBCC CHECKDB* to terminate in a variety of ways, depending on the corruption. For instance, if a file is created in the *FILESTREAM* log directory, *DBCC CHECKDB* fails, as shown here:

```
Msg 8921, Level 16, State 1, Line 1
Check terminated. A failure was detected while collecting facts. Possibly tempdb out of
space or a system table is inconsistent. Check previous errors.
Msg 5511, Level 23, State 10, Line 1
FILESTREAM's file system log record 'badlog.txt' under log folder '\\?\F:\Production\
FileStreamStorage\Documents\$FSLOG' is corrupted.
```

When *DBCC CHECKDB* starts, *FILESTREAM* garbage collection (GC) is prevented for the duration of the *DBCC CHECKDB* scan. *FILESTREAM* linkage facts are generated from the following:

- Table and index records that contain *FILESTREAM* columns

- The internal GC table, which contains information about which *FILESTREAM* files have been deleted logically (and hence do not have a linkage from a data/index record) but have not yet been deleted physically

- The per-rowset and per-column directories in the *FILESTREAM* container(s)

- The actual *FILESTREAM* data files

At fact-aggregation time, the following consistency checks are performed:

- A *FILESTREAM* file must have a parent link (from either a data/index record, or the GC table). If this check fails, error 7903 is reported.

- The *FILESTREAM* link from a data/index record, or the GC table, must point to a valid *FILESTREAM* file. If this check fails, error 7904 is reported. It is not uncommon for these two errors to be reported together, as shown here, if a manual change has been made to a *FILESTREAM* data file:

```
Msg 7903, Level 16, State 2, Line 1
Table error: The orphaned file "00000017-00000101-0003" was found in the FILESTREAM
directory ID 988dc26c-ab62-46a4-bc44-c1062b6f6f80 for object ID 2105058535, index ID
0, partition ID 72057594038779904, column ID 3.
Msg 7904, Level 16, State 2, Line 1
Table error: Cannot find the FILESTREAM file "00000017-00000101-0002" for column ID 3
(column directory ID 988dc26c-ab62-46a4-bc44-c1062b6f6f80) in object ID 2105058535,
index ID 0, partition ID 72057594038779904, page ID (1:169), slot ID 1.
```

- Each directory in the *FILESTREAM* data container directory structure must be part of the *FILESTREAM* storage structure. If the corrupt directory is in the top level of the

*FILESTREAM* data container, error 7905 is reported; otherwise, error 7907 is reported, as shown here:

```
Msg 7907, Level 16, State 1, Line 1
Table error: The directory "\988dc26c-ab62-46a4-bc44-c1062b6f6f80\BadDirectory" under
the rowset directory ID 7e23f5a2-9cc0-462f-82d3-03ff3eaec4c9 is not a valid FILESTREAM
directory.
```

- Each file in the *FILESTREAM* data container directory structure must be a valid *FILESTREAM* data file. If the corrupt file is in the top level of the *FILESTREAM* data container, error 7906 is reported; otherwise, error 7908 is reported, as shown here:

```
Msg 7908, Level 16, State 1, Line 1
Table error: The file "\988dc26c-ab62-46a4-bc44-c1062b6f6f80\corruptfile.txt" in the
rowset directory ID 7e23f5a2-9cc0-462f-82d3-03ff3eaec4c9 is not a valid FILESTREAM
file.
```

- Each *FILESTREAM* rowset or column directory should not be encountered more than once by the *DBCC CHECKDB* scan. If this check fails, error 7931 is reported.

- Each *FILESTREAM* rowset directory should be in the correct *FILESTREAM* container for a database. If this check fails, error 7932 is reported.

- Each *FILESTREAM* rowset directory must map to a valid partition in the database. If this check fails, error 7933 is reported.

- Each partition in the database for a table or index that contains *FILESTREAM* data must have a matching *FILESTREAM* rowset directory. If this check fails, error 7934 is reported. It is not uncommon for these two errors to be reported together (most likely with accompanying 7937 errors, as shown here) if a manual change has been made to a *FILESTREAM* data file:

```
Msg 7933, Level 16, State 1, Line 1
Table error: A FILESTREAM directory ID 6e23f5a2-9cc0-462f-82d3-03ff3eaec4c9 exists for
a partition, but the corresponding partition does not exist in the database.
Msg 7937, Level 16, State 1, Line 1
Table error: The FILESTREAM directory ID 988dc26c-ab62-46a4-bc44-c1062b6f6f80 for
column ID of object ID 2105058535, index ID 0, partition ID 72057594038779904 was not
found.
Msg 7934, Level 16, State 1, Line 1
Table error: The FILESTREAM directory ID 7e23f5a2-9cc0-462f-82d3-03ff3eaec4c9 for
object ID 2105058535, index ID 0, partition ID 72057594038779904 was not found.
```

- Each *FILESTREAM* column directory must match a column in a partition. If this check fails, error 7935 is reported.

- Each *FILESTREAM* column directory must match a *FILESTREAM* column in the partition. If this check fails, error 7936 is reported.

- Each *FILESTREAM* column in a partition must have a matching *FILESTREAM* column directory in the appropriate *FILESTREAM* rowset directory. If the parent rowset directory is corrupt in some way, all column directories in the rowset directory fail this check (as shown earlier), and error 7937 is returned.

- Each *FILESTREAM* data file should be encountered only once by the *DBCC CHECKDB* scan in a *FILESTREAM* column directory. If this check fails, it indicates file-system corruption and error 7938 is reported.

- Each *FILESTREAM* data file must be linked to by only a single record in the table or index partition. If this check fails, error 7941 is reported.

- The *FILESTREAM* log file should not be corrupt. If this check fails, error 7963 is reported.

## Nonclustered Index Cross-Checks

The last of the cross-page consistency checks to discuss concerns about nonclustered indexes. This has always been one of my favorite parts of the *DBCC CHECKDB* code base because of the intricacies of performing the checks efficiently.

The nonclustered index cross-checks verify that

- Every record in a nonclustered index (whether filtered or nonfiltered) must map to a valid record in the base table (that is, the heap or clustered index).

- Every record in the base table must map to exactly one record in each nonfiltered, nonclustered index, and one record in each filtered index, where the filter allows.

If a nonclustered index record is missing, errors 8951 and 8955 are reported. Error 8951 reports the table name and the name of the index missing a record. Error 8955 identifies the data record that is missing a matching index record plus the index keys of the missing index record.

If an extra nonclustered index record is present, errors 8952 and 8956 are reported. Error 8952 reports the table name and index name of the index with the extra record. Error 8956 identifies the index keys of the extra index record and the data record to which the index record links.

Commonly, a nonclustered index record is corrupt, so all four errors are reported as shown here:

```
Msg 8951, Level 16, State 1, Line 1
Table error: table 'FileStreamTest1' (ID 2105058535). Data row does not have a matching
index row in the index 'UQ__FileStre__3EF188AC7F60ED59' (ID 2). Possible missing or invalid
keys for the index row matching:
Msg 8955, Level 16, State 1, Line 1
Data row (1:169:0) identified by (HEAP RID = (1:169:0)) with index values 'DocId =
'7E8193B4-9C86-47C0-2207-BF1293BA8292' and HEAP RID = (1:169:0)'.
Msg 8952, Level 16, State 1, Line 1
Table error: table 'FileStreamTest1' (ID 2105058535). Index row in index 'UQ__
FileStre__3EF188AC7F60ED59' (ID 2) does not match any data row. Possible extra or invalid
keys for:
Msg 8956, Level 16, State 1, Line 1
Index row (1:171:1) with values (DocId = '7E8193B4-9C86-47C0-B407-BF2293BA8292' and HEAP RID
= (1:169:0)) pointing to the data row identified by (HEAP RID = (1:169:0)).
```

The mechanism to carry out these checks efficiently has changed in every release since SQL Server 7.0—becoming progressively more and more efficient. In SQL Server 2008, two hash tables are created for each partition of each nonclustered index—one hash table is for the actual records in that partition of the nonclustered index, and the other is for the records that *should* exist in that partition of the nonclustered index (as calculated from the existing data records in the table).

When a nonclustered index record is processed, all columns in the record are hashed together into a *BIGINT* value. This includes

- The physical or logical link back to the base table (known as the base table RID)
- All included columns—even LOB and *FILESTREAM* values) are hashed together into a *BIGINT* value

The resulting value is added to the master hash value for actual records for the nonclustered index partition of which the record is part.

*DBCC CHECKDB* knows which nonclustered indexes exist for the table and what the complete nonclustered index record composition should be for each. When a data record is processed, the following algorithm is run for each matching nonclustered index record that should exist for the data record (taking into account any filter predicates for filtered nonclustered indexes):

1. Create the nonclustered index record in memory (again, including the base table RID, plus included columns).

2. Hash all columns in the index record together into a *BIGINT* value.

3. Add the resulting value to the "should exist" master hash value for the relevant nonclustered index partition of which the index record is part.

The premise that this algorithm works on is that if no corruptions exist, the master hash values for the actual records and "should exist" records for each nonclustered index partition should match exactly at the end of the *DBCC CHECKDB* batch.

If they do not, however, there is a problem. The algorithm described here is not without loss. There is no way to tell exactly which record is corrupt in a nonclustered index partition if the two master hash values do not match (this has always been the case since SQL Server 2000). In that case, a deep-dive check must be performed where the table and its indexes are compared to find the exact corrupt record(s).

The deep-dive check can take a long time to run if it is triggered, which may significantly increase the run time of *DBCC CHECKDB*. If a deep-dive check is triggered, error 5268 is output to the SQL Server error log, along with an error 5275 for each table that was searched. An example is shown here:

```
2008-11-25 15:57:53.95 spid55     DBCC CHECKDB is performing an exhaustive search of 1
indexes for possible inconsistencies.  This is an informational message only. No user action
is required.
2008-11-25 15:57:53.96 spid55      Exhaustive search of 'dbo.FileStreamTest1, UQ__
FileStre__3EF188AC7F60ED59' (database ID 17) for inconsistencies completed.  Processed 1 of
1 total searches.  Elapsed time: 5 milliseconds.  This is an informational message only.
No user action is required.
```

The deep-dive check uses the query processor to perform matches between the table and the index of concern, basically doing two left-anti-semi-joins using internal-only syntax. The query involved takes the following form:

```
SELECT <all information needed for errors 8951 and 8955 for an unmatched data record>
FROM <tablename> tOuter WITH (INDEX = <base table>)
WHERE NOT EXISTS
(
        SELECT 1
        FROM    <tablename> tInner WITH (INDEX = <nonclustered index>)
        WHERE
        (
                (([tInner].<index columns> = [tOuter].<index columns>)
                OR ([tInner].<index columns> IS NULL AND [tOuter].<index columns> IS NULL))
        AND
                (([tInner].<base table RID> = [tOuter].<base table RID>)
                OR ([tInner].<base table RID> IS NULL AND [tOuter].<base table RID> IS NULL))
        )
)
UNION ALL
SELECT <all information needed for errors 8952 and 8956 for an unmatched index record>
FROM <tablename> tOuter WITH (INDEX = <nonclustered index>)
WHERE NOT EXISTS
(
        SELECT 1
        FROM    <tablename> tInner WITH (INDEX = <base table>)
        WHERE
        (
                (([tInner].<index columns> = [tOuter].<index columns>)
                OR ([tInner].<index columns> IS NULL AND [tOuter].<index columns> IS NULL))
        AND
                (([tInner].<base table RID> = [tOuter].<base table RID>)
                OR ([tInner].<base table RID> IS NULL AND [tOuter].<base table RID> IS NULL))
        )
)
```

Once the query has been executed for each nonclustered index partition where the two master hash values did not match, the batch is truly completed.

# Cross-Table Consistency Checks

Cross-table consistency checks involve validating nonphysical relationships between various tables in the database. Some examples are

- The metadata for a table must have matching metadata describing its columns (the two sets of data are stored in different system catalogs).

- A primary XML index must be an accurate representation of the XML column that it indexes (a primary XML index is stored as an internal table, separate from the table containing the XML column it indexes).

■ An indexed view must be an accurate representation of the view definition (an indexed view is stored as an internal table, separate from the tables referenced in the view definition).

These cross-table consistency checks cannot be run unless the tables involved have already been checked and have no consistency problems (or have had their consistency problems repaired).

For example, imagine a case where an XML index is based on an XML column in table *T1*. Table *T1* has a page that is damaged in such a way that it seems to be empty (that is, some records are inaccessible). If the XML index is checked before table *T1*, it might seem as though the XML index has extra information in it and is corrupt. In reality, however, the *T1* table is corrupt—the XML index needs to be rebuilt after any repair of table *T1*.

This may seem like a subtle difference, but *DBCC CHECKDB* needs to report the first-order consistency errors. The same logic holds for performing the other cross-table consistency checks, so depending on what consistency errors are found in earlier steps, some of the cross-table consistency checks may be skipped.

## Service Broker Consistency Checks

The Service Broker feature uses two types of tables in the database:

■ System catalogs that store metadata about Service Broker usage in the database (for example, conversations, endpoints, and queues)

■ Internal tables that are used to store the Service Broker queues

Both types of tables have the same physical structure as user tables but have different attributes governing their behavior and accessibility by users. Their physical structures are checked as part of the logical consistency checks described earlier.

Another level of checking is performed for the data contained with the Service Broker system catalogs and queues, similar to the system catalog consistency checks described earlier in the chapter. These checks validate things such as the following:

■ A conversation must have two endpoints.

■ A service must be related to a valid contract.

■ A service must be related to a valid queue.

■ A message must have a valid message type.

These checks are not performed by *DBCC CHECKDB*—instead, they are performed by the Service Broker subsystem itself, on the behalf of *DBCC CHECKDB*. If any consistency errors are found, they are reported back to *DBCC CHECKDB* for inclusion in the final set of user results as a 8997 error, with the same format as the 8992 cross-catalog consistency-check error.

## Cross-Catalog Consistency Checks

In SQL Server versions prior to SQL Server 2005, there was confusion about when *DBCC CHECKCATALOG* should be run to validate the relationships between the various system catalogs. To remove this confusion, the *DBCC CHECKCATALOG* functionality was included inside *DBCC CHECKDB* from SQL Server 2005 onwards.

The entire metadata subsystem in the Relational Engine was rewritten for SQL Server 2005 and as part of that effort, a new set of system catalog consistency checks was written, with some additions in SQL Server 2008. The checks are more comprehensive and efficient than the corresponding checks in SQL Server 2000 and earlier and are performed by the metadata subsystem on behalf of *DBCC CHECKDB* (they can also be performed using the *DBCC CHECKCATALOG* command).

These checks operate only on the system catalogs dealing with Relational Engine metadata. The storage engine metadata system catalogs are checked during the per-table consistency checks described earlier. Some examples of the checks include the following:

■ For all column metadata, the matching table metadata must exist.

■ All columns referenced in a computed column definition must exist.

■ All columns included in an index definition must exist.

If any consistency errors are found, they are reported back to *DBCC CHECKDB* for inclusion in the final set of user results as 8992 errors in the following format:

```
Msg 8992, Level 16, State 1, Line 1
Check Catalog Msg 3853, State 1: Attribute (object_id=1977058079) of row
(object_id=1977058079,column_id=1) in sys.columns does not have a matching row
(object_id=1977058079) in sys.objects.
Msg 8992, Level 16, State 1, Line 1
Check Catalog Msg 3853, State 1: Attribute (object_id=1977058079) of row
(object_id=1977058079,column_id=2) in sys.columns does not have a matching row
(object_id=1977058079) in sys.objects.
```

 **Note**  These checks are not run on the *tempdb* database.

## Indexed-View Consistency Checks

Even though an indexed view is a first-class object in the database, it is stored as if it were an internal table with a clustered index, so its physical structure is checked for corruptions as part of the per-table consistency checks. Those consistency checks do not check that the *contents* of the indexed view match the view definition (that is, that the internal table does not have any extra or missing rows).

The simple way to describe the indexed view consistency check is that it uses the *indexedcview* definition (which is stored in the system catalogs) to generate a temporary copy of the indexed view. It then uses the query processor to run two left-anti-semi-joins between the actual indexed view and the temporary indexed view. This query reports any missing or extra rows in the actual indexed view.

In reality, the temporary copy of the indexed view may not actually be created in its entirety— it depends which query plan the query processor uses when running the query. The query that *DBCC CHECKDB* uses is similar to the one used for the nonclustered index deep-dive cross-checking that was discussed earlier. The query format is

```
SELECT <identifying columns of missing rows>
FROM <materialize the view temporarily> tOuter WITH (NOEXPAND)
WHERE NOT EXISTS
(
        SELECT 1
        FROM <actual view> tInner WITH (INDEX = 1)
        WHERE
        (
                ([tInner].<view columns> = [tOuter].<view columns>) OR
                ([tInner].<view columns> IS NULL AND [tOuter].<view columns> IS NULL)
        )
)
UNION ALL
SELECT <identifying columns of extra rows>
FROM <actual view> tOuter WITH (INDEX = 2)
WHERE NOT EXISTS
(
        SELECT 1
        FROM <materialize the view temporarily> tInner WITH (NOEXPAND)
        WHERE
        (
                ([tInner].<view columns> = [tOuter].<view columns>) OR
                ([tInner].<view columns> IS NULL AND [tOuter].<view columns> IS NULL)
        )
)
```

The NOEXPAND hint used in the query instructs the query processor to perform an index scan of the indexed view rather than expanding it into its component parts. Any extra rows in the indexed view are reported as 8907 errors and any missing rows are reported as 8908 errors.

This check can be very time- and space-consuming. The more complex the *indexedcview* definition, and the larger the table(s) over which it is defined, the longer it takes to materialize a temporary copy of the indexed view and the more likely it is to take up space in *tempdb*. This check is not performed by default in SQL Server 2008 and must be enabled using the EXTENDED_LOGICAL_CHECKS option.

## XML-Index Consistency Checks

A primary XML index is stored as an internal table with a clustered index. A secondary XML index is stored as a nonclustered index on the primary XML index internal table. The consistency checks must validate that the XML indexes contain an accurate shredded representation of the XML values in the user table.

The mechanism for doing this is similar to that for the indexed-view consistency checks and can be visualized using the same style of query, although a T-SQL query is not used. In this case, the two left-anti-semi-joins can be thought of as between the actual XML index and a temporary copy of the XML index generated by the XML subsystem.

Any extra rows in the XML index are reported as 8907 errors and any missing rows are reported as 8908 errors.

This check can be very costly to run. The more complex the XML schema and the larger the XML column values, the longer it takes to generate the temporary copy of the XML index, and the more likely that it takes up space in *tempdb*. This check is not performed by default in SQL Server 2008 and must be enabled using the EXTENDED_LOGICAL_CHECKS option.

## Spatial-Index Consistency Checks

A spatial index is stored as an internal table with a clustered index. The consistency checks must validate that the spatial index contains an accurate decomposed representation of the spatial values in the user table.

The mechanism for doing this is similar to that for the indexed-view consistency checks and can be visualized using the same style of query, although a T-SQL query is not used. In this case, the two left-anti-semi-joins can be thought of as between the actual spatial index and a temporary copy of the spatial index generated by the spatial subsystem.

Any extra rows in the spatial index are reported as 8907 errors and any missing rows are reported as 8908 errors.

This check can be very time- and space-consuming, depending on how the spatial index was defined. The higher the number of cells at each grid level of decomposition inside the index bounding box and the higher the number of stored matching grid cells per spatial value, the longer it takes to generate the temporary copy of the spatial index and the more likely it is to take up space in *tempdb*. This check is not performed by default in SQL Server 2008 and must be enabled using the EXTENDED_LOGICAL_CHECKS option.

# *DBCC CHECKDB* Output

*DBCC CHECKDB* outputs information in four ways:

- Regular output, consisting of a list of errors and informational messages to the connection issuing the *DBCC CHECKDB* command
- A message in the SQL Server error log

■ An entry in the Microsoft Windows application event log

■ Progress reporting information in the *sys.dm_exec_requests* catalog view

## Regular Output

By default, *DBCC CHECKDB* reports the following:

■ A summary of the Service Broker consistency checks

■ A list of allocation errors, plus a count of these errors

■ A list of errors where the affected table cannot be determined, plus a count of these errors

■ For each table in the database (including system catalogs):

 ❑ The number of rows and pages

 ❑ The list of errors, along with a count of these errors

■ A summary count of allocation and consistency errors

■ The minimum repair level that must be specified to fix the reported errors

An example of *DBCC CHECKDB* output is given here, for a database containing some corruption:

```
DBCC results for 'CorruptDB'.
Service Broker Msg 9675, State 1: Message Types analyzed: 14.
Service Broker Msg 9676, State 1: Service Contracts analyzed: 6.
Service Broker Msg 9667, State 1: Services analyzed: 3.
Service Broker Msg 9668, State 1: Service Queues analyzed: 3.
Service Broker Msg 9669, State 1: Conversation Endpoints analyzed: 0.
Service Broker Msg 9674, State 1: Conversation Groups analyzed: 0.
Service Broker Msg 9670, State 1: Remote Service Bindings analyzed: 0.
Service Broker Msg 9605, State 1: Conversation Priorities analyzed: 0.
Msg 8909, Level 16, State 1, Line 1
Table error: Object ID 0, index ID -1, partition ID 0, alloc unit ID 0 (type Unknown), page
ID (1:158) contains an incorrect page ID in its page header. The PageId in the page header =
(0:0).
CHECKDB found 0 allocation errors and 1 consistency errors not associated with any single
object.
DBCC results for 'sys.sysrscols'.
There are 637 rows in 8 pages for object "sys.sysrscols".
DBCC results for 'sys.sysrowsets'.
There are 92 rows in 1 pages for object "sys.sysrowsets".
DBCC results for 'sys.sysallocunits'.
There are 104 rows in 2 pages for object "sys.sysallocunits".
DBCC results for 'sys.sysfiles1'.
There are 2 rows in 1 pages for object "sys.sysfiles1".
DBCC results for 'sys.syspriorities'.
There are 0 rows in 0 pages for object "sys.syspriorities".
DBCC results for 'sys.sysfgfrag'.
```

```
There are 2 rows in 1 pages for object "sys.sysfgfrag".

<some results removed for brevity>

DBCC results for 'sys.syssqlguides'.
There are 0 rows in 0 pages for object "sys.syssqlguides".
DBCC results for 'sys.sysbinsubobjs'.
There are 3 rows in 1 pages for object "sys.sysbinsubobjs".
DBCC results for 'sys.syssoftobjrefs'.
There are 0 rows in 0 pages for object "sys.syssoftobjrefs".
DBCC results for 'sys.queue_messages_1977058079'.
There are 0 rows in 0 pages for object "sys.queue_messages_1977058079".
DBCC results for 'sys.queue_messages_2009058193'.
There are 0 rows in 0 pages for object "sys.queue_messages_2009058193".
DBCC results for 'sys.queue_messages_2041058307'.
There are 0 rows in 0 pages for object "sys.queue_messages_2041058307".
DBCC results for 'sales'.
Msg 8928, Level 16, State 1, Line 1
Object ID 2073058421, index ID 1, partition ID 72057594038386688, alloc unit ID
72057594042384384 (type In-row data): Page (1:158) could not be processed.  See other errors
for details.
There are 4755 rows in 20 pages for object "sales".
CHECKDB found 0 allocation errors and 1 consistency errors in table 'sales' (object ID
2073058421).
DBCC results for 'sys.filestream_tombstone_2121058592'.
There are 0 rows in 0 pages for object "sys.filestream_tombstone_2121058592".
DBCC results for 'sys.syscommittab'.
There are 0 rows in 0 pages for object "sys.syscommittab".
CHECKDB found 0 allocation errors and 2 consistency errors in database 'CorruptDB'.
repair_allow_data_loss is the minimum repair level for the errors found by DBCC CHECKDB
(CorruptDB).
DBCC execution completed. If DBCC printed error messages, contact your system administrator.
```

Although this output is comprehensive, the informational messages are redundant. In regular operation, the important information concerns the corruptions that may be present in the database. I always recommend using the NO_INFOMSGS option to reduce the output only to the essential information. For example, here is the output from *DBCC CHECKDB* of the same corrupt database, but with the NO_INFOMSGS option specified:

```
Msg 8909, Level 16, State 1, Line 1
Table error: Object ID 0, index ID -1, partition ID 0, alloc unit ID 0 (type Unknown), page
ID (1:158) contains an incorrect page ID in its page header. The PageId in the page header =
(0:0).
CHECKDB found 0 allocation errors and 1 consistency errors not associated with any single
object.
Msg 8928, Level 16, State 1, Line 1
Object ID 2073058421, index ID 1, partition ID 72057594038386688, alloc unit ID
72057594042384384 (type In-row data): Page (1:158) could not be processed.  See other errors
for details.
CHECKDB found 0 allocation errors and 1 consistency errors in table 'sales' (object ID
2073058421).
CHECKDB found 0 allocation errors and 2 consistency errors in database 'CorruptDB'.
repair_allow_data_loss is the minimum repair level for the errors found by DBCC CHECKDB
(CorruptDB).
```

As you can see, this version of the output is easier to read.

There is a special case when *DBCC CHECKDB* is executed on the *master* database. In this case, *DBCC CHECKDB* is also run on the hidden resource database, *mssqlsystemresource,* and so the output contains the results for both databases.

If *DBCC CHECKDB* has to terminate prematurely for any reason, and the failure can be controlled by *DBCC CHECKDB*, error 5235 is output, containing an error state. The error states have the following meaning:

- **0**   A fatal metadata corruption was detected. One or more 8930 errors (described previously) accompanies the 5235 error.

- **1**   An invalid internal state was detected inside *DBCC CHECKDB*. One or more 8967 errors (described previously) accompanies the 5235 error.

- **2**   The primitive checks of the critical system tables failed. One or more of errors 7984 through 7988 (described previously) accompanies the 5235 error.

- **3**   The emergency mode repair failed because the database could not be restarted after rebuilding the transaction log. Error 7909 accompanies the 5235 error. This is described in more detail later in this chapter.

- **4**   An access violation or assert occurred (even though *DBCC CHECKDB* was re-engineered in SQL Server 2005 to avoid these occurrences).

- **5**   An unknown failure caused *DBCC CHECKDB* to terminate, although a graceful termination was possible.

### Error Reporting to Microsoft

In SQL Server 2008, whenever an error is found by *DBCC CHECKDB*, a dump file is created in the instance LOG directory, along with a textual summary of the errors in XML form and a copy of the current SQL Server error log file. If the instance has been configured to provide feedback to Microsoft, these files are uploaded automatically. The information contained within them is used by the SQL Server team to determine how common various corruptions are. This helps decide where engineering effort should be invested in future consistency-checking and repair functionality.

## SQL Server Error Log Output

Each time *DBCC CHECKDB* completes successfully, an entry is added to the SQL Server error log for the database that was consistency-checked. An example is shown below:

```
2008-11-03 00:51:11.08 spid56     DBCC CHECKDB (CorruptDB) executed by CHICAGO\
Administrator found 2 errors and repaired 0 errors. Elapsed time: 0 hours 0 minutes 0
seconds.  Internal database snapshot has split point LSN = 00000044:00000188:0001 and first
LSN = 00000044:00000187:0001.  This is an informational message only. No user action is
required.
```

Notice that the entry lists the elapsed time that *DBCC CHECKDB* took to complete. This is included so that database administrators can gain an understanding of the average run time of *DBCC CHECKDB* for a particular database without having to resort to manual timing. The entry also lists which options were specified. This can be useful to determine whether a database was previously repaired.

The entry also lists some metadata information about the database snapshot that *DBCC CHECKDB* created. This can be useful to Product Support when debugging corruption issues.

If *DBCC CHECKDB* terminates prematurely, an abbreviated entry is entered in the error log. If a high-severity error in the storage engine causes *DBCC CHECKDB* to terminate uncontrollably, there is no entry in the error log. The error-log-entry generation is one of the last things that *DBCC CHECKDB* does when it completes. This means that if an error occurs that, for instance, terminates the connection running the command, *DBCC CHECKDB* is unable to generate the error log entry.

## Application Event Log Output

*DBCC CHECKDB* generates a matching application event log entry each time it writes output to the SQL Server error log.

Each time *DBCC CHECKDB* completes successfully, an entry is added to the Application event log detailing the number of errors found and fixed. An example is shown in Figure 11-3.

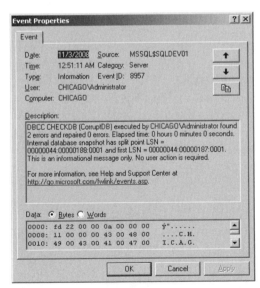

**FIGURE 11-3** Application event log entry when *DBCC CHECKDB* completes normally

If errors were found by *DBCC CHECKDB*, there may be three additional entries in the event log containing metadata for the error-reporting dump file described earlier.

In the event that *DBCC CHECKDB* decides to terminate prematurely, an abbreviated entry is entered into the event log. If the SQL Server error log entry is not generated because *DBCC CHECKDB* terminated uncontrollably, the application event log entry is also not generated.

## Progress Reporting Output

*DBCC CHECKDB, DBCC CHECKTABLE,* and *DBCC CHECKFILEGROUP* all report their progress in the *sys.dm_exec_requests* catalog view. The two columns of interest are *percent_complete,* which is self-explanatory, and *command,* which gives the current phase of execution of the DBCC command being executed. The various phases of *DBCC CHECKDB* are shown in Table 11-3 in order of execution. There is a similar list in the *SQL Server Books Online* topic "DBCC," but that list has several errors and omissions.

**TABLE 11-3 Progress Reporting Phases of Execution**

| Phase | Description | Granularity of Reporting |
|---|---|---|
| *DBCC ALLOC CHECK* | Allocation consistency checks | This step is considered a single unit of work (that is, progress starts at 0 percent and jumps to 100 percent when the step completes). |
| *DBCC ALLOC REPAIR* | Allocation repairs (if specified) | There is one unit of work per allocation error found in the previous step, and progress is updated when each repair operation completes. For example, with eight errors found, each repair will increment the progress by 12.5 percent. |
| *DBCC SYS CHECK* | Per-table consistency checks of critical system tables | Progress is calculated as a fraction of the total number of database pages that must be read and processed. Progress is updated after every 1,000 processed pages. |
| *DBCC SYS REPAIR* | Critical system table repairs, if specified and possible | As described for *DBCC ALLOC REPAIR.* |
| *DBCC TABLE CHECK* | Per-table consistency checks of all tables | As described for *DBCC SYS CHECK.* |
| *DBCC TABLE REPAIR* | User table repairs, if specified | As described for *DBCC ALLOC REPAIR.* |
| *DBCC SSB CHECK* | Service Broker consistency checks (and repairs if specified) | This step is considered a single unit of work. |
| *DBCC CHECKCATALOG* | Cross-catalog consistency checks | This step is considered a single unit of work. |
| *DBCC IVIEW CHECK* | Indexed-view, XML-index, and spatial-index consistency checks, if specified | There is one unit of work for each indexed view, XML index, and spatial index that is checked. |
| *DBCC IVIEW REPAIR* | Indexed-view, XML-index, and spatial-index repairs, if specified | As described for *DBCC ALLOC REPAIR.* |

**Note** There is no phase reported for primitive system table checks. This phase runs so quickly that when progress reporting was added into the *DBCC CHECKDB* code for SQL Server 2005, the development team did not think it worthwhile including a separate progress reporting phase.

For *DBCC CHECKTABLE*, the following phases are reported:

- *DBCC TABLE CHECK*
- *DBCC IVIEW CHECK* (if no errors were found by the previous step)
- *DBCC TABLE REPAIR* (if errors were found and a repair option was specified)

For *DBCC CHECKFILEGROUP*, the following phases are reported:

- *DBCC ALLOC CHECK*
- *DBCC SYS CHECK*
- *DBCC TABLE CHECK*

 **Note** *DBCC CHECKFILEGROUP* does not support repair operations.

## *DBCC CHECKDB* Options

The syntax diagram for *DBCC CHECKDB* from *SQL Server Books Online* is

```
DBCC CHECKDB
[
    [ ( database_name | database_id | 0
        [ , NOINDEX
        | , { REPAIR_ALLOW_DATA_LOSS | REPAIR_FAST | REPAIR_REBUILD } ]
        ) ]
    [ WITH
        {
            [ ALL_ERRORMSGS ]
            [ , EXTENDED_LOGICAL_CHECKS ]
            [ , NO_INFOMSGS ]
            [ , TABLOCK ]
            [ , ESTIMATEONLY ]
            [ , { PHYSICAL_ONLY | DATA_PURITY } ]
        }
    ]
]
```

The rest of this section explains these options, with additional information to that in *SQL Server Books Online*.

### NOINDEX

The NOINDEX option makes *DBCC CHECKDB* skip the nonclustered index cross-checks on user tables (that is, nonclustered index cross-checks are always performed on system tables when this option is specified). These checks are very CPU-intensive so turning them off can make *DBCC CHECKDB* run faster. This option is rarely used because the PHYSICAL_ONLY option does a much better job of disabling CPU-intensive checks and making *DBCC CHECKDB* run faster.

## Repair Options

You can specify three repair options, although the REPAIR_FAST option has been changed such that it does nothing in SQL Server 2005 and SQL Server 2008 and it exists only for backward compatibility.

The REPAIR_REBUILD option attempts to repair errors only where there is no possibility of data loss. The REPAIR_ALLOW_DATA_LOSS option attempts to repair all errors, including those where data is likely to be lost (the name of the option was carefully chosen). The repair process and specific repairs are discussed in much more detail later in this chapter.

> **Note** These options require the database to be in single-user mode. Running repair is usually used only as a last resort when restoring from a backup is not possible.

## ALL_ERRORMSGS

The ALL_ERRORMSGS option forces *DBCC CHECKDB* to give output for all corruption errors that it finds instead of the default, which is to output only the first 200 error messages. If there are more than 200 error messages, error 8986 is added at the end of the *DBCC CHECKDB* results and you need to rerun the command with the ALL_ERRORMSGS option to see the complete set of errors.

This means that by default, you get an incomplete view of the corruption in the database. You may think that 200 error messages is enough to decide what to do, but as discussed later in this chapter, it is important to see all error messages because the 201st error message may make you change your disaster recovery plan.

For example, consider a case where *DBCC CHECKDB* found 201 corruptions, but you use the default settings and see only the first 200. These 200 errors may all be in nonclustered indexes, meaning that you can rebuild those indexes to fix the corruptions. However, unbeknownst to you, the 201st error turns out to be a corruption in a clustered index data page that renders your nonclustered index rebuilds useless until that corruption is fixed.

> **Important** If you run *DBCC CHECKDB* using the ALL_ERRORMSGS option from within SQL Server Management Studio, it limits the number of errors to 1,000. To work around this, you must use *sqlcmd*. *SQL Server Books Online* incorrectly states that running *DBCC CHECKDB* multiple times allows you to see the complete list of error messages.

# EXTENDED_LOGICAL_CHECKS

The EXTENDED_LOGICAL_CHECKS option enables the cross-table consistency checks for indexed views, XML indexes, and spatial indexes. Because these checks are so expensive to run, they are switched off by default.

In SQL Server 2005 (when the indexed view and XML index checks were introduced), these checks were on by default. As such, when the database is set to the 90 compatibility level, the EXTENDED_LOGICAL_CHECKS option is ignored and these cross-table consistency checks are always performed.

# NO_INFOMSGS

When the NO_INFOMSGS option is specified, no informational messages are included in the output. This can make the output easier to read when errors are present. Although this is not the default, I recommend that this option is always specified.

# TABLOCK

The TABLOCK option forces *DBCC CHECKDB* to take database and table locks to obtain its transactionally consistent view of the database (that is, the consistency checks are performed offline and concurrent activity may be blocked). The locking behavior when this option is specified was described earlier in this chapter.

# ESTIMATEONLY

The ESTIMATEONLY option calculates how much space may be required in *tempdb* for the sort that holds the facts generated by the consistency-checking algorithms, taking into account all other specified options.

*DBCC CHECKDB* goes through the motions of building all the batches of objects to check (as described earlier in the chapter), but it does not actually check them. Instead, it uses the metadata that it has gathered about each table and index to produce an estimate of the number of each type of fact that it generates. The various numbers are multiplied by the size of each fact type and added together to form a total size for that batch. The batch with the highest total size is the one that is reported.

The estimation algorithms are very conservative in their calculations to ensure that an accurate maximum size is returned. The actual amount of *tempdb* space taken up may be considerably lower. For example, the estimation algorithm estimates the number of facts required to track forwarding and forwarded records by simply counting all the records in a heap and multiplying by two. This is almost never the case, but it is a sufficient estimation.

When the ESTIMATEONLY option is specified, the output does not contain any error or informational messages. Instead, the output has the following format:

```
Estimated TEMPDB space needed for CHECKALLOC (KB)
-------------------------------------------------
32

(1 row(s) affected)

Estimated TEMPDB space needed for CHECKTABLES (KB)
-------------------------------------------------
750

(1 row(s) affected)

DBCC execution completed. If DBCC printed error messages, contact your system administrator.
```

# PHYSICAL_ONLY

The PHYSICAL_ONLY option makes *DBCC CHECKDB* skip the CPU-intensive per-table and cross-table consistency checks. When this option is specified, *DBCC CHECKDB* does the following:

- Create a transactionally consistent, static view of the database.
- Perform low-level consistency checks of the critical system catalogs.
- Perform allocation consistency checks of the database.
- Read and audit all allocated pages from each table in the database.

*SQL Server Books Online* erroneously states that it also checks B-tree linkages, but it does not. It also skips all checks of *FILESTREAM* data.

By skipping all the CPU-intensive consistency checks, the PHYSICAL_ONLY option turns *DBCC CHECKDB* from a CPU-bound process into an I/O-bound process. This usually results in *DBCC CHECKDB* running significantly faster.

Because this option forces all allocated pages in the database to be read into the buffer pool, it is an excellent way to test all page checksums that exist.

The PHYSICAL_ONLY option has these restrictions:

- It is mutually exclusive with the DATA_PURITY option.
- It is mutually exclusive with any repair option.
- It switches on the NO_INFOMSGS option.

## DATA_PURITY

The DATA_PURITY option forces the per-column data purity checks to be run (as described earlier in this chapter). By default, these checks are run on databases that are marked as being pure. A pure database is one that was created on SQL Server 2005 or SQL Server 2008, or an upgraded database that has had *DBCC CHECKDB* with the DATA_PURITY option run without finding any corruptions (which irrevocably marks the database as pure).

For all other databases, the data purity checks are run only when this option is specified. The DATA_PURITY and PHYSICAL_ONLY options are mutually exclusive.

# Database Repairs

Apart from performing consistency checks on a database, *DBCC CHECKDB* can perform repairs of the majority of corruptions that it finds. I say "majority" and not "all" because there are some corruptions that *DBCC CHECKDB* cannot repair. This list includes:

- Corruption in the leaf level of a critical system catalog clustered index
- Corruption in a PFS page header
- Data purity errors (error 2570)
- Errors from system catalog cross-checks (error 8992)

If any of these corruptions are present, *DBCC CHECKDB* repairs as much as it can and indicates which corruptions cannot be repaired with a 2540 error ("The system cannot self repair this error").

This book is not the place to discuss when repair should be used, but suffice it to say that restoring from valid backups always allows data loss to be minimized and is usually the preferred course of action. Database repair functionality really exists as a last resort when backups are not available.

Repair should usually be viewed as a last resort for two reasons. First, the majority of the repairs that REPAIR_ALLOW_DATA_LOSS enables are to delete whatever is corrupt and fix up all linkages to and from the corrupt object. This is always the fastest, easiest to engineer, most easily proved, correct, and infallible way to remove a corruption. Second, not all corruptions can be repaired, as I explained previously.

However, if no backups are available, repair may be necessary. The necessary repair level to use is reported at the end of the *DBCC CHECKDB* output using an 8958 error, as shown here:

```
repair_rebuild is the minimum repair level for the errors found by DBCC CHECKDB
(ProductionDB).
```

The repairable corruptions fall into two groups—those that can be repaired without losing data (for example, corruptions in nonclustered indexes, indexed views, XML or spatial indexes, or in a forwarding <-> forwarded record linkage), and those that require data loss (that is, the majority of corruptions involving heaps and clustered indexes).

For those corruptions in the first group, the REPAIR_REBUILD option is sufficient. For those in the second group, the REPAIR_ALLOW_DATA_LOSS option is required. If not specified, some corruptions may not be repaired, and *DBCC CHECKDB* will explain that it is because a lower repair level was specified, using an 8923 error ("The repair level on the DBCC statement caused this repair to be bypassed").

## Repair Mechanisms

If a repair option was specified then once *DBCC CHECKDB* has completed each phase of the consistency checks, repairs are carried out at that point. This ensures that subsequent consistency checks and repairs are performed on a database without lower-level corruptions present.

When repair is required to run, the repair subsystem inside *DBCC CHECKDB* is passed the list of corruptions that the consistency checks found. The corruptions are not repaired in the order that they are found—instead, they are sorted according to how intrusive the repair is.

For instance, consider a nonclustered index that has a corrupt IAM page and a missing record. The repair for the corrupt IAM page is to rebuild the nonclustered index, and the repair for the missing record is simply to insert a new nonclustered index record. If the missing record was fixed before the corrupt IAM page, the insertion of the new record is wasted because the nonclustered index is then completely rebuilt to repair the corrupt IAM page.

Therefore, it makes sense to rank all corruptions by how intrusive their repairs are, and perform the most intrusive repairs first. This usually allows less intrusive repairs to be skipped because they may be repaired as a side effect of performing a more intrusive repair. Continuing the previous example, the nonclustered index IAM page corruption is ranked higher than the missing nonclustered index record. When the index is rebuilt to repair the corrupt IAM page, the new index includes the missing record, thus fixing the missing-nonclustered-index-record corruption as a side effect.

Repair ranking also prevents the repair system from inadvertently causing more corruption. For instance, consider a table that has a corrupt nonclustered index and a corrupt page at the leaf level of the clustered index. It is imperative that the more intrusive repair (deallocating the clustered index leaf-level page) is performed first. This guarantees that when the nonclustered index is rebuilt, the rebuild uses an error-free clustered index as its base. If the nonclustered index was rebuilt first, and *then* the clustered index leaf-level page was deallocated, the nonclustered index is corrupt.

Each repair is performed within a separate transaction. This allows *DBCC CHECKDB* to cope with a repair failing but then continue repairing other corruptions.

The output from *DBCC CHECKDB* contains details of the repair that was performed. The complete list of all corruptions with their repairs is well beyond the scope of this book, but example repairs include the following:

- Fixing incorrect record counts on a data or index page
- Fixing incorrect PFS page bytes
- Removing an extra record from a nonclustered index
- Inserting a single record into a nonclustered index (a much more efficient alternative than rebuilding a large nonclustered index to repair a single record)
- Moving a wrongly partitioned record to the correct partition
- Rebuilding a nonclustered index
- Rebuilding an indexed view, XML index, or spatial index
- Deleting orphaned off-row LOB values or *FILESTREAM* files
- Rebuilding a clustered index
- Deallocating a data record, with a consequent cascading delete of all nonclustered index records and off-row LOB or *FILESTREAM* values referenced by the record
- Deallocating an entire data page, with the consequent cascading deleted
- Setting or unsetting bits in the various GAM, SGAM, and IAM allocation bitmaps
- Fixing previous-page and next-page linkages in an IAM chain
- Truncating an IAM chain at a corrupt IAM page, stitching together the IAM chain remnants, and performing the consequent rebuilds and cascading deletes
- Resolving pages or extents that are allocated to multiple objects

Repairs that involve data loss have other possible consequences too. If a table affected by repair is involved in a foreign-key relationship, that relationship may be broken after running repair and so *DBCC CHECKCONSTRAINTS* should be performed. If a table affected by repair is part of a replication publication, the repairs are not replicated and so the subscription(s) should be reinitialized after running repair.

## Emergency Mode Repair

One additional piece of repair functionality is triggered only when the database is in EMERGENCY mode. EMERGENCY mode is used when the transaction log for the database has been damaged and no backups are available to restore from. In this case, regular repairs do not work—repairs are fully logged and this cannot occur if the transaction log is damaged.

In SQL Server 2000 and earlier, EMERGENCY mode was undocumented and was used to allow the transaction log to be rebuilt using the undocumented *DBCC REBUILD_LOG* command. Unfortunately, this procedure became publicized on the Internet but usually without all necessary steps. For this reason, I decided to add a documented and supported method of rebuilding a transaction log and recovering the database in SQL Server 2005. The feature is called *emergency mode repair* and its mechanism is unchanged for SQL Server 2008.

When the database is in EMERGENCY mode and SINGLE_USER mode, and *DBCC CHECKDB* is run with the REPAIR_ALLOW_DATA_LOSS option, the following steps are taken:

1. Force recovery to run on the transaction log (if it exists).

   This is essentially recovery with CONTINUE_AFTER_ERROR, in a similar vein to using CONTINUE_AFTER_ERROR with either BACKUP or RESTORE. The idea behind this is that the database is already inconsistent because either the transaction log is corrupt or something in the database is corrupt in such a way that recovery cannot complete.

   Given that the database is inconsistent and the transaction log is about to be rebuilt, it makes sense to salvage as much transactional information as possible from the log before it is discarded and a new one is created.

   This recovery with CONTINUE_AFTER_ERROR functionality is possible only from within *DBCC CHECKDB*.

2. Rebuild the transaction log if it is corrupt.

3. Run the full set of consistency checks on the database with the REPAIR_ALLOW_DATA_ LOSS option.

4. Bring the database online.

> **Tip** The vast majority of the time, this operation completes successfully, albeit with data loss. However I have seen it fail in production, especially on corrupt file systems, so again, backups are the recommended way to avoid data loss.

## What Data Was Deleted by Repair?

In the unfortunate case where you have no choice but to use the REPAIR_ALLOW_DATA_LOSS option, some data is inevitably lost, as explained previously. Your task becomes figuring out what data is lost so that it can be re-created or what other parts of the database are fixed up to reflect the loss.

Before running repair, you could try examining some of the pages that *DBCC CHECKDB* reports as corrupt to see if you can tell what data is on them. Consider the following error:

```
Server: Msg 8928, Level 16, State 1, Line 2
Object ID 645577338, index ID 0: Page (1:168582) could not be processed. See other errors
for details.
```

You can try using *DBCC PAGE* to examine page (1:168582). Depending on how badly the page is corrupt, you may be able to see some of the records on the page and figure out what data is lost when the page is deallocated by the repair operations.

After running repair, you may be able to tell what data has been deleted. Unless you are intimately familiar with the data in the database, you have two options:

■ Create a copy of the corrupt database before running repair so you can compare the prerepair and postrepair data and see what is missing. This may be tricky to do if the database is badly corrupt—you may need to use the WITH CONTINUE_AFTER_ERROR options of BACKUP and RESTORE to do this.

■ Start an explicit transaction before running repair. It is not very well known that you can run repair inside a transaction. After repair completes, you can examine the database to see what repair did, and if you want to undo the repairs, you can simply roll back the explicit transaction.

After the repair has completed, you may be able to query the repaired database to find out what data has been repaired. For instance, consider the case where a repair deleted a leaf-level page from a clustered index with an identity column. It may be possible to construct queries that find the range of records deleted, such as the following:

```
-- Start of the missing range is when a value does not have a plus-1 neighbor.
SELECT MIN(salesID + 1) FROM DemoRestoreOrRepair.dbo.sales as A
WHERE NOT EXISTS (
    SELECT salesID FROM DemoRestoreOrRepair.dbo.sales as B
    WHERE B.salesID = A.salesID + 1);
GO
-- End of the missing range is when a value does not have a minus-1 neighbor
SELECT MAX(salesID - 1) FROM DemoRestoreOrRepair.dbo.sales as A
WHERE NOT EXISTS (
    SELECT salesID FROM DemoRestoreOrRepair.dbo.sales as B
    WHERE B.salesID = A.salesID - 1);
GO
```

At the very least, after running a repair, you should perform a full backup and root-cause analysis of the corruption to find out what caused the problem.

# Consistency-Checking Commands Other Than *DBCC CHECKDB*

In this section, I explain what each of the *DBCC CHECK…* commands does. Historically, there has been much confusion about what all the different consistency-checking DBCC commands do, which ones should be performed, and in what order. *DBCC CHECKDB* includes the functionality of all *DBCC CHECK…* commands except *DBCC CHECKIDENT* and *DBCC CHECKCONSTRAINTS*.

## *DBCC CHECKALLOC*

*DBCC CHECKALLOC* performs the following:

- Primitive system-catalog consistency checks
- Allocation consistency checks on the database

It uses a database snapshot by default and has the same options as for *DBCC CHECKDB*, except for the following:

- PHYSICAL_ONLY
- REPAIR_REBUILD
- DATA_PURITY

None of these options make sense for allocation consistency checks.

If informational messages are allowed, it outputs comprehensive information about the number of pages and extents allocated to each allocation unit in the database, along with the first IAM page in the IAM chain and the root page. This information is not returned when the allocation consistency checks are performed as part of *DBCC CHECKDB*. Example output is shown here:

```
DBCC results for 'CorruptDB'.
******************************************************************
Table sys.sysrscols              Object ID 3.
Index ID 1, partition ID 196608, alloc unit ID 196608 (type In-row data). FirstIAM (1:188).
Root (1:189). Dpages 8.
Index ID 1, partition ID 196608, alloc unit ID 196608 (type In-row data). 10 pages used in 1
dedicated extents.
Total number of extents is 1.
******************************************************************
<some results removed for brevity>
******************************************************************
Table sys.syscommittab           Object ID 2137058649.
Index ID 1, partition ID 72057594038583296, alloc unit ID 72057594042580992 (type In-row
data). FirstIAM (0:0). Root (0:0). Dpages 0.
Index ID 1, partition ID 72057594038583296, alloc unit ID 72057594042580992 (type In-row
data). 0 pages used in 0 dedicated extents.
Index ID 2, partition ID 72057594038648832, alloc unit ID 72057594042646528 (type In-row
data). FirstIAM (0:0). Root (0:0). Dpages 0.
Index ID 2, partition ID 72057594038648832, alloc unit ID 72057594042646528 (type In-row
data). 0 pages used in 0 dedicated extents.
Total number of extents is 0.
File 1. The number of extents = 25, used pages = 174, and reserved pages = 195.
        File 1 (number of mixed extents = 18, mixed pages = 139).
    Object ID 3, index ID 1, partition ID 196608, alloc unit ID 196608 (type In-row data),
data extents 1, pages 10, mixed extent pages 9.
    Object ID 5, index ID 1, partition ID 327680, alloc unit ID 327680 (type In-row data),
data extents 0, pages 2, mixed extent pages 2.
    Object ID 7, index ID 1, partition ID 458752, alloc unit ID 458752 (type In-row data),
data extents 0, pages 4, mixed extent pages 4.
    Object ID 7, index ID 2, partition ID 562949953880064, alloc unit ID 562949953880064
(type In-row data), index extents 0, pages 2, mixed extent pages 2.
```

```
<some results removed for brevity>

   Object ID 2073058421, index ID 1, partition ID 72057594038386688, alloc unit ID
72057594042384384 (type In-row data), data extents 2, pages 23, mixed extent pages 9.
The total number of extents = 25, used pages = 174, and reserved pages = 195 in this
database.
        (number of mixed extents = 18, mixed pages = 139) in this database.
CHECKALLOC found 0 allocation errors and 0 consistency errors in database 'CorruptDB'.
DBCC execution completed. If DBCC printed error messages, contact your system administrator.
```

## DBCC CHECKTABLE

*DBCC CHECKTABLE* performs the following:

- Primitive system-catalog consistency checks
- Per-table consistency checks on the single table specified
- Cross-table consistency checks on indexed views that reference the specified table

The cross-table consistency checks are not performed if any corruptions were found in the table specified, even if the corruptions were repaired. This is slightly more restrictive behavior than for *DBCC CHECKDB*.

In addition, a nonclustered index ID can be specified that limits the nonclustered index cross-checks to only that nonclustered index. This cannot be specified if any repair options are used.

It uses a database snapshot by default and has the same set of options as *DBCC CHECKDB*, including repairs.

The output of the command is limited to the table being checked.

## DBCC CHECKFILEGROUP

*DBCC CHECKFILEGROUP* performs the following:

- Primitive system-catalog consistency checks
- Allocation consistency checks on the filegroup
- Per-table consistency checks on all tables stored in the filegroup
- Cross-table consistency checks, so long as the indexed views, XML indexes, and spatial indexes are stored within the filegroup and the tables on which they are based are also stored within the filegroup

It uses a database snapshot by default and has the same set of options as *DBCC CHECKDB*, except for the following:

- PHYSICAL_ONLY
- DATA_PURITY
- Any repair options

There are the following subtleties in the per-table consistency checks when a table and all its nonclustered indexes are *not* stored within the same filegroup:

- If a table is stored within the filegroup specified but one or more nonclustered indexes are stored in other filegroups, they are not checked for consistency.

- If a nonclustered index is stored within the filegroup specified, but the table (heap or clustered index) is stored in another filegroup, the nonclustered index is not checked for consistency.

The basic rule of thumb is that *DBCC CHECKFILEGROUP* does not perform cross-filegroup consistency checks.

The output of this command is the same as for *DBCC CHECKDB* except that it does not report any Service Broker details and only tables within the specified filegroup are checked.

## DBCC CHECKCATALOG

*DBCC CHECKCATALOG* performs the following:

- Primitive system catalog consistency checks
- Cross-catalog consistency checks

It uses a database snapshot by default and only has the NO_INFOMSGS option. If a database snapshot cannot be created, it requires an exclusive database lock to run. Given that neither a database snapshot nor an exclusive lock can be acquired on *tempdb*, *DBCC CHECKCATALOG* cannot be run on the *tempdb* database (either as part of *DBCC CHECKDB* or as the stand-alone command).

The output of this command is empty unless any corruptions are found.

## DBCC CHECKIDENT

*DBCC CHECKIDENT* checks that the identity value for the specified table is valid (that is, larger than the highest identity value contained in the table) and resets it automatically if necessary. It works by scanning the rows in the specified table to find the highest identity value and then comparing it with the next identity value stored in the table metadata.

The command can also be used to reset the identity value manually if required. Care should be taken when doing this so as not to produce duplicate values accidentally in the identity column.

If the command is just checking the identity value, then the table is locked with an intent-share lock, with minimal impact on concurrent operations. If a new value has been specified, the table is locked with a schema-modification lock for the short time it takes to modify the table metadata.

> **More Info**   The *SQL Server Books Online* topic for this command, "DBCC CHECKIDENT (Transact-SQL)," found at *http://msdn.microsoft.com/en-us/library/ms176057.aspx*, describes the various options and their effects.

### *DBCC CHECKCONSTRAINTS*

*DBCC CHECKCONSTRAINTS* checks the enabled FOREIGN KEY and CHECK constraints defined within the database. It can check a single constraint, all the constraints on a table, or all constraints in the database. If the ALL_CONSTRAINTS option is specified, it also checks any disabled FOREIGN KEY and CHECK constraints.

It works by creating a query to find all rows that violate the constraint being checked. The query uses an internal query hint to tell the query processor that *DBCC CHECKCONSTRAINTS* is running and that it should not short-circuit the query due to its knowledge of existing constraints.

It does not use a database snapshot and runs under whatever the session isolation level is set to. You must have the session option CONCAT_NULL_YIELDS_NULL set to ON; otherwise, the command fails with error 2507. If any rows violate a constraint, the row's keys are output along with the table name containing the row and the name of the violated constraint.

> **Tip**   *DBCC CHECKCONSTRAINTS* should be run after performing any kind of DBCC repair because the repairs do not take any constraints into account.

## Summary

As you can see from the descriptions in this chapter, the consistency checks that SQL Server 2008 can perform on a database are extremely comprehensive and have evolved significantly from earlier releases in terms of breadth, depth, and efficiency.

Also, you can see why *DBCC CHECKDB* can take such a long time to complete on a large, complex database. I've tried to include information on every corruption error that *DBCC CHECKDB* can report, as well as background on the consistency-checking mechanisms that it used to arrive at its conclusions.

Hopefully, this information will help you when you encounter corruption in real life.

# Index

## Symbols and Numbers

$FSLOG, 394–95
.trc file extension, 101
/3GB flag, 36
–k option, 33–34
@@IDENTITY function, 247–48
\Log subdirectory, 72
{HASH | ORDER} group, 514–15
{MERGE | HASH | CONCAT}
    UNION, 515
<filespec>, 176
32-bit operating systems
    buffer pool sizing, 36–38
    Max Worker Threads default
        settings, 66
64-bit operating systems
    buffer pool sizing, 36–38
    Max Worker Threads setting, 66

## A

accent sensitivity/insensitivity, 226
access methods
    code, 14–16
    database, 150, 170–71
    memory, NUMA, 19–20
    storage engine, 14–16
ACID properties, 16–17, 589–90
action columns, 495–96
actions, 114–15
Active VLF state, 187
active_workers_count DMO, 25
activity ID, 119–20
actual text facts, 669
Address Windowing Extensions
    (AWE) memory, 36
    allocation, 39
    AWE enabled option, 63
    buffer pool sizing, 36–38
    mapped, 562
    multiple server instances, 63
adhoc caching, 568
Adhoc objects, 555
adhoc queries, 528–30
Admin events, 110
AdventureWorks2008 database,
    128–29, 576–77, 581, 604, 625,
    631–32, 640, 648–49, 653
affinity, 26
Affinity I/O Mask setting, 64, 67

affinity mask configuration, 21, 23
    binding schedulers to CPUs,
        24–27
    dynamic affinity, 23–24
Affinity64 I/O Mask setting, 64, 67
aggregation
    fact, 669
    plan hinting, 515
    Query Optimizer, 488
    query processor, 671–72
aligned indexes, 442
ALL_ERRORMSGS option, 716
all-in-one insert, 494
allocation
    consistency checks, 679–83
    multipage, 570
    order, 675
    pages, 167
    storage engine, 15
    structures, heap modification,
        289–90
    unit ID, 668–70
    units, 606
ALLOCATION_UNIT locks, 606
Allow Updates option, 71
ALLOW_PAGE_LOCKS option,
    371, 628
ALLOW_ROW_LOCKS option, 628
ALLOW_SNAPSHOT_ISOLATION
    option, 635, 637, 639
    values, 641
    version store, 648–49
ALTER ANY SCHEMA permissions,
    175
ALTER ASSEMBLY command, 674
ALTER COLUMN clause, 283
ALTER DATABASE command, 77–78,
    142–43
    collation types, 225
    compatibility mode, 180
    database expansion, 136
    detaching databases, 175–76
    filestream filegroup file addition,
        390
    option setting, 148
    plan removal, 551–52
    Read Committed Snapshot level
        enabling, 638
    sample syntax, 143–44
    state options, 151
    termination options, 154–55
ALTER EVENT SESSION
    command, 121

ALTER INDEX command, 365–68
    constraint modification, 285
    fragmentation removal, 369–71
    index disabling, 366
    index rebuilding, 172–73
    locking, 628
    ONLINE option, 372–74
    options, 365–67
    row compression enabling,
        414–16
    Snapshot isolation level, 643
ALTER INDEX REBUILD command,
    200
ALTER LOGIN command, 171
ALTER PARTITION FUNCTION
    command, 643
ALTER permissions, 132, 175, 212
ALTER RESOURCE GOVERNOR
    command, 43
ALTER RESOURCE GOVERNOR
    DISABLE command, 52
ALTER RESOURCE GOVERNOR
    RECONFIGURE command, 52
ALTER TABLE command, 80, 83, 286
    column dropping, 285
    constraint modifications, 284–85
    lock escalation disabling, 630
    LOCK_ESCALATION option, 629
    partition-level lock escalation, 507
    row compression enabling,
        414–16
    Snapshot isolation level, 643
    SPARSE columns, 402–03
    SWITCH option, partitioning,
        439–42
    trigger disabling, 286
ALTER TRACE permission, 88
Analytic events, 110
anchor record, page
    compression, 428
AND clause, 469
And operator, 101
ANSI
    code pages, 232
    null default, 242
    nulls option, 242–43
    schema definition, 173
    SQL standard, 211–12
ANSI_DEFAULTS option, 243
ANSI_NULL_DEFAULT option, 156
ANSI_NULLS option, 156
ANSI_PADDING option, 157
ANSI_WARNING option, 157

729

# About the Authors

### Kalen Delaney

Kalen Delaney has been working with Microsoft SQL Server for over 21 years, and she provides advanced SQL Server training to clients around the world. She has been a SQL Server MVP (Most Valuable Professional) since 1992 and has been writing about SQL Server almost as long. Kalen has spoken at dozens of technical conferences, including every PASS Community Summit held in the United States since the organization's founding in 1999. Kalen is a partner and Director of Training for SQL Tuners (*www.sqltuners.net*), a SQL Server tuning and managed services company based in the northwestern United States.

Kalen is a contributing editor and columnist for *SQL Server Magazine* and the author or co-author of several Microsoft Press books on SQL Server, including *Inside Microsoft SQL Server 7*, *Inside Microsoft SQL Server 2000*, *Inside Microsoft SQL Server 2005: The Storage Engine*, and *Inside Microsoft SQL Server 2005: Query Tuning and Optimization*. Kalen blogs at *www.sqlblog.com*, and her personal Web site can be found at *www.SQLServerInternals.com*.

### Paul S. Randal

Paul is the managing director of SQLskills.com, which he runs with his wife, Kimberly L. Tripp. He is also a SQL Server MVP and one of the contributing editors of *TechNet Magazine*. Paul joined Microsoft in 1999 after spending five years at DEC working on the OpenVMS file system. He wrote various DBCC commands for SQL Server 2000 and then rewrote all of DBCC CHECKDB for SQL Server 2005 before moving into management on the SQL Server team. During SQL Server 2008 development, he was responsible for the entire Storage Engine.

Paul regularly teaches classes on topics such as database maintenance, high availability, disaster recovery, and SQL Server internals. He is a top-rated presenter at worldwide Tech·Ed and co-chairs the SQL Server Connections conferences. In the last year, Paul has written a large number of SQL Server 2008 materials, including white papers, and articles for *TechNet Magazine*. Paul's popular blog is at *www.SQLskills.com/blogs/paul*, and he can be reached at *Paul@SQLskills.com*.

## Kimberly L. Tripp

Kimberly is the president/founder of SQLskills.com, which she started in 1995 after leaving Microsoft, where she held multiple positions, including technical writer for the SQL Server Team and subject matter expert/trainer for Microsoft University. She is a SQL Server MVP, a Microsoft regional director, and a contributing editor of *SQL Server Magazine*. Since 1990, Kimberly has focused on many aspects of SQL Server availability, with emphasis on performance tuning and optimization.

Kimberly regularly teaches classes on topics such as database design, performance tuning, database maintenance, and SQL Server internals. She is a top-rated presenter at worldwide Tech·Ed conferences and the PASS Community Summit, and she co-chairs the SQL Server Connections conferences with Paul Randal. Kimberly has worked with all releases of SQL Server since version 1.0 and has written numerous resources, including online content and webcasts, white papers, and most recently, the Microsoft SQL 2008 JumpStart training class for DBAs. Kimberly's popular blog is at *www.SQLskills.com/blogs/kimberly* and she can be reached at *Kimberly@SQLskills.com*.

## Conor Cunningham

Conor Cunningham is principal architect of the SQL Server Core Engine Team, with over 10 years experience building database engines for Microsoft. He specializes in query processing and query optimization, and he designed and/or implemented a number of the query processing features available in SQL Server. Conor holds a number of patents in the field of query optimization, and he has written numerous academic papers on query processing. Conor blogs at "Conor vs. SQL" at *http://blogs.msdn.com/conor_cunningham_msft/default.aspx*.

## Adam Machanic

Adam Machanic is a Boston-based independent database consultant, writer, and speaker. He has been involved in dozens of SQL Server implementations for both high-availability OLTP and large-scale data warehouse applications, and he has optimized data access layer performance for several data-intensive applications. Adam has written for numerous Web sites and magazines, including SQLBlog, Simple Talk, Search SQL Server, *SQL Server Professional*, *CoDe*, and *Visual Systems Journal*. He has also contributed to several books on SQL Server, including *Expert SQL Server 2005 Development* (Apress, 2007) and *Inside SQL Server 2005: Query Tuning and Optimization* (Microsoft Press, 2007). Adam regularly speaks at user groups, community events, and conferences on a variety of SQL Server– and .NET-related topics. He is a SQL Server MVP, a Microsoft Certified IT Professional (MCITP), and a member of the INETA North American Speakers Bureau.

## Technical Reviewer: Benjamin Nevarez

Ben Nevarez has 15 years of experience with relational databases and has worked with SQL Server since version 6.5. He holds a master's degree in computer science and has been a speaker at several technology conferences, including the PASS Community Summit. Ben is currently a senior database administrator with the American International Group (AIG). When he is not working with SQL Server, Ben spends time with his wife, Rocio, and his three sons, David, Benjamin, and Diego.

# What do you think of this book?

We want to hear from you!

Your feedback will help us continually improve our books and learning resources for you.
To participate in a brief online survey, please visit:

**microsoft.com/learning/booksurvey**

...and enter this book's ISBN-10 or ISBN-13 number (appears above barcode on back cover).
As a thank-you to survey participants in the U.S. and Canada, each month we'll randomly
select five respondents to win one of five $100 gift certificates from a leading online merchant.
At the conclusion of the survey, you can enter the drawing by providing your e-mail address,
which will be used for prize notification only.*

Thank you in advance for your input!

**Where to find the ISBN on back cover**

ISBN-13: 000-0-0000-0000-0
ISBN-10: 0-0000-0000-0

90000

0   000000   000000

Example only. Each book has unique ISBN.

# Stay in touch!

To subscribe to the *Microsoft Press* Book Connection Newsletter—for news on upcoming
books, events, and special offers—please visit:

**microsoft.com/learning/books/newsletter**